QL681 .R66 1988
Root, Terry Louise.
Atlas of wintering North American birds

3 4369 00035808 8

W9-CJX-890

R66
.1988

WITHDRAWN

DATE DUE		
FEB 22 91'S		

ATLAS OF WINTERING
NORTH AMERICAN BIRDS

TERRY ROOT

With a Foreword by Chandler S. Robbins

ATLAS OF WINTERING
NORTH AMERICAN BIRDS

An Analysis of Christmas Bird Count Data

The University of Chicago Press / Chicago and London

Terry Root is assistant professor in the School of Natural Resources at the University of Michigan.

The University of Chicago Press, Chicago 60637
The University of Chicago Press, Ltd., London
© 1988 by The University of Chicago
All rights reserved. Published 1988
Printed in the United States of America

97 96 95 94 93 92 91 90 89 88   54321

Library of Congress Cataloging in Publication Data

Root, Terry Louise.
   Atlas of wintering North American birds.

   Bibliography: p.
   Includes index.
   1. Bird populations—North America—Geographical
distribution.   2. Birds—North America—Wintering—
Geographical distribution.   I. Title.
QL681.R66 1988   598.297   88-8591
ISBN 0-226-72539-1
ISBN 0-226-72540-5 (pbk.)

Illustrations of birds on the following pages are reprinted by permission of the publishers:

   Pages 3, 20, 22, 35, 37, 41, 42, 47, 100, 108, 111, 162, 181, 234, from Witmer Stone, *Bird Studies at Old Cape May,* copyright © 1937, 1965, Dover Publications, New York.

   Pages 4, 6, 65, 81, 121, 142, 147, 198, 210, 225, 232, 260, from George M. Sutton, *An Introduction to the Birds of Pennsylvania,* Harrisburg, Pennsylvania: The McFarland Company, 1928.

   Pages 45, 82, 90, 176, 236, from *A Guide to Bird Finding East of the Mississippi,* Second Edition, by Olin Sewall Pettingill, Jr. Copyright © 1951, 1977, 1979 by Olin Sewall Pettingill, Jr. Reprinted by permission of Oxford University Press, Inc.

   Pages 141, 144, 156, 161, 200, from *A Guide to Bird Finding West of the Mississippi,* Second Edition, by Olin Sewall Pettingill, Jr. Copyright © 1953, 1981 by Olin Sewall Pettingill, Jr. Reprinted by permission of Oxford University Press, Inc.

   Page 70, Reprinted from *North American Game Birds of Upland and Shoreline,* by Paul A. Johnsgard, by permission of University of Nebraska Press. Copyright © 1975 by the University of Nebraska Press.

   Pages 136, 169, 171, 224, from *Mexican Birds: First Impressions Based upon an Ornithological Expedition to Tamaulipas, Nuevo León, and Coahuila,* by George Miksch Sutton. Copyright © 1951 by the University of Oklahoma Press.

To the millions of people who have enjoyed and will enjoy the pleasures and pains of gathering Christmas Bird Count data, and to Mary Alice Root, who cultivated my curiosity about the world and took me on my first Christmas Bird Count

277962

Contents

Foreword

No other organized birding activity on earth can match the North American Christmas Bird Count in participation or continuity. From a modest beginning as a conservation measure at the turn of the century, the Christmas count has grown to be a major data-gathering, educational, and social event on the calendars of hundreds of nature organizations across the continent.

Over the decades, priorities and perspectives have changed. Shooting songbirds in North America is now prohibited by law. Other concerns have surfaced, however, including habitat loss through drainage of wetlands, the environmental effects of persistent pesticides, acid rain, and other pollutants, and trends toward more intensive agricultural and forestry practices.

Anecdotal evidence of declining bird populations abounds, but in this scientific age only firm documentation is taken seriously. Fortunately, the hours of field effort and miles traveled have been routinely recorded from the outset during Christmas Bird Counts. This foresight on the part of the originator, Frank Chapman, has provided a yardstick by which population changes can be measured over the decades. It also allows comparisons of populations throughout birds' winter ranges.

Christmas Bird Count data have largely remained dormant over the years because of the sheer bulk of the information and because the counts had not been entered into a computerized data bank. Overcoming this obstacle with a ten-year sample permitted Carl Bock to conduct several biogeographic studies and show the usefulness of the data in research and conservation.

The present volume demonstrates that Christmas count data can be used to show relative abundance on a broad geographic scale. Never before has relative abundance of North American birds in winter been plotted for a large number of species. I am confident that this landmark publication will ultimately provide the basis for comparisons with subsequent and prior decades. No other monitoring program (Breeding Bird Survey, nest record programs, bird banding, Breeding Bird Census, or Winter Bird-Population Study) covers nearly the time span of the Christmas Bird Count.

From time to time serious thought has been given to imposing stiffer rules on Christmas counters in an effort to make the results more amenable to rigid statistical analyses. It has been felt, however, that standardizing coverage, as by restricting participation to experienced counters in parties of specified size working along random transects, would destroy the educational and recreational aspects of the count. This in turn would lower the sample size to the point that the monitoring potential would be reduced rather than strengthened.

Despite stricter editing of the counts, some misidentifications are bound to occur. These generally involve only a tiny proportion of the total numbers of a species reported. Misidentifications are of primary concern when they occur outside the normal range of a species and distort the range limits.

Programming a computer to convert bird counts to relative density maps is at best a tricky operation. The reader should peruse the explanation of procedures followed and note especially that high counts are affected by counts from adjacent areas; that a few extralimital reports, whether valid or not, can distort the edge of the printed range; and that because the basic grid consists of 1° blocks of latitude and longitude, counts along the ocean (or a state line) may be displaced toward the center of the degree-block or even moved slightly out to sea.

Having participated in more than three hundred Christmas Bird Counts over the past fifty-five years, I have a special interest in these maps and their interpretation. The forty thousand observers who contribute to these counts each year will also find it fascinating to compare abundance of species in their local areas with that in other parts of the winter range.

Grid-based Breeding Bird Atlases are in progress in many states and provinces as cooperative programs between bird clubs and conservation departments. Some of these atlases will include relative abundance, others will show only presence or absence. The thousands of volunteer participants, as well as other users of these breeding-season atlases, will find it enlightening to compare breeding distribution with relative abundance in winter. The British have recently published a quantitative atlas of winter distriubtion by 100 km² blocks for all of Britain and Ireland, but it is unlikely that a similar study for an area as vast as North America will be undertaken in this century.

The present publication is much more than a collection of early winter distribution maps. It is an important research tool that shows at a glance where the major concentrations of each species are to be found. It makes it easy to compare distributions of closely related species, or species that flock together, or use the same habitats, or have similar food requirements. It also can call attention to areas that are of special conservation importance because they support sizable numbers of one or more species that are rare or declining.

The climatic and physiographic overlay maps will help the reader expand upon the author's interpretations and perhaps discover other factors that influence the winter distribution and abundance of North American birds. These overlays also permit comparison with similar parameters on the various state and provincial Breeding Bird Atlases that include similar overlays.

I hope that this first early winter atlas will stimulate more researchers to undertake serious studies with Christmas Bird Count data. As the Christmas count participants see their information being used in research and conservation, they should realize their responsibility to continually strive to improve the quality and continuity of the counts.

Chandler S. Robbins

Acknowledgments

I fortunately have been surrounded by people who understood that researching and writing this book took up most of my time, attention, and emotion. Many have provided encouragement, as well as constructive criticism and suggestions for improving various aspects of the study. In particular I thank Carl E. Bock for having the insight to put the Christmas Bird Count data into a computerized format, for instructing me on how to investigate biological questions using these data, and for possessing a trait all too rare among scientists—encouraging others to use the data he himself is working on. I thank the technical and support staff in the Contour Plotting System-1 division of Radian Corporation for providing the program CPS-1, computer time, and the technical assistance needed to generate the maps presented here; David Wood for helping me format the data for easier access; and Kenneth Parkes for reviewing a large portion of the book and making numerous suggestions on how to improve it. I am grateful to Chandler S. Robbins for writing the foreword and for all the useful recommendations he made after reviewing the initial proposal and the final draft of the book, and to an anonymous reviewer, David Bradley, Richard Bradley, John Fitzpatrick, Henry Horn, Burt Monroe, Scott Robinson, and John Terborgh for reviewing different portions of this project at various stages and making suggestions that greatly improved the analysis and the manuscript. I thank Robert May for encouraging me to take the time to write this book; the Princeton University Graduate Women's Group for reinforcing the skills needed to thrive in an academic career; Susan Abrams for encouragement from the inception of this project and for help in the initial design details; Deborah Hurry for reminding me that there is more to life than work; and Peg Johnson and David Johnson for listening to my tales of joy and woe. I am grateful to Mary Alice Root for encouragement throughout my life and to Joel Cracraft for helping to digitize the maps of environmental factors, for suggesting ways to improve the analysis and the writing, and for sharing the happy, sad, and frustrating times that the book has engendered. Partial funding came from the Biology Department of Princeton University, Radian Corporation of Austin, Texas, and the Museum of Zoology of the University of Michigan.

Introduction

Continentwide distribution and abundance patterns not only show where species are present and absent, but also identify the locations of concentrated populations. Such information is of great value to both amateur and professional ornithologists because it reveals where a particular bird can possibly be found (its range) and where it will probably be found (locations of high density). People who set environmental management policies also need to know the biogeographic patterns of species on a continental scale, to learn, for example, where concentrated populations of several species, including endangered ones, overlap. Once these locations are determined, policies can be devised to manage the areas appropriately.

Unfortunately, detailed large-scale studies of animals are rare (Brown and Gibson 1983). In the past two decades, most studies examining the abundance of species have been conducted within fairly small areas. Their findings have allowed us to develop a good understanding of the forces determining the distribution and abundance of species on small, localized scales, and this understanding provides much of the foundation of our ecological thought today. Biological processes, however, manifest themselves at various scales, and the results of studies conducted in restricted regions often cannot be directly extrapolated to much larger areas (Wiens 1981). Wardle (1981) suggested that within localized areas, biotic interactions such as competition and predation influence the details of species' range boundaries, whereas on a larger scale physiological tolerances for environmental characteristics such as climate and vegetation are the ultimate limiting factors.

To examine the importance of the environment, we need large-scale research, because patterns structured by such factors as ambient temperature can easily be overlooked in local studies. Studies that examine large regions directly do exist (e.g., McNab 1973), but there are very few (Brown and Gibson 1983). The main reason large-scale studies of species' biogeographic patterns are rare is that it takes a large group of investigators to collect the vast amounts of data needed. Fortunately, the National Audubon Society has established a protocol for mobilizing thousands of amateur and professional ornithologists. I have used these data to calculate and plot the continentwide distribution and abundance patterns of most birds wintering in North America. This atlas presents maps of these patterns, along with a brief analysis of each. The methods I used are explained here in the

Introduction; portions of the descriptions of my methods are taken from Root (1988a,b).

History of the Christmas Bird Counts

Frank Chapman was the editor of *Bird-Lore,* the first journal of the Audubon Society, when in 1900 he proposed the first Christmas Bird-Census, as it was then called (Chapman 1900). The census was promoted as a humane alternative to the horribly destructive Christmas side hunts, in which sportsmen would congregate on Christmas Day, choose sides, and then fan out through the countryside "killing practically everything in fur or feathers that crossed their path" (Chapman 1900, 192). The team that killed the most creatures, which included hundreds of nongame birds, won the contest and at one time was commended in the sportsmen's magazines. To help stop this gruesome tradition, Chapman called upon Audubon Society members to spend a portion of Christmas Day "with the birds," reporting the species and numbers of individuals seen, as well as the time of the census, the locality, and various weather parameters. These reports were then published in the February issue of *Bird-Lore.*

On 25 December 1900 twenty-seven people, at least twenty-one of whom were men, censused twenty-six localities, two in Canada and the rest scattered through thirteen states. The lowest absolute number of species seen was at Keene, New Hampshire, where three species were observed in three hours. In Toronto, Ontario, however, relatively fewer species were seen per hour, with four species recorded in five hours. By far the most species were seen in Pacific Grove, Monterey County, California, where thirty-six species were counted in two hours. (No census was held in Florida that first year.)

Since the turn of the century, the Christmas Bird Counts (CBC), as they are now known, have become an annual tradition and have significantly increased in popularity. In the eighty-sixth CBC (Winter of 1985–86) 38,346 people participated in 1,504 counts that covered all of the United States, most of Canada, and several localities in Middle and South America, Bermuda, and the West Indies (Leukering 1986). Guidelines for the counts have become more stringent over the years, but fortunately the methods have not changed enough to make the older counts incomparable with more recent ones. The counts are now restricted to specific locations, and each covers a circle 15 miles (24 km) in diameter. At least eight hours must be spent counting at each site. Rather than being held only on Christmas Day, the counts take place on any day within a two-week period around Christmas.

Background of the Analysis

This atlas contains maps drawn from CBC data, showing distribution and abundance patterns of species wintering in the conterminous United States and southern Canada. These maps differ from the standard species range maps (e.g., Peterson 1980; National Geographic Society 1983; Robbins, Bruum, and Zim 1983) because they incorporate abundance measures along with range information. This atlas is also different from other bird atlases, most of which are restricted to much smaller areas, usually within state and province boundaries (e.g., New York or Ottawa). Virtually all other atlases represent abundance information by using different-sized symbols—smaller dots indicate lower density. In this atlas computer-generated contour and three-dimensional maps present abundance data across the continent.

All range maps and maps representing both range and abundance patterns summarize analyzed data; they cannot portray raw data. Thus they are necessarily an interpretation, or best guess, of actual biogeographic patterns. Before plotting the distribution and abundance of species, one must decide how to define distributional edges and abundance patterns. The parameters used in drawing the maps in this atlas are explained below. They did not vary among species, and thus consistent and comparable interpretations of raw data are presented.

Data

The National Audubon Society Christmas Bird Count data were used to determine the continentwide biogeographic patterns of early wintering birds. The sites of these counts are not uniformly situated throughout North America. The density is high in the northeastern United States and low in Nevada and northern Canada, and only scattered locations are present in Central America. Because of the paucity of sites in the extreme northern portions of North America and throughout Central America, I restricted the area investigated to southern Canada and the conterminous United States. This area included 1,282 count sites (fig. 1) that were censused at least once during the ten-year period spanning the winters of 1962/63 to 1971/72 (references will be to the year a count was published; e.g., 1963 signifies the 1962/63 count). These ten years of data were chosen for study because they were available in computerized form. Carl E. Bock of the University of Colorado orchestrated their compilation, with funding from the National Science Foundation.

Maps of distribution and abundance patterns are by necessity static estimates of dynamic population parameters. At a continentwide scale, however, many changes in these parameters are not evident for most of the birds examined here. Species that have changed since 1972 primarily include those that use feeding stations. Feeding wild birds increased dramatically in popularity in the early 1970s (DeGraaf and Thomas 1974). With reliable, concentrated sources of food, "feeder" birds have been able to expand their ranges into harsh environments. As the data become available, maps showing species' more recent biogeographic patterns need to be constructed and compared with the maps presented here.

Some controversy exists about the usefulness of CBC data collected by thousands of people having a wide range of expertise (Kenage 1965; Robbins and Bystrak 1974). As with all data sets, errors do exist, but various analytic methods can diminish these problems or ameliorate their effects. The abilities of the participants, the miles traveled, the hours spent counting, and the size of the parties differ between count sites (Tramer 1974). Thus the species abundance data must be normalized by some measure of count effort (Raynor 1975; Bock and Root 1981). Weather may also cause variation in the data, because it affects the birds' detectability (Verner 1985) and the enthusiasm of the observers (Arbib 1967). For instance, the percentage of raptors soaring decreases with greater cloud over (Preston 1981), hawks are seen less often in strong winds (Enderson 1960), and woodland birds are much less conspicuous when the wind increases and the temperature drops (Grubb 1978). Another possible problem is that these counts occur in early winter, when individual birds may not have completed their migration, particularly in warm years (Graber and Graber 1983). Using average values, as I did in analyzing the large number of counts over ten years, reduces spurious effects due to weather or other

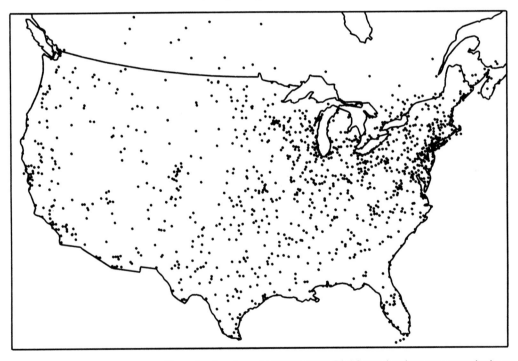

Figure 1. Locations of 1,282 Christmas Bird Count sites that were censused at least once during the winters of 1962/63 to 1971/72.

stochastic events such as movements of birds (Bock and Root 1981).

The CBC data adequately represent the average abundances of most of the birds reported. The exceptions are species that are extremely rare or unusually gregarious (Bock and Root 1981). The competitive nature of the counts is probably the main reason rare species are incorrectly recorded; everyone wants to see them, and often someone does "see" just one individual. The resulting distributions for these species often extend into areas outside these birds' actual ranges. The abundances of gregarious species also tend to be inaccurately recorded in the CBC data, for two reasons: first, flocks containing hundreds of birds are difficult to count accurately; second, chance movements of large flocks can significantly change the recorded abundance of a species. Thus maps of species with extremely high or low abundances (as defined below) are excluded from the main portion of the atlas but are included in appendix B.

Density Interpolation

I calculated the average density for the various species at each of the 1,282 site locations. Variation in count effort at the different sites was diminished by dividing the number of individuals (I) seen at a given site by the total number of hours (Hr) spent counting by the groups of people in separate parties at a given site. Averages at each site then were calculated by summing these values over the various years and dividing by the total number of years the count was held (Y). The mathematical expression for calculating this average density is:

$$\bar{X} = \left(\sum_{i=1}^{Y} (I/Hr)_i \right) / Y.$$

To aid in plotting, these density values were normalized to range between zero and one for each species by dividing the average values at each site for a given species by the average value at the site with maximum abundance. Frequently, however, some counts reported much larger abundances than other locations. For example, the highest average abundance of the Common Raven (*Corvus corax*) was 66.67 individuals seen per party-hour, while the next three highest abundances were 18.24, 15.76, and 13.02 individuals per party-hour. Therefore, instead of using the absolute maximum as the divisor in this normalization process, I used the average value that was greater than 99% of all the values for a given species (henceforth termed the maximum abundance). In the case of the Common Raven, which was seen on 329 sites, the maximum abundance used was 13.02 individuals per party-hour. The 1% of the resulting values that were greater than 1.0 were assigned the value of 1.0. These normalized abundance values were then plotted.

Plotting Method

The computer program CPS-1 (Contour Plotting System-1), distributed by Radian Corporation of Austin, Texas, was used to generate two-dimensional contour maps and three-dimensional fishnet maps for all the species (e.g., fig. 2). The two types of maps are different portrayals of the same data. An evenly spaced grid with each square about 1° of latitude or

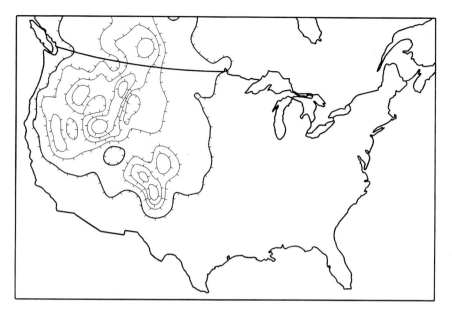

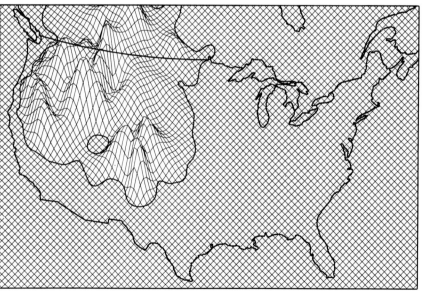

Figure 2. Contour and three-dimensional maps of the winter distribution and abundance patterns of the Black-billed Magpie (*Pica pica*). The four contour intervals are 20%, 40%, 60%, and 80% of the maximum abundance value used in the normalization process (see text). For the Black-billed Magpie this value is 18.30 individuals seen per party-hour (I/Hr). The tick marks point toward lower abundance values, and the bold line represents the edge of the range.

longitude on a side was interpolated from the irregularly located count sites. The abundance of a species at each grid point was calculated by finding the best linear least-squares fit plane that passed through the density values of at least four, and at most twenty-four, of the sites within a circle having a radius approximately 7.7° of latitude. If the sites were scattered fairly evenly around the grid point, then the height of the plane directly above the grid point provided the density value. If the sites were not evenly spaced around the grid point (if three or more consecutive octants of the circle surrounding the point were devoid of sites), then the grid-point value was determined in one of two ways. First, if a site was within roughly 0.1° of latitude of the point, then the point was assigned the value of that site. Second, weighted averages were taken of the sites within the circle, with the closest points dominating the average. Values could be determined at all grid points except a few in southwestern Canada and around James Bay. The interpolated grid values were smoothed using a biharmonic operator, an iterative process that reduced the overall curvature of the surface but retained its fit through the grid values. To further improve the smoothing process, the grid interval was reduced by half and the intermediate values were interpolated by weighted averages of the twelve surrounding grid points (Radian 1979).

The plots of the distribution and abundance patterns produced from these estimated densities (e.g., fig. 2) may seem difficult to interpret initially. However, all the species maps are constructed in an identical manner, and once one is understood they are all easy to interpret. On all the maps, the bold line indicates the edge of the species' distribution. This is defined to be 0.5% of the maximum abundance value, which is given in the accompanying text for each species. The contour intervals of each two-dimensional map are 20%, 40%, 60%, and 80% of the maximum abundance, and the tick marks point toward the lower abundance. The Great Lakes and James Bay are blanked out so that contour and distribution-edge lines are not drawn through them. These bodies of water are not blanked out on the three-dimensional maps; for these a hidden-line algorithm was used when drawing the three-dimensional net, but that algorithm did not apply to the boundaries of the study area or to the lines demarcating the edges of the distributions. The vantage point from which the three-dimensional maps are drawn is on the equator at the 95th meridian. All the maps use the Albers equal-area conic projection, with standard parallels at 29.5° and 45.5° north latitude and the origin at 23° north latitude and 96° west longitude.

Misleading Interpolations

Even though CPS-1 is a state of the art program for interpolating and plotting abundance data from irregularly spaced data points, some unusual situations in the CBC data resulted in misleading interpretations. One such instance occurred with localized data. The interpolation method uses data from several locations to determine the value at a given point. In most cases this method is superior to all others, but it tends to decrease the abundance of a localized peak and extend a localized distribution beyond its actual limits. An example of these effects can be seen in the maps of the Canvasback (*Aythya valisineria*; fig. 3). The data show that the mean abundance of the Canvasback at counts around Chesapeake Bay is equal to that at Bitter Lake National Wildlife Refuge in New Mexico. The maps, however, show a lower abundance in the vicinity of Chesapeake Bay, because numerous counts there recorded no Canvasbacks. Thus, when the interpolation process used the few high and numerous zero counts, the result was a lower peak abundance value. In New Mexico there are fewer counts (see fig. 1) and therefore fewer zero values considered in the interpolation, resulting in a higher calculated value. The extremely localized occurrence of Canvasbacks at Bitter Lake, and their absence from surrounding areas, is also not represented on the maps. The interpolation process depicts the abundance peak as covering southeastern New Mexico, because there were few nearby counts that would have had a density of zero. Thus the presence of such counts would have forced a more localized peak. These problems, however, occur only where there are localized populations and where count sites are sparse.

Another potentially misleading aspect of the mapping process is caused by the routine that smoothed the abundance patterns. Abrupt changes in slope were modified to avoid right-angle turns when the abundance pattern went from high to low values. The smoothing routine forced such turns to curve smoothly, producing a fishhook-shaped curve rather than an L-shaped one. This smoothing caused values to drop below zero if the low values themselves were close to zero, and as a consequence empty areas appear on the maps between areas of very high and very low abundance. This effect is probably contributing to the vacant area in west-central Arizona on the maps of the Sage Sparrow (*Amphispiza belli*; fig. 4). These smoothing and interpolation problems do occur on some of the maps, but the instances are few, and maps that are strongly misleading have been excluded from the body of the atlas and included only in appendix B.

Species

More than six hundred species were recorded in the ten years of CBC data examined. Those species that were seen at fewer than ten sites are not addressed in this atlas. This includes such species as the Boreal Owl (*Aegolius funereus*—seen at four locations), Cliff Swallow (*Hirundo pyrrhonota*—nine locations), and Blue-winged Warbler (*Vermivora pinus*—four locations). The exceptions to this rule are species that were recorded at fewer than ten sites but were seen regularly (in five or more years) at one or more of these sites (e.g., Whooping Crane [*Grus americana*], and White-tailed Ptarmigan [*Lagopus leucurus*]). In total, the distribution and abundance patterns of 508 species or subspecies are discussed. All the birds are listed in appendix A, along with the number of locations at which they were reported, their maximum abundances, and the reasons certain maps were excluded.

Figure 3. Contour and three-dimensional maps of the winter distribution and abundance pattern of the Canvasback (*Aythya valisineria*). Arrows indicate the high abundance areas discussed in the text. The four contour intervals are 20%, 40%, 60%, and 80% of 38.14 I/Hr, which is the maximum abundance value. The tick marks point toward lower abundance values, and the bold line represents the edge of the range.

Figure 4. Contour and three-dimensional maps of the winter distribution and abundance patterns of the Sage Sparrow (*Amphispiza belli*). The arrow indicates the void area discussed in the text. The four contour intervals are 20%, 40%, 60%, and 80% of the maximum abundance value (5.97 I/Hr). The tick marks point toward lower abundance values, and the bold line represents the edge of the range.

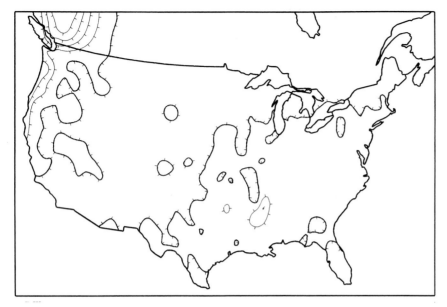

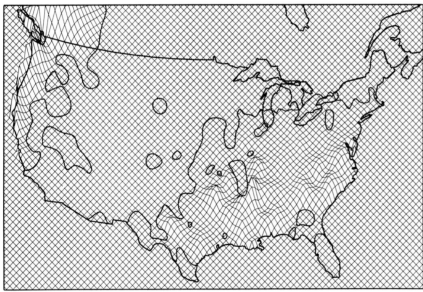

Figure 5. Misleading contour and three-dimensional maps of the winter distribution and abundance patterns of the Winter Wren (*Troglodytes troglodytes*). The maximum abundance value (0.58 I/Hr) inappropriately overshadows the entire abundance pattern. The arrow indicates the misleading abundance peak. The four contour intervals are 20%, 40%, 60%, and 80% of the maximum abundance value. The tick marks point toward lower abundance values, and the bold line represents the edge of the range.

Maps for 250 birds are provided in the body of the atlas. Appendix B includes 96 more maps that may present difficulties of interpretation for one reason or another. Included in appendix B are maps of 26 birds that are quite rare and 25 that are extremely gregarious. The rare species were defined as those with maximum abundances of fewer than 0.20 individuals (I) seen per hour (Hr), and extreme gregariousness was assumed when the maximum abundance was over 200.00 I/Hr. Other birds with maps included only in appendix B are 12 irruptive and 15 nomadic species. Birds in the former category have abundance patterns that change with the northern cone crop (e.g., Red-breasted Nuthatch [*Sitta canadensis*] and Red Crossbill [*Loxia curvirostra*]; Bock and Lepthien 1976d). The nomadic species have abundances that vary dramatically from year to year (e.g., Bohemian Waxwing [*Bombycilla garrulus*] and Snow Bunting [*Plectrophenax nivalis*]). Also excluded from the body of the text, but included in appendix B, are maps of the Northern Gannet (*Sual bassanus*), because its range is primarily pelagic, and the Semipalmated Sandpiper (*Calidris pusilla*), because most reports are due to misidentifications (see Phillips 1975).

Interpolation problems also prevented the maps of 14 species from being included in the body of the atlas, but they are in appendix B. The data for these maps were misinterpreted primarily because a low density of counts occurred in an area where the species was seen in high abundance, resulting in an unrealistic peak that overshadowed the entire abundance pattern. An example of such a map is that of the Winter Wren (*Troglodytes troglodytes;* fig. 5). In this case the high abundance along the coast of British Columbia, coupled with the lack of inland counts, caused an inappropriately high abundance peak. To emphasize that the maps of the 96 species in appendix B may be misleading, they are reduced in size, and only the contour maps are included.

Maps were not drawn for species with very restricted distributions—those seen at fewer than forty count locations (e.g., Trumpeter Swan [*Cygnus buccinator*] on fourteen sites, Gila Woodpecker [*Melanerpes uropygialis*] on sixteen sites, Smith's Longspur [*Calcarius pictus*] on twenty-one sites). A brief description of their distribution and abundance patterns, however, is given in the text. There are 162 such species. Two of these species, the Black-necked Stilt (*Himantopus mexicanus*) and the Painted Bunting (*Passerina ciris*), are included among the maps in appendix B. Even though these species were recorded at fewer than forty sites (thirty-eight and thirty-five, respectively), the patterns portrayed in their maps are informative.

Environmental Factors
I used the 250 maps in the main portion of the atlas to investigate associations between environmental factors and the distribution and abundance patterns of these birds (see also Root 1988a,b). To make direct comparisons easier, maps of environmental factors were generated at the same scale and on the same projection as the species maps. The factors examined include average minimum January temperature (fig. 6; USGS 1970; Canada, Department of Energy, Mines, and Resources 1974); mean length of frost-free

period (fig. 7; Baldwin 1973); mean annual precipitation (fig. 8; USGS 1970; Canada, Department of Energy, Mines, and Resources 1974); average annual general humidity or pan evaporation (fig. 9; Baldwin 1973); mean winter ocean-surface temperature (fig. 10; USGS 1970); elevation (fig. 11; USGS 1970; Canada, Department of Energy, Mines, and Resources 1974); and potential vegetation (figs. 12 and 13; Chapman and Sherman 1975). Snowfall was also examined in this analysis, but there were too few associations with species' biogeographic patterns to warrant including a figure here. Maps of all the environmental factors except snowfall are provided on transparent overlays in an envelope inside the back cover. These can be placed over the species maps, allowing direct comparison between these factors and the biogeographic patterns of each species. Also included are transparencies showing the locations of the count sites (fig. 1), the locations of national wildlife refuges in the United States (fig. 14; United States Fish and Wildlife Service 1982), the state and province boundaries with 5° latitude/longitude lines (fig. 15), the 1° latitude/longitude lines (fig. 16).

A transparent overlay of state and province boundaries, drawn to the same scale as the maps in appendix B, is also included inside the back cover.

Factors other than those directly examined in this study clearly influence winter distribution and abundance patterns. The availability of food, for example, is critical in determining whether birds occur in an area, but no large-scale mapping of food supplies is available.

Another factor that greatly influences species' winter abundance patterns is the location of their breeding grounds. For instance, a higher proportion of male than female Dark-eyed Juncos (*Junco hyemalis*) winter close to the breeding grounds (Ketterson and Nolan 1976). Though breeding grounds and other aspects of breeding biology are not directly addressed in this atlas, they often are important in understanding the occurrence of wintering birds.

In addition, that the winter ranges of many species extend south of the United States border is also important to understanding long-term trends in the abundance of some birds wintering in North America. The absence or inadequate development of conservation programs in southern countries adversely affects the total abundance of many North American migrants (Rappole et al. 1983). For example, game species often are not rigorously protected. In addition, the forests in Middle and South America are being cut at an alarming rate, which reduces the abundance of species dependent upon these valuable habitats (Rappole et al. 1983).

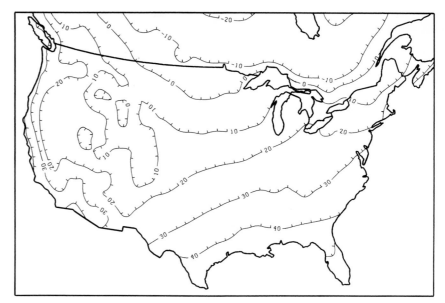

Figure 6. Contour map of average minimum January temperature, with contours at 10°F (5°C) intervals (after USGS 1970; Canada, Department of Energy, Mines, and Resources 1974). The tick marks point toward lower temperatures.

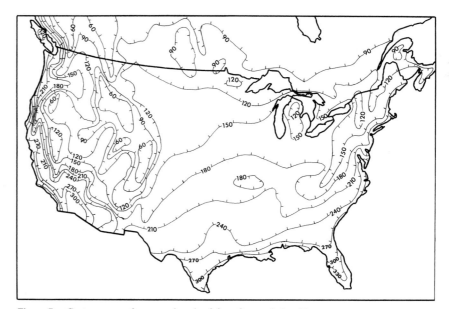

Figure 7. Contour map of average length of frost-free period, with contours at thirty day intervals (after Baldwin 1973). The tick marks point toward shorter periods.

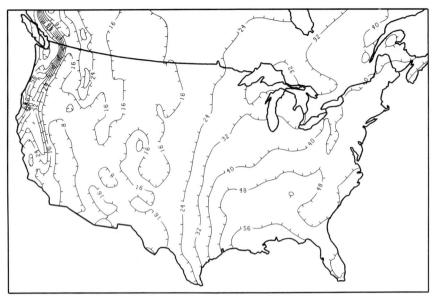

Figure 8. Contour map of mean annual precipitation, with contours at intervals of 8 inches (20 cm) (after USGS 1970; Canada, Department of Energy, Mines, and Resources 1974). The tick marks point toward less precipitation.

Figure 10. Contour map of mean winter ocean-surface temperature, with contour intervals every 2°F (1°C) (after USGS 1970). Tick marks point toward lower temperatures.

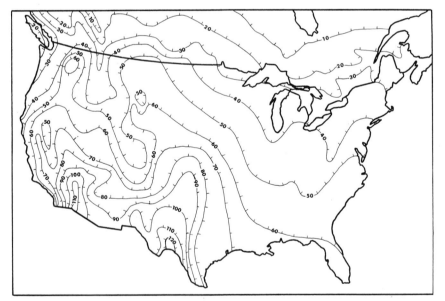

Figure 9. Contour map of average annual general humidity as measured by pan evaporation. Contours are drawn every 10 inches (25 cm) (after Baldwin 1973), and tick marks point toward smaller values.

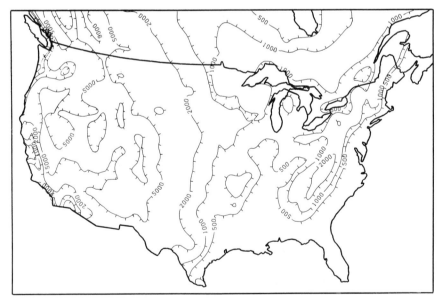

Figure 11. Contour map of elevation, with contour intervals at 500, 1,000, 2,000, 5,000, and 9,000 feet (152, 304, 608, 1,524, and 2,743 m) above sea level (after USGS 1970; and Canada, Department of Energy, Mines, and Resources, 1974). Tick marks point downslope.

Figure 12. Potential vegetation classified by species composition (after Chapman and Sherman 1975). The bold lines demarcate the same areas as indicated in figure 13 (**B**, boreal woodland and coniferous forest; **X**, mixed deciduous and coniferous forest; **M**, mixed mesophytic and deciduous forest; **G**, grassland; **S**, tree and shrub savanna; **A**, semiarid shrub and scrub steppes; **P**, dry-belt pine forest; **E**, mixed evergreen and deciduous forest; **C**, western temperate and coastal coniferous forest; **T**, tundra; **S**, swamp; **F**, floodplain forest; **D**, desert). The species types are as follows: **B1**, spruce and larch muskeg, spruce, larch, much bog, and lichen floor; **B2**, spruce and fir forest, and shaded floor; **X1**, spruce, pine, hemlock, maple, beech, and other northern hardwoods and rainy lake forest; **X2**, northern hardwoods; **M1**, rich forest and many hardwood species; **M2**, oak and hickory; **M3**, oak, hickory, and pine; **M4**, maple, beech, and other hardwoods; **M5**, mixed hardwoods; **M6**, southern mixed forest, sweet gum, beech, magnolia, pine, and oak; **M7**, mixed oak-conifer forest, oak, cedar, hemlock, and Douglas fir; **M8**, aspen groves, scattered spruce, and grassy openings; **M9**, aspen-oak groves and grassy openings; **M10**, maples and basswood; **M11**, prairie, oak, and hickory; **G1**, blackland prairie; **G2**, coastal prairie; **G3**, wheatgrass prairie; **G4**, bluestem prairie; **G5**, bluestem–grama grass prairie; **G6**, Nebraska sandhills prairie; **G7**, dry-belt prairie and steppe; **G8**, wheatgrass-needlegrass prairie; **G9**, grama–buffalo grass prairie; **G10**, foothills prairie; **G11**, Great Valley steppe; **G12**, plateau prairies, including meadow and fescue grasses; **S1**, oak, bluestem savanna; **S2**, savanna with mesquite-oak scrub and juniper; **S3**, mesquite scrub, some openings with oak, juniper, and buffalo grass; **S4**, mesquite-acacia scrub; **A1**, sagebrush steppe; **A2**, saltbush-greasewood scrub; **A3**, sagebrush scrub; **A4**, creosote bush scrub; **A5**, grama grass–creosote bush; **A6**, chaparral, golden chinquapin, manzanitas, and California lilacs; **A7**, shrub steppe, blackbrush, and creosote bush; **P1**, ponderosa pine forest; **P2**, pine, often with Douglas fir; **P3**, juniper, piñon, and other nut pines; **E1**, mixed evergreen forest, oak, Douglas fir, and other evergreen species; **E2**, oak, juniper woodland; **C1**, spruce, cedar, and hemlock rain forest; **C2**, northern subalpine forest, spruce, fir, and pine; **C3**, southern subalpine forest, spruce, fir, and Douglas fir; **C4**, Douglas fir forest with spruce, fir, hemlock, and larch; **C5**, grand fir and Douglas fir; **C6**, cedar, hemlock, and Douglas fir; **C7**, silver fir and Douglas fir; **C8**, cedar, hemlock, and pine; **C9**, mixed forest, fir, pine, and Douglas fir; **C10**, montane forest, pine, spruce, and Douglas fir; **T**, tundra; **S**, swamp; **F**, floodplain forest; **D**, desert.

Figure 13. Potential vegetation classified by the physiognomy of the species (after Chapman and Sherman 1975). The various types indicated include:

- Boreal woodland and coniferous forest
- Mixed deciduous and coniferous forest
- Mixed mesophytic and deciduous forest
- Grassland
- Tree and shrub savanna
- Semiarid shrub and scrub steppes
- Dry-belt pine forest
- Mixed evergreen and deciduous forest
- Western temperate and coastal coniferous forest
- Tundra

S Swamp

F Floodplain forest

D Desert

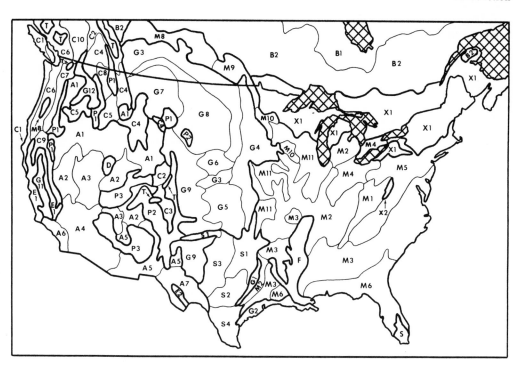

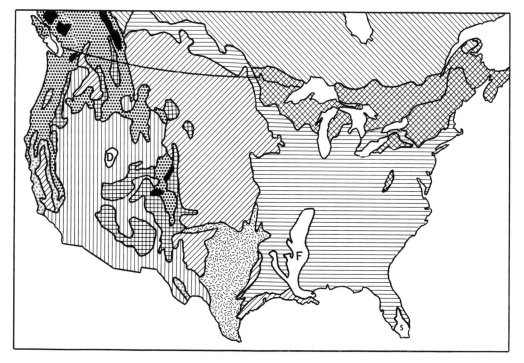

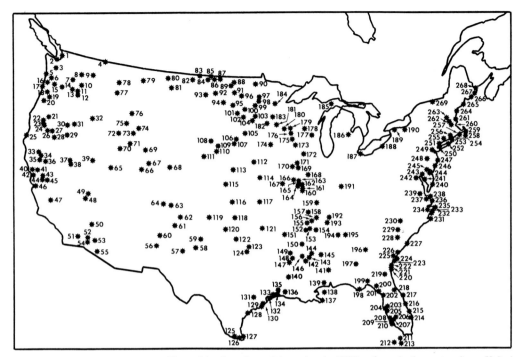

Figure 14. Locations of the national wildlife refuges in the conterminous United States (after United States Fish and Wildlife Service 1982). NGP—National Game Preserve; WMD—Wetland Management District.

46 Salinas River, CA
47 Kern, CA
48 Desert, NV
49 Pahranagat, NV
50 Havasu, AZ
51 Salton Sea, CA
52 Cibola, AZ
53 Kofa, AZ
54 Imperial, AZ
55 Cabeza Prieta, AZ
56 Bosque del Apache, NM
57 Bitter Lake, NM
58 Muleshoe, TX
59 Buffalo Lake, TX
60 Sevilleta, NM
61 Las Vegas, NM
62 Maxwell, NM
63 Alamosa, CO
64 Monte Vista, CO
65 Fish Springs, UT
66 Ouray, UT
67 Browns Park, CO
68 Arapaho, CO
69 Seedskadee, WY
70 Bear River, UT
71 Bear Lake, ID
72 Minidoka, ID
73 Grays Lake, ID
74 National Elk, WY
75 Camas, ID
76 Red Rock Lakes, MT
77 Lee Metcalf, MT
78 National Bison Range, MT
79 Benton Lake, MT
80 Bowdoin, MT
81 Charles M. Russell, MT
82 Medicine Lake, MT
83 Crosby WMD, ND
84 Lostwood, ND
85 Des Lacs, ND
86 Upper Souris, ND
87 J. Clark Salyer, ND
88 Sullys Hill NGP, ND
89 Devils Lake WMD, ND
90 Agassiz, MN
91 Arrowwood, ND
92 Audubon, ND
93 Lake Ilo, ND
94 Long Lake, ND
95 Kulm WMD, ND
96 Valley City WMD, ND
97 Tamarac, MN

98 Detroit Lakes WMD, MN
99 Fergus Falls WMD, MN
100 Tewaukon, ND
101 Sand Lake, SD
102 Waubay, SD
103 Morris WMD, MN
104 Big Stone, MN
105 Madison WMD, SD
106 Lake Andes, SD
107 Karl E. Mundt, SD
108 Lacreek, SD
109 Fort Niobrara, NE
110 Valentine, NE
111 Crescent Lake, NE
112 De Soto, IA
113 Rainwater Basin WMD, NE
114 Squaw Creek, MO
115 Kirwin, KS
116 Quivira, KS
117 Flint Hills, KS
118 Salt Plains, OK
119 Optima, OK
120 Washita, OK
121 Sequoyah, OK
122 Wichita Mountains, OK
123 Tishomingo, OK
124 Hagerman, TX
125 Rio Grande Valley, TX
126 Santa Ana, TX
127 Laguna Atascosa, TX
128 Aransas, TX
129 San Bernard, TX
130 Brazoria, TX
131 Attwater Prairie Chicken, TX
132 Anahuac, TX
133 McFaddin, TX
134 Texas Point, TX
135 Sabine, LA
136 Lacassine, LA
137 Delta, LA
138 Breton, LA
139 Mississippi Sandhill Crane Complex, MS
140 Catahoula, LA
141 Choctaw, AL
142 Panther Swamp, MS
143 Hillside, MS
144 Morgan Brake, MS
145 Noxubee, MS
146 Yazoo, MS
147 D'Arbonne, LA
148 Upper Ouachita, LA

1 San Juan Islands, WA
2 Dungeness, WA
3 Nisqually, WA
4 Kootenai, ID
5 Willapa, WA
6 Columbian White-tailed Deer, WA
7 Toppenish, WA
8 Columbia, WA
9 Turnbull, WA
10 McNary, WA
11 Cold Springs, OR
12 McKay Creek, OR
13 Umatilla, OR
14 Conboy Lake, WA
15 Ridgefield, OR
16 Lewis and Clark, OR
17 Cape Meares, OR
18 Baskett Slough, OR
19 Ankeny, OR
20 William L. Finley, OR
21 Klamath Forest, OR
22 Upper Klamath, OR
23 Bear Valley, OR

24 Lower Klamath, CA
25 Humboldt Bay, CA
26 Tule Lake, CA
27 Clear Lake, CA
28 Modoc, CA
29 Sheldon, NV
30 Hart Mountain National Antelope Refuge, OR
31 Malheur, OR
32 Deer Flat, ID
33 Sacramento, CA
34 Delevan, CA
35 Colusa, CA
36 Sutter, CA
37 Fallon, NV
38 Stillwater, NV
39 Ruby Lake, NV
40 San Pablo Bay, CA
41 Antioch Dunes, CA
42 San Francisco Bay, CA
43 Kesterson, CA
44 San Luis, CA
45 Merced, CA

(Figure 14 continued)

149 Felsenthal, AR
150 White River, AR
151 Holla Bend, AR
152 Wapanocca, AR
153 Lower Hatchie, TN
154 Hatchie, TN
155 Big Lake, AR
156 Lake Isom, TN
157 Reelfoot, TN
158 Mingo, MO
159 Crab Orchard, IL
160 Gilbert Lake, IL
161 Calhoun, IL
162 Batchtown, IL
163 Clarence Cannon, MO
164 Delair, IL
165 Mark Twain, IL
166 Gardner, IL
167 Swan Lake, MO
168 Chautauqua, IL
169 Keithsburg, IL
170 Louisa, IA
171 Big Timber, IA
172 Savanna, IL
173 Cassville, WI
174 Union Slough, IA
175 Lansing, IA
176 La Crosse, WI
177 Horicon, WI
178 Necedah, WI
179 Trempealeau, WI
180 Winona, MN
181 Minnesota Valley, MN
182 Litchfield WMD, MN
183 Sherburne, MN
184 Rice Lake, MN
185 Seney, MI
186 Shiawassee, MI
187 Ottawa, OH
188 Erie, PA
189 Iroquois, NY
190 Montezuma, NY
191 Muscatatuck, IN
192 Cross Creeks, TN
193 Tennessee, TN
194 Wheeler, AL
195 Blowing Wind Cave, AL
196 Piedmont, GA
197 Eufaula, AL
198 Saint Vincent, FL
199 Saint Marks, FL

200 Lower Suwannee, FL
201 Cedar Keys, FL
202 Chassahowitzka, FL
203 Pinellas, FL
204 Egmont Key, FL
205 Passage Key, FL
206 Caloosahatchee, FL
207 Matlacha Pass, FL
208 Island Bay, FL
209 Pine Island, FL
210 J. N. "Ding" Darling, FL
211 Great White Heron, FL
212 Key West, FL
213 National Key Deer, FL
214 Loxahatchee, FL
215 Hobe Sound, FL
216 Pelican Island, FL
217 Merritt Island, FL
218 Lake Woodruff, FL
219 Okefenokee, GA
220 Wolf Island, GA
221 Blackbeard Island, GA
222 Harris Neck, GA
223 Wassaw, GA
224 Tybee, GA
225 Savannah, SC
226 Pinckney Island, SC
227 Cape Romain, SC
228 Santee, SC
229 Carolina Sandhills, SC
230 Pee Dee, NC
231 Cedar Island, NC
232 Swanquarter, NC
233 Mattamuskeet, NC
234 Pungo, NC
235 Pea Island, NC
236 Mackay Island, NC
237 Great Dismal Swamp, VA
238 Back Bay, VA
239 Presquile, VA
240 Chincoteague, VA
241 Blackwater, MD
242 Mason Neck, VA
243 Eastern Neck, MD
244 Prime Hook, DE
245 Bombay Hook, DE
246 Brigantine, NJ
247 Barnegat, NJ
248 Tinicum, PA
249 Great Swamp, NJ
250 Oyster Bay, NY

251 Target Rock, NY
252 Morton, NY
253 Block Island, RI
254 Ninigret, RI
255 Salt Meadow, CN
256 Trustom Pond, RI
257 Sachuest Point, RI
258 Nantucket, MA
259 Monomoy, MA
260 Great Meadows, MA

261 Parker River, MA
262 Oxbow, MA
263 Wapack, NH
264 Rachel Carson, ME
265 Franklin Island, ME
266 Petit Manan, ME
267 Cross Island, ME
268 Moosehorn, ME
269 Missisquoi, VT

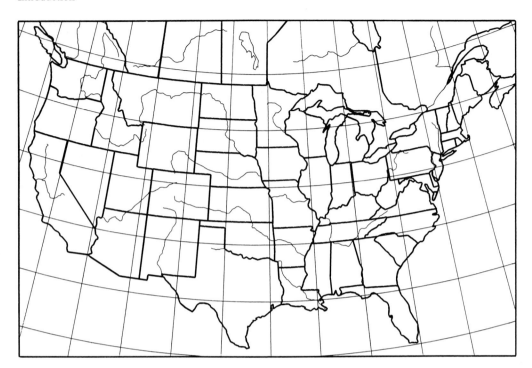

Figure 15.   State and province boundaries, along with the major rivers, and 5° latitude/longitude lines.

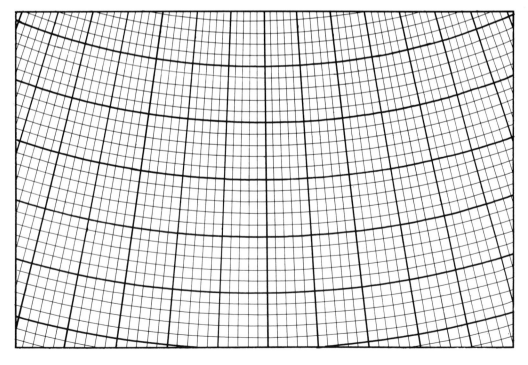

Figure 16.   Outline map of the area examined with 1° latitude/longitude lines.

Species Accounts

A description of the association between environmental factors and the biogeographic pattern of the species accompanies each map. A brief summary of the winter ecology of each bird is also included, but an exhaustive search of the literature on wintering ecology was not feasible. The highlights of the biogeographic patterns of birds without maps are also presented. When possible the species have been ordered according to the American Ornithologists' Union *Check-list of North American Birds* (AOU 1983). Rearrangements were sometimes necessary, but every attempt was made to keep phylogenetically related species together (Mayr and Short 1970; AOU 1983). Appendix A lists the species in the order presented in the text.

Overall Diversity

Knowing the continentwide distributions of virtually all birds wintering in North America provides a way to determine the diversity or species richness of birds across the continent. At each count site, I tallied the total number of species observed out of the 508 species examined and plotted these values. Figure 17 shows that most of the species occur in the warmer areas of the United States, with the highest densities in southern Florida and southwestern California.

Further Studies

Additional large-scale studies are needed; pervasive patterns due to environmental factors can be detected at a broad scale but are easily overlooked in spatially restricted studies. Such extensive studies are rare, but those available in the literature (e.g., McNab 1973; Root 1988a,b) indeed demonstrate that general patterns are present. For example, a large majority of species examined in this atlas have the northern, eastern, and western boundaries of their wintering ranges strongly associated with isopleths of various environmental factors (86.7% of the species examined, 70.5% and 80.0%, respectively). The three factors most often associated with birds' winter range limits are average minimum January temperature, mean length of frost-free period, and vegetation (Root 1988a). The northern boundaries of wintering passerines appear to be limited by the energy demands of cold ambient temperatures. Passerines seem to be expanding their ranges north only to the point where raising their metabolic rate to about 2.5 times their basal rate will allow them to keep warm through the night (Root 1988b). Thus, I strongly urge that more studies at a large scale be done, because as more evidence is amassed, we will better understand the factors that shape the distribution and abundance of species.

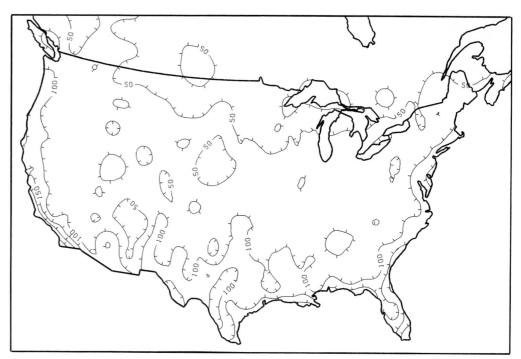

Figure 17. Contour map of the total density of wintering species, out of a possible 508 species. The contour interval is fifty individuals, and the tick marks point toward smaller values.

How to Read the Contour Maps

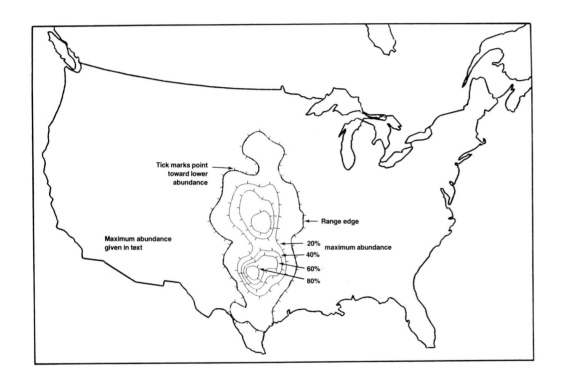

Tick marks point
toward lower
abundance

Range edge

Maximum abundance
given in text

20%
40%   maximum abundance
60%
80%

SPECIES ACCOUNTS

GAVIIDAE

Red-throated Loon (*Gavia stellata*) Maximum: 5.30 I/Hr

The Red-throated Loon winters along both the Pacific and Atlantic coasts, apparently where the average winter ocean-surface temperature is less than 62°F (16°C). On the eastern seaboard this incorporates the region from northern Georgia north to New Brunswick and Nova Scotia. In the West the water temperature along the entire length of the study area is less than 60°F (15°C), and this loon is present all along the Pacific coast. The winter range of the Red-throated Loon extends to northern Baja California (AOU 1983), about where the surface-water temperature rises above 62°F (16°C). The out-of-place population in Montana is due to a rare sighting of one individual at Glacier National Park in 1968.

Unlike the overall range of the Red-throated Loon, the abundance peaks do not seem to be strongly associated with either ambient or ocean-surface temperature. The population with the highest density is in southern North Carolina around Cape Fear, south of Wilmington. Less concentrated populations are found on the Atlantic coast around Delaware Bay and Albemarle Sound in northern North Carolina and between Point Arena and Point Reyes on the west coast.

The diet of the Red-throated Loon consists mainly of small fish, which it catches by pursuit underwater. This bird is a very good underwater swimmer, moving faster than a person can run along the beach. When it swims along the surface, its body can be either partly or wholly submerged. Observations in shallow, clear water show that this loon uses both its feet and its wings to propel itself underwater. It usually lands on water, using the water as a brake by plowing into it. In the fall individuals migrate along the coasts, usually alone (Bent 1919).

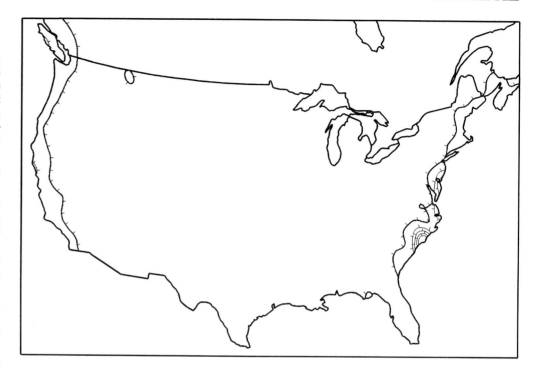

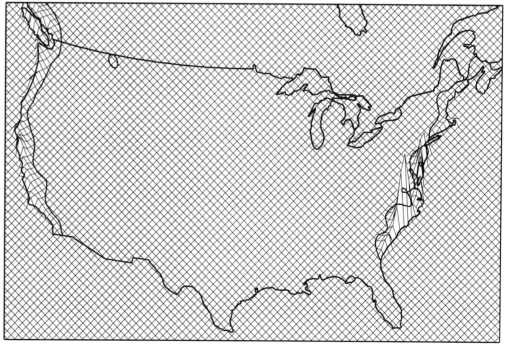

Red-throated Loon

GAVIIDAE

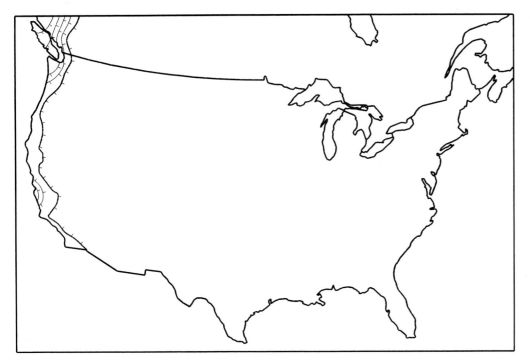

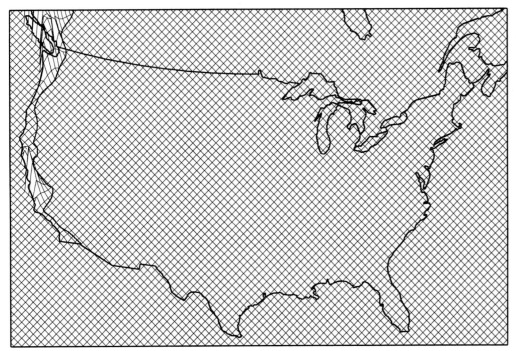

Pacific Loon (*Gavia pacifica*) Maximum: 5.40 I/Hr

The winter distribution of the Pacific Loon in North America stretches the entire length of the Pacific coast, with the northern limit extending into Alaska and the southern limit occurring in southern Baja California (AOU 1983). Thus, like the Red-throated Loon, this species frequents the cooler surface waters of the temperate regions rather than the warmer waters of more tropical areas.

The highest concentration of Pacific Loons in the United States and southern Canada is in British Columbia around Vancouver Island (5.40 I/Hr). In the area examined, this region has the coolest mean winter ocean-surface temperatures, with values below 40°F (4°C). A less concentrated population is found around Monterey Bay. Here a deep underwater canyon forces cooler water to the surface relatively near the shore. Pacific Loons migrate into Monterey Bay about mid-November and are then the most common loons in the area. They are usually solitary or in pairs and stay about 1 to 5 miles (2–8 km) offshore (Baltz and Morejohn 1977). The highest ten-year mean abundance recorded on a North American CBC was outside the study area, near Point Whiteshed, Alaska, where 26.40 individuals were seen per hour of count effort.

Like most loons, the Pacific Loon mainly eats small fish captured by underwater pursuit. A fish is brought to the surface between the mandibles, then swallowed headfirst. This loon uses both its feet and its wings when swimming underwater (Bent 1919).

Common Loon (*Gavia immer*) Map in Appendix B

The Common Loon winters regularly along all three coasts and exhibits sporadic wanderings throughout the interior of the continent. The most concentrated populations are found along the South Carolina coast (2.15 I/Hr), and other abundant populations occur along the coasts around Vancouver Island, in Humboldt National Wildlife Refuge in northern California, on the Florida panhandle, and along the Atlantic seaboard from Massachusetts to Maine. The numerous irregular sightings of this loon may provide misleading information about the distribution and abundance patterns for its wintering areas. Thus its map is included in appendix B.

Common Loon

Pacific Loon

PODICIPEDIDAE

Least Grebe (*Tachybaptus dominicus*) No Map

All nineteen site locations reporting the Least Grebe were in extreme southern Texas along the lower Rio Grande valley. This grebe was sighted in five or more years at only six of these locales. Of these sites, the La Sal Vieja count had the highest ten-year mean, with 0.39 Least Grebes seen for each hour the parties spent counting.

Pied-billed Grebe (*Podilymbus podiceps*) Maximum: 2.77 I/Hr

The Pied-billed Grebe uses freshwater habitats more often than any other grebe except the Least Grebe (Bent 1919). The winter distribution of the Pied-billed Grebe covers an extensive inland area. Besides freshwater habitats, ambient temperatures appear to strongly influence its winter distribution. Grebes are present chiefly where the temperature is warm enough to keep the lakes from freezing over completely. This includes areas where the average minimum January temperature is over 20°F (6°C). The major exception is the dense population on the Great Salt Lake in Utah, which rarely freezes because of its high salinity.

The densest populations occur chiefly on large lakes and on wide rivers. Both of the highest abundance peaks are in southern Texas: one is near San Angelo, by Twin Buttes Reservoir and O. C. Fisher Lake, the other is in the extreme southern corner of Texas along the lower Rio Grande valley. Northeast of these populations is a less dense concentration on Cedar Creek Reservoir southeast of Dallas. Less dense populations are also present on the Great Salt Lake in Utah, on Lake Mead along the border between Nevada and Utah, and in the San Joaquin valley of California.

This little grebe eats small fish, snails, frogs, and aquatic insects. When threatened, the bird escapes either by diving underwater or by hiding among vegetation. It rarely evades danger by taking flight, because it has some difficulty in getting airborne. Like the other grebes, it must run along the water to get enough power to take off. Taking off from land or ice is impossible because grebes' center of gravity is too far back for them to run along a hard surface (Bent 1919).

Western and Clark's Grebes (*Aechmophorus occidentalis* and *A. clarkii*) Map in Appendix B

The data for the Western Grebe and Clark's Grebe are grouped together in the CBC data examined. The combined winter distribution of these grebes stretches along the Pacific coast, with an inland population around Lake Mead. The highest abundances are near the Strait of Georgia and Lake Mead. Their joint densities, however, are highly variable in the winter. For example, the number of individuals seen per hour of count effort ranged from zero to 243.90 on the Henderson, Nevada, count, which includes Las Vegas Bay of Lake Mead. Thus, the resulting maps may be misleading and hence are included in appendix B.

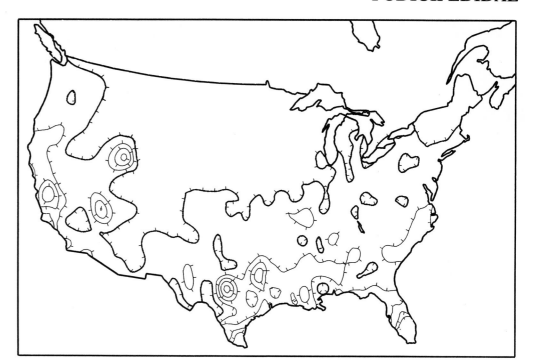

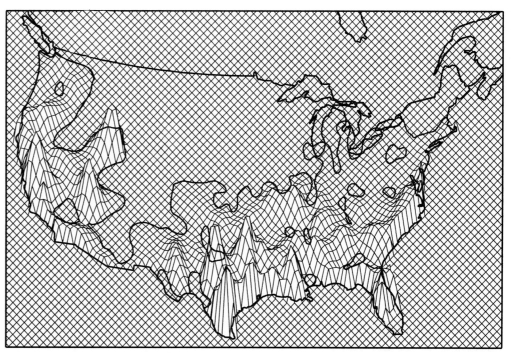

PODICIPEDIDAE

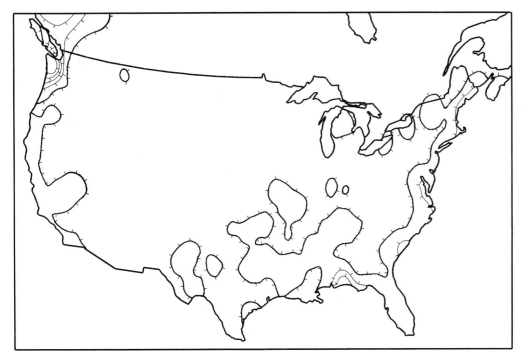

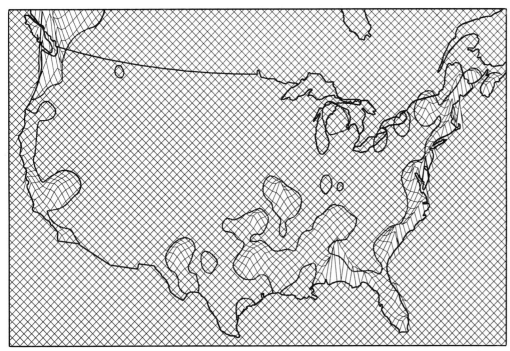

Horned Grebe (*Podiceps auritus*) Maximum: 6.00 I/Hr

Normally, in late November Horned Grebes migrate from their breeding areas to coastal wintering grounds (Eaton 1983). They usually travel singly or in small groups, and except for inland populations, the winter flocks are small (Bent 1919). The abundance maps show some wintering inland populations, but most, though certainly not all, are ephemeral. These inland populations are found along rivers or lakes where the minimum January temperature is over 30°F (-1°C). Ambient temperature, however, does not seem to determine the presence of Horned Grebes along the coasts.

All the most concentrated populations of this grebe are along the coasts, particularly in areas that are protected to some degree, such as around wildlife refuges or national seashores. The densest population is around Olympic National Park and Cape Flattery in the northwest corner of Washington State. The next most concentrated population is on the Gulf coast around the Gulf Islands National Seashore, just south of Pensacola, Florida. On the Atlantic coast there are a few low-density populations, which correspond to the locations of refuges. One is in South Carolina, centered on Cape Romain National Wildlife Refuge. Farther north there is a concentration along the southern shore of Chesapeake Bay. Even farther north, a slight concentration of Horned Grebes stretches from southern Cape Cod to Canada. The protection offered by the numerous wildlife refuges—Sachuest Point, Nantucket, Monomoy, Parker River, Rachel Carson, Franklin Island, Petit Manan Cross Island, and Moosehorn—undoubtedly contributes to this higher concentration. The Common Loon also has several abundance peaks that correspond in location to those of the Horned Grebe.

Horned Grebes' primary foraging behavior is underwater pursuit. Along the coasts they eat shrimp, various crustaceans, and minnows, whereas inland their diet is restricted to small fish. As with the other grebes, a large portion of their stomach contents consists of feathers, but the reason they ingest such nonnutritive material is an enigma. When alarmed this grebe escapes by diving, and it must run on open water to get airborne (Bent 1919). Because of this, many birds die if lakes freeze suddenly (Eaton 1983).

Horned Grebe

Horned Grebe

Red-necked Grebe (*Podiceps grisegena*) Maximum: 3.97 I/Hr

Unlike the other grebes, the wintering Red-necked Grebe is restricted to coastal habitats. The only exception shown on the map is a rare sighting of one individual on the Mason Valley count in Nevada in 1971. Within this count circle is a 220-acre cooling pond for the Fort Churchill power plant, which presumably is where the off-course grebe was seen. The more usual winter habitat is just beyond the waves (Bent 1919) of the colder water of the Atlantic and Pacific. On the Pacific coast it frequents waters with a mean surface temperature of 55°F (12°C) or less. This includes the area from Morro Bay northward. Along the Atlantic seaboard birds winter north of Chesapeake Bay, where the average surface water is colder than about 50°F (10°C). The Gulf of Saint Lawrence probably is avoided because fairly extensive areas normally are covered with ice.

Fairly calm, protected waters are optimal wintering areas for the Red-necked Grebe. There are two populations with very high abundances, both on the northern international border but along different coasts. One is around Vancouver Island in the Strait of Georgia, the other in the Bay of Fundy.

When foraging, the Red-necked Grebe pursues small fish, crayfish, and aquatic insects underwater, catching them between its mandibles rather than impaling them. For propulsion underwater, it uses just its feet, not its wings. To escape enemies, it swims away either on the surface or underwater (Bent 1919).

Eared Grebe (*Podiceps nigricollis*) Map in Appendix B

Unfortunately, at some locations the Eared Grebe congregates in extremely large flocks, making it impossible to achieve accurate density counts. When mapping these data, the few high counts overshadow the populations with fewer individuals. Thus, the map may be misleading and is included in appendix B. In general, the winter distribution of this grebe extends along the Pacific coast south of Vancouver Island and all along the Gulf coast. The highest concentration of birds is on Salton Sea.

PROCELLARIIDAE

Northern Fulmar (*Fulmarus glacialis*) No Map

This pelagic species was observed at seventeen sites along the Pacific coast south of the United States–Canada border and around the Gulf of Saint Lawrence. The count near Monterey Bay, California, recorded the highest average ten-year abundance of those sites where the Northern Fulmar was seen regularly; sightings from nine years resulted in an average abundance of 1.80 individuals per party-hour.

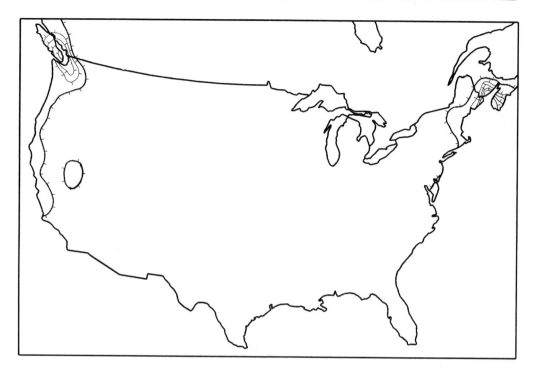

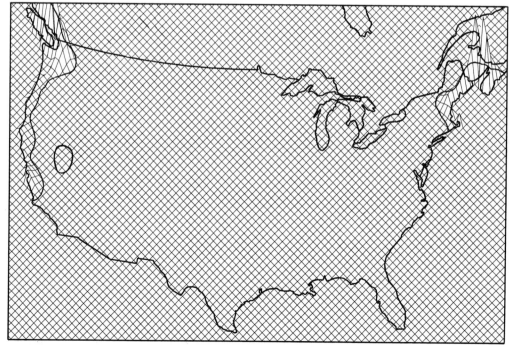

Red-necked Grebe

PROCELLARIIDAE / PELECANIDAE

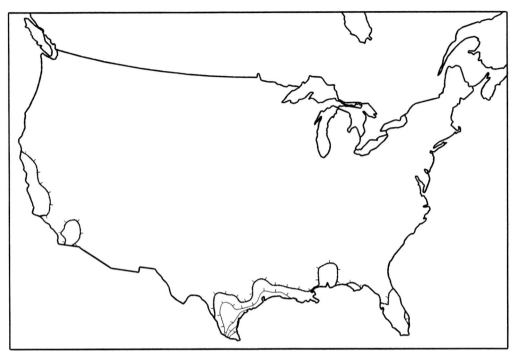

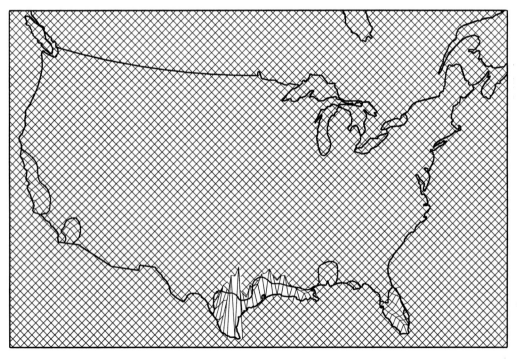

Sooty Shearwater (*Puffinus griseus*) No Map

The Sooty Shearwater was seen in very low numbers and at extremely irregular intervals. Of the fourteen sites reporting this pelagic species, only three California counts (San Clemente, Monterey, and Bodega Bay) reported it in five or more years. The highest average abundance was at San Clemente, with 0.03 individuals seen per hour of count effort.

Manx Shearwater (*Puffinus puffinus*) No Map

The count around Newport Beach, California, reported the Manx Shearwater in eight of the ten years examined, but the average abundance was very low—0.09 individuals seen per party-hour. Only three other sites reported this pelagic species, but at lower abundances and at much less regular intervals.

PELECANIDAE

American White Pelican (*Pelecanus erythrorhynchos*) Maximum: 23.34 I/Hr

Both the distribution and the abundance of the American White Pelican appear to be strongly influenced by temperature. Its range seems to be limited to the areas along the coastlines where the minimum January ambient temperature is over 40°F (4°C). This is true for the populations both on the southern Pacific coast and along the Gulf coast. In southern Florida its range covers areas where the average minimum winter temperature is over 50°F (10°C).

Besides a warm ambient temperature, a high mean ocean-surface temperature in winter seems to strongly influence the habitat preference of the American White Pelican. The highest density of this species is in southern Texas, where the ambient temperature is over 45°F (7°C) and the mean surface-water temperature is over 64°F (17°C). These same conditions occur in southern Florida, but its density is fairly low there, whereas the density of its congener the Brown Pelican is high.

The feeding behaviors of these two pelicans are very different (Bent 1922). The Brown Pelican dives from the air into the water after prey, whereas the American White Pelican forages collectively by swimming along the surface, sometimes in fairly large flocks (Schreiber, Woolfenden, and Curtsinger 1975).

The density of the American White Pelican dropped from the 1940s to the 1960s. Populations started increasing in the 1970s, probably because the United States banned several harmful pesticides (e.g., DDT) and increased protection at national wildlife refuges. The first complete and accurate survey of this pelican, conducted from 1971 to 1981, showed that there were about 18,500 nests in the United States, divided among 14 to 17 nesting colonies, and 33,000 nests in Canada at 50 nesting colonies (Crivelli and Schreiber 1984).

American White Pelican

Brown Pelican (*Pelecanus occidentalis*) Maximum: 6.50 I/Hr

The population density of Brown Pelicans fluctuates, possibly owing to changes in water temperature (Schreiber and Schreiber 1973) and changing density of fish (Anderson and Anderson 1976). Superimposed on these fluctuations was a dramatic decline in the 1940s and 1950s of populations along the California and Gulf coasts, particularly on the Florida shoreline (Schreiber and Schreiber 1973). Eggshell thinning caused by pesticides led to another drastic decline in the 1960s (Crivelli and Schreiber 1984). In 1972 DDT was finally banned, and populations increased until the 1980s, when the density regained pre-DDT levels (Crivelli and Schreiber 1984).

The data examined here were collected primarily when the populations of the Brown Pelican were very low. During this time, the species' distribution extended along the coastlines of both the Pacific Ocean and the Atlantic Ocean where the average surface-water temperature was at least 52°F (11°C). Even though the surface water of the Gulf coast was certainly warm enough for this pelican, with the lowest reading dropping to 62°F (16°C), only one individual was recorded along the coast of Texas (in 1967). Before the population decline in the 1940s and 1950s, birds used to winter along the coasts of the Florida panhandle, Texas, and Louisiana (Schreiber and Schreiber 1973), and a brief examination of more recent CBC data for this region shows they are again present there.

In the 1960s and early 1970s the Brown Pelican's density was depressed, and its highest winter populations were in southern Florida. Like that of the American White Pelican, the Brown Pelican's optimum habitat appears to be determined by temperature not only of the ocean, but also of the air. The peak abundance in peninsular Florida is in a region where the minimum January ambient temperature is over 50°F (10°C) and the water-surface temperature is over 66°F (18°C). The only other place in the United States having these conditions is southern Texas, where the American White Pelican is most abundant.

The foraging behavior of the two species is very different, with the American White Pelican feeding from the surface of the water and the Brown Pelican feeding underwater. The latter plunges for fish, diving into the water from 10 to 50 feet (3–15 m) above the surface (Bent 1922). When foraging, the Brown Pelican will sight and select a prey item, dive for it, chase the prey underwater with its bill closed, open its bill to distend the pouch, then close its bill, trapping the fish (Schreiber, Woolfenden, and Curtsinger 1975). Its diet consists entirely of fish (Bent 1922).

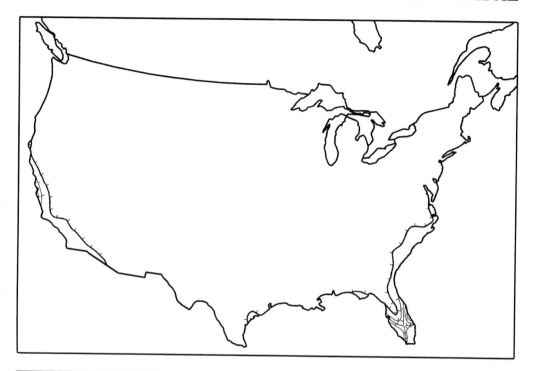

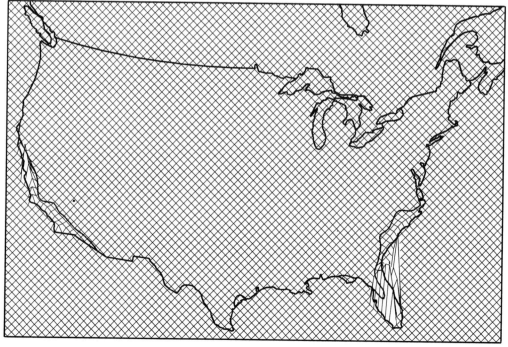

SULIDAE / PHALACROCORACIDAE

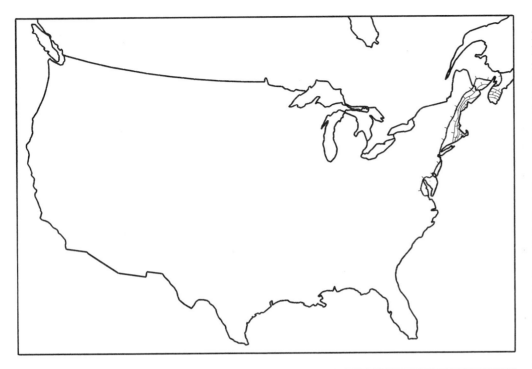

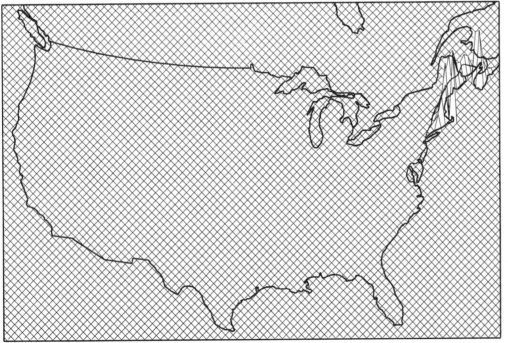

SULIDAE

Northern Gannet (*Sula bassanus*) Map in Appendix B
Even though the Northern Gannet is a pelagic species (AOU 1983), it was recorded at 63 localities along both the Pacific and Atlantic coasts. Its abundance at any one location was highly variable, which reflects its nomadic behavior but unfortunately precludes drawing a meaningful map. Thus, the map is included only in appendix B. The highest average abundance (10.46 I/Hr) was recorded in eastern North Carolina on the Pea Island National Wildlife Refuge count.

PHALACROCORACIDAE

Great Cormorant (*Phalacrocorax carbo*) Maximum: 9.53 I/Hr
The winter distribution of the Great Cormorant is restricted to areas along the Atlantic coast from Chesapeake Bay north. This is where the surface of the Atlantic is coldest, with the average temperature ranging from 42°F (5°C) along the Virginia coast to 30°F (1°C) in the Bay of Fundy.

The surface temperature of the ocean apparently influences where this cormorant winters. The highest abundance of Great Cormorants occurs along the coasts where the mean ocean-surface temperature is between 32°F and 38°F (0°C and 3°C). This encompasses the area from Long Island Sound to the northern end of the Bay of Fundy and also the ocean off the southern tip of Nova Scotia.

The abundance of this species has probably not been greatly affected by humans, because its eggs and meat are unpalatable. Eskimos, however, did use its primary feathers to stabilize their arrows (Bent 1922).

This cormorant's diet consists entirely of fish, which it pursues underwater, using its legs for propulsion (Bent 1922).

Brandt's Cormorant (*Phalacrocorax penicillatus*) No Map
The Brandt's Cormorant was seen on thirty-nine sites, ranging along the Pacific coast from San Diego to Canada. Several of these sightings were sporadic, with birds seen in fewer than half of the ten years examined. Of those sites where it was seen most regularly, the count near Bodega Bay had the highest ten-year average, with 45.29 individuals seen per party-hour.

Pelagic Cormorant (*Phalacrocorax pelagicus*) Map in Appendix B
Even though the Pelagic Cormorant was observed at forty sites, maps are included only in appendix B, because this species is very nomadic. The highest mean abundance was recorded on the Farallon Islands, with 60.15 individuals seen per party-hour, but over the ten years the abundances at this site ranged from 3.40 to 181.80 individuals for each hour of count effort.

Great Cormorant

Double-crested Cormorant (*Phalacrocorax auritus*) Maximum:
33.32 I/Hr

During the period examined, the Double-crested Cormorant wintered primarily along the Pacific, Gulf, and southern Atlantic coasts, with a few extensions inland. Since that time its winter range has extended north to New York, and it occurs irregularly along the Massachusetts coast (K. Parkes, pers. comm.). Ambient temperature seems to influence the presence of this cormorant, which helps explain why it occurs much farther north along the Pacific coast than on the Atlantic seaboard. The areas where the maps indicate it is present and the regions into which it apparently is extending its winter range all have a minimum January temperature over 30°F (−1°C). This even includes the population in eastern New Mexico at the Bitter Lake National Wildlife Refuge.

Temperature is also associated with concentrated populations of the Double-crested Cormorant. The population with the highest density is on the southern tip of Florida, where the ambient and ocean-surface temperatures are both high; the minimum January air temperature is over 50°F (10°C), and the average winter temperature is higher than 66°F (18°C). Temperature, however, is not the only determining factor, because these same warm conditions occur on the southern coast of Texas, where the cormorant is present only in relatively low numbers. Less concentrated populations occur along the coast of North Carolina and upper South Carolina and along the lower Colorado River valley. These high densities apparently are encouraged by the presence of national wildlife refuges.

The Double-crested Cormorant eats fish almost exclusively (Bent 1922). It pursues both bottom and reef fish, catching them between its mandibles. Before eating a fish, a bird comes to the surface and repositions the prey so it can be swallowed headfirst (Owre 1967). The cormorant spends much time swimming on the surface and usually dives for fish from the surface (Bent 1922). Rather than landing on branches or the ground, this bird normally lands on water, dragging its tail as a brake. To take off from the water, it runs along the surface (Owre 1967).

Olivaceous Cormorant (*Phalacrocorax olivaceus*) No Map
Only eighteen sites along the Texas coast and the extreme lower portion of the Rio Grande valley reported the Olivaceous Cormorant. The La Sal Vieja count recorded this species in the most years and at the highest densities. This site encompasses the La Sal Vieja Lakes and is just west of Raymondville in southern Texas. The cormorant was recorded in nine of the ten years, and its density was a mean abundance of 6.46 individuals seen per party-hour.

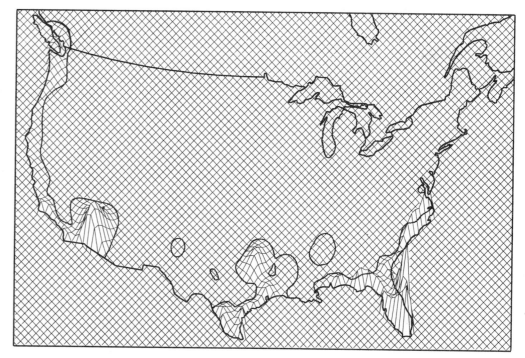

ANHINGIDAE / FREGATIDAE

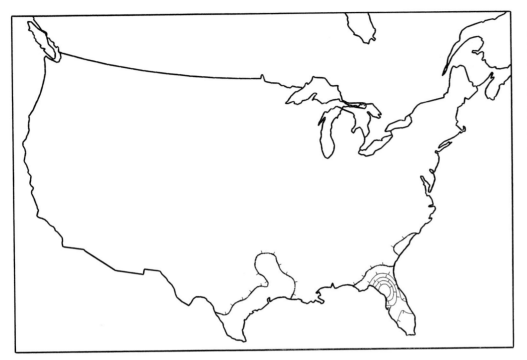

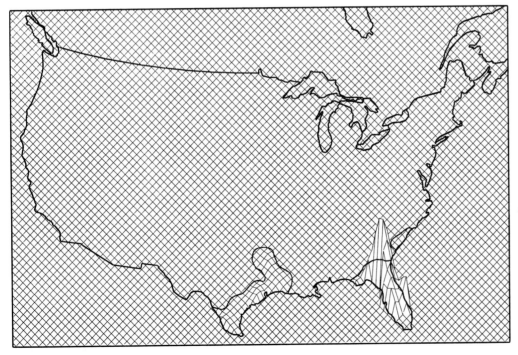

ANHINGIDAE

Anhinga (*Anhinga anhinga*) Maximum: 3.91 I/Hr

Even though the distribution shows the presence of the Anhinga along coastlines, it rarely is found in salt water. This is probably due more to the lack of exposed perches than to an aversion to brackish water, because the species does frequent mangrove marshes in Florida (Owre 1967). The Anhinga occurs in the warmest part of the country; it avoids areas where the average minimum January temperature drops below 40°F (4°C). The exceptions are the populations along the Texas-Louisiana border and along the South Carolina coast. The former is due to rare sightings of one individual in 1972 on the Palestine, Texas, count and twelve individuals in 1963 near Marshall, Texas. The South Carolina populations are not ephemeral and may be influenced by the presence of several national wildlife refuges. The peak abundance around Gainesville, Florida, indicates the optimal nature of the swampland habitat.

The snakebird, as the Anhinga is often called, has that nickname because it frequently is seen swimming with all but its head and neck submerged. When foraging underwater it stalks its prey rather than pursuing it. It mainly eats fish that are laterally flat because it impales its prey. It avoids fish that have thick scales, are bottom dwellers, or swim quickly. The bird's cervical vertebrae and muscles are modified to allow rapid forward motion of the head and bill necessary in capturing prey. The bill is usually held slightly open while hunting, which probably makes it easier to remove impaled fish (Owre 1967). Fish are brought to the surface before being eaten and are repositioned so they can be swallowed headfirst. If need be, large fish are taken to shore and beaten to death. Rather than taking flight when it leaves the water, the Anhinga crawls out on land or onto a branch. To get airborne, birds dive from trees, and instead of alighting in the water they usually land on exposed branches. Once in the air they are good fliers and often can be seen soaring on thermals. The tail has a large surface area that provides lift during flight and is also used as a rudder, a brake, and a prop in a tree.

FREGATIDAE

Magnificent Frigatebird (*Fregata magnificens*) No Map

Of the twenty-three sites reporting the Magnificent Frigatebird, only three were not on the peninsula of Florida, and each of these reported observations only once in the ten years examined. The most reliable place to see this frigatebird is near Vero Beach, Florida. Here the average ten-year abundance was the highest of all the sites, with 0.86 individuals seen per party-hour, and the bird was recorded in each of the ten years.

ARDEIDAE

American Bittern (*Botaurus lentiginosus*) Maximum: 0.23 I/Hr
The American Bittern undergoes an extensive postbreeding dispersal and also migrates out of regions where the temperature frequently dips below freezing (Hancock and Elliott 1978). The abundance maps indicate that this species winters along the coasts, where the oceans moderate the climate. The enigmatic disjunct populations in Texas and New Mexico, and extending inland from the western border, are due to sporadic sightings in regions where temperatures frequently drop below freezing. These individuals probably have not completed their migration. The small population at the west end of Lake Erie centers on the Ottawa National Wildlife Refuge.

National wildlife refuges and marshes strongly affect this bittern's abundance pattern. The highest concentrations are in the Everglades at the southern tip of Florida and in the tule marsh of the San Joaquin River in California. Other marshes where it is at least fairly common include the wetlands near the coast of North Carolina, Okefenokee Swamp on the border between Georgia and Florida, and the swamps along the Louisiana coast. The latter includes the Sabine and Lacassine national wildlife refuges and the Rockefeller and Russell Sage state refuges. The rather dense population in southern California is associated with the Salton Sea National Wildlife Area. The slight peak in northern California is near Honey Lake, and the peak in Mississippi centers on the Noxubee National Wildlife Refuge. Obviously, protected and managed areas with open water are important in determining where the American Bittern winters.

The foraging tactics of this bittern are restricted to standing and waiting for prey to wander close enough to capture or walking slowly and looking for prey. This is the most restricted repertoire of all the North American herons except the Yellow-crowned Night-Heron (Kushlan 1976). The American Bittern is almost exclusively a carnivore, eating small fish, frogs, crayfish, mollusks, snakes, lizards, grasshoppers and other insects, and a few mice (Bent 1926). It usually feeds in shallow, muddy freshwater ponds surrounded by tall reeds and vegetation, but it can be found near salt water and even in meadows (Hancock and Elliott 1978). This is normally a difficult species to census because it usually forages alone (Hancock and Elliott 1978), and its cryptic markings and behavior of pointing its bill in the air allow it to blend in with the reeds around it (Bent 1926).

Least Bittern (*Ixobrychus exilis*) Map in Appendix B
The low densities of the Least Bittern in North America in winter make them difficult to count, which may have caused inaccurate abundance data to be recorded. Thus, maps are included only in appendix B. This bittern winters in southern California and along the Gulf and southern Atlantic coasts. The densest population (0.06 I/Hr) is around the dammed Colorado River between California and Arizona.

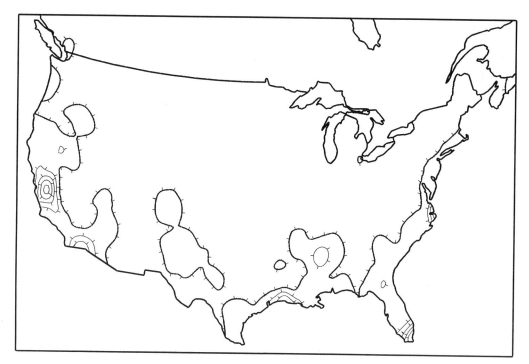

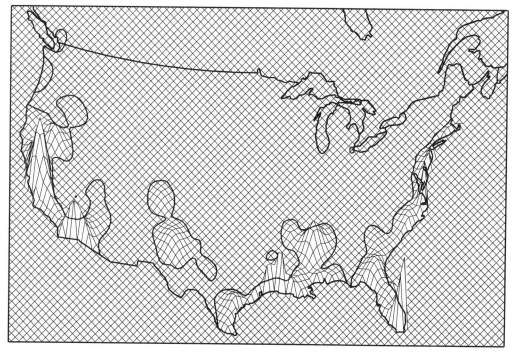

American Bittern

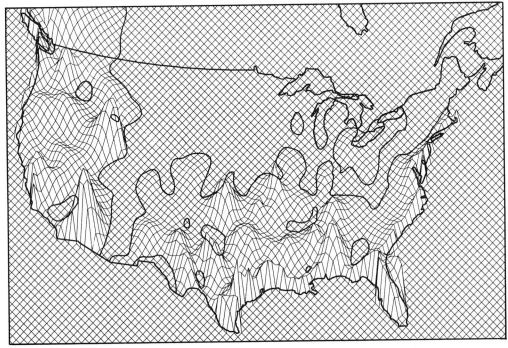

Great Blue Heron, Blue and White Races (*Ardea herodias herodias* and *A. h. occidentalis*) Maximum: 2.45 I/Hr

The Great Blue Heron is probably the best-known heron in North America, because it has such a wide distribution, is so large, and forages in fairly open areas (Bent 1926). The northern limit of the Great Blue Heron's distribution is strongly associated with temperature; this bird generally avoids areas that average colder than 20°F (−6°C) in January. The exceptions are the populations extending north along the Mississippi and Wabash rivers and the two disjunct populations associated with Necedah National Wildlife Refuge in Wisconsin and Ottawa National Wildlife Refuge at the southern tip of Lake Erie. The inland area in southwestern Canada is chiefly an artifact of the interpolation method, because of the high abundance on the coast and few inland counts. This bird does winter in British Columbia, but only along the coast (AOU 1983).

Along with other sources of open water, national wildlife refuges are important in shaping the abundance pattern of the Great Blue Heron. The densest population occurs near the Imperial and Cibola national wildlife refuges on the southern Colorado River. The next highest densities occur around the Great Salt Lake and near Aransas National Wildlife Refuge on the Texas coast.

The density of herons at the southern tip of Florida does not include data on the white race, which was previously considered a separate species. White individuals were seen throughout central and southern Florida, but more regularly around the Keys. The densest population was around Cape Sable on Florida Bay, where 1.88 individuals were seen each party-hour.

Even though they roost in large groups, Great Blue Herons usually feed alone (Bovino and Burtt 1979). Foraging tactics include the standard heron behaviors of standing and waiting and walking slowly. Added to these is wing flicking—suddenly extending and retracting the wings several times while walking slowly. Often a bird will stop after a few flicks to stand and watch (Kushlan 1976). When a fish is caught, the heron tosses it in the air and catches it headfirst to swallow it (Bent 1926). Other foods include frogs, eels, salamanders, tadpoles, grasshoppers, dragonflies, and other insects (Bent 1926). Although some vegetable matter is eaten, this is believed not to contribute nutrients but to help form pellets, which contain fish scales, bones, and the like (Hancock and Elliott 1978). Foraging is more active and successful on overcast days, provided it is not raining or snowing. On sunny days the heron's dark body may be more visible to its prey (Bovino and Burtt 1979).

Great Egret (*Casmerodius albus*) Maximum: 12.98 I/Hr

The fairly high abundance and perhaps even the very existence of the Great Egret are due to efforts of the National Audubon Society and other conservation groups to stop the slaughter of these birds by plume hunters around the turn of the century. The aigrettes—the long, flowing feathers present during the breeding season—were used extensively in the millinery trade in Europe and America. For example, at a London auction in 1902, 1,608 packages of plumes were sold, representing 192,960 birds killed and two to three times as many eggs and chicks left without parents. After extensive education campaigns, primarily by the Audubon Society, laws were passed to protect this egret and its rookeries. By the 1920s the colonies were increasing significantly (Bent 1926).

This egret's distribution, like that of most other herons, is limited to warm areas with open water. Most of its range is in regions that average at least 240 consecutive days a year without frost. The disjunct population around Lake Texoma on the border of Texas and Oklahoma and the extension along the Mississippi-Alabama border are in areas where the frost-free period is a bit shorter: 210 days.

National wildlife refuges play an important role in shaping the Great Egret's abundance pattern. The highest abundance peaks center on the Chassahowitzka refuge on the Gulf coast of Florida and the Sabine refuge on the coast near the Louisiana-Texas border. There is a fairly high peak on the southern Colorado River near the Imperial and Cibola refuges, a preferred area for several other herons as well, including the Least Bittern, Great Blue Heron, Snowy Egret, and Black-crowned Night-Heron. The Great Egret is also rather common around Humboldt Bay National Wildlife Refuge on the California coast.

In the winter this rather shy heron frequently forages with several other individuals and roosts in large groups (Hancock and Elliott 1978). Its foraging activities include the normal heron behaviors of standing and waiting and walking slowly, along with more aggressive actions like hopping, which involves jumping into the air and flying a short distance to catch prey, leapfrog feeding—a variation on hopping that includes flying over other foraging individuals and landing at the front of the flock—and wing flicking, described in the Great Blue Heron account (Kushlan 1976).

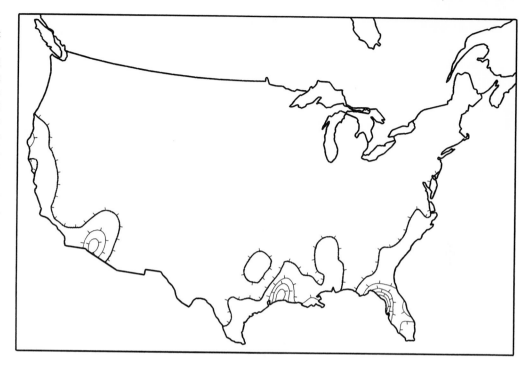

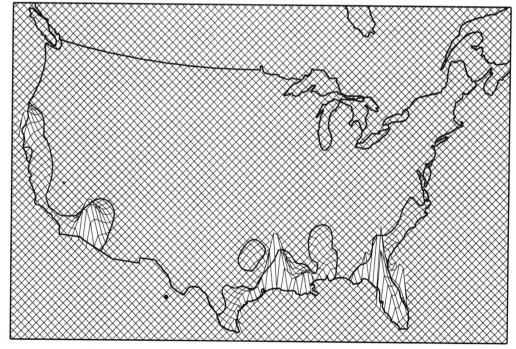

Great Egret

ARDEIDAE

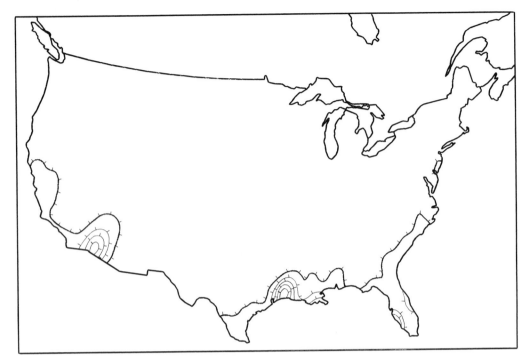

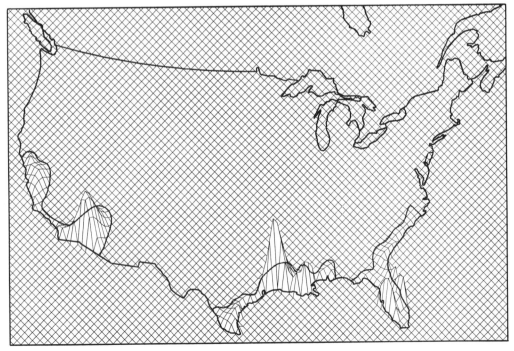

Snowy Egret (*Egretta thula*) Maximum: 14.14 I/Hr

Like the Great Egret, this species was decimated by plume hunters just before the turn of the century. Even more Snowy Egrets than Great Egrets were killed; their plumes were in more demand because they are shorter and softer, individuals were easier to find because they are not as shy, and Snowy Egrets were more abundant. Using extensive education campaigns in the United States and Europe, the National Audubon Society was able to end this senseless "fashion" slaughter before any of the herons became extinct (Bent 1926).

The Snowy Egret is present in regions that have a frost-free period of more than about 260 days a year. This includes the populations on the Pacific coast, in the San Joaquin valley, and around the border between California and Arizona. The small but fairly regular populations in New Jersey, however, are where the frost-free period is only 210 days. Another anomaly in the species' distribution is that it avoids the swampland in eastern North Carolina. This area offers what appears to be an adequate environment for this heron as well as the White Ibis, Green-backed Heron, and Least Bittern, but they all avoid this region. The American Bittern, Great Blue Heron, and Black-crowned Night-Heron, however, are present.

The areas of high abundance show that the Snowy Egret frequents wet, swampy habitats in winter. The highest peak is near the Louisiana-Texas border around the Sabine National Wildlife Refuge and the Rockefeller State Refuge. To the east of this area along the coast, the density of Snowy Egrets stays fairly high, and it reaches a lesser peak around the mouth of the Mississippi River near the Delta National Wildlife Refuge. Another rather high peak is attained at the inland, freshwater location at the southern end of the Colorado River around the Imperial and Cibola national wildlife refuges. In Florida dense populations occur around Charlotte Harbor near the Island Bay refuge, and there is a lesser peak on the east coast around Cocoa Beach.

Around salt water, the Snowy Egret feeds primarily on shrimp. Its diet also includes fish, snails, crabs, frogs, lizards, grasshoppers, and cutworms (Bent 1926). Its foraging activities are variable. Inland it can be found capturing prey disturbed by foraging cattle (Hancock and Elliott 1978). Around water, it often uses White Ibis to flush prey (Courser and Dinsmore 1975). More typical foraging behaviors include standing and waiting and walking slowly, along with more active methods like running and hopping and using its light-colored feet to disturb prey by stirring, raking, probing, and paddling (Kushlan 1976).

Snowy Egret

Little Blue Heron (*Egretta caerulea*) Maximum: 20.41 I/Hr

Even though plume hunters were not killing Little Blue Herons for their feathers, they caused the abundance of this and other nonpersecuted herons to decline by disturbing the multispecies breeding areas. Adult herons were forced to leave their nests, exposing eggs and chicks to the elements and opportunistic crows (Bent 1926; Hancock and Elliott 1978). The encroachment of civilization has also negatively affected this fairly shy heron (Bent 1926). It needs extensive areas of shallow water where it can forage for fish, crayfish, crabs, frogs, lizards, snakes, spiders, and insects, but such wetlands are being drained (Hancock and Elliott 1978). During the breeding season this heron frequents, perhaps even prefers, freshwater inland habitats (Bent 1926; Hancock and Elliott 1978). Its wintering grounds in the United States, however, are primarily coastal, including the Gulf and Atlantic coasts. The Little Blue Heron's distribution is in areas having at least 210 consecutive days a year without frost.

The most concentrated population of wintering Little Blue Herons is in the southern Louisiana bayous, around the mouth of the Mississippi River. The protected and managed region of the Delta National Wildlife Refuge has probably influenced this high abundance. This peak is much higher than those at other locations and consequently overshadows them. The three-dimensional map shows a few increases in abundance that are too low to appear on the two-dimensional contour map. These slight peaks indicate a tendency for this heron to be more common along the west coast of Florida from around Perry to Citrus Springs and from Tampa Bay to Naples, and along Florida's east coast around Daytona Beach.

Of all the herons except the Snowy Egret and the Tricolored Heron, the Little Blue Heron uses the most diverse foraging behaviors. These include the standard methods of standing and waiting and walking slowly, along with more active pursuit of prey by walking quickly, running, hopping (jumping in the air and flying a very short distance), leapfrog feeding (similar to hopping but the position in the feeding flock changes), and diving feet first. It also performs various aerial feeding behaviors such as dipping, where a bird catches its prey near the surface of the water while flying; hovering, which is similar except that it does not move forward; and dragging one or both feet through the water while flying. Another active, prey-disturbing method is raking the substrate with a foot while walking. Wings may also be used in foraging by flicking or by opening them completely (Kushlan 1976).

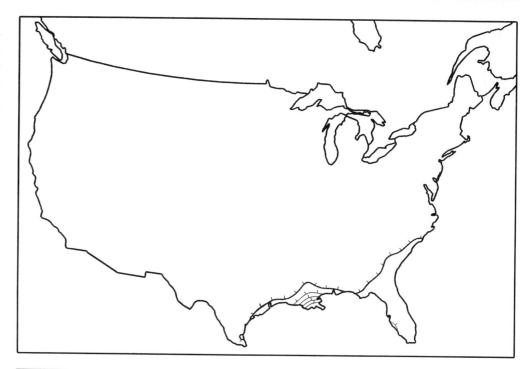

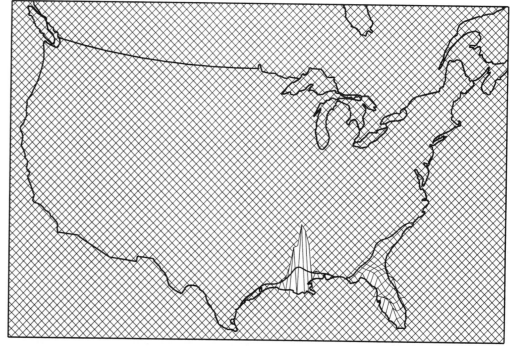

Little Blue Heron

ARDEIDAE

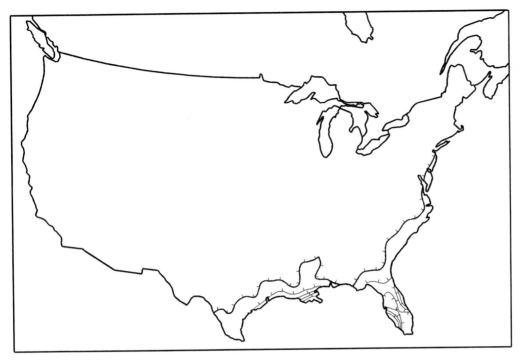

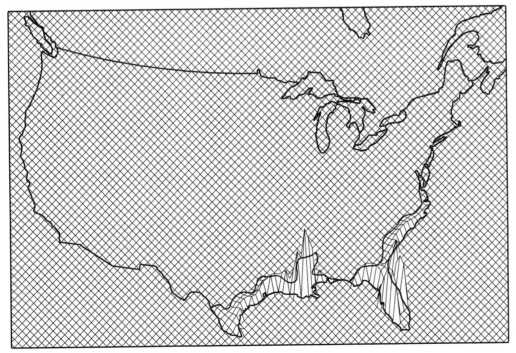

Tricolored Heron (*Egretta tricolor*) Maximum: 4.81 I/Hr
The overall distribution of the Tricolored Heron reflects its need for warm coastal environments. It is present where the ocean moderates the climate so that the frost-free period is at least 240 days long.

This bird has been reported as the most common heron in Florida (Hancock and Elliott 1978), but the abundance pattern shows the densest population in the Louisiana bayous, extending from the mouth of the Mississippi River along the coast to Anahuac National Wildlife Refuge in Texas. The region of high abundance encompasses several national and state refuges, including Sabine, Lacassine, Rockefeller, Russell Sage, Shell Keys, and Delta. In Florida this heron occurs in high abundance around Cocoa Beach and on the Gulf coast around Charlotte Harbor near Fort Myers. It is basically common throughout the Florida peninsula, except at the southern tip in the Everglades and in the area from Crystal River inland to just west of Orlando and south to Tampa Bay. It is uncommon in the latter region because the environment is fairly dry, with few marshy habitats. The reasons it is uncommon in the Everglades are not so obvious. Perhaps high abundances of other heron species restrict it. More intense fieldwork is needed to determine what factors deter it from this area.

Throughout its distribution the Tricolored Heron is found foraging in shallow water (Hancock and Elliott 1978) in marshes, ponds, rice fields, bays, or estuaries (Bent 1926). It eats fish, amphibians, crustaceans, gastropods, leeches, worms, spiders, and grasshoppers (Hancock and Elliott 1978). Apart from the Snowy Egret, this heron employs more foraging behaviors than any other. They include those utilized by the Little Blue Heron plus feeding while swimming, stirring the sediment while hovering or standing, feeding in the shadow of outstretched wings (Kushlan 1976), and feeding on prey flushed by the White Ibis (Courser and Dinsmore 1975).

Reddish Egret (*Egretta rufescens*) No Map
This actively feeding heron occurs sporadically from Texas to Florida along the Gulf coast and along the Atlantic south of the Florida-Georgia border. Its densest populations are around Laguna Largo (0.63 I/Hr), which is just south of Corpus Christi, Texas, and in southern Florida (0.59 I/Hr) near Tavernier on the Florida Keys.

Tricolored Heron

Cattle Egret (*Bubulcus ibis*) Maximum: 66.67 I/Hr

The Cattle Egret has become "one of the great avian success stories" because it has recently expanded its range throughout the world (Hancock and Elliott 1978). It was first recorded on Christmas counts in 1958, with an average of about 0.20 birds seen per party-hour in the United States. By 1972 the average had increased exponentially to about 1.20 individuals per party-hour (Bock and Lepthien 1976a). During this time of general increase, its numbers were negatively affected by cold weather in Florida and Louisiana in 1962, 1963, and 1968. Although other cold winters occurred in these two states in 1958 and 1964, they did not have a negative impact on the egret's abundance, probably because its density was already so low that the relatively few birds were able to concentrate in warmer areas farther south (Bock and Lepthien 1976a).

The overall distribution of this species shows that this egret indeed requires warm areas that are not too swampy. Most of the range is in regions where the temperature rarely falls below 40°F (4°C) in January. The exception is the extension on the coastal plains of Texas as far north as the Dallas–Fort Worth area. Cattle Egrets are seen fairly regularly there and are somehow able to endure the colder temperatures.

The two densest populations occur on the Florida peninsula. One is near Perry, stretching inland around Gainesville and south to Tampa Bay. The other is at the southern tip of Florida around Miami and in the Everglade swamps. The next most dense population is in the warm, dry areas of the Salton Sea. Another warm, dry area where this egret is fairly common is the low coastal plains of southern Texas. An equally dense population occurs in the swampy bayous at the mouth of the Mississippi River in Louisiana.

This egret prefers to forage in open habitats that are drier than those used by other herons wintering in North America. Cattle Egrets primarily eat grasshoppers and other insects but also feed on lizards, frogs, and small mammals. They need water nearby because they often drink (Hancock and Elliott 1978). Foraging tactics include the normal heron behaviors of standing and waiting and walking slowly, along with active pursuit by walking quickly, running, hopping, gleaning, and aerial and standby fly catching (Kushlan 1976). Heatwole (1965) found that by foraging around cattle this egret obtains 50% more food while expending two-thirds less energy. Perhaps the birds around Dallas–Fort Worth are making use of this foraging method, thereby reducing the energy needed to find food.

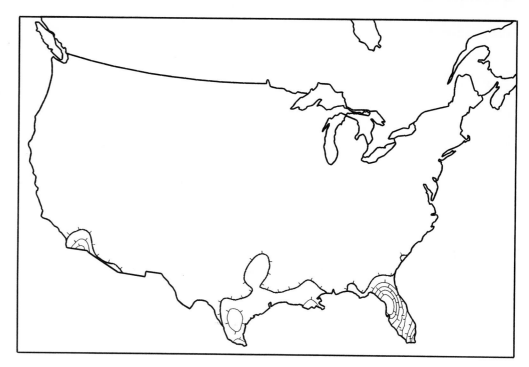

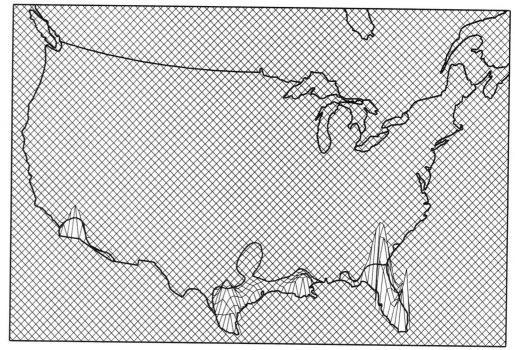

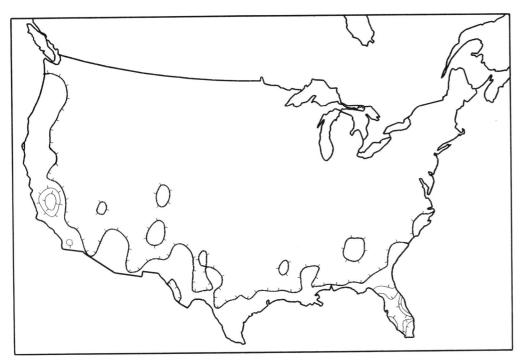

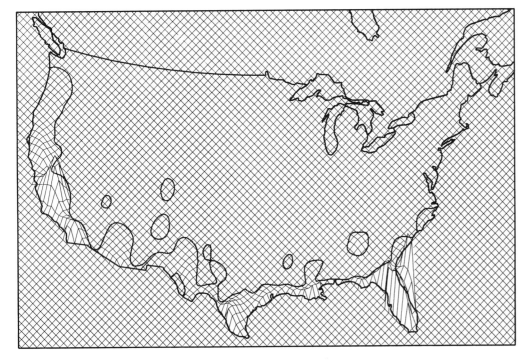

Green-backed Heron (*Butorides striatus*) Maximum: 1.01 I/Hr

The Green-backed Heron has a very convoluted border to its range. There are several extensions away from the main distribution and many disjunct populations that result because very few individuals are observed in only one or two years. These birds presumably have not yet started to migrate or are in the process. Warmth apparently helps determine where this species winters, since it is present where the average length of the frost-free period is 240 days or more.

The densest populations of Green-backed Herons winter throughout most of peninsular Florida. Particularly high abundances occur on the east coast from around Cocoa Beach to West Palm Beach and on the west coast around Charlotte Harbor, near Fort Myers. There are fairly low numbers in the Everglades. In California this heron is fairly common in the tule marsh between Fresno and Bakersfield. The Kern and Pixley national wildlife refuges have played an important role in protecting marsh habitat, which attracts large numbers of Green-backed Herons. Unlike several other herons, the Green-backed Heron has not been recorded around the dammed area of the southern Colorado River.

This heron prefers to forage at least partially concealed in dense vegetation around ponds, lakes, and lagoons. In saltwater environments it chooses mangrove-lined coastlines and estuaries, where its feeding times are determined by the tides (Hancock and Elliott 1978). Along the coasts it primarily eats fish. Inland its diet is more diverse, consisting of fish, crayfish, tadpoles, snakes, water bugs of different sorts, earthworms, crickets, grasshoppers, and even a few small mammals (Bent 1926; Hancock and Elliott 1978). The Green-backed Heron's foraging tactics include the usual standing and waiting and walking slowly behaviors used by all herons, but it adds a variation; instead of standing erect, it crouches. It also uses its feet to stir and rake the substrate looking for prey, as well as actively pursuing prey by diving, swimming, and jumping from a perch into the water. This particular species uses baiting—attracting prey by placing an object in the water while it stands and waits (Kushlan 1976).

Green-backed Heron

Green-backed Heron

Black-crowned Night-Heron (*Nycticorax nycticorax*) Maximum: 1.98 I/Hr

Worldwide, the Black-crowned Night-Heron is probably the most abundant heron, and it is certainly the most cosmopolitan (Hancock and Elliott 1978). In the United States its winter distribution and abundance appear to be primarily associated with warm temperatures and national wildlife refuges. The core area of its distribution occurs in regions where at least 240 consecutive days a year are free of frost. All the disjunct populations are in colder areas, but those around San Antonio, Texas, in southern Indiana, and in eastern Kentucky are due to sporadic sightings of a few individuals. Some censuses in colder areas did record this heron regularly—on Lake Erie, where a regular population occurs near Toledo, Ohio, around several national wildlife refuges (Cedar Point, Ottawa, and West Sister Island)—but other sightings north of there are sporadic. There is also a regular population at Bitter Lake National Wildlife Refuge on the Pecos River in New Mexico, but most other sightings in this region are irregular. The populations extending inland from the coasts of eastern Texas and Oregon are also irregular.

Almost all the abundance peaks are around national wildlife refuges. Unexpectedly, the highest peak is inland along the border between Oregon and California, where temperatures fall below freezing in January. There are several wildlife refuges in the area, including Upper Klamath, Lower Klamath, Tule Lake, and Clear Lake. Just west of here on the California coast, a slighter peak is attained around the Humboldt Bay refuge. The next most dense population is in a tule marsh on the San Joaquin River in central California. Still lower peaks occur along the California-Arizona border near the Imperial and Cibola refuges along the southern Colorado River, around the Anahuac refuge near Galveston Bay, Texas, and along the coast by Jacksonville, Florida.

As its name implies, this heron feeds at dusk, at dawn, and through the night (Bent 1926; Hancock and Elliott 1978). When competing species are absent, however, it will feed during the day (Hancock and Elliott 1978). It is a carnivore, primarily eating live fish, frogs, snakes, insects, small mammals, and birds (Bent 1926), but it will also eat animals that have recently died (Hancock and Elliott 1978). Its foraging techniques include, of course, the standard standing and waiting and walking slowly, plus hovering, plunging, feet-first diving, swim feeding, and bill vibrating—standing with the tip of the bill in the water and rapidly opening and closing it to attract prey to the disturbance (Kushlan 1976). These behaviors usually occur on mud flats during low tide or along streams or ponds (Hancock and Elliott 1978).

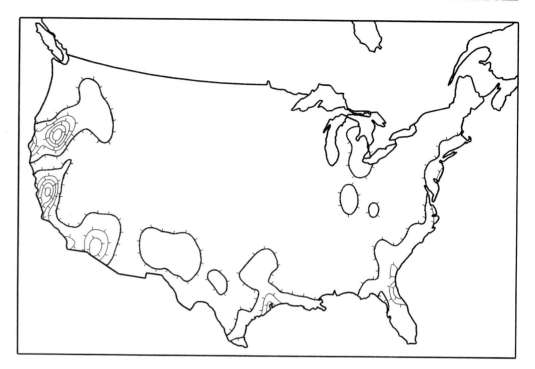

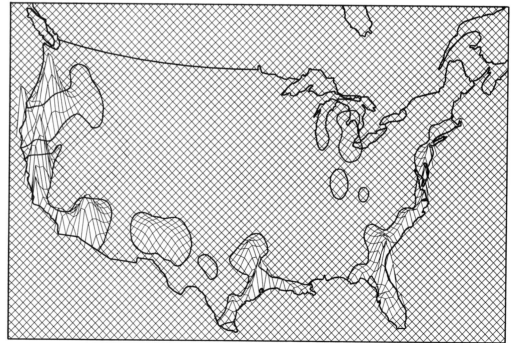

ARDEIDAE

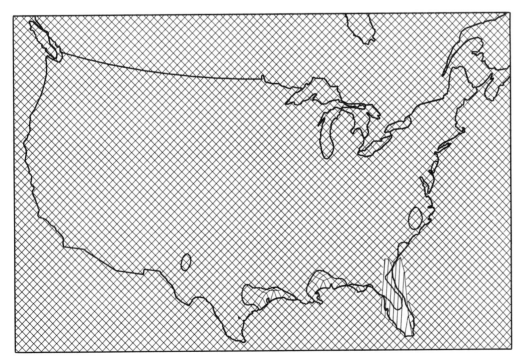

Yellow-crowned Night-Heron (*Nycticorax violaceus*) Maximum: 0.99 I/Hr

The Yellow-crowned Night-Heron is primarily a coastal species (Hancock and Elliott 1978), as is reflected in the CBC data, with regular sightings occurring only along the Gulf and Atlantic coasts. Ambient temperature is probably the most important factor influencing where it winters; the frost-free period must be at least 270 days long. Unexpectedly, this heron is absent from the coast of southern Texas. Further study is needed, since it is not obvious why it avoids this area.

The western Florida environments are optimal for this night-heron. The densest population centers roughly on Naples. On the coast, it extends from around Tampa Bay to Cape Sable and stretches inland almost to Lake Okeechobee. Corkscrew Swamp Sanctuary, owned by the National Audubon Society, is within this area of high abundance.

The diet and foraging habits of the Yellow-crowned Night-Heron are much more restricted than those of other herons. It eats a few fish, frogs, grasshoppers, and the like when they are readily available, but it specializes in crustaceans such as crayfish and crabs (Bent 1926; Hancock and Elliott 1978). For stalking and capturing these prey it uses only two methods—standing and waiting, and walking slowly—the basic foraging methods for all herons. The American Bittern is the only other heron with such a restricted foraging repertoire (Kushlan 1976). Contrary to its name, this night-heron is frequently found foraging in daylight (Bent 1926). Its crepuscular and nocturnal feeding habits may have evolved because it was excluded from its foraging areas by other herons during the day. Diurnal observations are normally of solitary individuals (Hancock and Elliott 1978).

Yellow-crowned Night-Heron

Yellow-crowned Night-Heron

THRESKIORNITHIDAE

White Ibis (*Eudocimus albus*) Maximum: 6.65 I/Hr

The White Ibis is a year-round resident along the Gulf and southern Atlantic coasts (Bent 1926; AOU 1983). Some birds do wander inland (AOU 1983), reflected in the maps by the extension of the distribution into the interiors of Mississippi and Georgia. This ibis undoubtedly prefers the moderated climate along the coastlines; most of its range is in areas where temperatures infrequently fall below 40°F (4°C) in January. The main exception is the population in northern Georgia and southern South Carolina, where the temperature drops to about 30°F (−1°C).

The area with the highest concentration is in western Florida, centered on Charlotte Harbor and running from about the Chassahowitzka National Wildlife Refuge in the north to Naples in the south. A lesser peak is found north of this dense population in the swamplands from Crystal River and continuing north to around Perry. Another short abundance peak is on the Atlantic coast around Cocoa Beach, just east of the most abundant population. The bayous around the mouth of the Mississippi River and a bit west show another slight increase in abundance. Owing to the constraints of the computer program used to map abundance, the high densities of White Ibis on the Florida Keys are not represented.

When foraging, this species relies mainly on touch rather than vision to locate its prey, placing its partly open bill in the water or bottom sediment. Prey is caught in the tweezerlike bill; undoubtedly the shape of the mandibles, with a gap about halfway up so only the tips meet when the bill is closed, provides a precision grasp (Kushlan 1977). The White Ibis is a fairly active forager and uses several feeding methods. Besides the most common behavior of probing, this ibis moves the tip of its partly opened bill through the bottom sediment by swinging its head from side to side (Kushlan 1977). Snowy Egrets, Tricolored Herons, and Laughing Gulls often forage with this ibis, using it as a "beater" to flush prey for them (Courser and Dinsmore 1975).

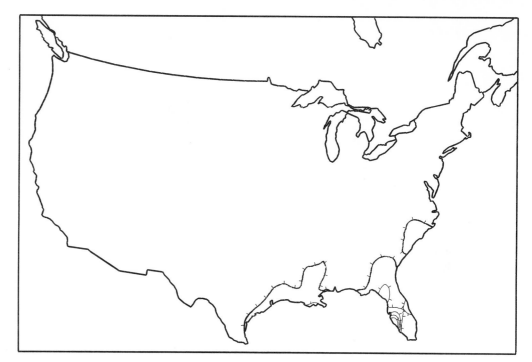

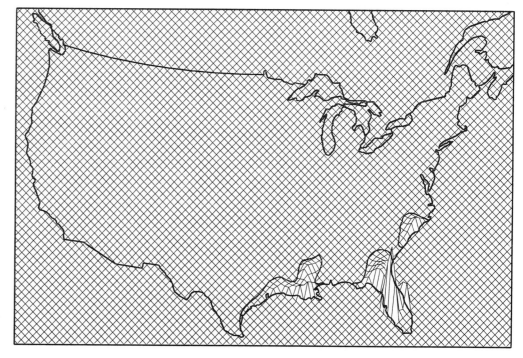

White Ibis

THRESKIORNITHIDAE

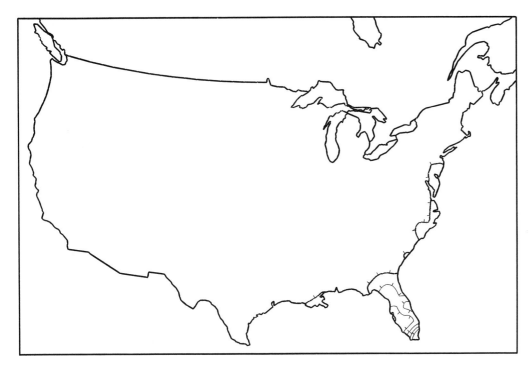

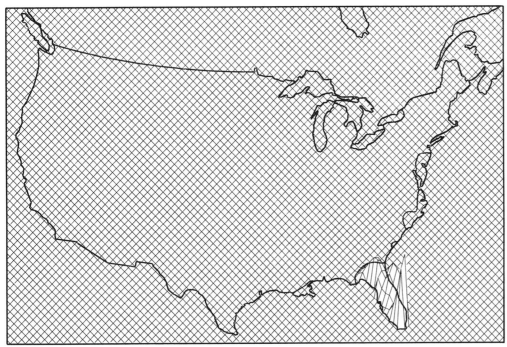

Glossy Ibis (*Plegadis falcinellus*) Maximum: 1.50 I/Hr

The two factors that apparently influence where the Glossy Ibis winters in the United States are swampland and warm temperature. The maps show that this species occurs in the Louisiana bayous, throughout the Florida peninsula, in the wetlands of eastern North Carolina, and into New Jersey. Only two of the sites outside Florida regularly recorded sightings. These two exceptions are counts held near Chincoteague National Wildlife Refuge in Virginia and around the Pea Island refuge in North Carolina. Sightings at all the other locations outside Florida occurred only in one, two, or three years out of the ten examined. Many of the observations of wandering individuals were in 1972, perhaps because an abnormally high number of young were fledged the previous breeding season or because the climate in these other areas was unusually warm that winter.

The highest concentration of Glossy Ibis is in peninsular Florida, with the densest population in the Everglades and a lesser concentration around Cocoa Beach. Enigmatically, a low abundance occurs from Tampa Bay south to the northern border of the Everglades.

Very few studies have been done on this ibis, and little is known about its behavior or ecology (Cramp 1977). Most of the information available is anecdotal. The Glossy Ibis seems to prefer shallow-water habitats, such as lake edges, lagoons, deltas, rivers, and estuaries. Infrequently it can be found along coastlines in saltwater sloughs (Cramp 1977). Rarely is an individual found alone; at night the birds roost communally with herons and other ibis, and during the day they form small foraging flocks (Cramp 1977). Its diet consists chiefly of insects, but it also eats leeches, mollusks, worms, crayfish, and small snakes (Bent 1926; Cramp 1977).

White-faced Ibis (*Plegadis chihi*) No Map

The White-faced Ibis is the western counterpart of the Glossy Ibis, at least in the United States. It winters along the Pacific coast of southern California and in Texas and Louisiana along the Gulf of Mexico (AOU 1983). It was observed on both of these coastlines during the Christmas counts but was seen regularly only around San Diego, California, and on the Texas and western Louisiana coasts. The densest population was recorded at the Sabine National Wildlife Refuge in Louisiana, with an average of 24.65 individuals seen per party-hour.

Roseate Spoonbill (*Ajaia ajaja*) No Map
This exotic-looking bird is locally resident on the Gulf coast of Texas and western Louisiana and in southern Florida (AOU 1983), the same locations where it was observed regularly on the Christmas counts. Two counts recorded relatively high numbers of spoonbills; at Sabine National Wildlife Refuge in Texas (2.36 I/Hr) and on Florida Bay near Cape Sable (2.32 I/Hr).

CICONIIDAE

Wood Stork (*Mycteria americana*) Maximum: 6.65 I/Hr
In the United States, peninsular Florida is the primary wintering ground for the Wood Stork. Only irregular sightings were recorded outside this area, in the protected marshes of national wildlife refuges. The largest numbers of nomadic birds occurred in Texas at the Anahuac refuge, in South Carolina at the Cape Romain refuge, and on the panhandle of Florida at the Saint Vincent refuge.

This stork becomes relatively common in the region of Florida where the average minimum January temperature is 50°F (10°C) or above. The highest peaks occur on the Gulf coast from the tip of Florida to around Fort Myers, which is roughly the northern extent of swampy land. An equally high peak is on the Atlantic coast, but it is not as extensive, reaching only from West Palm Beach to around Miami. A smaller peak occurs around Pelican Island National Wildlife Refuge, just north of Vero Beach. There is a relative low peak in abundance around Lake Okeechobee.

The Wood Stork is a permanent resident of hot, moist bottomlands, where it feeds in shallow, muddy ponds, marshes, sloughs, and infrequently saltwater mud flats (Bent 1926). Its diet consists mainly of fish, but it will also eat other living animals that it can catch and some plant matter. Foraging is usually diurnal, but some night feeding has been reported. Foraging flocks are normally found in water 6 to 20 inches (15–51 cm) deep. The bird uses touch rather than vision to find and capture prey. Where there is little underwater vegetation, it walks slowly forward with the bill open about 3 inches (8 cm) at the tip and submerged to the external nares. When it feels a prey item, the bill snaps shut. Where underwater vegetation is present, the Wood Ibis modifies its behavior to include foot stirring— pumping its foot up and down about five times in the water just above the vegetation as it steps forward. The prey flee from its moving foot, making them easier to catch and significantly increasing the number captured per unit of time (Kahl 1964).

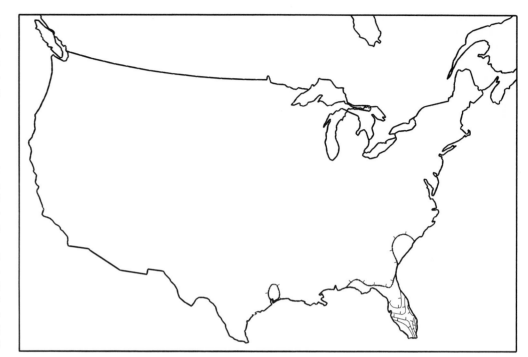

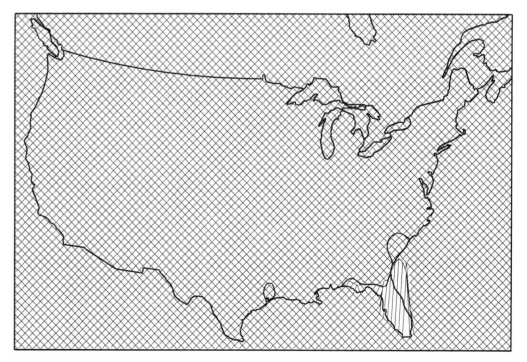

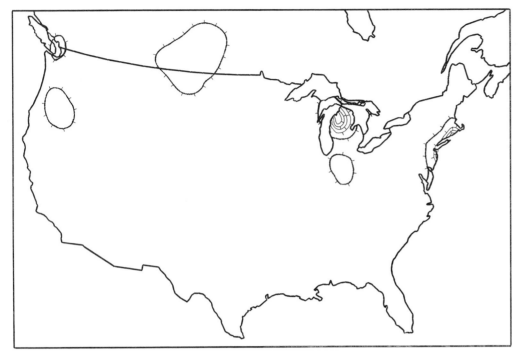

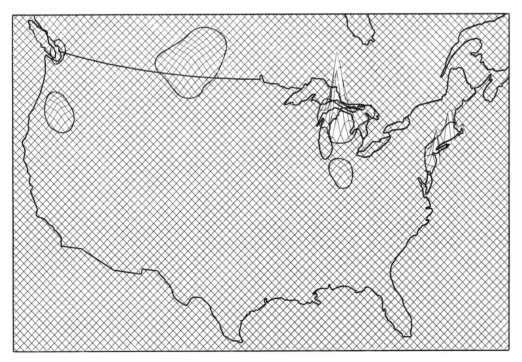

ANATIDAE

Mute Swan (*Cygnus olor*) Maximum: 4.31 I/Hr

The Mute Swan is not a native North American species. Birds were first introduced into southeastern New York in 1910 and on Long Island, New York, in 1912 (Bull 1974). In 1916 a young bird that apparently had dispersed from a New York population was recorded in Elizabeth, New Jersey (Stone 1937). The first pair was imported to Michigan in 1919. By about 1945 this population had increased to 47 individuals, and by 1974 those had multiplied to 500 (Bellrose 1980). The maps show that the highest concentration of Mute Swans in North America is in Michigan. The next densest population occurs along the eastern seaboard, stretching from Delaware to Massachusetts. All the other populations throughout the country are deliberate or accidental introductions. Swans were recorded on the Duncan count and other Vancouver Island counts only after 1967. The population at Regina, Saskatchewan, was established earlier; birds were observed in all ten years, starting in 1963. The map shows a much larger distribution for this Saskatchewan population than actually exists because of the lack of counts in this area, which allowed nonzero interpolated values to extend farther than they should. An artificial spreading also occurs, but to a lesser extent, for the populations around Bend, Oregon, and New Castle, Indiana.

Unlike those in the Old World, the Mute Swans in North America are not migratory (Bellrose 1980). During the winter, particularly in the areas with harsher climates, their survival depends on human intercession. In Regina, Saskatchewan, where the minimum January temperature averages −10°F (−23°C), the swans winter on a lake that is kept open by hot-water discharge from a power plant. In Michigan the birds' diets are supplemented with corn and table scraps. In fact, 20 tons (20,320 kg) of corn were fed to these swans in 1971. A more natural diet consists primarily of submerged aquatic plants, supplemented to some degree with crustaceans, fish, and aquatic insects (Bellrose 1980).

Tundra Swan (*Cygnus columbianus*) Map in Appendix B

Because of the nomadic tendency of the Tundra Swan in winter, maps of ten-year abundance averages may be misleading and thus are included only in appendix B. The 222 sites recording this swan are along the Atlantic coast from northern South Carolina to southern New Jersey, around the Great Salt Lake, and on the California coast from Monterey to the northern border. The highest ten-year average abundance was recorded in northwestern Utah, with 140.76 individuals observed per party-hour. The yearly values used in calculating this average, however, fluctuated from 0.11 individuals per party-hour in 1968 to 2,111.00 in 1963.

Trumpeter Swan (*Cygnus buccinator*) No Map

National wildlife refuges have a major influence on the abundance of the Trumpeter Swan. Of the eleven sites recording this swan, only four had regular sightings, and three of these were on wildlife refuges. Reporting this species in seven years were the counts around National Elk National Wildlife Refuge in western Wyoming and near the Powell River in western British Columbia. Sightings in eight years occurred at Malheur National Wildlife Refuge in southeastern Oregon and at the Red Rock Lakes refuge in southwestern Montana. The National Elk count in Wyoming had the highest abundance, with 0.63 birds seen per party-hour.

Fulvous Whistling-Duck (*Dendrocygna bicolor*) No Map

The winter range of the Fulvous Whistling-Duck in the United States encompasses the Gulf coast and southern Florida (AOU 1983). Only two Christmas counts in eastern Florida regularly recorded this duck; one was just south of West Palm Beach, where on average 0.12 individuals per party-hour were observed in eight years, and the second was on Merritt Island, where 0.05 individuals per party-hour were seen in six years. The other twenty-four localities reporting this bird were scattered along the coast of Texas and in southern Florida.

Black-bellied Whistling-Duck (*Dendrocygna autumnalis*) No Map

The Black-bellied Whistling-Duck is a very irregular visitor to the United States in winter. It was seen at only twelve CBC sites, all along the southern coast of Texas. Eleven of these localities reported this duck in only one or two years. The one exception was a count near Corpus Christi, Texas, where it was observed in three years at the very low average abundance of 0.03 individuals per party-hour.

Greater White-fronted Goose (*Anser albifrons*) Map in Appendix B

The abundance of the Greater White-fronted Goose at various sites fluctuates radically over time. In 1963 and 1966 no individuals of this species were seen on the count near Chico, California, but 30,040 individuals were recorded in 1970, resulting in an average of 937.50 birds per party-hour for that year. Such large variability may make the abundance information misleading, and thus the maps are included only in appendix B. The distribution shows that this goose is present along the Texas coast and in California from Morro Bay to around Arcata in the northern part of the state.

Snow Goose, White and Blue Morphs (*Chen caerulescens*) Map in Appendix B

During the time when the data for this study were collected, the Snow Goose and Blue Goose were considered different species, and thus the data were collected separately. Maps are included only in appendix B for both color phases, because the yearly number of individuals seen per hour of count effort for both ranged from zero to several hundred. This is probably because in some years the Christmas counts occurred before migration was over, but in other years cold weather forced migration to be completed by the middle of December (F. Cooke, pers. comm.).

The maximum abundance is 500.00 per party-hour for the white morph and 419.89 for the blue morph. Both color phases have their densest populations along the Missouri River in Missouri and their second densest on the Mississippi River where Nebraska, Iowa, Kansas, and Missouri meet. Both morphs occur along the coast and marshlands of North Carolina, on the Texas and Louisiana coasts, along the Arkansas River in Oklahoma and Arkansas, and in Illinois. The white phase is present and the blue is low in numbers or absent in western locations such as central New Mexico at the Bosque del Apache National Wildlife Refuge and in California's Imperial and Sacramento valleys.

Ross' Goose (*Chen rossi*) No Map

All thirty count sites where the Ross' Goose was recorded are west of the 95th meridian, and most of the observations were in warmer areas, including southern Texas, southern New Mexico, southern Arizona, and California. This small and fairly rare goose was seen in five or more years at only five locations: on the east coast of Texas, around Tucson, Arizona, at the Bosque del Apache National Wildlife Refuge in central New Mexico, in western New Mexico at the Bitter Lake National Wildlife Refuge, and at the southern end of the Sacramento valley in California near Sacramento. The count at the last location not only had the highest average abundance value, 0.27 individuals per party-hour, but also had the most regular sightings, with Ross' Geese seen in nine of the ten years.

Brant, Black Race (*Branta bernicla nigricans*) No Map

The data for the Atlantic and Black races of the Brant were recorded separately in the Christmas count data. All thirty-two locations reporting the Black race were along the Pacific seaboard, stretching from San Diego to southern Canada and beyond. The sightings at all but four of these locations were sporadic. These four included areas around Morro Bay, Point Reyes, Humboldt National Wildlife Refuge, and the Cape Meares and Three Arch Rock national wildlife refuges. Of these sites, Morro Bay had the highest mean abundance, with 14.06 individuals seen each party-hour.

ANATIDAE

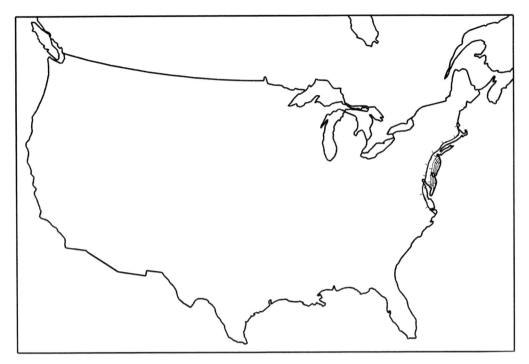

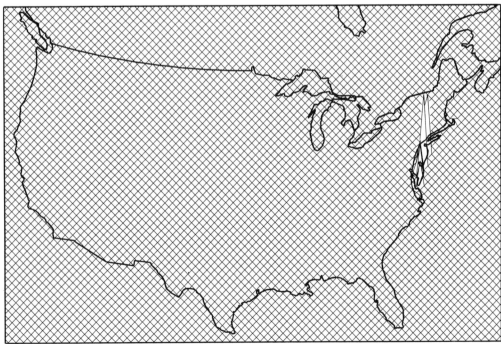

Brant, Atlantic Race (*Branta bernicla hrota*) Maximum: 319.75 I/Hr
Even though the maximum abundance for the Atlantic race of the Brant is over 200 individuals per party-hour, the map is reliable because this goose is not nomadic; instead, it uses basically the same wintering areas in roughly the same abundances year after year. The high maximum does have the unfortunate consequence of overshadowing the lower values. Thus, the distribution mapped is probably somewhat more restricted than it should be. Comparing these maps with Bellrose's (1980) wintering maps, however, shows little discrepancy between the two. The maps provided here show that the Atlantic Brant winters along the coast from New York to North Carolina. The highest concentrations are around the two national wildlife refuges on the New Jersey coast—Barnegat and Brigantine.

In the winter, Brant are primarily maritime, feeding on mud flats according to the timing of the tide (Owen 1980). The preferred food is eelgrass, but in the 1930s there was a dramatic decline in the abundance of this plant, at least partially owing to heavy grazing by this goose. In turn there was a drastic drop in the abundance of Brant, ameliorated to some extent when the geese switched to foraging on sea lettuce (Bellrose 1980), cordgrass, and cultivated grass (Smith, Vangilder, and Kennamer 1985). Often Brant will join feeding flocks of diving ducks, eating the algae and eelgrass the ducks dislodge (Owen 1980). Along with the demise of eelgrass, severe weather on the breeding ground causes fairly large fluctuations in abundance. Populations ranged from 266,000 birds in 1961 to 42,000 in 1973 (Bellrose 1980).

Canada Goose (*Branta canadensis*) Map in Appendix B
The combined effects of the gregariousness and nomadic behavior of this widespread species may have contributed to making the abundance pattern generated from the Christmas count data unreliable. Thus, its map is provided only in appendix B. The Canada Goose was seen at over 744 locations, but at many of these sites the number seen per party-hour ranged from zero to thousands.

In general, the distribution of the Canada Goose covers the entire continent from the Pacific to the Atlantic. The northern range limit appears to be influenced by ambient temperature; this goose avoids areas where the minimum January temperature drops below an average of 10°F (−12°C). The area with the highest concentration of Canada Geese is in the center of the country and includes the southern tip of Illinois, Kansas, Missouri, western Texas, the border between Texas and Oklahoma, and northern Alabama along the Tennessee River. There is an outlier group in North Carolina and Maryland.

Wood Duck (*Aix sponsa*) Maximum: 6.08 I/Hr

The winter distribution of the Wood Duck shows that in general it is absent in colder areas and at higher elevations. Except for a few cases this duck is present only where the average minimum January temperature is over 25°F (−4°C). Within these warmer areas, though, it avoids mountainous regions, including the Appalachians and the Ozarks. Outside the warmer areas, the populations are chiefly influenced by the protection and management offered by wildlife refuges. This is true of the population at the Kirwin National Wildlife Refuge in Kansas, at the Mingo refuge in Missouri, around the Killdeer Plains Wildlife Area of Ohio, and on the Willow Slough Fish and Wildlife Area in Indiana. The remaining two populations are near the Chinalake area of California and around Guelph, Ontario.

The highly concentrated populations also seem to be strongly associated with the protected and managed areas of national wildlife refuges. The highest abundance peak is in western Mississippi around Jackson, stretching north and east to the Noxubee refuge. North of there on the Mississippi River is a lesser peak, along the border between Tennessee, Missouri, and Kentucky near the Reelfoot and Lake Isom refuges. On the Atlantic coast there is an equally low peak in Virginia around the Peroquile refuge.

The Wood Duck has delicious meat, making it a desirable quarry for hunters (Bent 1923), and thus its population was decimated before 1918. Unfortunately, the habitats the Wood Duck frequents are accessible, and before the early 1900s hunting seasons were long and the bag limit was high. The main reason this duck is prized is its vegetarian winter diet of acorns, other nuts, berries, waste corn (Bellrose 1980), rice, and other seeds (Bent 1923). After 1918 the Migratory Bird Act helped protect this species, allowing the populations to recover (Bellrose 1980).

Green-winged Teal (*Anas crecca*) Map in Appendix B

The yearly variation in the abundance of Green-winged Teal was large at many of the count sites. For example, at one site the average number of individuals seen per party-hour ranged from zero to 1,563.00. Mapping average abundances of these data may be misleading, and thus, the map is included in appendix B. The most concentrated populations are associated with national wildlife refuges, including the Muleshoe refuge in western Texas, Bear River refuge in northern Utah, Quivira refuge in Kansas, and Yazoo refuge on the border between Mississippi and Arkansas. An abundance peak not associated with a refuge occurs in southeastern North Carolina.

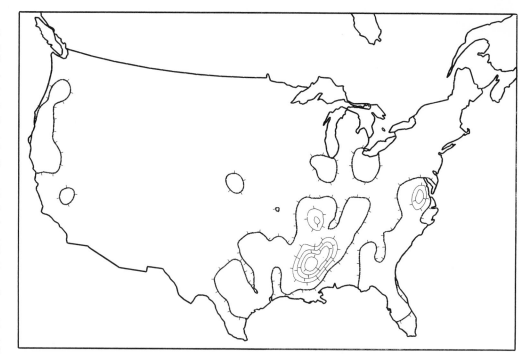

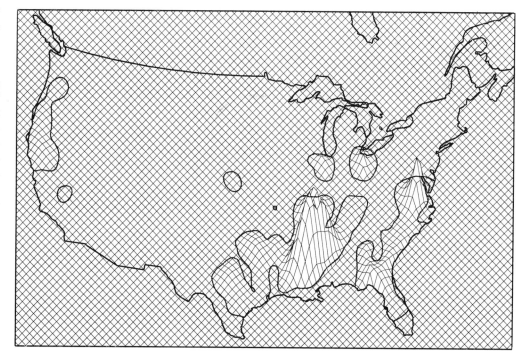

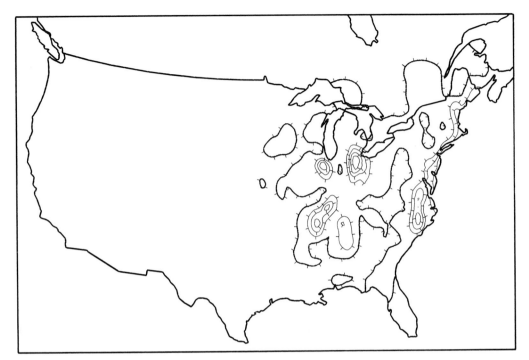

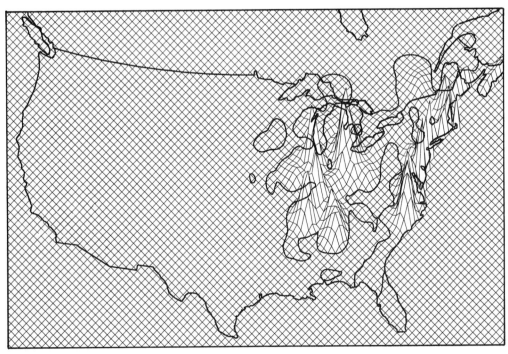

Green-winged Teal, Common Race (*Anas crecca crecca*) No Map
The North American wintering grounds of the Common Teal, now considered conspecific with the Green-winged Teal, are on the Aleutian Islands (AOU 1983). Rare sightings of this duck, however, were reported at fourteen count locations in the United States and southern Canada. It was most often reported on the Glenolden, Pennsylvania, count, where it was sighted in three years.

American Black Duck (*Anas rubripes*) Maximum: 11.75 I/Hr
The environmental factors influencing the range limits of the American Black Duck are something of an enigma. The western range of this eastern species does not extend much farther than the Mississippi River, but what causes this duck to avoid more western regions is not obvious. The same is true for the northern and southern range boundaries. Possibly the reason there is no obvious association between these range limits and environmental factors is that its range may be contracting. Christmas count data from 1940 to 1964 have been used to document that the ratio of Black Ducks to Mallards has dramatically decreased in Georgia, Pennsylvania, Maryland, West Virginia, and Ontario. Johnsgard and DiSilvestro (1976) have hypothesized that the change in the ratio is due to a decrease in the American Black Duck, which they attribute primarily to increased competition and hybridization with the Mallard. More study is needed to determine how much of the ratio change is due to an increase in the Mallard population and how much is due to a decrease in the American Black Duck population. One environmental factor that obviously influences the American Black Duck is elevation; it avoids the higher altitudes of the Appalachians.

The densest populations occur primarily along rivers. The highest concentration is on the Maumee River, southwest of Toledo, Ohio. West of there a slightly less dense population winters on the Kankakee River south of Chicago. Relatively high abundances occur along the Mississippi River bordering Tennessee, stretching up the Ohio River in southwestern Indiana. In this area peak abundances are present in Reelfoot National Wildlife Refuge in Tennessee and near John J. Audubon State Park in Kentucky. Relatively high abundances are found in east-central North Carolina and extend north along the coast to Maine. A lesser peak is present around Bledsoe Creek State Park in Tennessee and continues south to Northern Alabama.

By mid-December, approximately 98% of female American Black Ducks are members of breeding pairs, but courtship behavior continues through February (Hepp and Hair 1983). The gender ratio is not equal: there are about 1.23 drakes per hen (Bellrose 1980), which may help explain why courtship continues after pairing.

Mottled Duck (*Anas fulvigula*) Maximum: 8.88 I/Hr

Migration in the Mottled Duck consists of shifting positions within the breeding range, except in Florida where birds are resident (Bellrose 1980). Thus, the winter and summer ranges of this duck are basically the same, and as the maps show, the area it occupies is fairly restricted. The environmental factor that seems to strongly influence where the species is present and what areas it avoids is the average minimum January temperature. This duck occurs where the temperature rarely drops below 40°F (4°C).

On the other hand, the locations of the densest populations do not seem to be strongly influenced by temperature. The optimum habitats of the Mottled Duck are on or near national wildlife refuges, where the environment is both protected and managed. The highest abundance peak is around the Aransas refuge, on the southern coast of Texas. From here relatively high concentrations extend along the coast to the Anahuac refuge and on to the Louisiana coast, where there are two state refuges, Rockefeller and Russell Sage. In southern Florida there is another relatively dense population, apparently associated with the Caloosahatchee National Wildlife Refuge and Myakka River State Park.

The Mottled Duck population has not been severely depressed by hunting pressures because it is not migratory. It frequents relatively inaccessible habitats (Howell 1932), and before the early 1900s when hunting pressure was at its peak, few hunters entered its range (Bent 1923). Also, it eats both vegetable and animal matter, including insects, fish, snails, crayfish, wild millet and rice, delta duck potato, spike rush, and pondweed (Bellrose 1980), which makes its meat less attractive.

Mallard (*Anas platyrhynchos*) Map in Appendix B

The Mallard was seen at 1,059 sites throughout the United States and southern Canada, with a maximum abundance of 2,142.86 individuals seen per party-hour. The gregariousness and wandering of this duck make it very difficult to assess its density accurately. In general, the range of the Mallard covers the continent from coast to coast. The highest concentrations occur between the 90th and 110th meridians and from the 33rd to the 45th parallel.

Northern Pintail (*Anas acuta*) Map in Appendix B

The Northern Pintail's maximum abundance was 714.29 individuals per party-hour. The differential between this maximum and the low abundances was fairly large, resulting in a misleading, spotty map showing only relatively abundant populations. The high abundances were all strongly associated with national wildlife refuges, with the most concentrated populations at the Bear River refuge in Utah and the Muleshoe refuge in western Texas.

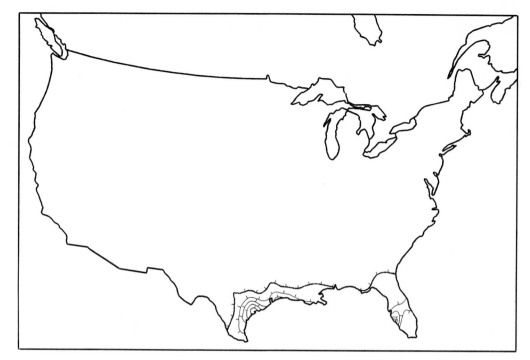

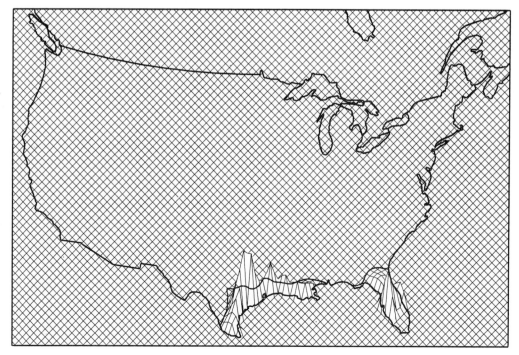

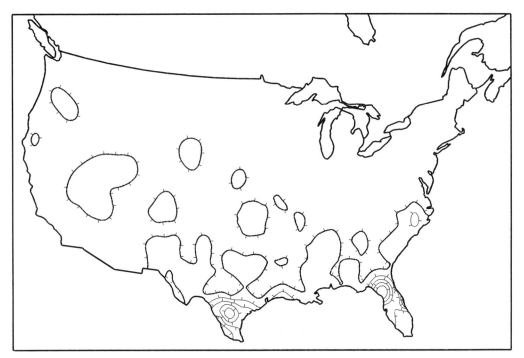

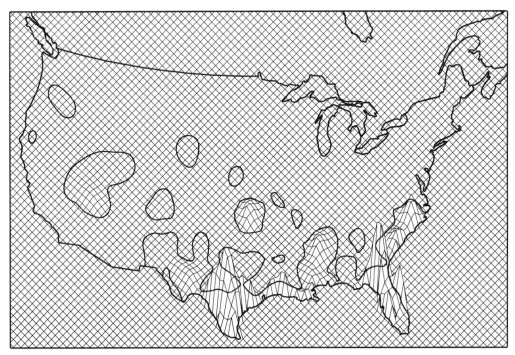

Blue-winged Teal (*Anas discors*) Maximum: 15.25 I/Hr

The winter range of the Blue-winged Teal extends from the southern United States through Middle America to northern South America. In North America one of the more striking aspects of its winter distribution is the spotty, disjunct populations, all due to unusual sightings recorded in only one or two years. Almost all the populations in areas where the minimum January temperature drops below 40°F (4°C) are ephemeral. Birds in these areas are probably stragglers that migrated late, which also helps explain why these sporadic sightings are not localized in one region. Unlike most migrants, the Blue-winged Teal does not congregate in large flocks before migrating, and the routes it takes are more complex than is usual (Bellrose 1980).

The highest abundance peaks of the Blue-winged Teal are in the extreme southern part of Texas and on the peninsula of Florida. The reason these areas are optimal for this teal is probably the warm temperature. The actual peaks center on San Antonio, Texas, and Gainesville, Florida. There is a smaller peak near the national wildlife refuge on Merritt Island on the Atlantic coast of Florida.

The Blue-winged Teal is a dabbling duck; it spends most of its time foraging on the surface or only a few inches below. Its diet consists mainly of aquatic plants supplemented with grain and rice and a few animals such as snails (Bent 1923). This teal is reported to have the highest annual mortality of all the dabbling ducks, reaching 65% (Bellrose 1980). At least three factors contribute to this elevated death rate. First, this teal is a favorite of hunters because it is an early migrant and therefore vulnerable when their enthusiasm is highest, and it is a fast flier, which makes killing it an added challenge (Bent 1923). Second, most of the population migrates over the oceans to South America, certainly a high-risk endeavor (Bellrose 1980). Third, the hunting regulations in Middle and South America are vary lax. As late as the 1960s this species was still being hunted for market in these areas (K. Parkes, pers. comm.).

Cinnamon Teal (*Anas cyanoptera*) Map in Appendix B

The primary wintering area for the Cinnamon Teal stretches from the southern coast of Texas inland, paralleling the United States–Mexico border, and up the California coast to the Oregon border. In 1963 a large concentration of this teal, 1,050 individuals, was reported on the Bear River Migratory Bird Refuge count in northwestern Utah, certainly an odd location for these birds at the end of December. This must have been an unusual year for teal in general, because 57,600 Green-winged Teal were recorded that year at the same location. Unfortunately this anomalous sighting of Cinnamon Teal strongly overshadows all other observed abundances, making the resulting maps uncharacteristic of its general winter abundance pattern. Thus, the map is presented in appendix B.

Northern Shoveler (*Anas clypeata*) Map in Appendix B

As with many ducks and geese, flocks of Northern Shovelers can be very large and nomadic, causing the abundance on some counts to vary dramatically over the years. On the Benicia, California, counts, for example, the annual mean number of individuals seen per party-hour ranged from zero to 833.30. In general this duck winters where the average minimum January temperature rarely drops below 20°F (-7°C). The exception is areas where humans intercede to help the birds survive harsher environments—for example, at wildlife refuges. The highest concentrations were associated with refuges in warm regions, including California's San Joaquin and Imperial valleys, the Bitter Lake refuge in New Mexico, and the Clear Lake refuge in northern California.

Gadwall (*Anas strepera*) Maximum: 25.06 I/Hr

In the United States, the primary wintering grounds of the Gadwall cover the area where the average minimum January temperature is over 20°F (-7°C). It avoids the Appalachians. Where this duck is able to survive in western areas with colder climates, it is probably frequenting wildlife refuges and lakes warmed by hot-water discharge from power plants.

Besides being important to the western range of the Gadwall, protected and managed areas are strongly associated with high-abundance populations. Both of the densest populations center on national wildlife refuges; one is in northwestern Utah at the Bear River Migratory Bird Refuge, and the other is in southeastern Missouri around the Mingo refuge. Somewhat less dense populations are present just south of Mingo on the Mississippi River around the Yazoo refuge. A similarly dense population is present on the Louisiana coast around the Sabine and Lacassine national refuges and the Rockefeller and Russell Sage state refuges. To the northwest, there is an equally abundant population on the Red River, with slight concentrations stretching southwest to the San Angelo area and back up to the Muleshoe and Bitter Lake refuges. Another rather high abundance peak is in the San Joaquin valley near several refuges.

Although the Gadwall population has been increasing since the late 1950s (Bellrose 1980), in the early 1920s its abundance was decreasing (Bent 1923). This may have been due to hunting pressure, since some hunters prize this duck for its tasty meat. Others, however, contend that the Gadwall is not fit to eat (Bent 1923). This discrepancy probably arose because different populations have different diets. The Gadwall primarily eats aquatic plants, preferring stems and leaves to seeds, but when these are not available it will graze on grassy pastures if they are close by (Bellrose 1980) or eat small aquatic animals (Bent 1923), which can impart a strong, unsavory flavor to its meat.

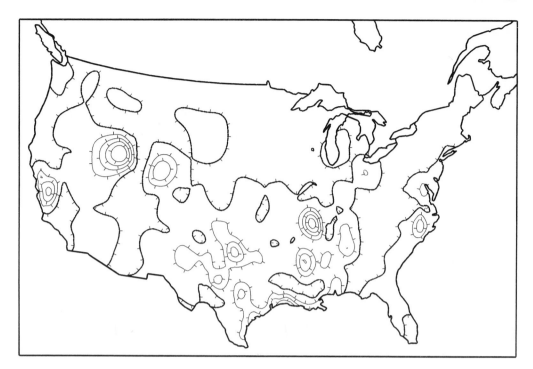

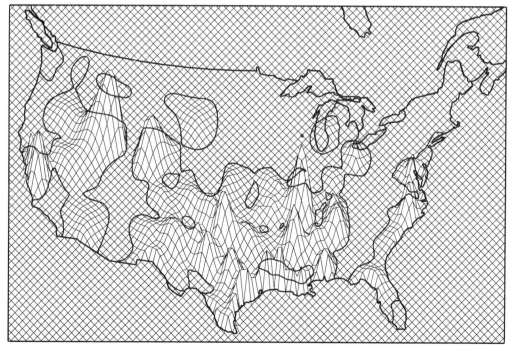

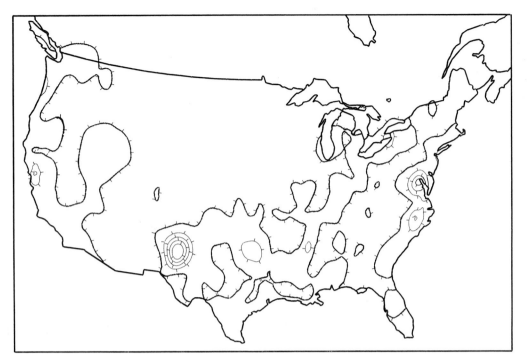

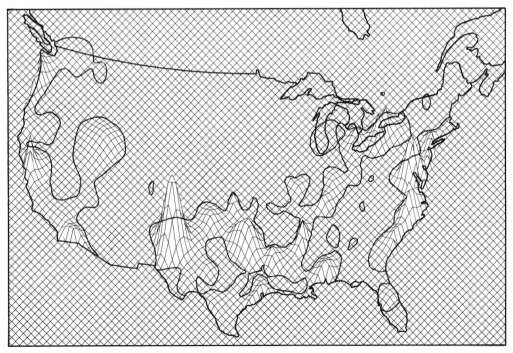

Eurasian Wigeon (*Anas penelope*) Map in Appendix B
The low abundance of the Eurasian Wigeon is the reason its abundance pattern is shown only in appendix B. The highest average abundance was 0.09 birds per hour of count effort. The two counts having that density value were on the Florida Keys and at the western end of the Columbia River in the Northwest. Of the fifty-seven sites reporting this duck, only seven sighted it five or more times.

American Wigeon (*Anas americana*) Map in Appendix B
The winter abundance of the American Wigeon shows wide yearly fluctuations at several of the count sites. An example is the count at Tyler, Texas, where the yearly average number seen per party-hour ranged from zero to 6,250.00. The map is thus included only in appendix B. The most concentrated populations generally occur in the Northwest along the Pacific coast and around Vancouver Island, also in the Southwest at the Muleshoe and Bitter Lake national wildlife refuges along the New Mexico–Texas border.

Canvasback (*Aythya valisineria*) Maximum: 38.14 I/Hr
The overall distribution of the Canvasback shows that it is present primarily where the minimum January temperature is over 20°F (−7°C). The major exceptions are that it avoids the higher elevations of the Appalachians, regardless of temperature, and that it is present in areas where the effects of harsh, cold climate are to some extent ameliorated by humans, as in northwestern Utah at the Bear River Migratory Bird Refuge.

The highest concentration of this duck is at Bitter Lake National Wildlife Refuge in eastern New Mexico. The maps show a lesser peak surrounding Chesapeake Bay. The actual ten-year means from which these maps were generated, however, show that the counts in the Chesapeake Bay area were as high as the one at Bitter Lake. The interpolation used in the mapping process generated this discrepancy for the following reason: inland sites close to the bay recorded no Canvasbacks, and these zero values were used in calculating the estimates around the bay, thereby decreasing its abundance. Zero values were also used in the interpolation process for the Bitter Lake population, but they were farther away and therefore weighed less in the calculations.

The abundance of the Canvasback at times in the past has been so low that without protection and management it might have become extinct. This exceptionally good-tasting duck was severely hunted before the early 1900s (Bent 1923). Even after being protected, Canvasbacks wintering in the United States and southern Canada declined by 53% from 1955 to 1974 (Bellrose 1980). Poisoning and the scarcity of its preferred food may also be negatively affecting its survival. The diet of the Canvasback is about 80% vegetable matter, preferably wild celery. The abundance of this plant has declined dramatically, forcing the Canvasback to switch to other foods (Bellrose 1980).

Redhead (*Aythya americana*) Maximum: 47.89 I/Hr

The overall distribution of the Redhead is fairly spotty. Most of the western populations are ephemeral, and the locations west of the 104th meridian have an unequal sex ratio, with more males in the North and more females in the South (Alexander 1983). The more permanent wintering areas are in the East, and here the sex ratio is equal. These regions include areas along the eastern half of New Mexico and the western portion of Texas; stretching east from the panhandle of Texas along the Red River, the boundary between Texas and Oklahoma; along the Gulf coast; on the Atlantic coast from southern New Jersey to North Carolina; on the Atlantic coast of Florida; and around Lakes Erie and Ontario. Thus, two factors apparently influence where Redheads winter: the mild climate with warmer temperatures along the coast, and national wildlife refuges.

The presence of wildlife refuges is strongly associated with the concentrated populations of Redheads. This duck is most abundant at Laguna Atascosa on the Gulf coast in south Texas. There are less dense populations on the eastern coast of Florida around the Merritt Island refuge, on the coast of the Florida panhandle near the Saint Vincent refuge, and at the Bitter Lake refuge in New Mexico.

The plight of the Redhead has been very similar to that of the Canvasback. Although not as low in abundance as the Canvasback, the Redhead is scarce enough to need protection. Before the early 1900s, hunting pressure was fairly severe, but all hunting of Redheads was banned in 1936 and 1937 and again from 1960 to 1963. In 1972 and 1973 a limit was set of only one or two individuals. Even so, its annual mortality is higher than that of most other birds, with 80% of first-year birds dying and a 40% death rate in the second year (Bellrose 1980).

Although the Redhead is a diving duck, it often is found feeding in shallow marshes and ponds. In such habitats it feeds by tipping up like a dabbling duck. Most of its diet consists of vegetable matter such as pondweeds (Bellrose 1980).

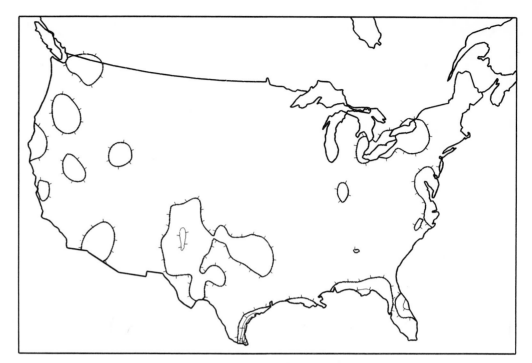

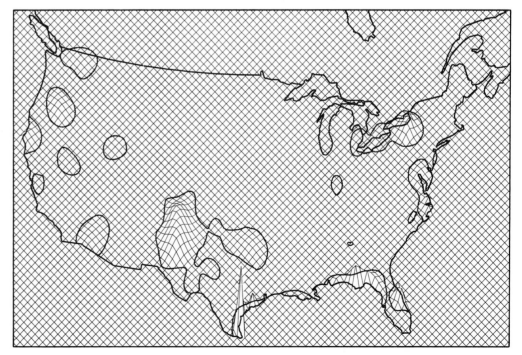

Redhead

ANATIDAE

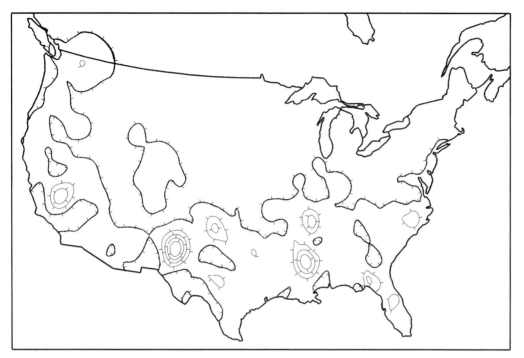

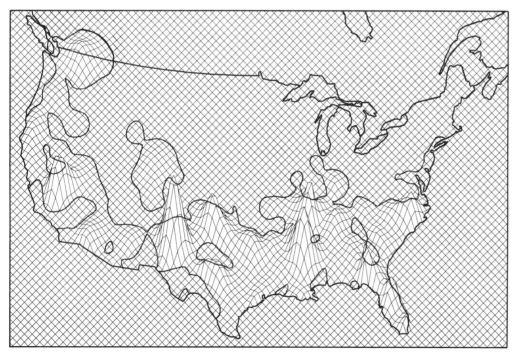

Ring-necked Duck (*Aythya collaris*) Maximum: 33.86 I/Hr

Like that of most other anatids, the distribution of the Ring-necked Duck is apparently associated with two main factors: temperature and managed and protected areas. Most of this species' range is where the average minimum January temperature rarely drops below 20°F (−7°C). The exception is the disjunct population in Colorado, Utah, and Wyoming, which encompasses the following national wildlife refuges: Monte Vista and Alamosa in southern Colorado, Arapaho and Browns Park in northern Colorado, Ouray in northeastern Utah, Seedskadee in southwestern Wyoming, and National Elk in west-central Wyoming.

National wildlife refuges are also strongly associated with denser populations of Ring-necked Ducks. The highest concentration is at the Bitter Lake refuge in east-central New Mexico. The next most abundant population is on the Mississippi River in central Mississippi, where there are four refuges: Panther Swamp, Hillside, Morgan Brake, and Yazoo. Two of the lesser abundance peaks are also associated with the Lake Isom and Reelfoot refuges on the border between Missouri and Tennessee and the Saint Marks refuge in the panhandle of Florida. Not associated with wildlife areas are the similarly dense populations on the eastern edge of the Texas panhandle and at the southern end of the San Joaquin valley.

The Ring-necked Duck prefers freshwater inland habitats to coastal or even brackish inland marshes. Birds close to the coast may spend their nights out at sea but come in at dawn to feed in fresh water. Generally, they frequent marshes and sloughs more often than large open, unprotected lakes (Bent 1923). The ring-neck is a diver, but it normally dives much less deep than other diving ducks, usually less than 6 feet (2 m). It eats primarily vegetable material, such as seeds of bulrush and sedge, pondweeds, wild rice, and tubers of the water bulrush in the autumn. Clams, snails, and insects supplement its diet (Bellrose 1980). This duck is an important game bird. A. H. Howell (quoted in Bent 1923) gives the following account of hunting this species in 1911, before protection for birds was available. In Arkansas at Big Lake, "In November and December it is often the most abundant duck, and gunners there frequently kill as many as 50 birds in a few hours. A few remain all winter."

Greater Scaup (*Aythya marila*) Maximum: 130.78 I/Hr

The wintering grounds of the Greater Scaup are primarily along the northern portions of both the Atlantic and Pacific coasts and around the Great Lakes. The distributions on both coasts are coincident with mean ocean-surface temperatures of less than 55°F (13°C). The exceptions are the disjunct populations in South Carolina and on the panhandle of Florida. The population in Florida is fairly regular, with individuals seen in seven years (1966 to 1972) on the Bay County count. Birds along the border between Illinois and Missouri are not seen nearly as consistently. This species was sighted in three years—1964, 1966, 1971—at Pere Marquette State Park, which encompasses part of the Mark Twain National Wildlife Refuge. These birds were probably late migrants, because this area is within the Mississippi flyway along which 1,600 to 5,000 individuals migrate (Bellrose 1980).

The most abundant population of Greater Scaup is in the calm waters around Vancouver Island of British Columbia. There is a less dense population around Long Island Sound, New York. As with the Canvasbacks in Chesapeake Bay, the Christmas count data show that the abundance of Greater Scaup in this latter area is higher than indicated on the maps. The interpolation process used to generate the maps depressed the values in this region, because nearby inland sites (where there were no Greater Scaup) were weighted heavily in the calculations.

The name "scaup" may come from the call of this duck, but one report states that it was derived from a local term used in Europe for beds of broken shellfish, which is where the Scaup, as the Greater Scaup is called in Europe, feeds (Bent 1923). Its principal food, in winter at least, is clams (Bellrose 1980), supplemented by crustaceans, crabs, starfish, mollusks, and a bit of wild celery, eelgrass, and other succulent plants. When feeding it often dives fairly deep in the ocean (Bent 1923).

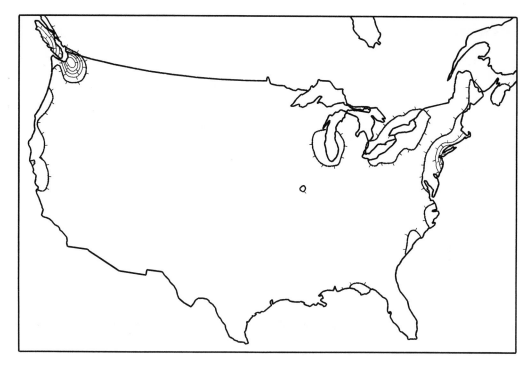

Greater Scaup

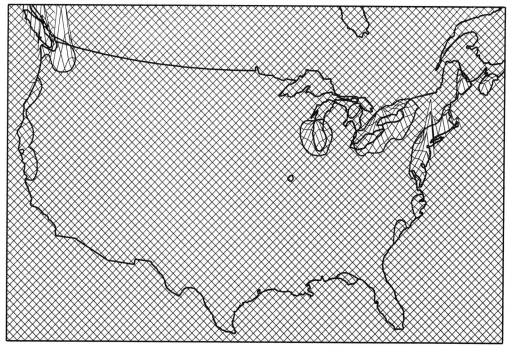

ANATIDAE

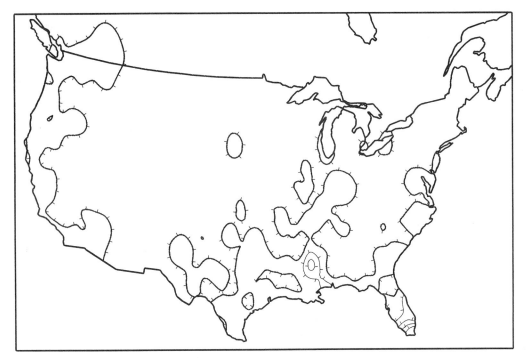

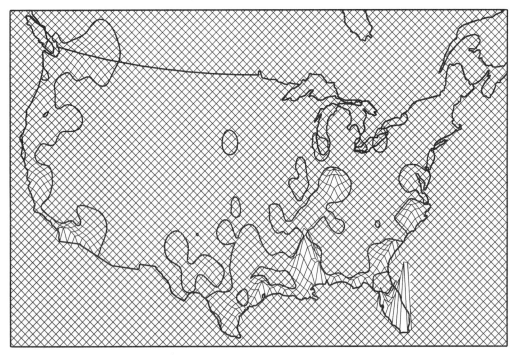

Lesser Scaup (*Aythya affinis*) Maximum: 78.43 I/Hr

In winter the Lesser Scaup frequents fresh water much more than its congener. The winter range of this smaller species covers basically all the area in the eastern United States that is lower than 500 feet (152 m) above sea level. This encompasses most of the coastal plains, which includes the area along the Gulf and Atlantic coasts, and up the Mississippi valley to the confluence of the Ohio River. In the West this scaup ranges throughout the warmer areas along the seaboard from the lower Colorado River valley to the Columbia River in southern British Columbia.

The highest concentration of Lesser Scaup is on the marshes and ponds in the Everglades at the southern tip of Florida. The next most dense population is on Ross Barnett Reservoir near Jackson, Mississippi. The reason it frequents these areas probably is related to available water and the warm climate.

The Lesser Scaup is classified as a diving duck, and except for sea ducks, it feeds at greater depths than any other diver. It is often found where the water is 10 to 25 feet (3–8 m) deep, and usually in fresh water. The amount of animal and vegetable matter it eats varies with location. In North Carolina most of the diet is vegetation, while on the Mississippi River roughly 90% is animal matter. In fact, the type of food eaten at any one location changes, presumably with shifts in the abundance of prey. At Keokuk Pool on the Mississippi River in 1948, 92% of the diet was snails (Rogers and Korshgen 1966), but in 1967 the staple had changed to clams (Thompson 1973). In southwestern Louisiana and southeastern Texas, the Lesser Scaup feeds in rice lakes, gleaning grains from the muddy bottom (Bent 1923).

Common Eider (*Somateria mollissima*) Map in Appendix B

There are two reasons the map of the Common Eider is included only in appendix B. First, this duck's distribution within the area examined is very restricted. Second, it occurs in such high abundance that census takers, particularly those who are not trained, have difficulty counting the individuals in large assemblages.

The winter distribution of this sea duck extends from the border between Connecticut and Rhode Island to the northern coast of Maine and the southern tip of Nova Scotia. The highest concentrations are around Cape Cod, Massachusetts, and near Penobscot Bay in Maine. The maximum average abundance was 266.67 individuals seen per hour of count effort, but unlike most other species with such high average abundance, the density of Common Eider at each of the given locations was very consistent, implying that this species is not nomadic.

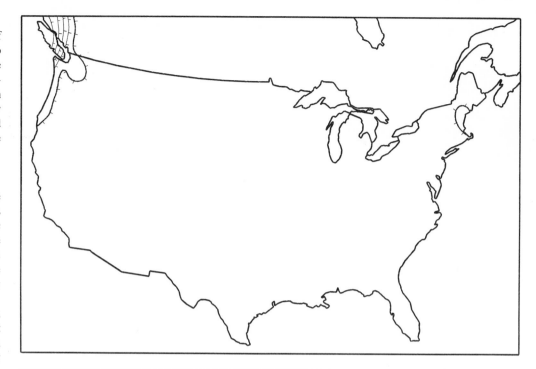

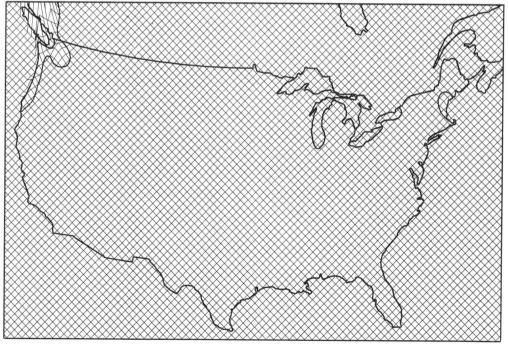

King Eider (*Somateria spectabilis*) Map in Appendix B
Only two counts in the study area had an average ten-year abundance of over 0.20 individuals per party-hour. This species was consequently too rare to ensure the reliability of the abundance pattern generated from these data. The highest abundance (7.33 I/Hr) was due solely to an aberrant observation on Cape Cod, Massachusetts, in 1967. The next highest mean abundance was 0.21, recorded at Montauk Point on Long Island, New York, where this eider was observed in eight years. This duck was reported in six years on the coastal sites in New Jersey and New York, and in one year in New Hampshire.

Harlequin Duck (*Histrionicus histrionicus*) Maximum: 3.35 I/Hr
The winter distribution of the Harlequin Duck is fairly restricted. On the Pacific coast it extends from the Pribilof Islands and Aleutian Islands (AOU 1983) south to the Oregon-California border, and on the Atlantic coast from Cape Cod Bay to near Portland, Maine. The temperature of the ocean surface does not seem to have much effect on the presence of this duck. A rocky coast may be the most important factor dictating where the species winters, given its ecology and its preference for feeding in fairly rough waters around rocks (Bellrose 1980).

The Christmas count data show that the highest number of Harlequin Ducks is at the western end of the Aleutians on Adak Island. Here, at 51.88° north latitude and 176.65° west longitude, it was observed at an average rate of 27.60 individuals per hour of count effort. Within the study area the highest abundance was around Vancouver Island, stretching up the southwestern coast of British Columbia. The density of birds here, however, is only about one-ninth of that farther north.

Because of the relatively inaccessible areas where the Harlequin Duck occurs, humans have had little effect on its density. Severe weather, on the other hand, may be important in depressing population size. This duck does not migrate to avoid the harsh northern winters, but in the spring and fall birds do move laterally between their inland breeding sites and coastal wintering areas (Bellrose 1980). They are usually found in single-species flocks, and when they are found with Oldsquaws the two species may just be using the same feeding areas (Bent 1925). The Harlequin Duck eats primarily animal material, including crustaceans, mollusks, aquatic insects, echinoderms, and fish (Bellrose 1980). The local name for this duck in Maine is the sea mouse, because of its high, squeaky call (Bent 1925).

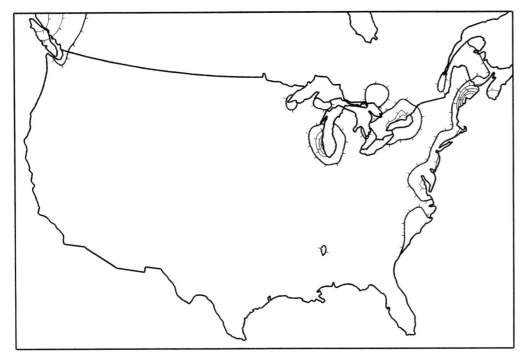

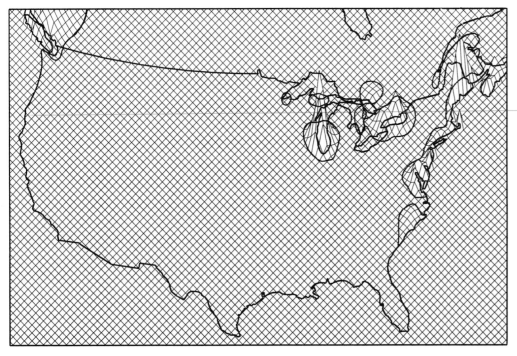

Oldsquaw (*Clangula hyemalis*) Maximum: 106.03 I/Hr

Oldsquaws winter in areas with fairly harsh climates; around the Great Lakes the average minimum January temperature ranges between 10°F and 20°F (−2°C and −7°C), and on the Gulf of Saint Lawrence the minimum temperature drops to 0°F (−18°C). From the eastern coast of Nova Scotia and the Bay of Fundy, the range extends down the eastern seaboard to the upper portion of the South Carolina coast. On the Pacific coast, only the southern end of the range protrudes into the study area around Vancouver Island. From this area the wintering range stretches along the coastline to the Bering Sea (AOU 1983).

The densest Oldsquaw population, between 700,000 and 1,000,000 individuals, occurs along the chain of the Aleutian Islands. The next densest population is on the Gulf of Saint Lawrence, where there are about half a million birds (Bellrose 1980). This high number does not show on the maps because of the lack of counts there and because much of the region is outside the mapped area. Within the area examined, the highest abundance peaks are around Lake Michigan and along the coast of Maine. A lesser peak is on Lake Ontario, and a still less dense population is present along the southern coast of British Columbia.

The Oldsquaw dives for its food. In Lake Michigan, where people often fish with gill nets, Oldsquaws are caught in nets placed 60 to 150 feet (18–46 m) deep. That the nets are placed on the bottom of the lake and are only about 5 feet high (1.5 m), and about 25% of the stomach contents is sand and grit, implies that the birds are feeding on bottom-dwelling creatures (Peterson and Ellarson 1977). About 90% of this duck's diet is animal matter (Bellrose 1980). The particular prey species depend on what is available and abundant (Peterson and Ellarson 1977), but it eats crustaceans, mollusks, fish (Bellrose 1980), shrimp, and aquatic insects (Bent 1925). In the early 1950s when gill nets were used more extensively in the Great Lakes, massive numbers of Oldsquaws were killed. Between fall 1951 and spring 1952, 15,500 were caught, and 19,600 died over the same period a year later. Other than these massacres, humans have had little effect on their numbers. Oldsquaws have tough, fishy-tasting flesh (Bent 1925), so hunting pressure has been low. This was confirmed by fluoroscoping 643 birds; only 1% had shot embedded in their flesh, compared with 36% of 3,341 individuals of the often-hunted Mallard (Bellrose 1980).

Black Scoter (*Melanitta nigra*) Maximum: 27.31 I/Hr

The Black Scoter winters primarily on coastal waters, with a few inland populations frequenting large lakes and rivers (AOU 1983). In the United States and southern Canada, its winter range extends along the Atlantic seaboard from the eastern coast of Nova Scotia and the Bay of Fundy to the northern coast of Florida. On the Pacific coast, it stretches from the shores of British Columbia to around Morro Bay in California. The distributions on both coasts stop approximately where the average minimum ocean-surface temperature is above 50°F to 52°F (10°C–11°C). The inland extension into British Columbia is an artifact of the interpolation process owing to the lack of counts in this area and the high abundance along the coast.

The densest concentrations of Black Scoters are strongly associated with national wildlife refuges. On the Atlantic coast the most abundant populations are on the New Jersey shore around the Barnegat and Brigantine refuges and on the South Carolina coast around the Cape Romain refuge. In the Northwest, the calm waters between Vancouver Island and the mainland harbor a very large population of this species and the other two scoters. Jones Island, San Juan Islands, and Dungeness national wildlife refuges and Desolation Sound Provincial Marine Park are situated here. The population in North Carolina is much less dense and is not associated with any refuges.

All three scoters form fairly large mixed-species flocks, particularly around extensive beds of mollusks. Eiders and Oldsquaws may also join these groups. The Black Scoter dives to depths of about 40 feet (12 m) or less in search of mussels, clams, scallops (Bent 1925), and oysters (Bellrose 1980). Except for the inland populations, which eat a lot of vegetable matter (Bent 1923), 90% of this duck's diet is animal prey (Bellrose 1980). Since about 1955, all the scoters have been experiencing an unexplained decline in total population (Bellrose 1980).

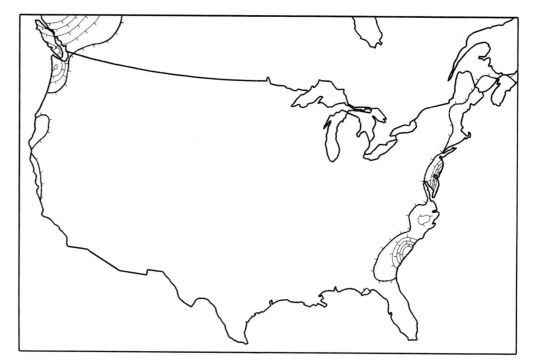

Black Scoter

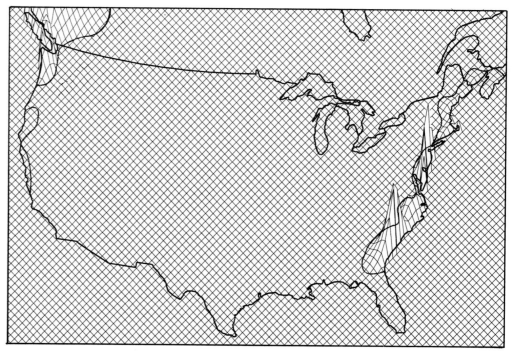

ANATIDAE

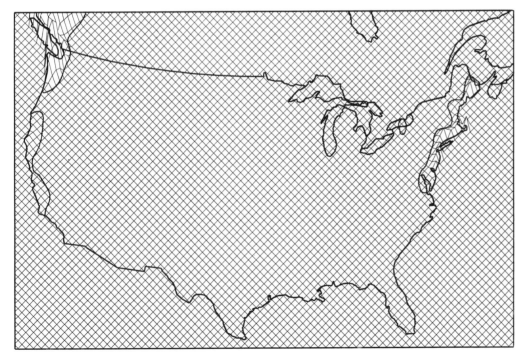

White-winged Scoter (*Melanitta fusca*) Maximum: 85.00 I/Hr

The winter distribution of the White-winged Scoter is very similar to those of the other scoters, except that it is more restricted on the Atlantic coast, with only rare sightings south of Chesapeake Bay. On the Pacific coast the distribution extends from the Aleutian Islands (AOU 1983) to around Santa Barbara, California. The southern limits on both coasts coincide with a mean winter ocean-surface temperature of about 56°F (13°C). This apparent preference for cold water is also reflected in the only relatively dense and regularly occurring inland population, on Lake Ontario near Rochester, New York.

Like the other two scoters, the White-winged Scoter has a highly concentrated population around Vancouver Island. Again, this is probably due to the calm waters, the high productivity of the many estuaries in the area, and the protected refuge areas. On the Atlantic coast there are a few less concentrated populations in areas around Long Island Sound, on Cape Cod Bay, and along the northern coast of Maine, where there are numerous bays. All these areas provide a habitat somewhat protected from the rough swells of the sea.

On migration, White-winged Scoters follow the coast (Bent 1925), normally flying in small flocks that stay about 4 miles (6 km) offshore (Bellrose 1980). Instead of flying around the hook of Cape Cod, birds fly over the cape at approximately the same place each year. This crossing, which extends from near Barnstable Harbor to Craigville, is purported to be the narrowest point on the cape (Bent 1925). In winter this scoter's diet consists almost entirely of marine organisms. On the Atlantic coast the staple is mollusks, and in the West it is rock clams. In both locations it also eats crustaceans and aquatic insects (Bellrose 1980).

White-winged Scoter

White-winged Scoter

Surf Scoter (*Melanitta perspicillata*) Maximum: 62.22 I/Hr

Of the three scoters in North America, the Surf Scoter is the only one indigenous to the area. Its breeding range extends from the Northwest Territories and western Alaska around Hudson Bay to Labrador, while in the winter it ranges along the Pacific coast from the Aleutians to central Baja California, along the Atlantic coast from the Bay of Fundy to Florida, and on the Great Lakes (AOU 1983). For the area examined, the maps show this same winter pattern except that the number of individuals on the Great Lakes and along the Georgia and Florida coasts is not indicated because their densities are too low relative to the high counts around Vancouver Island and San Diego, California.

The densely concentrated populations in the Northwest and Southwest occur in relatively calm waters and around estuaries. The sandy substrate at the mouth of rivers is the ideal habitat for clams—a major component of the Surf Scoter's diet (Bellrose 1980). Many rivers and streams empty into the Strait of Georgia in British Columbia and Puget Sound in Washington, and Vancouver Island itself abates the turbulence of the sea. In southern California a similar situation occurs near San Diego, where the Sweetwater River spills into San Diego Bay.

The feeding behavior of the Surf Scoter is similar to that of other sea ducks. It dives to depths of 6 to 30 feet (2–9 m), seeking and capturing prey. About 90% of its diet is animals (Bellrose 1980), including mollusks, mussels, clams, scallops, and small razor clams (Bent 1925).

Barrow's Goldeneye (*Bucephala islandica*) Map in Appendix B

In winter the Barrow's Goldeneye frequents the coast of Maine, the Gulf of Saint Lawrence, and the Pacific coast from Washington northward, and occurs inland in the area of the Montana-Wyoming border and in southern Idaho and northern Nevada and Utah. The highest numbers of this duck are restricted to the western part of the country, including the calm waters around Vancouver Island in British Columbia, the warm-water lakes of Yellowstone National Park, and the protected and managed environments of the Minidoka Game Refuge near Rupert, Idaho. Unfortunately, the number of Christmas counts in the west-central region, particularly Nevada, is low. Thus, the interpolated values there were strongly influenced by the nearby high counts, making the maps in this area misleading. Hence, only the contour map is included in appendix B.

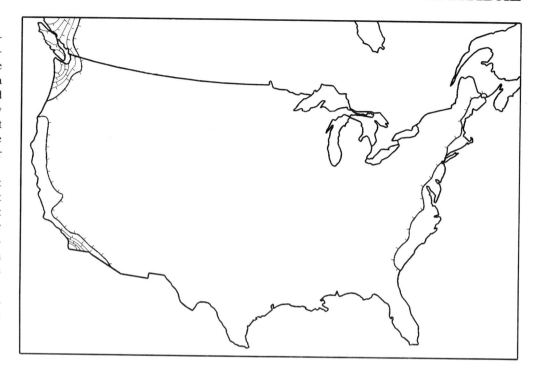

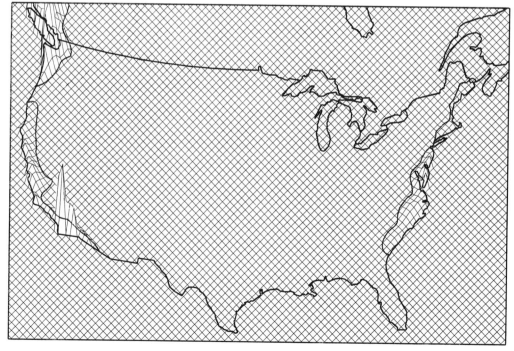

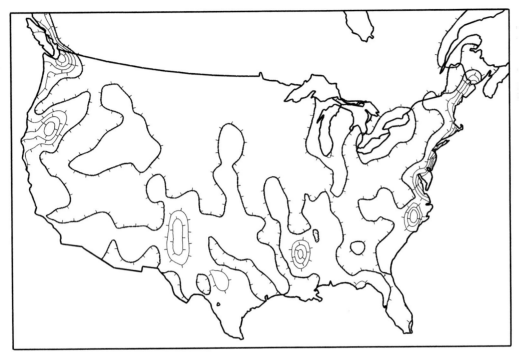

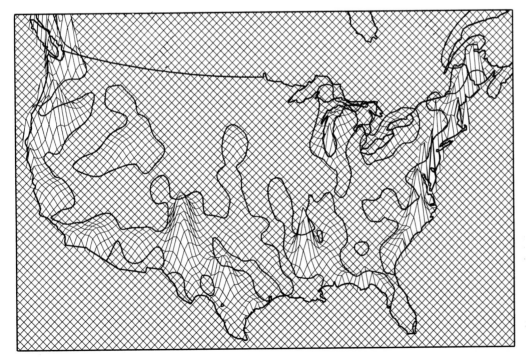

Common Goldeneye (*Bucephala clangula*) Map in Appendix B

The Common Goldeneye winters along the Pacific coast from the Aleutians to southern California; on the Great Lakes stretching south along the Mississippi and Ohio valleys to the Gulf coast; and along the Atlantic coast from Nova Scotia to Florida (AOU 1983). The density recorded on CBCs near the Saint Lawrence River was extremely high, which unfortunately overshadowed the rest of the abundance data. Except for providing information about the location of this highly concentrated population, the resulting abundance map may be misleading. Therefore it is included only in appendix B. The dense populations seem to be associated with national wildlife refuges—for example, Browns Park in northwestern Colorado and the Karl E. Mundt refuge in South Dakota.

Bufflehead (*Bucephala albeola*) Maximum: 24.69 I/Hr

The winter distribution of the Bufflehead extends along both coasts and encompasses the Great Lakes and other inland areas where open water is available. The latter locations include lakes and ponds in southern areas where the average minimum January temperature is over 20°F (7°C) and also bodies of water warmed either by geothermal energy, as in the Yellowstone area, or by hot-water discharge from power plants. Of course the Great Lakes are large and deep enough that they freeze over completely only during unusually cold winters.

One of the most concentrated wintering populations occurs around Vancouver Island. To the south there is a less abundant population along the border of Oregon and California. The presence of five national wildlife refuges in this region (Upper Klamath, Bear Valley, Lower Klamath, Tule Lake, and Clear Lake) probably influences the high number of Buffleheads. Along the Atlantic coast there are several dense populations. The highest is on the New Jersey coast around the Barnegat and Brigantine refuges, but high concentrations of Buffleheads basically run the length of the coast from the Bay of Fundy to Chesapeake Bay. In Mississippi a dense population is present around the Yazoo refuge, and in New Mexico a somewhat less dense population extends along the Pecos River and encompasses the Bitter Lake refuge.

The diet of this small duck depends upon the location. On fresh or brackish water, between 65% and 85% of its diet is animal prey, mainly aquatic insects. On salt water, however, 90% is crustaceans and mollusks (Erskine 1972). Feeding flocks of Buffleheads are generally small, frequently only two or three individuals of the same species (Bellrose 1980), though other species may happen to be feeding in close proximity to them (Bent 1925). Bellrose (1980) has found that Buffleheads increased in the Northeast from 1927 to 1966. Over the same period slight increases were noted in the Great Lakes region and the Southeast, with a decline in the West. The increase in the Northeast is corroborated by Bent (1925), who reported that Buffleheads no longer wintered on the New England shore because hunters had extirpated them, but the maps provided here show large concentrations of Buffleheads in this region.

Hooded Merganser (*Lophodytes cucullatus*) Maximum: 2.80 I/Hr
The Hooded Merganser normally winters on fresh water, but it is regularly seen in salt water in a few sheltered bays and estuaries (AOU 1983). Inland the range is fairly continuous throughout the eastern United States, but it becomes more disjunct in the West. This bird chiefly winters in areas where the average minimum January temperature does not drop much below 20°F (−7°C). The western boundary of this continuous eastern distribution is concomitant with the isopleth of an average of 16 inches (41 cm) of annual precipitation. In drier regions, populations do exist around national wildlife refuges, including Bear River in northern Utah, Minidoka in southern Idaho, Browns Park and Arapaho in Colorado, Seedskadee in Wyoming, and Karl E. Mundt in eastern South Dakota. On the Pacific coast this merganser is present from south coastal Alaska (AOU 1983) to San Francisco.

The most concentrated population of Hooded Mergansers is on the western border of central Mississippi. Here the White River, Morgan Brake, Yazoo, Hillside, and Panther Swamp national wildlife refuges provide optimal winter habitat. To the east is a smaller concentration around Wheeler refuge, on the Tennessee River, and rather dense populations stretch northwest from here to western Kentucky around Lake Barkley, also near the Tennessee River. There are also rather high abundance peaks in central Missouri around Lake of the Ozarks and around Lake Tawakoni, just east of Dallas, Texas.

The Hooded Merganser is the only merganser indigenous to North America. Flocks of this elegant duck usually consist of fewer than ten individual. It eats mainly fish, crustaceans, and aquatic insects obtained by diving (Bellrose 1980). This diet imparts a fishy taste to its meat, and thus, this merganser is not a valued game bird. Also, it is small and a fast flier, making it difficult to hit on the wing (Bent 1923). The number of Hooded Mergansers, however, has been on the decline, apparently because of increased drainage of wetlands in the United States. Besides the direct effect of the decreasing water levels, draining makes the remaining water more turbid, so it is difficult to find prey (Bellrose 1980).

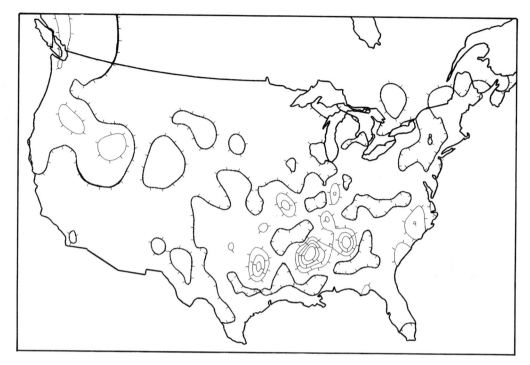

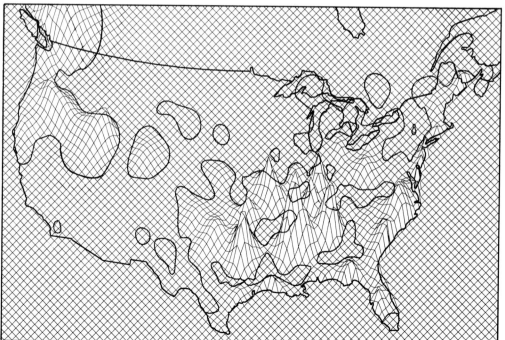

Hooded Merganser

ANATIDAE

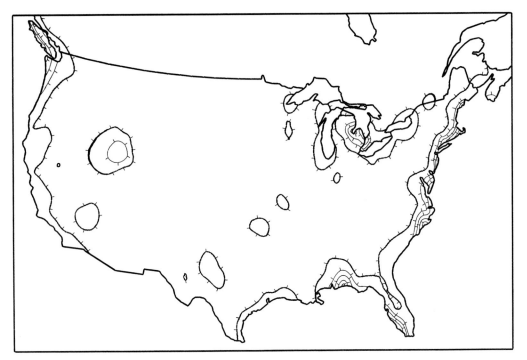

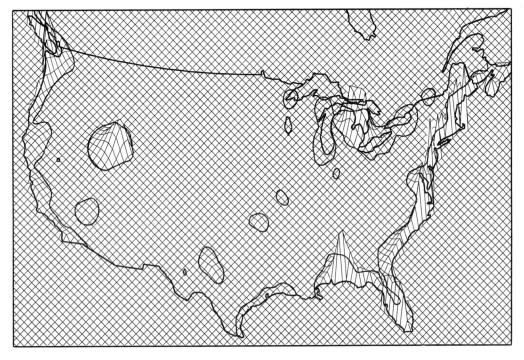

Common Merganser (*Mergus merganser*) Map in Appendix B

The Common Merganser is one of the last ducks to migrate south in the fall (Bellrose 1980). This and its very large flocks cause its abundance pattern to vary dramatically at given sites over the years. For example, in southern Oklahoma around Wichita Mountains National Wildlife Refuge the number of individuals seen per party-hour varied from 0.08 to 1,056.00. In general, the early-winter distribution stretches from coast to coast in a band across the center of the country. The highest abundances are in Kansas, Oklahoma, Missouri, around the southern border of South Dakota, and in southwestern Idaho. The maximum abundance at the 703 sites recording this duck was 58.33 individuals per party-hour.

Red-breasted Merganser (*Mergus serrator*) Maximum: 22.22 I/Hr

In winter the Red-breasted Merganser is primarily found in marine environments, and thus its range extends the full length of the coasts. There are several inland populations, however, most notably on the Great Lakes. The other interior populations are strongly associated with national wildlife refuges or large lakes. The refuges include Sequoyah in eastern Oklahoma; Muleshoe in western Texas; Havasu around the border of California, Nevada, and Arizona; Bear River in northwestern Utah; and the many refuges along the Mississippi River where it divides Minnesota and Wisconsin. Other populations are found on Lake of the Ozarks in central Missouri and around Indianapolis.

The most concentrated populations of Red-breasted Mergansers occur at wildlife refuges and along the coasts in fairly protected areas with calm seas. There are only two rather abundant inland populations, which encompass the Shiawassee refuge at the southern end of Lake Huron and the Bear River Migratory Bird Reserve in Utah. All other abundance peaks are along the coasts. The abundance of this merganser is elevated along the Atlantic coast from Penobscot Bay in Maine to North Carolina. Within this region are two of the densest concentrations; one around Cape Cod in Massachusetts and the other near Cedar Island National Wildlife Refuge in North Carolina. The remaining maximum abundance peak is on the Gulf coast at the southern end of the Florida panhandle near Choctawhatchee Bay.

Like the other sea ducks, the Red-breasted Merganser forages by diving. Sometimes it will herd a school of fish into shallow water, making capture much easier. It eats chiefly herring and sculpins, supplemented by shrimp and crabs (Bellrose 1980). This duck is a strong, fast flier once in the air, but to take off it must run along the water or ground, especially in calm weather. One pair of mergansers left footprints in the sand for 87 feet (26.5 m) before getting airborne (Bent 1923).

Red-breasted Merganser

Ruddy Duck (*Oxyura jamaicensis*) Maximum: 153.49 I/Hr

In North America 55% of the Ruddy Ducks winter along the Pacific coast, and 85% of those are in California. Of the total winter population, 25% are found on the Atlantic coast, with 70% around Chesapeake Bay. This leaves 20% that winter inland (Bellrose 1980). The Atlantic coast population extends from New York to South Carolina. The range on the Pacific coast stretches from the Canadian border to San Diego. As is true for most ducks, the inland populations depend on protected and managed areas. These include Bitter Lake National Wildlife Refuge in New Mexico, several refuges along the Mississippi River, and three refuges and a couple of state parks along the Rio Grande valley in southern Texas.

The populations with the highest concentrations are similarly associated with wildlife refuges. These include the Imperial Valley of southern California around the Salton Sea refuge and an area on the Mississippi River along the border between Arkansas and Mississippi between the Yazoo and White River refuges.

In most locations the Ruddy Duck primarily eats vegetation. It dives for its main staples, widgeon grass and pondweed, which it supplements by a small amount (about 5%) of animal prey, primarily shrimp. When plant food is not available, however, the Ruddy Duck will eat more animal items (Bellrose 1980). Because it is primarily vegetarian, this duck has fairly tasty flesh and therefore is valued as a game bird. In the 1890s, when the abundance of Redheads and Canvasbacks was low because of hunting pressure, the Ruddy Duck soon became the choice in the markets. From 1899 to 1920 this duck's population on Wenham Lake in Massachusetts was reduced 70% by hunters (Phillips 1926). For its small size, the Ruddy Duck lays incredibly large eggs, comparable in size to those of the Great Blue Heron (Bent 1925).

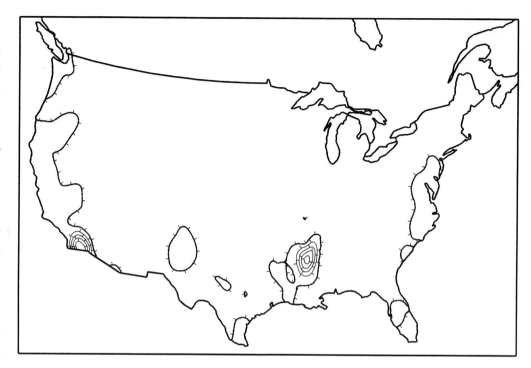

Ruddy Duck

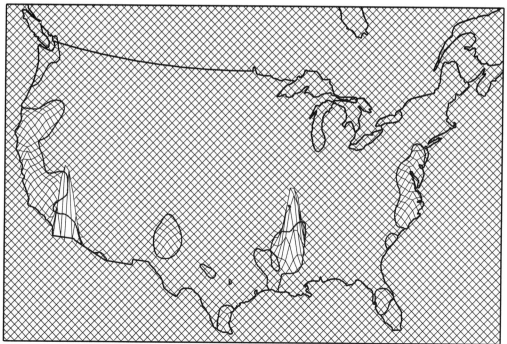

CATHARTIDAE

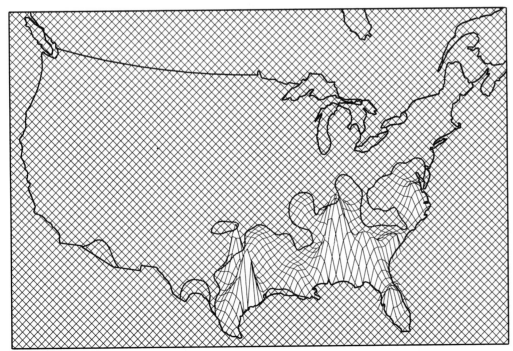

CATHARTIDAE

Black Vulture (*Coragyps atratus*) Maximum: 7.79 I/Hr

Most of the area where the Black Vulture occurs has an average minimum January temperature above 30°F (−1°C). The exceptions are along the Mississippi valley up to the southern edge of Illinois and on the interior low plateau of Tennessee and Kentucky. Both these areas have altitudes less than roughly 500 feet (152 m) above sea level. This species avoids the higher elevations of the Appalachians and the Ozarks. The population that is farthest west centers on Organ Pipe Cactus National Monument along the southwestern border of Arizona, where the temperature remains above freezing in winter.

Most of the high concentrations of this raptor are associated with lakes or reservoirs; perhaps the lakes attract other animals, increasing the supply of carrion, the staple of the vulture's diet. The open habitat around lakes may also make it easier to detect food. The highest abundance peak is in Alabama near the William Dannelly Reservoir, with a high concentration of vultures extending to Lake Seminole in Georgia and on over to the coast. Somewhat less concentrated populations occur in eastern Texas, one around Lake Whitney and the other centered on Aransas National Wildlife Refuge along the Gulf coast. An even less dense population is in central Tennessee, near Tims Ford Lake. Slight increases in abundance occur in North Carolina around Lake Gaston and in Florida from Tampa to Fort Myers on the Gulf coast and inland around Lake Kissimmee.

Brown and Amadon (1968) report that the Black Vulture "probably has a larger population than any other bird of prey in the Western Hemisphere." This species is certainly ecologically beneficial because it eats carrion, thereby removing decaying and perhaps diseased carcasses. Thousands of Black Vultures and Turkey Vultures have been destroyed, primarily by ranchers, because these scavengers are mistakenly believed to kill young livestock and to spread diseases like anthrax from dead animals to healthy ones. The Black Vulture prefers large carcasses, and as many as 300 birds may feed on the same item. It often uses its tail as a brace, so the feathers become quite worn (Brown and Amadon 1968). Unlike the Turkey Vulture, the Black Vulture does not have a well-developed sense of smell, and where their distributions overlap the Black Vulture is attracted to carrion by congregations of Turkey Vultures (Heintzelman 1979). The two species have similar diets and roost together (Yahner, Storm, and Wright 1986).

Turkey Vulture (*Cathartes aura*) Maximum: 7.56 I/Hr

In the Southeast, the Turkey Vulture is sympatric with the Black Vulture. The range of the Black Vulture, however, extends only to areas where the average minimum January temperature is over 30°F (−1°C), while the Turkey Vulture is present where it drops to 25°F (−4°C). The latter species tends to avoid the higher elevations of the Appalachians and Ozarks, and its western distribution is bounded by the high peaks of the Sierra Nevada. The range extends into the region along the Wabash River in Indiana where the temperature drops below 25°F (−1°C).

Dense populations of Turkey Vultures are recorded in the same regions where the Black Vulture occurs in fairly high concentrations—around Aransas National Wildlife Refuge on the Texas coast and inland near Whitney Lake. From these areas the Turkey Vulture's abundance stretches over to Lake Texoma on the Red River. There are also high concentrations of this vulture throughout most of Florida, with apexes stretching from Naples to Vero Beach and east of Tallahassee. There is even a peak in the colder northern region along the Wabash River in Indiana.

This cathartid is not truly migratory in North America (Brown and Amadon 1968), but it is nomadic. It leaves summer roosts after cold fronts, and on warmer days it drifts back on southerly winds. It can survive without food for seventeen days (Hatch 1970) and can drop its body temperature from 100°F to 93°F (38°C to 34°C) when sleeping (Brown and Amadon 1968). About thirty individuals of Black and Turkey Vultures normally roost together. The Turkey Vulture usually forages alone. Small-mammal carrion makes up the largest portion of its diet, but it also eats very rotten fruit and will kill mice and snakes (Brown and Amadon 1968). Food items change depending on availability (Yahner, Storm, and Wright 1986). An autumn analysis of pellets from Virginia showed a high proportion of opossum, sheep, and bird remains, along with those of freshly killed moles and shrews. Unexpectedly, one pellet was 70% plant material (Paterson 1984). Extensive trapping and killing of vultures in Texas has contributed to a dramatic decline in the abundance of both species (Brown and Amadon 1968).

California Condor (*Gymnogyps californianus*) No Map

The California Condor was a resident of the California Coast Range (AOU 1983). The wild populations declined dramatically because young could not be added to the population fast enough to compensate for the death rate. The age of first reproduction is six to eight years; only one egg is laid, and birds nest only every other year (Amadon 1984). The death rate increased because of poisoning from lead shot ingested with carrion from animals wounded by hunters (Ensley 1984). The condor was recorded on the Sespe Wildlife Area Christmas count since its inception in 1967. Unfortunately these data do not accurately represent the number of condors, because individuals travel long distances while foraging and because the rarity of the species makes count participants overzealous (Bock and Root 1981).

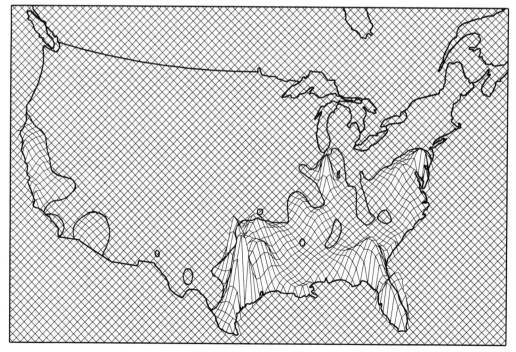

ACCIPITRIDAE

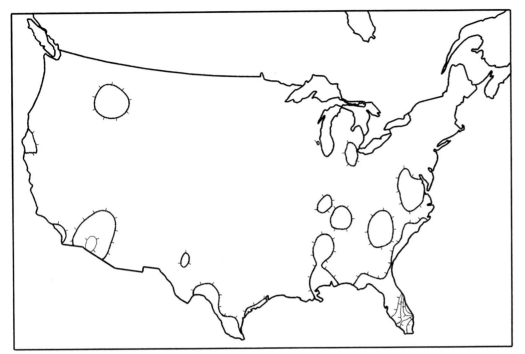

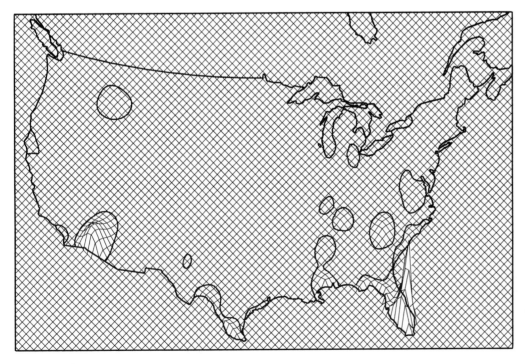

Osprey (*Pandion haliaetus*) Maximum: 1.02 I/Hr

Except on unusual occasions during migration, the Osprey is always asso-ciated with water, whether fresh or salt (Brown and Amadon 1968). This association is reflected in the maps—even the sightings in eastern New Mexico were along the Pecos River. The primary wintering grounds in the United States include central California, southern Texas, the Gulf coast, and southern Florida (AOU 1983). On the Christmas counts, regular sight-ings were reported as far north on the California coast as Laguna Beach, along the Gulf coast, and up the Atlantic coast to Hilton Head Island in southern South Carolina. The populations outside these areas are due to irregular sightings, presumably of late migrants. There was no consistent pattern in the years of these irregular observations, implying that they are chance events rather than being synchronized by something like weather. In 1905 most of the birds shot by hunters outside their primary wintering grounds were immatures (Bent 1937).

The highest concentration of Ospreys is in southern Florida around Vero Beach, extending inland to Lake Okeechobee and on over to Naples on the Gulf coast. A much less concentrated population is found along the Colorado-Arizona border above Imperial Dam near the Imperial National Wildlife Refuge. The overall abundance of the Osprey has dropped dra-matically over the years. Henny and Wight (1969) reported a 12.9% de-crease per year in the population on Gardiners Island, New York, from 1945 to 1965, and other populations have shown an annual decline of 14.1%. Persecution of this raptor has been slight, since farmers and ranchers realize it is not a threat to their livestock and have even aided the Osprey by putting up nesting platforms. The dramatic decline has been caused primarily by poisoning from DDT and other pesticides (Grossman and Hamlet 1964).

The Osprey's diet consists almost exclusively of live-caught fish. When foraging it flies 50 to 100 feet (15–30 m) above the water. When it detects a fish, it hovers and then drops to catch it in its talons (Brown and Amadon 1968). Bottom-feeding fish are most easily caught, and piscivorous fish (those that feed on other fish) are most difficult for the Osprey to capture, probably because the former may not see an attacker from above, whereas the latter are particularly agile (Swenson 1979). Foraging time decreases on cloudy days and when the surface is choppy (Grubb 1977), presumably be-cause visibility in the water is much poorer then. When an Osprey catches a fish, as it does on about 90% of the attempts, it carries the prey to a perch in its talons, holding it parallel to its own body with the head pointing into the wind (Brown and Amadon 1968).

ACCIPITRIDAE

Black-shouldered Kite (*Elanus caeruleus*) Maximum: 1.22 I/Hr
The maps show that the distribution of the Black-shouldered Kite in the United States is fairly restricted. It occurs throughout the Coast Range of California, extending east to the higher peaks of the Sierra Nevada and north to the Klamath Mountains. In southern California its eastern edge is restricted by the San Bernardino and Chocolate mountains. The harsh desert environment of inland Texas apparently constrains it to the coastline and the extreme southern end of the Rio Grande valley.

About 1925 the Black-shouldered Kite appeared to be on its way to extinction; its hovering in open country made it an easy target. It was legally protected in 1957, however, after a massive education drive in California that warned of the impending disaster and explained how beneficial the kite was to farmers because of its diet of mice. Since then the persecution of this raptor has drastically declined, permitting a significant increase in its abundance. By 1970 it was again common on the grassy, oak-scattered foothills and in the open, cultivated bottomland (Eisenmann 1971). The most concentrated population is in the Central Valley of California at the confluence of the Sacramento and San Joaquin rivers. A much slighter abundance peak occurs around San Diego.

The Black-shouldered Kite normally feeds alone or in pairs. It sits on an exposed perch or hovers watching for prey. Late afternoon is its most productive foraging time, because this is when its prey is most active. Meadow mice and a few house mice make up the main portion of this kite's diet. Birds may be added occasionally. Because its gape is large, this species usually eats its prey in only three bites, more like an owl than a hawk. At night up to forty-five individuals will roost together (Brown and Amadon 1968).

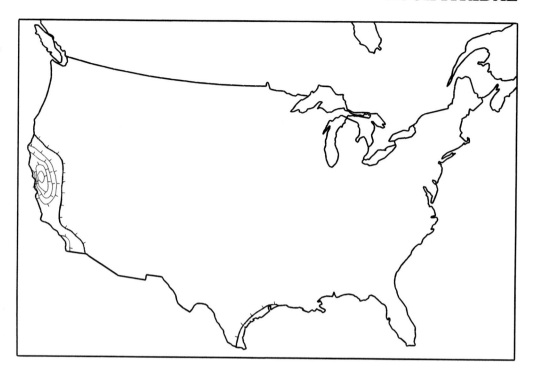

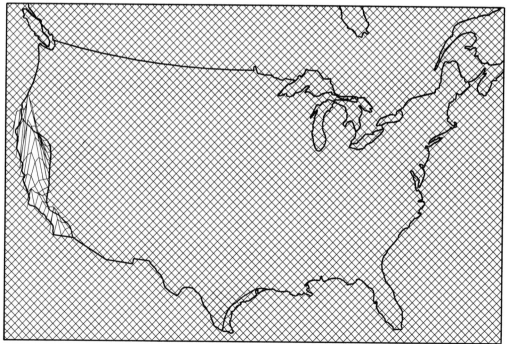

ACCIPITRIDAE

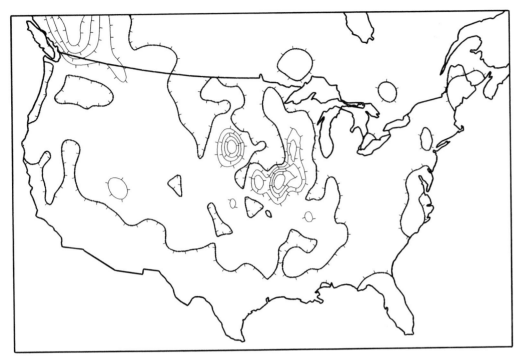

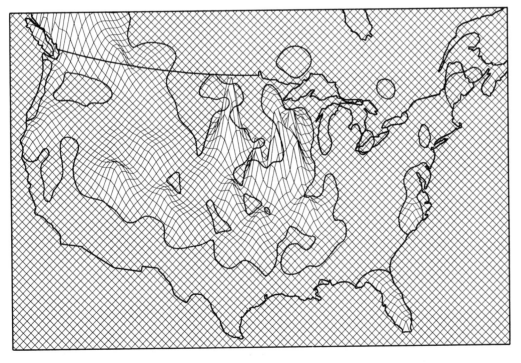

Bald Eagle (*Haliaeetus leucocephalus*) Maximum: 3.87 I/Hr

The environmental conditions constraining the winter distribution of the Bald Eagle are not obvious from the maps; there is no clear association between the range limits and temperature, precipitation, snowfall, pan evaporation, or vegetation. The concentrated populations, on the other hand, show a high correspondence with rivers, particularly around wildlife refuges and electric plants. Both areas attract waterfowl, the former through management and feeding programs and the latter warmed by hot-water discharge, keeping them free of ice all winter. Bald Eagles in turn come to prey on the congregations of ducks and geese (Brown and Amadon 1968). Before 1953, when the first multipurpose dam was built on the Missouri River, there were no wintering populations of Bald Eagles in South Dakota, but since that time they have been found regularly (Spencer 1976). One of the two densest populations in the United States is along the Missouri River on the South Dakota–Nebraska border, where there is a hydroelectric plant; it is also fairly close to the Karl E. Mundt and Lake Andes refuges. The other abundant population is farther south along the Missouri River in northern Missouri. Slighter concentrations extend west to the Kansas border and north on the Mississippi River to Wisconsin. Again there are national wildlife refuges as well as electric plants, primarily coal-burning, in these locations. The abundant population in southwestern Canada is at least partially an artifact of the analysis; there are few counts in this region. Although high numbers of Bald Eagles are recorded in British Columbia and western Alberta, the peak to the east is exaggerated. An intensive winter census in the conterminous United States conducted by the National Wildlife Federation from 1979 to 1982 revealed dense populations of Bald Eagles in northwestern Washington, along the Missouri and Mississippi rivers, and in northern Arkansas (Millsap 1986). All but the last of these locations are roughly the same ones found in this study.

There seems to be a vague tendency for this eagle to avoid the densely forested regions in the eastern mixed mesophytic and deciduous forest and the dry, harsh areas of the Southwest and western Nevada. The northern population extending along the Mississippi River into Minnesota shows an affinity for rivers. There are several disjunct populations, both inland and along the Atlantic coast.

Bald Eagles are often found in pairs. At times it appears that two birds may be hunting cooperatively, with one taking over the chase when the first tires, but this may be by coincidence rather than design. They eat fish, birds, mammals, and carrion, with dead or dying fish the primary staple (Brown and Amadon 1968). Waterfowl and mammals are the main prey items when water levels are high or there is extensive ice (Lingle and Krapu 1986). Eagles often steal fish from Ospreys, and they are capable of catching a goose on the wing (Brown and Amadon 1968). They frequently use other eagles as a cue to the location of food (Knight and Knight 1983).

Northern Harrier (*Circus cyaneus*) Maximum: 1.53 I/Hr

West of the 100th meridian, the northern distribution of the Northern Harrier is coincident with areas where the temperature drops below 5°F (−15°C). The exception is the extension of the range into Saskatchewan and Alberta, which is due to irregular sightings at two Canadian locations and one in Montana. In the East its range coincides with the dense mixed deciduous and coniferous forest. This raptor also avoids the higher elevations of the Appalachians and Ozarks.

Even though the distribution of the Northern Harrier stretches across North America, the abundance pattern shows that it is primarily a raptor of the Great Plains and Great Basin. Its most concentrated populations are restricted to areas with low, unobstructive vegetation of the semiarid shrub and scrub steppe, and to grassland. Also, abundant populations in general do not occur in habitats where the average minimum January temperature drops below 10°F (−12°C). The population in the Great Plains is extensive, with a peak along the Pecos River in southwestern Texas and eastern New Mexico that encompasses the Muleshoe, Bitter Lake, and Buffalo Lake national wildlife refuges. Smaller concentrations extend west to the Bosque del Apache and Sevilleta refuges along the Rio Grande valley, and others occur on the same river in southern Colorado around the Monte Vista and Alamosa refuges. These refuges undoubtedly influence Northern Harrier abundance by attracting numerous ducks as well as duck hunters, who provide wounded waterfowl. There are accounts of brazen harriers' taking injured ducks right in front of hunters (Brown and Amadon 1968). Northeast of the most extensive abundance peak, a more localized concentration occurs in the shinnery vegetation on the border between Texas and Oklahoma. Continuing in the same direction, another equally dense population occurs on the Arkansas River near the Quivira refuge. The high abundance in eastern Oklahoma is around Eufaula Reservoir near the Sequoyah refuge. In the Great Basin the highest peak occurs around the Great Salt Lake, with a slighter peak in Oregon around the Malheur and Hart Mountain refuges, and there is a depression in abundance in northwest Nevada. There is also a large concentration in the grassland habitat of the San Joaquin valley, with a peak around the Kesterson, San Luis, and Merced refuges. The only other area with a somewhat high abundance peak is along the Texas and Louisiana coast, also a grassland habitat.

The Northern Harrier roosts on dry mounds on the ground (Weller, Adams, and Rose 1955), usually in groups of fewer than ten, and sometimes with Short-eared Owls. During the day a harrier spends about 40% of its time on the wing, systematically quartering the same hunting ground, flying an estimated 100 miles (161 km) a day. In winter the size of this feeding territory ranges from 40 acres to one square mile (4–2,590 km²). It eats primarily small mammals and a few birds, frogs, reptiles, crustaceans, and insects (Brown and Amadon 1968). During a "good" *Microtus* year these mice make up 95% of the harrier's diet, while in a "bad" year they constitute only 75% (Weller, Adams, and Rose 1955).

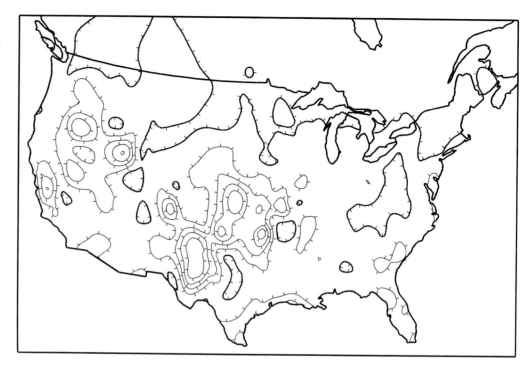

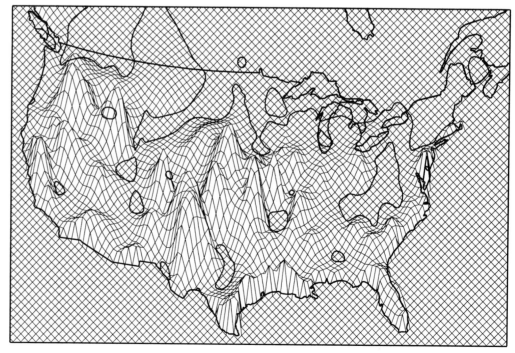

ACCIPITRIDAE

Sharp-shinned Hawk (*Accipiter striatus*) Map in Appendix B
The general low abundance of this widespread species brings into question the reliability of the mapping of its distribution and abundance patterns. Therefore, the contour map is included only in appendix B. The maximum mean abundance for this hawk was 0.12 individuals per party-hour, with peaks in northern Nevada, southwestern Texas, and central New Mexico and Arizona. In general the northern distributional limit shows that this raptor is absent from areas that get colder than 0°F (−18°C) in winter.

Cooper's Hawk (*Accipiter cooperii*) Map in Appendix B
Like the Sharp-shinned Hawk, the Cooper's Hawk is a widespread, rare species. Therefore, the Christmas count data may not provide an accurate representation of its biogeographic patterns. In general its northern range limit indicates that it avoids areas where the average minimum January temperature is below 10°F (−12°C). Concentrations are present around the northern California-Nevada border, in southern New Mexico, and in the southwestern corner of Utah, but the maximum average abundance was only 0.15 individuals per party-hour.

Northern Goshawk (*Accipiter gentilis*) Map in Appendix B
Like its congeners, the Northern Goshawk may be too rare and widespread for the Christmas count data to provide accurate abundance information. The maximum abundance was 0.09 goshawks seen per party-hour. The distribution shows that this species avoids the southeastern United States and ranges from western Texas north to Arkansas and east to the Atlantic coast.

Broad-winged Hawk (*Buteo platypterus*) Map in Appendix B
Irregular winter sightings of the Broad-winged Hawk occurred at seventy-seven count locations throughout the mixed mesophytic and deciduous forest of the East, and two additional reports came from the Monterey Bay region of California. This dense-woodland hawk was seen regularly only on the Florida Keys. The highest abundance was recorded west of Key Colony Beach, with a ten-year average of 0.37 individuals seen per party-hour. Besides southern Florida, the primary wintering ground for this raptor includes Guatemala on south through Middle America to eastern Peru, Bolivia, and southern Brazil (AOU 1983).

Short-tailed Hawk (*Buteo brachyurus*) No Map
In the United States, this raptor is restricted to southern Florida. It was recorded on eight Christmas counts from the Keys to near Zephyrhills, northwest of Lakeland. There was only one count where the Short-tailed Hawk was seen regularly, just off Florida Bay on Cape Sable, and even there the abundance was very low, with only 0.02 individuals seen per party-hour. Apart from Florida, this hawk can be found wintering throughout Mexico to eastern Peru, Bolivia, and northern Argentina (AOU 1983).

Swainson's Hawk (*Buteo swainsoni*) Map in Appendix B
The normal wintering grounds for the Swainson's Hawk are on the pampas of South America (AOU 1983), but a few birds are seen irregularly at sporadic locations on Christmas counts primarily in the west-central United States, from northern Montana to southern inland Texas. This raptor was seen most regularly on counts at Cape Sable, Florida (six years), and near Sinton, Texas (five years), just north of Corpus Christi. The average ten-year abundance at both these locations was less than 0.01 individuals seen per party-hour.

White-tailed Hawk (*Buteo albicaudatus*) No Map
The White-tailed Hawk is resident from southern Arizona and southeastern Texas through Middle America and South America to extreme eastern Peru and central Argentina (AOU 1983). It was recorded on only eleven count sites in the United States, but most regularly (six or more years) on the Texas Gulf coast. These sites included Laguna Atascosa National Wildlife Refuge, where the highest abundance was recorded (0.06 I/Hr), at the northern end of Padre Island National Seashore, around Copano Bay, and in Aransas National Wildlife Refuge. Concentrations of this hawk can be found around fires, because these birds are attracted to the small mammals exposed in the ashes (Tewes 1984).

Red-tailed Hawk, Harlan's Race (*Buteo jamaicensis harlani*) Map in
  Appendix B
The data were recorded separately for the Harlan's Hawk and Red-tailed Hawk, because at the time they were collected these races were considered separate species. I have not combined these data, because they provide insights into the ecology and evolution of the two taxa. The Harlan's Hawk is present in basically the same region where the Red-tailed Hawk is common: in the center of the United States between the 90th and 110th meridians. Peak abundances are in northeastern Arkansas and stretch over to a lesser peak in central Oklahoma and a separate peak in central Missouri. The overall abundance of this hawk was very low, however, reaching a maximum of only 0.12 individuals seen per party-hour.

Red-tailed Hawk (*Buteo jamaicensis*) Maximum: 1.80 I/Hr

The Red-tailed Hawk is present throughout North America except where the average minimum temperature drops below 5°F (−15°C) in January, including northwestern Wyoming and Idaho. The indicated presence of an abundant population of this raptor in British Columbia and western Alberta is unreliable because there is a lack of counts in this area, which forced the interpolation process to use only the high coastal values.

The major concentrations of this hawk are disjunct; one is primarily in the more fertile regions of California and the other is in the farming and ranching area of the central United States. The former peak is higher and extends from Kerns National Wildlife Refuge in the south to around the Clear Lake refuge in the north, with a projection into western Nevada near the Fallon and Stillwater refuges. The main area of concentration in the central United States is in eastern Oklahoma, eastern Nevada, northern Missouri, and southern Iowa. The edges of this area are concomitant to the east with the increasing altitude of the Appalachians, to the north with temperatures below 10°F (−12°C), and to the west with the arid regions receiving less than 24 inches (61 cm) of precipitation annually. This area encompasses the Central Feed, Grain, and Livestock land-resource region, where the land use is classified as arable with grazing. The abundance of grain in this area may support a large population of rodents and other animals (e.g., House Sparrow), which in turn supports a high concentration of Red-tailed Hawks. In central New York at least, the abundance of this hawk indeed correlates with the abundance of *Microtus* (Bart 1977). In the central United States, the highest concentrations appear to be associated with protected areas: on the eastern border of the Texas panhandle near Blackettle National Grassland, in northeastern Oklahoma near the Sequoyah refuge, and in northern Missouri around the Swan Lake refuge. As happened with several other raptors, the abundance of the Red-tailed Hawk decreased noticeably from 1903 to at least 1955 in Illinois (Graber and Golden 1960).

After the northern-breeding birds have migrated into the southern portion of the range, this raptor becomes more aggressive, and territories are defended, particularly by nonmigrating pairs (Brown and Amadon 1968). Soaring flight is used in defense, because an entire territory can be seen better from high altitudes and diving on an intruder from above is probably less costly and more intimidating (Ballam 1984). In winter the bird's diet may consist exclusively of mice, but when possible fairly large ground-dwelling birds, such as meadowlarks and quail, are added to its menu. Like owls, and unlike most other hawks, the Red-tailed Hawk will eat small mammals in one bite (Brown and Amadon 1968).

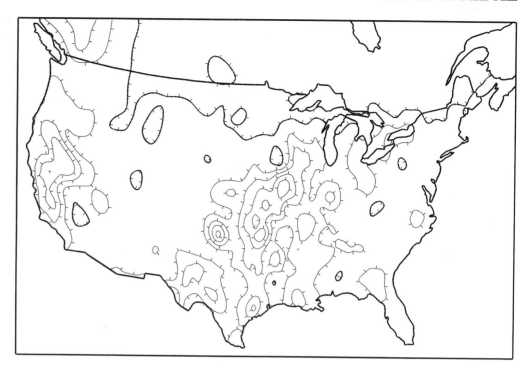

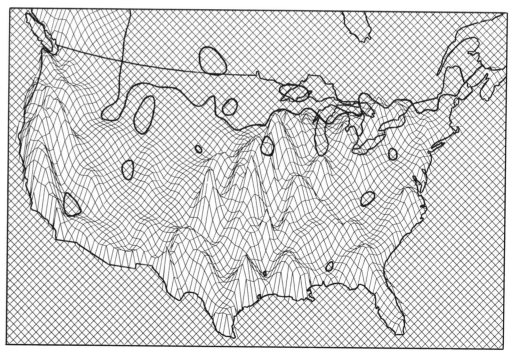

ACCIPITRIDAE

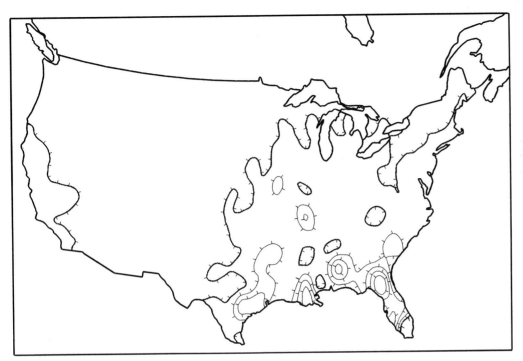

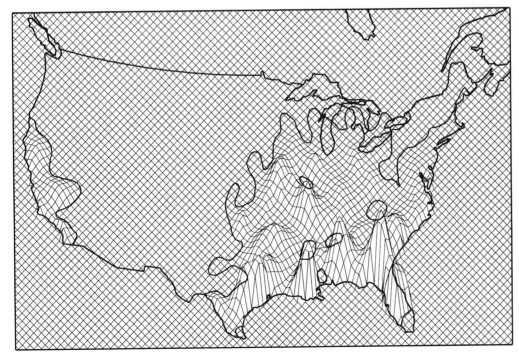

Red-shouldered Hawk (*Buteo lineatus*) Maximum: 0.56 I/Hr

In the West the Red-shouldered Hawk occurs chiefly in the area west of the higher peaks of the Sierra Nevada and the San Bernardino Mountains. Except in the grassland along the San Joaquin valley, this area is covered by the moist mixed evergreen and deciduous and coastal coniferous forests. In the East this hawk is primarily a species of the mixed mesophytic and deciduous forest, avoiding the much drier mixed deciduous and coniferous forest to the north and the grasslands to the west. The convoluted western range limit shows that this buteo extends its range into the grasslands along the galeria forests of the Missouri, Arkansas, and Mississippi rivers. The range in both the East and the West occurs in areas that have an elevation less than 1,000 feet (305 m) above sea level. This hawk avoids the higher elevations of the Appalachians and the Sierras. Most of its distribution is in areas that receive over 32 inches (81 cm) of precipitation annually.

Most of the concentrations are in regions of the country that have an average minimum January temperature over 40°F (4°C). This includes the most concentrated population, which extends from the Okefenokee Swamp and wildlife refuge to the swamp around Perry, Florida. Slighter concentrations stretch south of there, with an apex around Charlotte Harbor, and also west from the highest peak with a dense concentration around the William Dannelly Reservoir in Alabama. An abundant population occurs along the Louisiana bayous and a short distance up the Mississippi River. A less numerous population is on the coastal plain in eastern Texas, with an abundance peak in front of the Edwards Plateau. Two slight concentrations occur in a colder region of the country, just east of the Ozarks, and in Missouri on the Missouri River.

The Red-shouldered Hawk is more sedentary than the other buteos, normally staying within an area only about one-quarter mile in diameter. Here it sits and waits for unsuspecting prey, which in the winter consists mainly of mice, though it will not ignore other small mammals, birds, reptiles, and insects. It captures prey by dropping from its perch, which in winter is usually at the edge of a woodlot or a swampy area. Even in the summer it avoids the centers of large stands of forest (Brown and Amadon 1968). Logging undoubtedly is increasing its available habitat by making mosaics of the larger forest tracts. This may help explain the unusual finding that from 1903 to 1955 there was no decrease in abundance of this hawk in Illinois (Graber and Golden 1960).

Ferruginous Hawk (*Buteo regalis*) Maximum: 0.75 I/Hr

The Ferruginous Hawk spends more time soaring than any of the other buteos (Brown and Amadon 1968), which helps explain why it is present almost exclusively in areas over 2,000 feet (610 m) above sea level, but it avoids the high altitudes of the Rocky Mountains. This raptor is absent from the Great Plains and the lower altitudes of the Imperial Valley and from the area around and inland from Monterey Bay. It also avoids harsh, dry areas such as the Sonoran Desert and most regions that get less than 8 inches (20 cm) of precipitation a year. Except for the population around Billings, Montana, all the disjunct populations north and east of the main distribution are ephemeral, with individuals observed only in a few years. In fact the occurrence in Mississippi was due to a light-phase bird seen on the Moon Lake count in 1965. The editor commented that this was "amazing, probably the first Mississippi report" (Cruickshank 1965). The Montana population is near the Greycliff Prairie Dog Town State Monument. The Ferruginous Hawk undoubtedly is attracted to this location because prairie dogs are one of the main items in its diet (Brown and Amadon 1968).

Like many hawks and eagles that have been relentlessly persecuted, the Ferruginous Hawk is becoming rare and needs protection (Brown and Amadon 1968). The abundance pattern shows that it is fairly uncommon throughout most of its winter range, except around the panhandle and western regions of Texas and in southwestern Texas. Two populations have dense concentrations: one is southwest of the Davis Mountains, along the Rio Grande valley, and the other is around Amarillo and Dalhart, Texas. From the latter region, rather high abundances of this hawk stretch from northeastern New Mexico and the panhandle of Oklahoma along the New Mexico–Texas border to a much slighter peak around Midland and Odessa, Texas. This lower peak is in the region where several other hawks are abundant.

Besides prairie dogs, this raptor preys upon other small to medium-sized mammals like mice and ground squirrels. Pairs of hawks have been reported to hunt cooperatively for larger prey such as jackrabbits. When they are available, it will also eat snakes and larger insects (Brown and Amadon 1968). When not soaring, this open-country buteo perches on badger mounds or, if available, trees or posts (Brown and Amadon 1968). In the evening, along the northern part of the winter distribution, it has been found to roost with Bald Eagles, and this apparently is not due to a shortage of roost sites (Steenhof 1984). The birds that nest in the northern extremes of the breeding area are migratory, moving into the warmer southern areas to winter (Brown and Amadon 1968).

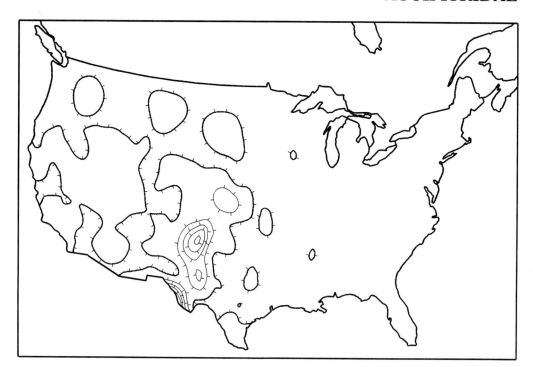

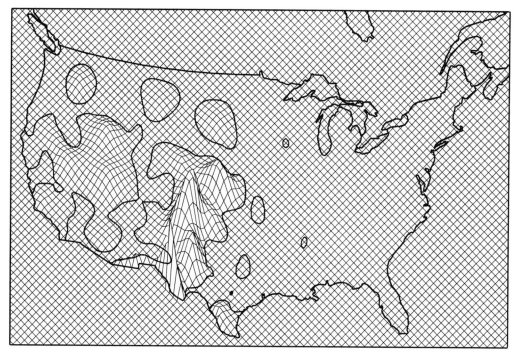

ACCIPITRIDAE

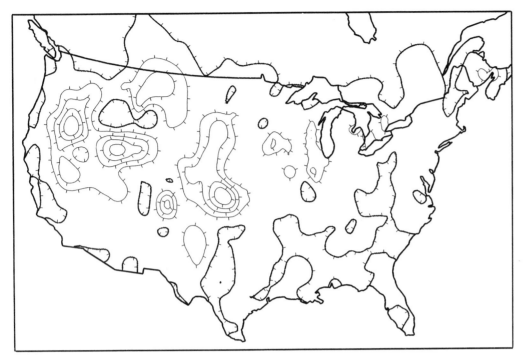

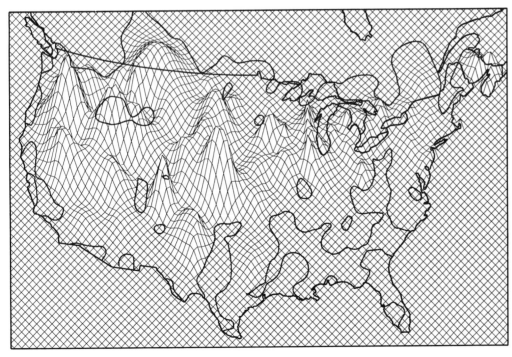

Rough-legged Hawk (*Buteo lagopus*) Maximum: 1.02 I/Hr

The distribution of the Rough-legged Hawk appears to correlate most strongly with climatic factors, specifically precipitation and temperature. To the north this raptor is absent from regions where the average minimum January temperature drops below $-10°F$ ($-23°C$). It also tends to avoid the western coastline and the southeastern corner of the United States, perhaps because it prefers areas that get less than 40 inches (102 cm) of annual precipitation.

The abundance pattern of the Rough-legged Hawk shows that it occurs throughout the United States but is most common in the Great Basin and northern Great Plains. The most concentrated populations are strongly associated with national wildlife refuges, which provide a protected and managed environment for both the hawk and its prey. In the Great Plains, the rather extensive peak in Montana encompasses the Benton Lake, Bowdoin, and Charles M. Russell refuges. There are no refuges in the corridor of low abundance extending from northwestern South Dakota through western Wyoming. The abundance increases from central South Dakota on south into the northeastern corner of Colorado, reaching its apex in western Kansas. Just to the west of this peak is a lower one in the San Luis Valley of Colorado. In the Great Basin the increased population covers a very large area stretching from western slope of the Cascades and Sierra Nevada through Oregon and northern Nevada to southwestern Wyoming and central Utah. National wildlife refuges are scattered throughout this area, except in north-central Nevada, where the abundance significantly decreases, and in central Oregon. Peaks are reached in northern Utah around the Bear River refuge and in south-central Oregon near the Malheur, Hart Mountain, and Sheldon refuges. Outside the Great Basin and Great Plains, fairly dense concentrations exist in northeastern Illinois and southeastern Wisconsin, which do not correspond with any refuges, and in northern Iowa around the Union Slough refuge.

Brown and Amadon (1968) report that migration out of the northern breeding areas depends on the availability of food, primarily lemmings. When the lemmings are abundant, Rough-legged Hawks remain in the North, provided the snow is not so deep that the lemmings are difficult to catch. (During the ten years of Christmas counts examined, this hawk was seen on about the same number of southern counts each year.) Besides lemmings, the Rough-legged Hawk eats other small mammals and an occasional bird. All of its prey, including birds, is captured on the ground (Brown and Amadon 1968). Individuals are territorial in the winter (Watson 1986), but mated pairs often remain together throughout the winter, and in the evening several birds will roost together (Brown and Amadon 1968). Flying frequency is affected by various weather conditions. The hawks fly less when the wind velocity is low, the skies are overcast, there is a falling barometer, the relative humidity is high, and the temperature is low (Schnell 1967).

Harris' Hawk (*Parabuteo unicinctus*) Maximum: 1.49 I/Hr

General dryness of the environment and certain types of vegetation are apparently associated with the range of the Harris' Hawk. The maps show that it lives in areas where the pan evaporation is over 100 inches (256 cm) but avoids the harshest areas, which include the deserts of southeastern California and southern Nevada, where the pan evaporation is over 130 inches (330 cm). Even though the general humidity is near the appropriate levels, the Harris' Hawk avoids the Rio Grande valley in southern New Mexico, probably because the vegetation is inappropriate. This region contains a shrub steppe habitat of grama and tobosa grass, quite different from the vegetation in regions where this raptor is present. In southwestern Arizona this bird occurs in an environment of creosote bush and bur sage, with paloverde and cactus shrub mixed in. In southern Texas the vegetation consists of mesquite and acacia scrub, and in western Texas it comprises buffalo grass and mesquite.

The abundance pattern of the Harris' Hawk shows two populations with equally high concentrations, one in western Texas around the Midland-Odessa area and the other in southern Texas on the Nueces Plains in front of the Edwards Plateau. The human population in both these regions is relatively low.

The Harris' Hawk occurs in seasonally dry deserts and savannas that have fairly complex vegetation structure, with saguaro and other cacti, paloverde, ironwood, and shrubs (Mader 1978). It needs a moderate amount of tall vegetation (or telephone poles) for perches (Grossman and Hamlet 1964). Compared with other buteos in the area, the Harris' Hawk has shorter wings and a longer tail, allowing agile flying through fairly dense vegetation in pursuit of prey (Grossman and Hamlet 1964; Mader 1978). Its diet is varied, consisting of mammals, birds, reptiles, and possibly carrion (Grossman and Hamlet 1964), and changes in its menu depend on the abundance of the prey (Mader 1978). Snakes, however, are rarely eaten, perhaps because their sluggish behavior makes them difficult to detect, or because this hawk's talons are too long to instantly kill deadly prey (Mader 1978). When it eats birds, including teal, flickers, rails, and gallinules, it first plucks their feathers (Brown and Amadon 1968). Harris' Hawks are normally found in pairs (Brown and Amadon 1968) and, in Arizona at least, often in trios (Mader 1978), probably because of their extended breeding season, which begins in February and runs through December. Bonds between individuals sometimes last longer than one breeding season, and one trio is known to have remained together from 1973 to 1975 (Mader 1978). Where they are not persecuted, Harris' Hawks become very tame (Brown and Amadon 1968).

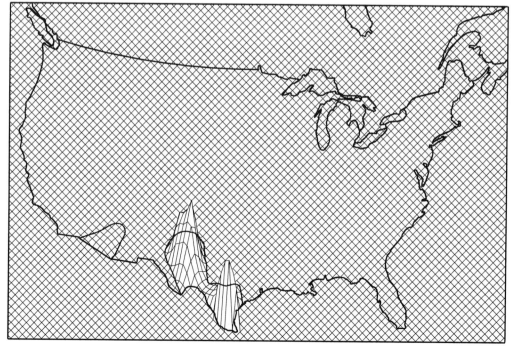

Harris' Hawk

ACCIPITRIDAE

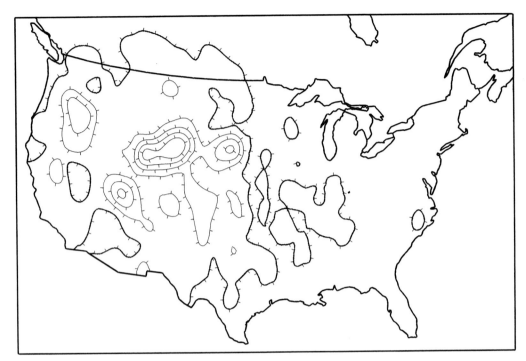

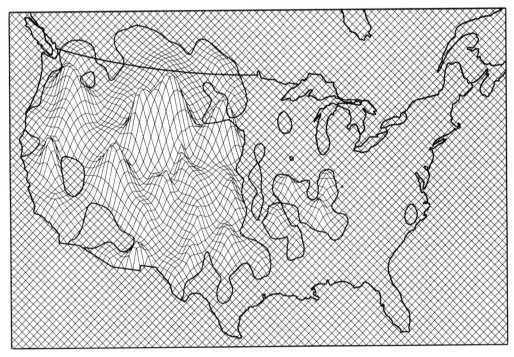

Golden Eagle (*Aquila chrysaetos*) Maximum: 0.58 I/Hr

Describing the Golden Eagle as the mountain eagle (Brown and Amadon 1968) is quite appropriate, as is indicated by its distribution on the maps. Besides a few disjunct populations east of the 95th meridian, which are due to irregular sightings, this bird of prey frequents only western areas that are over about 1,500 feet (457 m) in elevation. This holds true for the low elevations of the Imperial Valley, the northern coastline, and the Columbia basin, all of which this eagle avoids. Other areas where it is absent are the harsh, dry areas of the Sonoran Desert and central Nevada, which receive less than 8 inches (20 cm) of precipitation annually. East of the Canadian Rockies the northern distribution limit skirts the northern edge of the grasslands, with this eagle avoiding the mixed mesophytic and deciduous forest. In the Rockies and on west, the bird is absent from the western temperate forests, but it does extend north into eastern Washington, where there is a small area of grassland.

Like the distribution pattern, the abundance pattern is associated with elevation. Most of the highly concentrated populations occur near the foothills of mountains, where there are excellent updrafts. This eagle is an accomplished soarer (Brown and Amadon 1968). The densest population, which covers a large area, is in the Wyoming basin around Casper, Wyoming, and extends over to the Green River in the Flaming Gorge National Recreational Area. A slight abundance continues over to another peak that is away from the mountains on the border of South Dakota and Nebraska near Fort Niobrara National Wildlife Area and the Lake Andes refuge on the Missouri River. From the former peak, a slight abundance continues south along the eastern foothills of the Rocky Mountains. There is also a slight peak in abundance in the San Luis Valley of southern Colorado and a rather high concentration in southwestern Utah, west of the Hurricane Cliffs. In the Great Basin, a somewhat dense population occurs east of the Cascades in Oregon.

The Bald Eagle Act of 1940 protected the national bird from persecution (Boeker and Ray 1971) and apparently aided the Golden Eagle indirectly, because there was an increase in wintering Golden Eagles in Illinois from the early 1940s to at least 1955 (Graber and Golden 1960). In 1962 the Bald Eagle Act was officially amended to protect the Golden Eagle (Boeker and Ray 1971), but this majestic bird is still persecuted.

In winter the staple of its diet is carrion. When hunting, it usually slowly quarters slopes and occasionally stoops at speeds measured at 150 to 200 miles (24–32 km) an hour to catch prey. It prefers mammals but will take game birds too. It usually captures prey on the ground, but cranes and geese are infrequently caught in the air. There is apparently some correlation between the density of prey and the size of this eagle's home range, which in California varies from 20 to 60 square miles (51,800–155,400 km^2), with a mean of 35 square miles (90,650 km^2) (Brown and Amadon 1968).

FALCONIDAE

Crested Caracara (*Polyborus plancus*) No Map

The Crested Caracara is resident from southern Arizona, central Texas, and central Florida south through Middle America and most of South America (AOU 1983). On the Christmas counts, it was recorded at twenty-seven sites: one in southwestern Arizona, four in Florida, and twenty-two in southern Texas. All six sites reporting this falcon most regularly were in southern Texas.

Prairie Falcon (*Falco mexicanus*) Maximum: 0.22 I/Hr

As its name suggests, the Prairie Falcon prefers nonforested habitats. It occurs throughout the West in the semiarid and scrub steppes, dry-belt pine forest, and grasslands and avoids the mixed mesophytic and deciduous forest to the east, the tree and shrub savanna to the southeast, the boreal woodland to the north, the western temperate forest in Idaho, and the coastal coniferous forest along the Pacific coast. The vacant area along the 110th meridian from southern Montana to northern New Mexico may reflect the bird's avoidance of scattered stands of western temperate forest.

The peak abundances are chiefly in the Great Plains and Great Basin. In the former, dense concentrations are strongly associated with protected areas. The highest abundance is on the border between South Dakota and Nebraska near the Fort Niobrara and Valentine national wildlife refuges. Lesser abundance peaks occur near Great Bend, Kansas, on the Arkansas River, around the Kiowa National Grasslands of New Mexico, in Colorado on the Pawnee National Grasslands, and throughout the San Luis Valley of Colorado. The concentrated populations in the Great Basin show no obvious association with protected or managed areas. The two highest abundances are in the northwestern corner of Utah and on the northern part of the border between California and Nevada, with a lesser concentration extending north through central Oregon to south-central Washington.

The Prairie Falcon cannot fly quite as fast as the Peregrine Falcon, but it is still able to catch rapidly flying birds, such as White-throated Swifts. Most of its prey, however, is caught on the ground. While hunting, it will fly 50 to 300 feet (15–91 m) above the ground looking for prey. When it detects an item, the falcon descends on a long, sloping stoop. It usually takes small to medium-sized mammals, such as rabbits and ground squirrels, but birds of the same size will not be ignored when available. In the winter, territories become linear, extending along telephone wires for about 6 miles (10 km). Birds can often be seen perched on telephone poles, but windy weather may force them to perch on grass hummocks. This falcon frequently harries other raptors in the area (Brown and Amadon 1968).

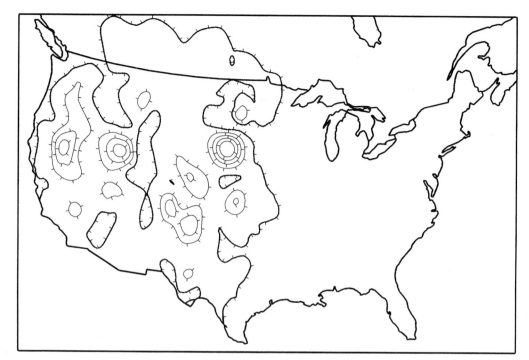

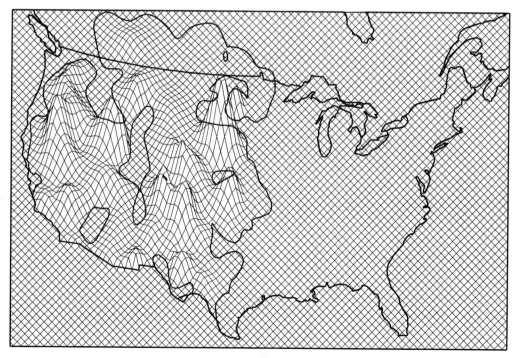

Prairie Falcon

FALCONIDAE

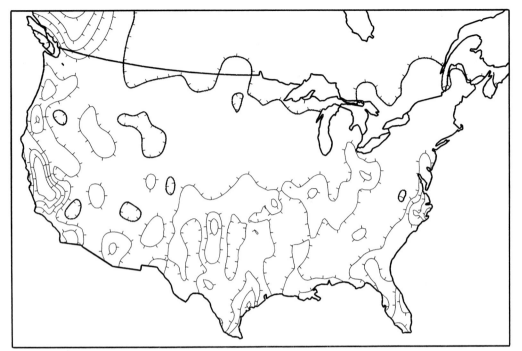

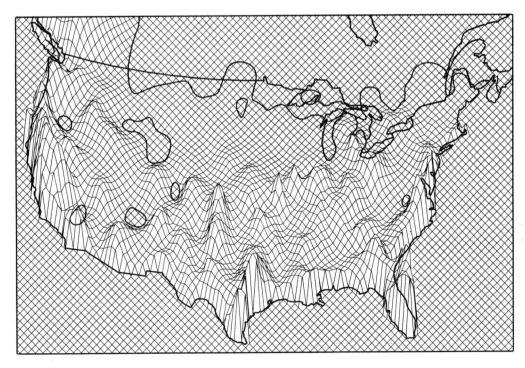

American Kestrel (*Falco sparverius*) Maximum: 2.04 I/Hr

Unfortunately, the lack of counts in southwestern Canada and the rather high density of kestrels along the Strait of Georgia have both contributed to an artifactual abundance peak in British Columbia and an extended distribution limit in western Alberta. The interpolation process undoubtedly overestimated the number of kestrels in this area, and therefore this peak should be ignored. The rest of the map, however, appears to accurately represent the number of American Kestrels wintering in the United States.

Temperature is the primary environmental factor associated with the distribution and abundance patterns of the American Kestrel. The northern range limit coincides with the average minimum January temperature isotherm of 0°F (−18°C), and most of the more concentrated populations are in areas where the January temperature rarely gets below 20°F (−7°C). The distribution pattern also shows that this falcon is absent around the higher peaks of the Rocky Mountains, in the Mojave Desert, and in northeastern Arizona where less than 8 inches (20 cm) of precipitation falls annually. The vacancy in these last two regions is unexpected, given that this species has two characteristics that would help it survive harsh desert environments: an elevated body temperature, which allows it to radiate heat in hot environments, and a diet that makes drinking unnecessary (Brown and Amadon 1968).

The American Kestrel is relatively common throughout most of the country where the minimum January temperature is over 20°F (−7°C). The only major exception is the area around the Appalachians. There are several locations where the densities reach a maximum of 2.04 individuals seen per party-hour. The most extensive of these populations is in the Sacramento and San Joaquin valleys of California. All of southern Florida has a rather high concentration, but the areas along the Atlantic coast from Cocoa Beach to West Palm Beach and on the Gulf coast from Naples to the southern tip have the highest density. Another population of high density occurs on the Atlantic coast around Pamlico Sound in North Carolina. The only other equally high peak is on the Texas coast near Port Lavaca.

The American Kestrel is usually solitary and even roosts alone (Brown and Amadon 1968). The females normally frequent open habitats that are sparsely vegetated, whereas the males stay in areas with denser vegetation, though usually near a clearing (Mills 1976). Individuals maintain territories throughout the winter. This falcon prefers elevated perches such as telephone poles and wires. From these vantage points, or sometimes while hovering, it searches for prey, which it captures by diving on them. In the winter it eats primarily mice and a few birds, except in areas with heavy snow cover, where the kestrel is a connoisseur of House Sparrows and mice (Brown and Amadon 1968). From 1903 to 1955 the American Kestrels wintering in Illinois declined (Graber and Golden 1960), and this trend probably has continued.

American Kestrel

Merlin (*Falco columbarius*) Map in Appendix B

This falcon is seen throughout North America, but nowhere is the abundance very great; the maximum was only 0.11 Merlins per party-hour. Because it is so rare, the Christmas counts may not give an accurate representation of this species' abundance pattern, and thus, its map is included in appendix B. The Merlin is seen throughout the West and only sporadically in the East. According to the AOU (1983), it winters in North America west of the Rocky Mountains, locally in southern Canada, and from South Carolina to southern Texas along the Gulf coast, extending south through Middle America to northern South America.

Peregrine Falcon (*Falco peregrinus*) Map in Appendix B

The Peregrine Falcon is present in low numbers over most of the United States, and owing to its rarity (maximum abundance of 0.11 I/Hr) the Christmas count data may not give an accurate portrayal of its abundance pattern; thus, its map is provided in appendix B. Its abundance began to decline about 1954, and ten years later DDT was determined to be the major cause. In 1969 this falcon was officially placed on the endangered-species list, and a captive-breeding program was started. DDT was finally restricted in this country in 1972 (Cade 1983). Besides occurring in the United States, this falcon winters throughout Middle and South America (AOU 1983), where the pesticide restrictions are not strict. The captive-breeding program has been successful, and the three breeding centers are raising more than two hundred young a year. Between 1975 and 1984, these three facilities, along with private and Canadian breeders, have released a thousand Peregrine Falcons into the wild (Cade 1983).

Gyrfalcon (*Falco rusticolus*) No Map

This large falcon winters in the northern half of the southern provinces of Canada and in southern Alaska, with only a few birds, primarily immatures, wandering far enough south to be in the area examined in this study (Cramp 1980). The Gyrfalcon was observed at only twenty Christmas count locations, all north of the 40th parallel. At eighteen of these locations this falcon was seen in only one year. The remaining two locations recorded it in only two years.

CRACIDAE

Plain Chachalaca (*Ortalis vetula*) No Map

This noisy but fairly secretive bird ranges throughout parts of northeastern Mexico, with its northern limit along the lower Rio Grande valley in southern Texas (AOU 1983). In the United States the density is greatest at the Santa Ana National Wildlife Refuge, with an average of 2.77 birds seen per hour of census effort. The introduced and established population on Sapelo Island off the Georgia coast was recorded in four years. The density declined from a high of 0.16 birds per party-hour in 1963 to 0.03 in 1966, and thereafter none were recorded.

PHASIANIDAE

Spruce Grouse (*Dendragapus canadensis*) No Map

This grouse is rarely seen on Christmas counts, partly because of its arboreal habits and partly because it frequents dense coniferous forests when snow covers the ground (Johnsgard 1975). The populations near cities have been reduced too, because these rather tame birds were killed in fairly large numbers (Bent 1932). Of the nine counts reporting Spruce Grouse, the highest abundance was in southern Nova Scotia, with roughly one individual seen for every 6.7 hours of searching.

Blue Grouse (*Dendragapus obscurus*) No Map

Like the Spruce Grouse, this species is difficult to locate in the winter. It avoids snow on the ground by becoming arboreal and moves up in elevation to the upper spruce forests, which have denser foliage and provide greater protection from harsh weather (Bent 1932). It was reported on sixteen counts in the southern and central Rockies and the northern Cascades, with the most abundant population (0.37 I/Hr) recorded in the Colorado Rockies.

Sage Grouse (*Centrocercus urophasianus*) No Map

The Sage Grouse, largest of all the grouse in the United States and Canada, is a western species, occurring only in scrub steppe communities. It relies on sagebrush for both cover and food, particularly in winter (Johnsgard 1983b), when sage makes up 100% of its diet. During the fall migration this species travels down from the mountain peaks to the foothills. All ten count sites recording this grouse were in the foothills. The densest population was in the southwest corner of North Dakota near Bowman, where on average 3.93 birds were seen every party-hour.

PHASIANIDAE

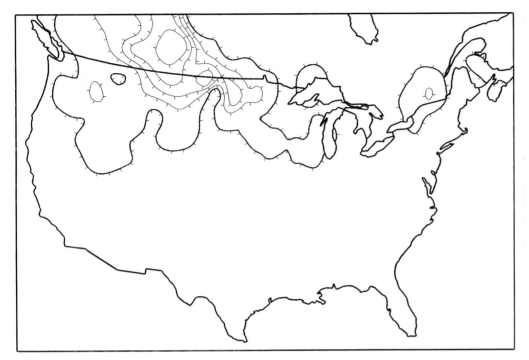

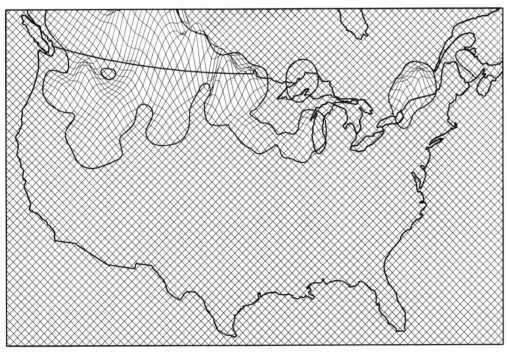

Gray Partridge (*Perdix perdix*) Maximum: 4.00 I/Hr

This species was first introduced to North America in New Jersey by Benjamin Franklin's son-in-law in the late 1700s. Other introductions of a few individuals were tried, and in 1907 an extensive transplanting effort was undertaken in the Atlantic coast states. None of these were successful. A release program in 1908 near Calgary did succeed, however, and the birds introduced from Hungary quickly established themselves. These and individuals from subsequent introductions dispersed throughout southwestern Canada and the northwestern United States (Bent 1932).

The maps show that vegetation strongly influences where this partridge survives. Essentially the species avoids dense coniferous, mixed coniferous, and deciduous forests. Temperature and snowfall do not overtly dictate where it exists.

Vegetation is also important in determining where the Gray Partridge occurs in high numbers. All the high-density populations are in grasslands. The eastern edge of this high-abundance area is coincident with the border between the grasslands and the mixed mesophytic and deciduous forests. To the west, this partridge occupies the grasslands of the plains in front of the foothills of the Canadian Rocky Mountains. This entire region of high abundance is coincident with the area where spring wheat is grown. The harvested wheatfields contain dropped grains, and these, along with weed seeds from fencerows and abandoned pastures, provide food in the winter (Bent 1932). The disjunct region in the West where partridges are somewhat common also occurs in a segregated grassland habitat of the plateau prairie.

Chukar (*Alectoris chukar*) No Map

This species was introduced into forty-two states and six provinces, but it established itself only in ten states and one province (Johnsgard 1973). It was recorded on only thirty-five counts, scattered primarily throughout the western United States. Most birds were seen in northern Oregon, with an average of 2.09 individuals seen per hour of censusing. The factors probably limiting its distribution and abundance are its preference for rocky slopes in sagebrush-grassland communities and its need for open water (Johnsgard 1973).

Gray Partridge

Ring-necked Pheasant (*Phasianus colchicus*) Maximum: 15.47 I/Hr
Ring-necked Pheasants from Shanghai, China, were first introduced to
North America in Oregon in 1881. The first eastern introduction was in
1887 in New Jersey. There were numerous subsequent introductions, and
by 1928 this adaptable bird had spread from coast to coast. It was so pro-
lific in its new environment that hunters had shot about 1 million individuals by 1926 and 1.5 million by 1927 (Bent 1932).

The factors shaping the range of the Ring-necked Pheasant are somewhat obscure because it is extensively managed as a game bird, but some
patterns do emerge. Its southern limit coincides with the 20°F (−7°C)
isotherm of average minimum January temperature. Thus, this pheasant
frequents cold areas but avoids regions where the climate is too cold; its
northern range limit coincides with the −10°F (−23°C) isotherm. This
northern limit also shows that the Ring-necked Pheasant is absent from the
boreal-coniferous forest, which is too dense to allow much seed-producing
undergrowth to survive.

Four of the five areas with the highest densities of Ring-necked Pheasants are grassland habitats where the pheasants easily find grains and seeds.
The fifth peak is in the lowlands to the northwest of the Great Salt Lake,
where the forest is fairly open, with grassy undergrowth in which this bird
forages. In the northern part of this abundant area spring wheat is grown,
and waste grain in the field and weed seeds along the fencerows are an
excellent source of food.

In the winter this pheasant requires protected roosting locations, particularly during harsh weather. The bushes and trees along rivers and creeks,
shelterbelts, and fencerows provide such protection. Even though it is a
ground-foraging species, deep snow cover does not seem to deter its feeding. It just uses its powerful legs to scratch through the snow (Johnsgard
1973). In fact, the southern edge of its distribution shows that it lives in
areas that receive two feet of snowfall annually.

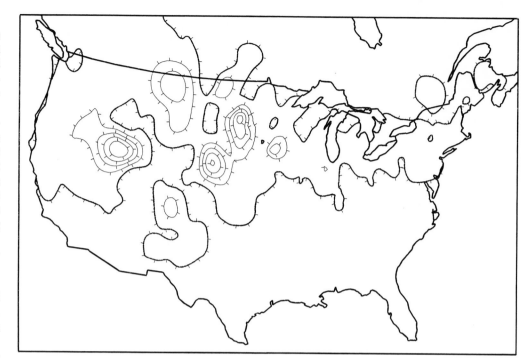

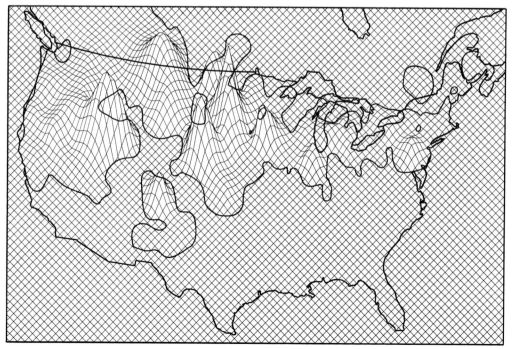

Ring-necked Pheasant

PHASIANIDAE

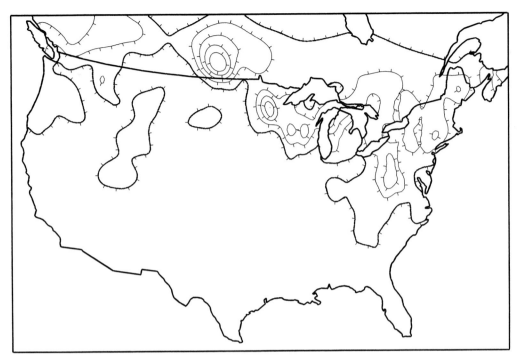

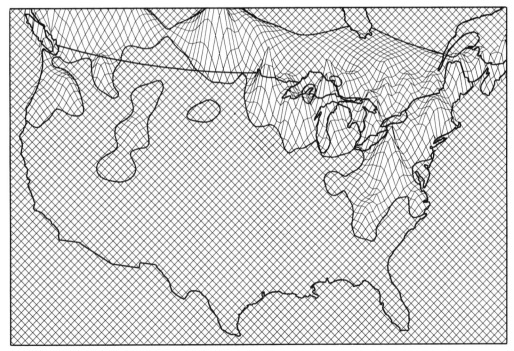

White-tailed Ptarmigan (*Lagopus leucurus*) No Map
This ptarmigan, which occurs at various locations throughout the Rocky Mountains (AOU 1983), was recorded at only two Christmas count sites. Its preferred habitat is stunted willow thickets on windswept mountains above treeline. The buds and twigs of the willows make up its entire winter diet (Johnsgard 1975). The two sites recording this bird were in the Colorado Rockies, with the higher abundance (0.18 I/Hr) and more regular sightings (six years) in Rocky Mountain National Park.

Ruffed Grouse (*Bonasa umbellus*) Maximum: 0.81 I/Hr
The Ruffed Grouse is primarily a resident of dense forests; it prefers deciduous trees to pines (Johnsgard 1975), and vegetation is strongly associated with its range limits. The distribution skirts grasslands, semiarid scrub, and dry-belt pine forest habitats, which do not provide the necessary dense arboreal environment. This bird does occur in the mixed mesophytic and deciduous, mixed deciduous and coniferous, western temperate, and coastal coniferous forests. The disjunct population that extends from Montana to Utah is in the northern Rocky Mountains where the forest consists of Douglas and true fir species, spruces, and pines. Without its preferred habitat of deciduous trees, except for a few scattered aspens, this population remains relatively uncommon.

The southern range limit along the Pacific coast is concomitant with the area where the forest gets drier and more open and where the California oaks begin. The southern edge of the distribution that occurs within the mixed mesophytic and deciduous forest indicates that altitude influences where this species lives. It appears to occur only at elevations above 1,000 feet (305 m), including the Appalachian Mountains, where the bird is relatively common.

The areas of high abundance are also strongly associated with deciduous forests. The peak in the Appalachians occurs in the northern hardwood forest community. The other peaks are in the mixed mesophytic and deciduous forest.

When the ground is snow covered this grouse become arboreal, eating buds and twigs from poplars, aspens, apple trees, birches, oaks, and cherry trees (Johnsgard 1975), along with the berries of poison ivy and sumac (Bent 1932). When the weather becomes severe, it makes a snow cave, just large enough to accommodate one bird, by flying into a snowbank (Bent 1932). Cold weather, therefore, is not a major factor limiting this species' distribution unless there is little snow cover.

Ruffed Grouse

Sharp-tailed Grouse (*Tympanuchus phasianellus*) Maximum:
12.86 I/Hr

The range limit of the Sharp-tailed Grouse is strongly associated with vege-tation. This bird thrives in most types of grasslands, but in the South it completely avoids the bluestem prairie and even the mixed bluestem–grama grass prairie. The rift shown in the grasslands separating the two regions where this species is most abundant is at least in part an artifact of the interpolation program and the lack of counts in this area. The rift in Minnesota and Manitoba, however, is real and not an artifact. It shows that the grouse does not live in mixed mesophytic and deciduous forests. The disjunct population in Wisconsin is in an ecotone of oak savanna and blue-stem prairie. The disjunct population in Washington centers on a grassland habitat of the plateau prairies.

The abundance peaks are in grassland habitats. Two high-density popu-lations occur along the Missouri and Saskatchewan rivers; the former is associated with an extensive galeria forest. These peaks, along with the entire area where this grouse is somewhat abundant, are in the area where spring wheat is grown.

This grouse occupies several diverse vegetation types, including grass-lands, western temperate forests, and dense spruce-fir forests. In winters when there is deep snowcover, the birds in the forests become arboreal to avoid the snow and eat the buds of willows, aspens, and larches (Bent 1932). In the grasslands, the species forages on grains and seeds and prob-ably makes use of galeria forests and farmer-planted shelterbelts during particularly harsh weather.

Greater Prairie-Chicken (*Tympanuchus cupido*) No Map

As pioneers moved west and started growing small-grain crops, this game bird expanded its range (Johnsgard 1983b), but as farms increased it began declining. With the human takeover of the habitat, and with extensive hunting, the birds decreased almost to extinction. Game preserves and na-tional wildlife refuges played an important part in preserving this species (Bent 1932). It was recorded at twenty CBC sites, all in the west-central lowlands of the Interior Plains, the region roughly between the 95th and 100th meridians. The area of highest abundance (2.80 I/Hr) occurred around the Kansas-Missouri border.

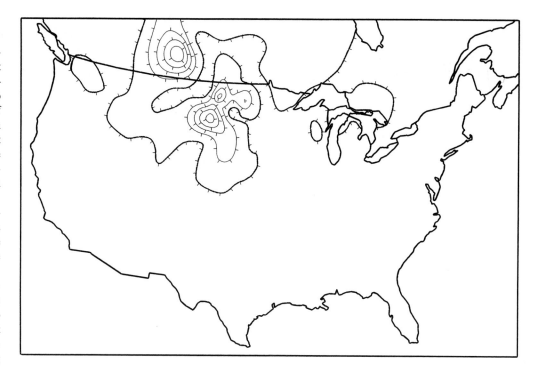

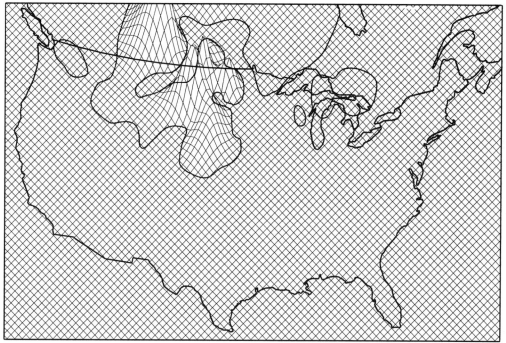

Sharp-tailed Grouse

PHASIANIDAE

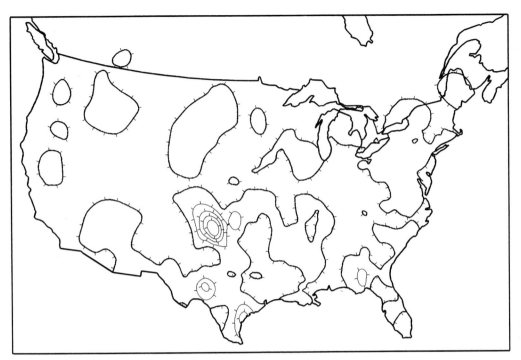

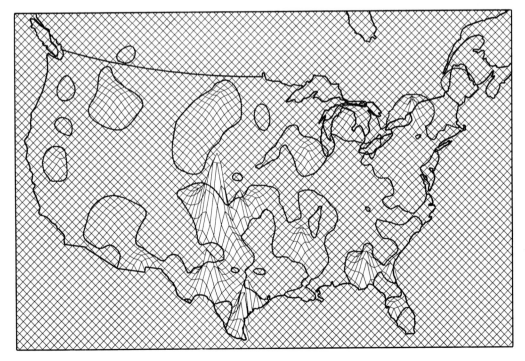

Lesser Prairie-Chicken (*Tympanuchus pallidicinctus*) No Map
Like the Greater Prairie Chicken, this slightly smaller species has been decimated by humans. As its habitat has been taken over for farming and ranching, the seeds on which it feeds have become more and more scarce. Now it strongly relies on cultivated grains and cereals for survival, particularly in the winter (Johnsgard 1973). The three counts where it was recorded, one in eastern New Mexico and two in western Oklahoma, are in the region where corn, winter wheat, and sorghum are cultivated. It was seen most regularly in the Gypsum Hills of the Oklahoma panhandle region (seven years, 7.58 I/Hr).

Wild Turkey (*Meleagris gallopavo*) Maximum: 3.28 I/Hr
The biogeography of this species has been greatly affected by humans. Its original range included most of the eastern, central, and southern United States, but with the introduction of firearms the abundance of this tasty bird plummeted. The last nonintroduced individuals were shot out of Connecticut in 1813, and it vanished from the mountains of Massachusetts in 1851 (Bent 1932). Numerous reintroductions have been tried, as well as introductions into areas where it previously did not occur, such as the Pacific coast states. Several of these have been unsuccessful owing to poaching and the lack of adequate habitat. This present-day distribution and abundance pattern is determined almost totally by management programs.

All but one of the more abundant populations occur near protected environments. The highest abundance is in the Texas-Oklahoma panhandle region where the Howe Wildlife Management Area is situated, along with three national grasslands: Black Kettle, Rita Blanca, and Kiowa. The lesser peak in north-central Oklahoma centers on the Great Salt Plains National Wildlife Refuge. In southern Texas, Wild Turkeys are fairly common in and around Aransas National Wildlife Refuge. The rather dense population near Tallahassee, Florida, is probably able to survive because of the protection it receives in the Apalachicola National Forest. The only fairly abundant population that is not obviously associated with a wildlife preserve is in a very sparsely populated area of south-central Texas near the Pecos and Devils rivers.

Many of the disjunct populations scattered around the United States do not have a very high density of Wild Turkeys. Even in these areas the turkey is undoubtedly managed to some degree, either by introductions or by providing supplemental grain in the winter. These management practices are necessary, since most of this species' suitable habitat has been eliminated by "human progress."

Montezuma Quail (*Cyrtonyx montezumae*) No Map
The United States distribution of this comical-looking quail primarily includes south-central Arizona, at the northern end of the Sierra Madre Occidental of Mexico. This quail lives on rocky foothills in the oak-juniper woodlands. Within this habitat it feeds primarily on the bulbs of wood sorrel and on nut-grass tubers (Johnsgard 1973). In the winter it also eats acorns, piñon nuts, and fruit of various types (Bent 1932). The densest population was recorded on the count near Patagonia, Arizona, where on average one quail was seen every 2.25 party-hours. Disjunct populations were recorded in western New Mexico in a piñon-juniper community and southwestern Texas in an oak-juniper habitat.

Northern Bobwhite (*Colinus virginianus*) Maximum: 5.20 I/Hr
The Northern Bobwhite is a favorite game bird, so its abundance is extensively managed throughout the year. This quail frequently has been introduced and established outside its native range (AOU 1983). The effects of introductions on the biogeographic pattern may be obvious, as they are in Oregon and Idaho, or subtle and manifested only as range extensions (e.g., northwestern Wyoming) (Johnsgard 1973).

The distribution of the Northern Bobwhite shows that it avoids certain types of vegetation. The southwestern half of the range limit coincides with the eastern edge of the semiarid scrub and scrub steppe, and north of that with the dry-belt pine forest. From approximately the Great Lakes on east, the northern limit shows that this quail avoids the mixed deciduous and coniferous forest. The northern edge in the Great Plains probably is determined not by natural vegetation but by the northern limit of the Central Great Plains Winter-Wheat and Range-Land resource region.

Very dense concentrations also occur in the Central Great Plains Winter-Wheat and Range-Land resource area. This region grows primarily winter wheat and some sorghum, important foods for this quail, especially in winter. Most of the other fairly abundant populations occur in regions where sorghum is raised. The western range edge and, more certainly, the western limit of the more abundant populations are apparently influenced by the occurrence of the Scaled Quail. This and other such interactions between various quail are discussed in greater detail in the text for the Gambel's Quail.

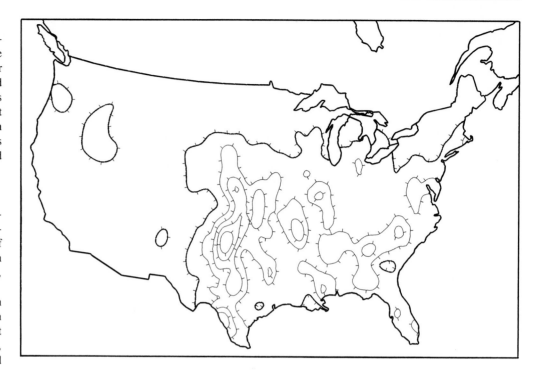

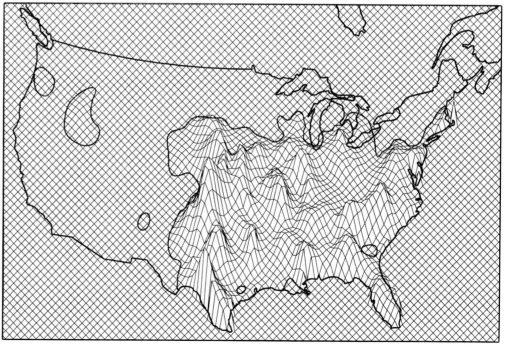

PHASIANIDAE

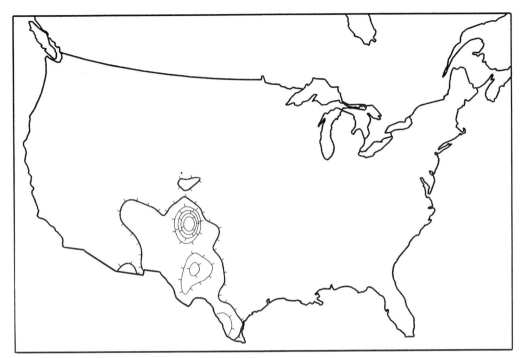

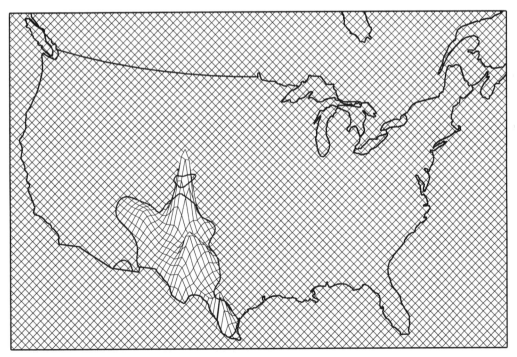

Scaled Quail (*Callipepla squamata*) Maximum: 19.65 I/Hr

Like most quail, the Scaled Quail is a managed game bird, which makes the factors affecting its distribution and abundance difficult to decipher. For example, birds were introduced into southern Colorado and spread along the riparian environment of the Arkansas River. This population merged with the native group, creating a more northerly range limit. This quail has also been artificially established in the plains of northern Colorado (Bent 1932).

The Scaled Quail's range encompasses the Chihuahuan Desert and some of the Colorado Plateaus. The cold and wetter climate farther north probably prevents it from expanding in that direction. This species frequents sandy washes in arid habitats consisting of cactus, mesquite, sagebrush, and scrub oak (Bent 1932). The eastern and western range edges are associated to some extent with vegetation. To the east the distributional edge coincides with the beginning of the tree and shrub savanna vegetation type, except in southern Texas, where this quail extends into the mesquite-acacia scrub. To the west the distribution basically follows that of the semiarid scrub and scrub steppe vegetation, primarily avoiding regions with dry-belt pine forest.

The occurrence of other quail probably affects the distribution and, especially, abundance of this species. Except for the small abundance peak in southern Texas, the regions where the Scaled Quail is abundant are parapatric with high concentrations of the Northern Bobwhite. To the west the same occurs with the abundance peaks of the Gambel's Quail. When we examine only the distributions of these species, there is fairly extensive overlap, especially between the Scaled Quail and Gambel's Quail, but the locations of abundance peaks suggest possible interspecific interactions. The abundance patterns of all three quail exhibit density-dependent segregation. Their evolution and interspecific aggression probably explain in large part why the separations occur. The account of the Gambel's Quail gives a brief explanation of the evolutionary relation between this bird and the Scaled Quail.

Scaled Quail

Scaled Quail

Gambel's Quail (*Callipepla gambelii*) Maximum: 10.24 I/Hr

Established populations of introduced Gambel's Quail have, for the most part, fused with those in the native range, making it difficult to determine the species' original range limits. Certainly this desert bird is not native as far north as Colorado and Idaho, as the maps show. The birds in these northern regions are stressed during the winter months by heavy snowfall and low temperatures (Johnsgard 1973). Without management, particularly in extremely harsh winters, these populations would not survive.

The extended distribution does not obscure all the information about the biogeography of this species. The void between the two fingers radiating north roughly corresponds with the location of the Colorado Plateaus. A more obvious correspondence is between the eastern limit of the distribution and the edge of the semiarid scrub and scrub steppe vegetation, showing that this quail avoids grasslands and savannas, which are frequented by the Scaled Quail.

The Gambel's Quail apparently avoids the Scaled Quail, which can be seen by looking at concentrated populations of both species. In fact, the peak abundances of all four quail for which maps were provided (Northern Bobwhite, Scaled Quail, Gambel's Quail, and California Quail) are, with rare exception, contiguous. The evolution of these species helps us understand this pattern. Hubbard (1973) theorized that the three western species arose from a common ancestor that occupied approximately the same region as the combined distribution of these three modern species during the Yarmouth interglacial period of the Pleistocene. During both the Illinoian and the Wisconsin glacial periods the ancestral species was forced into three disjunct and decidedly different environments; the pre-*squamata* birds were sequestered in the Chihuahuan refugium in the Chihuahuan arid lands of central Mexico, the pre-*gambelii* birds retreated into the Sonoran refugium in the Sonoran Desert of western Mexico, and the pre-*californica* birds were pushed into the California refugium of the chaparral areas of California and Baja California. As the glaciers receded, the species migrated north. Even though their distribution became contiguous—overlapping in some cases—only limited hybridization has occurred (Johnsgard 1971), and the individual species have remained wedded to the basic habitat types of their glacial refugia. The areas of highest abundance therefore may be juxtaposed because the preferred habitats of the quail are parapatric, and interspecific interactions may play only a small part in segregating them.

The preferred habitat of the Gambel's Quail is the Sonoran Desert, where it finds a warm, dry environment with adequate brush for cover, as well as seeds, leaves, and shoots for food (Bent 1932). In desert valleys the brush is mainly mesquite, saltbush, and tamarish, and in the upland desert habitats, from 3,000 to 4,500 feet (914–1,372 m) above sea level, there are acacia, creosote bush, and yucca (Johnsgard 1973).

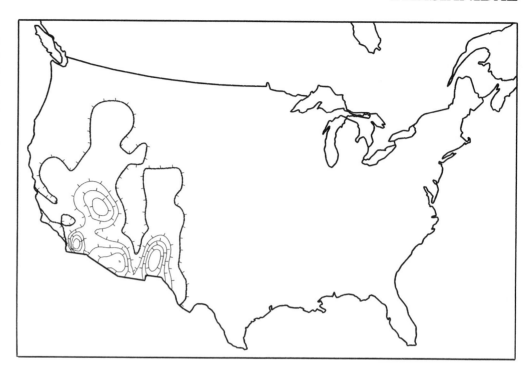

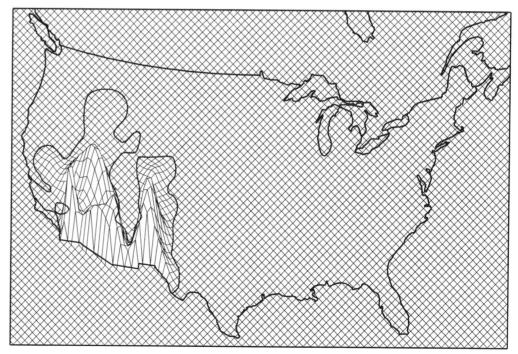

PHASIANIDAE

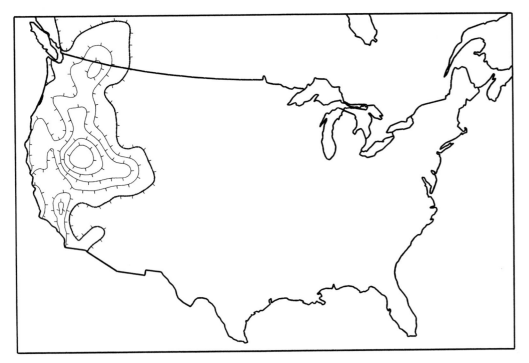

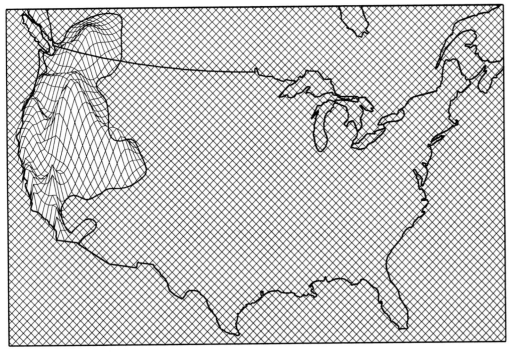

California Quail (*Callipepla californica*) Maximum: 17.20 I/Hr
Introductions outside its original range have expanded this quail's distribution. Once primarily restricted to California, it now extends into the Great Basin. The original distribution was contained within the border of California, except for the extreme southern part of Oregon and an extension into Baja California. In the mid-1800s this quail was introduced and established in Oregon, Washington, Nevada, and Utah (Leopold 1973). In Canada, birds were released in British Columbia and on Vancouver Island (Bent 1932). Release programs are still being implemented in Nevada as late as 1971 (Leopold 1973), and thus, the abundance patterns in the accompanying maps may reflect some recently introduced but not yet established populations, thereby distorting the patterns to some extent.

Even with extensive management, this species cannot survive in the harsh climates of the Mojave Desert and Death Valley, as is evidenced by the southern edge of the range. It also avoids the hot southern part of the Colorado Plateaus. The distribution encompasses most of the Great Basin, skirting the western edge of the Rocky Mountains, except in British Columbia, where introductions presumably helped establish it on the eastern side of the Canadian Rockies.

Within its distribution, climate is the primary factor determining this quail's preferred habitat. California Quail are relatively common throughout regions that are fairly warm and have moderate precipitation; that is, areas with annual pan evaporation of 50 to 90 inches (127–229 cm). The denser populations are in even more climatically moderate habitats, where the yearly pan evaporation has the narrow range of 60 to 80 inches (152–203 cm). As was explained for the Gambel's Quail, the densest populations of the two quail are allopatric. Their evolutionary history is probably the most parsimonious explanation for this separation.

This quail primarily occurs in semiarid scrub and scrub steppe vegetation of the Great Basin. Unlike most other quail, it seeks cover in herbaceous vegetation rather than in brush (Johnsgard 1973). Coveys forage for seeds in open, grassy areas, particularly in the winter (Gutierrez 1980). Birds also eat legumes and the leaves of forbs, clover, and grass, and when succulent plants are not available they must have access to open water (Johnsgard 1973).

Mountain Quail (*Oreortyx pictus*) No Map
The Mountain Quail is somewhat more secretive than other North American quail. It occupies mountain habitats in the Pacific states and provinces. Introductions into Washington and British Columbia in the 1800s artificially extended its range north, and releases were still occurring in 1965, when several pairs were introduced on the Uncompahgre Plateau in Colorado (Johnsgard 1973). The Christmas count data do not reflect this recent introduction; all thirty of the counts recording this species were in the Cascades and the Sierra Nevada. The densest population of Mountain Quail (2.04 I/Hr) was in the Trinity Mountains at the northern end of the Sacramento valley.

California Quail

ARAMIDAE

Limpkin (*Aramus guarauna*) No Map

The Limpkin is reported to be resident in southeastern Georgia and Florida, except on the Keys and the panhandle (AOU 1983). During the Christmas counts it was observed only in Florida. The densest population was also the most northerly, around Apalachee Bay near Saint Marks, at the eastern edge of the panhandle. The average number of individuals seen was 0.37 per party-hour.

RALLIDAE

Black Rail (*Laterallus jamaicensis*) No Map

This rail, one of the most difficult to find and census, is purported to winter along the California and Gulf coasts and in the Imperial Valley and the lower Colorado River valley (AOU 1983). CBC reports on this rail were irregular in these areas and along the Atlantic coast as far north as New Jersey. The densest and most regular population was reported near Titusville, Florida, with an average of 0.01 individuals seen per party-hour over five years.

Clapper Rail (*Rallus longirostris*) Maximum: 1.43 I/Hr

The overall distribution of the Clapper Rail is influenced most strongly by the salinity of water (Ripley 1977) and by ambient temperatures. This bird occurs in saltwater marshes (Bent 1926; Johnsgard 1975), particularly those traversed with tidal sloughs (Ripley 1977), and in mangrove swamps, where the average salinity is about 7,480 ppm (Ripley 1977). In areas with about 5,670 ppm, this rail may come in contact with its freshwater counterpart, the King Rail. Hybrids between these two species have been recorded in these moderately salty regions (Ripley 1977). The climate of these saltwater marshes is tempered by the warmth of the oceans, so that the coastal environments have a frost-free period lasting 210 days or more and January temperatures that rarely drop below 20°F (−7°C). Although the climate along most of the Pacific coast is warm enough, this species occurs only locally around San Diego and San Francisco, California. Within its distribution the Clapper Rail is primarily resident. Crawford and co-workers (1983) have found evidence through banding records that birds in the Southeast show some movement, which is probably migration but could be due to dispersal or wandering.

During the time when Audubon was studying the avifauna of North America, the Clapper Rail was quite abundant. He reported collecting seventy-two dozen eggs of this species in one day, and professional eggers were said to take one hundred dozen a day. In a series of marshes extending roughly 20 miles (32 km), he estimated that one or two Clapper Rails were seen about every 30 feet (9 m) (Bent 1926). Because of persecution by hunters and eggers and the draining of marshes, the abundance of this rail has dropped significantly. In the present study only 1.43 individuals were seen per party-hour in the densest populations, which stretch from Titusville, Florida, to Camp Lejeune in North Carolina and almost the entire length of the South Carolina coast. In these and other coastal marshes it usually feeds during low tide on crabs, snails, fish, insects, and plants (Bent 1926).

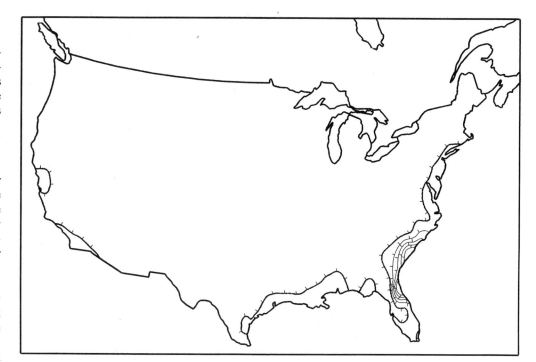

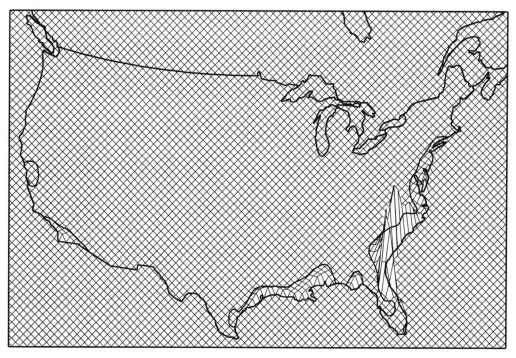

Clapper Rail

RALLIDAE

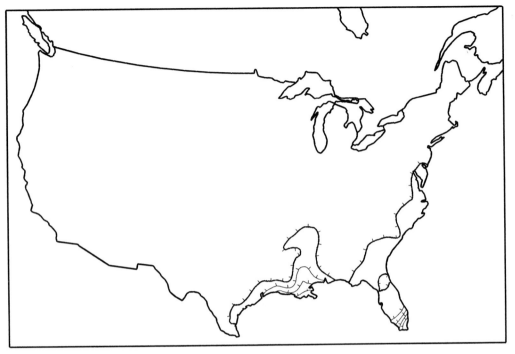

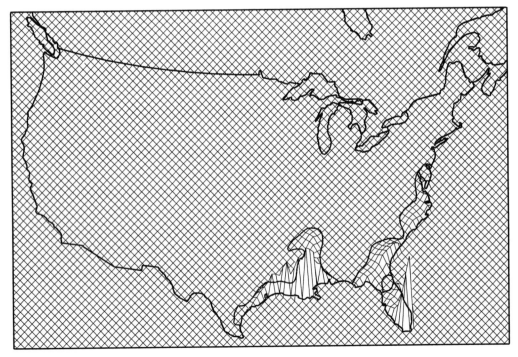

King Rail (*Rallus elegans*) Maximum: 0.27 I/Hr

Temperature is important in determining the winter distribution of the King Rail. Areas must be warm enough to keep the birds from expending too much energy staying warm and to prevent the marshes from freezing. The entire distribution of this rail occurs in regions that rarely drop below 30°F (−1°C) in January, which includes the inland extension into Mississippi. Most of the Mississippi River is avoided because the water is too fast and deep. The other factor that influences where this species occurs may be dense populations of Clapper Rails, an ecologically similar species that may be excluding the King Rail from the area around Saint Augustine, Florida, and Cape Romain National Wildlife Refuge in South Carolina. Because the Clapper Rail's distribution and abundance pattern does not appear to be affected by that of the King Rail, the former seems to be excluding the latter. These maps, however, can provide only circumstantial evidence about competition. Field studies are needed to test this exclusion hypothesis.

The abundance of the King Rail, like that of the Clapper Rail, has been drastically reduced by hunting and other human activities (Bent 1926). Today the most abundant population occurs throughout the southern tip of Florida in the Everglades. A slightly less abundant population occurs in the Louisiana bayous around the mouth of the Mississippi River. This peak extends west to the Anahuac National Wildlife Refuge in Texas, encompassing the McFaddin, Texas Point, Sabine, and Lacassine national refuges and the Rockefeller and Russell Sage state refuges. This population also stretches east to the Alabama border and north up the Pearl River to just below Jackson, Mississippi.

Ecologically and physiologically the King Rail is very similar to the Clapper Rail; there are records of their interbreeding. Such strong similarity prompted Ripley (1977) to consider them conspecific. The AOU (1983), however, disagreed with his conclusion and retained the species status of both. Besides many other differences, the King Rail prefers freshwater rather than saltwater marshes (Bent 1926; Johnsgard 1975). The marshes frequented usually have a salinity less than 3,700 ppm (Ripley 1977). This rail is primarily a crepuscular forager (Bent 1926), feeding on aquatic insects (Johnsgard 1975), tadpoles, crayfish, slugs, and seeds (Bent 1926).

Virginia Rail (*Rallus limicola*) Maximum: 0.20 I/Hr

The maps show that the Virginia Rail is present in both coastal and inland localities. The environmental factors most strongly associated with its occurrence are freshwater marshes and a warm climate. In most of the regions it frequents, the temperature rarely drops below 20°F (−7°C), which ensures that the marshes will only occasionally, if ever, be frozen. There are populations in some areas, however, where the temperature dips below freezing. Perhaps birds in these locations are wintering on ponds warmed by hot-water discharge from power plants. For example, there is a hydroelectric plant on the Snake River in eastern Idaho, a coal-fired plant on the Platte River in Wyoming, and several types of electric plants in Colorado, all coincident with the disjunct populations of rails. Other disjunct populations in colder areas that appear to be associated with plants generating electricity include the ones in western Nevada and north-central New Mexico. More study is needed to determine if power plants actually do affect the occurrence of this rail. Other disjunct populations occur around Lake Meredith in Texas, throughout the eastern Great Lakes, and near the Felsenthal National Wildlife Refuge on the Arkansas-Louisiana border. The inland extension into Mississippi and Tennessee is apparently influenced by the occurrence of wildlife refuges and the Cumberland and Mississippi rivers. In Washington the Columbia River basin provides an adequate inland environment for this rail. This species also extends up the Colorado River and throughout the Pahranagat refuge near the borders of California, Arizona, Nevada, and Utah.

The densest population is in the lower Colorado River valley, around the Imperial, Cibola, and Havasu national wildlife refuges. Lesser peaks occur near Morro Bay in California and in the Louisiana bayou country near the mouth of the Mississippi River and extend along the coast to the Anahuac refuge in Texas. Even lower peaks are found around Lake Meredith in Texas, east of Mobile Bay in Alabama, and in the swamps of eastern North Carolina extending up the coast to Chesapeake and Delaware bays.

The preferred habitat of this rail is freshwater marshes with rushes, sedges, and cattails (Ripley 1977), where it feeds on earthworms, insect larvae, slugs, snails, fish, caterpillars, and some vegetable matter such as the seeds of marsh plants. Foraging primarily entails probing the mud with its bill (Bent 1926). It frequently shares its wetland haunts with Soras, but the Virginia Rail normally occurs in the drier areas of the marshes (Ripley 1977).

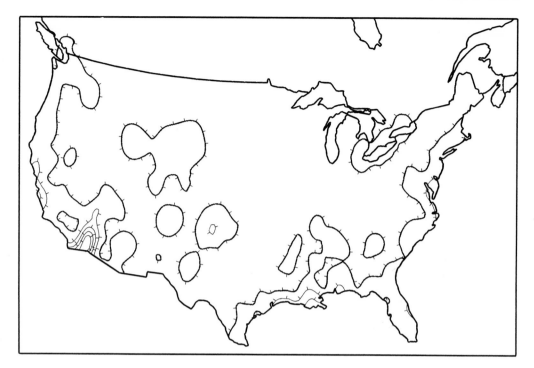

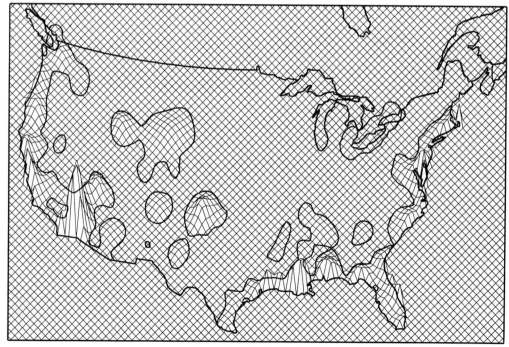

RALLIDAE

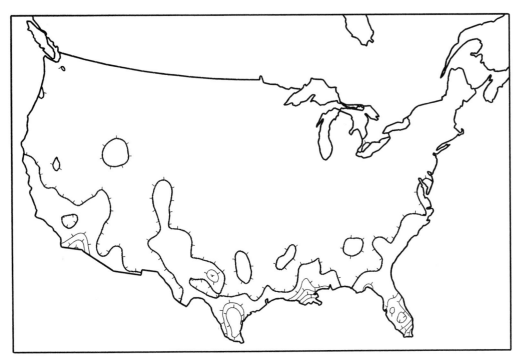

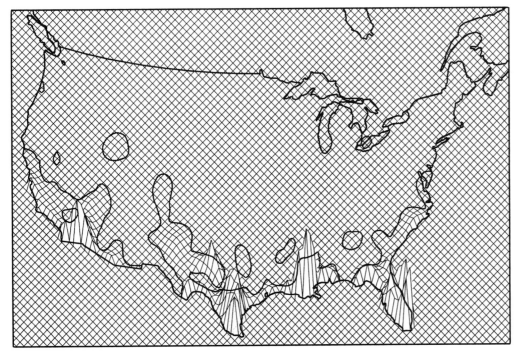

Sora (*Porzana carolina*) Maximum: 0.66 I/Hr

The maps reflect the Sora's preference for warmer wintering areas. Most of its range is in regions that have a minimum January temperature above 30°F (−1°C). There are two localities where populations extend into much colder regions: up the Colorado River into Arizona, and along the Rio Grande into Colorado. Standing water, which this species requires, normally would freeze in these colder areas, but both locations have a number of large electric plants, which may be discharging hot water into ponds and thereby creating adequate habitats. There are three disjunct populations in colder regions: Washington, Nevada, and Utah. Birds were observed at these locations only in 1967, suggesting that either that particular winter was abnormally warm, allowing for a wider-ranging distribution, or an unusually high number of offspring were fledged the preceding breeding season, resulting in more extensive dispersal.

All but one of the dense populations occur in regions that basically never get colder than 40°F (4°C) in January, and one of the highest abundance peaks is in the area of the United States that is usually over 50°F (10°C). This latter population is in peninsular Florida, with the most birds observed in the Everglades. In Florida, lesser peaks occur around Cocoa Beach and Bartow, and there is a depression in the relative abundance around Lake Okeechobee. The other of the highest peaks is in the bayous of Louisiana, where the Mississippi River opens into the Gulf of Mexico. Lesser peaks occur on the coastal plains of southern Texas, along the lower Colorado River valley on the border of Nevada and Arizona, and around San Angelo, Texas. This last peak is in an area that is fairly cold, having an average minimum January temperature of about 30°F (−1°C). There is a power plant in approximately this same location, which may be positively influencing the abundance of this rail.

The Sora is the easiest North American rail to census, because it is the tamest and least secretive. These traits, along with its being a poor flier, made it easy game for hunters, who significantly decreased its abundance. In 1846, before there was a limit to the number that could be killed, on average one hundred birds per day were shot by each hunter over a thirty-four-day period (Bent 1926). The draining of wetlands and the encroachment of civilization have also taken their toll, not only on this denizen of the marshes but on all wetland species. The Sora needs shallow standing water (Ripley 1977) in which to forage for small mollusks, dragonflies, mosquitoes, and seeds (Bent 1926). It is fairly sensitive to cold (Bent 1926), and in winter it migrates into warmer areas with mud flats, though it usually avoids saltwater marshes (Ripley 1977).

Purple Gallinule (*Porphyrula martinica*) No Map
In the United States the primary wintering grounds of the Purple Gallinule include southern Texas, Louisiana, and Florida, but this species does wander widely (AOU 1983). Christmas count records show it at sporadic locations along the Gulf coast and more continuously on the Atlantic coast of Florida. The densest population was recorded at Delray Beach, Florida, where 0.11 individuals were seen per party-hour.

Common Moorhen (*Gallinula chloropus*) Maximum: 3.33 I/Hr
Like that of most other marsh and wetland birds, the winter distribution of the Common Moorhen is limited primarily to the availability of open water. Warm climates as well as ponds and marshes, therefore, are the primary environmental factors shaping its range. It is associated with the region of the country that has a frost-free period of at least 240 days. This includes the areas along the Gulf, southern Atlantic, and Pacific coasts, as well as those inland populations along the Sacramento, San Joaquin, and Colorado river valleys. Its apparent occurrence throughout Arizona is partly an artifact of the interpolation method used to generate the maps, owing to the lack of counts in the area and to several individuals being seen on the Phoenix count. The disjunct population in northeastern Texas represents a small number of birds seen regularly around Dallas.

The most individuals, by far, are seen on the northwestern portion of the Florida peninsula around Tallahassee. The maps show that farther south, around Lake Okeechobee, the abundance drops significantly and rises only slightly in the Everglades. Other populations about as dense as the one in the Everglades occur in the Louisiana bayous around Lacassine National Wildlife Refuge and Rockefeller State Refuge and in California at two locations—on the San Joaquin River in the tule marshes, and near Porterville, presumably on Lake Success.

The Common Moorhen is almost cosmopolitan in its distribution and is resident wherever freshwater habitats do not freeze in the winter. It prefers wetland environments with reeds or cattails for cover (Ripley 1977). Most of its diet is vegetable matter, such as the soft parts of succulent water plants, seeds, roots (Bent 1926), duckweed, grasses, leaves of pond weeds, berries, and fruits (Ripley 1977). Snails, mollusks, grasshoppers, and worms make up the small amount of animal matter consumed (Bent 1926). Its foraging methods include swimming and diving in relatively shallow water, and walking about in grassy areas (Bent 1926; Ripley 1977).

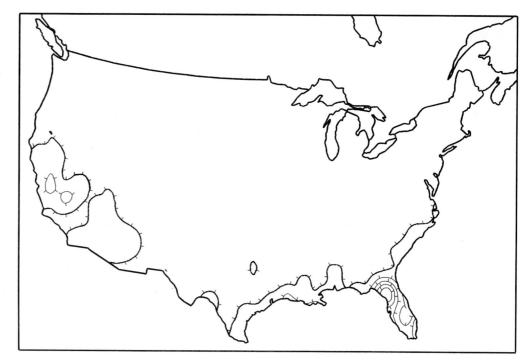

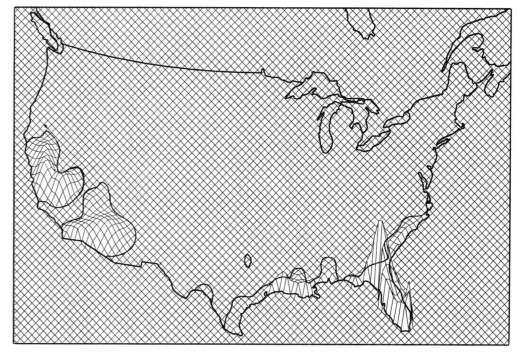

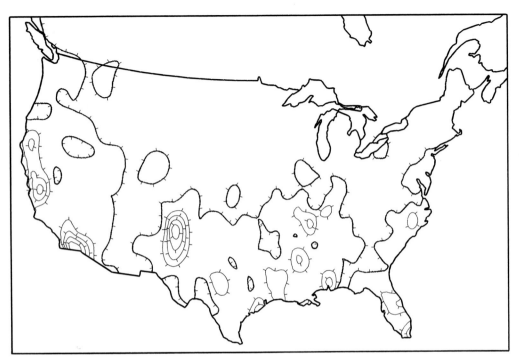

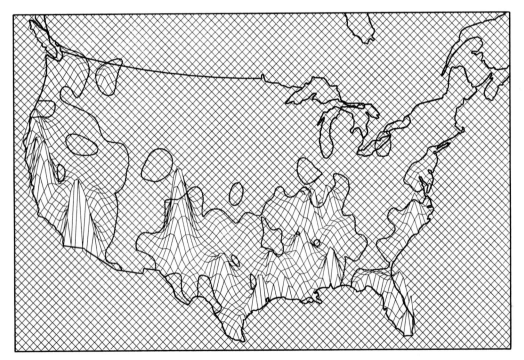

American Coot (*Fulica americana*) Maximum: 183.20 I/Hr

Of all the members of the Rallidae that winter in the United States and Canada, the American Coot has the most extensive distribution. It occurs throughout most of the southern United States, and its northern range limit apparently is influenced by cold temperatures. Except for a few disjunct populations, birds east of the 100th meridian are in regions with an average minimum January temperature greater than 20°F (−7°C). In the West the correspondence with temperature is not as obvious, because of more irregular and sporadic sightings, but the primary western wintering areas are also in locations that are warmer than 20°F (−7°C) in January. Disjunct populations are found around Coeur d'Alene in Idaho, at Browns Park National Wildlife Refuge on the Wyoming-Colorado border, on the Arkansas River in Kansas, near Chautauqua, Illinois, and around the Erie refuge on Lake Erie. This coot avoids the higher altitudes of the Appalachians and the dry areas of Arizona and Utah.

The highest concentrations of the American Coot are on and around Conchas Lake in New Mexico and in the Imperial Valley of southeastern California. The next highest abundance peak is in the San Joaquin valley, with a slighter concentration extending up the Sacramento valley and a lesser peak around Shasta Lake. Other lesser peaks are primarily associated with national wildlife refuges.

Most aspects of its ecology indicate that the American Coot is a generalist. Even though underwater plants are its staple food (Ripley 1977), it is an omnivore, eating leaves, fronds, seeds, and roots of aquatic vegetation along with fish, tadpoles, worms, snails, insects, and even carrion and algae off dead vegetation (Bent 1926). Its foraging activities are also diverse, including picking items off the water surface, submerging its entire head and neck, tipping up like a dabbling duck, diving, and walking on land (Ripley 1977). Often it forages close to ducks, such as the Canvasback, catching prey they disturb (Ripley 1977). Large rafts of coots may also enhance foraging by disturbing prey (Ripley 1977). This bird prefers fresh to salt water (Bent 1927).

GRUIDAE

Sandhill Crane (*Grus canadensis*) Map in Appendix B

The Sandhill Crane forms very large flocks, which are difficult to count. The population around Muleshoe National Wildlife Refuge in western Texas, extending southeast to Big Springs and west to the Bitter Lake refuge in New Mexico, is so dense (2,331.31 I/Hr) that it overshadows the rest of the biogeographic pattern of this species. For instance, the population in northern Florida, which comprises between 600 and 1,800 birds (Williams and Phillips 1972) is not dense enough to be recognized when compared with the maximum peak. Thus, the contour map is provided only in appendix B.

Whooping Crane (*Grus americana*) No Map
The abundance of the Whooping Crane has been severely decreased by humans. In 1937 Aransas National Wildlife Refuge was established to protect its primary wintering grounds. Since that time, small populations outside this area have become extinct (Olsen et al. 1980). The Aransas CBC is the only count recording this crane in the ten years examined. To increase abundance and perhaps establish another population, a cross-fostering program was started in 1975 using Sandhill Cranes that breed at Gray's Lake, Idaho, and winter at Bosque del Apache National Wildlife Refuge in New Mexico (Olsen et al. 1980).

CHARADRIIDAE

Black-bellied Plover (*Pluvialis squatarola*) Maximum: 6.16 I/Hr
The Black-bellied Plover primarily winters along the coasts, except for a few inland populations. It occurs continuously along the Atlantic coast from Florida to as far north as northern New Jersey. The northern limit is probably partly dictated by temperature; the minimum January temperature drops below 20°F (−7°C) at the New Jersey–New York border. The distributions along the Gulf and Pacific coasts are more discontinuous than those in the East. On the Pacific coast, the distribution is continuous from the Mexican border north to Point Reyes National Seashore. To the north there is a strong association between national wildlife refuges and the presence of this plover.

National wildlife refuges also seem to influence where high densities of this plover occur. The highest abundance is on the northern California coast, around the Humboldt Bay refuge. The next densest population is in the Imperial Valley around the Salton Sea refuge. The Cape Romain refuge in South Carolina is in the center of the highest peak on the Atlantic coast. Two lower peaks are in southern Florida around Naples and in northern North Carolina.

This cosmopolitan shorebird is the largest plover in North America (Bent 1929), measuring 11.5 inches (29 cm) from bill to tail (National Geographic Society 1983). It usually occurs in small, mixed-species flocks and is the dominant member of such groups (Bent 1929). The birds' small flock size meant that hunters at the turn of the century could not kill large numbers with just one or two shots, and because Black-bellied Plovers learn to avoid decoys, the abundance of this species did not significantly decline even though it was a favorite quarry (Bent 1929). Within a flock, plovers are not randomly spaced, but there is a great variation in the distance between individuals. This "personal space" is maintained through avoidance rather than aggression (Stinson 1977). In winter this plover is found on tidal sand or mud flats of oceans, bays, and estuaries, where it eats crabs, shrimp, marine worms, mollusks, and insects (Johnsgard 1981). Occasionally it frequents sand dunes, hunting for cutworms and grasshoppers (Bent 1929). Foraging entails three sequential behaviors—running, pausing, and pecking—repeated time and again. The main variation is that a side flick may be added to the pecking (Johnsgard 1981). Prey is detected visually (Bent 1929).

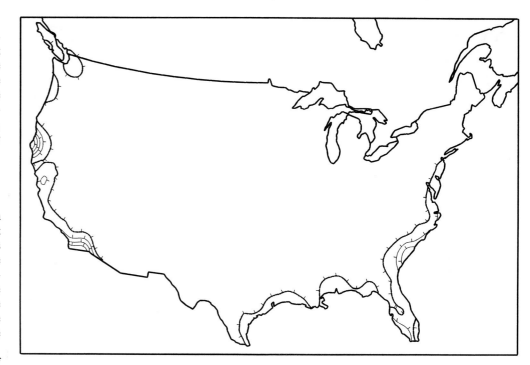

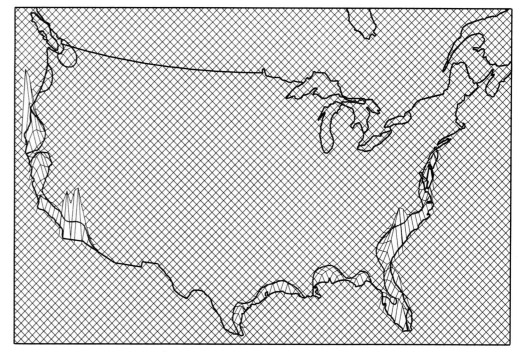

CHARADRIIDAE

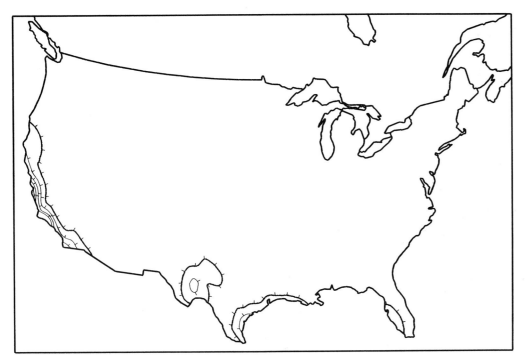

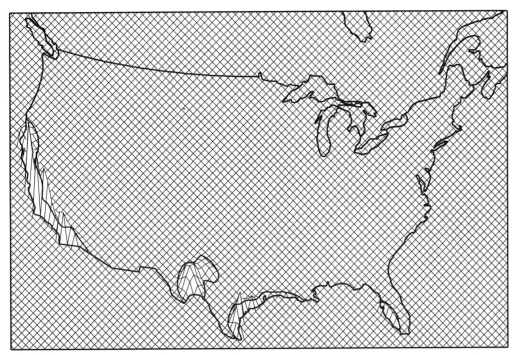

Lesser Golden-Plover (*Pluvialis dominica*) No Map
This plover was recorded at scattered locations along the Gulf coast and on the Atlantic coast of Florida. The most regular sightings were on the Pacific coast from Humboldt Bay National Wildlife Refuge south to the Mexican border, with the count around San Diego recording it in the most years (seven out of ten), but in very low abundances (0.01 I/Hr).

Mountain Plover (*Charadrius montanus*) No Map
The wintering grounds of the Mountain Plover stretch from central California, southern Arizona, and central Texas south into northern Mexico and southern Baja California (AOU 1983). During the ten years examined, it was observed sporadically in southern Texas and more regularly in central and coastal California. It was seen most consistently (nine out of ten years) around Newport Beach, California, with an average abundance of 0.75 individuals seen per party-hour.

Snowy Plover (*Charadrius alexandrinus*) Maximum: 0.94 I/Hr
This plover, which is the Pacific coast counterpart of the Piping Plover, winters primarily on the western seaboard from the southern border of Oregon to the Mexican border. Its also frequents the Gulf coast from Louisiana to southern Texas and the western coast of peninsular Florida. The fairly extensive inland population shown in southwestern Texas near the Pecos River is due to birds occurring here only in 1966, 1967, and 1968. All the populations of this plover are in areas that are warmer than 30°F (−1°C) in January. The southern Florida population occurs in an area that has a minimum January temperature over 50°F (10°C). The factors keeping the distributions from extending farther north on the Pacific coast or east on the Gulf coast are difficult to determine because of the large scale of this study.

The highest concentration of Snowy Plovers is on the California coast from San Francisco continuing south to the Mexican border, with peaks around Monterey Bay, Santa Barbara, and San Diego. Much lesser peaks occur around Corpus Christi and near Fort Stockton, Texas. The locations of these peaks and of the overall distribution do not appear to be associated with wildlife refuges. This is unexpected, given that the abundance of this plover is declining and the refuges protect both the bird and its habitat. The species has been on the National Audubon Society's Blue List since the list's inception in 1972 (Johnsgard 1981).

The Snowy Plover is the smallest of all the North American plovers, measuring only 6.25 inches (16 cm) from bill to tail (National Geographic Society 1983). It is normally found feeding at the water's edge on sparsely vegetated, broad sandy beaches (Bent 1929; Johnsgard 1981). When foraging, it runs and pecks in the typical plover manner and at times pats the ground with one foot to disturb its prey. Its diet consists of crustaceans, mollusks, annelids, and insects (Johnsgard 1981).

Semipalmated Plover (*Charadrius semipalmatus*) Maximum: 3.13 I/Hr
In winter the Semipalmated Plover occurs along all three coasts where the ambient temperature rarely drops below freezing. There are, however, areas with temperatures above freezing where this plover is absent. The distribution on the Gulf coast is the most discontinuous; the bird avoids the regions around Port Lavaca, Texas; near the mouth of the Mississippi River; at the west end of the Florida panhandle; and in Florida from around Crystal River to Perry. On the Atlantic coast the distribution extends as far north as North Carolina. There is a continuous population along the California coast and a disjunct population farther north in southern Washington and northern Oregon. The surface temperature of the ocean may influence where this species is found, because the northern limit of the population on the Atlantic coast and that of the more extensive population on the Pacific coast are coincident with where the mean winter surface temperature drops below 52°F (11°C).

The numbers of Semipalmated Plovers, which had been dropping since 1890 because of hunting, increased dramatically after the Migratory Bird Act was enacted in 1918 by both Canada and the United States. The most concentrated winter populations occur along the coast of South Carolina and at the extreme southern tip of Florida around Everglades National Park and on the Keys. There are lesser concentrations around Tampa Bay on the Gulf coast of Florida and near Saint Augustine on the east coast.

The Semipalmated Plover eats mollusks, crustaceans, worms, insects, and some seeds. During the 1873–76 locust outbreak in the United States, an individual plover ate an average of thirty-eight locusts a day (Bent 1929). When feeding the bird runs and pauses and also uses foot trembling to entice prey to move (Johnsgard 1981). It usually feeds at low tide (Bent 1929) on muddy, sandy, or pebbly coasts (Johnsgard 1981), and it rests and sleeps on the beach (Bent 1929).

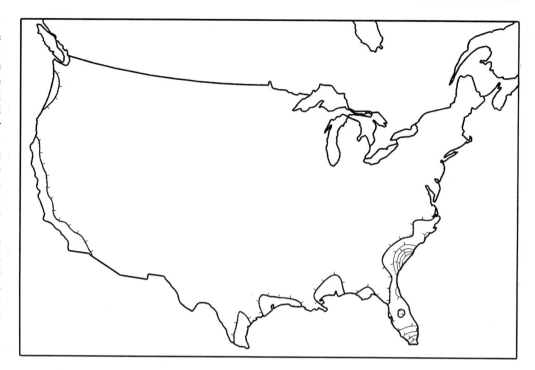

Semipalmated Plover

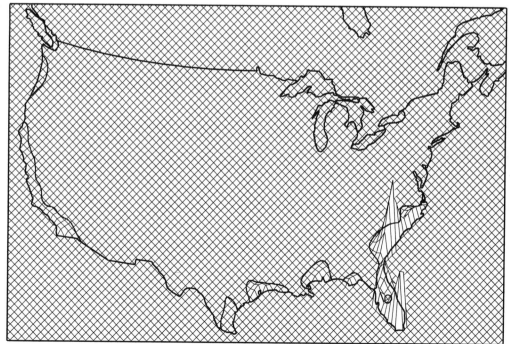

CHARADRIIDAE

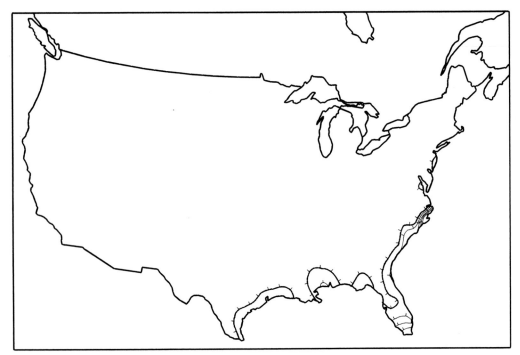

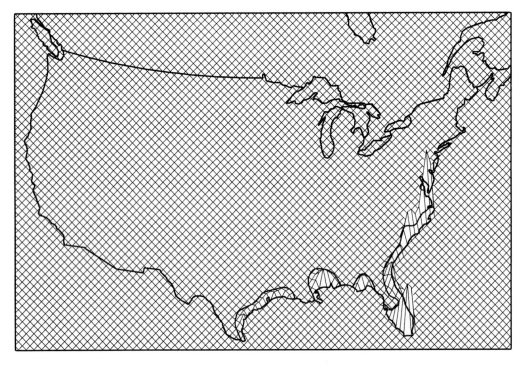

Piping Plover (*Charadrius melodus*) Maximum: 2.12 I/Hr

The distribution of the Piping Plover is very similar to the eastern distributions of the Semipalmated Plover and Black-bellied Plover, except that the first species occurs farther north on the Atlantic coast than the other two. The sightings of the Piping Plover in New Jersey were sporadic, but those around Chesapeake Bay were regular. On the Gulf coast, all three plovers avoid the area just west of the mouth of the Mississippi River, the western end of the Florida panhandle, and the part of Florida from Perry to around Crystal River. Why it avoids these areas is an enigma at this time. There are high concentrations of Killdeer near these regions, which suggests either that these areas do not offer the appropriate habitat for other plovers or perhaps that the Killdeer is excluding them. Because the Killdeer uses grassier habitats in winter than the other plovers (Bent 1929), competitive exclusion probably does not contribute significantly to the separation of species. More study is certainly needed on the winter habitat use of these plovers.

The Piping Plover's abundance was greatly decreased by hunting around the turn of the century (Bent 1929), and it is on the National Audubon Society's Blue List because of declining numbers throughout its range (Johnsgard 1981). The highest concentration of Piping Plovers is in eastern North Carolina near the Pea Island, Mattamuskeet, Swanquarter, Cedar Island, and Pungo national wildlife refuges, which protect both the birds and their habitats. A fairly high abundance of this plover extends south into South Carolina to around the Cape Romain refuge. Another dense concentration occurs at the southern tip of Florida, and there are much smaller concentrations around the borders between Georgia and Florida and Mississippi and Alabama.

The Piping Plover frequents beaches and the edges of lagoons in winter (Johnsgard 1981), where it forages in loose flocks (Bent 1929). Its foraging behavior consists of repeatedly running forward, stopping, looking around, and then picking prey off the ground. Probing is seldom if ever used. Marine worms, beetles, insects, crustaceans, and mollusks make up this shorebird's diet (Bent 1929).

Piping Plover

Piping Plover

Killdeer (*Charadrius vociferus*) Maximum: 12.66 I/Hr

Temperature is the factor most strongly associated with the Killdeer's winter distribution. East of the Rocky Mountains this plover avoids areas that get colder than 20°F (−7°C) in January. In the West it can survive where temperatures drop to about 10°F (−12°C), but not much below. The harsh environments of the Colorado Plateaus, the higher peaks of the Colorado and Wyoming Rockies, and the Harney basin in Oregon are all avoided. The presence of other plovers may also be limiting the Killdeer's distribution; it apparently avoids southern Mississippi and Florida, though other plovers are prevalent there. A smaller-scale study is needed to determine whether competition, habitat variation, or some other factor is causing the Killdeer to avoid these areas.

Temperature also apparently strongly influences where concentrated populations of this plover occur. In the East, abundant populations are found in regions where the temperature rarely drops below 40°F (4°C) in January, and in the West all these populations are in regions with temperatures above 20°F (−7°C). National wildlife refuges also apparently influence where the peak abundances occur. In the West the highest concentration of Killdeer occurs around the Humboldt Bay refuge, with lesser peaks in northern Oregon around the Baskett Slough, Ankeny, and William L. Finley refuges and in central California at the confluence of the Sacramento and San Joaquin rivers. Fairly high numbers of Killdeer occur from south Texas to eastern Louisiana, with a very high peak in southern Louisiana and a lesser peak near Houston. In Alabama there is a fairly dense population around the William Dannelly Reservoir. In California predation may be suppressing its abundance. An estimated 6.9% of the Killdeer population is eaten by raptors (Page and Whitacre 1975).

In winter the Killdeer is the most widely distributed plover in the United States and also the most abundant by at least a factor of two, partially because it adapts easily to human modifications of the environment (Johnsgard 1981). It actively feeds in pastures, meadows, and parks on insects (primarily beetles), which make up about 98% of its diet. In winter it can be found flocking with other shorebirds on beaches and mud flats (Bent 1929). When feeding in water, it normally returns to shore to defecate, presumably either because water deeper than toe depth inhibits defecation (Brackbill 1970), to prevent the spread of parasites, or to avoid fouling and clouding its foraging area. It forages by the typical plover method of running forward, pausing to look for prey, and then seizing an insect from the surface of the ground, with very little probing into the soil. The large eyes of this plover allow it to be a crepuscular and nocturnal, as well as a diurnal, forager (Johnsgard 1981).

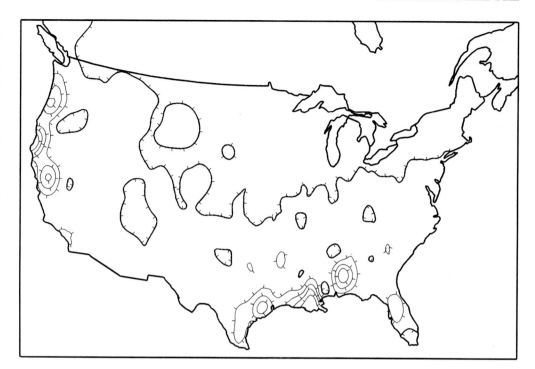

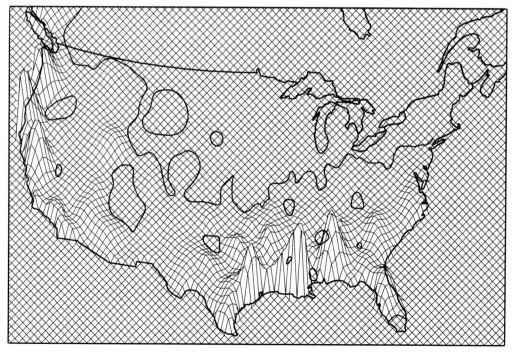

CHARADRIIDAE / HAEMATOPODIDAE

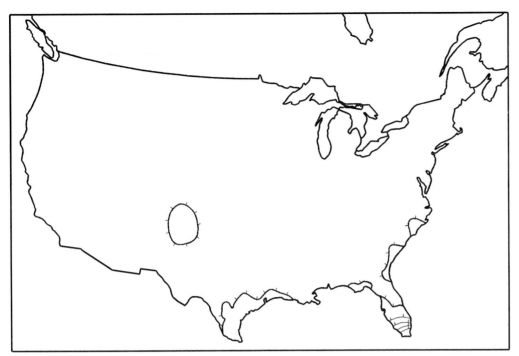

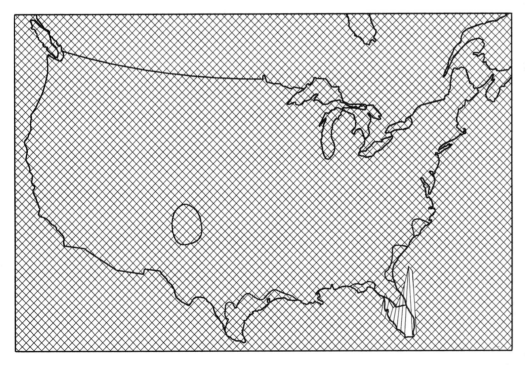

Wilson's Plover (*Charadrius wilsonia*) Maximum: 1.33 I/Hr

The Wilson's Plover migrates south out of the colder parts of its breeding range, which extends as far north as the New Jersey shore, to the warmer regions of the Atlantic and Gulf coasts in the United States and on south into northern South America (AOU 1983). The maps show that most of its wintering area is south of the 31st parallel. Those populations north of this line in North and South Carolina are due to sporadic sightings of what were probably late migrants or wandering individuals. This bird is regularly seen on both coasts of Florida, particularly in the south, and on the Texas and western Louisiana Gulf coasts. All these areas have a minimum January temperature of at least 45°F (7°C) and a mean ocean-surface temperature of 64°F (18°C). Other factors, such as prey productivity, must be influencing the distribution, because there are numerous places where the temperatures are sufficiently warm but the plover is absent. This is true for the areas from central Louisiana to the Florida panhandle, on the western coast of Florida from Crystal River to Perry, and on Florida's Atlantic coast from Cocoa Beach to the Georgia border.

The highest concentration of Wilson's Plovers occurs in southern Florida, with the peak on the northern Keys. Ambient temperature undoubtedly has some effect on where this plover is most abundant, because in southern Florida the temperature rarely falls below 50°F (10°C).

Open sand flats are this plover's preferred habitat, including sandbars and sandy islands (Bent 1929). It forages by standing and watching for its prey, then running after it. Rarely if ever will it wade while foraging. Its prey consists primarily of fiddler crabs (Johnsgard 1981), supplemented by other invertebrates such as marine insects, shrimp, and mollusks (Bent 1929). Normally this plover is found alone or in very loose and widely distributed flocks (Bent 1929).

HAEMATOPODIDAE

American Oystercatcher (*Haematopus palliatus*) No Map

This shorebird was observed regularly at thirty-two scattered locations along the Gulf coast and on the Atlantic coast from the tip of Florida to around Chesapeake Bay. The most abundant population was at Cape Romain National Wildlife Refuge in South Carolina, where on average 41.15 individuals were seen per party-hour. Dense populations also occurred near Morehead City, North Carolina, and around Cape Charles, Virginia.

Black Oystercatcher (*Haematopus bachmani*) No Map

The Black Oystercatcher is resident throughout its breeding range, which extends from the Aleutians to Baja California (AOU 1983). On the counts examined, however, the species was not observed in extreme southern California, since it ranges only from Juneau, Alaska, to Morro Bay. The most birds seen on average over the ten-year period were on the Farallon Islands off the California coast, where 3.26 individuals were seen per party-hour.

RECURVIROSTRIDAE

Black-necked Stilt (*Himantopus mexicanus*) Map in Appendix B
In the United States the winter distribution of the Black-necked Stilt is restricted to small, localized areas on the southern coast of Texas and in southern and central California. The most concentrated populations were in southern California along the San Diego coast and in the Imperial Valley. Even though only thirty-eight sites recorded this long-legged wader, the contour map is included in appendix B because it provides accurate biogeographic information.

American Avocet (*Recurvirostra americana*) Maximum: 47.68 I/Hr
The distribution of the American Avocet is similar to that of the Black-necked Stilt. Both are present in southern and central California and on the western Gulf coast. The main exceptions are that the avocet occurs farther east along the Gulf coast of Texas and Louisiana and is present along the California coast from Point Conception to above Point Reyes. The Imperial Valley in southern California contains the highest concentration of both avocets and stilts, but unlike the stilt, which is also very abundant around San Diego, the avocet is restricted in peak abundance to the Salton Sea area and its adjoining valley.

Like the stilt, the avocet is a long-legged wader that forages in relatively shallow water. The latter, however, has webbed feet and swims well (Bent 1927). Because its legs are shorter than those of the stilt, the avocet prefers shallower water. It also can frequently be found foraging on land; its shorter legs allow it to reach the ground with its bill more easily than can the stilt. The avocet prefers mud flats and more alkaline and saline pools with barren edges (Hamilton 1975). Besides vision, it uses tactile stimulation to detect prey. Its visual foraging behaviors are the same as those described for the stilt. Its tactile methods are rather diverse, with various scything behaviors the most frequent. Single scything is the most common feeding method in mud and also is used sometimes in water. It involves putting the recurved tip of the slightly opened bill on the substrate at one side and then rapidly moving it to the other side. When rapidly repeated, this behavior is called multiple scything. Dabble scything is single scything done while the body is tipped up like a dabbling duck's. By extending its neck, the avocet can move its bill forward about 2 to 8 inches (5–20 cm) along the substrate, which is usually mud. When the bill is open, this is called scraping. A much rarer feeding method is bill pursuit: the bill is erratically moved along the surface of the water while it is repeatedly opened about 0.5 inch (1 cm) and closed rapidly (Hamilton 1975). Besides brine shrimp and flies (Hamilton 1975) the avocet's diet, which is about 65% animal matter, includes fish, crustaceans, snails, various insects, and carrion (Bent 1927). Like several other shorebirds, the avocet goes ashore to defecate (Hamilton 1975).

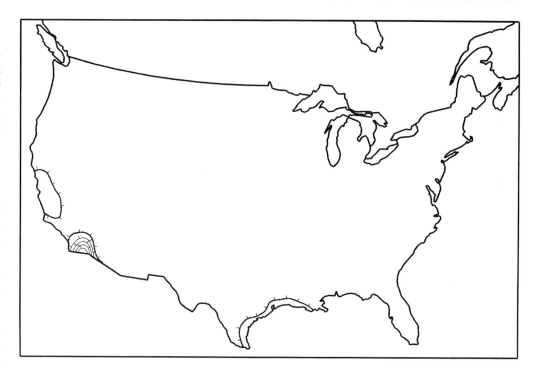

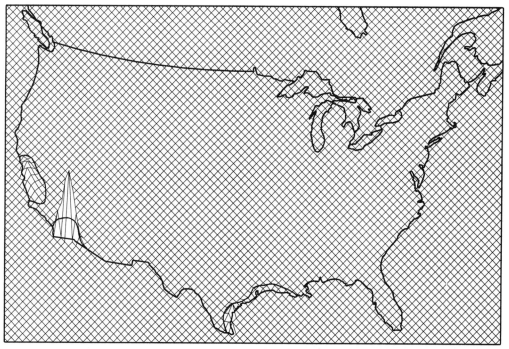

American Avocet

SCOLOPACIDAE

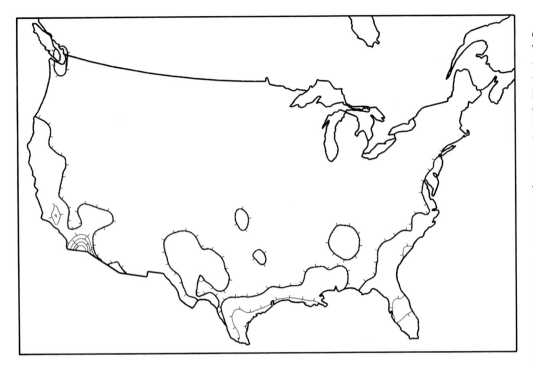

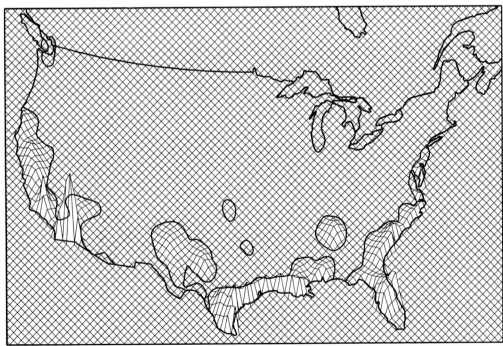

Greater Yellowlegs (*Tringa melanoleuca*) Maximum: 2.72 I/Hr

Temperature seems to be an important environmental factor determining where this yellowlegs winters. Its distribution in the East occurs primarily where temperatures rarely drop below 30°F (−1°C) in January. In the West, however, a large portion of its range gets as cold as 20°F (−7°C). In several of these colder areas the birds are in protected valleys. Included are the Pecos River valley, which extends from southwestern Texas on north to eastern New Mexico, and along the southern Colorado River up to Lake Mead in Nevada. In California the distribution extends from the Sierra Nevada to Humboldt Bay National Wildlife Refuge on the coast. Several disjunct populations occur in colder regions too, including the areas around the Great Salt Plains Lake on the Arkansas-Oklahoma border, Lake Texoma on the Texas-Oklahoma border, Guntersville Lake and the Cumberland River in Alabama, and the Strait of Georgia and Puget Sound in northwestern Washington.

As with the avocet and stilt, which are also long-legged waders, the highest peak abundance of the Greater Yellowlegs occurs in the Imperial Valley around Salton Sea, where its concentration is quite a bit denser than at other locations. Less abundant populations occur at the southern end of the San Joaquin valley near Bakersville, California, and around Aransas National Wildlife Refuge near Corpus Christi, Texas. Lesser abundance peaks occur along the Gulf coast from southern Texas to the mouth of the Mississippi River. Accompanying this slight concentration on the coast is an extension inland along the Nueces River in Texas. All of central peninsular Florida and the area around the Cape Romain refuge in South Carolina have roughly the same concentration of this yellowlegs as the western Gulf coast.

Hunting of this shorebird, which was still legal in 1925, probably caused a contraction of its distribution (Bent 1927). Its preferred habitat includes shallow water (Bent 1927) with accompanying mud flats. When the water is too deep, it will fly rather than swim (Johnsgard 1981). It forages for fish and aquatic insects, which it finds by running about with its head and neck down (Bent 1927). When there is a high concentration of fish, it occasionally is seen plowing the surface, a tactile foraging method that involves running forward with its bill open and the lower mandible in the water (Zusi 1968). Myers and Myers (1979) found that in Argentina the Greater Yellowlegs winters alone or in small flocks on ponds with emergent vegetation and in littoral areas of tidal flats. Here individuals may defend small feeding territories. These same conditions are probably true for birds wintering in the United States, but further study is needed.

Lesser Yellowlegs (*Tringa flavipes*) Maximum: 1.43 I/Hr

As with the Greater Yellowlegs, temperature apparently is the major environmental factor dictating where the Lesser Yellowlegs winters. Its distribution along the Atlantic, Pacific, and Gulf coasts covers areas where the average minimum January temperature is above 30°F (−1°C). This includes the extensions in southern Texas onto the Edwards Plateau and in Louisiana along the Red River. All the disjunct, interior populations, however, are in areas where the temperature drops far below 30°F (−1°C). This yellowlegs was seen only sporadically in all these areas. The coldest region is in Utah around the Great Salt Lake, where the average minimum January temperature drops below 10°F (−12°C). Other disjunct populations are along the Pecos River in eastern New Mexico, around Lubbock, Texas, and on the Arkansas River in Kansas. On the Pacific coast the distribution is discontinuous, with separate populations in extreme southern California around Salton Sea in the Imperial Valley and extending west to San Diego, along the coast from about Santa Barbara to Monterey, around the confluence of the Sacramento and San Joaquin rivers, and on the Humboldt Bay National Wildlife Refuge.

Temperature apparently also affects the location of the abundant populations of this yellowlegs. All the most concentrated populations are in regions where the temperature infrequently drops below 40°F (4°C) in January. The highest abundance peak occurs in the Louisiana bayous, just west of the mouth of the Mississippi River, and lesser concentrations stretch from this peak along the entire length of the western Gulf coast to southern Texas. Lesser concentrations also occur in central Florida, extending inland from Tampa Bay, and around Cocoa Beach.

The Lesser Yellowlegs is normally found in marshy areas with short grass, shallow pools (Bent 1927), and mud flats (Johnsgard 1981). In these environs it flocks mainly with small waders rather than with its congener (Bent 1927). It actively forages in shallow water for insects (Johnsgard 1981), fish, and crustaceans that it gleans off the surface of the water or mud (Bent 1927). It seldom probes in the mud (Bent 1927) or skims its bill side to side as does the Greater Yellowlegs (Johnsgard 1981). On the wintering grounds in Argentina, this yellowlegs is usually found foraging in small flocks, but each individual defends a feeding territory about 0.1 to 0.5 hectares in diameter (Myers and Myers 1979).

Solitary Sandpiper (*Tringa solitaria*) Map in Appendix B

The Solitary Sandpiper is a rare species in North America in the winter. Only 0.10 individuals per party-hour were seen in the densest population, which was on the coastal plain in southern Texas near the city of Alice. Temperature apparently influences where this species winters; all the concentrated populations were in areas where the minimum ambient temperature was over 45°F (7°C), and its range extends into regions warmer than 30°F (−1°C), which includes the Gulf coast and the coast of southern California.

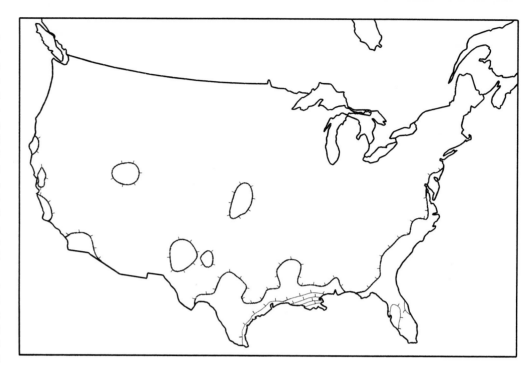

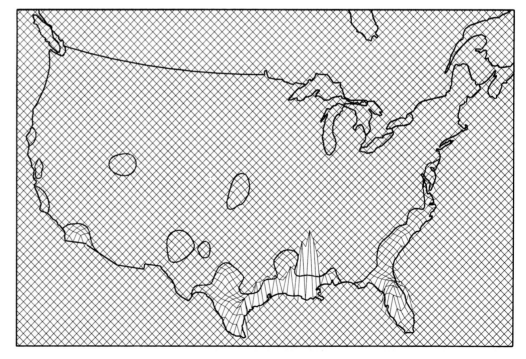

SCOLOPACIDAE

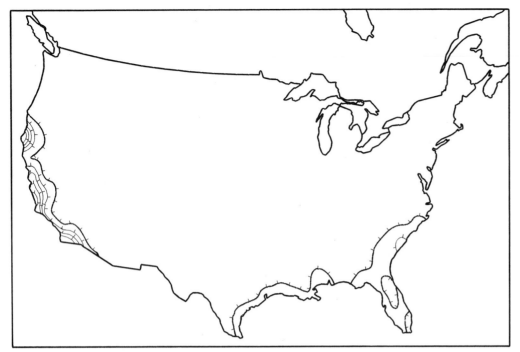

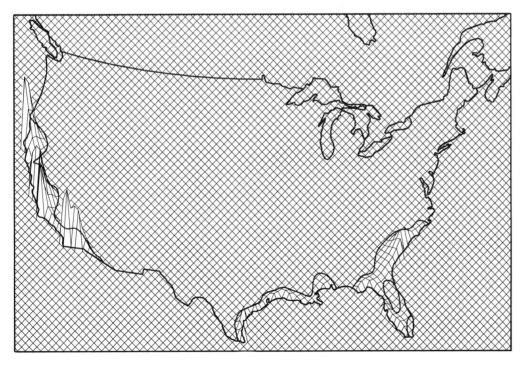

Willet (*Catoptrophorus semipalmatus*) Maximum: 28.96 I/Hr

The Willet winters along all three coasts in the United States. In the West it occurs from around Port Orford, Oregon, in the north to the Mexican border in the south. The distribution along the Gulf coast is not as continuous, stretching from extreme southern Texas to around Pensacola, Florida, then picking up again near Panama City and continuing around the tip of Florida. On the Atlantic coast this wader ranges south from New Bern, North Carolina, to around Fort Pierce and is absent in central Florida from Gainesville to Lake Istokpoga. Certainly it seeks out warm areas; the temperatures in all the areas where it winters rarely fall below 30°F (−1°C) in January. The reasons it avoids certain areas, however, are not obvious at present. The maps of several species, not just waders, show that the area around the west end of the Florida panhandle is avoided. I do not believe this is an artifact of the analysis method used in this study. More intense fieldwork is needed to determine why so many species avoid this region of the Gulf coast. The Willet's northern limits on both coasts may occur where they do because of cold mean winter ocean-surface temperatures. On both coasts the northern range edges occur approximately where the surface temperature drops below about 50°F (10°C).

Two of the more concentrated populations of Willets are associated with national wildlife refuges. These areas offer protection to this species, which was declining around the turn of the century because of hunting, removal of eggs, and the destruction of suitable habitat (Bent 1929). One of the most abundant populations is in California's Humboldt Bay National Wildlife Refuge, and the lowest abundance peak occurs around the Cape Romain refuge in South Carolina. Other high peaks are in California, with the most abundant population stretching north from around Morro Bay to Monterey and in a lesser concentration on up to San Francisco. There is a lower peak around San Diego that extends into the Imperial Valley around Salton Sea.

The Willet is usually found on mud flats or sand flats of bayous, bays, or estuaries (Bent 1929) and in marshes or pastures (Stenzel, Huber, and Page 1976). It typically feeds on tidal flats during low tide and moves inland at high tide. Prey detection is completely visual and is done primarily while walking or by turning over rocks or debris with the bill. The bird has five methods of prey capture, though the first two are used 93% of the time: pecking, multiple pecking, probing, multiple probing, and stealing from other waders, which on the California coast are mainly Long-billed Curlews. Its winter diet consists of fish, worms, gastropods, clams, and tube-dwelling amphiphods (Stenzel, Huber, and Page 1976). Page and Whitacre (1975) found that on the California coast raptors, particularly Northern Harriers and Cooper's Hawks, ate about 6.2% of the Willet population.

Wandering Tattler (*Heteroscelus incanus*) No Map

This shorebird occurs only on the Pacific coast from the United States through Mexico to Panama, Colombia, and Peru and on several South Pacific islands (AOU 1983). On the Christmas counts, the Wandering Tattler was observed at twenty sites along the Pacific coast from southeastern Vancouver Island to San Diego, but the only regular observations occurred south of the California-Oregon border. The highest abundance in California was on the Farallon Islands, with 0.79 individuals seen per party-hour.

Spotted Sandpiper (*Actitis macularia*) Maximum: 0.41 I/Hr

During the summer the Spotted Sandpiper is the most widely distributed scolopacid in North America, ranging coast to coast from Alaska and the Yukon in the north to central Arizona and Texas in the south (AOU 1983). It may also be the most abundant North American member of this family (Johnsgard 1981). In the fall birds migrate south to warmer areas. East of the 100th meridian it winters only in regions that have an average minimum January temperature above 30°F (−1°C), and to the west of this line it occurs in areas with temperatures over 20°F (−7°C). As well as along the coastlines, wintering birds are found in meadows and along the sandy shores of inland ponds and rivers (Bent 1929). The maps indicate that it occurs along the Colorado, Rio Grande, Red, Cumberland, and Alabama rivers and around several lakes near Atlanta, Georgia. The small "population" in Tennessee was due to an unusual sighting of one individual in 1968. The northern range limit along the Atlantic coast occurs just south of the marshes in northern North Carolina. It may avoid this wetland habitat in North Carolina because it lacks sandy or rocky shores, which are necessary for a species that wades infrequently (Bent 1929). This sandpiper also is absent in the marshes in northwestern peninsular Florida.

The highest concentration of wintering Spotted Sandpipers is found in the Everglades of southern Florida. All the other abundance peaks are inland except a small one in the Louisiana bayous around the mouth of the Mississippi River. The entire southern Rio Grande valley from Big Bend National Park on south to the Gulf of Mexico contains high numbers of Spotted Sandpipers, as does the area around the Colorado River and Lake Mead in Nevada. There are lesser peaks in California at the southern end of the San Joaquin valley and the northern end of the Sacramento valley just west of Redding.

The overall abundance of this sandpiper was not greatly affected by hunting around the turn of the century, primarily because it is usually solitary, which prevented hunters from killing large numbers with one shot (Bent 1929). The Spotted Sandpiper forages by pecking food items from the substrate and by slowly stalking its prey. In meadows it frequently can be found carefully approaching winged insects (Johnsgard 1981). It also eats fish and various aquatic and terrestrial insects (Bent 1929).

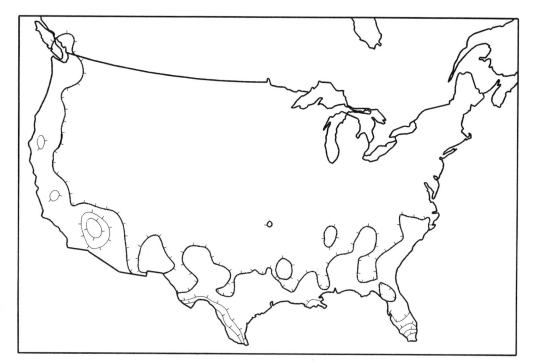

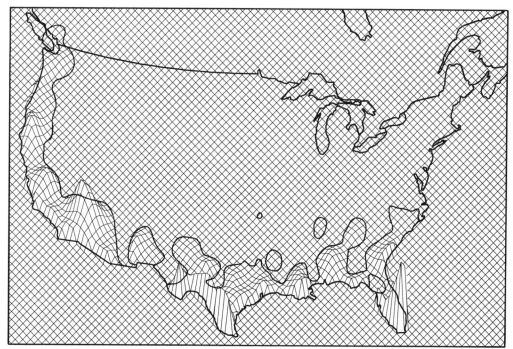

Spotted Sandpiper

SCOLOPACIDAE

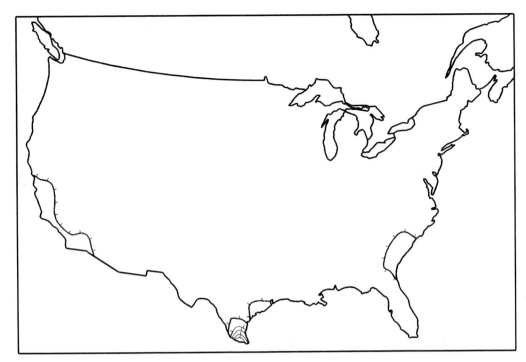

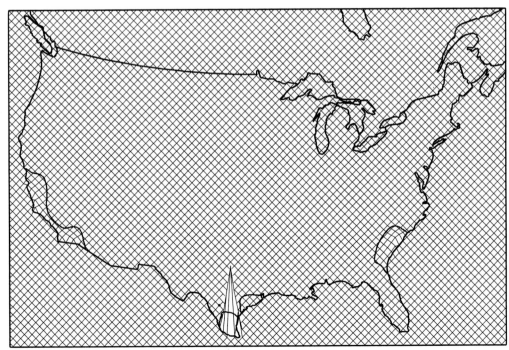

Whimbrel (*Numenius phaeopus*) Maximum: 7.57 I/Hr

The Whimbrel has a very limited winter distribution in the United States. It occurs on the Pacific coast from San Francisco Bay south to the Mexican border and on the Atlantic coast from the North Carolina–South Carolina border to the Georgia-Florida border. The most southerly distribution in the United States is along the Texas Gulf coast from Anahuac National Wildlife Refuge to the Aransas refuge, and then the species is present again from around Corpus Christi on south to the Rio Grande valley. Certainly the warm climate of all these areas attracts Whimbrels, but the reason this species is present only in these areas, and not other warm locations, cannot be determined in a study of this type.

The densest population is near the mouth of the Rio Grande. This may be an aberrant peak, though, because the average ten-year mean was strongly influenced by a large number of birds recorded in 1966. That year 3,119 individuals were seen, a "new national record" (Cruickshank 1966). This peak overshadows less concentrated populations that appear on the three-dimensional map as slight bulges around Cape Romain National Wildlife Refuge in South Carolina, near Salton Sea in California, and near Morro Bay in southern California.

In recent years the Whimbrel has been increasing its winter range. As late as 1929, Bent reported that its only occurrence in North America was on its breeding range in Greenland. Since that time the birds that presumably breed in Iceland have begun wintering in the southern United States (Cramp 1983). Not much is known about this species in its relatively new wintering areas, and it is assumed to have an ecology similar to that of the large curlews (Johnsgard 1981). The Whimbrel usually feeds at tideline, where it forages by probing, but not deeply. It eats mainly marine organisms and fiddler crabs (Cramp 1983).

Whimbrel

Whimbrel

Long-billed Curlew (*Numenius americanus*) Maximum: 7.62 I/Hr

The Long-billed Curlew can be found foraging in shallow-water habitats both inland and along coastlines (Johnsgard 1981). The maps of the distribution show that it occurs along the Pacific and Gulf coasts but avoids the Atlantic seaboard. In the West it winters from just north of San Francisco to southwestern Arizona and from western Louisiana to southern Texas on the Gulf coast. Inland this shorebird can be found in western Texas, where there are regular populations around Midland and San Angelo. In California its inland range is bounded by the Sierra Nevada and the more southern San Bernardino Mountains.

Like the Whimbrel, the Long-billed Curlew has its most concentrated population in southern Texas where the Rio Grande empties into the Gulf of Mexico. A slight concentration of this species extends from this population up the coast and joins with a less dense population on the Colorado River in Texas. There is a moderate abundance peak in the southern San Joaquin valley and an even less dense population in the Imperial Valley around the Salton Sea National Wildlife Refuge.

The Long-billed Curlew is the largest of all the shorebirds, measuring 23 inches (59 cm) from bill tip to the end of the tail (National Geographic Society 1983). Because of its size, it was a prize game bird around the turn of the century. It was easy prey for hunters because it readily responded to decoys and whistles, and the flock would circle above wounded members (Bent 1929). This, plus the encroachment of civilization on its breeding grounds, resulting in its extirpation from Kansas, Iowa, Minnesota, Wisconsin, and Illinois, has caused a general decline in the abundance of this species (Johnsgard 1981).

Along the California coast the Long-billed Curlew feeds on tidal flats during low tide and roosts in inland marshes during high tide. It uses three foraging methods: probing burrows in the mud, using tactile stimulation to sense prey; standing motionless in shallow water for about five to ten seconds with its open bill slightly submerged and moving slowly to within striking distance before quickly capturing its prey; and pecking items visually detected on the substrate. The third method is used infrequently. The winter diet in a California marine habitat consisted of 63% mud crabs, 20% ghost shrimp, and 7% mud shrimp (Stenzel, Huber, and Page 1976), and presumably this is representative of wintering Long-billed Curlews in general.

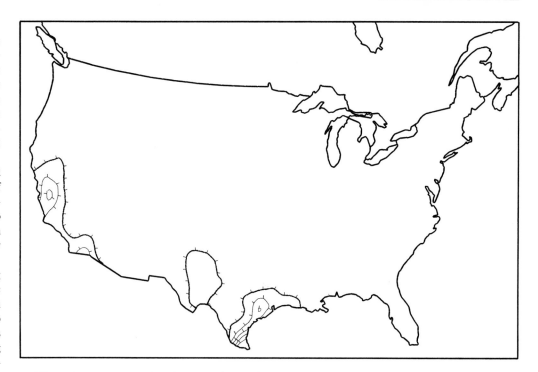

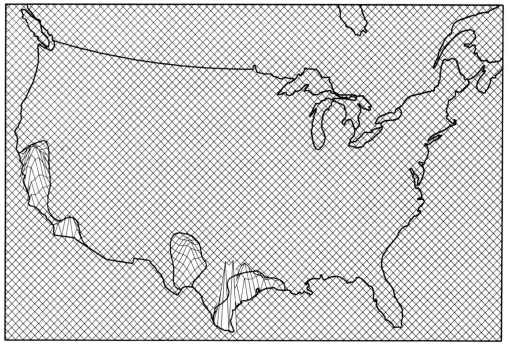

SCOLOPACIDAE

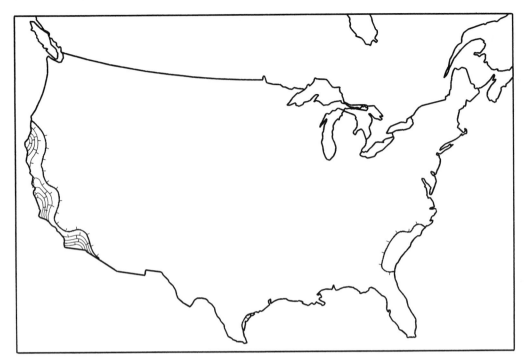

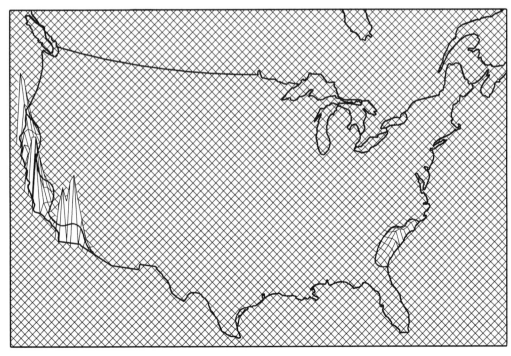

Marbled Godwit (*Limosa fedoa*) Maximum: 27.32 I/Hr

The winter distribution of the Marbled Godwit resembles that of the ecologically similar Whimbrel. Both are present on all three coasts in roughly the same locations. On the Atlantic coast the Marbled Godwit frequents only the area from central North Carolina to central Georgia. As with the Whimbrel, it is not obvious why areas farther south into Florida are not occupied or why the wetlands of North Carolina are avoided. The Marbled Godwit is much more restricted on the Gulf coast than is the Whimbrel. The former occurs only on the Texas shoreline around Aransas National Wildlife Refuge. Again, why it is present in such a small region is not currently understood. The western distribution of this species is more extensive than that of the Whimbrel. The godwit ranges continuously from the Imperial Valley along the Mexican border to just beyond Oregon Island National Wildlife Refuge in southern Oregon. Certainly warm temperatures are a major impetus for the species to winter in all these coastal areas, but other factors, such as the availability of prey and appropriate habitat, undoubtedly also influence its selection of wintering grounds. More in-depth field studies are needed before we can understand all the limiting factors.

The accompanying maps show that the densest populations of Marbled Godwits occur in California. There are three concentrated populations, all equally dense. One is associated with the Humboldt Bay National Wildlife Refuge near Cape Mendocino. To the south, one peak stretches from around Monterey Bay to Santa Barbara, with its apex near San Luis Obispo. The third peak extends from the San Diego coast to the Imperial Valley and Salton Sea, spilling over into the Colorado River valley and southwestern Arizona.

Coastal mud flats that adjoin wet savannas or meadows are the preferred habitat of the Marbled Godwit (Johnsgard 1981). Here it feeds on insects, mollusks, snails, crustaceans, worms, and leeches (Bent 1927), capturing its prey either by pecking along the surface of the substrate or by probing into the mud. The abundance of this shorebird in the East has greatly decreased over time. In 1832 Audubon reported seeing "an immense number of these birds on an extensive mud bar" near one of the Florida Keys (cited in Bent 1927), but about ninety years later Bent (1927) found only one individual during a five-month stay in Florida. This decline undoubtedly has been at least partly caused by hunting and the takeover of prairie breeding grounds for agriculture (Bent 1927).

Marbled Godwit

Ruddy Turnstone (*Arenaria interpres*) Maximum: 3.17 I/Hr

In the United States the wintering grounds of the Ruddy Turnstone include all three coastlines. On the Pacific coast it is present from San Diego to northern Washington around Grays Harbor, but it avoids the area around Humboldt Bay. The distribution on the Atlantic coast extends from as far north as Bangor, Maine, to the southern tip of Florida around West Palm Beach. This species appears to avoid heavily populated regions such as around Miami, Florida, and New York City. It is absent from several locations along the Gulf coast, including the mouth of the Mississippi River, the western panhandle of Florida to Panama City, and the northeastern shore of Florida from Perry to Crystal River. The last area is avoided by several other waterbirds, including some shorebirds, gulls, and herons. The reasons for the lack of diversity in this region are not currently understood.

Temperature seems to have some effect in determining where this species occurs in high densities. All the peak abundances, except a very slight peak around Cape May, New Jersey, are in areas where the average minimum temperature rarely drops below 40°F (4°C) in January. The highest concentration reaches from Jacksonville, Florida, south to Daytona Beach. A slight concentration continues north from Jacksonville and meets a fairly high concentration around Charleston, South Carolina, and Cape Romain National Wildlife Refuge. On the Gulf coast of Florida a rather dense population occurs from around Sarasota to Cape Romano.

The Ruddy Turnstone is almost exclusively a maritime species, frequenting rocky and stony beaches. As its name suggests, one of its primary foraging behaviors is to turn stones over with its bill and eat the prey hiding underneath. If a particular stone is too heavy to turn with a flip of its bill and head, the bird may use its weight to displace it by pushing the stone with its breast (Bent 1929). Besides turning stones when searching for prey, this species roots around in seaweed and often digs holes in wet sand as large as a human fist. When foraging it looks for sand fleas, worms, insects (Bent 1929), crustaceans, mollusks, human food scraps, and carrion, which make up most of its diet (Johnsgard 1981). Individuals are usually solitary or occur in mixed flocks of shorebirds (Bent 1929). Immature members of this cosmopolitan species usually stay on the wintering grounds their first summer (Johnsgard 1981).

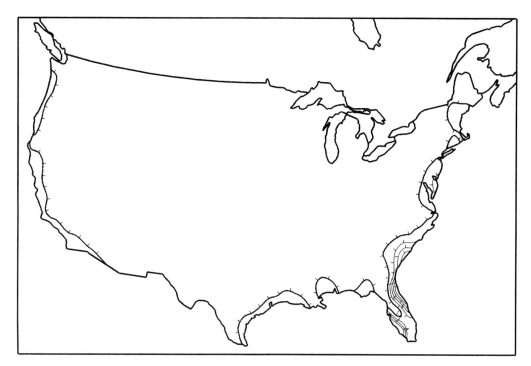

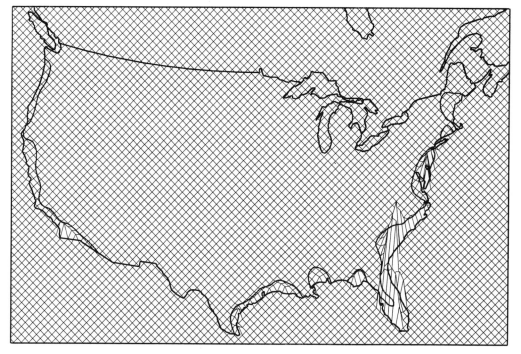

SCOLOPACIDAE

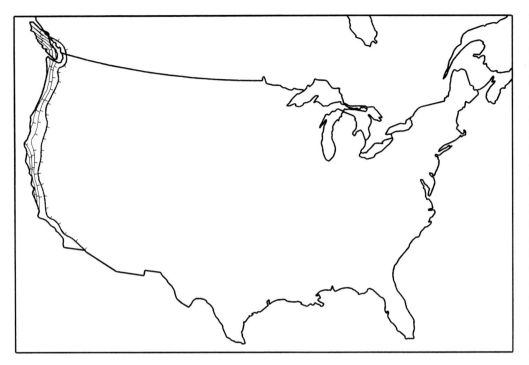

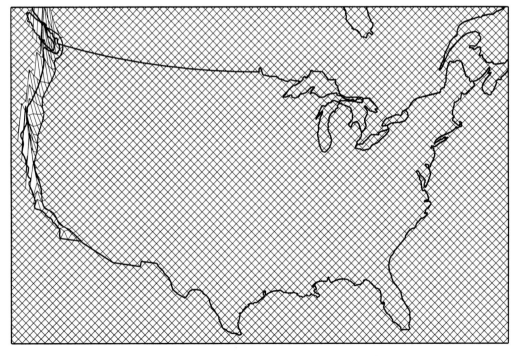

Black Turnstone (*Arenaria melancephala*) Maximum: 7.50 I/Hr

Maps are included for the Black Turnstone even though this species was recorded at only thirty-eight count sites. Those sites are spread fairly evenly along the length of its range, and thus much information can be gleaned from them.

Unlike its congener, the Black Turnstone winters only on the Pacific coast. The maps show that its distribution covers the entire length of the coastline from San Diego to around Powell River, British Columbia, and includes all of Vancouver Island. In fact this species prefers the isolated habitats of outlying islands (Bent 1929). Temperature may be limiting its distribution in the North, because it is absent from areas where January temperatures drop much below 30°F (−1°C).

The most concentrated population is on the southwest side of Vancouver Island, the location of Pacific Rim National Park. This is probably not a coincidence, because the park protects both the bird and its habitat. High densities of the Black Turnstone continue south from Vancouver Island to the mainland of Washington, around Cape Flattery. Fairly high concentrations extend all along the coast to around Humboldt Bay, the only location on the United States' Pacific coast that the Ruddy Turnstone seems to avoid. South of there, near Point Arena, the concentration of the Black Turnstone again increases, reaching a peak around Monterey Bay. The density then drops off significantly south of Morro Bay.

Rocky shorelines, jetties, and barnacle-covered reefs are the preferred habitat for this turnstone (Johnsgard 1981). In such environments it follows waves and gleans prey from the surface of the rocks, turns over seaweed searching for hidden food, or digs in wet sand for animals that burrow (Bent 1929). Like its congener, it turns over stones to capture prey hiding underneath. If a stone is too heavy to move with its bill, it often uses its body as a battering ram. It uses these various methods to capture crustaceans, barnacles, sea slugs, mollusks (Bent 1929), and shrimp (Johnsgard 1981).

Surfbird (*Aphriza virgata*) No Map

The wintering grounds of the Surfbird are extensive, stretching the entire length of the Pacific coast from Alaska to the Strait of Magellan at the southern tip of South America (AOU 1983). Only twenty-eight Christmas counts reported it, and that number includes sites as far north as Juneau, Alaska. North of Vancouver Island the locations recording the bird have varied over the years. The highest abundance was recorded around Point Saint George near the California-Oregon border, with 2.01 individuals seen per party-hour.

Red Knot (*Calidris canutus*) Maximum: 5.34 I/Hr

Instead of being uniformly spread along the coastlines, Red Knots are concentrated in a few local areas (Johnsgard 1981). This is reflected in the maps, which show the species' discontinuous distribution along all three coasts. On the Pacific coast there are two disjunct populations, one centered on Monterey Bay and roughly covering the area from Bodega Bay to Morro Bay, the other extending from Santa Monica to San Diego and the Imperial Valley. The most continuous population on the Gulf coast runs from the mouth of the Rio Grande to the eastern edge of the Sabine National Wildlife Refuge in western Louisiana. Much smaller populations are found along the short expanse of the Mississippi coast and around Cape Saint George on the panhandle of Florida. Along the Gulf coast of peninsular Florida, knots are present from the Crystal River area to just south of Naples. This population has by far the highest concentration, and the peak substantially overshadows all the other populations. On the Atlantic coast this species extends farther north into colder regions than most other shorebirds. The northern limit along the southern border of Maine occurs where the mean minimum temperature drops below 15°F (−9°C). This northernmost population covers all of Cape Cod and Rhode Island. The Red Knot is also present along the coast of New Jersey and Maryland. It occurs infrequently in the area from the Chesapeake Bay to the southern edge of the marshes in North Carolina but is present from here to Saint Augustine, Florida. Finally, there is a small population around Cocoa Beach.

The Red Knot is normally found in compact flocks ranging from five to one hundred individuals. It forages on sandy beaches and mud flats (Johnsgard 1981), feeding on marine insects and their larvae. In fall it migrates out of the breeding areas as both the insect population and the temperature drop (Bent 1927). The abundance of this species was strongly declining around the turn of the century owing to hunting. Several factors contributed to its demise: it was considered a "good table bird"; it gathered in large, compact flocks, so many birds could be killed with one or two shots; and it was easy to decoy and whistle in. Large numbers were killed during "fire lightings." Two people hunting at night, one carrying a lantern of some sort, would sneak up on extremely large roosts of these birds. While one person held the light, blinding the birds, the other would catch them with bare hands, then bite their necks to kill them. At one time people could get ten cents a dozen—easy money.

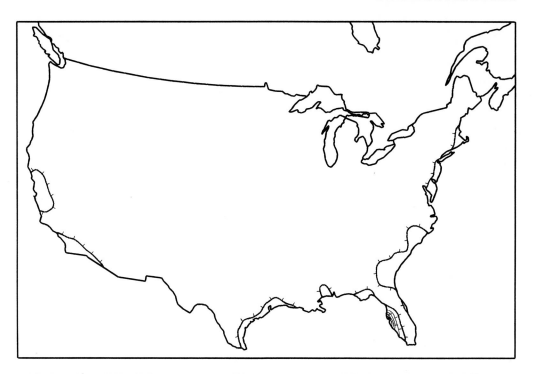

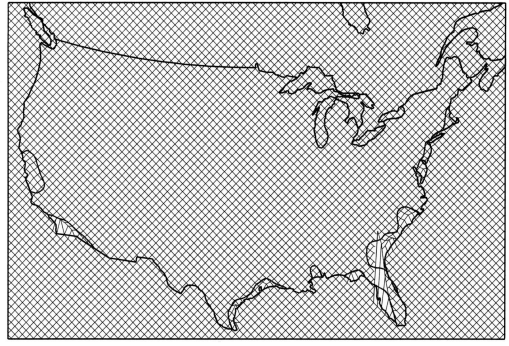

SCOLOPACIDAE

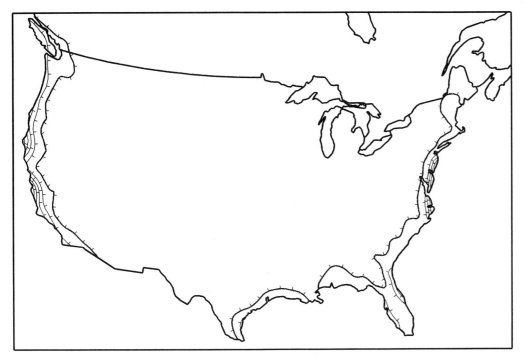

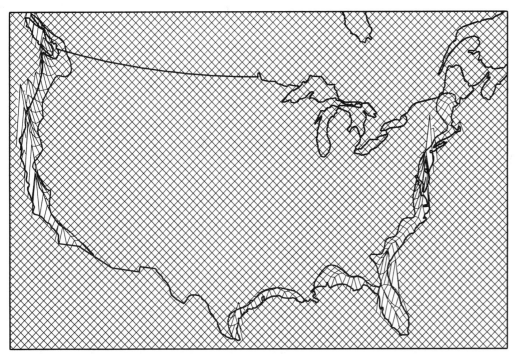

Sanderling (*Calidris alba*) Maximum: 12.68 I/Hr

The Sanderling is probably the most widespread maritime shorebird wintering in North America. It occurs along all coasts except from northern Maine and farther north, around the mouth of the Mississippi River, and at the tip of Florida. Given that most other shorebirds avoid the northwestern coast of Florida from Perry to Crystal River, it is interesting that the Sanderling is present there. The western range extends the length of the Pacific coast, and sporadic observations were recorded as far north as Alaska.

Sanderling abundance is relatively high all along the Pacific coast except between Point Arena and Point Reyes and around Los Angeles. The most concentrated populations are around Humboldt Bay and Monterey Bay. The densest populations on the Atlantic coast, which are slightly lower than those on the Pacific coast, are in New Jersey near the Brigantine refuge and farther south in northern North Carolina. There is a lower abundance peak along Canaveral National Seashore and the Merritt Island refuge. On the Gulf coast of Florida a slight abundance peak is present from Crystal River to around Naples. Another slight peak occurs around the Aransas refuge near Corpus Christi, Texas.

The predominant foraging behavior of the Sanderling is to follow receding waves, picking up prey items washed ashore or probing for burrowing animals in the wet sand (Bent 1927). When probing, it makes a series of quick, shallow, almost stitching jabs into the sand (Johnsgard 1981). It hunts for sand flies, mollusks, ostracods, and polychaete worms. Normally it forages in intraspecific flocks (Bent 1927) of about ten birds (Johnsgard 1981). During stormy weather it is a much more active feeder, in part because more prey items are washed ashore (Bent 1927). Page and Whitacre (1975) found that the Sanderlings themselves are prey for raptors, which ate 6.8% of their population in a lagoon just north of San Francisco.

Semipalmated Sandpiper (*Calidris pusilla*) Map in Appendix B

Phillips (1975) did an exhaustive study of the winter distribution of the Semipalmated Sandpiper using study skins. He found that the bill size and various plumage characteristics of this shorebird overlap significantly with those of the Western Sandpiper. A protracted search for Semipalmated Sandpipers collected in the United States in the winter found only one individual, from southern Florida. Phillips concludes, and the AOU apparently agrees, that in the United States the winter range of this sandpiper encompasses only the southern tip of Florida. The maps from the CBC data show an extensive distribution of this sandpiper stretching along the Gulf and Atlantic coasts. Presumably this pattern has been generated because of misidentifications. Therefore the map is misleading and consequently provided only in appendix B.

Western Sandpiper (*Calidris mauri*) Maximum: 45.90 I/Hr

The winter distribution of the Western Sandpiper shows that, contrary to its name, it is not restricted to the West. Besides being found on the Pacific coast, it is present on the Gulf and Atlantic coasts. In addition, the abundance along these latter two coasts should be even greater than shown here. Western Sandpipers along both of these coasts, except in southern Florida, have in all likelihood been misidentified as Semipalmated Sandpipers (Phillips 1975). The distribution of the former species would not radically change if the misidentified individuals were included, but the range would extend a bit farther north along the Atlantic coast.

Temperature apparently affects the general winter range of the Western Sandpiper, because it winters primarily in areas that stay above freezing. Several disjunct populations occur where the ambient temperature is much colder than along the southern coasts. Only one of these is ephemeral—the one around the junction of Nevada, Utah, and Idaho. Individuals are seen regularly at the other sites. These locations include the area around Puget Sound in Washington, throughout the Midland–Big Spring region of western Texas, and near El Paso, Texas.

Adding the abundance information of those individuals misidentified as Semipalmated Sandpipers to that of the correctly identified Western Sandpipers might change the abundance pattern. The peaks on the maps of the Western Sandpiper show that its concentration is much higher in the West; all the densest populations are along the Pacific coast. The highest abundance peak centers on the Humboldt Bay National Wildlife Refuge in northern California. The next densest population is in the San Diego area and stretches into the Imperial Valley, encompassing Salton Sea. Temperature probably influences where this sandpiper occurs in large concentrations, because all the abundance peaks are in regions where the minimum January temperature is about 40°F (4°C).

Western Sandpipers usually form fairly large and noisy flocks, which made them easy prey for hunters in the later 1800s (Bent 1927). Apart from the Semipalmated Sandpiper, this is the only *Calidris* with partially webbed toes. In a study in Argentina on the interactions between these two similar sandpipers, Ashmole (1970) found that they allocate their time differently among foraging behaviors. Whereas the Semipalmated Sandpiper spends only 21% of its foraging time probing the mud, the Western Sandpiper spends 70%. The latter is usually found on mud flats that are covered with moist mud or shallow water (Ashmole 1970).

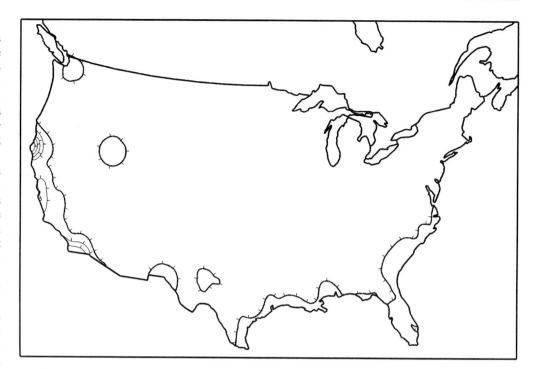

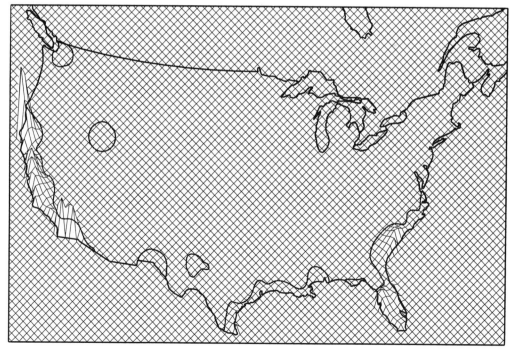

SCOLOPACIDAE

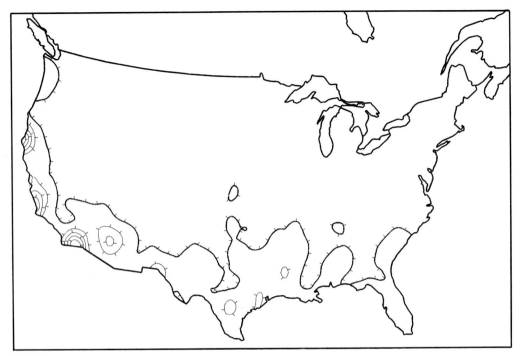

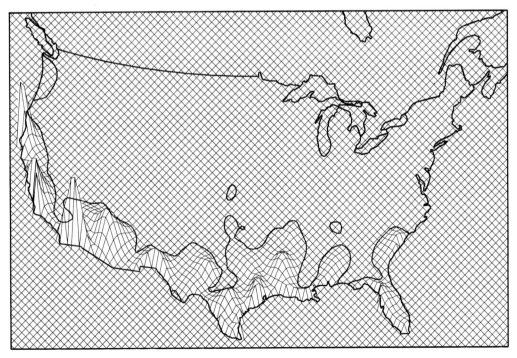

Least Sandpiper (*Calidris minutilla*) Maximum: 12.53 I/Hr

The distribution of the smallest North American sandpiper shows that in winter it frequents inland environments as well as maritime habitats. The range edge is convoluted and defies easy explanation of the factors limiting it. Temperature certainly has some influence. In the East, most of the distribution occurs in places that are warmer than 30°F (−1°C) in January, while the western range extends into areas that get no colder than 20°F (−7°C). Vegetation type may also have an influence; this species occurs in the warmer parts of the swamp forest of the Mississippi valley. There are three disjunct populations, all ephemeral. Birds were observed along the Washington and northern Oregon coasts only in 1969 and 1972, on the Arkansas River in Kansas in 1969 and 1971, and in central Tennessee in 1970 and 1972.

All the higher abundance peaks are in the western part of the country. Humboldt Bay National Wildlife Refuge is the site of one of the highest concentrations, and the other peak of comparable height is in the Imperial Valley near the Salton Sea refuge. The next most concentrated population is also in California, extending from Monterey Bay to Point Conception, with its apex around San Luis Obispo. A less abundant peak centers on Phoenix, Arizona. Four slight concentrations occur on the Mexican border near El Paso, Texas, in front of the Edwards Plateau around San Antonio, Texas, along the Texas coast near the San Bernard and Brazoria national wildlife refuges, and on the Red River in Louisiana.

Descriptions of the foraging behavior of the Least Sandpiper are not consistent. Johnsgard (1981) reports that it pecks at prey either singly or multiply and rarely if ever probes, whereas Bent (1927) states that it normally is found probing in the mud of marshes or tidal flats. Its diet consists of crustaceans, worms, insects, and some seeds (Bent 1927). Predation by raptors on Least Sandpipers in a wintering California population was 7% (Page and Whitacre 1975). Natural predators may cause a slight decrease in abundance, but the impact of human hunting was much more severe and stopped only when protection was legislated in 1913 (Bent 1927). Until this time Least Sandpipers, despite their small size, were prize game birds because they taste good, form fairly large flocks, making them easy to kill, and are easily fooled by decoys and whistling (Bent 1927).

Baird's Sandpiper (*Calidris bairdii*) No Map

The primary wintering ground for the Baird's Sandpiper is in South America, from central Peru to Tierra del Fuego (AOU 1983). In the United States during the ten years of data examined, sixteen sightings were made, chiefly along the Gulf and Pacific coasts, with only two of these occurring at the same location.

Pectoral Sandpiper (*Calidris melanotos*) No Map

As for the Baird's Sandpiper, only ephemeral sightings of the Pectoral Sandpiper were reported in the United States, all on the Gulf coast and along the Atlantic coast as far north as Connecticut. All but one site reported this sandpiper in only one year, and the exception reported it in only three years. Its main wintering ground is in southern South America from Peru and southern Brazil to central Chile and southern Argentina (AOU 1983).

Purple Sandpiper (*Calidris maritima*) Maximum: 222.22 I/Hr

Even though the Purple Sandpiper occurs in large flocks in certain areas of its distribution, a set of maps has been included because this species is not nomadic. Thus the location of the highest abundance was constant over the years examined. Unfortunately, the abundance peaks are probably shown lower than they should be, because most birders have difficulty estimating the number in a large flock, but this should not substantially affect the general distribution and abundance patterns.

Unlike most other shorebirds, the Purple Sandpiper occurs in cold environments. A disjunct distribution occurs along the Atlantic coast, but its presence in the South is limited. Much of its range is where the minimum January temperature is below freezing. The exceptions include the small groups around the Florida-Georgia border, near Cape Fear in North Carolina, and from central North Carolina around the Swanquarter National Wildlife Refuge to Chesapeake Bay.

The species' most concentrated population extends from Cape Cod and Massachusetts Bay to the southern end of the Bay of Fundy, including the coasts of Maine and Nova Scotia. The apex stretches along the coast of Maine from Bar Harbor to Bath.

The species name *maritima* certainly is appropriate in the winter, because this sandpiper frequents only wave-washed, rocky coastlines. In this environment it obviously does not probe but pecks at prey exposed on the rocks. Although it can often be seen swimming between foraging areas, it does not feed while swimming (Johnsgard 1981). Shrimp, crabs, marine insects, mollusks (Bent 1927), marine gastropods, and fish (Johnsgard 1981) make up most of its diet.

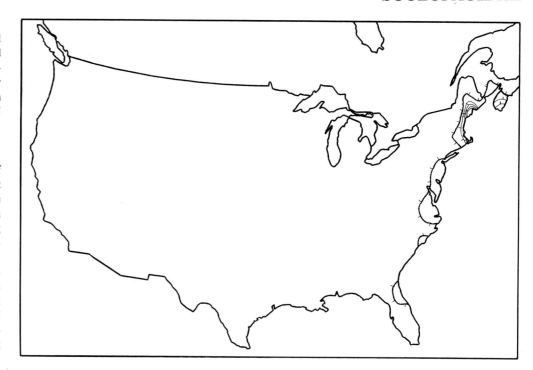

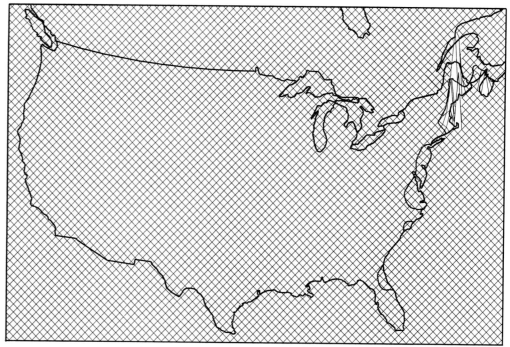

SCOLOPACIDAE

Rock Sandpiper (*Calidris ptilocnemis*) No Map
The Rock Sandpiper's winter distribution reaches from southern Alaska to central California (AOU 1983). It was recorded on Christmas counts as far south as Santa Monica, California, but the more regular sightings extended north from Tillamook Bay in northern Oregon. The northernmost sighting was at Kachemak Bay, Alaska, and there was even a record from the extreme western end of the Aleutian Island chain. Tillamook Bay had the most frequent sightings (seven out of the ten years) in the study area, with an average of 0.41 individuals seen each party-hour.

Dunlin (*Calidris alpina*) Map in Appendix B
The number of Dunlins seen per party-hour at some count sites differed dramatically from year to year, ranging from zero to hundreds. Because of the transient behavior of these flocks, the abundance pattern resulting from the ten-year means may be misleading. Thus, the set of maps for the Dunlin has been included only in appendix B. In general this shorebird ranges along the Atlantic coast from northern New Jersey to the southern tip of Florida and on the Gulf coast. The distribution is much more discontinuous on the Pacific coast, with populations occurring only in the San Diego region, from Monterey Bay to the California-Oregon border, and in the areas around Vancouver Island and Puget Sound.

Stilt Sandpiper (*Calidris himantopus*) No Map
The Stilt Sandpiper is present in the United States only along the Gulf coast and as far north as South Carolina on the Atlantic coast, but the most regular sightings occur below the 31st parallel. The count near Key West, Florida, recorded sightings in more years than those from any other site (eight out of the ten years), and the highest mean abundance was at the Santa Ana National Wildlife Refuge in Texas (0.35 I/Hr). This sandpiper's chief wintering ground extends from Bolivia and south-central Brazil to northern Chile and northern Argentina (AOU 1983).

Wilson's Phalarope (*Phalaropus tricolor*) No Map
The Wilson's Phalarope was seen at only thirteen Christmas count locations, and maximum average abundance was only 0.02 individuals seen per party-hour. All but two of the sites were south of the 35th parallel, ranging along the Gulf and Pacific coasts, and at various inland locations. Newport Beach, California, reported this species in the most years (four out of ten). The primary wintering ground is in western South America from Peru through Chile and Argentina (AOU 1983).

Red-necked Phalarope (*Phalaropus lobatus*) No Map
This phalarope normally winters at sea on the Pacific Ocean (AOU 1983), but individuals were observed at eleven Christmas counts along the Pacific coast, two on the Gulf coast, and one inland. It was most regularly seen (seven out of ten years) around San Diego, with an abundance of 0.25 individuals per party-hour.

Red Phalarope (*Phalaropus fulicaria*) No Map
Even though the Red Phalarope winters chiefly at sea on the Pacific Ocean, off the coast of South America from Colombia to Chile, and on the South Atlantic off Patagonia, it is regularly seen in southern California (AOU 1983). Christmas counts reported this species along the Pacific coast from San Diego to northern Oregon and sporadically on the northern Atlantic coast from Maryland to Maine. The most regular sightings were at San Diego, with an abundance of 1.10 individuals per party-hour averaged from reports in six out of the ten years.

Stilt Sandpiper

Short-billed Dowitcher (*Limnodromus griseus*) Maximum: 14.10 I/HR
The entire distribution of the Short-billed Dowitcher is in regions where the minimum January temperature rarely drops below 30°F (−1°C), and most of its range is normally warmer than 40°F (4°C). Included is the area along the California coast from Stewarts Point to San Diego. The distribution is discontinuous on the Gulf coast, with the dowitcher present from Corpus Christi, Texas, to the Sabine National Wildlife Refuge, around Mobile Bay, Alabama, and from Panama City, Florida, to the southern tip of Florida. A disjunct pattern also occurs on the Atlantic coast; this species avoids the Miami, Florida, area but is present from West Palm Beach to southern South Carolina and skips over to the Cape Romain refuge, where it extends north to Albemarle Sound in North Carolina.

There are populations with high concentrations on all three coasts, with the highest ones encompassing Tampa Bay, Florida, and San Diego, California, and extending over to the Imperial Valley–Salton Sea area. The next highest peaks are on Florida's eastern coast, stretching from Daytona Beach to Saint Simons Island, with the apex around Jacksonville, and covering almost the entire length of the North Carolina coast. There are small concentrations near Galveston, Texas, and around San Luis Reservoir, just east of Monterey Bay, California.

The Long- and Short-billed Dowitchers are so similar in appearance that many studies do not attempt to differentiate them. Indeed, no convincing argument as to their separate species status was shown until 1950 (Pitelka 1950). The bill lengths do vary between the two species, but there is overlap. The length of the Short-bill's culmen ranges between 51 and 62 mm for the male and 56 and 68 mm for the female, while the measurements for the Long-billed are 57 to 69 mm and 64 to 76 mm (Johnsgard 1981). The Short-billed Dowitcher is purported to prefer saltier water than its congener and often feeds on tidal flats during low tide by probing the mud with its bill as it walks or stands (Johnsgard 1981).

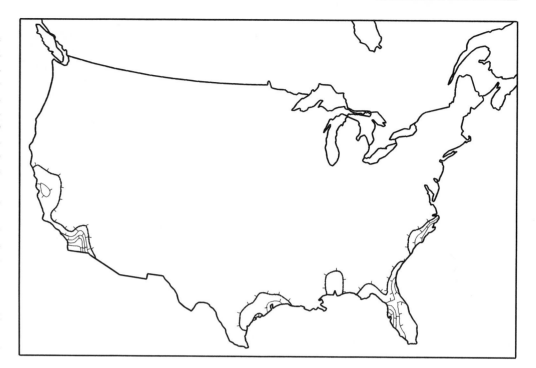

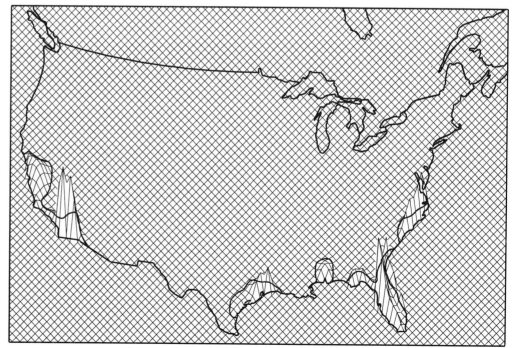

SCOLOPACIDAE

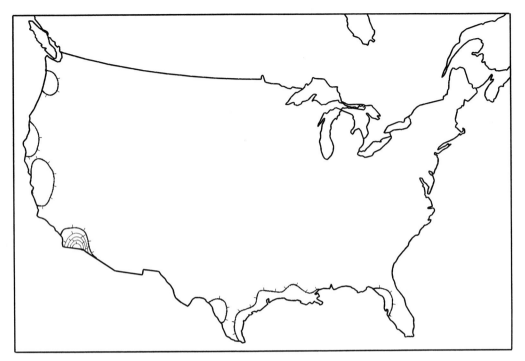

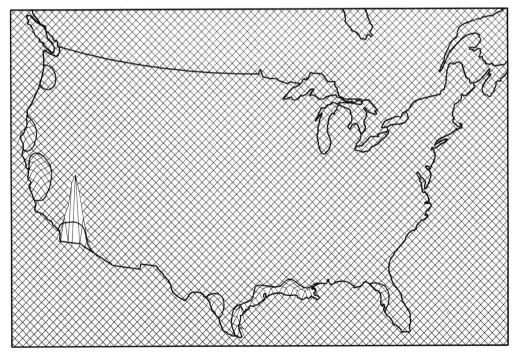

Long-billed Dowitcher (*Limnodromus scolopaceus*) Maximum: 11.62 I/Hr

The distribution of the Long-billed Dowitcher is quite different from that of its congener. The Long-billed is not present on the Atlantic coast, has a disjunct distribution on the Pacific coast, and ranges more continuously along the Gulf coast. Along the Pacific coast, the Long-billed Dowitcher occurs from Grays Harbor in Washington to Cape Meares and Three Arch Rock refuges in Oregon, around Humboldt Bay in California, from Point Reyes to Morro Bay, California, and along the San Diego coast. An inland population was observed regularly in the Rio Grande valley between Eagle Pass and Laredo, Texas. On the Gulf coast this dowitcher occurs from southern Texas to the Louisiana-Mississippi border, and on the Florida coast it is found from Steinhatchee to Crystal River. This latter area is avoided by several other shorebirds.

The abundance patterns of the two congeners show that high concentrations of the Long-billed Dowitcher are less frequent than those of the Short-billed. The former has only one peak, in the Imperial Valley of California around Salton Sea, while the latter has several peaks, one of which is also in the Imperial Valley.

The Long-billed Dowitcher is normally found in fresher water than its short-billed congener. Because of its longer bill (see the Short-billed Dowitcher account for measurements), it is reported to feed in deeper water. While walking or standing, it probes the mud with its bill, often immersing its head. The foraging behavior of both dowitchers is best described as including jabs—brief thrusts of the bill into mud with quick withdrawal—and probes, which are basically deeper and prolonged jabs, usually accompanied by a rapid up-and-down quiver (Burton 1972). The two congeners have basically the same diet, except that the Long-billed Dowitcher eats more insects (Johnsgard 1981). Both species have been reported to feed on mud and sand flats, where they eat aquatic bugs, fish eggs, mollusks, leeches, marine worms, various insects, and some seeds and roots. They form fairly large flocks with other shorebirds, such as plovers and sandpipers, which made them relatively easy prey for hunters in the previous century. They fly in tight groups, making it possible to kill many with one shot, and uninjured individuals return to the calls of the injured birds, giving the hunter another opportunity to kill them. This resulted in a dramatic decline in dowitcher abundance until such hunting was outlawed (Bent 1927). As for natural predators, Page and Whitacre (1975) found that in a California population, 15.5% of the dowitchers were eaten by raptors.

Common Snipe (*Gallinago gallinago*) Maximum: 2.95 I/Hr

The northern limit of this widespread species apparently is influenced by temperature and, to a lesser extent, by elevation and the presence of protected river valleys. East of the 100th meridian the Common Snipe avoids regions that have a minimum January temperature lower than 20°F (−7°C), except along the Mississippi River, where it extends into areas where the temperature drops below 10°F (−12°C). It avoids the Appalachians completely. In the West the Common Snipe occurs where the temperature drops to about 10°F (−12°C). There are vacant areas in Idaho and Wyoming because the species avoids the higher, colder peaks of the Rocky Mountains. The snipe also is absent in the Ozarks, the drier areas of the Colorado Plateaus, the harsh environment of the Mojave Desert, and the waterlogged habitat of the Florida Everglades.

Temperature apparently is also important in determining the snipe's optimal habitat. All the dense populations are in areas where the January temperature rarely drops below 40°F (4°C). The highest concentration is in the Louisiana bayous, encompassing the mouth of the Mississippi River. In Alabama there is a somewhat smaller concentration around the William Dannelly Reservoir. A population of approximately the same concentration is present around Gainesville, Florida, extending into the region between Perry and Crystal River. Humboldt Bay National Wildlife Refuge is the location of a rather high concentration of Common Snipes. Lesser abundance peaks are scattered throughout the distribution, all but one in areas that are usually warmer than 30°F (−1°C) in January. These warmer regions include the area on the coast around the California-Oregon border, inland from Corpus Christi and Galveston, Texas, around Eufaula Lake in Oklahoma, along the Mississippi River between Arkansas and Mississippi, and inland from the North Carolina coast. The slight abundance peak near the Las Vegas National Wildlife Refuge in eastern New Mexico is in an area that gets as cold as 10°F (−12°C) in January.

Even in dense populations, Common Snipes are usually found foraging alone in moist meadows (Bent 1927). They probe the organic soil, primarily searching for insects but rounding out their diet with earthworms, crustaceans, snails, and a bit of vegetable matter. When probing, they normally work intensively on a fairly small area (Johnsgard 1981). Until the early 1900s, the numbers of this game bird dropped significantly owing to hunting (Bent 1927). Predation by raptors was only 2% in a California population (Page and Whitacre 1975).

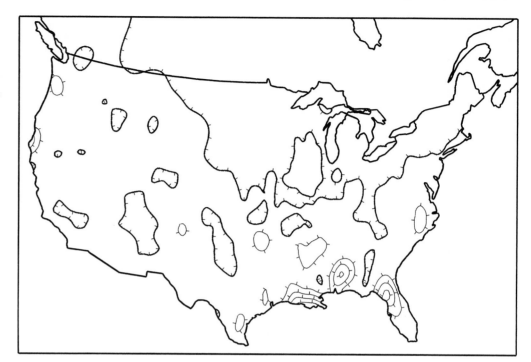

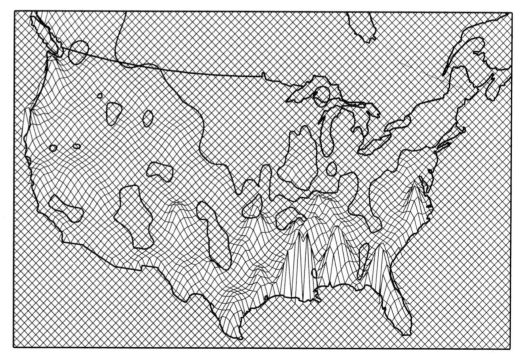

SCOLOPACIDAE

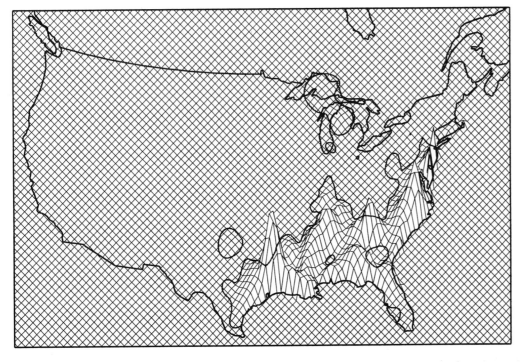

American Woodcock (*Scolopax minor*) Maximum: 0.34 I/Hr

Elevation apparently influences the overall distribution of the woodcock. This bird is present in areas less than five hundred feet (152 m) above sea level except in the Appalachians, where it avoids only the higher peaks. Most of its distribution is also in regions that are warmer than 30°F (−1°C) in January, but there are extensions into colder areas—those in the low altitude of the coastal plains along the Mississippi River and along the Atlantic coast above Chesapeake Bay. There are several disjunct populations, all ephemeral.

The dense concentrations of woodcocks occur in areas that have moist but not wet soil. The highest abundance peak is in eastern Texas around Sam Rayburn Lake, which is in the Angelina National Forest, and near the Toledo Bends Reservoir in the Sabine National Forest. Undoubtedly these managed areas protect the habitat this species prefers. The next most concentrated population is inland in North Carolina between the Neuse and Roanoke rivers, but the species avoids the wet soil close to the coast. An extension of that population continues up to the Brigantine refuge in New Jersey. In Georgia there is an abundance peak in Oconee National Forest and around neighboring Lake Sidney Lanier. The importance of soil type to the woodcock is evident in the increase of abundance that runs east along the Mississippi River. The location of this population corresponds with an equally narrow band of gray-brown podzolic soil.

This cryptically colored, wetland forest bird has eyes set far enough back on its head to allow a 360° field of vision (Cramp 1983). It is normally found in poorly drained, young forests with scattered openings, where it roosts at night. When the vegetation becomes too thick, or taller than 6 feet (2 m), the area is abandoned. Ideal habitats include burned or previously grazed fields, or abandoned or infrequently used homesites in pine forests (Johnsgard 1981). This bird is a crepuscular feeder, foraging primarily for earthworms, of which it can eat its weight in twenty-four hours (Bent 1927). Foraging sites are selected by the color of the soil, which reflects moisture and organic content, and thereby probable earthworm presence (Rabe, Prince, and Beaver 1983). Earthworms are detected tactilely by probing the soil with its sensitive bill. At times the bird stamps the ground, perhaps to coax the worms to surface. During dry times when earthworms are rarely near the surface, woodcocks will forage in dead leaves for various insects (Bent 1927).

LARIDAE

Pomarine Jaeger (*Stercorarius pomarinus*) No Map

This species, the largest of the jaegers, is chiefly pelagic in winter. On the Pacific it ranges from central California south to South America, and on the Atlantic from Florida to northern South America and Africa (AOU 1983). During the ten years examined, the Pomarine Jaeger occurred sporadically along the coasts. It was seen more consistently, in three or more years, along the California coast near Newport Beach and Monterey Bay and around Cocoa Beach, Florida. The highest average abundance was 0.01 individuals seen per party-hour on the coast of California.

Parasitic Jaeger (*Stercorarius parasiticus*) No Map

This "gull-like bird, with hawk-like characteristics" (Bent 1921) winters mainly offshore, ranging from southern California to Chile on the Pacific Ocean and from Maine to southern Brazil on the Atlantic (AOU 1983). There were scattered CBC sightings along the coasts and fairly regular sightings, in three or more years, at the same locations where the Pomarine Jaeger was seen with some regularity. The highest abundance of 0.03 individuals seen per party-hour was recorded on the California coast.

Heermann's Gull (*Larus heermanni*) No Map

After breeding on the Gulf of California and along the Pacific coast of Mexico, the Heermann's Gull ranges south to Guatemala and north to Canada (AOU 1983). The twenty-six CBCs recording this gull show that it winters regularly all along the Pacific coast of the United States and irregularly in southern Canada. It is most abundant in California's Monterey Bay, reaching an average density over the ten years of 50.00 individuals seen per hour of observation. Here it forages on northern anchovies and market squid that it obtains by plunging into the water (Baltz and Morejohn 1977).

Franklin's Gull (*Larus pipixcan*) No Map

Franklin's Gull is the only gull that breeds exclusively in freshwater marshes and, other than Sabine's Gull, the only Holarctic gull to winter south of the equator (Cramp 1983), primarily on the Pacific coast of South America (AOU 1983). Christmas counts recorded it sporadically along the North American Pacific coast, the Gulf coast of southern Texas, and inland roughly between 95° and 100° west longitude south of Kansas. It occurred with some regularity, in at least three years, at three locations in Texas: at Corpus Christi, Galveston, and Dallas–Fort Worth. The abundance was highest at the last location—0.27 individuals per party-hour.

Iceland Gull (*Larus glaucoides*) Map in Appendix B

The CBC data show that the Iceland Gull is most common in the far Northeast, around the Gulf of Saint Lawrence. Unfortunately, few censuses are held in this region, resulting in the interpolation of misleading abundance patterns. The data show that the densest populations were recorded in Nova Scotia on the northeastern side of Cape Breton Island near Glace Bay and Louisbourg, around Bonne Bay in Newfoundland north of Corner Brook, and at the extreme southeast point of New Brunswick. The average abundances there were 9.47, 9.17, 9.21, and 7.86 individuals per party-hour, respectively. This gull's distribution indicates that it occurs in low numbers throughout the Great Lakes and along the Atlantic coast from Newfoundland to New Jersey.

Lesser Black-backed Gull (*Larus fuscus*) No Map

The Lesser Black-backed Gull was recorded on only fourteen counts during the ten years examined. Sightings were scattered along the Atlantic coast from Canada to North Carolina, but each location reported it in only one or two years. An exception was the count at the south end of one of the Finger Lakes near Ithaca, New York, which reported this gull in six years. The average abundance here, however, was only 0.01 individuals per party-hour. These unusual sightings may be connected with the small, but apparently regular and increasing, numbers of an inland population of this gull around the Great Lakes (AOU 1983).

Western Gull (*Larus occidentalis*) Map in Appendix B

In winter the Western Gull is the only gull resident in Monterey Bay, California (Baltz and Morejohn 1977). The density here is very high, with 1,500.00 individuals seen per party-hour in 1971 and 1,800.00 in 1972. The mean abundance at this location was 969.54 individuals per party-hour, which precludes drawing an accurate abundance map. In general, the distribution shows that the Western Gull indeed deserves its name. It is restricted to the Pacific coast, ranging from San Diego to Vancouver Island.

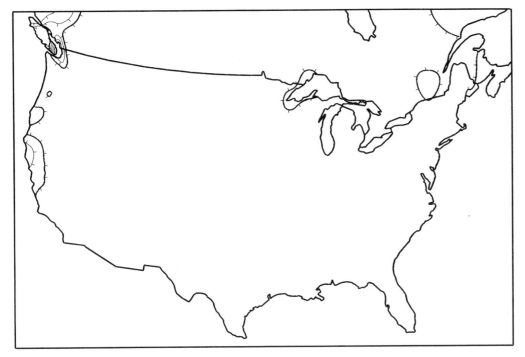

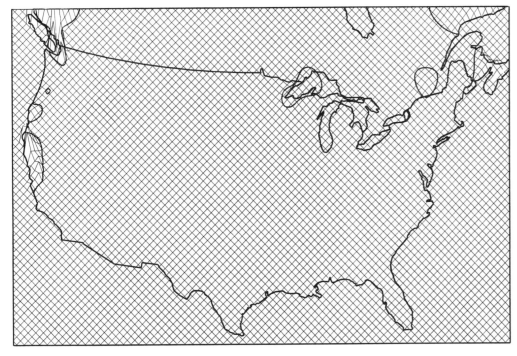

Glaucous-winged Gull (*Larus glaucescens*) Map in Appendix B

This large gull winters along the Pacific coast as far north as it can find open water (Bent 1921) and as far south as southern Baja California (AOU 1983). Its densest population (163.57 I/Hr) was recorded on the mainland side of Vancouver Island along the Strait of Juan de Fuca near Port Angeles and on the Strait of Georgia near Vancouver and Point Roberts. These high values, coupled with the very few inland counts in southern British Columbia, resulted in misleading maps. Therefore they are included only in appendix B.

Glaucous Gull (*Larus hyperboreus*) Maximum: 8.00 I/Hr

The distribution shows that the Glaucous Gull occurs on the Pacific coast and northern extremes of the Atlantic coast, along the Gulf of Saint Lawrence, and around the Great Lakes. On the Pacific coast it is present from just south of Monterey Bay, California, to just north of Eureka, Oregon, but this species avoids the area in northern California where the Klamath Mountains protrude near the coastline. There are two disjunct populations associated with the Great Lakes, one on the western tip of Lake Superior and the other on the east end of Lake Ontario. Another population is present farther east on the Saint Lawrence River. The Gulf of Saint Lawrence is also frequented, and several birds were recorded on Prince Edward Island, in northern Nova Scotia, and in Newfoundland. Many scattered counts on the Atlantic coast south of Maine reported Glaucous Gulls fairly regularly. There were so few individuals, however, that the relative abundance was below 0.01.

The Glaucous Gull is relatively rare throughout most of its North American winter range; its most concentrated population averaged only 8.00 individuals per party-hour, which is low because the value for all other gulls examined is 50.00. The densest Glaucous Gull population is northeast of Vancouver Island on the Strait of Georgia near San Juan, Galeano, and Salt Spring islands. This area provides a marine habitat that is well protected by Vancouver Island from the harsh oceanic environment. The map indicates a highly abundant population north of Vancouver, which is partly an artifact of the interpolation process owing to lack of counts in this region and high abundances along the coast. A slight concentration of this gull occurs around Monterey Bay, extending north to the coastal town of Fort Bragg.

Although the Glaucous Gull is relatively rare, it forages in large multi-species flocks consisting of Herring Gulls and other gulls (Bent 1921). Its feeding behavior is similar to that described for the California Gull (Ashmole 1971). It is omnivorous, and more than half its diet is animal matter (Cramp 1983).

Herring Gull (*Larus argentatus*) Maximum: 279.32 I/Hr

The winter distribution and abundance patterns of the Herring Gull show a strong association with either fresh or salt water. The range is fairly continuous along all three coasts, and the irregular inland pattern coincides with rivers and lakes. In the north this gull is prevalent around the Great Lakes and along the Saint Lawrence Seaway. The distribution extends into southern Illinois along the Mississippi River, east into West Virginia along the Ohio River, and on south into Tennessee and Alabama along the Cumberland River. The population along the Gulf coast protrudes north up the Mississippi valley, but not far enough to fuse with the more northerly group. The reasons for this void are not evident at this scale of examination. A rather diffuse, disjunct population is present in the central Great Plains, where it is apparently making use of the Pecos, Red, Cimmaron, Arkansas, Platte, and Missouri rivers that transect this region. The two small disjunct populations that occur between this and the more extensive eastern group are around Harry S. Truman Lake in Missouri and on the Arkansas River near Little Rock, Arkansas. To the west, the small group along the foothills of the Colorado Rocky Mountains is not associated with a large body of water, but it may be attracted to smaller lakes that are kept open by hot-water discharge from hydroelectric plants. The other two inland populations are around the Great Salt Lake, and around Lake Mead in Nevada. The distribution in Washington extends from the coast along the Columbia and Snake rivers into the Columbia basin. The overall northern limit of the distribution apparently is defined by temperature, since this gull occurs only in areas that usually are warmer than 10°F (-12°C).

A large proportion of immature Herring Gulls occurs throughout most of the species' southern winter range. In contrast, most adults remain on or near their breeding range (Cramp 1983), which is in the Great Lakes region and along the Atlantic coast from northern South Carolina on north (AOU 1983). All the peak abundances are in these areas, where this gull is resident year-round.

The Herring Gull's foraging behavior is similar to that of the California Gull (Ashmole 1971). (A more detailed description is given for that species.) It fishes, scavenges, and pirates the various items of its diet, and it also breaks clams by dropping them on hard surfaces. Ingolfsson and Estrella (1978) found that adults are more efficient at breaking open clams, taking an average of 1.6 drops, while a first-year bird needs 2.3 drops.

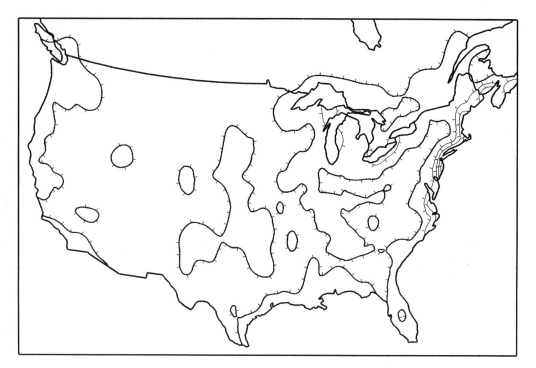

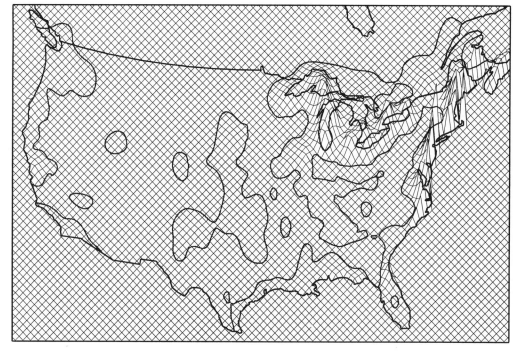

Herring Gull

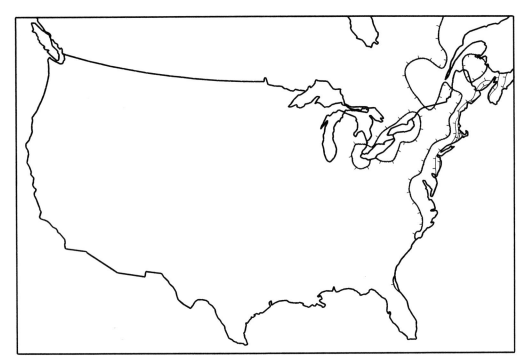

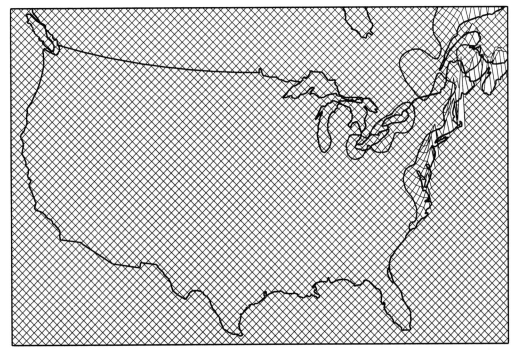

Great Black-backed Gull (*Larus marinus*) Maximum: 42.91 I/Hr

Except for the far northern breeding areas, the winter range of this gull overlaps most of its summer range (Cramp 1983). It is present in cold, open water along the Atlantic coast from Newfoundland to North Carolina, around the coast of the Gulf of Saint Lawrence, along the Saint Lawrence Seaway, and on Lakes Erie and Ontario. Some individuals winter as far south along the Atlantic coast as Florida, but most of these southern sightings are sporadic and of few individuals. The southern limit of the main distribution may be influenced by surface-water temperature; south of North Carolina, the mean ocean-surface temperature rises above 60°F (16°C). In the interior of New Brunswick, this gull avoids the area around the higher peaks at the northern end of the Appalachians.

High abundances of Great Black-backed Gulls extend the length of the Atlantic coast from Delaware Bay north to the Bay of Fundy. Apexes occur within this region around Sandy Hook Bay in New Jersey and the Massachusetts Bay and Bigelow Bight areas near Boston. The data show that the densest population is outside the area examined, in Nova Scotia on the southeast side of Cape Breton Island, with 57.29 individuals seen per party-hour.

The Great Black-backed Gull is the largest gull in North America, measuring 30 inches (76 cm) in length (National Geographic Society 1983). It usually flocks with Herring Gulls and is always the dominant member of a group (Bent 1921). Despite disturbance by humans during the breeding season, it has significantly benefited from an increase of human-created refuse, and consequently its winter range has extended farther south (Cramp 1983). It winters on or near its breeding areas (Cramp 1983), but some birds, probably immatures, move farther south. It feeds in the same manner as described for the California Gull (Ashmole 1971), usually foraging along the coast, but it can be found as far offshore as 95 miles (150 km) (Cramp 1983).

Great Black-backed Gull

Great Black-backed Gull

California Gull (*Larus californicus*) Maximum: 75.56 I/Hr
The distribution of the California Gull reflects a strong association with water, and elevation apparently influences the location of inland populations. Away from the coast this gull winters in areas that are less than 5,000 feet (1,524 m) above sea level. This includes the extension of the range into Washington around the Columbia basin and the disjunct population in the Snake River valley, which borders Oregon, Idaho, and Nevada. The eastern extension in southern Canada is partly an artifact owing to a lack of counts in the area. During the interpolation process, the extremely high values along the coast necessarily were used, which artificially inflated the results in this region.

The densest population of wintering California Gulls is not in California but in northwestern Washington along the Strait of Juan de Fuca. Jewett and co-workers (1953) reported that California Gulls in Washington are usually on salt water, and that they eat insects and even catch rodents now and then. In western British Columbia the density of California Gulls is high, but the abundant populations primarily are restricted to the saltwater habitats along the seaboard. Again, the inland extension on the map is chiefly due to interpolation problems. A fairly dense population is present in California, around Monterey Bay.

The California Gull migrates south and west from its inland breeding areas in western Canada and the United States to winter along the Pacific coast (AOU 1983). Here it opportunistically feeds offshore, inshore, and on land (Ashmole 1971) in flocks made up of many gull species (Bent 1921). Its foraging methods include dipping, which entails flying and catching prey an inch or two above or below the surface; surface seizing, which is similar to dipping except that the gull is sitting on the water rather than flying; plunging into the water from the air in pursuit of prey; and scavenging dead organic matter (Ashmole 1971). In general, its diet consists of fish, invertebrates, and carrion (Ashmole 1971), but its staples are northern anchovies and market squid on Monterey Bay (Baltz and Morejohn 1977). After hard inland rains, the California Gull has been known to eat newly sprouted barley exposed by the rain (Behle 1944).

Mew Gull (*Larus canus*) Map in Appendix B
This wide-ranging gull winters from southern California to Anchorage, Alaska. Like the Heermann's Gull, the Mew Gull reaches its highest abundance on Monterey Bay, where on average 80.04 individuals are seen each party-hour. The birds flock with other gulls (Bent 1921) and feed by scavenging, fishing, and dropping clams on rocks (Jewett et al. 1953). This is the commonest gull wintering in the Puget Sound area (Jewett et al. 1953), and this high population on the coast of Washington is the reason maps are not provided in the text. A sufficient number of counts recorded it, but the sparseness of counts in inland southwestern Canada and the high values on the coast resulted in misleading interpolated values.

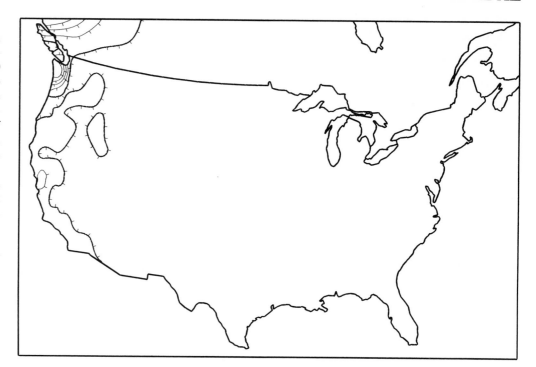

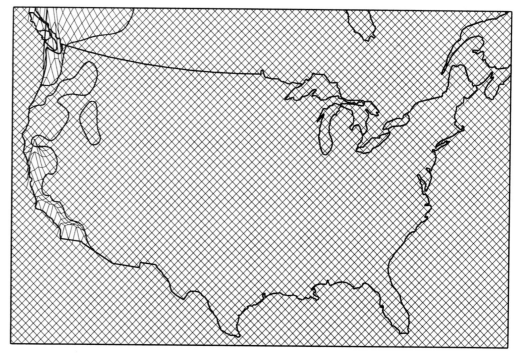

LARIDAE

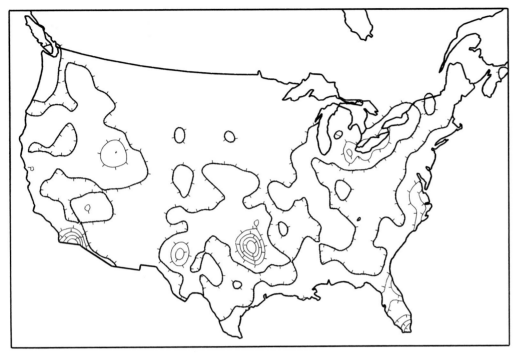

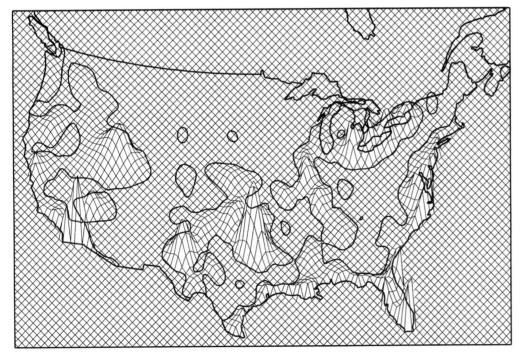

Ring-billed Gull (*Larus delawarensis*) Maximum: 91.95 I/Hr

The Ring-billed Gull's distribution seems most strongly associated with elevation, ambient temperature, and open water. The effects of elevation are evident throughout the continent. In the East the species is absent in areas higher than about 500 feet (152 m) above sea level. This includes the Appalachian and Ozark mountains. Regions higher than 5,000 feet (1,524 m) above sea level are avoided in the West, which includes the Rocky Mountains and the Colorado Plateaus. The northern range limit indicates that this gull winters primarily where the average minimum January temperature is over 20°F (−7°C). In colder areas bodies of water freeze, making the environment inhospitable. The Great Lakes, however, are too deep to freeze except occasionally, and in the West, hot-water discharge from electric plants keeps lakes open. Gulls frequent both these habitats.

All the areas where the concentration of this gull is more than 20% of the maximum abundance are strongly associated with large bodies of water. The two highest peaks occur on Lake Texoma, which is on the border between Oklahoma and Texas, and in the California desert at Salton Sea. The locations of the lesser peaks include the Great Salt Lake, Lake Mead in Nevada, the Pecos River and its associated Lake McMillan in eastern New Mexico, Lake Erie, the swampland of the North Carolina coast, and Florida around Daytona Beach and in the Everglades.

Audubon called this species "the Common American Gull," but from that time to the early 1900s its density significantly decreased owing to persecution by egg collectors and the encroachment of human settlement (Bent 1921). Today it again is fairly common, and its distribution covers a large portion of the United States. It is migratory, moving south from the northern extremes of its breeding range. There are two fairly discrete breeding populations, one in the western interior and the other around the Great Lakes and the Saint Lawrence Seaway. These populations remain roughly segregated in the winter, with the 96th meridian the approximate dividing line (Cramp 1983). This gull is omnivorous, eating everything from human scraps to food pirated from other birds (Bent 1921). Grace (1980) found that ring-bills force diving ducks to relinquish their catch by flying at them and threatening to land on their backs. This makes waterfowl release their prey and dive.

Laughing Gull (*Larus atricilla*) Maximum: 61.13 I/Hr

This gull occurs along the Gulf coast and on the shores of North Carolina, Georgia, and eastern Florida. There are undoubtedly some Laughing Gulls on the South Carolina coast and the upper northwest coast of Florida also, but not enough to appear in these relative-abundance plots. The reason there are so few is probably climate. Its distribution shows that this gull is absent from regions, including these two areas, where the annual frost-free period is shorter than about 285 days. The temperature of the ocean also may affect the species' distribution somewhat; it occurs only on oceans with a mean winter surface temperature of at least 50°F (10°C).

The densest Laughing Gull populations apparently are concomitant with warm ambient temperatures. Concentrated populations occur in the warmest areas in the country; the southern coasts of Texas and Florida both have frost-free periods lasting at least 330 days, and more often than not frost never occurs at all in these regions.

The Laughing Gull is primarily a maritime species (Cramp 1983). It joins flocks of other gulls, Royal Terns, and Brown Pelicans and forages on prey pirated from other flock members or on small fish caught on the surface of the water. The Laughing Gull is not as efficient a scavenger as many other gulls, but it will follow boats to eat scraps thrown overboard (Bent 1921).

Little Gull (*Larus minutus*) No Map

This is the smallest of the North American gulls (Bent 1921), with a length of only 11 inches (28 cm) and a wingspan of 24 inches (61 cm) (National Geographic Society 1983). It forages much as terns do (Cramp 1983). The CBC data show that it winters around Lakes Erie and Ontario and along the Atlantic coast from Maine to North Carolina, but not consistently in any one spot. Only on the southwestern shore of Lake Erie and at the west end of Long Island Sound was it seen at the same location in three years.

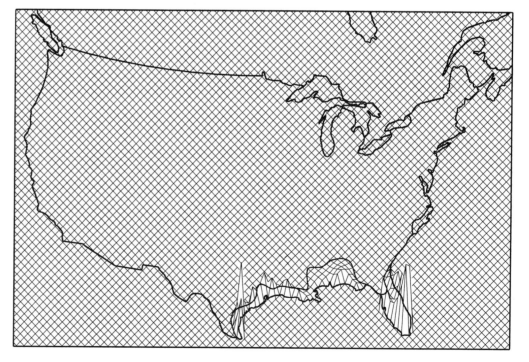

Laughing Gull

LARIDAE

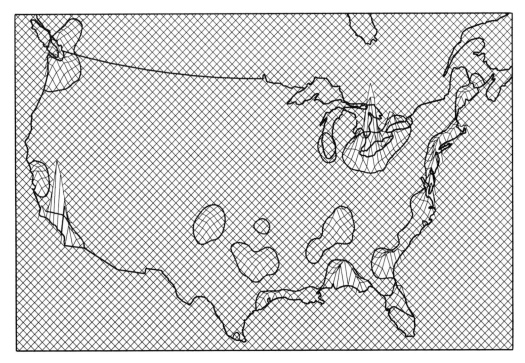

Common Black-headed Gull (*Larus ridibundus*) No Map
The Common Black-headed Gulls that winter in North America probably breed in Iceland, because increases in wintering populations correspond to rises in the breeding population there (Cramp 1983). In winter this species is seen along the Saint Lawrence River and on the Atlantic coast from Virginia to Nova Scotia. It is most regularly recorded on the coast from New Jersey on north, and the most abundant population is on the southeastern coast of Nova Scotia (0.29 I/Hr).

Bonaparte's Gull (*Larus philadelphia*) Maximum: 66.06 I/Hr
The Bonaparte's Gull occurs in a variety of habitats, ranging from offshore to freshwater rivers and lakes (Baltz and Morejohn 1977). The maps show that it is present along the coasts with disjunct populations inland, all associated with fairly large bodies of water. These latter locations include the Red, Cumberland, and Arkansas rivers, Lake Meredith in the Oklahoma panhandle, and the Great Lakes. All the coastal and inland locations, except the ones around Lakes Michigan and Ontario and along the coast north of Maine, occur where the frost-free period lasts longer than 180 days a year. Ambient temperature, therefore, seems to affect where this gull winters. Elevation may also influence its presence in winter, because areas along the seaboard where it is absent correspond to regions of high elevation in the Coast Range. The three disjunct communities occur in valley regions of low elevation; the Columbia basin, the San Joaquin valley, and the basin to the west of the San Bernardino Mountains.

The most concentrated populations of the Bonaparte's Gull are in very different habitats. One is in the warm coastal area around Los Angeles, California. The other is in the relatively colder and harsher inland habitat near Cleveland, Ohio, on Lake Erie, which is large enough that it does not usually freeze over.

Black-legged Kittiwake (*Rissa tridactyla*) Map in Appendix B
The Black-legged Kittiwake sometimes occurs in large, nomadic flocks, which precludes mapping its abundance pattern. The data show that this species occurs at scattered locations along both the Pacific and Atlantic coasts. It is found regularly in good numbers in the West near San Diego, around Monterey Bay, and on the coast of Oregon. In the East it is often found on the coasts of North Carolina, New Jersey, and Massachusetts on up to southern Nova Scotia. Over 1,000 individuals per party-hour were seen in 1969 around Passamaquoddy Bay on the border between the United States and Canada, but two years later fewer than 20 were recorded at this same site.

Gull-billed Tern (*Sterna nilotica*) No Map

The Gull-billed Tern occurs regularly, but in low numbers, along the Gulf coast. The densest population is around Aransas National Wildlife Refuge, where on average 0.21 individuals were seen per hour of count effort. Other dense populations occur at the southern tip of mainland Florida and around Brownsville, Texas. Its wintering area generally extends south from the Gulf coast through Mexico and to northern Argentina, and on the Pacific coast it occurs from Oaxaca, Mexico, to Peru (AOU 1983).

Caspian Tern (*Sterna caspia*) Maximum: 1.32 I/Hr

The distribution of the Caspian Tern covers the Gulf coast and the southern parts of both the Atlantic and Pacific coasts. The northern limits on the latter two coasts show that this tern avoids regions where the mean average ocean-surface temperature falls below 55°F (13°C). Ambient temperatures may also influence its distribution, because all the areas where it is present rarely get below freezing in January. Besides seacoasts, it frequents bays, estuaries, lakes, marshes, and rivers (AOU 1983), and the distribution shows that it does occur inland along the Guadalupe, Colorado, and Trinity rivers in Texas, up the Tombigbee River in Alabama, and on the Oconee River in Georgia.

The highest abundances are on the east coast of Florida, just south of Cocoa Beach, and on the Gulf coast of Texas from a bit north of Houston to south of Corpus Christi. Lower concentrations of Caspian Terns stretch along the Gulf coast from the mouth of the Mississippi River to southern Texas and along all of the Atlantic coast of northern and central Florida, and a more localized population is present around San Diego Bay.

The Caspian Tern is the largest and most aggressive North American tern. It is usually seen foraging alone or occasionally in groups of up to three individuals (Bent 1921). Its diet consists primarily of small fishes, normally caught by plunging into the water from a fairly high altitude. Infrequently it also catches fish by dipping its bill about an inch below the surface of the water while flying (Ashmole 1971). The abundance of this tern is strongly tied to the availability of fish. From 1925 to 1957 the breeding population around the Great Lakes dramatically declined as pollution killed off the fish. In 1957 the alewife invaded the region, providing much more food for the tern (Ludwig 1965). The average life span of a Caspian Tern in this breeding area is 8.8 years, with about 25% of the population being shot or collected (Ludwig 1965).

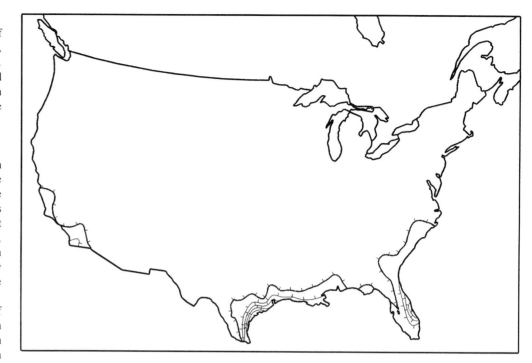

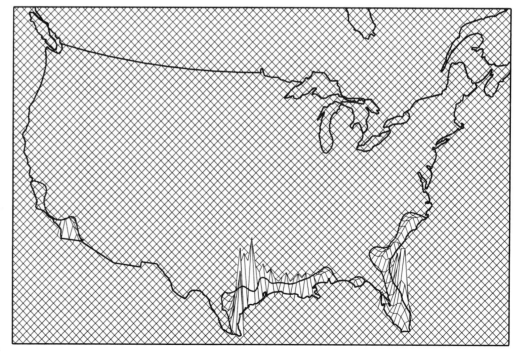

Caspian Tern

LARIDAE

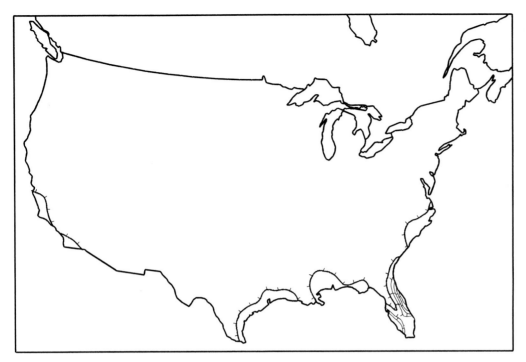

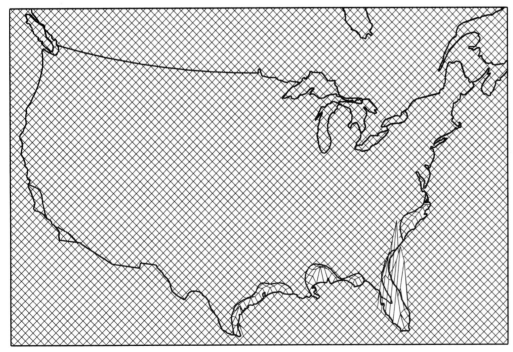

Royal Tern (*Sterna maxima*) Maximum: 7.92 I/Hr

The winter distribution of the Royal Tern is similar to that of the Caspian Tern; both species are present along the Gulf coast and the southern coastlines of the Pacific and Atlantic. Their northern limits differ a bit. On the Atlantic coast the Royal Tern occurs somewhat farther north, and it is absent along the South Carolina coast and around the mouth of the Mississippi River. The mean surface temperatures of the ocean at the northern range limits along the Atlantic and Pacific coasts are similar, with the edges occurring near the 55°F (13°C) isocline. The Royal Tern rarely frequents lakes and ponds as the Caspian Tern does. Instead it remains along the coastlines, lagoons, and estuaries (AOU 1983). This is reflected in its distribution, which does not extend far inland except in Mississippi.

The densest populations occur on both coasts of the Florida peninsula. The one on the east is only slightly south of the densest population of the Caspian Tern. The high concentration on the Gulf coast encompasses the area roughly from Sarasota to Fort Myers. The numerous national wildlife refuges in these regions may be attracting this tern. The Merritt Island refuge is on the east coast, and the Pinellas, Egmont Key, Passage Key, Island Bay, Pine Island, Matlacha Pass, and J. N. "Ding" Darling refuges are on the west coast.

The foraging behavior and diet of the Royal Tern and the Caspian Tern are very similar. Both feed primarily on small fish that they capture by plunging or dipping (Ashmole 1971). (See the Caspian Tern account for further explanation of these foraging methods.) The winter foraging behavior of the adult Royal Tern is much more efficient than that of the juveniles; adults make twice as many dives and catch more prey per unit time. Members of both age groups recatch dropped prey, but the juveniles make fourteen times as many drops. The adults spend more time roosting than the juveniles. Small flocks of juveniles often form, but the adults never flock and in fact avoid all others except their own offspring (Buckley and Buckley 1974).

Elegant Tern (*Sterna elegans*) No Map

The Elegant Tern winters along the Pacific coast from Guatemala to central Chile, but birds regularly wander along the coast as far north as central California (AOU 1983). Until about 1951, however, the bird was only an erratic visitor north of Mexico (Monroe 1956). During the ten years examined, this tern was seen at only six count sites that ranged between the northern border of Mexico and San Francisco Bay. Four of these sites recorded Elegant Terns only once during the ten years, and near Santa Barbara it was recorded in three years. It was most regularly reported around San Diego (seven years), but even there it was exceedingly rare (0.01 I/Hr).

Common Tern (*Sterna hirundo*) Maximum: 0.48 I/Hr

The Common Tern is present in winter along all the southern coastlines in the United States. The northern limit on the Pacific coast occurs around San Francisco Bay, and on the Atlantic coast it is at the southern end of Chesapeake Bay. Temperatures, both ambient and water-surface, coincide with both these limits. This tern is present only in areas with a mean minimum January temperature above freezing. On both coasts it is absent from colder oceans—those with a maximum average surface temperature lower than 58°F (14°C) in the winter. The distribution map also shows that this species forages around lakes, rivers, and marshes as well, and along coasts, estuaries, and bays. It extends inland along the San Antonio River in Texas, the Pearl River in Mississippi, and the San Joaquin valley in California, to name a few areas. The relative abundance of this species drops to zero around the Mississippi River, which is also true for the Royal Tern. The reason these two species are not present there is not apparent from this study.

There are three populations with high densities, all on the Gulf coast. One straddles the Texas-Louisiana border, with Anahuac National Wildlife Refuge at the approximate center. Undoubtedly this protected and managed area is important to the location of this peak. Another dense population is present along the Gulf coast, from Mobile Bay, Alabama, to Cape San Blas, Florida. The least of the three highest abundance peaks stretches from roughly Tampa Bay to below Naples, Florida. Protection of this tern has allowed significant increases of its abundance in the past. In the first half of the nineteenth century the species was persecuted for its feathers, used to decorate hats, and for its eggs. After it was protected, the breeding colony on Muskeget Island, between Nantucket and Martha's Vineyard, almost doubled from 1894 to 1898 (Bent 1921).

The diet and foraging strategy of the Common Tern are similar to those described for the Caspian Tern. The main difference is that besides small fish this tern eats some crustaceans (Ashmole 1971), small squid, and insects (K. Parkes, pers. comm.). In the breeding season at least, this tern feeds primarily on the most abundant small, inshore fish. It forages in a diversity of habitats ranging from inland to pelagic (Bent 1921; Ashmole 1971; AOU 1983).

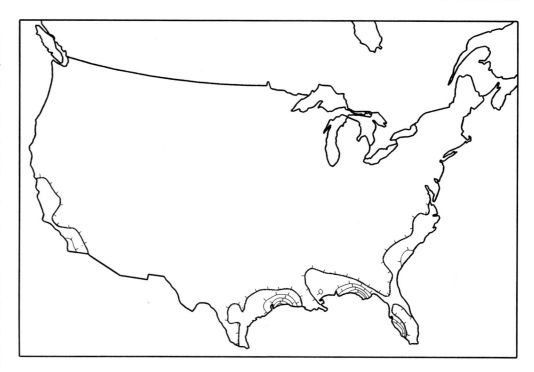

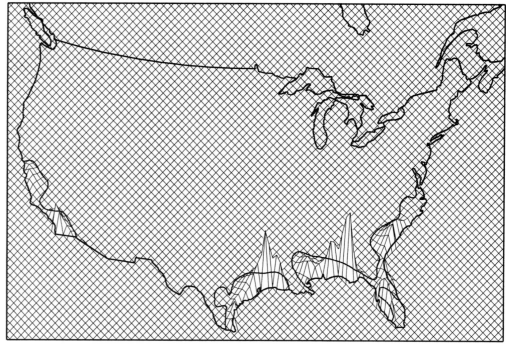

LARIDAE

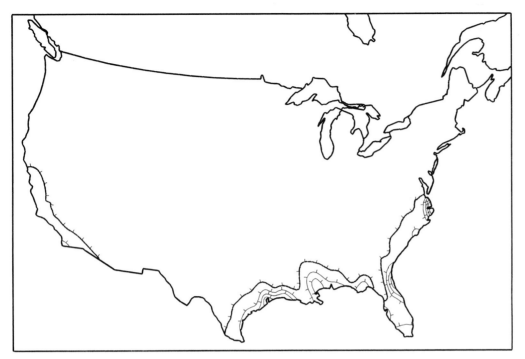

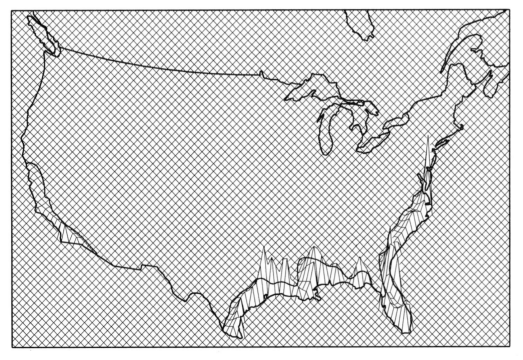

Sandwich Tern (*Sterna sandvicensis*) No Map
The Sandwich Tern forages around seacoasts, bays, estuaries, and mud flats and rarely if ever ventures inland (AOU 1983). In the United States it winters primarily along the coastline of the Gulf of Mexico and is irregular and rare along the Atlantic coast in southern Florida. Of the thirty-four counts recording this tern, the highest abundances were in Florida around Sarasota and Key West, with 2.96 and 1.65 individuals seen each party-hour, respectively. The northernmost area along the Atlantic coast where this tern was seen regularly was near Cocoa Beach. Here it was recorded 90% of the time, but at an average of only 0.02 individuals per party-hour.

Forster's Tern (*Sterna forsteri*) Maximum: 7.12 I/Hr
Bent noted in 1921 that the winter distribution of the Forster's Tern extends farther north than that of any other North American tern. The maps show that even decades later this is still true, particularly on the Atlantic coast. Cape May, New Jersey, is the northernmost location where this tern occurs fairly regularly on the Atlantic coast. Here it was seen in five out of the ten years examined, but the number observed was very low, with an average of only 0.01 birds seen per party-hour. This tern is rare at all locations north of the mouth of Chesapeake Bay. Along the Pacific coast the distribution stops just north of San Francisco Bay. The entire range is in regions that have a minimum January temperature warmer than 30°F (−1°C), suggesting that this tern prefers to winter in a relatively warm environment.

The highest abundances are in roughly the same locations as the coastal breeding areas (AOU 1983). They also occur around national wildlife refuges, which offer year-round protection and management. The densest population straddles the Virginia–North Carolina border, the site of the Pea Island, Black Bay, and Great Dismal Swamp refuges. In Texas there is a somewhat lesser concentration along the Galveston coast and Galveston Bay near Anahuac National Wildlife Refuge and extending to the Sabine refuge. A population of equal density occurs near Jacksonville, Florida, and a less dense population is present in Mississippi along the Pearl River.

Besides foraging along seacoasts, bays, and estuaries, this tern also feeds inland around lakes and rivers (AOU 1983), as is reflected in the distribution that extends inland along the Pearl River in Texas, for example. It eats fish up to 4 inches (10 cm) long (Salt and Willard 1971) and some crustaceans (Ashmole 1971). It prefers to feed in calm water that is not too deep. Even though the Forster's Tern usually forages in a flock, each bird defends a few feet of private airspace around itself (Salt and Willard 1971).

Least Tern (*Sterna antillarum*) No Map

During winter the Least Tern is only a transient in the United States. Its entire winter range is not well known, but it does occur regularly from Baja California to southern Mexico and on the Atlantic coast of South America from Colombia to Brazil (AOU 1983). It was recorded at seventeen locations scattered along the Gulf and Atlantic coasts, reaching as far north as southern North Carolina. Only two of these locations recorded this tern in two years, and it was recorded only once at the remaining sites.

Black Skimmer (*Rynchops niger*) Maximum: 19.27 I/Hr

In the United States the Black Skimmer winters along the Gulf and southern Atlantic coasts, reaching as far north as North Carolina. It is present where the mean winter surface temperature of the ocean is warmer than 60°F (16°C) and where the ambient temperature in January rarely drops below 40°F (4°C). This includes the areas where the distribution extends inland along rivers, such as in Texas along the San Antonio River and in Mississippi along the Pearl River.

There are two regions where the Black Skimmer is common. The denser population winters along central Florida's eastern coastline near Daytona Beach. Part of the reason it is present here may be the warm ambient temperature; the edge of this abundance peak is coincident with the minimum January temperature isocline of 50°F (10°C). More study is needed to determine just how important ambient temperature is in determining the location of this peak. The other area where this species is common is inland on the tip of Florida in the Everglades, where the marsh channels provide excellent habitat for foraging.

The foraging behavior of the Black Skimmer is unique; the bird flies several inches above the water surface with its bill open and the lower mandible cutting through the water. It normally eats small fish, primarily because that is what it usually finds, but it will eat larger ones if they are caught (Erwin 1977). In winter it forages in water that is 4 to 8 inches (10–20 cm) deep and within 7 feet (2 m) of land (Black and Harris 1983), usually along bays, estuaries, lagoons, mud flats (AOU 1983), and marsh channels (Erwin 1977). Foraging occurs mainly at night (Bent 1921; Erwin 1977) and also during diurnal low tides when tide pools and mud flats are exposed (Erwin 1977). It forages alone but roosts in flocks on sandbars and beaches (Bent 1921).

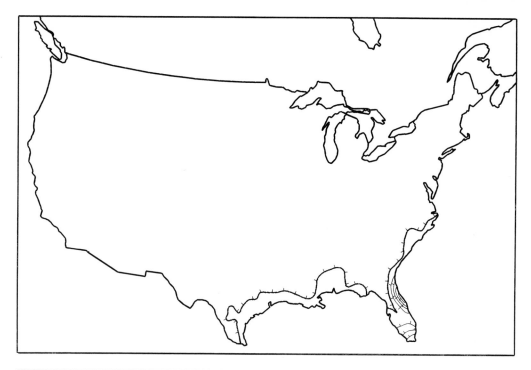

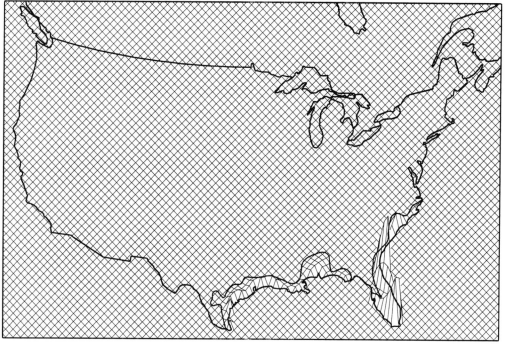

ALCIDAE

Dovekie (*Alle alle*) Map in Appendix B

Even though the Dovekie is mostly pelagic, it is frequently seen along the Atlantic seaboard (AOU 1983). Of the forty-six sites reporting this bird, regular observations were made only in Massachusetts around Cape Cod, on the coast of Maine around Portland, and on the Gulf of Saint Lawrence. There were sporadic sightings along the Atlantic coast as far south as central Florida. The count showing the highest mean abundance was just south of Bangor, Maine, where 29.69 Dovekies were seen each party-hour.

Common Murre (*Uria aalge*) Map in Appendix B

The Common Murre was recorded at many sites along the Pacific coast from San Diego to Alaska and at only seven sites on the Atlantic coast, from New Jersey to the Gulf of Saint Lawrence. Regular sightings were reported from Vancouver Island to as far south as Santa Barbara, California. The highest average abundance of these regular sites was near Cape Meares National Wildlife Refuge, on the coast directly west of Portland, Oregon. Here on average 226.70 individuals were seen per party-hour. At this location a count of 50,000 birds in 1969 was reported to be a "conservative estimate."

Thick-billed Murre (*Uria lomvia*) No Map

The Thick-billed Murre's winter range extends into the study area from the Gulf of Saint Lawrence south to New Jersey. This mostly pelagic bird (AOU 1983) was reported at only seventeen sites in this area, and most of these recorded it in only one year. The one place in the study area where it was recorded in four years was around Acadia National Park, just south of Bangor, Maine, where the average abundance was 0.83 individuals per party-hour.

Razorbill (*Alca torda*) No Map

Sporadic sightings were recorded all along the Atlantic coast from North Carolina to New Brunswick. Of the twenty-two sites reporting the Razorbill, only two had observations in five or more years. These were on Cape Cod in Massachusetts and just south of Bangor, Maine, around Acadia National Park. The highest average abundance was at the latter location, with 12.29 individuals seen per party-hour, but the number varied from year to year; 30.00 individuals were seen per party-hour in 1968 and only 1.33 in 1971.

Black Guillemot (*Cepphus grylle*) No Map

The Black Guillemot ranges along the Atlantic coast north of New Jersey. It was recorded at twenty-eight count sites inside the study area and at seven others in extreme western and northwestern Canada. This species occurred in fairly constant densities at eight sites where it was seen in five or more years. These sites are on Cape Cod, along the coast of Maine, and around the Gulf of Saint Lawrence. The highest number of birds was seen off Cape Cod, with an average of 7.61 individuals observed per party-hour.

Pigeon Guillemot (*Cepphus columba*) No Map

The Pigeon Guillemot is the western counterpart of the Black Guillemot. The former ranges along the Pacific coast from Santa Barbara, California, north to Alaska. A total of thirty-eight Christmas counts reported this guillemot, but nine were north of Vancouver Island and outside the area examined. There were several locations where this species was seen regularly, and of these the area with the highest abundance was near the south end of the Strait of Georgia. Here guillemots were seen in all ten years, and the average abundance was 0.73 individuals per party-hour.

Marbled Murrelet (*Brachyramphus marmoratus*) No Map

Of the two murrelets recorded on the Christmas counts, the Marbled Murrelet was seen at the most sites. There were observations at thirty-four locations, seven of which were along the coastline north of the study area. The more southern sites stretched as far south as San Diego, California, but the most regular sightings were in the Strait of Georgia around Vancouver Island. The abundance was the highest in this location too, with 1.95 individuals seen per hour of count effort.

Ancient Murrelet (*Synthliboramphus antiquus*) No Map

The Ancient Murrelet was seen sporadically all along the Pacific coast; nineteen sites reported it from San Diego to Vancouver Island, and one additional count reported it on the coast north of the study area. This murrelet was seen regularly at only two locations, Monterey Bay and the Strait of Georgia. The most regular observations and the densest concentration were in the latter location, where it was observed in nine years, with an average of 1.29 individuals seen each party-hour.

Cassin's Auklet (*Ptychoramphus aleuticus*) No Map

Of all the alcids, the Cassin's Auklet was recorded on the fewest counts, fourteen sites between San Diego and Vancouver Island. It was seen regularly, in more than five years, at three separate locations: Monterey Bay, California; around Seattle, Washington, on Puget Sound; and in the Strait of Georgia. Of these three locations, the densest population occurred in the Monterey Bay area, with 0.95 individuals seen per party-hour.

Rhinoceros Auklet (*Cerorhinca monocerata*) No Map

The winter sightings of the Rhinoceros Auklet, like those of the other alcids, stretch along the Pacific coast. Seventeen sites, all within the boundaries of the study area, reported this auklet over the ten years, but it was observed regularly at only five of these. Those five locations include the waters around Morro Bay, California; around Monterey, California; off Point Reyes, California; on Puget Sound around Seattle, Washington; and at the southern end of Vancouver Island near Victoria. The most regular sightings (nine years) and highest density of this auklet (4.99 I/Hr) were around Monterey, California.

COLUMBIDAE

Rock Dove (*Columba livia*) No Map

The domesticated Rock Dove occurs throughout the world, with its highest abundances in large cities like New York and Los Angeles (Goodwin 1983b). It feeds on the ground in open areas, eating a wide variety of seeds and human food scraps (Goodwin 1983a). Birds learn to recognize particular people who feed them and will solicit food specifically from those individuals. In small towns flocks may fly together into the countryside to feed, but they return in the evening to roost among the buildings (Goodwin 1983b).

White-crowned Pigeon (*Columba leucocephala*) No Map

The White-crowned Pigeon is very gregarious and almost exclusively an arboreal feeder, eating fruits, grains, and snails (Goodwin 1983b). It winters in southern Florida and on islands in the Caribbean (AOU 1983). Five Christmas counts recorded sightings of this pigeon. The highest mean abundance was near Tavernier, just south of Key Largo, Florida, with an average of 0.41 birds seen per party-hour.

Band-tailed Pigeon (*Columba fasciata*) Maximum: 40.63 I/Hr

In the winter, birds in the northern and eastern reaches of this pigeon's breeding range migrate into the southwestern areas of the summer range in the Cascades and the Sierra Nevada. The Band-tailed Pigeon frequents the more hospitable parts of this region, those that are not too hot and dry. This includes areas that have an annual pan evaporation measurement of 80 inches (203 cm) or less and that do not get over 100°F (38°C) during the summer. Summer temperature probably is important, because the winter distribution is coincident with this species' southwestern breeding range, which certainly is affected by summer heat.

Flocks of Band-tailed Pigeons wander from one abundant food supply to another (Bent 1932), eating mainly acorns, madrona and mountain ash berries, and pine nuts (Neff 1947). The species prefers mountain-slope environments where oaks are present (Goodwin 1983b). Indeed, the maps reflect this preference, because the southern portion of the distribution encompasses the scrub oaks of the California chaparral and the mixed evergreen and deciduous forest, which contains oaks. The population farther north in Washington and British Columbia occurs in coastal coniferous forests.

This pigeon is most common in the more moderate environments in the Sierra Nevada and the San Gabriel Mountains, areas that get no hotter than an average of 75°F (24°C) in July and have fairly high humidity (pan evaporation of 40 inches [102 cm] annually).

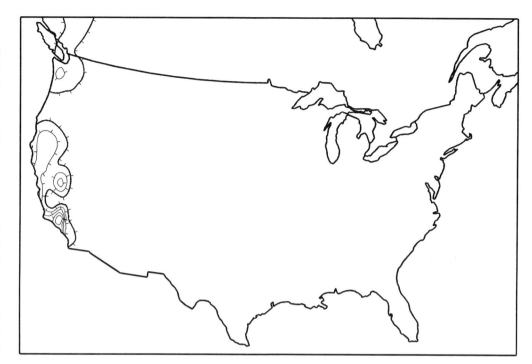

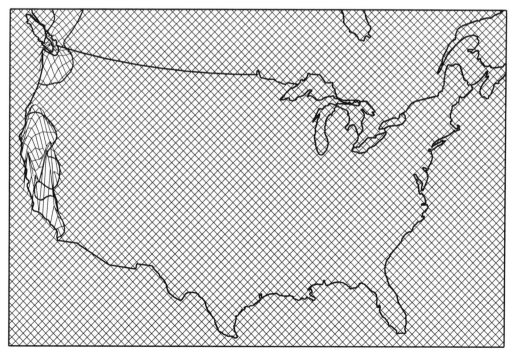

COLUMBIDAE

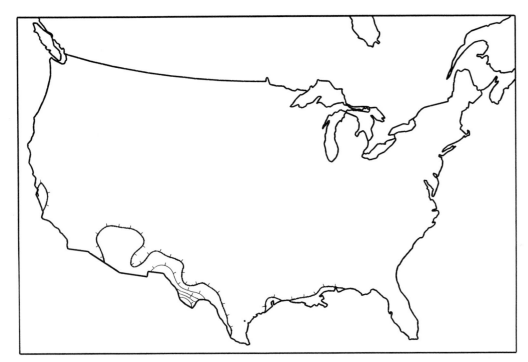

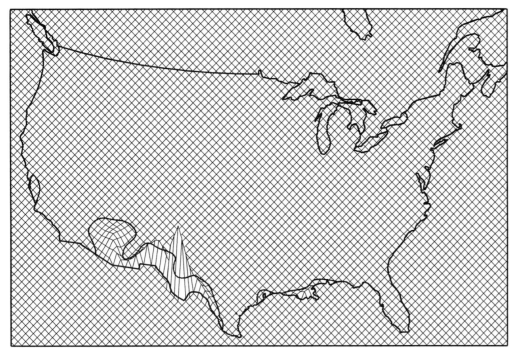

Ringed Turtle-Dove (*Streptopelia risoria*) No Map
This long-domesticated species is probably a form of the African Collared Dove (*Streptopelia roseogrisea*) (Goodwin 1983b). The Ringed Turtle-Dove is very tame. There are four regions in the United States that recorded it in at least two of the ten years: in southwestern California; near Tucson, Arizona; in west-central Florida; and around Panama City, Florida. The California and west-central Florida populations appear stable, being recorded since 1963. The Arizona population became established in 1970 and was present in the remaining two years examined. The Florida panhandle population is more dubious, since it was recorded only in 1968 and 1972.

Spotted Dove (*Streptopelia chinensis*) No Map
The Spotted Dove was introduced to North America from India, Ceylon, and the Indo-Malayan region (Goodwin 1983b). It occurs regularly only in southwestern California from San Diego to Santa Barbara. The most concentrated population was recorded in San Bernardino, with 4.14 birds seen per party-hour.

White-winged Dove (*Zenaida asiatica*) Maximum: 1.64 I/Hr
White-winged Doves that breed in the northern parts of their summer range migrate into the more southern breeding areas and along the Gulf coast (AOU 1983). These southern breeding areas include the Chihuahuan Desert and extend west to part of the Sonoran Desert. The maps show that in this region the dove frequents the semiarid scrub and scrub steppes, and it apparently avoids tree and scrub savannas and dry-belt pine forests. It forages on the ground for seeds, berries, and even cactus fruits (Goodwin 1983b). It also forages in stubble fields for waste grain such as corn, wheat, and sorghum (Cottam and Trefethen 1968). Outside the southern breeding area, the wintering locations along the coast stretch from the San Bernard and Brazoria National Wildlife refuges south of Galveston, Texas, to the western end of the Florida panhandle. Throughout this range the average minimum January temperature rarely drops below 45°F (7°C).

The most concentrated population of White-winged Doves is in the Big Bend area of Texas. Johnsgard (1975) reported that the preferred habitat of this dove is semiarid woodlands with fairly short but densely foliaged trees and open ground cover, which precisely describes the oak-juniper woodlands of southwestern Texas.

White-winged Dove

Mourning Dove (*Zenaida macroura*) Maximum: 24.67 I/Hr

Ambient temperature appears to strongly influence both the distribution and the abundance pattern of the wintering Mourning Dove. During the breeding season its distribution covers basically all of the United States and southern Canada (AOU 1983). In the fall, individuals that breed in the Great Basin, Rocky Mountains, and northern Great Plains migrate out of these colder areas into regions with more favorable climates. The Mourning Dove winters only where the average minimum January temperature is over 10°F (−12°C).

Temperature also apparently has a strong effect on where this dove is most common. Although it can survive temperatures as low as 10°F (−12°C), it concentrates in regions where the January temperature remains above 20°F (−7°C). The densest population is in south-central Arizona around Phoenix and extends south to the Mexican border. Less dense, but fairly extensive populations occur throughout southern Texas, with an apex around San Angelo, and also south of the Great Lakes to northern Alabama and Georgia. The availability of open water also seems to influence where this species is common, since it needs a ready source of water, particularly in arid regions (Goodwin 1983b). The peak abundances, even outside the drier areas, correspond somewhat to the location of rivers, including the Gila, Pecos, Mississippi, Wabash, Cumberland, and Hudson.

The diet of this widespread species includes a large variety of seeds and grain and little animal matter such as insects. Foraging flocks of about twelve birds move from site to site, often searching fields for waste wheat and buckwheat (Bent 1932). They also frequent second-growth environments of open woods with some trees, bushes, and pastures (Goodwin 1983b). This species has increased tremendously in the Northeast in recent years (K. Parkes, pers. comm.).

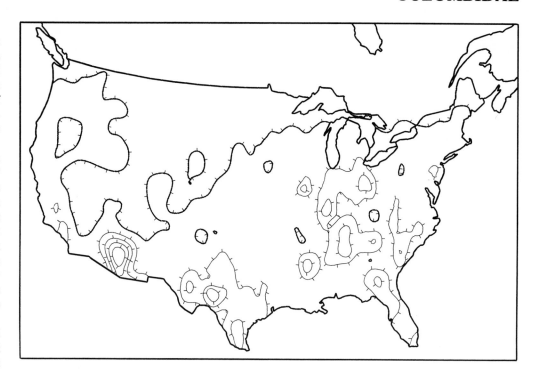
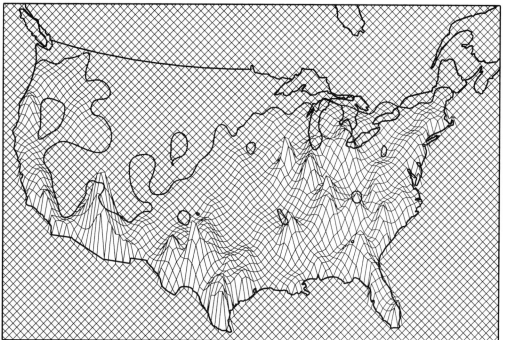

Mourning Dove

COLUMBIDAE

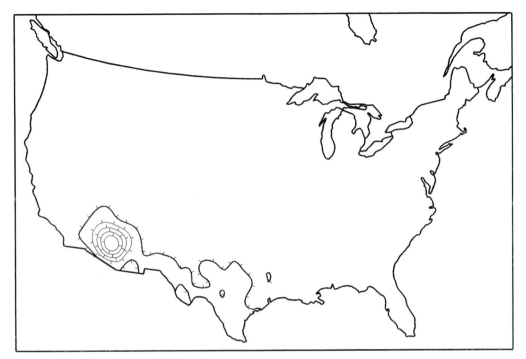

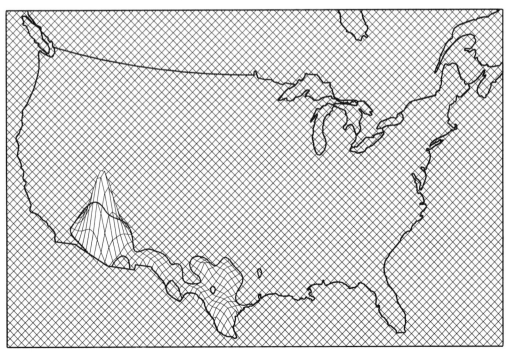

Inca Dove (*Columbina inca*) Maximum: 8.38 I/Hr

The distribution of the Inca Dove encompasses both the Sonoran and Chihuahuan deserts, plus the area between these two harsh environments and the region south and east of the latter. The small disjunct population in east-central Texas is due to the rare sighting of eleven individuals on the Nacogdoches, Texas count in 1972. Its range does not obviously associate with any of the environmental factors examined. Unlike the Mourning Dove, this smaller dove is not restricted by temperature. Several birds keep warm on chilly nights by roosting close together with their bodies touching, then a second row of birds roosts on the backs of the first (Johnston 1960; Bent 1932). Such a mass of heat-generating bodies creates a fairly warm micro-climate.

This dove lives in urban areas where numerous parks and yards provide an open habitat for foraging. The most concentrated population centers on Phoenix and covers most of southern Arizona. The high density of birds in this region overshadows the abundance in other regions. The three-dimensional map shows slight concentrations in southern and central Texas and in southern New Mexico.

The Inca Dove is nonmigratory (AOU 1983), and thus its winter range may be indirectly determined by factors influencing the summer range. It occurs in arid and semiarid regions, but it needs open water (Bent 1932). Normally it forages in open woodlands and savannas with trees scattered throughout and avoids grasslands. A wide variety of small weed seeds and waste grain like sorghum make up its diet (Goodwin 1983b).

White-tipped Dove (*Leptotila verreauxi*) No Map

The White-tipped Dove is usually solitary, contrary to the flocking behavior of most doves in the United States. It is fairly secretive, even though it is rather large, and prefers the cover of brushy country, where it primarily eats seeds and berries found on the ground along forest edges, groves, or open woodlands (Goodwin 1983b). The eight CBC sites recording this dove are in the Rio Grande Valley, with the densest population occurring at Santa Ana National Wildlife Refuge, where on average 0.38 doves were seen per party-hour.

Common Ground-Dove (*Columbina passerina*) Maximum: 27.27 I/Hr
At first the distribution of the Common Ground-Dove appears incongruous because it shows this dove occurring both in arid deserts and on the humid Florida peninsula. However, these are the areas in the United States that have 240 consecutive days with temperatures above freezing. The distribution is also coincident with the areas that have no snowfall throughout the year. The short legs of this sparrow-sized bird would certainly preclude its foraging in snow, particularly since the staple of its diet is small seeds that it picks off the ground (Goodwin 1983b; Bent 1932).

The Common Ground-Dove is the smallest columbid in the United States. It is fairly tame but not nearly as common in cities and towns as the Inca Dove. The maps show that the densest populations are not in cities, but in areas with open woodlands. The highest density, near the Salton Sea National Wildlife Refuge in southern California, is in piñon-juniper woodlands with scattered creosote bush and bur sage. In south Texas a relatively abundant population is present in the mesquite savanna.

CUCULIDAE

Yellow-billed Cuckoo (*Coccyzus americanus*) No Map
The primary wintering grounds of the Yellow-billed Cuckoo range from northern South America to Peru, Bolivia, and Argentina (AOU 1983). The fifteen Christmas count sites reporting this species are scattered along the Gulf and Atlantic coasts, but most are in Florida. The most regular sightings were around Cape Sable at the southern tip of Florida and west of Fort Lauderdale, where this cuckoo was observed in three and four years, respectively, though the average abundance at each site was less than 0.01 individuals seen per party-hour.

Mangrove Cuckoo (*Coccyzus minor*) No Map
This uncommon cuckoo was seen in six years near Cape Sable, Florida, but the average abundance was only 0.01 individuals seen per party-hour. Birds were observed in only one year at four other counts scattered along the Gulf coast.

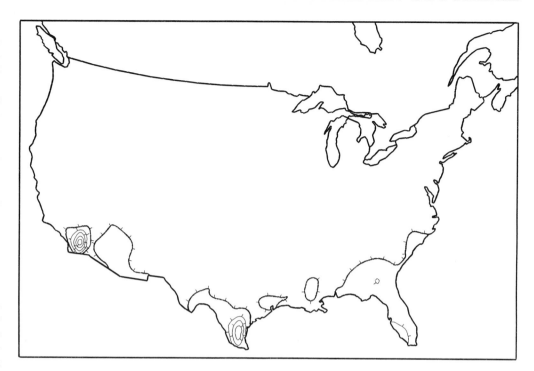

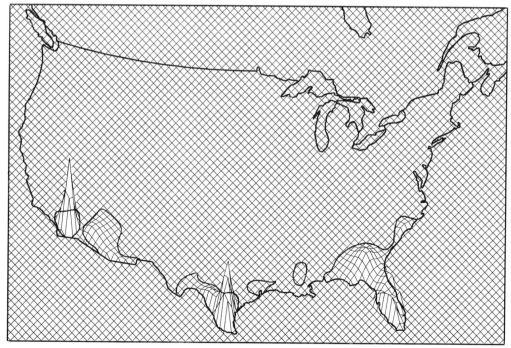

CUCULIDAE

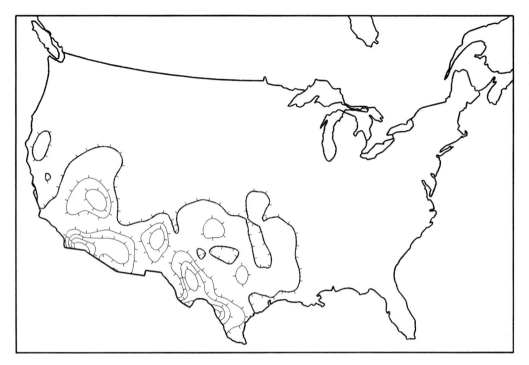

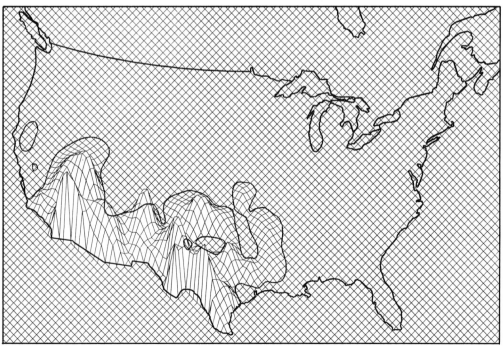

Greater Roadrunner (*Geococcyx californianus*) Maximum: 0.32 I/Hr
The Greater Roadrunner is probably the most caricatured nonpasserine bird in North America. It is resident in the warm semiarid and arid regions of the Southwest where the annual pan evaporation, an inverse measure of general humidity, is greater than 80 inches (203 cm). The abundance peaks are in even drier areas, with measures over 100 inches (254 cm). The amount of sunshine also seems to affect where this roadrunner is present; its range is roughly coincident with the region in the United States that annually gets at least 140 clear days from sunrise to sunset. Sunshine is certainly important to this species, since it can frequently be found sunning itself early in the morning or on cool days. It positions itself so its feathers are perpendicular to the sun rays, exposing its black or dark gray skin. This sunning has been found to raise its body temperature by about 5°F (3°C) (Ohmart and Lasiewski 1971). Neither temperature nor precipitation seems to have a direct effect on its distribution.

The Roadrunner is basically a carnivore, and 90% of its diet is animal material (Bent 1964). Prey items include lizards, small snakes, scorpions, grasshoppers, crickets, mice, birds, seeds, and fruit (Oberholser 1974). It has been persecuted by quail hunters because it eats quail eggs and young birds, but the number it consumes is negligible (Bent 1964).

Smooth-billed Ani (*Crotophaga ani*) No Map
This cuckoo is resident in central and southern Florida (AOU 1983) and was recorded on nineteen Christmas counts in this region. The counts near Boynton Beach, which is just north of Boca Raton and inland from Fort Lauderdale, recorded it each of the ten years examined. Fort Lauderdale reported the densest population, with a mean of 3.02 birds seen per party-hour.

Groove-billed Ani (*Crotophaga sulcirostris*) No Map
This cuckoo resides in Texas and south along both slopes of Middle America and along both coasts of South America (AOU 1983). It was seen at scattered CBC locations along the Texas and Louisiana coasts and up the Rio Grande valley. Counts in Texas near Bentsen State Park, Corpus Christi, and Freeport reported it in at least 50% of the years examined. Of these, the highest abundance was 0.09 individuals per party-hour at Corpus Christi.

Greater Roadrunner

TYTONIDAE

Common Barn-Owl (*Tyto alba*) Map in Appendix B

Even though this widespread species was seen on 292 Christmas counts, the abundances at all but two of these locations were under 0.20 individuals seen per party-hour. Thus, its rarity precluded presenting maps of its abundance pattern in the text. The data also strongly suggest that the locations of the abundant populations reflect the presence of dedicated census takers rather than revealing the actual biogeographic pattern of the Common Barn-Owl. The distribution, however, suggests that this bird is present where the average minimum January temperature is above 10°F to 20°F (−12°C to −7°C), and that it avoids the Mississippi valley and the higher peaks of the Rockies.

STRIGIDAE

Eastern and Western Screech-Owls (*Otus asio* and *O. kennicottii*)
Maximum: 0.31 I/Hr

At the time the CBC data examined were collected, these two owls were considered the same species, so the data were grouped together. The distributions of these nonmigratory birds overlap very little and abut roughly along the western side of the Great Plains (AOU 1983). The eastern species frequents the mixed mesophytic and deciduous forest and the tree and shrub savanna of Texas and Oklahoma, with extensions into the grasslands along the galeria forests of the Mississippi, Platte, and Arkansas rivers. The range of the western species is also closely linked with vegetation. It occurs in the southern California chaparral and the coastal stands of mixed evergreen and deciduous forest, and in the coastal coniferous forest. Populations are also present in the semiarid scrub and scrub steppe of the Great Basin and southern Arizona.

The densest population of the eastern species is much more abundant than that of its western congener, and thus the abundance pattern of the Eastern Screech-Owl overshadows that of the Western Screech-Owl. The three-dimensional map indicates that the most concentrated population of the western species is in the California Sierra Madre between San Luis Obispo and Santa Barbara. The most concentrated population of the eastern owl is around the Prairie Dog Town Fork of the Red River in the panhandle of Texas, in the grassland-savanna ecotone. Other abundant populations occur around Boone, Iowa, in northern Indiana and northwestern Ohio, and in the wetlands of eastern North Carolina.

The diet of the screech-owl varies depending on the availability of small animals. Prey are caught in the bill if an owl is flying, and with the feet otherwise (Burton 1984). Insects, other arthropods, and vertebrates are all included in the diet, but vertebrates are the staple in colder regions during winter (Earhart and Johnson 1970). An experiment with captive wild-caught owls showed that hungry birds prefer smaller rather than larger mice, presumably because they are easier to capture (Marti and Hogue 1979). Surplus food is cached in the winter roosting cavities (Burton 1984), and cached items are not hoarded but are eaten and replaced with fresh prey (Phelan 1977).

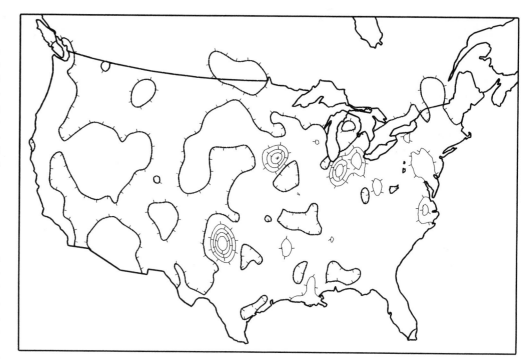

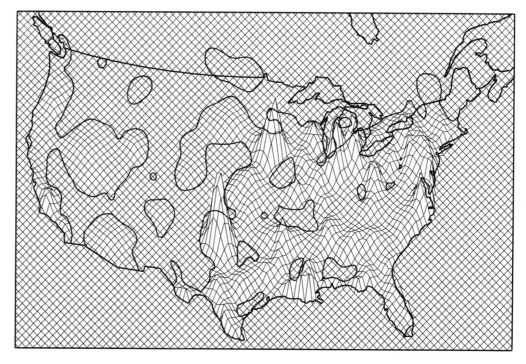

Eastern and Western Screech-Owls

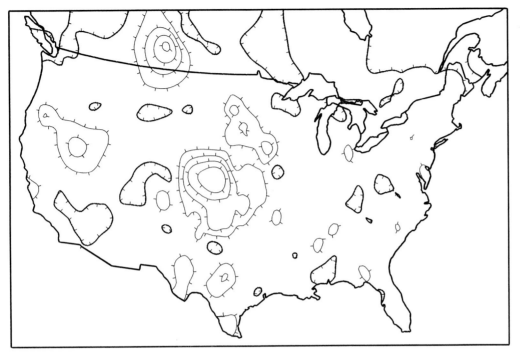

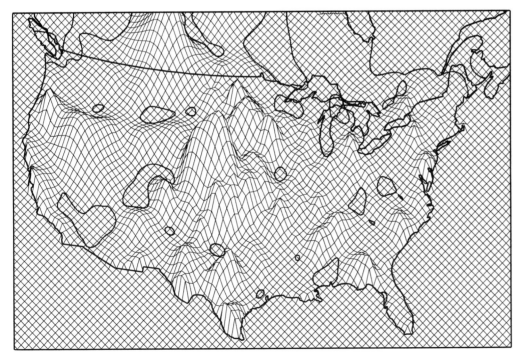

Great Horned Owl (*Bubo virginianus*) Maximum: 0.43 I/Hr
The range of the Great Horned Owl covers most of the area studied. The vacancies in southern Canada are questionable because of the lack of counts there. The vacant areas within the United States are more reliable and indicate that this large predator tends to avoid the Appalachian and Rocky mountains and the Mojave and Sonoran deserts between California and Arizona. Throughout the range individuals vary in size, with larger birds occurring at high latitudes and altitudes. For example, owls in Alaska are about 20 inches (51 cm) long, while those in Central America measure about 18 inches (46 cm) (Burton 1984).

The densest populations occur outside forests. The more extensive of the two most abundant populations is in the grassland–agricultural region of Nebraska, Kansas, and eastern Colorado. Fairly high concentrations continue south into northern Oklahoma. The other population with maximum abundance is in southern Saskatchewan along the Saskatchewan River at the northern edge of the grassland, next to the mixed mesophytic and deciduous forest. Also along this vegetational border is a rather extensive area where this owl is common, stretching diagonally from southeastern North Dakota to central Iowa. Equally abundant populations are in northern Nevada, with an extension into south-central Oregon, and in the savanna habitat of southern Texas.

The foraging behavior of this owl requires a habitat that is fairly open, because it sits on a perch and waits until it detects prey, then flies out and captures it. The owl remains on the same perch only three to five minutes (Marti 1974). Its staple is small mammals, but it also eats small birds, amphibians, reptiles, and insects when they are available (Earhart and Johnson 1970).

Snowy Owl (*Nyctea scandiaca*) Map in Appendix B
This northern species was recorded on 235 sites, but at only one of these was the abundance over 0.20 individuals seen per party-hour. Also, every four or five years the Snowy Owl irrupts into the South because of low availability of lemmings and Arctic hares (Burton 1984). The maps thus were excluded from the text. The range generally covers the areas north of the southern tip of the Great Lakes. The highest abundance of 0.21 individuals per party-hour was recorded near Green Bay, Wisconsin, where Snowy Owls were seen in 80% of the years examined.

Northern Saw-whet Owl (*Aegolius acadicus*) Map in Appendix B
This small owl was seen on 165 Christmas counts, primarily in areas north of the 35th parallel and south of the 50th. The highest recorded abundances were in the Columbia basin and in southern Iowa. The maximum average abundance was only 0.12 individuals per party-hour, so this owl is too rare to ensure that the CBC data are reliable.

Burrowing Owl (*Athene cunicularia*) Map in Appendix B
The ninety-eight sites reporting this long-legged owl stretch along the coast of California, inland from southern California to southern Texas, and along the Gulf coast of Louisiana and the Florida panhandle. Only three of these sites recorded an average abundance greater than 0.20 individuals per party-hour, and this high average at one of these sites was due to several individuals seen in only one year. The highest average abundances were around Plainview and Lubbock, Texas, probably concentrated on black-tailed prairie dog towns (Butts 1976).

Spotted Owl (*Strix occidentalis*) No Map
This owl has been on the National Audubon Society's Blue List since 1980 because of its declining numbers (Tate 1986). The average abundance near Point Reyes Bird Observatory, where it was observed in the most years (40%), was only 0.01 individuals seen per party-hour. Most of the thirteen sites recording this owl were in southern California. The sightings at ten locations occurred in only one year and at two locations in only two years.

Barred Owl (*Strix varia*) Maximum: 0.26 I/Hr
Even though the maximum abundance of the Barred Owl is low, the average abundance at several locations was over 0.20 individuals seen per party-hour. This owl prefers dense forests with mature trees, particularly locations near swamps and streams (Burton 1984). The range shows a strong association with the mixed mesophytic and deciduous forest. The northern range limit is not concomitant with any obvious vegetation boundary, which may be due to the lack of count locations in this area or to some factor not examined. The disjunct population reflects one individual seen on the Pinawa, Manitoba, count in 1970.

The most concentrated populations are in the warm South, stretching from around the Gulf coast to the southern Tennessee border. The abundance peaks in this region are associated with Homochitto National Forest in southwestern Mississippi and Tombigbee National Forest and Noxubee National Wildlife Refuge in the northeastern portion of that state. Another fairly abundant population is present in southwestern Georgia, where the average minimum January temperature is over 40°F (4°C). Populations of equal abundance are in Illinois, stretching north and south along the Mississippi River and east along the Ohio River.

The Barred Owl rarely eats insects (Earhart and Johnson 1970). Instead, its diet consists primarily of mice, but it also eats squirrels, rabbits, shrews, fish, amphibians, and birds. It often hunts in open areas at night or on cloudy days. It uses sound to locate prey and thus can hunt in complete darkness (Burton 1984).

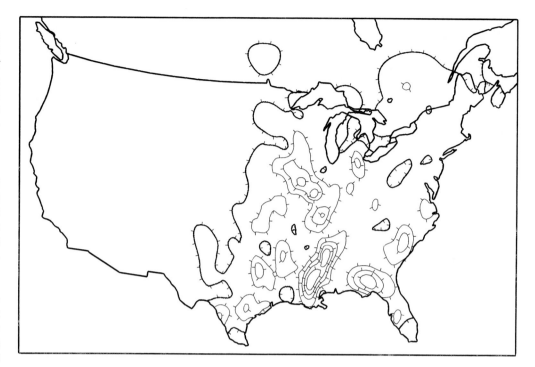

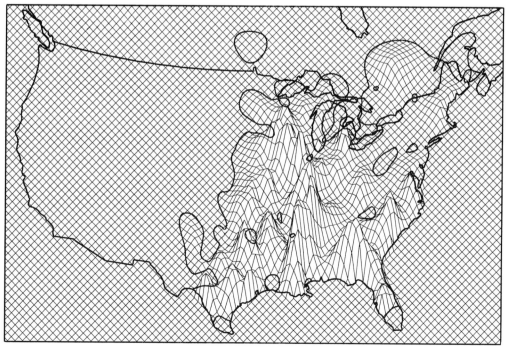

Barred Owl

STRIGIDAE

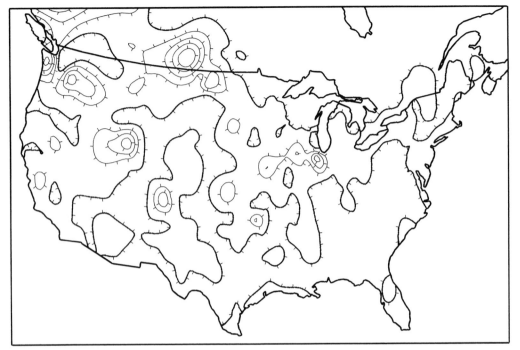

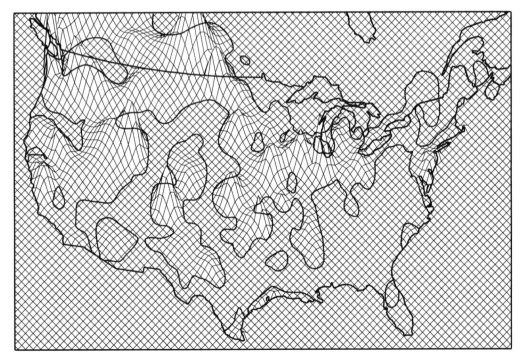

Northern Hawk-Owl (*Surnia ulula*) No Map
Only eighteen Christmas counts reported this owl. Most of these were east of the Great Lakes and north of the southern tip of Lake Michigan. Only the census near Sault Sainte Marie on the United States–Canada border recorded it in three years, and the abundance there was only 0.03 individuals seen per party-hour. All the other sites reported it in only one or two years.

Northern Pygmy-Owl (*Glaucidium gnoma*) Map in Appendix B
Maps for this owl were not included in the text because the most concentrated population recorded an average of only 0.17 individuals seen per party-hour, in the Columbia basin of Washington. Sightings were reported all along the Pacific coast and around the foothills of the Rocky Mountains.

Short-eared Owl (*Asio flammeus*) Maximum: 0.44 I/Hr
The distribution of the Short-eared Owl is rather discontinuous, but less so than that of the Long-eared Owl. Both these species are absent in the Southeast, but the Short-eared Owl does occur south along the Mississippi River. The Short-eared Owl also avoids the western half of the Great Plains and the western foothills of the Rocky Mountains. In the North this owl is absent from the mixed deciduous and coniferous forests and the boreal forests.

Most of the concentrated Short-eared Owl populations occur near protected and managed areas. The most obvious exception is the extensive population of maximum abundance in south-central Saskatchewan. The densest population of Great Horned Owls is just west of this location. The other extremely abundant Short-eared population is in northwestern Washington. West of there is a slightly less dense population along the Columbia River. An equally dense population is in northern Utah and southern Idaho near the Bear River and Bear Lake refuges. The population of comparable abundance in northeastern Illinois is not associated with a refuge. Less dense populations occur in Colorado near the Monte Vista and Alamosa refuges, in eastern Oklahoma in the Sequoyah refuge, and in North Dakota around the Des Lacs, Upper Souris, and J. Clark Salyer refuges.

Unlike most owls the Short-eared Owl is diurnal, and its flight is more buoyant because of its longer and narrower wings (Burton 1984). It roosts at night on the ground in tufts of dense grass less than 1 foot (0.3 m) high (Weller, Adams, and Rose 1955). Small birds and mammals, including voles and mice, make up most of its diet (Graber 1962; Burton 1984). When *Microtus* are abundant they constitute as much as 95% of its food, but this percentage drops to 75% when these rodents are relatively rare (Weller, Adams, and Rose 1955).

　　　　　　　Short-eared Owl

Long-eared Owl (*Asio otus*) Maximum: 0.24 I/Hr

The distribution of the Long-eared Owl is spotty, but the reason is not obvious. It is absent in the Southeast except along the Tennessee River, in areas where the average minimum January temperature drops below $0°F$ ($-18°C$), and in several regions in the West except for some riparian habitats.

One of the densest populations is in northeastern Colorado, just west of a high abundance peak of the Great Horned Owl. Apparently this high concentration of Long-eared Owls is associated with the galeria forest along the South Platte River. The other population with maximum density is less extensive and occurs in the southeastern corner of Iowa, along the Des Moines River.

Besides being "one of the most nocturnal owls in the world," it is also one of the "most effective mousers" (Burton 1984). Over 95% of its diet consists of mammals (Marti 1974, 1976). Indeed, of twenty-nine species of prey eaten, all were either *Microtus, Peromyscus,* or *Mus* (Graber 1962), but the staple is normally *Microtus* (Earhart and Johnson 1970). Hunting occurs primarily in the open near forest edges. This owl locates prey by sound, so it can hunt in total darkness. During the day birds prefer to roost near the trunk of coniferous trees (Burton 1984), which makes them difficult to find and census.

CAPRIMULGIDAE

Common Nighthawk (*Chordeiles minor*) No Map

Northern and central South America are the main wintering grounds of the Common Nighthawk (AOU 1983). Fifteen sightings were reported at sporadic locations in Florida, along the Texas coast, up the Rio Grande valley, and in southern Alabama. The most regular sightings were in four years in Florida around Fort Myers and inland from Fort Lauderdale. The average abundance at both these locations was less than 0.01 individuals per party-hour.

Common Pauraque (*Nyctidromus albicollis*) No Map

This caprimulgid is resident from southern Texas, across Mexico, and into South America (AOU 1983). It was recorded on eighteen Christmas counts throughout the coastal plain of Texas, reaching as far north as San Antonio. Several sites reported the Common Pauraque in at least 50% of the years examined. The densest population was recorded at Bentsen State Park on the Rio Grande, with an average of 0.45 individuals seen per party-hour.

Common Poorwill (*Phalaenoptilus nuttallii*) No Map

The Common Poorwill purportedly winters throughout the southern part of its breeding range in California, Arizona, and Mexico (AOU 1983). Of the nineteen CBCs reporting it, however, the most frequent sightings were on the count near Monterey, California, where it was seen in only three of the ten years. The average abundance here was less than 0.01 individuals per party-hour.

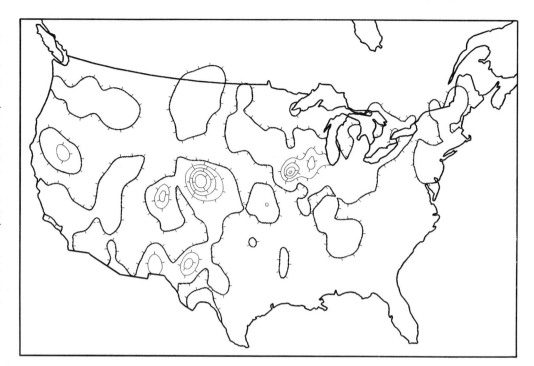

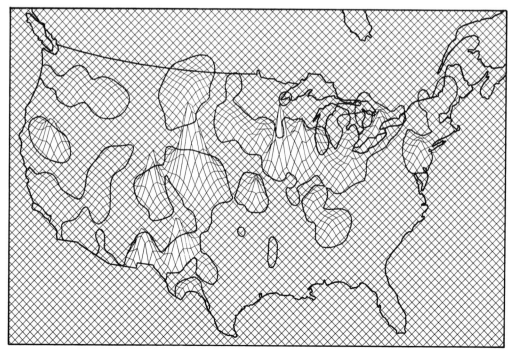

CAPRIMULGIDAE / APODIDAE / TROCHILIDAE

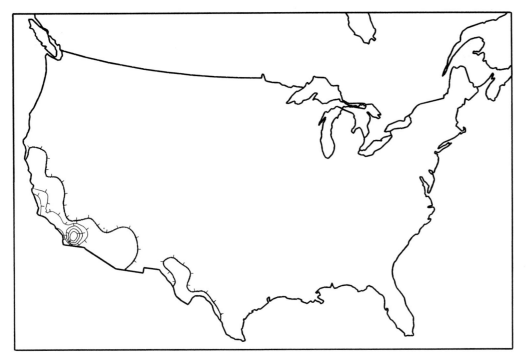

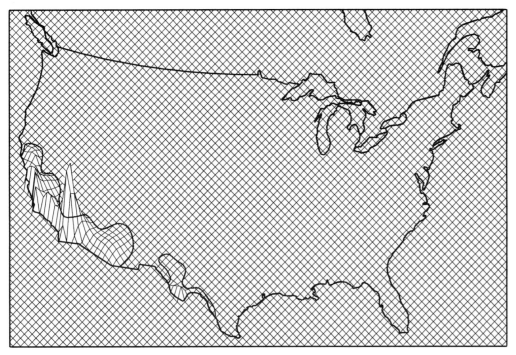

Chuck-will's-widow (*Caprimulgus carolinensis*) No Map
The Atlantic coast of Florida was where the Chuck-will's-widow was seen on Christmas counts with the most regularity, but it also was reported sporadically along both the Gulf and Atlantic coasts. Six counts along Florida's east coast recorded this caprimulgid in at least six of the ten years. The densest population occurred near Vero Beach, with 0.03 birds seen each party-hour.

Whip-poor-will (*Caprimulgus vociferus*) No Map
The wintering ground of the Whip-poor-will stretches from southern Texas along the Gulf coast and into southeastern South Carolina and continues on south into Mexico and Panama (AOU 1983). The twenty-nine Christmas counts recording this species were primarily in Florida, and all six counts where it was observed in at least 70% of the years examined were on the Atlantic coast of Florida. Of these six, the average abundance was the highest on the Vero Beach count, where 0.03 individuals were seen per party-hour.

APODIDAE

White-throated Swift (*Aeronautes saxatalis*) Maximum: 9.09 I/Hr
The winter distribution of the White-throated Swift includes most of California, southern Arizona, and southwestern Texas. Elevation and ambient temperature are the factors most strongly associated with the limits of its distribution. This swift is present west of the higher peaks of the Sierra Nevada, south of the Mojave Desert, and south of the Mogollon Rim in Arizona, which is over 6,500 feet (1,980 m) above sea level. In Texas it ranges throughout the Davis, Guadalupe, and Delaware mountains. The temperature in most of these areas rarely falls below freezing in January.

The White-throated Swift occurs in high concentration around the valleys and foothills between Salton Sea and the San Bernardino Mountains. Here the air is warm, and presumably the mountains create air currents that carry prey up into the atmosphere where this agile bird feeds.

As its genus name suggests (*Aeronautes*), the White-throated Swift is an adept flier. Groups of these highly specialized birds feed on aerial plankton throughout the year (Brooke 1970). The individuals that breed in the North migrate down to the southern regions of their breeding range, and their longer wings may have developed to aid their migration (Behle 1973).

TROCHILIDAE

Ruby-throated Hummingbird (*Archilochus colubris*) No Map
The Ruby-throated Hummingbird was observed at thirty-one sites scattered along the Rio Grande valley, on the Gulf coast in Texas and Louisiana, and up the Atlantic coast to North Carolina. All observations outside southern Florida were ephemeral. The counts in the South near Cape Sable and just east of Key West reported the highest concentration of Ruby-throated Hummingbirds, with 0.01 individuals seen per party-hour at both sites. Outside the United States, its primary wintering grounds extend through Mexico to Costa Rica (AOU 1983).

White-throated Swift

Black-chinned Hummingbird (*Archilochus alexandri*) No Map
The twenty-two sites reporting this hummingbird were scattered along the lower Rio Grande valley from the Big Bend region to the Gulf coast and from southeastern Arizona to southern California and up the coast to San Luis Obispo. Observations in five or more years occurred, however, only at four of these sites (three in California and one in southern Arizona). The densest population was near San Bernardino, California, where on average 0.02 birds were seen per party-hour.

Anna's Hummingbird (*Calypte anna*) Maximum: 2.57 I/Hr
The distribution of the Anna's Hummingbird is strongly associated with chaparral in California and creosote bush/bur sage scrub in southern Arizona. The most extensive area of chaparral is in southern California, where this species reaches its highest abundance. North of here, disjunct and smaller chaparral areas occur around the San Joaquin and Sacramento valleys, up to about Redding, California. There is a disjunct population on the California-Oregon border that corresponds with another small patch of chaparral.

The Anna's Hummingbird is unusual in many respects. It is the only hummingbird whose winter range is primarily in the United States, it eats more insects than other North American hummingbirds (Oberholser 1974), and it is the only bird of the chaparral region that breeds before the winter solstice (Stiles 1973). Breeding begins after the onset of the heavy winter rains in November or December causes the *Ribes* and eucalyptus to bloom. Males defend these nectar sources, with the size of the breeding territory proportional to the quantity of food available and the level of competition (Stiles 1971). On colder days the birds spend proportionally less time defending these areas and more time feeding, and on rainy days, when nectar may be diluted, they catch more insects (Wheeler 1980).

Costa's Hummingbird (*Calypte costae*) No Map
The northern portion of the range of the Costa's Hummingbird extends into southern California and southern Arizona, and this species is seen irregularly in all the Pacific coast states and British Columbia, central Nevada, northern Utah, and eastern Texas (AOU 1983). All the twenty-two CBCs recording this species, whether regularly or irregularly, were in southern California and southern Arizona. Of the five sites with regular observations, the count at Organ Pipe Cactus National Monument showed the highest abundance (0.06 I/Hr).

Rufous Hummingbird (*Selasphorus rufus*) No Map
This is a sporadic winter visitor in the Rio Grande valley of Texas, along the coast from southern Texas to Alabama, and on the Pacific coast from southern California up to Washington. It was seen most regularly around Long Beach, California, where it was reported in five of the ten years at an abundance of 0.01 individuals seen per party-hour. Its main wintering ground extends through Mexico from Oaxaca to western Veracruz (AOU 1983).

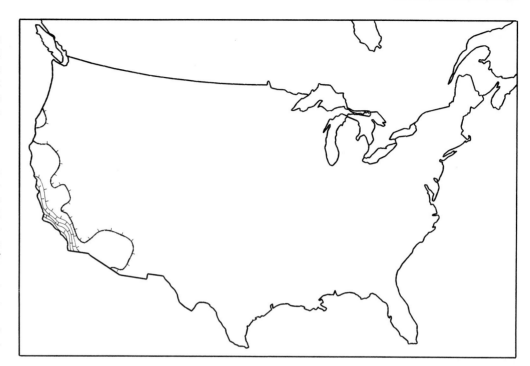

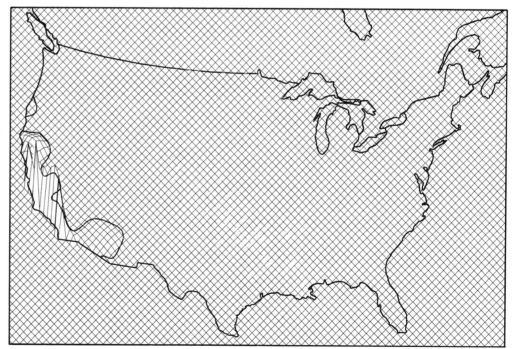

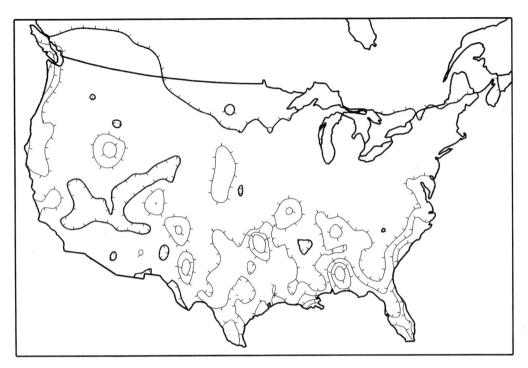

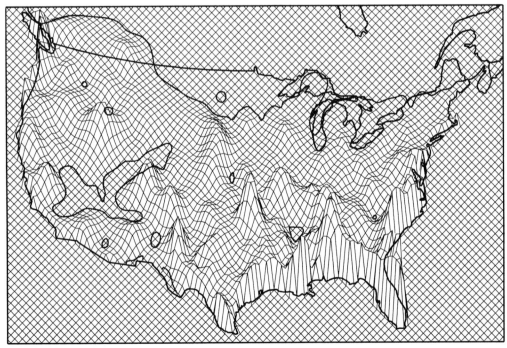

Allen's Hummingbird (*Selasphorus sasin*) No Map
There were scattered, irregular sightings of the Allen's Hummingbird from the southern border of California to San Francisco. Long Beach and Santa Barbara were the only sites where it was seen regularly (six out of the ten years), and Long Beach had the higher abundance (0.42 I/Hr). It is reported to be resident on the Channel Islands and the Palos Verdes peninsula, but its main wintering region is in Baja California and from Sinaloa to Mexico City (AOU 1983).

ALCEDINIDAE
Ringed Kingfisher (*Ceryle torquata*) No Map
The Ringed Kingfisher is resident from southern Texas to Tierra del Fuego (AOU 1983). It was reported on the Falcon Dam count in Texas every year it was held, with an average of 0.10 individuals seen per party-hour.

Belted Kingfisher (*Ceryle alcyon*) Maximum: 0.90 I/Hr
The winter range of the Belted Kingfisher extends from the coast of Alaska, through the contiguous United States and Mexico, and south to northern South America (AOU 1983). In Arizona it is reported to winter wherever there is open water (Phillips, Marshall, and Monson 1983), which, on a continentwide scale, would presumably limit it to areas that remain free of ice. West of the Great Lakes, however, this kingfisher occurs in regions that get as cold as 0°F (−18°C) in January. East of the Great Lakes it avoids areas with an average minimum January temperature colder than 10°F (−12°C). Perhaps it is using ponds kept open by hot-water discharge from power plants.

This kingfisher is relatively common where the frost-free period is longer than 180 days a year. Within this region the apexes are not centered on large rivers like the Mississippi, Arkansas, and Missouri, which presumably are too muddy and probably have few perches over the water. Concentrated populations do occur on the Sacramento, San Joaquin, Snake, Pecos, and Platte rivers. Some abundance peaks, such as those in western Colorado, northern Texas, Missouri, Tennessee, Oklahoma, and Alabama, are associated with smaller rivers.

The Belted Kingfisher normally forages alone. It sits on a perch over the water and waits for its prey, usually fish less than 6 inches (15 cm) long. It therefore needs convenient perches over clear water, so it can see the prey. It dives directly from its perch to capture fish (Bent 1964). When fish are not available it will eat crabs, crayfish, clams, lizards, frogs, mice, and even seeds. Several birds have been observed with their bills caught between the shells of clams (Bent 1964).

Green Kingfisher (*Chloroceryle americana*) No Map

This kingfisher is resident primarily in the lowlands from central Texas south to central Argentina (AOU 1983). It was observed regularly on counts in Texas near Sheffield on the Pecos River (eight years) and near Falcon Dam (five years) and Del Rio (six years) on the Rio Grande. The most abundant population was recorded at Falcon Dam, with an abundance of 0.29 birds per party-hour.

PICIDAE

Lewis' Woodpecker (*Melanerpes lewis*) Maximum: 1.32 I/Hr

The overall distribution of the Lewis' Woodpecker is coincident with two general vegetation types: coastal coniferous forest and dry-belt pine forest. Thus, it apparently avoids grasslands, solid stands of semiarid scrub and scrub steppe, tundra, and coniferous forests. The disjunct population in southern California occurs in the California oaks that are interspersed in the chaparral. The other two disjunct populations farther east are ephemeral. The eastern edge of the main distribution abuts the western limit of the Red-headed Woodpecker. These species are basically western and eastern ecological equivalents in that both prefer open habitat, store food, and rarely excavate in wood for insects (Bock, Hadow, and Somers 1971). Each is probably influencing the edge of the other's distribution, because, at least in the breeding season, interspecific aggression occurs (Bock, Hadow, and Somers 1971).

Concentrated populations of the Lewis' Woodpecker occur only in localized areas in the northern Rio Grande valley and in the coastal forest of southern Oregon. This woodpecker is also fairly abundant in California's San Joaquin valley. The vegetation at all these locations consists of fairly open forests in which this flycatching woodpecker finds exposed perches where it sits and watches for flying insects. The ecology of the Lewis' Woodpecker and that of the Acorn Woodpecker are fairly similar, and this may influence the location of their abundance peaks in California. Interspecific interactions may cause their abundance peaks to be juxtaposed, with the Lewis' Woodpecker's being farther north than the Acorn's. More study is needed to determine how much these two species do interact in the winter.

Like all members of the genus *Melanerpes,* the Lewis' Woodpecker caches food, such as acorns, corn, pine seeds, and juniper berries, to use in winter when fresh food is scarce. It rarely if ever drills holes specifically for storing items (Bock, Hadow, and Somers 1971) but uses natural crevices. Rarely does it excavate insects from the trunks and branches of trees in the usual woodpecker style; rather, it catches insects on the wing (Bent 1939).

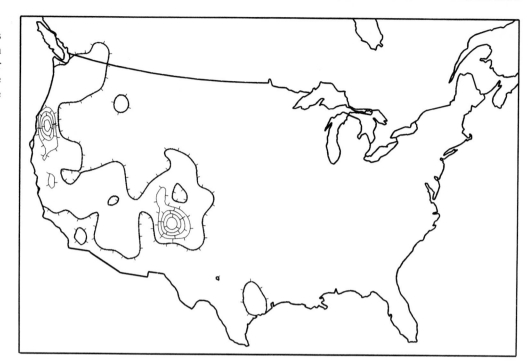

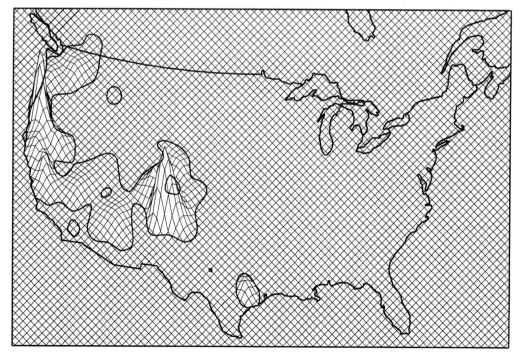

Lewis' Woodpecker

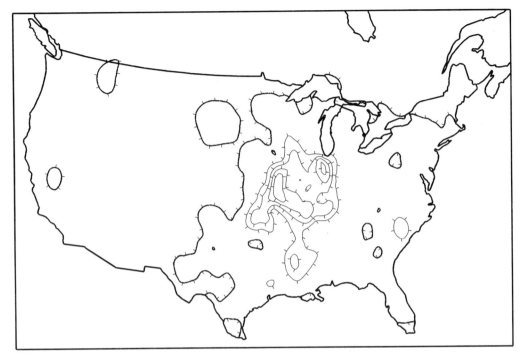

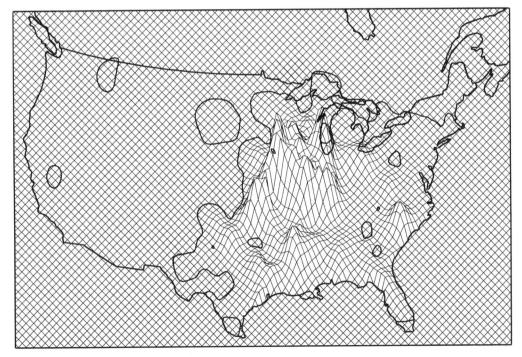

Red-headed Woodpecker (*Melanerpes erythrocephalus*) Maximum: 2.54 I/Hr

The Red-headed Woodpecker occurs primarily in open-canopy habitats of the mixed mesophytic and deciduous forest and the tree and shrub savanna. To the west it avoids the grasslands, including the galeria forests along river valleys that are scattered throughout the prairie habitat. The northern range limit indicates that it is absent in the mixed deciduous and coniferous forest, which has a fairly closed canopy. Also, in this area the average minimum January temperature drops below 10°F (−12°C). The southwestern range edge may be determined to some extent by the occurrence of this woodpecker's western ecological equivalent, the Lewis' Woodpecker. Field studies have shown that these species do behave aggressively toward each other (Bock, Hadow, and Somers 1971).

The open forests of the central Midwest provide the optimal wintering habitat for the Red-headed Woodpecker. The areas where it is most common include parts of the riparian forests along the Mississippi, Missouri, and Arkansas rivers. There is also an extension of this abundant population into the area south of Lake Michigan. The apexes of the areas where the Red-headed Woodpecker is common may be partially determined by dense populations of Red-bellied Woodpeckers. The abundance peaks of these two species show complementarity, which provides circumstantial evidence for interspecific interactions. In a smaller-scale study, Willson (1970) reported aggressive behavior between these two species. The eastern edge of the general area where the Red-headed Woodpecker is fairly common coincides with the foothills of the Appalachians; in fact, it completely avoids the higher elevations of these mountains. This species is also uncommon in the Ozarks. The northern and western edges of the region where the Red-headed Woodpecker is common indicate that it frequents areas receiving at least 32 inches (81 cm) of precipitation annually.

The ecology of the Red-headed Woodpecker helps explain why it prefers open-forest environments. Instead of excavating insects from the trunks and branches of trees, it sits on exposed perches and waits for flying insects, then sallies out to capture them. In the winter particularly, it also forages on the ground and in trees for berries and concealed insects. To some extent this species also stores food, such as corn, berries, and even grasshoppers, for later use. Sometimes it seals the opening to the storage area with a twig or the like, and storage locations are aggressively defended in the winter (MacRoberts 1975).

Acorn Woodpecker (*Melanerpes formicivorus*) Maximum: 7.96 I/Hr

As its name suggests, the Acorn Woodpecker is strongly associated with oaks. Its distribution in California and Oregon occurs in the California oakwoods, chaparral with oaks interspersed, and the Oregon oakwoods. It avoids the redwood forest along the coast. The population in southern Arizona and New Mexico is limited to the area with scattered oak-juniper woodlands. In northern Arizona, birds live around the ecotone of oak-juniper woodlands and mountain mahogany–oak scrub. Another population occurs in the oak forest in southwestern Texas. Temperature, as well as oaks, apparently determines the location of these populations, since this woodpecker is present only in oak forests where the average minimum January temperature is above 20°F (−7°C).

The most concentrated population of the Acorn Woodpecker is in the northern portion of the most extensive stand of oaks in California. The southern part of this woodland is much drier than that farther north, receiving less than 16 inches (40.6 cm) of rain annually. The summer temperatures, which possibly influence the wintering site of this nonmigrating species, are much hotter in the south; the normal daily temperature in July is 10°F (−12°C) higher than that in the northern area. The presence of a concentrated population of Lewis' Woodpeckers on the California-Oregon border also may be keeping the abundance peak of the Acorn Woodpecker from extending farther north. Certainly closer examination of the interaction between these two species is warranted.

Acorn Woodpecker offspring remain with the family group even after they are capable of breeding, so groups contain between two and twelve birds. The young will remain with their families as nonbreeding helpers until a breeding bird in another group dies (Koenig 1981a). The competition to fill such a vacancy is intense, and the battle may be fought together by several same-sex siblings. If victorious, all these siblings become breeders in their new group (Koenig 1981b). A group therefore may comprise a pair of breeders and their helpers or several breeding pairs and their helpers. The limited availability of suitable storage trees may be the reason offspring remain with their family groups (Koenig 1981a). Storage trees are used to hold caches of acorns, grains, fruit, and the like, which are collected while in high abundance and used when fresh food becomes scarce (Bent 1939).

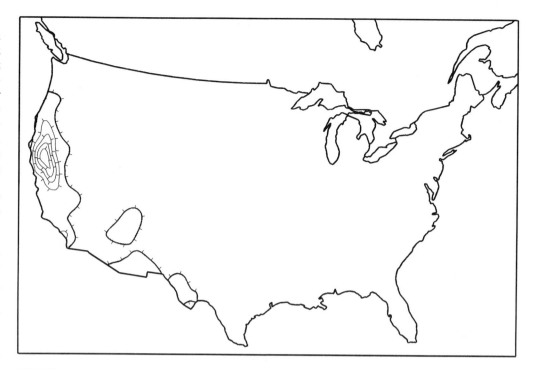

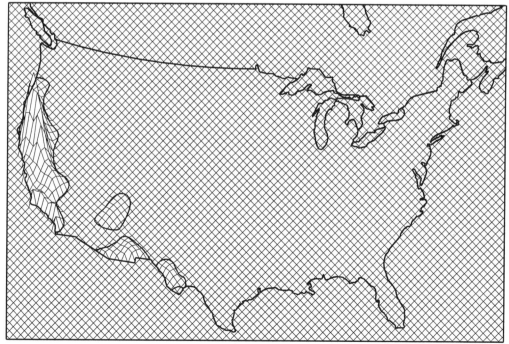

PICIDAE

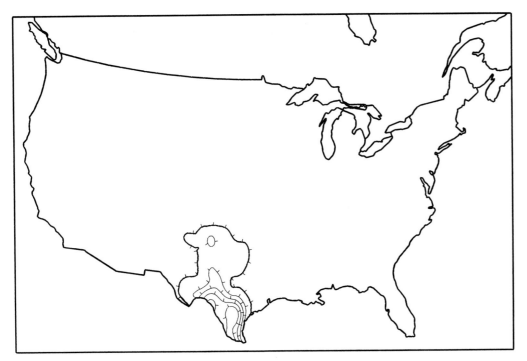

Gila Woodpecker (*Melanerpes uropygialis*) No Map
Appropriately, the Gila Woodpecker's restricted distribution encompasses the Gila River south of Phoenix, Arizona. The density of this species is fairly high throughout its range, with a slight peak near Tucson, where 2.60 birds were seen per party-hour. This Sonoran Desert species forages for insects primarily in riparian habitats and among mesquite trees. In the winter it breaks open galls to retrieve their insect occupants. It also eats berries from mistletoe and other plants (Bent 1939).

Golden-fronted Woodpecker (*Melanerpes aurifrons*) Maximum:
   1.75 I/Hr
The Golden-fronted Woodpecker is rarely seen outside Texas. It lives in the drier regions of the tree and shrub savanna vegetation zone. This type of vegetation extends farther east than the range of the woodpecker, but this eastern area receives over 35 inches (89 cm) of precipitation a year, which apparently creates too moist an environment. In the drier regions, the species forages for insects on mesquite and oaks and in pecan groves, and it also eats acorns, corn, and berries when available (Bent 1939).

The highest abundance of this species occurs throughout the mesquite-acacia savanna of southern Texas. In the 1930s and perhaps beyond, it was significantly affected by hunting. This species was classified as a pest because it was ruining the newly installed telephone poles, which were made of soft pine. These poles provided excellent nesting sites because it was easier to drill cavities in them than in the native hardwoods. In fact, some poles contained several nest holes. The hunting of this "pest" noticeably decreased its density (Bent 1939).

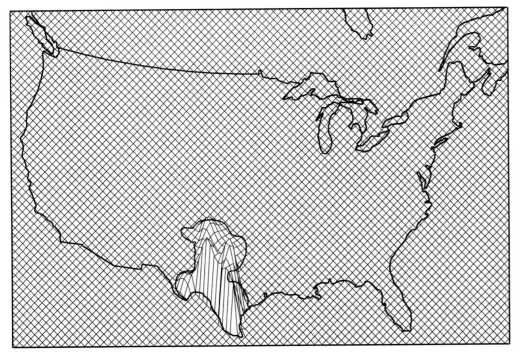

Golden-fronted Woodpecker

Golden-fronted Woodpecker

Red-bellied Woodpecker (*Melanerpes carolinus*) Maximum: 1.89 I/Hr
The distribution pattern indicates that the Red-bellied Woodpecker occurs primarily at elevations lower than 1,000 feet (305 m) above sea level. This includes the entire coastal plains and radiations along various river valleys. The Appalachians and Ozarks have fewer birds than the surrounding areas. In fact, the Appalachians are more than 1,000 feet (305 m) higher than the Ozarks, and the density of Red-bellied Woodpeckers is correspondingly lower in the Appalachians. The western edge of the distribution reflects this species' avoidance of areas higher than 2,000 feet (610 m). This woodpecker does, however, frequent various river valleys (e.g., Platte, Arkansas, Red, Mississippi, and Souris in Canada and Sheyenne in North Dakota), undoubtedly attracted by the galeria forests along these rivers. The southwestern edge of the distribution coincides with the eastern distributional edge of the Lewis' Woodpecker. This probably is not coincidental, because these species are ecologically very similar (Bent 1939).

Concentrations of the Red-bellied Woodpecker are probably influenced by the occurrence of dense populations of Red-headed Woodpeckers. In a field study, Willson (1970) found that these two species behaved aggressively toward each other. The maps of their abundances show that they rarely occur together in high densities.

The Red-bellied Woodpecker is fairly common throughout its entire range. River valleys, including the Mississippi, Ohio, Missouri, Arkansas, Red, and Cumberland valleys, and the eastern coastal plains support exceptionally dense concentrations. These habitats primarily contain deciduous trees in open forests that are usually moist or swampy. Here the species excavates wood-boring beetle larvae from trunks and branches. This is not a shy bird; it uses parks, visits bird feeders to feast on suet, and sometimes eats oranges and other fruits from orchards. It also stores nuts, fruits, and some insects for later consumption. When both fresh and stored foods become scarce, birds migrate south (Bent 1939).

Vegetation appears to be another factor influencing the distribution and abundance pattern of this species. The Red-bellied Woodpecker is present in mixed mesophytic and deciduous forests and is very common in swamp forests. It is completely absent in the mixed deciduous and coniferous forests, which occur along the northern edge of the species distribution. It also avoids the prairies to the south along the coast of Louisiana and to the west, except for extensions along galeria forests in river valleys.

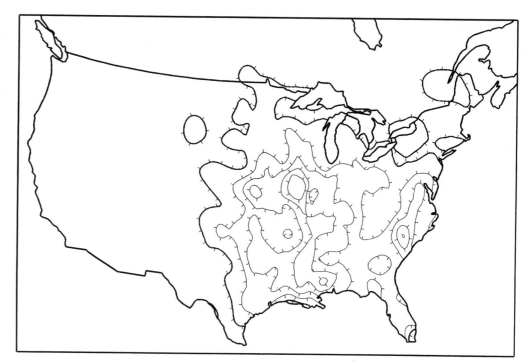

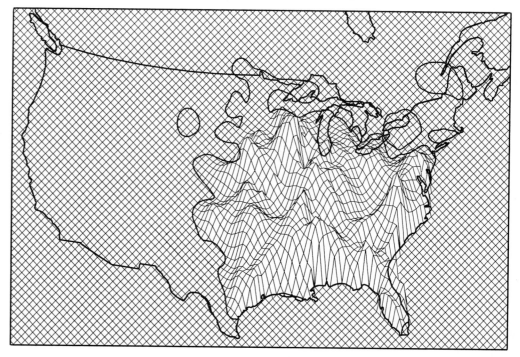

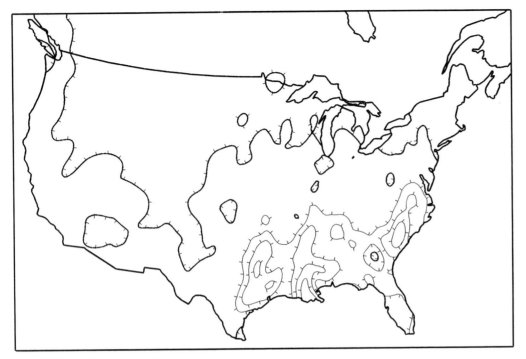

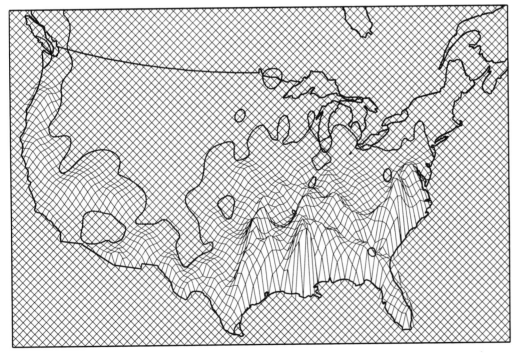

Yellow-bellied and Red-breasted Sapsuckers (*Sphyrapicus varius* and *S. ruber*) Maximum: 0.87 I/Hr

Until 1983 the Red-breasted Sapsucker was considered conspecific with the Yellow-bellied Sapsucker (AOU 1983). Thus, the records of these two species were grouped together in the CBC data examined and the maps show the combined abundance pattern. The Red-breasted Sapsucker winters west of western Nevada (AOU 1983). The maps show that its range encompasses the coastal conifer forest west of the Cascade Mountains, the Sierra Nevada and on west, and the semiarid scrub of the Sonoran Desert. Other than a slight overlap in southern California (AOU 1983), the remainder of the map reflects the distribution of the Yellow-bellied Sapsucker. Its distribution shows that it is absent from the mixed deciduous and coniferous forests in the North, and it circumvents the Rocky Mountains.

The northern range limit indicates that both species winter only in regions with an average minimum January temperature above 15°F (−9°C). The foraging habits of these unusual woodpeckers must influence where they winter. They feed on sap, which flows less copiously when trees are cold; these woodpeckers must therefore avoid cold climates. They tap the sap either by drilling a row of small holes along the trunk or a branch or by stripping off an entire patch of outer bark (Spring 1965).

The abundance pattern of the Yellow-bellied Sapsucker obscures that of the Red-breasted Sapsucker, because the former is much more common. The abundance pattern of the Yellow-bellied Sapsucker, however, provides much information about its biology and ecology. This species is common where the temperature rarely drops below freezing. The most abundant population is in the swamp forest of the southern Mississippi valley. The western edge of the abundant population probably is affected by two factors. First, this edge coincides with the 32 inch (81 cm) isocline of annual precipitation; second, the area of highest abundance of the Ladder-backed Woodpecker abuts that of the Yellow-bellied Sapsucker. The abundance of both species drops abruptly in this area. This separation of abundant populations may mean changes in habitat are being tracked by the birds, or these species may be excluding each other from otherwise suitable regions. Field studies are needed to determine the factors separating their dense populations.

Williamson's Sapsucker (*Sphyrapicus thyroideus*) No Map
This sapsucker was recorded at only twenty-six locations: scattered throughout the regions west of the Cascades near Eugene, Oregon; along California's Sacramento valley and extending into the Sierra Nevada; on the eastern side of the southern Rockies in New Mexico, and stretching south from there to the region of Douglas, Arizona. Observations at most sites occurred only in one or two years, but the count in the northern San Bernardino Mountains recorded this sapsucker in six years, with an average abundance of 0.03 individuals seen per party-hour. Like the other sapsuckers, the Williamson's feeds on subcortical phloem, but it prefers to remove patches of bark from the trunks of pines to stimulate drainage instead of drilling rows of small holes (Stallcup 1968).

Ladder-backed Woodpecker (*Picoides scalaris*) Maximum: 1.55 I/Hr
The overall distribution of the Ladder-backed Woodpecker is associated with general humidity. This woodpecker inhabits areas in the United States with very dry air, where the mean annual pan evaporation is 80 inches (203 cm) or more.

This small woodpecker is resident in the deserts and semiarid regions of North America. It frequents several habitats such as oak woodlands, pine forests, shrub savanna, and cholla-grassland prairie. The highest density occurs in regions where it rarely gets below freezing in January, which includes the Sonoran and Chihuahuan deserts. Besides being warm, these areas are dry; they receive less than 32 inches (81 cm) of rain a year.

In southern California the occurrence of the similar Nuttall's Woodpecker apparently affects the distribution of the Ladder-backed Woodpecker. In various parts of its range, the Ladder-backed frequents oak woodland habitats, but in California the Nuttall's Woodpecker successfully excludes this congener from foraging in oaks (Short 1971). In fact, from closer evaluation than is possible with these Christmas count data, Short found that the two species are indeed allopatric in California, with the Nuttall's Woodpecker occurring in the moist west-facing slopes of the Sierra Nevada while the Ladder-backed was present on the dry east-facing slopes. Owing to the mathematical smoothing done in these analyses of the Christmas count data and because the count sites encompass both habitat types, the distributions of these two species do not appear totally parapatric, but the overlap is slight. Short also found that the Ladder-backed Woodpecker was allopatric with the Hairy Woodpecker in that the former occurs in riparian habitats and apparently forces the latter into coniferous forests. The maps of these two species show that the Hairy is relatively rare in locations overlapping the distribution of the Ladder-backed and totally absent where the Ladder-backed is most common. The maps also suggest interspecific interactions occur between the Ladder-backed Woodpecker and the Yellow-bellied Sapsucker, because their areas of high abundance in Texas are juxtaposed. However, evidence obtained from the maps is circumstantial, and fieldwork is needed to determine if interactions are actually causing exclusions.

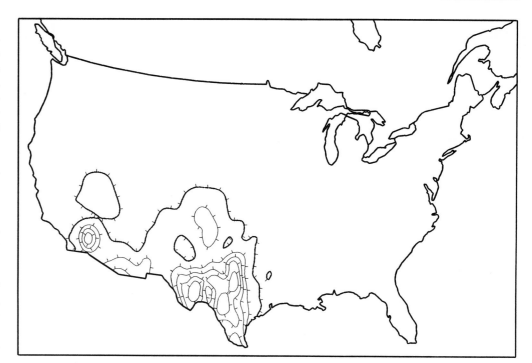

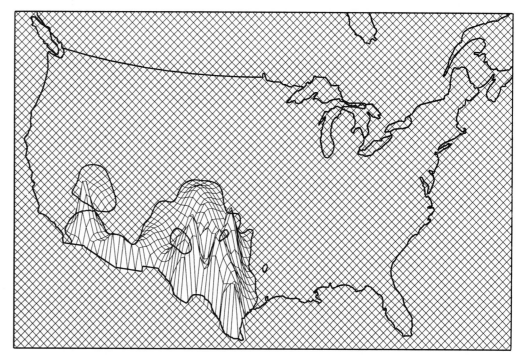

PICIDAE

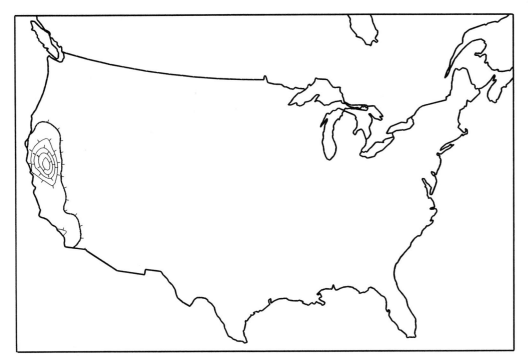

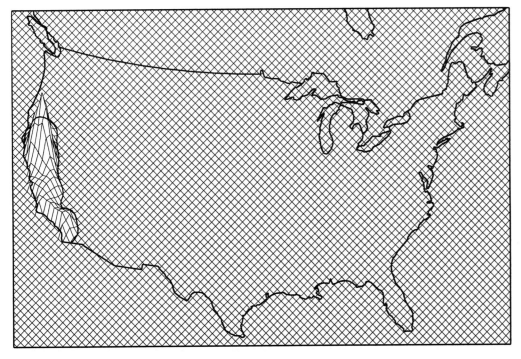

Nuttall's Woodpecker (*Picoides nuttallii*) Maximum: 1.27 I/Hr

The physical appearance and ecology of the Nuttall's Woodpecker closely resemble those of the Ladder-backed Woodpecker. One of the major ecological differences is that the Nuttall's occurs in moister environments in the southern Pacific mountain system. Although both species occur in the same mountain range, their distributions are parapatric, with the Nuttall's present only on the moister west-facing slopes and the Ladder-backed on the drier east-facing slopes (Short 1971). Even with the coarse-grained examination provided by the CBC data, the maps show only a slight overlap of these distributions.

The range of the Nuttall's Woodpecker, which is almost completely within the state of California, is strongly defined by vegetation, mainly oaks and chaparral. In the north this species is restricted to the California oak woodlands. The Lewis' Woodpecker, which is abundant in the Oregon oak woodlands, may be limiting the Nuttall's northern range. In the south the Nuttall's distribution is coincident with chaparral, which is liberally sprinkled with oak scrub. The eastern distributional limit indicates that this woodpecker is absent in the sagebrush scrub in Nevada and creosote bush scrub in eastern California.

The Nuttall's Woodpecker is most common in the northern California oak woodlands. Even though extensive stands of oaks extend much farther south, other factors such as low precipitation apparently make this southern region less than optimal. The small area of high abundance in the chaparral environment is in a fairly extensive stand of oak scrub.

This woodpecker usually does not eat acorns even though it is common in oaks. Its foraging behavior resembles that of a large nuthatch in that it often hangs upside down under limbs. Wood-boring beetle larvae, wild fruits such as blackberries, and poison oak seeds make up most of its diet. This foraging behavior and diet are similar to those of the Downy Woodpecker, and Short (1971) found that these two species do indeed affect each other's biogeography. This, however, cannot be detected in the maps except that the Downy Woodpecker is in low abundance throughout the West.

Nuttall's Woodpecker

Downy Woodpecker (*Picoides pubescens*) Maximum: 2.25 I/Hr

Although the Downy Woodpecker is most common in the eastern United States, it is present throughout basically the entire study area. This woodpecker is absent from the harsh environments of the Sonoran Desert and southwestern Texas. The vacant area in southeastern Canada, however, must be viewed with skepticism, because very few counts are held there. Aggressive behaviors have been reported between the Downy Woodpecker and the Nuttall's (Short 1971), Red-cockaded (Ligon 1968), and Red-headed Woodpeckers (Willson 1970), but neither the distributions nor the abundance patterns of these species show any obvious signs of these interactions.

The Downy Woodpecker is abundant only in the East, in the more humid regions where the annual pan evaporation is less than 65 inches (165 cm), and these areas are conjoined with regions where the average minimum January temperature is warmer than $-10°F$ ($-23°C$). The density also decreases as the vegetation changes from forest to grasslands. Curiously, the areas of moderately high density in the Great Plains prairies are not in the galeria forests along river valleys. In fact, this species seems to avoid the Missouri, Arkansas, and Platte rivers, since densities are high on either side of these valleys. It also avoids the Ozarks and Appalachians.

While foraging, the Downy Woodpecker usually moves with a flock of chickadees, nuthatches, and titmice throughout moderately open woodland habitat. Like other members of the flock, it is attracted to feeders and suet put out by humans. Primarily, however, its diet consists of beetles and wood-boring larvae (Bent 1939) that it excavates from tree limbs (Bock and Lepthien 1975). Because it eats insects that live inside the trees rather than on the surface, this woodpecker can find prey where the winters are severe (Bock and Lepthien 1975). In the colder portions of its range roosting cavities, usually excavated in tree limbs, provide protection from harsh weather (Bent 1939).

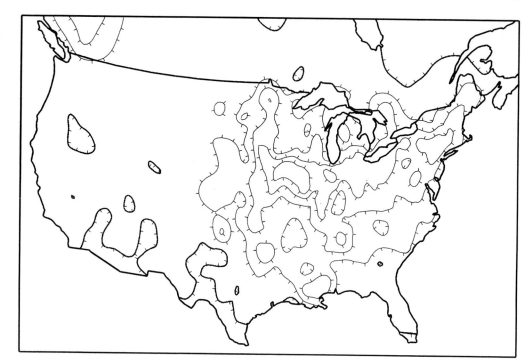

Downy Woodpecker

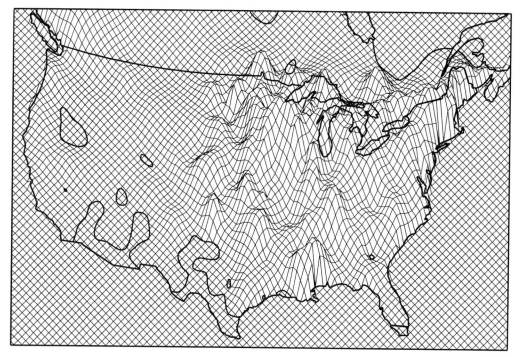

Downy Woodpecker

PICIDAE

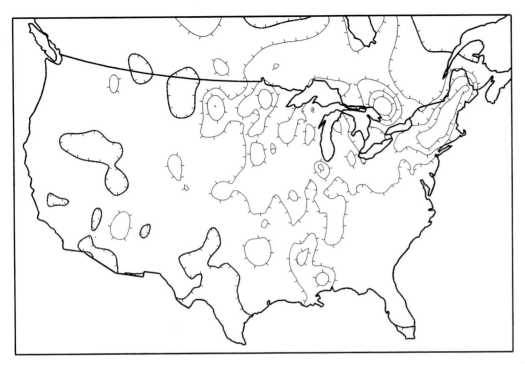

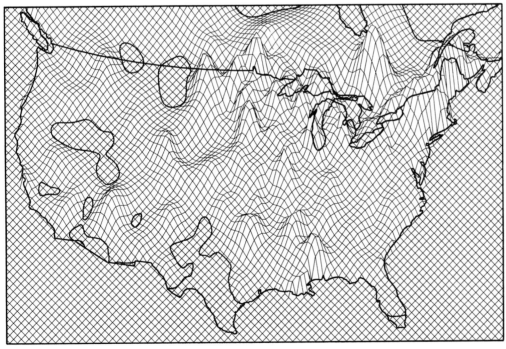

Hairy Woodpecker (*Picoides villosus*) Maximum: 1.11 I/Hr

A few places within the range of the Hairy Woodpecker, all in the West, are devoid of this bird. The two most northerly ones and the small one in New Mexico are not coincident with any obvious environmental factor. The other empty areas occur roughly in the hottest parts of the United States, where the average maximum July temperature is over 95°F (35°C). Since this species is somewhat nomadic in winter and not necessarily wedded to a particular breeding ground (Bent 1939), the hot summer weather may have an indirect rather than a direct effect on its wintering locations. The range of the Strickland's Woodpecker, in Arizona, and that of the Golden-fronted Woodpecker, in Texas, are coincident with these empty areas, and interactions with these species may be keeping the Hairy Woodpecker out. Field studies are needed to examine this possibility. Short (1971) has shown that the Ladder-backed Woodpecker does indeed force the Hairy Woodpecker out of riparian habitats and into coniferous forests. Various studies (Spring 1965; Short 1971; Morse 1972) have shown that the similar Downy Woodpecker does not influence the abundance of the Hairy, because the former feeds on the limbs of trees and the latter on the lower trunks. The Hairy Woodpecker is able to winter in areas where winters are harsh and tree-surface insects are scarce because it excavates wood-boring insects (Bock and Lepthien 1975). Berries and acorns are also included in its diet, as are seeds and suet from feeders (Bent 1939).

This species is an ecological generalist, as is evident from its wide distribution. It is present at most locations throughout the contiguous United States and southern Canada. (As with the Downy Woodpecker, the pattern in southeastern Canada must be viewed with skepticism because so few counts are held there.) Dense mixed deciduous and coniferous forest appears to be its optimal habitat. The areas of high density occur in this type of mixed forest, except for the fairly dense population on the southern coastal plains of Mississippi and those along the Mississippi, Missouri, and Illinois rivers. The birds are attracted to the dense riparian habitat of these river valleys. This woodpecker is less common in the Appalachians and Ozarks.

Hairy Woodpecker

Hairy Woodpecker

Strickland's Woodpecker (*Picoides stricklandi*) No Map
This species, also known as the Arizona Woodpecker, occurs primarily in oaks and to a lesser extent in pine-oak woodlands and riparian habitats (Davis 1965). It was recorded on only seven Christmas counts in the Tucson-Nogales region of Arizona. The count just west of Nogales on the United States–Mexico border averaged the highest abundances, with 0.13 individuals seen per party-hour.

Red-cockaded Woodpecker (*Picoides borealis*) Maximum: 0.41 I/Hr
The range limits show that the Red-cockaded Woodpecker is absent from areas with minimum temperatures much below freezing. Precipitation also apparently affects where this woodpecker lives; it occurs in areas with at least 40 inches (102 cm) of annual precipitation but not more than 50 inches (127 cm). This woodpecker is also absent from the higher elevations of the Appalachians.

The most concentrated population of Red-cockaded Woodpeckers is on the border between Louisiana and Arkansas around the Felsenthal National Wildlife Refuge. In fact wildlife refuges and national forests are associated with all the locations where this species reaches high densities. These managed areas undoubtedly have protected the larger and older pine trees, which are more susceptible to red-heart disease, and have provided sheltered environments for the woodpecker. This species primarily forages in live pines and prefers trees that are over 9 inches (23 cm) in diameter at breast height. The males feed in the crown and middle trunk, while females restrict their foraging to the middle and lower trunk (Hooper and Lennartz 1981).

This woodpecker is endemic in mature pine and pine-oak forests (Mengel and Jackson 1977). Its biogeographic pattern is dictated by the availability of pines that have red-heart disease, which contain 90% of all nesting cavities (Jackson 1977). Because the Red-cockaded Woodpecker does not migrate (AOU 1983), the presence of diseased trees dictates its winter distribution. Red-heart disease is caused by a fungus that weakens the heartwood and makes excavating nest holes easier. The nests are relatively easy to locate because the area around the hole is covered with sap. When it is excavated, the tree oozes sap, and birds also drill a ring of bill-sized holes around the tree above and below the hole, causing the trunk to become covered with sticky sap that probably helps prevent the tree-climbing rat snake from invading the nest (Jackson 1974).

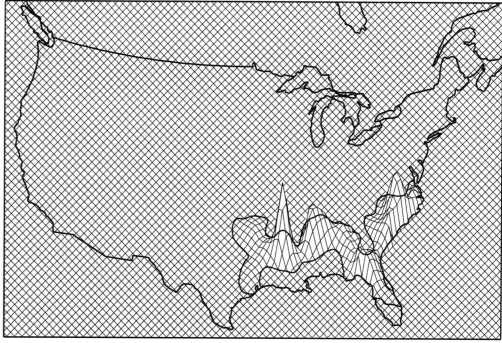

Red-cockaded Woodpecker

PICIDAE

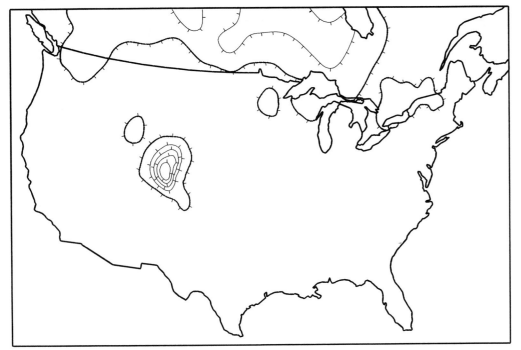

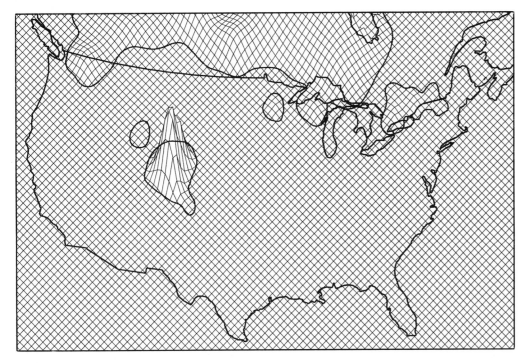

White-headed Woodpecker (*Picoides albolarvatus*) No Map
This woodpecker was recorded at only sixteen count sites, most in the Sierra Nevada or the Cascades. Even where it is most common, this species is seen infrequently. The densest population occurred in southern Oregon near the town of Fort Klamath, where only 0.56 individuals were observed per party-hour. The population with the next highest density also occurred in the Cascade Mountains, near Lassen Peak in northern California, with an average abundance of 0.24 individuals per party-hour.

Three-toed Woodpecker (*Picoides tridactylus*) Maximum: 0.29 I/Hr
The distribution of the Three-toed Woodpecker is strongly associated with vegetation; the species is present in coniferous forests. In the South the population is chiefly in spruce, fir, and pine forests. In the North the distribution edge skirts the grasslands of the Great Plains; in the West it dips south into the forests of the Rockies; and in the East it descends into the mixed deciduous and coniferous forest. The small disjunct population along the border between Idaho and Wyoming is in Douglas fir forests of the Rocky Mountains, which is curious because Bent (1939) reported that this woodpecker rarely forages in Douglas firs. Like the Black-backed Woodpecker, the Three-toed forages on burnt trees, but more often it frequents live trees (Bent 1939). It obtains 85% of its food by excavating insects from trees (Spring 1965).

This woodpecker is fairly widespread throughout the North but not very abundant anywhere within its range. The most individuals recorded on the Christmas counts were outside the area mapped, near Kenai, Alaska, where on average 0.33 birds were seen per party-hour. Within the study area, the highest abundance occurs in the Colorado Rocky Mountains, and high densities also occur in southern Canada. Because of the sparseness of counts in the northern part of the mapped region, the pattern seen in this area was determined by interpolation and extrapolation, using fairly distant count locations. The map is a good approximation based on the data available, but more counts are needed in this area to obtain more accurate distribution and abundance patterns.

Three-toed Woodpecker

Three-toed Woodpecker

Black-backed Woodpecker (*Picoides arcticus*) Map in Appendix B
The Black-backed Woodpecker is resident in the coniferous forest from western Alaska throughout Canada. More southern populations occur in the Cascades and the Sierra Nevada as far south as central California and stretch across the northern tier of states (AOU 1983). Throughout its range this woodpecker is fairly rare. Of the fifty-four CBC sites reporting this species, the highest abundance was only 0.03 individuals seen per party-hour, on a count in New Hampshire.

Northern Flicker, Yellow-shafted Race (*Colaptes auratus auratus*)
  Maximum: 2.77 I/Hr
During the time these data were collected, the various races of the Northern Flicker were considered separate species. For this reason and because more biogeographic information can be gleaned by plotting the abundance pattern of each, the maps of the major races are presented separately.

The overall distribution of the Yellow-shafted race apparently is associated with vegetation. In the North, it is present in the mixed mesophytic and deciduous forest and absent from the mixed deciduous and coniferous forest. This race does not extend into the dry-belt pine forest of the West. There are fingerings into these otherwise vacant environments along the hospitable riparian habitats of the Arkansas, Platte, Missouri, Red (the border between North Dakota and Minnesota), and Saint Croix rivers.

The Yellow-shafted race of the Northern Flicker is abundant in the East in areas lower than 1,000 feet (305 m) above sea level. The most concentrated populations are exclusively along river valleys (Red, Mississippi, and Missouri rivers) and on the coastal plains. The density of this woodpecker is low in the Ozarks, which are over 1,000 feet (305 m), and even lower in the Appalachians and on the Edwards Plateau, both of which are over 2,000 feet (610 m) in elevation.

The foraging habits of this unusual woodpecker help explain why the species occurs where it does. Instead of excavating for wood-boring insects like most other woodpeckers, the flicker forages on the ground looking for ants, in areas with a ground cover that is not too thick and overgrown (Short 1965), and in winter it prefers areas without much snow cover. Except for the peak abundance along the Missouri River, this species is most common in areas receiving less than 12 inches (30 cm) of snowfall a year. It can survive where there is heavier snowfall, but it is much less common and must supplement its diet with berries and other fruits.

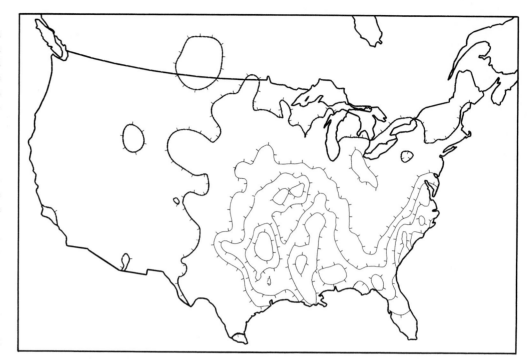

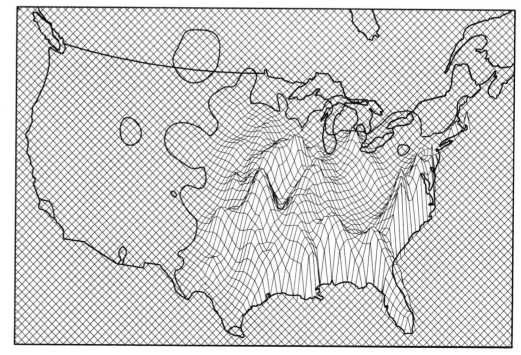

PICIDAE

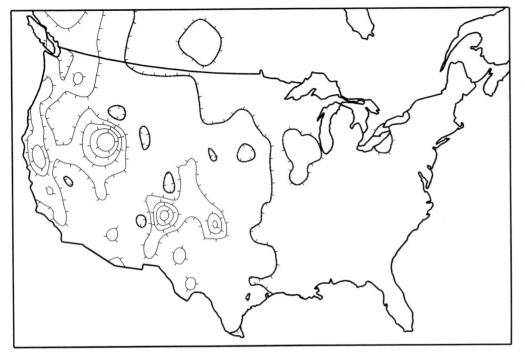

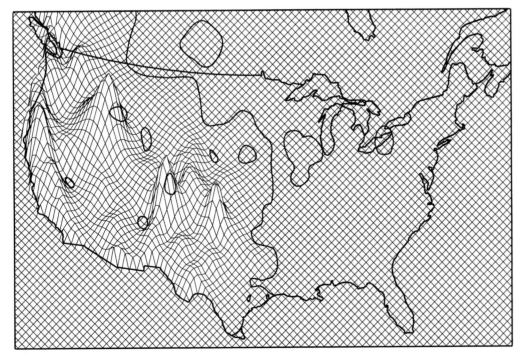

Northern Flicker, Red-shafted Race (*Colaptes auratus cafer*)
   Maximum: 4.72 I/Hr

Like the Yellow-shafted race, the Red-shafted Flicker tends to populate areas of low elevation. The trend is not as ubiquitous, however, because some concentrated populations in New Mexico and on the southern edge of Idaho occur at about 5,000 feet (1,524 m). All the peak abundances occur along river valleys (Sacramento, Snake, Columbia, Rio Grande, and Canadian in the Texas panhandle), indicating that this race prefers a riparian habitat.

The occurrence of Red-shafted Flickers in western Canada was mapped by interpolating values derived from few and distant count sites. No Christmas counts are conducted in inland British Columbia or western Saskatchewan, so estimates in those regions were based partly on the relatively high values along the coast and on Vancouver Island. This is the best estimate, but certainly more counts are needed.

Temperature seems to determine where members of this race can survive. The northern distributional edge is concomitant with the 0°F (−18°C) average minimum January temperature isocline. Temperature also affects where this race is most common in the winter; in most areas of higher abundance the average minimum January temperature is above 10°F (−12°C). The eastern edge of the range overlaps with the western boundary of the distribution of the Yellow-shafted race, and here many individuals are intergrades between the red and yellow races. In these areas flickers are relatively rare except along the Red River, where they occur in fairly high abundances.

Several locations within the main distribution of the Red-shafted race are devoid of this species. High peaks of the Rocky Mountains occur at three of these locations, in Colorado, Idaho, and Wyoming, suggesting that this subspecies avoids high elevations.

Northern Flicker, Gilded Race (*Colaptes auratus chrysoides*) No Map
The Gilded race was recorded at only twelve count sites, all in southern Arizona. The densest population was reported on the Santa Catalina Mountains count, just west of Tucson, where 1.66 individuals were seen per party-hour.

Pileated Woodpecker (*Dryocopus pileatus*) Maximum: 0.70 I/Hr

From the Great Lakes eastward, the northern range boundary of the Pileated Woodpecker follows the boundary between the boreal forest, where this woodpecker is absent, and the mixed coniferous and deciduous forest. The distribution edge skirts the area of the western United States containing grasslands, semiarid scrub, and dry-belt pine forest. The Pileated Woodpecker avoids all these environments and is present in the surrounding deciduous and western temperate forests. This species also avoids extremely wet areas along the Washington, California, and Louisiana coasts and in south-central Alabama, where the average annual precipitation is over 56 inches (142 cm).

This woodpecker is fairly rare throughout its entire range. As with the Ivory-billed Woodpecker (*Campephilus principalis*), large size undoubtedly has influenced its abundance in that it is a fairly easy target for poachers. Also, logging has removed the larger trees it needs for nesting (Bent 1939). The area of greatest abundance is east of the Great Plains, primarily where the average minimum January temperature is warmer than 20°F (−7°C). The Pileated Woodpecker avoids the mountains, as is seen by the low abundance on the eastern slopes of both the Appalachians and the Ozarks. The most concentrated populations are along river valleys (Sabine, Red, Missouri, Mississippi, and Tennessee rivers) and on the coastal plains. The location of the abundant population on the coastal plains of South Carolina also has high densities of the Northern Flicker, Red-cockaded Woodpecker, Yellow-bellied Sapsucker, Red-bellied Woodpecker, and Red-headed Woodpecker. The reason this environment is optimal for so many woodpeckers is currently an enigma.

The Pileated Woodpecker does not migrate, and in the winter males defend territories, with fights usually occurring within the territory rather than at the edges. Pairs often forage together, and the more abundant the prey, the closer together they will forage. Feeding habits are similar between the sexes (Kilham 1976). In colder areas, birds roost in cavities to avoid harsh weather (Bent 1939).

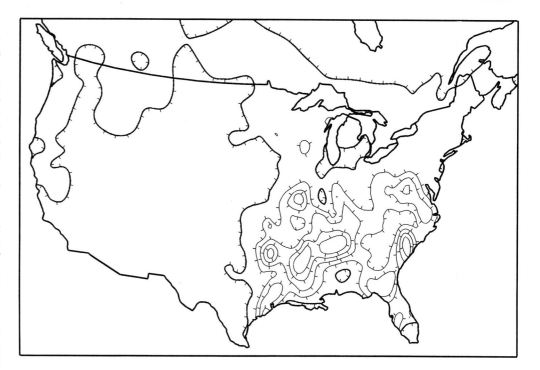

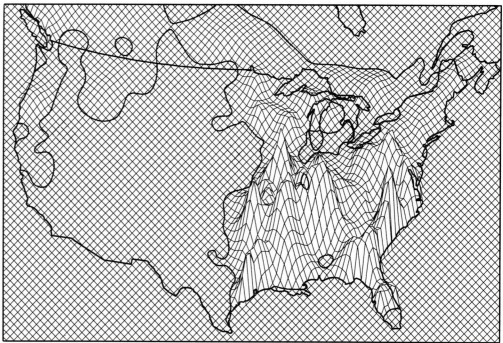

Pileated Woodpecker

TYRANNIDAE

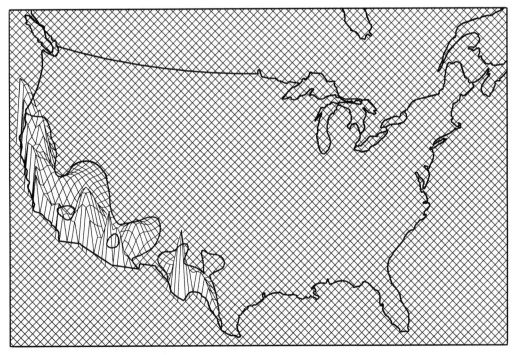

Eastern Wood-Pewee (*Contopus virens*) No Map

The Western Wood-Pewee (*Contopus sordidulus*) was reported irregularly at only eight sites, too few to warrant examining these data. Its eastern counterpart, however, was seen at eighteen sites, all east of the 100th meridian in the warmer areas along the Gulf and Atlantic coasts. Seventeen of these sites reported the Eastern Wood-Pewee in just one or two years, and at the remaining location sightings occurred in only three years. The abundance was very low, with the highest average value being 0.03 individuals seen per party-hour.

Black Phoebe (*Sayornis nigricans*) Maximum: 1.45 I/Hr

The maps show that the Black Phoebe is present in the warmer areas of semiarid shrub and scrub steppe and extends north into the Central Valley of southern California. The presence of coastal coniferous forest north of Redding may help restrict the northern limit of this flycatcher in California.

The highest densities of the Black Phoebe are at the northern and southern extremes of its distribution. High concentrations extend from an apex around Humboldt National Wildlife Refuge south along the coast to lesser abundance peaks along the Colorado River and in the area south of Tucson, Arizona. The other highly concentrated population is in Big Bend National Park in southwestern Texas, with a lesser concentration extending southeast along the Rio Grande valley.

The winter distributions of the Black Phoebe and Say's Phoebe overlap, but within these areas they inhabit fairly different environments. Plumage color reflects the habitat each prefers; the sandy brown Say's Phoebe occurs in drier and more exposed areas, while the Black Phoebe frequents dark, shady areas, which in the Southwest are normally around water. In fact, the Black Phoebe is more strongly associated with water than any of the other western flycatchers (Bent 1942). This phoebe is not resident in Arizona, but it winters in areas where water is available throughout the season (Phillips, Marshall, and Monson 1983). Over the years, its distribution has increased with the establishment of towns, cities, and irrigated fields. It is very tame, occurring in barnyards, parks, and even "the artificial canyons of downtown Los Angeles" (Bent 1942). Like the other phoebes, it forages from a low perch, watching for insects flying only a few inches off the ground. In the winter it is solitary and territorial, so one of the mated pair must leave the breeding territory. Winter territories are larger than summer ones, and higher perches are used (Verbeek 1975). Except for birds in California that eat some pepperberries in the winter, the Black Phoebe is strictly carnivorous. More than a third of its diet consists of bees and wasps, but it avoids honeybees, and the remainder of the diet is made up of beetles, true bugs, flies, grasshoppers, crickets, moths, caterpillars, dragonflies, and spiders. The indigestible portions of these prey items are regurgitated as pellets 0.28 to 0.32 inches (7–8 mm) in diameter (Bent 1942).

Eastern Phoebe (*Sayornis phoebe*) Maximum: 1.38 I/Hr

With the onset of frost, the Eastern Phoebe migrates south, and solitary individuals set up feeding territories and defend them both intra- and inter-specifically (Bent 1942). The importance of a warm climate is obvious from its winter distribution. This phoebe occurs only where the average minimum January temperature is over about 25°F (−4°C). An exception is a slight northern extension along the Mississippi River. The small disjunct population in Pennsylvania is due to a rare sighting of one individual in 1966 on the Thompson count.

The strong effect of temperature on the Eastern Phoebe is also reflected in the areas of highest concentration, all of which have a minimum temperature of 40°F (4°C). The peak abundances center on the Aransas National Wildlife Refuge and the swamplands west of Gainesville, Florida. Rather low abundances occur in the Great Smoky Mountains at elevations over 3,000 feet (914 m), probably because of the colder temperatures at this altitude (Stupka 1963). Marked population fluctuations have been noted in this flycatcher, probably when unusually cold winters in the South bring high mortality (Hall 1983). Another possible cause of population fluctuations is brood parasitism. Among the species most often parasitized by the cowbird, the Eastern Phoebe ranks fifth (Friedmann 1963).

Like the other phoebes, this species is very tame, frequenting barnyards, orchards, parks, and the yards of homes. Its diet consists of about 10% vegetable matter throughout the year, a much higher percentage than the other phoebes. Most of the small fruits, berries, and seeds are eaten during the winter months. The rest of its diet is insects and spiders. The most common prey items are bees and wasps; it eats fewer beetles, grasshoppers, crickets, moths, and caterpillars (Bent 1942). Assuming that the beetles it eats are roughly the same size as other food items, most prey range in size from 0.08 to 0.5 inches (2–13 mm) (Hespenheide 1971).

The Eastern Phoebe was the first bird banded in North America. About 1840, in Pennsylvania, John J. Audubon tied silver wire loosely around one leg of nestlings about to fledge. The next year he found several nesting pairs in the vicinity of the original nest, and two contained a member with silver wire around one leg (Bent 1942). This finding suggests that this migratory species exhibits strong breeding-site tenacity.

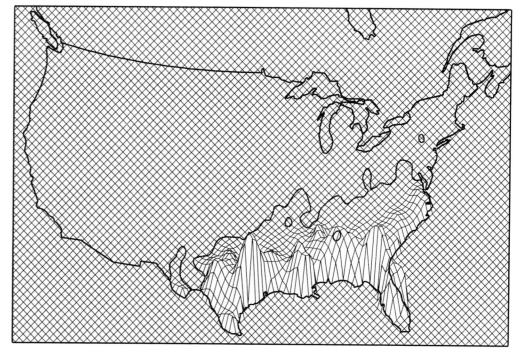

TYRANNIDAE

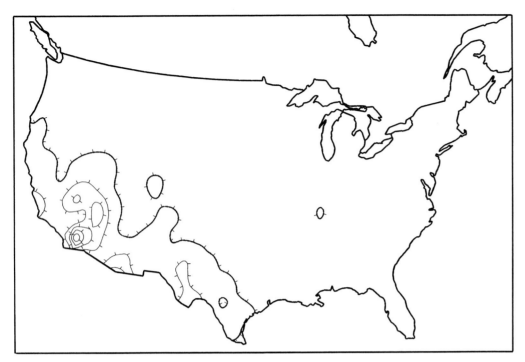

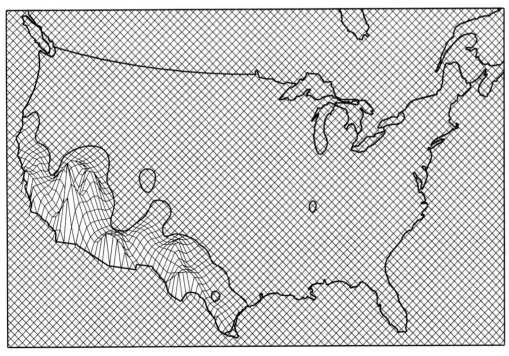

Say's Phoebe (*Sayornis saya*) Maximum: 7.27 I/Hr

The winter ranges of the Black Phoebe and Say's Phoebe are very similar, except that the latter extends farther north into the Great Basin and up along the Rio Grande valley in New Mexico. The maps show that vegetation and warm temperature are the factors most strongly associated with the presence of the Say's Phoebe, which occurs in the shrub steppe of the Southwest, where the average minimum January temperature does not drop below 20°F (−7°C). Besides the physiological stress cold places on this bird, insects and spiders are much less abundant and more difficult to detect in colder environments (Young 1982).

The two disjunct populations, which occur in uncharacteristic habitats, are due to rare sightings of one individual at each location. These were reported in 1967 on the Mermet Public Hunting and Fishing Area count on the Ohio River in southern Illinois and at Hotchkiss, Colorado, in 1969.

The highest concentration of Say's Phoebes wintering in the United States occurs in the Salton Sea area of the Imperial Valley in southern California. A fairly high density of this phoebe extends from this location north along the lower Colorado River valley and turns northwest to encompass a rather abundant population around Death Valley National Monument. A population of roughly the same concentration as these latter two is present just south of Tucson, Arizona. Populations with lesser densities are present along the Pecos River in southwestern Texas and southeastern New Mexico and south of Monterey, California.

This species, the largest of the phoebes, frequents open country (Phillips, Marshall, and Monson 1983) such as the sagebrush plains, dry foothills, badlands, and desert borders of the Southwest and avoids wooded areas (Bent 1942). The Say's Phoebe forages by waiting attentively on fence posts or low branches, preferably in flat, open country with stunted vegetation (Bent 1942); less frequently, it can be seen hovering like an American Kestrel (Phillips, Marshall, and Monson 1983). It is exclusively carnivorous, catching most of its prey on the wing. Almost a third of its diet consists of bees and wasps, but it selectively avoids honeybees. Beetles, flies, grasshoppers, and crickets make up about 4.5% of the diet, with true bugs and dragonflies filling out the rest. The Say's Phoebe ejects pellets formed from the indigestible portions of its prey (Bent 1942).

Ash-throated Flycatcher (*Myiarchus cinerascens*) No Map

Sightings of the Ash-throated Flycatcher were restricted to the southwestern United States. Of the thirty-one sites reporting this flycatcher, only two observed it in at least 50% of the years examined. These included a site in the area of Big Bend National Park, where it was reported in five years, and the Green Valley–Madera Canyon count in southeastern Arizona, where it was reported in six years. The highest average abundance, 0.18 individuals per party-hour, was in the Big Bend area.

Say's Phoebe

Great Crested Flycatcher (*Myiarchus crinitus*) No Map
Most of the thirty-two sites reporting the Great Crested Flycatcher were in southern Florida, stretching from the Keys to around Merritt Island on the east coast and to Saint Petersburg on the Gulf coast. The densest population occurred around the town of Flamingo in Everglades National Park. Here this flycatcher was seen in each of the ten years examined, at an average abundance of 0.47 individuals per party-hour.

Vermilion Flycatcher (*Pyrocephalus rubinus*) Maximum: 1.11 I/Hr
The maps show that the Vermilion Flycatcher winters where the average minimum January temperature rarely drops below 30°F (−1°C). There are several extensions of its winter range into ostensibly colder areas, but all these extensions are along protected river valleys, including the Mississippi, Brazos, Pecos, Rio Grande, and Colorado rivers. Although it apparently seeks out warm areas, this flycatcher avoids dry-belt pine forests. The disjunct population in Florida appears to be fairly regular, with four sites reporting this species.

The wintering areas most frequented by the Vermilion Flycatcher are in southern Texas and around Nogales, Arizona. Given the scale of this study, the factors combining to make these habitats desirable are not obvious. For example, these areas do not have the same type of vegetation. Study on a smaller scale is clearly needed to determine what is attracting the birds.

The translation of the scientific name is "red like fire head" (Gotch 1981), certainly an apt description of this unusually colorful flycatcher. The Vermilion Flycatcher is fairly tame and easy to see. It often sits on exposed perches watching attentively for flying insects, then sallies out and catches them on the wing. The flycatcher's diet consists of all types of flying insects including honeybees, which reportedly are avoided by other flycatching species (e.g., phoebes). When it catches a large prey item, the Vermilion Flycatcher carries it back to its perch, beats it to death, and then eats it. Some insects are caught on the ground—for example, grasshoppers, crickets, and ground beetles (Bent 1942). In the fall this flycatcher moves into the moister areas of its breeding grounds, such as protected valleys. Individuals show great site tenacity in these wintering areas (Phillips, Marshall, and Monson 1983), which frequently have willows and cottonwoods and an understory thicket of smaller trees and underbrush (Bent 1942). Phillips, Marshall, and Monson (1983) have noted fluctuations in the abundance of this flycatcher from year to year, which are probably due to die-offs during severe winters.

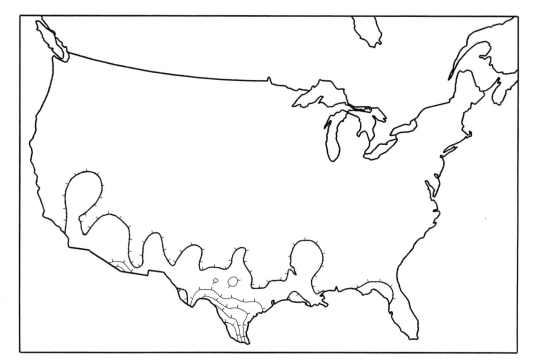

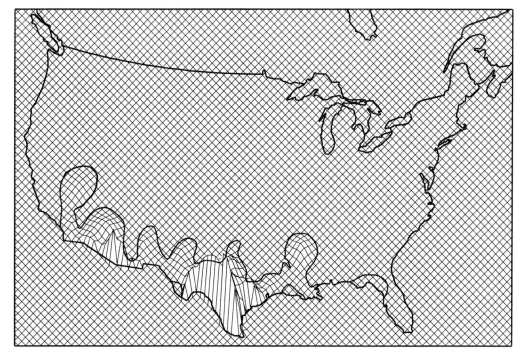

Vermilion Flycatcher

TYRANNIDAE

Dusky Flycatcher (*Empidonax oberholseri*) No Map
Sightings of the Dusky Flycatcher on the Christmas counts were limited to areas in southeastern Arizona and around Big Bend National Park in southwestern Texas. Only five locations reported this flycatcher, and only one recorded it in more than two years. The regular sightings were on the Green Valley–Madera Canyon census in Arizona, where it was seen in six years. Even at this location the abundance was low, with only 0.01 individuals seen each party-hour.

Gray Flycatcher (*Empidonax wrightii*) No Map
The environment in and around the Green Valley–Madera Canyon area in Arizona appears to be particularly suitable for western flycatchers. Along with the Dusky Flycatcher, the Gray Flycatcher was seen fairly regularly only at this Christmas count site. The latter was observed at eight locations, but all except the site mentioned above reported this species in 30% or fewer of the years examined. On the Arizona count where it was recorded regularly, the abundance of this flycatcher was only 0.12 individuals seen per party-hour.

Western Flycatcher (*Empidonax difficilis*) No Map
The Western Flycatcher was observed at twelve locations extending from the area around Big Bend National Park in southwestern Texas to southern California and up the coast to Monterey. Sightings were made at these locations in only one, two, or three years, except in the Green Valley–Madera Canyon area, where it was seen in four years. At all locations, even in southeastern Arizona, the abundance was low, with only 0.01 individuals seen per party-hour.

Great Kiskadee (*Pitangus sulphuratus*) No Map
The Great Kiskadee is resident throughout its range, which extends from southern Texas through Middle America to southern South America (AOU 1983). The range in the United States is very restricted; only eleven counts, which were between the 97th and 100th meridians and south of Houston, reported this flycatcher. At all but a few of these locations, birds were seen in more than 50% of the years examined. The most abundant population occurred in the southern Rio Grande valley, where on average 2.08 individuals were observed each party-hour.

Tropical Kingbird (*Tyrannus melancholicus*) No Map
The Tropical Kingbird was reported at fifteen sites scattered from the southern tip of the Rio Grande valley to the California coast and to San Francisco, but only three of these sites reported this flycatcher in five or more years. All these sites were at the extreme southern tip of Texas, along the Rio Grande valley. The most concentrated population was observed around the Santa Ana National Wildlife Refuge, where the average abundance was 0.22 individuals per party-hour.

Cassin's Kingbird (*Tyrannus vociferans*) No Map
In winter the Cassin's Kingbird is in fairly low abundance, even at sites where it is seen regularly year after year. The highest average abundance (0.14 I/Hr) occurred around Newport Beach, California. Fifteen Christmas count sites reported this flycatcher, but only six recorded it in five or more years. All fifteen sites were in southern California, ranging from San Diego to Los Angeles.

Western Kingbird (*Tyrannus verticalis*) Map in Appendix B
In the United States the Western Kingbird has the most extensive winter range of all the tyrannid flycatchers. It was observed at forty-seven count locations throughout the warmer regions of the country: in the South, along the Atlantic coast as far north as New Jersey, and up the Pacific coast to the Canadian border. The sightings at all but four of the locations occurred in fewer than 50% of the years examined. The four with regular sightings were in Florida: near Tavernier on the Keys, around Fort Lauderdale, at the southern end of Merritt Island, and near Delray Beach. The highest abundance occurred at the first of these locations, with 0.06 individuals seen per party-hour.

Eastern Kingbird (*Tyrannus tyrannus*) No Map
The Eastern Kingbird was observed at twenty-six sites in the warm regions east of the 100th meridian, but it was not seen at any of them in more than three years. These irregular sightings occurred along the Gulf coast, throughout Florida, and up the eastern seaboard to New Jersey. The highest average abundance (0.15 I/Hr) was recorded around Saint Mark's National Wildlife Refuge in the Florida panhandle.

Scissor-tailed Flycatcher (*Tyrannus forficatus*) No Map
The winter range of the Scissor-tailed Flycatcher extends from southern North America through Middle America, primarily on the Pacific slope, and into central Costa Rica (AOU 1983). The sightings on Christmas counts in the United States were restricted to the Gulf coast region and throughout Florida up to the Georgia border. Of the twenty-one sites reporting this flycatcher, it was seen regularly at only four. All of these were in southern Florida, with the count near Key West having the highest average abundance, 0.05 individuals seen per party-hour.

ALAUDIDAE

Eurasian Skylark (*Alauda arvensis*) No Map

The Eurasian Skylark is a very local resident on Vancouver Island, British Columbia, where it was introduced in the early 1900s (National Geographic Society 1983). It was reported on the Victoria count during each of the ten years examined and at Duncan, British Columbia, in 1971 and 1972, the only years that count was held between 1963 and 1972. The highest average abundance was 2.77 individuals per party-hour at Victoria. Other introductions have been tried in North America, but fortunately none have been successful (Bent 1942).

Horned Lark (*Eremophila alpestris*) Maximum: 58.40 I/Hr

The distribution of the Horned Lark stretches across the continent, with vegetation apparently influencing where it is absent. It occurs in grassland, scrub steppe, savanna, and deciduous forests, but it avoids coniferous and mixed deciduous and coniferous forests. This is evident to the north, where its range edge does not extend into the western temperate and coniferous forest in the West, the mixed deciduous and coniferous forest in the East, or the boreal forest between these two. In the Southeast, the southern mixed forest, which contains pines, and the oak-hickory-pine forest are both avoided. The vacant area in northeastern Wyoming is coincident with the Black Hills pine forest. Besides the presence of pines, harsh conditions appear to affect the limits of this species' distribution, because it is absent from the arid environments of the Sonoran Desert in southern Arizona.

The highest concentrations of this lark are in the Great Basin and the central Great Plains. These two abundant populations are divided by the Rocky Mountains, where the concentration drops dramatically. In the Great Plains, the main concentration occurs where winter wheat and sorghum are grown (Chapman and Sherman 1975). There are smaller peak abundances in the Imperial Valley of southern California, along the Columbia River in Washington, and along the Missouri River in North and South Dakota.

The ecology of the Horned Lark helps explain why concentrated populations occur in the Great Plains and the Great Basin. When foraging it primarily walks through open fields eating grass and weed seeds and waste grain (Bent 1942). It prefers habitats with very little cover and relies on large flocks to protect it from predators (when attacked, the flock flies up and forms a tight group). A high abundance of seed is needed, however, to satisfy the requirements of such large flocks (Grzybowski 1983). Humans have had a significant effect on both the distribution and the abundance of this species, which has extended its range as people have cleared the forests and cultivated the land (Mumford and Keller 1984). For example, it has become more abundant and widespread over the years in Kentucky, with flocks frequenting flat, cleared areas such as cornfields (Mengel 1965). Golf courses, airports, and pastures also are often used by this lark.

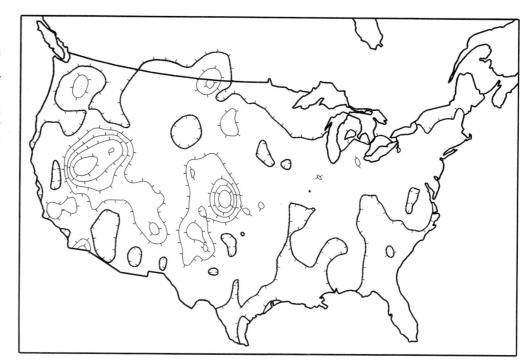

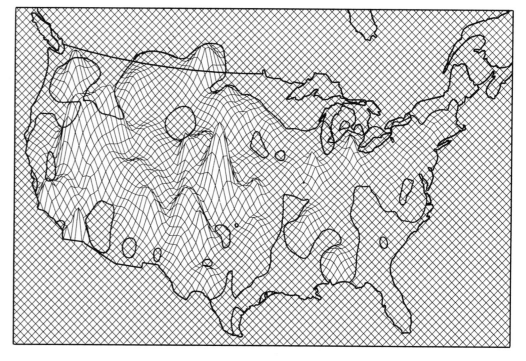

Horned Lark

HIRUNDINIDAE

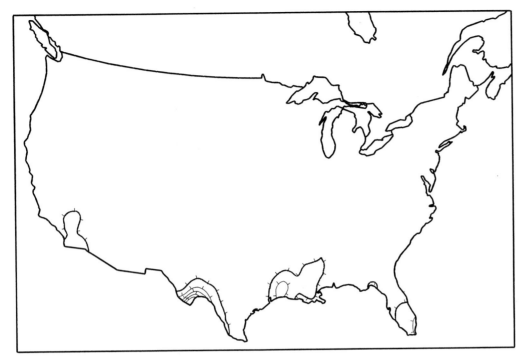

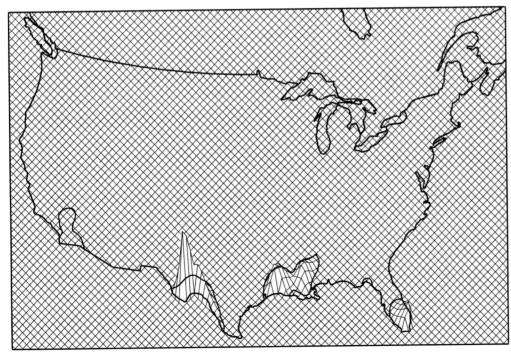

HIRUNDINIDAE

Tree Swallow (*Tachycineta bicolor*) Map in Appendix B
Meaningful information about the abundance of the Tree Swallow cannot be obtained from averaging ten years of data; sometimes these swallows form extremely large flocks, which are fairly nomadic. The locations of the sites reporting this species indicate that it primarily winters down the Atlantic coast from New Jersey on south, along the Gulf coast, and south of San Francisco on the Pacific coast. These areas are preferred because of their warm climates. During unusual years when there are severe freezes in these areas, thousands of Tree Swallows die (Bent 1942).

Violet-green Swallow (*Tachycineta thalassina*) No Map
Of the thirty-seven sites recording the Violet-green Swallow, only three reported it regularly. These three sites, each of which reported this swallow eight times in the ten-year period, are in California on the Monterey Peninsula, in Contra Costa County, and near Santa Rosa. Of these the Santa Rosa count averaged the highest abundance, with 0.05 individuals seen per party-hour. Almost all thirty-seven sites were along the California coast and in the Imperial Valley in southern California.

Northern Rough-winged Swallow (*Stelgidopteryx serripennis*)
   Maximum: 2.92 I/Hr
The Northern Rough-winged Swallow was reported from only forty count sites and was not regularly seen at some of these. This is true for the population in the Imperial Valley of southern California and the one along the Gulf coast of Louisiana. Every year, however, these swallows were reported on at least one census in each of these regions. This species is thus a regular visitor to these areas, though not to particular sites within them. Consistent sightings were made both in the Rio Grande valley at Big Bend National Park and on the peninsula of Florida. The reason the winter distribution is limited to these areas undoubtedly is partly that the average minimum January temperature there is above freezing.

The highest average concentration of this swallow is in Big Bend National Park in Texas. A much less abundant population occurs around West Palm Beach in eastern Florida. The number of birds present around the Sabine National Wildlife Refuge, on the border between Louisiana and Texas, is also fairly high.

The Northern Rough-winged Swallow got its name because the leading edge of the outer primary in adult males is serrated (Phillips, Marshall, and Monson 1983). About a third of its diet is flies, with spiders, beetles, bees, wasps, ants, and true bugs completing the menu. This swallow migrates into warmer areas in winter (Bent 1942), partly because of the decrease in insects in colder areas (Young 1982).

Barn Swallow (*Hirundo rustica*) No Map
The Barn Swallow was reported only sporadically within the United States. Most of these sightings were along the Gulf coast, with a few in southern California. The Salton Sea South count reported this swallow most frequently, with sightings in four years. This was also the location with the highest average abundance (0.03 I/Hr).

CORVIDAE

Gray Jay (*Perisoreus canadensis*) Maximum: 1.48 I/Hr
The distribution of the Gray Jay shows a strong association with coniferous forests. In the North the range stops when the vegetation changes from mixed deciduous and coniferous forest to mixed mesophytic and deciduous forest. The range does not extend into southwestern Canada, which may be partly an artifact of the few counts in this area; the only count sites are along the coast and in the mixed mesophytic and deciduous forest, and this jay avoids both these habitats. More counts in coniferous forests are needed to give a more accurate representation of the distributions of this bird and others. A bit farther south, where the density of counts is higher, the maps show that the Gray Jay lives in the coniferous forests of the Cascades and the Rocky Mountains. Disjunct populations are in the pine forests of the Black Hills near the western border of South Dakota and those of the northern Colorado Plateaus in Utah.

Dense populations in the south of the range occur in the spruce-fir forests of the Colorado Rockies and the fir-hemlock forests near Mount Rainier in Washington. The general high abundance in the Northeast is certainly feasible, given this species' propensity for dense coniferous forests, but the exact details of the pattern are dubious because of the lack of counts in the region.

One of the Gray Jay's nicknames, "camp robber," accurately portrays its curious nature. It frequently scavenges both table scraps and shiny objects from campsites. The name "Whiskey Jack" does not come from a propensity for alcohol. The American Indians called this species Wiss-ka-chon or Wis-ka-tjou, modified by English-speaking people to Whiskey John and further corrupted to Whiskey Jack (Bent 1946). Besides table scraps, this jay feeds on a wide variety of native foods such as insects, young fir needles, and when other resources are scarce, lichen. Like most jays, the Gray Jay stores food for later use, but not in the ground like other corvids. It has the unique behavior of forming the food into a bolus and then permeating and coating this with saliva, making it into a sticky mass that adheres to needles and twigs (Goodwin 1976).

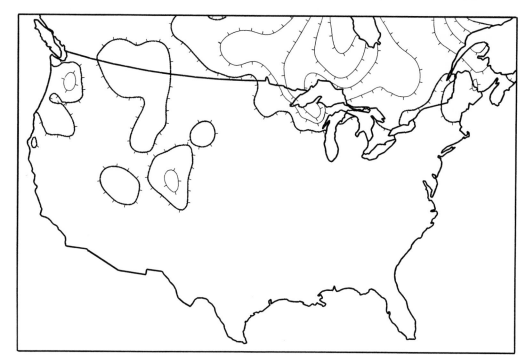

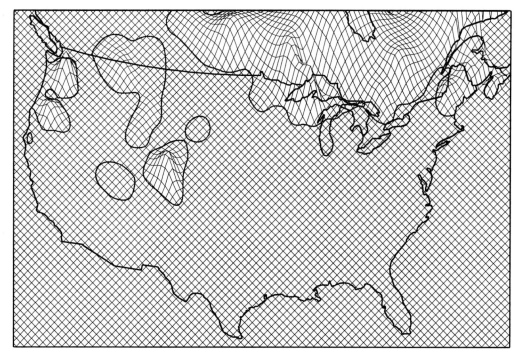

CORVIDAE

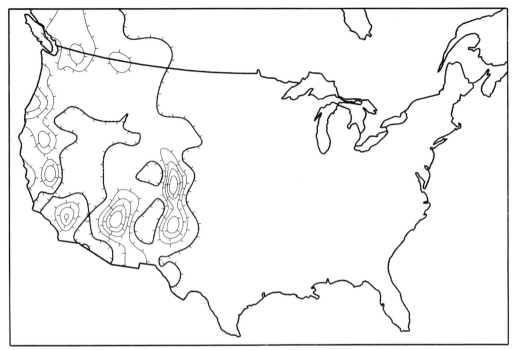

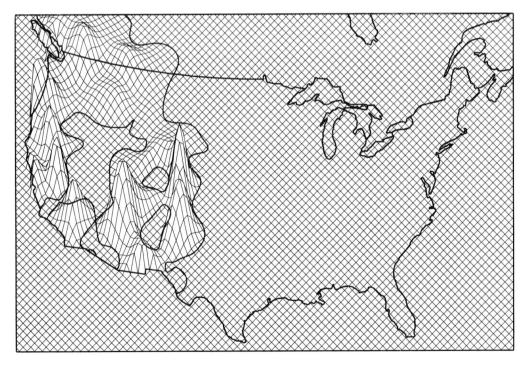

Steller's Jay (*Cyanocitta stelleri*) Maximum: 3.12 I/Hr

The Steller's Jay is the western counterpart of the eastern Blue Jay. Their distributions are basically parapatric, primarily because the former prefers deciduous woodlands and the latter coniferous, and mixed coniferous and deciduous forests (Goodwin 1976). In Boulder, Colorado, ornamental deciduous trees planted in residential yards interlace with the conifers of the Rocky Mountain foothills. Hybrid jays have been reported here, but they were not as fit as their parents and rapidly died out (Williams and Wheat 1971).

The major environmental factor associated with the distribution of the Steller's Jay is vegetation. This bird ranges throughout most of the western coniferous forests. The eastern range edge is bounded by the grasslands and even indicates an avoidance of the galeria forests along the Platte and Arkansas rivers. This species is absent in the Great Basin and the Sonoran Desert, where there are only a few small dry-belt pine forests scattered throughout the semiarid scrub and scrub steppe vegetation. Not surprisingly, it also avoids Death Valley.

Vegetation is also coincident with where this jay is most common. Concentrated populations occur wherever there are extensive coniferous forests, except in the Douglas fir forests of Wyoming and Montana. This includes the western spruce–fir and pine–Douglas fir forests of New Mexico and Colorado, the Arizona pine and spruce-fir–Douglas fir forests in Arizona, the mixed conifer forests in southern California and along the Sierra Nevada, the spruce-cedar-hemlock and cedar-hemlock–Douglas fir forests of western Oregon, and the fir-hemlock and western spruce–fir forests on the border between Washington and British Columbia and between Montana, British Columbia, and Alberta.

In these forests the Steller's Jay eats pine nuts, insects, weed seeds, acorns, table scraps, and birdseed from feeders. When food is available in large quantities, this jay caches it in crevices and in holes dug in the ground (Goodwin 1976).

Steller's Jay

Steller's Jay

Blue Jay (*Cyanocitta cristata*) Maximum: 11.72 I/Hr

Along with the Bald Eagle and the Northern Cardinal, the Blue Jay is probably among the best-known birds endemic to the United States. It readily comes to feeders, has an aggressive personality, and is relatively common throughout most of its range.

This corvid dwells primarily in deciduous forests, preferring the mixed woodlands with oaks and beeches (Goodwin 1976) of the eastern mixed mesophytic and deciduous forests, and also the galeria forests, planted parklands, and shade trees throughout the grasslands (Goodwin 1976). The western distribution stops abruptly along the edge of the dry-belt pine forest and semiarid shrub and scrub steppes, which are occupied by the Steller's Jay. This western jay in turn avoids deciduous forest, and consequently these congeners have parapatric distributions. The Blue Jay avoids the swamps of southern Florida.

Within the Blue Jay's distribution, vegetation and elevation dictate where this species is common. This jay frequents areas in the mixed mesophytic and deciduous forest that are lower than 1,000 feet (305 m) above sea level. This describes most of the habitat in the East, and thus the Blue Jay is common throughout a large proportion of its range. The exceptions are the higher peaks of the Appalachians and Ozarks, where the jay occurs only in low numbers. The western border of the area where this jay is common occurs in the Central Lowlands of the Great Plains, where the elevation rises above 1,000 feet (305 m).

The most concentrated populations are in northern Missouri and in the Northeast. Bock and Lepthien (1976b) noted that Blue Jays have increased in the Northeast in recent years, probably owing to an increase in bird feeders. Kendeigh's classic study (1939) shows that metabolic heat generated during digestion helps birds survive colder environments. Feeders provide an opportunity for Blue Jays to gorge themselves, thereby producing additional heat.

Green Jay (*Cyanocorax yncas*) No Map

Most of the distribution of this spectacular jay occurs in Mexico and South America (AOU 1983), with only the northern tip of the distribution reaching as far as the lower Rio Grande valley. All eleven Christmas counts recording the Green Jay were in this valley. The population near Bentsen State Park had the highest abundance, with an average of 2.29 birds seen per party-hour.

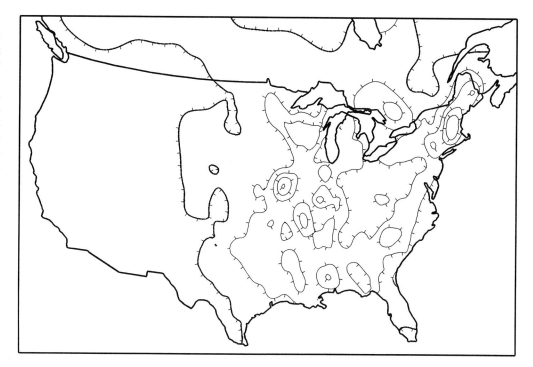

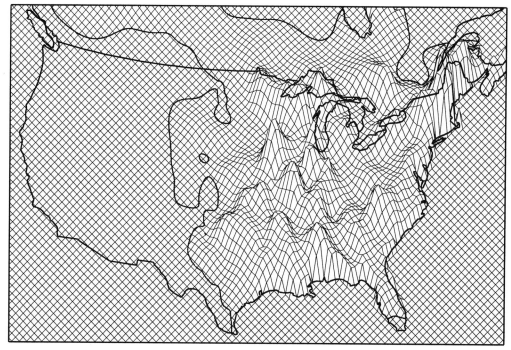

CORVIDAE

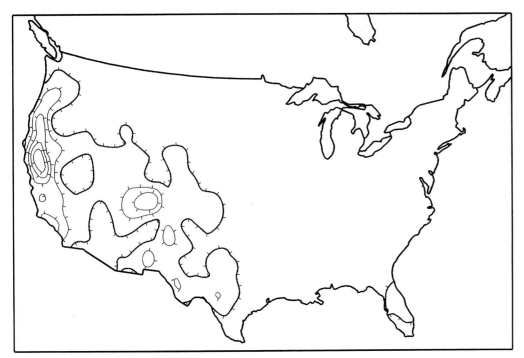

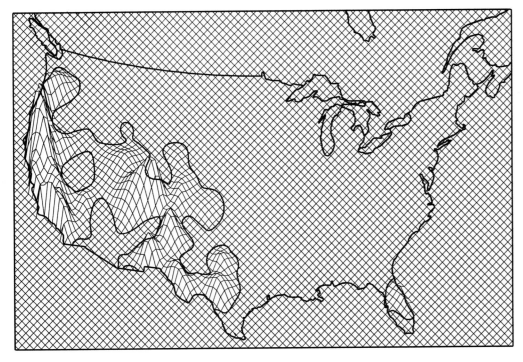

Scrub Jay (*Aphelocoma coerulescens*) Maximum: 5.75 I/Hr

The Scrub Jay is aptly named, since it occurs in stunted trees such as mesquite and scrub oak (Goodwin 1976) and in fairly thick, low brush (Bent 1946). There are four subspecies (AOU 1983), and vegetation defines their distributions. The ranges of the two western groups encompass all the large tracts of oaks in the West. The *californica* group lives in the Oregon and California oak woodlands, from southern Washington to the California-Arizona border. The *woodhouseii* race intermingles with the former race in Nevada and continues on east in scrub oak and oak-juniper woodlands. It avoids the Columbia basin, the central Great Basin, and the Sororan Desert. The eastern edge of its distribution stops when the vegetation changes from dense brushy habitat to grassland. The disjunct Florida population (*A. c. coerulescens*) is in oak scrub with dense thickets that are less than 9 feet (3 m) tall (Goodwin 1976) and contain many sandy, open spaces (Woolfenden 1973). The fourth subspecies, *insularis,* inhabits the vegetation on the island of Santa Cruz (AOU 1983).

Vegetation also strongly affects the locations of dense populations of Scrub Jays. This jay reaches its highest abundance in California's Sacramento valley, in the extensive stand of California oaks. The lower peak in the Four Corners area, where Arizona, New Mexico, Colorado, and Utah meet, is coincident with the occurrence of mountain mahogany–oak scrub.

The abundance of the Scrub Jay has been adversely affected by human encroachment. The overall density in Florida has decreased with the building of beach houses and the consequent destruction of habitat. In California as late as 1935, massive, competitive shoots were organized in the name of protecting crops. During that year's hunt, over 1,350 Scrub Jays were killed (Bent 1946). Woolfenden (1975) found that nest failure or the death of fledglings can influence the future breeding success of the parents. Breeding pairs with helpers produce more offspring than those without. Basically, all one-year-old birds help their parents, as do about half of the two-year-olds. Therefore the effects of a nesting failure will be felt one and perhaps two years later.

Gray-breasted Jay (*Aphelocoma ultramarina*) No Map
There are two disjunct populations of Gray-breasted Jays in the United States, one in southeastern Arizona and southwestern New Mexico, the other in the Big Bend area of Texas. The birds in both these populations are social, having helpers at the nest (Ligon and Husar 1974; Brown 1963). As Brown (1963) put it, they have a "tendency toward a communistic society." These two populations are connected by a U-shaped distribution that extends south in Mexico along the Sierra Madre Occidental and back north along the Sierra Madre Oriental (Ligon and Husar 1974). In the United States the highest density occurs near Nogales, Arizona, where 4.54 individuals were seen per party-hour.

Pinyon Jay (*Gymnorhinus cyanocephalus*) Maximum: 16.06 I/Hr
The presence of piñon-juniper forests is strongly associated with the distribution of the Pinyon Jay. This jay avoids the creosote bush scrub of the Sonoran Desert, the sagebrush steppe of the Great Basin, and the scattered areas of grama-galleta steppe in New Mexico. Other environmental factors like climate or elevation do not seem to have a direct effect. The roosting behavior of these jays helps them endure cold climates; the flock roosts together and probably chooses the location with the warmest microclimate (Balda, Morrison, and Bement 1977).

The abundance pattern of the Pinyon Jay is also strongly associated with piñon pines. Piñon-juniper forests on the foothills of western mountains are its preferred habitat, and the densest population occurs in the most extensive tracts of this forest type, around the Four Corners area, where New Mexico, Arizona, Utah, and Colorado meet. The concentrated population on the eastern slopes of the New Mexico Rockies is also in a fairly large piñon-juniper forest. A smaller, less extensive forest of the same type on the eastern slope of the Sierra Nevada is the site of another dense population.

Not surprisingly, the staple food of the Pinyon Jay is piñon nuts, supplemented in winter by cedar berries (Bent 1946). The jay forages in flocks of 200 to 250 individuals (Balda and Bateman 1971). The flocks, which are socially definable for many years (Balda, Morrison, and Bement 1977), are locally nomadic and will wander within a specific home range in response to the fluctuating food supply. In years when no nuts or berries are available, they abandon their home range (Goodwin 1976).

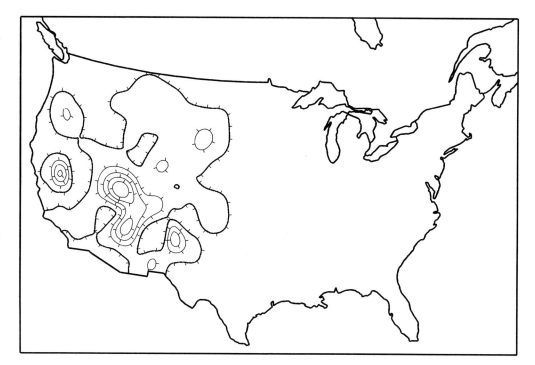

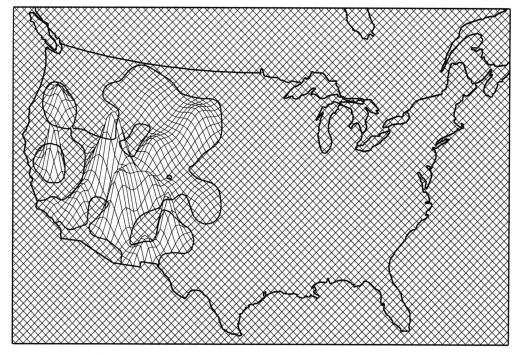

Pinyon Jay

CORVIDAE

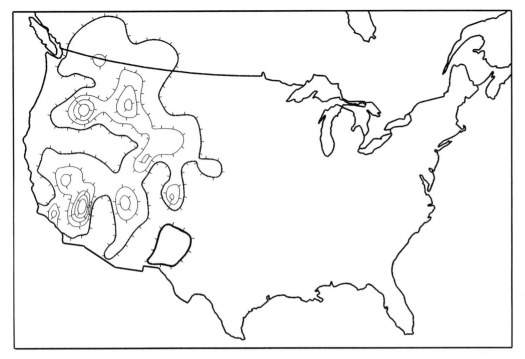

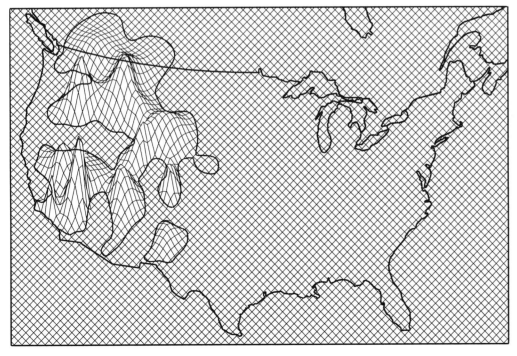

Clark's Nutcracker (*Nucifraga columbiana*) Maximum: 3.50 I/Hr

The distribution of Clark's Nutcracker shows that this western species usually occurs at elevations over 5,000 feet (1,524 m) and nearly always is found above 2,000 feet (610 m). It avoids the central Great Basin, the harsh environment of the Sonoran Desert, and the lowlands of the Columbia basin in Washington State.

All the dense populations are in dry-belt pine forests at fairly high elevations, including the foothills of the Rockies. The most highly concentrated population, on the California-Nevada border, appropriately centers on Clark Peak. The next highest density of this nutcracker is in Oregon's Blue Mountains.

The Clark's Nutcracker was named for William Clark of the Lewis and Clark expedition, who first described this species, mistakenly calling it a woodpecker (Bent 1946). It does not excavate insects from trees but instead specializes on seeds from ponderosa, white-bark, limber, piñon, and Jeffrey pines and Douglas fir (Giuntoli and Mewaldt 1978). The type of seeds eaten depends on production; Douglas fir seeds will be used if they are abundant and ponderosa pines have a low seed output. When seeds are abundant, the birds store them for later use when fresh supplies are scarce, so pine seeds can be their staple diet year-round (Tomback 1977). Nutcrackers carry seeds to their caches in a unique sublingual pouch, a diverticulum of the floor of the mouth. Individuals have been reported to carry seventy-two pine seeds in the pouch at one time (Goodwin 1976). When caching Jeffrey pine seeds, birds put about four seeds in a shallow trench scraped in the ground with the bill, then cover them (Tomback 1977). These food stores are used during particularly harsh winters and, more usually, in late spring when seeds from cones on the trees are depleted.

These food caches are probably the reason temperature and even snow cover do not limit this species' distribution. The stored food allows birds to gorge themselves before cold spells. As in the Blue Jay, the metabolic heat produced during digestion helps satiated individuals survive cold temperatures. Snow cover does not present much of a problem, because birds can dig through the snow to retrieve seeds (Bent 1946).

Clark's Nutcracker

Black-billed Magpie (*Pica pica*) Maximum: 18.30 I/Hr

Several factors influence the Black-billed Magpie's distribution. The most obvious is the species' avoidance of harsh environments; the southern border skirts the Mojave, Sonoran, and Chihuahuan deserts. This avoidance is due to a direct effect of heat on the magpie itself, which is physiologically adapted to colder habitats and cannot survive in hot environments (Hayworth and Weathers 1984). This physiological requirement is also reflected in its propensity for higher elevations. The species is present in areas higher than about 1,600 feet (488 m) in elevation, which means it occurs in the Great Plains but avoids the Central Lowlands. The eastern range boundary also does not extend to areas that receive more than 24 inches (61 cm) of rain annually, implying that this species does not like moist environments. The western edge of the distribution also reflects this avoidance, since this species stays on the dry side of the Coast Range.

This magpie is relatively common throughout most of the mountains in the West. The most abundant populations are where the elevation is less than 10,000 feet (3,048 m) above sea level. This includes the foothills of the Sangre de Cristo Mountains in New Mexico, the San Juan Mountains in southern Colorado, the Columbia Plateau south of the Snake River in Washington and Oregon, the Big and Little Belt Mountains south of Great Falls, Montana, and the Blue Mountains of Oregon. The Black-billed Magpie tends to avoid high mountains; it is rare in the Absaroka and Wind River ranges in northwestern Wyoming, the Lost River and Lemhi ranges in Idaho, and the Sawatch Range and the higher peaks of the Front Range in northern Colorado. Except in the Uinta Mountains of eastern Utah, the low abundances in Utah and Nevada are due not to mountain peaks, but to the hot, dry desert environments.

The Black-billed Magpie is omnivorous, mainly feeding on the ground in open areas and eating insects, particularly maggots in carrion, but it also eats grains and human food scraps (Goodwin 1976). In winter 60% of its diet is vegetable matter (Bent 1946) such as seeds, fruit, and grains.

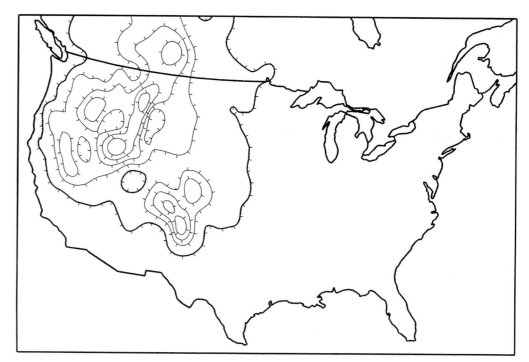

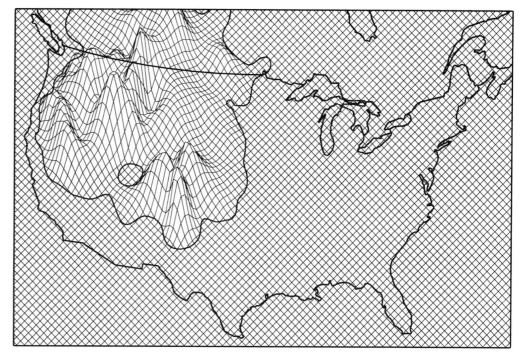

Black-billed Magpie

CORVIDAE

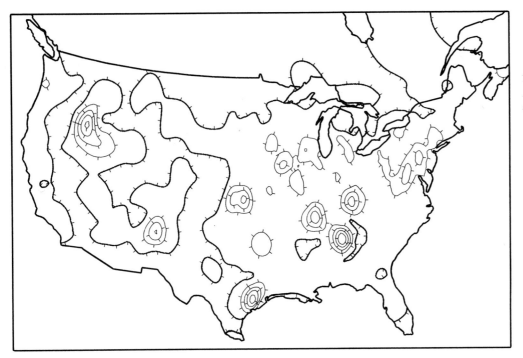

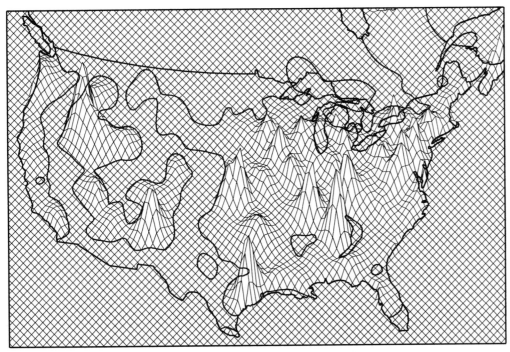

Yellow-billed Magpie (*Pica nuttalli*) No Map
The distribution of the Yellow-billed Magpie is entirely within California. The nineteen Christmas counts recording this species indicate that it ranges from near Redding in the north to around San Bernardino in the south, frequenting the parklike country of the Sacramento and San Joaquin valleys. This magpie is fairly social and pairs for life, and a pair defends its territory throughout the year (Verbeek 1972). The highest density recorded on the Christmas counts was an average of 17.74 birds seen per party-hour near Beale Air Force Base.

American Crow (*Corvus brachyrhynchos*) Maximum: 98.91 I/Hr
The range of the American Crow shows an unusual, disjunct pattern. The distribution is continuous in the East from the Atlantic coast to the grasslands. Even though this crow usually feeds on the ground (Goodwin 1976), it needs trees for roosting. Thus, it is absent from areas in the grasslands where trees are scarce. The species does occur in the dry-belt pine forest, but it avoids the harsh climates of the Mojave, Sonoran, and Chihuahuan deserts in the South. The rain shadow of the Coast Range, where less than eight inches of precipitation is recorded annually, is too dry an environment. This bird is also absent in the northern Rocky Mountains and the Colorado Plateaus. To the north, the American Crow is absent from areas where the average minimum January temperature drops below 0°F (−18°C).

Most of the highly concentrated populations of the American Crow occur along river valleys, including the Snake, Rio Grande, Arkansas, Mississippi, and Cumberland rivers, which provide both open areas for foraging and large riparian trees for roosting.

The American Crow is one of the most persecuted of all passerines. Farmers and ranchers have blamed it for everything from killing young sheep to destroying nut, fruit, and grain crops. In the winter crows may roost in groups of thousands, which has made them easy targets for bombing. In 1926 over 10,000 American Crows were killed in one week by dynamiting their roosts (Bent 1946).

American Crow

American Crow

Northwestern Crow (*Corvus caurinus*) No Map

The Northwestern Crow can be found in the mountains along the Pacific coast from slightly north of Eugene, Oregon, continuing north through Canada and Alaska. It is a fairly social species and is abundant in villages, where it finds scraps to supplement its more natural diet of fish, crabs, and mussels (Goodwin 1976). Within the area examined, the highest abundance was an average of 31.25 individuals seen per party-hour near Vancouver, British Columbia. However, a higher ten-year mean of 42.74 was recorded in Alaska on the east side of Prince William Sound.

Fish Crow (*Corvus ossifragus*) Maximum: 38.32 I/Hr

The Fish Crow associates strongly with open water, occurring near coasts, marshes, rivers, and lakes. The distribution extends along the Atlantic coast from just north of Chesapeake Bay down through Florida and along the Gulf coast to around Houston, Texas. The northern extent of the range is apparently influenced by freezing temperatures; this corvid frequents areas where the ambient temperature rarely drops below an average of 32°F (0°C) in January, ensuring that bodies of fresh water will not freeze. The reason the distribution stops near Houston is not obvious from the maps. It could be that the areas to the southwest are too dry, since they have a low general humidity (annual pan evaporation of more than 70 inches [178 cm]).

The most abundant populations again show that the Fish Crow prefers environments where there is open water. The dense population in Louisiana occurs in the swamp and marsh area of the Mississippi Delta. The abundance peak just north and a bit west of Tallahassee, Florida, centers on Lake Seminole, which feeds the Apalachicola River. The high density at the southern tip of Florida is in the Everglades.

This crow does form fairly large flocks (Bent 1946), and it roosts communally, particularly in winter (Goodwin 1976). In semiaquatic habitats it feeds on fiddler crabs and other crustaceans (Bent 1946). Birds usually feed on the ground and infrequently eat garbage (Goodwin 1976).

Chihuahuan Raven (*Corvus cryptoleucus*) No Map

The Chihuahuan Raven's range retracted as Europeans established settlements in the West. The disappearance of the buffalo decreased the amount of carrion, a major food source for this raven (Bent 1946). This is a bird of the Sonoran and Chihuahuan deserts, where it forages for insects, grain, and carrion on open plains and arid farmlands (Goodwin 1976). From 1963 to 1972 its range was fairly restricted, and only thirty-nine southwestern counts recorded it. The most individuals reported were on the count west of Big Spring, Texas, where on average 59.29 individuals were seen per party-hour.

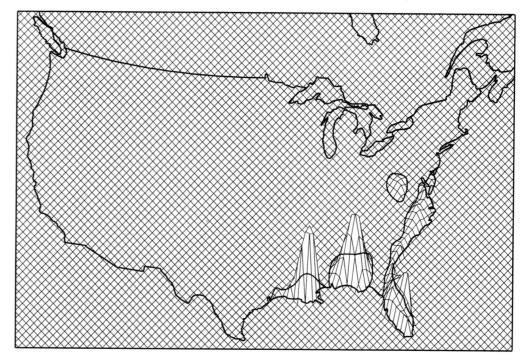

CORVIDAE

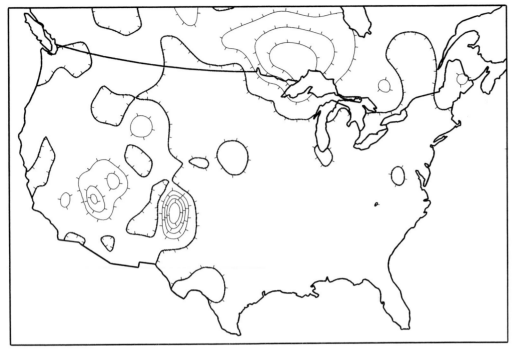

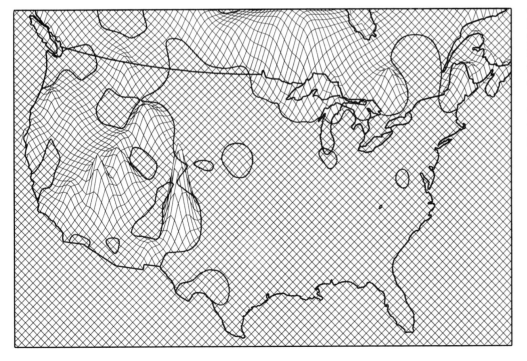

Common Raven (*Corvus corax*) Maximum: 13.02 I/Hr

The maps show that the Common Raven winters throughout southern Canada and the western United States, with some scattered populations along the Platte River, on the Edwards Plateau, and in the Appalachians. Historically the range was much more extensive, particularly in the eastern mountains, where this raven frequented areas from the Allegheny Mountains in northern Georgia to the Adirondacks in northern New York. Within the past century, it has been eliminated from Alabama and Kentucky. The widespread reduction has been attributed to poisons, baited traps, and the disappearance of the buffalo, which drastically reduced the carrion available (Knight and Call 1980).

Several environmental factors seem to be associated with the distribution of this raven; in the West, elevation appears to be the most important. This species basically occurs only in areas at least 5,000 feet (1,524 m) above sea level. This excludes the Columbia basin in Washington, and in California the depression around Salton Sea and the Sacramento and San Joaquin valleys. There is a disjunct population on the Edwards Plateau in Texas and another farther east in the higher elevations of the Appalachians.

The concentrated populations in the southwestern part of its range are all associated with mountains and heavy snowfall. The dense population in Wyoming is in the Wind River Mountains, where there is at least 96 inches (244 cm) of snow yearly. In New Mexico a dense population occurs in the Sangre de Cristo Mountains and their foothills, which receive about 60 inches (152 cm) of snowfall a year. The abundance peaks in Nevada, Arizona, and Utah are on the western Colorado Plateaus. In California the peak is near the Inyo Mountains, which also receive a heavy snow each year. The peak abundances in the North are based on good approximations calculated from just a few count-site records. These areas are not associated with mountains, but they do get over 96 inches (244 cm) of snow each year.

The Common Raven is a generalist, both in what it eats and in its habitat. Its winter diet consists primarily of carrion, human food scraps, and waste grain from harvested fields (Knight and Call 1980). Mammalian carrion makes up about 90% of the food eaten by a wintering population in the Appalachians (Harlow et al. 1975). This corvid usually feeds on the ground (Goodwin 1976), sometimes in flocks with gulls and crows, where it is dominant (Bent 1946).

Common Raven

PARIDAE

Black-capped Chickadee (*Parus atricapillus*) Maximum: 13.46 I/Hr
The overall winter distribution of the Black-capped Chickadee is apparently influenced by both environmental factors and biotic interactions. The southeastern boundary is undoubtedly affected to some degree by the presence of the Carolina Chickadee (Tanner 1952; Merritt 1981). Snowfall may also infuence this chickadee's distribution; it occurs in areas averaging more than 20 inches (51 cm) of snow each year. At its northern boundary, this species frequents the boreal spruce and fir forest but avoids the spruce and larch forests farther north. Even though the number of counts in southeastern Canada is low, the interpolated northern distribution limit corresponds with that from several other sources (AOU 1983; National Geographic Society 1983; Robbins, Bruum, and Zim 1983; Peterson 1980).

Temperature and precipitation apparently influence the abundance of the Black-capped Chickadee, which frequents areas where the average minimum January temperature is 20°F to −10°F (−7°C to −12°C) and that receive more than 20 inches (51 cm) of precipitation annually. Small abundance peaks occur outside these climatic boundaries in the Oregon oak woodland, the Black Hills of South Dakota, the northern floodplain forest of the Great Plains, and the western temperate forest in western Canada. This last peak may be partly an artifact due to the lack of counts in the area.

In the Southeast, the Black-capped is replaced geographically by the Carolina Chickadee. The breeding ranges of these two species are allopatric, but the width of the gap between them varies from about 18.5 miles (30 km) in Indiana (Merritt 1981) to only 600 feet (183 m) in the Appalachians (Tanner 1952). In winter, however, Black-capped Chickadees move into the range of the Carolina Chickadee (Tanner 1952; Merritt 1981). The maps demonstrate this overlap in distributions, yet they also show that in areas of higher abundance these two species are parapatric. No obvious environmental factors seem to influence this abrupt change from one abundant species to another. Therefore these species, when in high densities, appear to be excluding one another even in winter. The Black-capped Chickadee seems to have a stronger effect on the Carolina Chickadee than vice versa, because the abundance of the Carolina rises more steeply along the border of contact between the two dense populations.

From four to eight Black-capped Chickadees, most of which are paired for life (Brewer 1961), form the nucleus of winter foraging flocks that may include other species such as the White-breasted and Red-breasted Nuthatches and the Golden-crowned Kinglet (Morse 1970; Kilham 1975). Chickadees search the foliage and small branches of trees for insects, eggs, and pupae, which together make up more than half their diet (Bent 1946). In cold and windy weather the birds descend to feed in low, dense shrubs that offer protection from the elements (Grubb 1975).

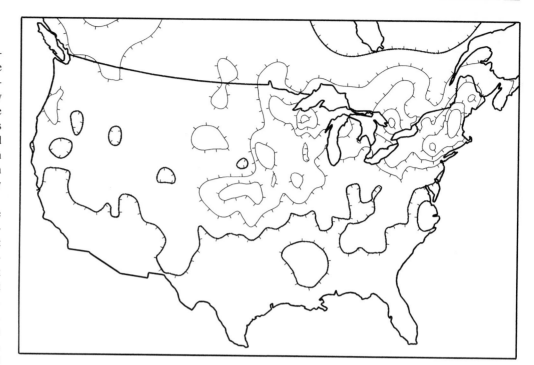

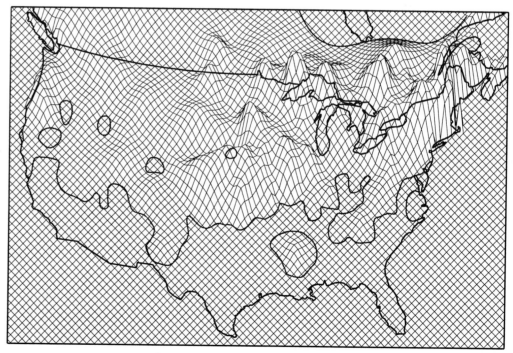

Black-capped Chickadee

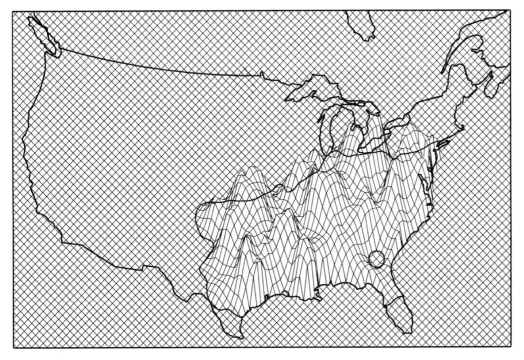

Carolina Chickadee (*Parus carolinensis*) Maximum: 4.91 I/Hr

The Carolina Chickadee is the southeastern counterpart of the Black-capped Chickadee. These two species apparently influence each other's abundance patterns, because the locations of their densest populations abut (see discussion of the Black-capped Chickadee). The Carolina Chickadee is more likely the one excluded, since the Black-capped is common up to its range limit. The resulting steep change in the abundance of the Carolina implies that some abrupt, external factor is limiting this species (Terborgh 1971; Terborgh and Weske 1975; Terborgh 1985), but no obvious physical boundary, such as a major change in habitat type, occurs at the range edge. An association exists between the northern edge of the range and temperature, showing that this species does not occur in areas that get much colder than 20°F (−7°C). Yet temperature does not provide an abrupt boundary, inasmuch as the change in temperature is gradual across this region. Thus the sudden change in abundance of the Carolina Chickadee is probably precipitated by competition with the Black-capped Chickadee, with temperature exerting a secondary or indirect effect. More fieldwork is needed, however, to corroborate this circumstantial evidence.

The Carolina Chickadee's western distribution edge shows that this species is present throughout the tree and shrub savanna of the southern Great Plains but avoids the grasslands and dry-belt pine forests. Around the panhandle of Texas, however, its range does extend through the grasslands along the shinnery, which is a savanna habitat of oaks and bluestem grass.

The abundance pattern shows that the bird is relatively common throughout most of its range, except at higher elevations of the Appalachians and Ozarks. To the west it becomes relatively rare, and no Carolina Chickadees are found above 2,000 feet (610 m).

Carolina Chickadees forage in flocks made up of individuals paired for life. Other species, such as White-breasted Nuthatches, Brown Creepers, Red-bellied Woodpeckers, and Downy Woodpeckers, forage along with the chickadee flocks (Brewer 1961). At night and during inclement weather, these chickadees roost alone in small cavities scattered throughout the flock's home range (Pitts 1976).

Mountain Chickadee (*Parus gambeli*) Maximum: 16.25 I/Hr
Mountains are an integral part of the distribution and abundance pattern of the Mountain Chickadee. In the breeding season it prefers areas between 6,000 and 11,000 feet (1,829 and 3,353 m) above sea level, but in winter it migrates downward and at times can be found foraging in the foothills with flocks of Black-capped Chickadees (Bent 1946).

The maps show that even in winter Mountain Chickadees live primarily in regions higher than about 5,000 feet (1,524 m) above sea level; the eastern edge of the range shows that this chickadee occurs in the foothills of the Rocky Mountains but not in the Great Plains. Throughout the West, it avoids most regions that are under 3,000 feet (914 m). The areas excluded are the Columbia River valley in Oregon, the lower Colorado River valley in Arizona, the regions along the California coast and in the Sacramento and San Joaquin valleys, and the northern border of Nevada in the Harney basin. The absence of Mountain Chickadees in the Chiricahua Mountains in southeastern Arizona may be due to the presence of the Mexican Chickadee (*Parus sclateri*), whose distribution is coincident with the void in the Mountain Chickadee range. A more intensive study is needed to test this possibility. The disjunct Mountain Chickadee population centered on the J. Clark Salyer National Wildlife Refuge near the Canadian border in North Dakota is due to fourteen individuals seen in 1971.

All the concentrated populations of the Mountain Chickadee are appropriately associated with mountains. Dense populations occur in the Oregon Cascade Mountains near Upper Klamath Lake and in the Front Range of the Rocky Mountains in Colorado and Wyoming. A third abundance peak, not as high as the previous two, is in the San Bernardino Mountains and Spring Mountains and surrounding areas in southern California and Nevada.

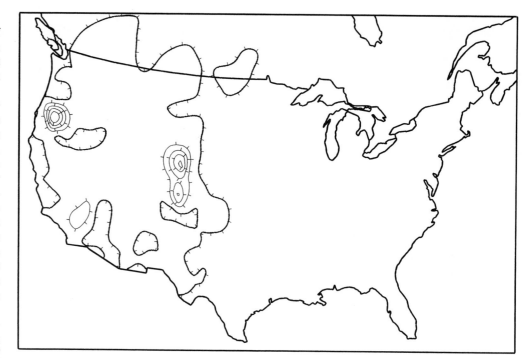

Boreal Chickadee (*Parus hudsonicus*) Map in Appendix B
The Boreal Chickadee is primarily associated with black spruce and balsam fir (McLaren 1976). In these forests it feeds on pine seeds and insect eggs gleaned from foliage and the tips of branches (Bent 1946). Bock and Lepthien (1976d) found that eight pine-seed-eating birds of the boreal forest show a synchronous pattern of winter irruptions and that these invasions are associated with fluctuations of the pine-seed crop. The Boreal Chickadee was not one of the species included in their study, but Yunich (1984) has shown that irruptions of this species occur in New York. Upon examining the Christmas count data, I found a continentwide irruptive pattern. I determined the number of counts recording this chickadee each year and divided that by the total number of counts held for the given year that ever recorded a Boreal Chickadee in the ten years studied. The results show irruptions in 1964, 1966, 1969, 1970, and 1972, the same years as those Bock and Lepthien found for other boreal species. Because of this irruptive behavior, maps of abundances averaged over ten years are of questionable use and thus are not included in the text. In general the distribution indicates that the Boreal Chickadee lives in the northern spruce and fir forests and avoids the western temperate forests.

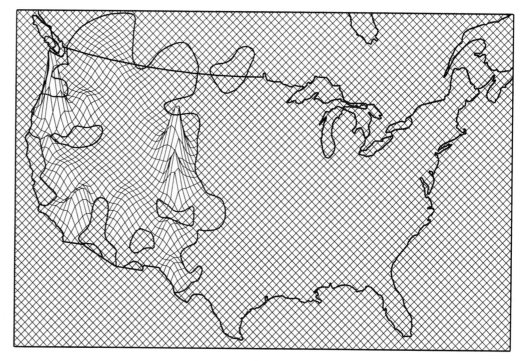

PARIDAE

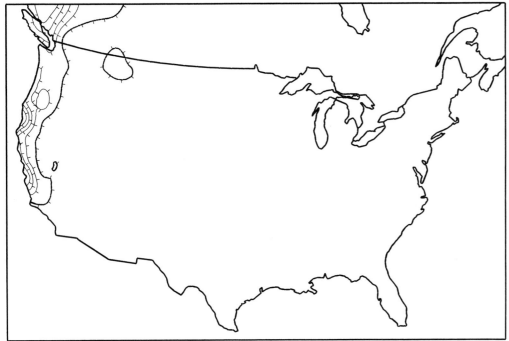

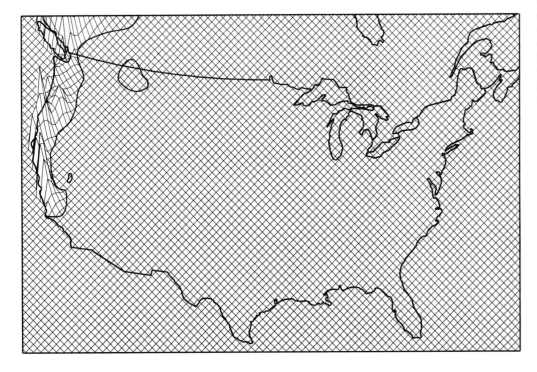

Chestnut-backed Chickadee (*Parus rufescens*) Maximum: 7.94 I/Hr
The Chestnut-backed Chickadee's distribution is primarily restricted to the mountainous areas near the Pacific coast. In this region it occurs mainly at altitudes lower than 5,000 feet (1,524 m) above sea level. To the east its range is bounded by the higher peaks of the Sierra Nevada. Fairly recently its breeding range expanded into south-central California because of the planting of orchards and shade trees (Dixon 1954). In the winter some birds wander as far south as Bakersfield, but again this range edge is limited by the peaks of the Sierra Nevada that curve west toward the Coast Range. In northern California near Redding, the Pit and McCloud river valleys provide a low-altitude pass to the eastern side of the Cascade Mountains. North of here the range encompasses both the Coast Range and the Cascades. This chickadee is also fairly common on Vancouver Island. Unfortunately, the high abundance values along the coast and the few counts held in British Columbia and Alberta have made the interpolated values in inland British Columbia unrealistically high. However, this chickadee has been reported in western Alberta, and in winter it wanders into southeastern British Columbia (AOU 1983). The distribution also shows two disjunct populations, both in national parks—one in Yosemite and the other in the Lewis Mountains of Glacier International Peace Park.

This chickadee is relatively common throughout practically all the western part of its range. This is primarily in the Coast Range, at elevations lower than 3,000 feet (914 m) above sea level. It is not common in the Olympic Mountains west of Seattle, Washington, which reach an altitude of over 3,000 feet (914 m). The dip in the chickadee's abundance around San Francisco Bay coincides with the location of the Plain Titmouse's most concentrated population. The reason for this juxtaposition is at least partly historical; the chickadee invaded this region only about 1940, and until that time the titmouse was the only *Parus* there (Dixon 1954). Competitive exclusion is probably not a major factor. Interspecific interactions between these two species are rather rare, because they have fairly different ecologies. The titmouse forages about half the time in evergreen oaks and uses its larger bill to hammer open acorns, whereas the chickadee spends about 67% of its time gleaning insects from eucalyptus and laurels (Dixon 1954). Root (1964) found that titmice prefer drier habitats, whereas the chickadee likes mesic coniferous forests at low elevations.

Chestnut-backed Chickadee

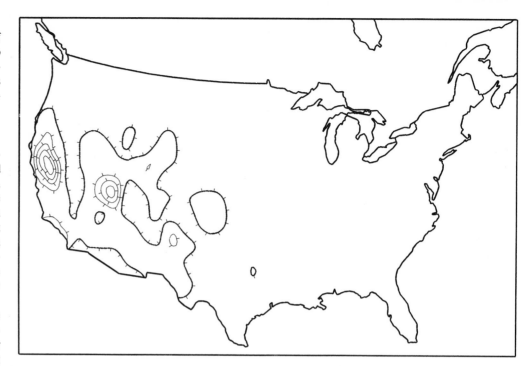

Bridled Titmouse (*Parus wollweberi*) No Map

This titmouse is primarily a Mexican species, with only the northern tip of its range extending into the United States (AOU 1983). It is restricted to southeastern Arizona and southwestern New Mexico. Fourteen sites reported it in the Tucson area, the Chiricahua Mountains, and as far north as the Mogollon Mountains near Silver City, New Mexico. The densest population was recorded in the Chiricahua Mountains (2.37 I/Hr).

Plain Titmouse (*Parus inornatus*) Maximum: 4.78 I/Hr

The Plain Titmouse is a bird of the warm, dry environments of the Southwest, where it frequents stunted, open habitat of the semiarid scrub and scrub steppe, which includes the sagebrush, greasewood, saltbush steppes, and piñon-juniper forests. It avoids fairly dense stands of trees. Along the Pacific coast this titmouse occurs in the California steppe, in the San Joaquin and Sacramento valleys, and on the foothills in the California oak woodlands. This species avoids the Sonoran Desert in southern Arizona and the extremely dry areas on the Colorado Plateaus and in western Nevada, both of which are in the rain shadow of the Sierra Nevada and receive less than 8 inches (20 cm) of annual precipitation. The two more easterly disjunct populations are due to sightings in 1967 only.

The densest population is in the Sacramento valley. The vegetation there is similar to that in the San Joaquin valley, but the climate is more favorable, with lower temperatures in the summer and more precipitation over the year. In California this titmouse feeds in live oaks (Root 1964), using its large bill to chip away bark and expose insects or to hammer open acorns (Dixon 1954). In the winter, 84% of its diet is vegetable matter (Dixon 1954). The summer temperature is important to the winter distribution because this species does not migrate. Individuals pair for life, and both mates defend their territory throughout the year (Dixon 1956). Plain Titmice are common in western Utah too, where the population is in a piñon-juniper forest, the same habitat type of the small abundance peak in New Mexico on the eastern side of the southern Rockies. Another small peak is in the oaks of the California chaparral along the southern California coast.

Bridled Titmouse

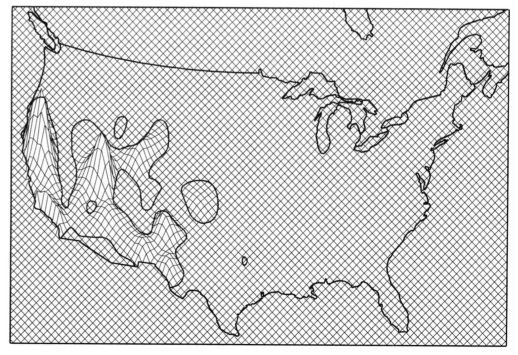

PARIDAE

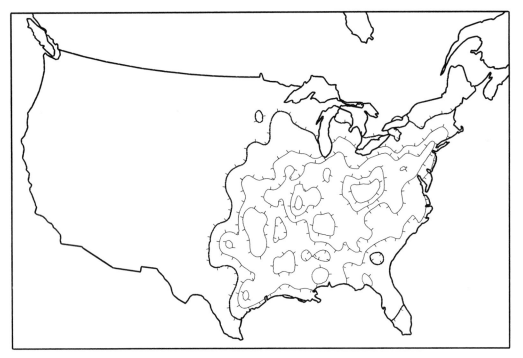

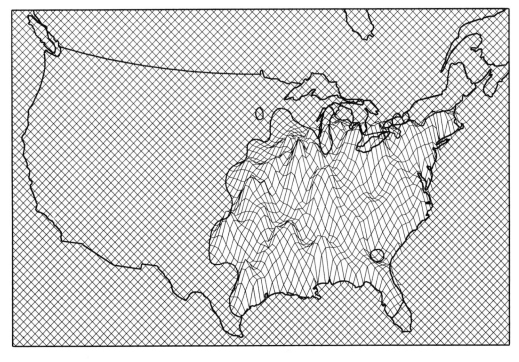

Tufted Titmouse (*Parus bicolor*) Maximum: 4.26 I/Hr

Both precipitation and elevation seem to influence the Tufted Titmouse's western distribution. This range limit, which extends south from Nebraska and skirts the Balcones Escarpment of the Edwards Plateau in Texas, shows that the species is absent from areas higher than 2,000 feet (610 m) above sea level. The association with precipitation can be seen in the western edge of both the distribution and the region where this titmouse is common. This species is present only in areas receiving more than 24 inches (61 cm) of rain annually and is most common where there is at least 32 inches (81 cm).

The Tufted Titmouse's abundance pattern is very similar to that of the Carolina Chickadee. Both have southeastern distributions with dense populations along the Ohio, Cumberland, Arkansas, and Mississippi rivers and lows in the Ozark and Appalachian mountains. The major difference between the two is that the range of the Tufted Titmouse extends farther north, and it is common in this region.

The Tufted Titmouse expanded its range rather recently; the first breeding record in Wisconsin was in 1944–45. A range extension also took place in the Northeast at roughly the same time, with the first nests being recorded in Connecticut in 1946 and in eastern Massachusetts in 1958 (Beddall 1963). This species frequents feeders, and an increase in the number of feeding stations certainly has contributed to its expansion. In fact, it is the dominant species at feeders, subjugating all but the Blue Jay (Bent 1946). In the winter two to five Tufted Titmice form feeding flocks, and most are also members of mated pairs. The dominant female and male are usually paired and will establish their breeding territory within the flock's wintering range (Brawn and Samson 1983). Species that frequently join the foraging flocks include the Carolina Chickadee, Northern Cardinal, Carolina Wren, Dark-eyed Junco, and various sparrows and woodpeckers (Bent 1946).

Tufted Titmouse, Black-crested Race (*Parus bicolor atricristatus*)
    Maximum: 11.25 I/Hr
The black-crested race of the Tufted Titmouse was considered a separate species during the time these data were collected. Separate maps were generated for this race because more information can be obtained from the two sets of maps than from the combined data.

   In North America the Black-crested Titmouse is almost totally restricted to Texas, except for extreme southern New Mexico and southwestern Oklahoma. This entire area is the hottest region of the Great Plains in summer; the temperature regularly reaches 95°F (35°C) or above in July. These high summer temperatures have a direct effect on the winter distribution of this race, because the birds do not migrate out of their breeding range in the winter (Phillips, Marshall, and Monson 1983). Other factors associated with this distribution are vegetation and precipitation. The range is restricted to tree and shrub savanna and shrub steppe. This titmouse completely avoids the forests of the East and the grasslands. Its range extends east through arid habitats and stops abruptly where annual precipitation exceeds 45 inches (114 cm).

   The densest Black-crested Titmouse populations occur on the Edwards Plateau, in the species' preferred habitat of hillsides with scrub oak and cedars (Bent 1946). There is a smaller abundance peak west of Fort Worth near Mineral Wells, along the escarpment. These highest peaks are juxtaposed with the peaks of its conspecific, which shows that these groups do segregate in a fairly distinctive manner. The oak woodlands of the Davis Mountains also support a rather dense population of Black-crested Titmice.

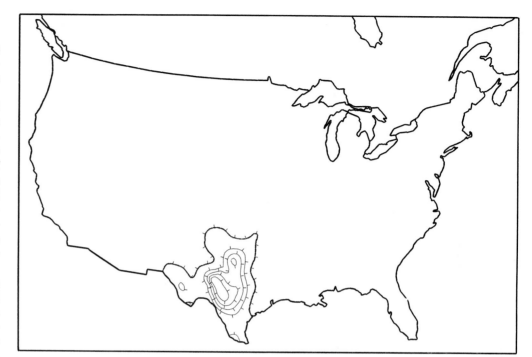

Black-crested Titmouse

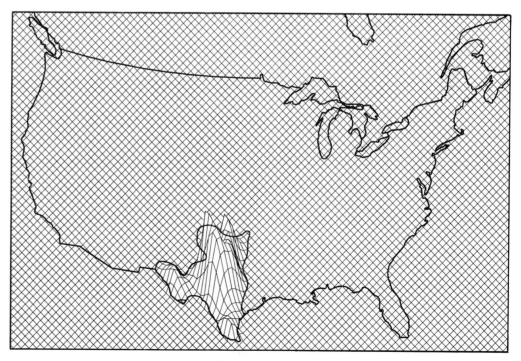

REMIZIDAE

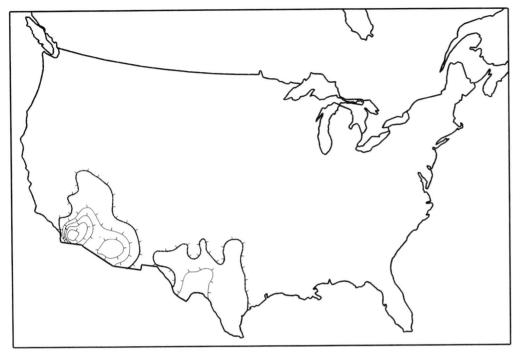

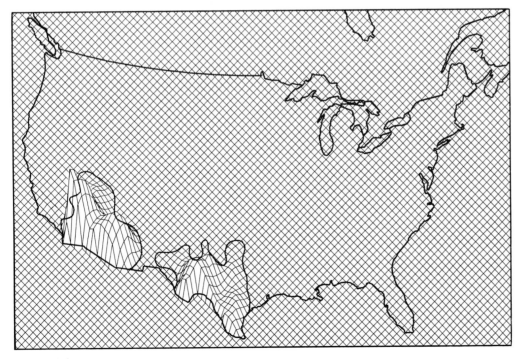

REMIZIDAE

Verdin (*Auriparus flaviceps*) Maximum: 4.52 I/Hr

The Verdin resides in the harshest, most arid environments in the United States, including the Mojave and Sonoran deserts and south-central Texas. Vegetation apparently is most strongly associated with its range; throughout the distribution there are thorny brushlands, which include mesquite, cholla, creosote bush, and paloverde.

The densest population of Verdins in the United States is in the Mojave Desert. Low elevation as well as hot climate define where the species is common. This bird is abundant in the lower elevations of the Salton Sea area, which are below sea level. The more widespread region where the Verdin is fairly common is marked by an average maximum July temperature of 100°F (38°C) or more. This same region rarely gets below freezing during the winter. Other areas with less concentrated populations occur in southwestern Texas on the Stockton Plateau and in southern Arizona between Phoenix and Tucson.

The Verdin feeds on creosote bush—one of the few birds that does—by pecking "minute objects" from the bark of twigs (Phillips, Marshall, and Monson 1983). The stiff twigs of the thorny desert bushes are used in placing and constructing its nest, which is spherical like those of all members of the family Remizidae (Harrison 1979). The Verdin builds its nest 2.5 to 10 feet (1–3 m) above the ground with an entrance near the bottom leading to the interior cup, which is lined with grasses, leaves, and feathers bound together with spider silk (Harrison 1979). When the bird builds in a cholla, it first clips off the spines in the immediate area (Phillips, Marshall, and Monson 1983). The Verdin does not migrate out of its breeding area in the winter, and it may use its nest for roosting in the nonbreeding season (Bent 1946) or may build a separate roosting nest (Harrison 1979).

Verdin

AEGITHALIDAE
Bushtit, Common and Black-eared Morphs (*Psaltriparus minimus*)
Maximum: 9.86 I/Hr

Vegetation is the main factor associated with the range of the Bushtit. This small bird is present in the savannas of the lower Great Plains and in the southwestern semiarid scrub and scrub steppe. It avoids the western temperate forests to the north, the grasslands, and the mixed mesophytic and deciduous forest to the southwest. It also avoids the harsh environment of the Sonoran Desert, where summer temperatures reach over 100°F (38°C), which undoubtedly affects the winter distribution of this non-migratory species (AOU 1983). The high elevations of the Davis Mountains in southwestern Texas, the grassland prairie in eastern New Mexico and western Texas, and the coniferous forests in the eastern foothills of the Rocky Mountains are small areas within its range where the Bushtit is absent.

Concentrated populations occur in the California oak woodlands of the Sacramento valley and along the Coast Range. Near the California-Oregon border there is an area of low density where an abundant population of Mountain Chickadees occurs. More study is needed to determine if these species are excluding each other or if a change in habitat causes this avoidance pattern. There are several less concentrated Bushtit populations, along the Chehalis River valley in Washington, in the Great Basin, on the western foothills of the Colorado Rockies, in the piñon-juniper forest of the eastern foothills of the lower Rocky Mountains, and in the Glass Mountains of southwestern Texas. The abundance is low throughout the Sierra Nevada and in the dry region of their rain shadow.

The Bushtit forms rather large and active foraging flocks that move rapidly through live oak and shrubby thickets, gleaning insects from branches and foliage. Several species such as kinglets, wrens, and chickadees join these flocks, but they do not remain with them continuously because the Bushtits move through an area too quickly (Bent 1946).

When the data examined in this study were collected, Bushtits with black ear marks were considered a separate species, the Black-eared Bushtit. The difference between the two forms is now considered a polymorphism (AOU 1983). The data for these dark-phase birds were not grouped together with those for their conspecifics. The dark-phase birds occur in southern Texas, with the most abundant (0.67 I/Hr) and most frequently observed (five years) population in Big Bend National Park in southern Texas.

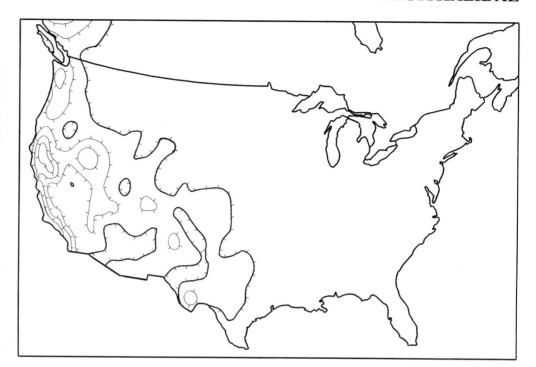

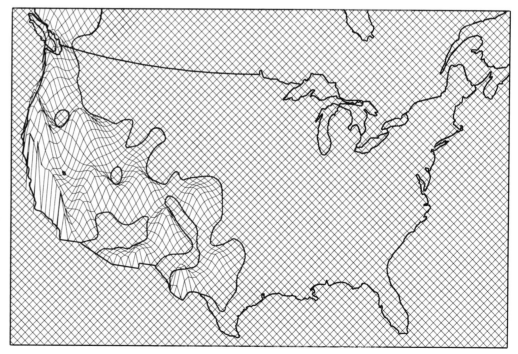

SITTIDAE

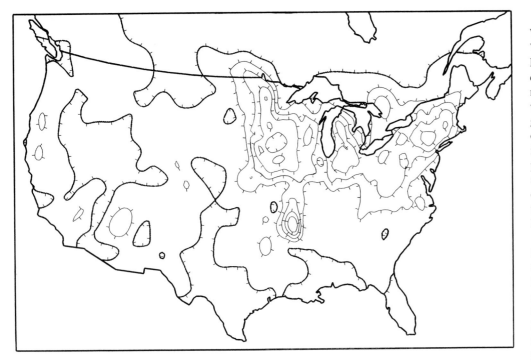

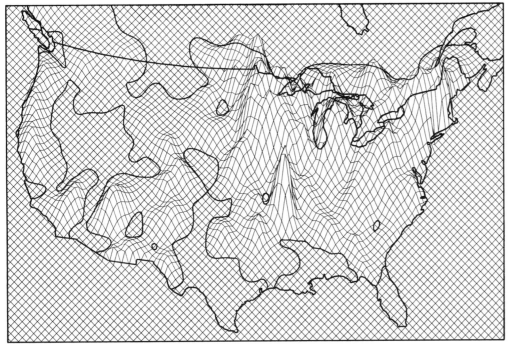

White-breasted Nuthatch (*Sitta carolinensis*) Maximum: 2.59 I/Hr

Vegetation shows a strong association with the range of the White-breasted Nuthatch. The northern boundary in central and eastern Canada is coincident with the boreal forest, which this species avoids. The vacant areas in northern Montana and southern Saskatchewan and from southern Texas to west-central Nebraska indicate that this nuthatch does not frequent the grasslands of the Great Plains—understandably, since it forages in crevices of tree bark. Its occurrence on the prairies of South Dakota and Wyoming is undoubtedly due to sightings in riparian habitats and scattered ponderosa pine groves. This species is absent from the semiarid shrub and scrub steppe of the Great Basin and the Sonoran Desert. The reason for the vacant area in the Southeast is undetermined, but it may be at least partly due to interactions with the Brown-headed Nuthatch. Where these two nuthatches are sympatric, hostility does occur (Morse 1967).

Although it is not nearly as obvious, vegetation also is associated with the dense populations of White-breasted Nuthatches. This bird is fairly common throughout most of the northeastern part of its distribution, showing that the nuthatch frequents mixed deciduous and coniferous forest and some areas of mixed mesophytic and deciduous forest. Dense populations occur on the Ozark Escarpment east of the Ozark Mountains, along the Mississippi River in Minnesota, and in the ecotone between the two major forest types in New York and Massachusetts. Several smaller concentrations occur in the foothills of various mountains.

Even though the White-breasted Nuthatch is normally found on pines (Morse 1967; Stallcup 1968; Kilham 1975; Anderson 1976) and eats mostly vegetable matter (Bent 1948; Williams and Batzlie 1979), it does not show irruptive cycles as does its more colorful congener the Red-breasted Nuthatch. In fact the White-breasted Nuthatch is nonmigratory (AOU 1983), and pairs may even retain feeding territories of 25 to 50 acres (101 to 202 km^2) throughout the winter (Bent 1948). In Colorado this nuthatch feeds on pine seeds (Stallcup 1968), and in New Hampshire it eats hemlock seeds, but it also uses acorns, wheat, corn, and sunflower seeds along with a wide range of insects such as adult beetles, adult orthopterans, and lepidopteran larvae (Williams and Batzlie 1979). It normally forages on the bark of tree trunks and limbs, usually head downward. When it finds nuts or seeds, it often stores them in cracks or holes in bark, sometimes covering them with bark or lichen (Kilham 1974).

White-breasted Nuthatch

Red-breasted Nuthatch (*Sitta canadensis*) Map in Appendix B

During years when the pine-seed crop is low, Red-breasted Nuthatches in the northern portion of their winter range move south in search of food (Bock and Lepthien 1972, 1976d). Thus the distribution and abundance patterns of this nuthatch vary from year to year, and plotting average abundance does not provide information about its specific presence or absence, so the maps were not included in the text. In general, the distribution covers most of the United States and southern Canada, but this nuthatch does avoid southern Florida and the arid regions of the Southwest. The most consistently concentrated populations are in the dense forests in the Northeast, along the Michigan-Wisconsin border, and in northeastern Washington.

Pygmy Nuthatch (*Sitta pygmaea*) Maximum: 7.12 I/Hr

As with the White-breasted Nuthatch, vegetation is the chief factor corresponding with the Pygmy Nuthatch's range. Its range roughly coincides with the combined distributions of the Jeffrey and ponderosa pines (Brockman 1968) except in Montana, where presumably the average minimum January temperature of less than 10°F (−12°C) is too low for this small bird. Reportedly, cold causes it to descend from its summer mountain habitats of 3,500 to 10,000 feet (1,067–3,048 m) (Bent 1948), but it does not migrate latitudinally (AOU 1983).

The location of mountains appears to influence where highly concentrated populations of the Pygmy Nuthatch occur. One of the two densest populations is in the western ponderosa forest near Charleston Peak of the Spring Mountains in southern Nevada, and the other population is in the same type of forest on the foothills around Spokane, Washington. A slightly lower abundance peak is in the pine–Douglas fir forest on the foothills of the Colorado Rockies, between Colorado Springs and Denver. Of equal height is the abundance peak near Monterey, California. This population departs from the pattern of being in ponderosa pines in the mountains, but there are redwoods nearby, and it is at the northern end of the Santa Lucia Range. On the coast just north of Monterey, near Albion, is a slight concentration of Pygmy Nuthatches in the redwood forest west of the Coast Range, and another population is present in the San Francisco Mountains around Flagstaff, Arizona.

This small nuthatch travels in noisy flocks of up to one hundred birds and often joins foraging flocks of chickadees, titmice, warblers, creepers, small woodpeckers, and White-breasted Nuthatches (Bent 1948). In Colorado the Pygmy Nuthatch forages on ponderosa pines by flaking bark, and it retrieves seeds dropped on the ground (Stallcup 1968; Bock 1969). In pines it forages over the entire tree, including under branches, on twigs and needles, and on the trunk. Pine seeds constitute 17% of its diet, and insects and spiders make up 83% (Bent 1948).

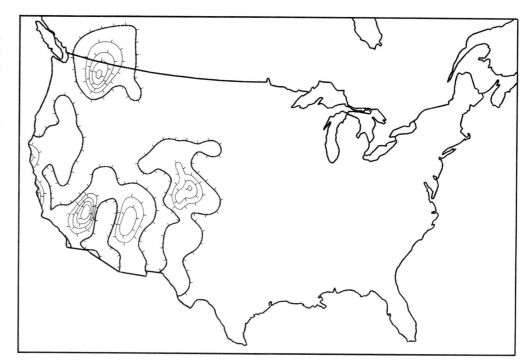

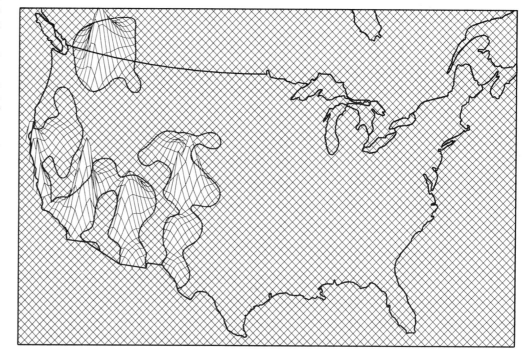

Pygmy Nuthatch

SITTIDAE

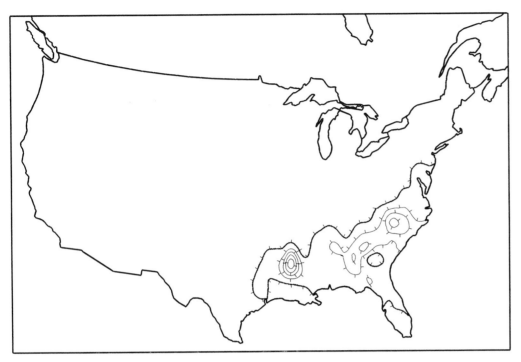

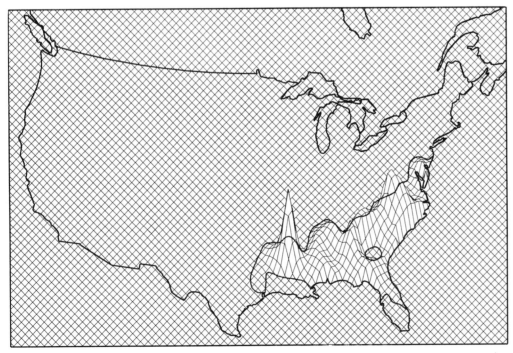

Brown-headed Nuthatch (*Sitta pusilla*) Maximum: 3.20 I/Hr

The Brown-headed Nuthatch occurs in the oak-hickory-pine forest, the southern mixed forest, and the swamp forest of the Mississippi valley, which transects the other two forests. Its range skirts the strip of grassland habitat along the Louisiana and Texas coasts. North of the southeastern corner of Tennessee, the edge of this nuthatch's distribution coincides with the edge of the area where the White-breasted Nuthatch is fairly common. This, plus the fact that these two congeners show much hostility toward each other (Morse 1967), suggests that interspecific interactions may influence the biogeographic patterns of both.

The Brown-headed Nuthatch is fairly common throughout a large portion of its range, and high densities occur in the oak-hickory-pine forest. Within this region, concentrated populations tend to be found in protected areas. One of these populations is in the Uwharrie National Forest of North Carolina. A less dense population is south and west of there around Atlanta, Georgia, and a bit farther in the same direction is another population in the Pine Mountains north of Columbus near Franklin Delano Roosevelt State Park. The highest concentration of Brown-headed Nuthatches is in the swamp forest of the Mississippi River near the Felsenthal National Wildlife Refuge in Louisiana.

The ecology of this nuthatch is interesting because the bird uses tools. When foraging it sometimes employs a scale of pine bark as an extension of its bill, using it as a wedge to remove other bark scales that hide insects (Morse 1968). This bird often hangs upside down while searching for prey in the needles and bark of pines (Bent 1948). It forages on the distal limbs and twigs primarily when it is associated with an interspecific flock (Morse 1967). The species is fairly sociable, traveling in intraspecific flocks of six to twenty-four birds, often joined by kinglets, titmice, bluebirds, small woodpeckers, Pine Warblers (Bent 1948), and Carolina Chickadees (Morse 1968). Most of the Brown-headed Nuthatch's diet is insects and spiders, but it will also eat pine seeds (Bent 1948), particularly when the seeds are abundant (Morse 1967).

Brown-headed Nuthatch

Brown-headed Nuthatch

CERTHIIDAE

Brown Creeper (*Certhia americana*) Maximum: 0.62 I/Hr

The Brown Creeper occurs throughout most of North America. The northern boundary of its range, in southeastern Canada, suggests that this small bark-gleaning species avoids the boreal woods except around Lake Winnipeg. Other environments where this species is absent include the higher peaks of the Rocky Mountains and the dry, harsh environment of the Sonoran Desert.

The abundance pattern of the Brown Creeper is one of the most complex among wintering North American birds. This small, cryptically colored insectivore is fairly common throughout most of the mixed mesophytic and deciduous forest in the East, the tree and shrub savanna of Texas, and the western coastal coniferous forest. It also appears to be common in the grasslands, but closer examination indicates that the creeper is frequenting galeria forests along river valleys, such as the Platte River in Nebraska. A high concentration of Brown Creepers occurs in the panhandle of Texas along the Prairie Dog Town Fork of the Red River. Southeast of there in the ecotone between the bluestem prairie and oak-hickory forest around Bastrop and Buescher state parks an equally dense population occurs. In central Iowa there is another dense population in a similar ecotone. Another highly concentrated population occurs just south of Lakes Michigan and Huron, with peak abundances between Lafayette and Indianapolis, Indiana, and Dayton and Toledo, Ohio. The habitats at both of these spots are localized occurrences of types of bluestem prairie and oak-hickory forest. This pattern strongly suggests that the ecotone between these two vegetation types is the Brown Creeper's optimal habitat. Low abundances in the eastern half of the study area occur in the swamp forest of the Mississippi valley, in the southern mixed forest in the South, and in central Oklahoma. The abundance in the West is generally low except that concentrated populations do occur in dry-belt pine forests, such as in the foothills of the Colorado Rockies, and in the coastal conifers. The abundance peak on the border between Montana and Alberta is in the Waterton–Glacier International Peace Park area.

In the winter creepers often join foraging flocks of chickadees, titmice, nuthatches, kinglets, and small woodpeckers (Bent 1948), but they eat many more insects than most, if not all, of these species. A large proportion of their diet consists of ants, small homopterans, adult hemipterans, and spiders, along with small amounts of acorns and corn (Williams and Batzlie 1979). This creeper forages primarily on tree trunks (Willson 1970), starting near the ground and usually spiraling up to the top. Suet and seeds at feeders attract the Brown Creeper (Bent 1948).

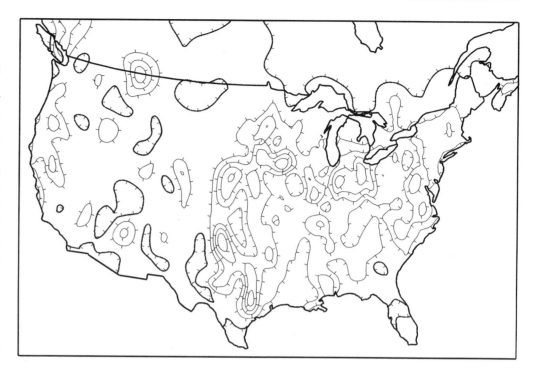

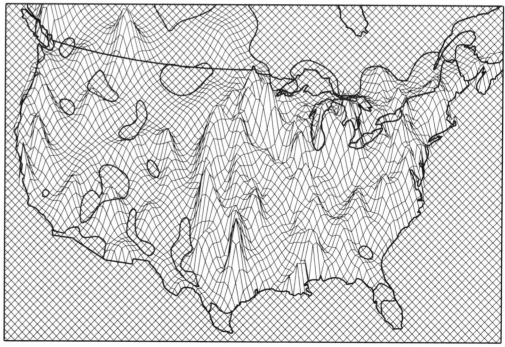

Brown Creeper

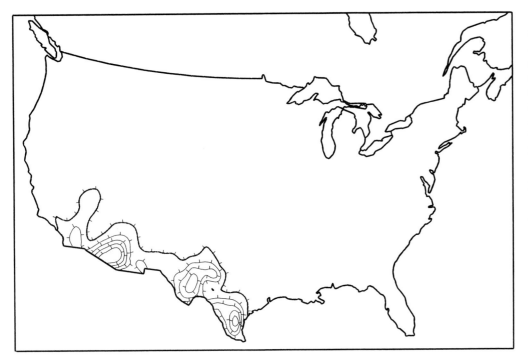

TROGLODYTIDAE

Cactus Wren (*Campylorhynchus brunneicapillus*) Maximum: 4.09 I/Hr
Aside from its being present in the mesquite-acacia scrub of the tree and shrub savanna of extreme southern Texas, the range of the Cactus Wren is strongly coincident with the distribution of creosote bush. This includes southern California and southern Arizona, where paloverde and cactus scrub are scattered throughout the range of the creosote bush; southeastern Arizona and southern New Mexico, where grama grass is mixed in with the creosote bush; and the shrub steppe of southwestern Texas, which is made up of blackbrush and creosote bush.

The Cactus Wren occurs in high abundance over a large portion of its distribution, but all the most concentrated populations are in regions that have minimum January temperatures higher than 30°F (−1°C). One of the two highest abundance peaks is in the mesquite-acacia scrub of southern Texas around Alice, and the other stretches through southern Arizona from Organ Pipe Cactus National Monument to Tucson. A slightly less dense population is in the shrub steppe of Texas from between Santiago Peak and the Glass Mountains to the Midland-Odessa area, with a lesser concentration extending over to San Angelo. There are slight concentrations in both southwestern New Mexico and the Imperial Valley of southern California.

The Cactus Wren builds its nest in thorny shrubs, including cacti (Bent 1948). Early in the breeding season when the desert is still cool, the entrance of the nest is built away from the cold prevailing winds. Late-breeding individuals orient the entrance to face the wind, which helps dissipate the heat inside the nest during the late summer (Ricklefs and Hainsworth 1969), making breeding more successful (Austin 1973). Besides a nest for raising young, each wren has a roosting nest, particularly in the winter. These nests are enclosed and pouch shaped, with the entrance away from the bush (Anderson and Anderson 1957). In the winter small flocks form, consisting of a paired female and male, their offspring of the past summer, and perhaps a few outsiders. The roosting nests of the mated pair are usually built close together, frequently in the same cholla (Anderson and Anderson 1957). The group forages throughout a 15 acre (61 km²) area (Anderson and Anderson 1957), searching under organic litter on the ground for beetles, ants, weevils, grasshoppers, bugs, and a few spiders. Only about 17% of this wren's diet is vegetable matter, such as cactus fruit and berries (Bent 1948).

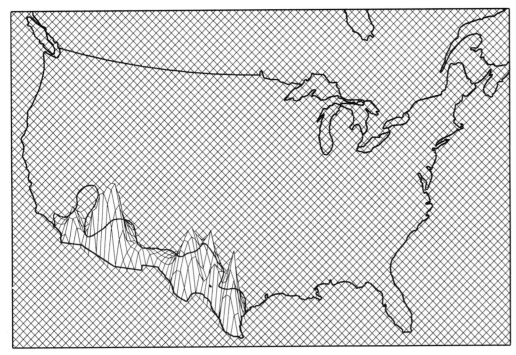

Rock Wren (*Salpinctes obsoletus*) Maximum: 1.42 I/Hr

As its name suggests, the Rock Wren frequents exposed and bare rocky outcrops within its distribution, which encompasses the drier areas of the United States. Throughout most of its range the general humidity is low, with a pan evaporation measure of over 80 inches (203 cm), and except along the Pacific coast, the annual precipitation is under 24 inches (61 cm). Throughout most of the range, but again not in central California, the vegetation consists mainly of creosote bush and paloverde-cactus scrub. In California this wren occurs in mixed evergreen and deciduous forest. Except for the disjunct populations, the regions frequented are fairly warm, with the minimum January temperature rarely falling below 20°F (−7°C).

Sparse vegetation appears to be the chief factor determining where concentrated populations of Rock Wrens occur. The highest abundance peaks are in southwestern Texas in the shrub steppe of blackbrush and creosote bush west of the Davis Mountains and east of the Chisos Mountains in Big Bend National Park. Fairly high concentrations also occur around San Angelo, Texas, in southern Arizona from Nogales to about Organ Pipe Cactus National Monument, and in the canyon lands of the Colorado River in southern Utah.

Unfortunately, little research has been done on this wren. It probably is exclusively an insectivore, eating spiders, beetles, worms, and grasshoppers that it finds in the crevices of rocks (Bent 1948). It rarely if ever drinks water, probably getting the necessary fluid from the insects it eats and decreasing the loss of body moisture by frequenting cooler microhabitats in the deserts (Smyth and Bartholomew 1966).

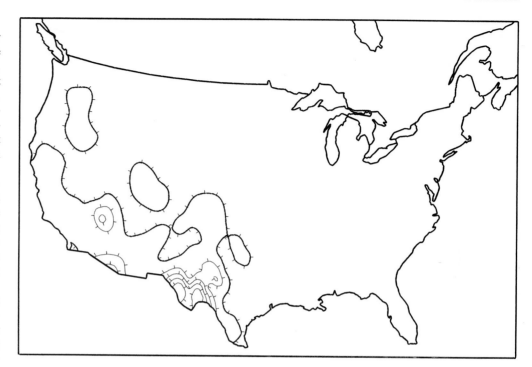
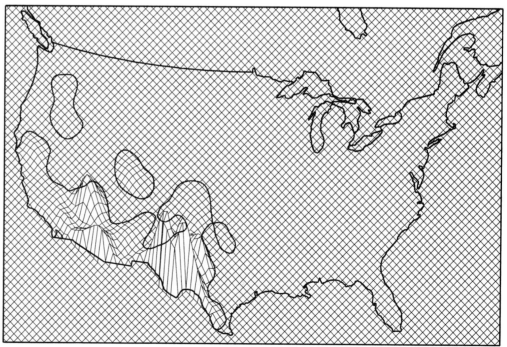

TROGLODYTIDAE

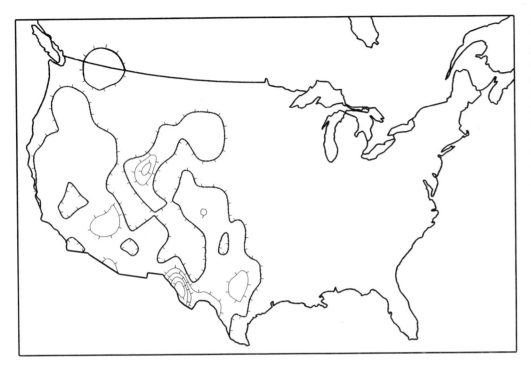

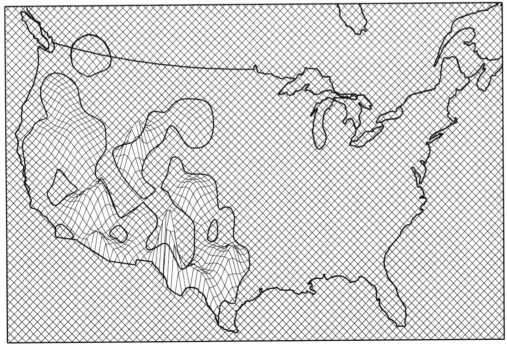

Canyon Wren (*Catherpes mexicanus*) Maximum: 0.96 I/Hr

The distribution of the Canyon Wren indicates its apparent predilection for elevations roughly over 1,000 feet (305 m) but under 9,000 feet (2,743 m) and shows that it frequents areas with low general humidity (a pan evaporation rate of more than 75 inches [190 cm]). The high precipitation on the Pacific coast, over 40 inches (102 cm) annually, apparently precludes its occurrence along the seaboard north of Monterey Bay. The eastern limit of this wren's distribution runs along the edge of the Edwards Plateau and then shifts westward with the drier climate. In South Dakota there is an extension into the Black Hills. Vacant areas in Colorado, New Mexico, and Wyoming may be due to this bird's avoiding the higher elevations of the Rocky Mountains. The small disjunct population is made up of individuals regularly seen in the mountains outside Spokane, Washington.

High concentrations of this wren are restricted to a very small portion of the overall distribution, and several of these are in managed locations such as national parks and recreational areas. The highest abundance is in the Chihuahuan Desert of southwestern Texas, the apex covering the area between two national parks—Guadalupe Mountain and Big Bend—with high counts in the Guadalupe, Davis, and Chisos mountains. A slighter concentration continues southeast in the Chihuahuan Desert along the Rio Grande. All the birds in this concentrated population are members of the white-throated race of Canyon Wren (*C. m. albifrons*) (Bent 1948; AOU 1957). A lesser abundance peak is associated with the Flaming Gorge National Recreation Area on the border between Utah and Wyoming. Lower concentrations occur along the Colorado River in Grand Canyon National Park and Lake Mead National Recreational Area, around Organ Pipe Cactus National Monument, in southeastern Colorado and northwestern Oklahoma near Black Mesa, the highest point in Oklahoma, and in central Texas on the eastern side of the Edwards Plateau along the escarpment carved by the Colorado River.

Like that of most wrens, the ecology of the Canyon Wren has not been well studied. Its diet probably consists chiefly, and perhaps entirely, of insects and spiders gleaned from rocks and low-growing plants (Bent 1948).

Canyon Wren

Carolina Wren (*Thryothorus ludovicianus*) Maximum: 2.45 I/Hr

Temperature is the factor most strongly associated with both the distribution and abundance patterns of the Carolina Wren. The northern range limit shows that this wren is absent where the average minimum January temperatures drops below 10°F (−12°C). Examination of the data from individual counts shows that regular sightings were recorded only where this winter temperature is above 20°F (−7°C). The irregular sightings in colder areas are probably of young individuals that disperse into these regions and survive relatively warm winters but die during colder years (Bent 1948). Subsequently, dispersing young reinhabit these colder areas, and the cycle begins again. The extension into these colder northern regions was first noted in the early 1900s (Bent 1948). The disjunct population around Quebec City, Quebec, was due to a rare sighting of one individual in 1972. The western side of the distribution indicates that this wren occurs in areas receiving at least 20 inches (51 cm) of precipitation annually.

The Carolina Wren is fairly abundant throughout most of its distribution. Most of the areas with higher concentrations have an average minimum January temperature over 25°F (−4°C). Elevation is also associated with the abundance pattern, because this wren is fairly common around the Ozarks but in low abundance at the higher elevations. The highest and most extensive population is in the area of the eastern United States that receives more than 56 inches (142 cm) of precipitation annually. This abundant population stretches from around the William Dannelly Reservoir in Alabama to near Baton Rouge, Louisiana. Another equally high, but much less extensive, peak is on the northern Louisiana border.

Unlike the House Wren, the Carolina Wren is not often found around houses but prefers the more secluded environment of the forests. It is shy but curious and often responds to "pishing." It is an active bird that usually makes only short flights and often climbs trees much as Brown Creepers do. Its diet consists primarily of hemipterans—including stinkbugs and leafhoppers—caterpillars, beetles, ants, bees, wasps, grasshoppers, and spiders, along with a few seeds and berries (Bent 1948).

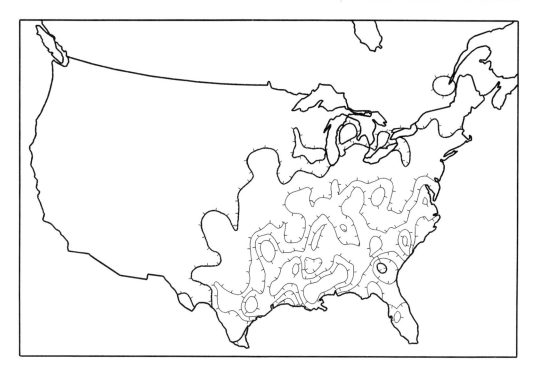

Carolina Wren

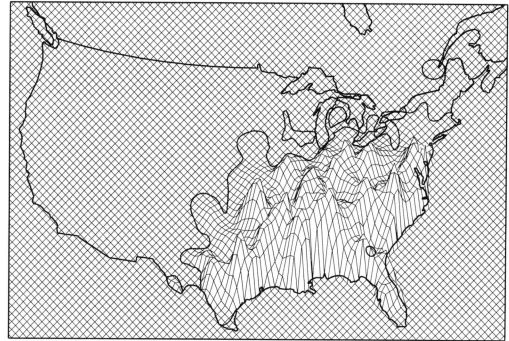

TROGLODYTIDAE

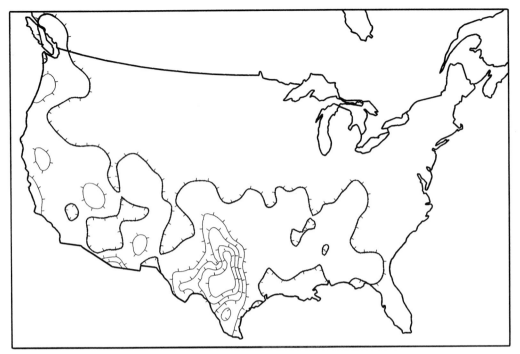

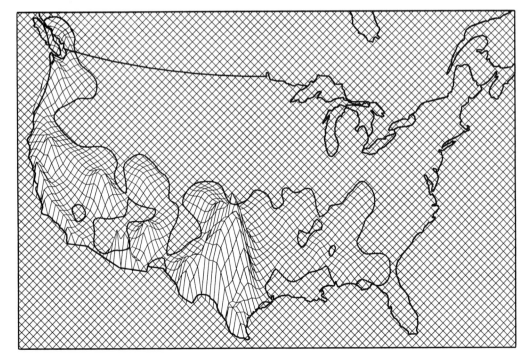

Bewick's Wren (*Thryomanes bewickii*) Maximum: 1.62 I/Hr

It is easier to name the factors not correlated with the distribution of the Bewick's Wren than to name those that are. Temperature, precipitation, snowfall, and vegetation show no obvious association with the range of this species, though it is absent from higher elevations like the Rocky Mountains and the Colorado Plateaus. Part of the eastern range limit appears to abut the Appalachians.

The abundance pattern of the Bewick's Wren is dominated by a large and extensive concentration of birds in central Texas, on the western side of the tree and scrub savanna and spilling over into the shrub steppe of southwestern Texas. This wren appears to avoid the grasslands and the eastern part of the tree and scrub savanna, where the high concentrations of Carolina Wrens are found. A less concentrated population of Bewick's Wrens occurs in the desert around Nogales, Arizona, and populations with even lower abundance are present along the California coast, in the northern part of the Central Valley of California, along the coast of northern Oregon and southern Washington, and in the deserts of western New Mexico and southern Nevada.

The Bewick's Wren shows aggression toward both the Carolina Wren (Bent 1948) and the House Wren (Bent 1948; Root 1969). The maps for those species show some evidence of these biotic interactions. The Bewick's Wren avoids Florida and southern Louisiana and shows a depression in abundance in southern Texas, the same locations where the House Wren is most abundant. A similar replacement of these two species in winter was seen in a finer-scale study, where it was noted that the Bewick's Wren moved into the habitat left vacant by the migrating House Wren. In these areas the former would construct nests in the spring only to be driven out into adjacent areas when the House Wrens returned. In years of low House Wren abundance these two species would co-occur during the breeding season (Root 1969). Bent (1948) reports that when the House Wren is not present the Bewick's Wren occurs in open woodlands, near houses, in fencerows and the like, but when the House Wren is present the Bewick's Wren is relegated to swampy woodlands. The western end of the area where the Carolina Wren is more concentrated roughly abuts the eastern edge of the range of the Bewick's Wren. More study is needed before interspecific interaction and not some other factor, such as habitat preference, can be shown to cause this juxtaposition.

Like the other wrens, the Bewick's Wren is an insectivore that frequents the lower branches of trees and bushes (Bent 1948). When foraging, it gleans insects from branches and foliage, turns over dead leaves on the ground, and sometimes digs for insects in bark crevices. It remains territorial throughout the year and often roosts in cavities (Miller 1941).

Bewick's Wren

House Wren (*Troglodytes aedon*) Maximum: 1.06 I/Hr

The major part of the House Wren's distribution occurs where the winter temperature is over 30°F (−1°C). Exceptions include the disjunct populations and the individuals a bit inland from the Pacific coast, most of which are in regions where the average minimum January temperature is at least 20°F (−7°C). All the disjunct populations that are regularly reported are in protected valleys. These include the Rio Grande valley in New Mexico, along the Columbia River on the border between Oregon and Washington, and what was previously the Colorado River valley and is now Lake Mead in southern Nevada. This last population appears more extensive on the maps than it probably is because of the lack of census sites in Nevada. There were reports from several sites in both of the two disjunct distributions in the East, but not one of these reported this wren regularly.

All the higher concentrations of the wintering House Wren are in areas where the January temperature is normally over 40°F (4°C), and all the highest peaks are near regions where 50°F (10°C) is usually the low. One of the densest populations is on the coast of southeastern Florida, from around West Palm Beach on south. The other extremely concentrated population is on the southern coast of Louisiana, in the bayous just west of the mouth of the Mississippi River. A much smaller abundance peak is in southern Texas. Two very slight concentrations occur on the Pecos River near the Texas–New Mexico border and along the coast near the border between North and South Carolina.

This is by far the most familiar wren to the general populace, because of its propensity to nest in wren boxes and to forage in ornamental bushes planted in yards and parks. This relationship between the House Wren and people is mutualistic, because the wren eats stinkbugs, leafhoppers, grasshoppers, caterpillars, beetles, and spiders. In winter it becomes shier and more quiet, and besides migrating south into warmer climates, it also moves away from human populations into the undergrowth of forests or, in Florida, into palmetto thickets. Large numbers of migrating birds die en route because they run into tall structures such as buildings and bridges. The overall abundance declined as the House Sparrow became established, because this more aggressive passerine was able to displace the wren from nest holes (Bent 1948).

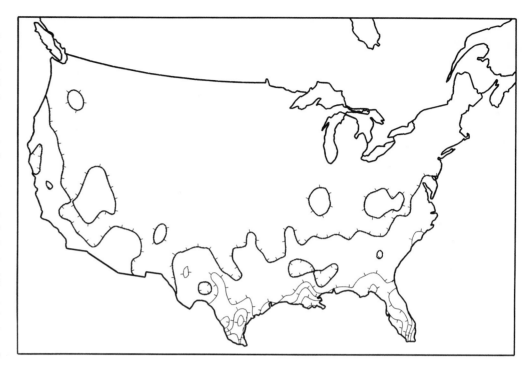

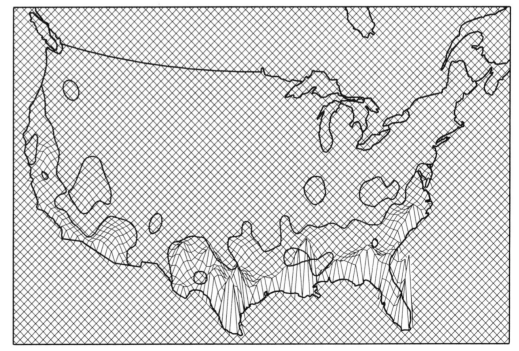

TROGLODYTIDAE

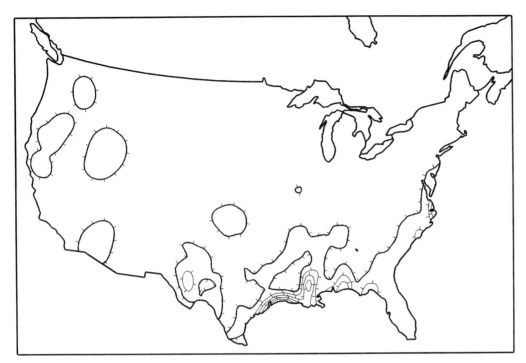

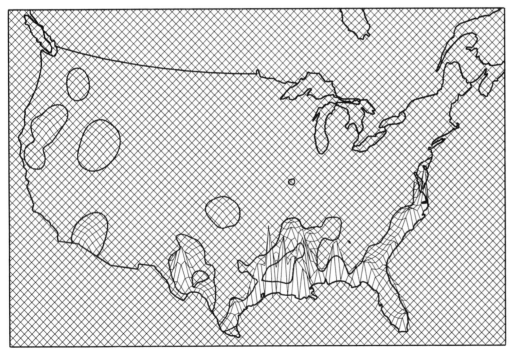

Winter Wren (*Troglodytes troglodytes*) Map in Appendix B

An inordinate abundance of Winter Wrens occurs along the Pacific coast from San Francisco north into northern Canada and Alaska, with an apex on the coast just west of Portland, Oregon. This concentrated population, with an average of 0.58 individuals seen per party-hour, overshadows all other populations, and these high values coupled with the lack of census sites in southwestern Canada caused unrealistic abundance values to be interpolated in locations throughout southern British Columbia. Therefore, the maps are confusing and thus not included here. The contour map, however, is shown in the Introduction as an example of a misleading map. In general the distribution pattern shows that this wren occurs only in areas that receive over 32 inches (81 cm) of precipitation yearly. The northern border of the distribution east of the 100th meridian shows that the Winter Wren is present in the mixed mesophytic and deciduous forest but avoids the mixed deciduous and coniferous forest.

Sedge Wren (*Cistothorus platensis*) Maximum: 0.78 I/Hr

There are two striking aspects of the Sedge Wren maps; first is the number of disjunct populations, and second is the restriction of the distribution east of the 100th meridian to warmer areas below 500 feet (152 m) above sea level. Except for the population in western Texas, all the disjunct populations reflect rare or unusual sightings in one or two years, and all are along river valleys. There was no synchrony in the years of these sightings; thus a warm winter or an overall population increase during a particular year cannot be implicated. The 1972 record in Illinois, however, was accompanied by the statement that sightings of Sedge Wrens are "not unusual [in] mild winters" (Cruickshank 1972).

The most concentrated populations occur in regions warmer than 40°F (4°C) in January: the region along the Gulf coast of Texas and Louisiana, with an inland extension to the northeastern border of Louisiana. Slighter abundance peaks are present in the marshy lowlands along the North Carolina coast and around Pensacola, Florida. Even lesser concentrations are in the marshes on the Florida Gulf coast east of Pensacola, along the Pecos River in western Texas, and in the Green Swamp near Wilmington, North Carolina.

This wren requires dense cover and prefers moist but not wet environments. It is often found in moist meadows and in the drier areas of marshes with tall, thick cover, avoiding cattails that grow in 2 to 4 feet (0.5–1 m) of standing water, which are frequented by Marsh Wrens. The Sedge Wren is fairly difficult to see because of its habit of remaining in dense growths of tall grass and *Carex,* and its lack of curiosity severely decreases the chance of enticing it into the open by "pishing." Its diet consists of spiders and insects such as ants, bugs, weevils, beetles, caterpillars, and grasshoppers (Bent 1948).

Marsh Wren (*Cistothorus palustris*) Maximum: 1.29 I/Hr

The wintering grounds of the Marsh Wren may have been changing recently, because in 1957 the AOU reported that the subspecies *C. p. waynei* wintered only as far south as southeastern South Carolina. Kale (1975), however, reported it in Georgia and Florida. The overall distribution of the Marsh Wren, like that of the Sedge Wren, appears to be correlated with elevation and to a lesser extent with temperature. East of the 100th meridian, the Marsh Wren frequents only areas that are under 500 feet (152 m) in elevation and have an average winter temperature over 30°F (−1°C), while in the West it occurs in areas that are under 5,000 feet (1,524 m) and get no colder than 10°F (−12°C). Most of the western sightings in areas colder than about 20°F (−7°C), however, are irregular, occurring in four or fewer of the ten years examined.

The high concentrations of Marsh Wrens are all where the minimum January temperature is over 25°F (−4°C). Undoubtedly these are areas where the water in their marshy environment rarely freezes. The highest abundance peak is in the low altitude and warm environment of the Imperial Valley in southern California. A continuation of this concentration extends north along the Colorado River, with an apex near Havasu National Wildlife Refuge and a high concentration in the canyon lands of Utah around Zion National Park. There is a slightly lower peak in the tule marshes of the San Joaquin River in southern California and at San Luis National Wildlife Refuge and another peak of equal concentration around San Angelo, Texas. Even less concentrated populations are present on the Pecos River in southwestern Texas and on the northeastern border of Louisiana, where the Sedge Wren reaches a fairly high concentration. The smallest abundance peaks of the Marsh Wren are near Goose Lake on the border between California and Oregon, around Bear River National Wildlife Refuge on the Idaho-Utah border, and near Canton Lake in Oklahoma.

The Marsh Wren is found in much wetter environments than the Sedge Wren, but because the former is much more curious it is easier to see. Normally the Marsh Wren is found in dense cattails and rushes growing in standing water and in tall reeds and grasses in saltwater marshes. Finding this wren can be more difficult in winter than in summer because it stops singing (Bent 1948), abandons its territories, and moves in secretive small groups (Kale 1965). Around the coasts, this wren will glean insects off the vegetation as they climb up to escape rising waters at high tide, and it will pick marine organisms off the ground during low tide. Most of the winter diet consists of homopterans, supplemented with hymenopterans, coleopterans, hemipterans, and dipterans and a few spiders, mollusks, lepidopterans, and orthopterans (Kale 1965).

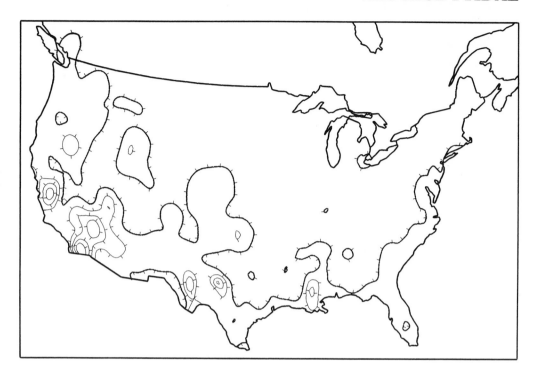

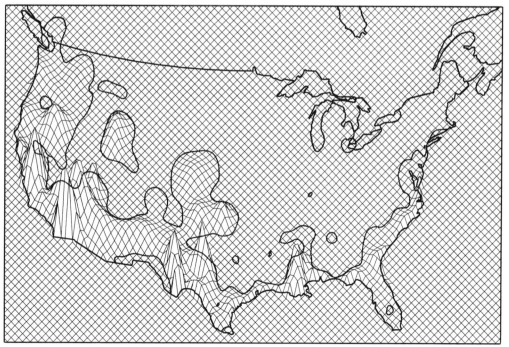

CINCLIDAE

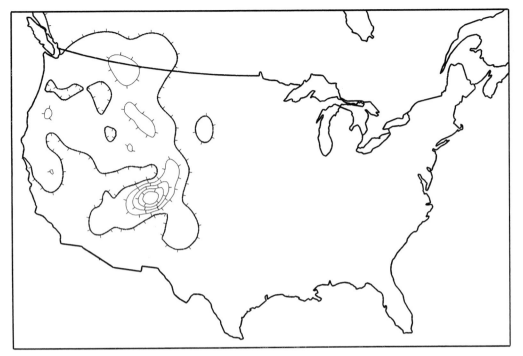

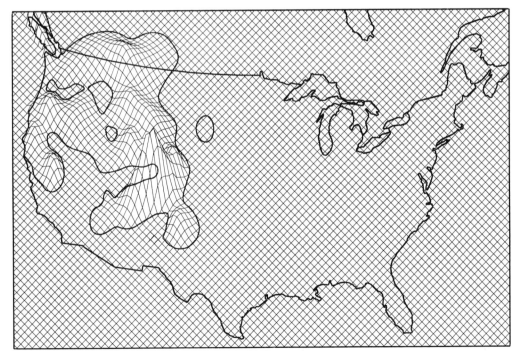

CINCLIDAE

American Dipper (*Cinclus mexicanus*) Maximum: 0.97 I/Hr

The American Dipper's distribution reflects its preference for fast-flowing mountain streams; it occurs in areas that are above 5,000 feet (1,524 m) in elevation, including the region in the West around the Rocky Mountains, Colorado Plateaus, and Pacific mountain system and a disjunct population in the Black Hills of South Dakota. This bird avoids the low, relatively flat lands of the Columbia basin and Snake River plains. Cold temperatures are usually not a limiting factor, because a thick undercoat of down between the feather tracts allows the dipper to maintain normal body temperature even when the ambient temperature drops to $-22°F$ ($-30°C$) (Murrish 1970b).

In winter the American Dipper is concentrated on ice-free stretches of fairly wide rivers that have high food density and sufficient roosts. Site-dependent territories are not set up, because the presence of ice is too unpredictable. Yet individuals are aggressive toward each other, resulting in a site-independent dominance hierarchy (Price and Bock 1983). The highest concentration of dippers in North America occurs in the western drainages of the Colorado Rockies. Less abundant populations are strongly associated with national parks, presumably because in these protected areas the rivers are not dammed and the habitat is preserved. These abundance peaks are in Glacier International Peace Park, Yellowstone, Crater Lake and Yosemite national parks, and along the drainage of the Absaroka Mountains in southwestern Montana and northwestern Wyoming.

The dippers are the only truly aquatic passerines (Murrish 1970a). They obtain most of their food by searching around and under stones on the bottom of rushing mountain streams, and their diet consists of aquatic insect larvae, such as midge larvae and case-bearing caddis larvae, as well as snails, aquatic beetles, stonefly nymphs (Thut 1970), and small fish (Bent 1948; Murrish 1970a). Several anatomical modifications enable them to dive, including nasal flaps that prevent water from entering, modifications of the muscles that adapt the wings for swimming, a uropygial gland that secretes large quantities of oil for waterproofing feathers, and more hemoglobin per red blood cell, giving the blood greater oxygen capacity. Upon submerging the dipper undergoes bradycardia, a lowering of the heart rate, and when it surfaces it experiences tachycardia (Murrish 1970a).

American Dipper

MUSCICAPIDAE

Golden-crowned Kinglet (*Regulus satrapa*) Maximum: 2.71 I/Hr

The Golden-crowned Kinglet winters in most major vegetation types throughout the East, Great Plains, and extreme West. The slight fluting along the range limit in the central Great Plains and the extension into northern Minnesota indicate that this small insectivore also occurs along the galeria forests of the Arkansas, Platte, and northern Mississippi rivers. It avoids the northern boreal woodlands and coniferous forests of Canada and the dry-belt pine forest, semiarid scrub, and scrub steppes of the intermontane plateau region of the West. Two disjunct populations, however, do not fit this pattern. One is in the oak-juniper woodland of the Davis Mountains in southwestern Texas, continuing north to the piñon-juniper forest east of the Sacramento Mountains in New Mexico. The other is around the San Bernardino Mountains of California and the Spring Mountains of Nevada. The areas that these populations inhabit, particularly the latter, may appear more extensive on the maps than they actually are because the lack of count sites in these regions necessitated protracted interpolation.

Lepthien and Bock (1976) found that various temperature and precipitation factors correlated with the distribution and abundance patterns of this kinglet. These patterns were produced from the same Christmas count data used in this study, but they were grouped into 5° latitude-longitude blocks. The maps presented here show no obvious association between distribution and precipitation, but both the distribution and abundance patterns certainly are coincident with temperature. The northern range limit indicates that this species avoids areas with January temperatures colder than 0°F (−18°C), and all the highest abundance peaks occur in regions where it rarely gets below freezing.

The densest populations are west of the Cascades in the Coast Range of southern Washington, Oregon, and northern California, on the coastal plains from northern Virginia to South Carolina, and throughout Mississippi and extending along the Arkansas-Louisiana border. Lower peaks are scattered throughout the distribution, with two in the Foothill Range of the Colorado and Wyoming Rocky Mountains, one in the Warner Mountains of northern California, another along the Columbia River in Washington and British Columbia, and the last along the Ohio-Michigan border.

This kinglet readily joins winter foraging flocks of chickadees, creepers, and Downy Woodpeckers. It actively gleans insects and insect eggs and pupae from foliage, branches, and trunks (Bent 1949). Usually it feeds in the upper canopy (Franzreb 1984).

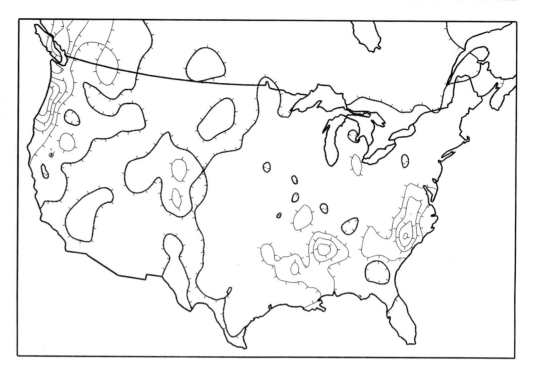

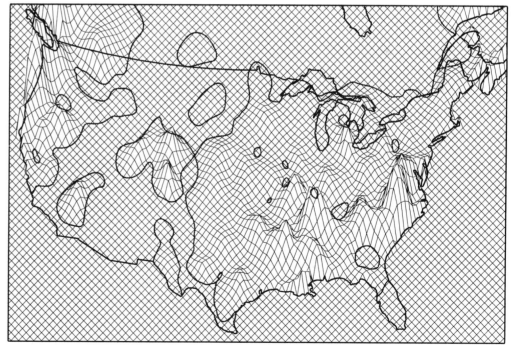

Golden-crowned Kinglet

MUSCICAPIDAE

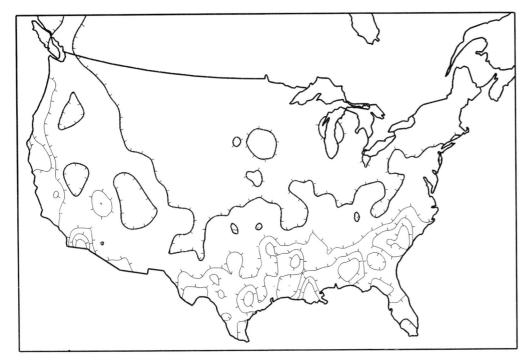

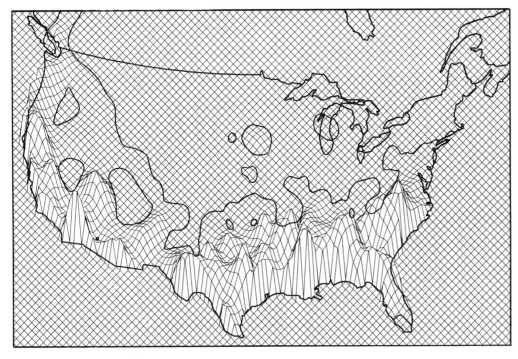

Ruby-crowned Kinglet (*Regulus calendula*) Maximum: 3.84 I/Hr

The distribution of the Ruby-crowned Kinglet is associated most strongly with temperature and elevation, not vegetation as is that of the Golden-crowned Kinglet. In fall the former species migrates both altitudinally and latitudinally out of the colder areas of its breeding range. East of the Rocky Mountains, it remains only where temperatures infrequently drop below 25°F (−4°C) in January. It also avoids the higher altitudes of both the Appalachians and the Ozarks. In the West, the edge of its distribution skirts the western foothills of the Rocky Mountains. It also avoids the Colorado Plateaus in Arizona and Utah, the Harney basin in Oregon, and southwestern Nevada. A few disjunct populations do occur in areas that normally would be too cold, but birds apparently survive in the protected valleys of the Missouri, Big Sioux (at the South Dakota–Minnesota border), and Big Blue (along the Nebraska-Kansas border) rivers and near Lakes Michigan and Erie.

This kinglet is fairly common in virtually all parts of the country where the January temperature rarely drops below freezing. This includes areas in the southeastern coastal plains from North Carolina to Texas, along the Pacific coast from southern California to southern Washington, in the Imperial Valley of southern California, and in southern Arizona around Tucson and Nogales. In a quantitative analysis of the same data examined in this study, but grouped into 5° latitude-longitude blocks, Lepthien and Bock (1976) also found that temperature correlated significantly with this kinglet's distribution and abundance patterns.

In winter the Ruby-crowned Kinglet forages in loose flocks that contain Golden-crowned Kinglets, titmice, nuthatches, and creepers. Like its congener, the Ruby-crowned Kinglet actively forages on branches and foliage of trees (Franzreb 1984). The diets of both kinglets consist almost exclusively of insects and are virtually identical (Bent 1949). Even though the species are ecologically similar, their distribution and abundance patterns show no obvious signs of competitive exclusion. Their distributions overlap extensively, and sympatric abundance peaks occur near the Louisiana-Arkansas border and the North Carolina–South Carolina border.

Ruby-crowned Kinglet

Blue-gray Gnatcatcher (*Polioptila caerulea*) Maximum: 2.32 I/Hr

The environmental factor most obviously influencing the distribution of the Blue-gray Gnatcatcher is ambient temperature. This small passerine cannot survive many more than three consecutive days of freezing weather, and thus in the fall birds in northern parts of the breeding range migrate south to warmer areas (Bent 1949). It winters primarily where the average maximum daily January temperature is at least 60°F (15°C). It does occur in a few areas that do not stay this warm, but most of these are in the protected valleys of the Rio Grande, Red, Mississippi, and Colorado rivers. Even though the temperature is high enough, this gnatcatcher avoids the harsh environments of the western Chihuahuan Desert and western New Mexico.

Temperature is also strongly associated with this gnatcatcher's abundance pattern. High densities occur in regions having an annual frost-free period of at least 270 consecutive days. It is common over extensive areas, including all of central peninsular Florida, with the peak inland from Tampa Bay; the entire area from the mouth of the Mississippi River west along the Gulf coast to around Port Lavaca, Texas; and southern Texas in front of the Edwards Plateau, with the peak around San Antonio. A smaller peak occurs in the Imperial Valley in southern California.

The presence of low numbers of the Black-tailed Gnatcatcher does not seem to influence the distribution of its congener. Dense populations of these two species, however, may affect one another. Their peak abundances in California and Arizona are juxtaposed, and the absence of Blue-gray Gnatcatchers in southwestern Arizona corresponds with an abundance peak of the Black-tailed Gnatcatcher. More intensive fieldwork needs to be done before we understand the precise role of interspecific interaction.

The Blue-gray Gnatcatcher is one of the smallest passerines, weighing only 5.8 grams (Root 1967) and measuring 4.5 inches (11 cm) from the tip of the bill to the end of its disproportionally long tail (National Geographic Society 1983). Because of its small size, its diet is limited to relatively small prey items, all of which, in the western population at least, are arthropods (Root 1967). The gnatcatcher is an active forager, gleaning insects from twigs and leaves while it jumps or hovers around the foliage chasing insects flushed during all foraging activities, but it never feeds upside down. In Arizona it roosts in trees in moist canyons but moves out of these protected areas as soon as the morning sun warms the paloverde, mesquite, and bur sage where it feeds (Root 1967).

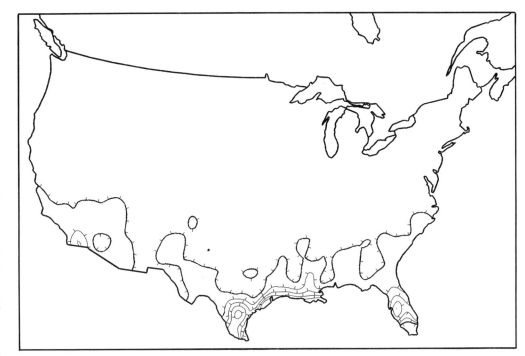

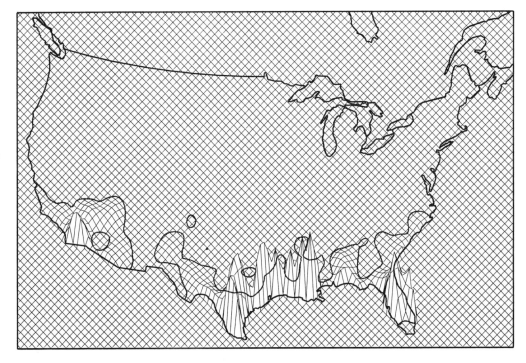

MUSCICAPIDAE

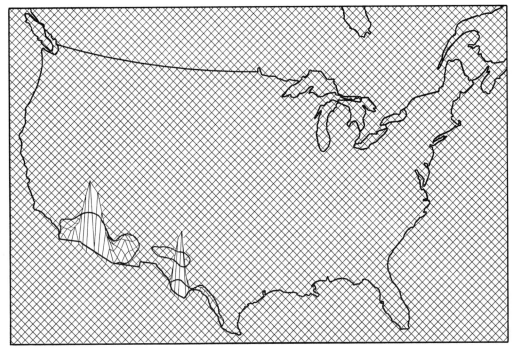

Black-tailed Gnatcatcher (*Polioptila melanura*) Maximum: 1.91 I/Hr
Throughout its range, which includes the Sonoran Desert and the western part of the Chihuahuan Desert, the Black-tailed Gnatcatcher frequents the mesquite, acacia, and creosote bush of semiarid scrub environments and avoids the taller growth of dry-belt pine forests. Along with vegetation, several climatic factors associate with this species' distribution. Temperature is the most obvious. This gnatcatcher is found in the region of the country where temperatures rarely drop below freezing in January and where the frost-free period is longer than 240 days. These high temperatures are beneficial to this bird in at least two ways: first, the direct energy demand of keeping warm is less; second, insects are more active and therefore easier to find. The eastern edge of the range in Texas is apparently associated with precipitation, for this species is absent from regions receiving more than 24 inches (61 cm) of rain annually.

Precipitation also is associated with the abundance pattern of this gnatcatcher. The two abundance peaks occur in the most arid regions in the United States—those receiving an annual average of less than 8 inches (20 cm) of rain and having an annual pan evaporation greater than 105 inches (267 cm). These locations are in the Big Bend region of southern Texas and around the Cabeza Prieta National Wildlife Refuge in southwestern Arizona. The presence of dense populations of its congener may influence where this bird is common, because the abundance peaks of the two species in Arizona are juxtaposed. If this is true, then the Black-tailed Gnatcatcher probably affects the Blue-gray more than the other way around, because the abundance of the latter drops to zero where the former is most common. Obviously this circumstantial evidence alone can only suggest the possibility of competition. More detailed fieldwork is needed.

Like its congener, the Black-tailed Gnatcatcher is one of the smallest passerines in the United States, measuring 4.5 inches (11 cm) from its bill to its unusually long tail (National Geographic Society 1983). Its foraging habits are very similar to those of the Blue-gray Gnatcatcher; insects, which make up 98% of its diet, are actively gleaned from branches and foliage of shrubs. It feeds primarily near the ground because of the stunted desert vegetation. Contrary to its name, it does little "gnatcatching" (Bent 1949). Unlike the Blue-gray Gnatcatcher, this species is resident throughout its range (AOU 1983), and individuals are sedentary, with mated pairs defending the same territory year-round (Bent 1949).

Black-tailed Gnatcatcher

Eastern Bluebird (*Sialia sialis*) Maximum: 4.56 I/Hr

Temperature is strongly correlated with the limits of the Eastern Bluebird's range. In the North its distribution infrequently extends into regions with an average minimum January temperature lower than 20°F (−7°C). On particularly cold, clear evenings, Frazier and Nolan (1959) found that five to fourteen of these birds roosted communally in a protected cavity, with their heads together in the middle. The body heat accumulated in a closed area helps sustain them through fairly cold nights.

The western edge of the distribution indicates that this bluebird occurs in habitats that receive over 16 inches (41 cm) of precipitation annually. The presence of the other two bluebirds to the west may also affect its range limit. The ranges show significant overlap, but in an earlier study my colleagues and I found that the abundance of these species shows an abrupt change from the Eastern Bluebird to its two western congeners (Root, Holmgren, and Andrews 1981). The rapid transition from eastern to western species occurs within the short distance of two degrees of latitude (from the 100th to the 102nd meridian). The disjunct population in California was due to nine individuals seen in 1967, which might have been the "first record for southern California" (Cruickshank 1967).

The highly concentrated populations of the Eastern Bluebird occur in areas that are warm and moist. This bird is common throughout most of the region where the frost-free period averages at least 180 days and there is more than 24 inches (61 cm) of precipitation a year. It is fairly uncommon at higher elevations (in the Ozarks and Appalachians) and in the swamp forest of the upper Mississippi River valley.

Much concern has been raised in the past two decades about the dramatic drop in the Eastern Bluebird's abundance throughout most of its range (Zeleny 1976). This decline has been attributed to a combination of several factors, most of them either directly or indirectly connected with humans. The most publicized is the lack of nesting cavities caused by people removing the dead trees and limbs in which these cavities occur, or owing to the takeover of nest holes by the more aggressive House Sparrow and Starling. This has resulted in a massive effort to provide adequate nest boxes (Zeleny 1976). Other causes of declining populations include the destruction of native berry plants, a major source of food in the winter, pesticides (Zeleny 1976), removal of perch sites (Pinkowski 1977), and severe winter weather with dramatic die-offs in unusually long freezing periods (James 1962; Zeleny 1976).

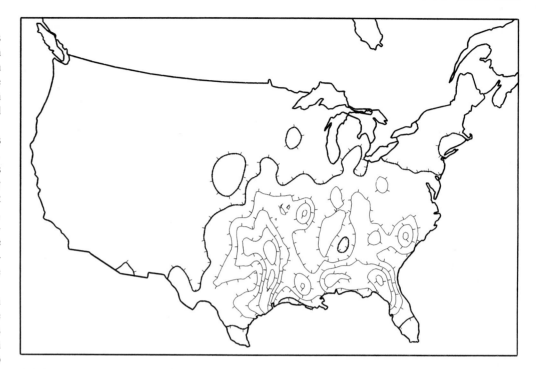

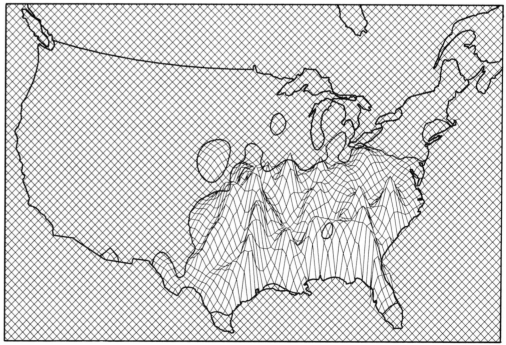

MUSCICAPIDAE

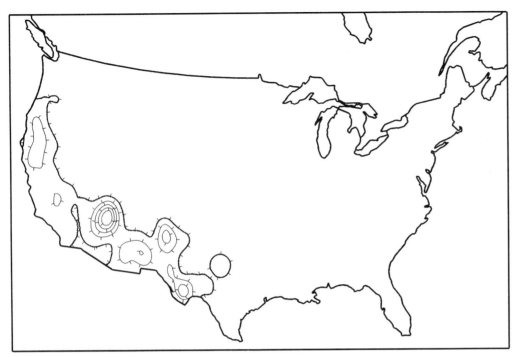

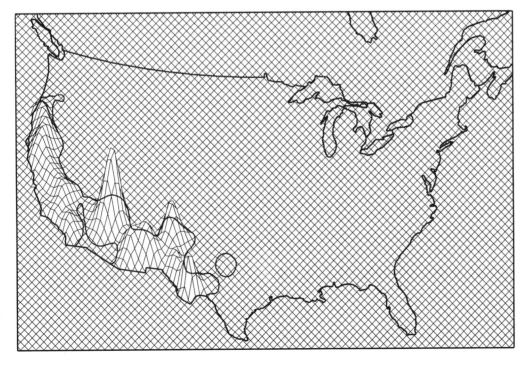

Western Bluebird (*Sialia mexicana*) Maximum: 8.82 I/Hr

The Western Bluebird occurs throughout most of the Southwest. It survives in habitats within fairly narrow limits of temperature and moisture, and temperature is the factor most strongly associated with its distribution. Like the Eastern Bluebird, it inhabits areas that are usually warmer than 20°F (−7°C) in January. On a gross scale, this association does not appear to be as strong as for its eastern congener, but a closer examination of the microhabitats created by the diverse topography of the West shows that the correspondence is good. The southern boundary reflects the Western Bluebird's absence from the harsh environments of the Sonoran and Mojave deserts and Death Valley, which apparently are too hot and dry, particularly in the summer, since this species shows little latitudinal migration (AOU 1983). The general humidity in these deserts is the lowest in the country, with annual pan evaporation values over 110 inches (279 cm). The far northern boundary is also associated with pan evaporation, but to the other extreme, with the low value of 30 inches (76 cm). Here the environment is apparently too humid for the Western Bluebird. The eastern edge of the distribution shows that it frequents the semiarid shrub, shrub steppe, and dry-belt pine forest communities and avoids grasslands and savannas. The presence of the Eastern Bluebird may also affect this eastern border to some degree. As was explained for its eastern congener, these species abruptly replace each other near the 101st meridian (Root, Holmgren, and Andrews 1981).

Abundance peaks are scattered throughout the range of the Western Bluebird. All but one of the higher peaks occur in piñon-juniper forest. These include the densest population, along the Colorado River on the Colorado Plateaus in Arizona, and two lesser peaks: on the eastern side of the southern Rocky Mountains and in the dry-belt pine forest near Silver City, New Mexico. The remaining high peak and some of the lesser ones are associated with oaks. Two of these are in the California oak woodlands in the Sacramento and San Joaquin valleys, and another is in the juniper-oak forests of the Davis Mountains in southwestern Texas.

This bluebird apparently prefers open, scrubby forests. In winter it migrates down from higher elevations into foothill and canyon habitats, where it feeds almost exclusively on mistletoe berries throughout the winter (Bent 1949). Frequently it joins foraging flocks made up of House Finches and an occasional Yellow-rumped Warbler (Audubon's race) (Bent 1949).

Mountain Bluebird (*Sialia currucoides*) Maximum: 19.02 I/Hr

The Mountain Bluebird is more strongly associated with mountains in summer than in winter. Its fall migration takes it south into the southern United States and Mexico (AOU 1983) and down in elevation, so it avoids the more severe weather in the mountains (Bent 1949). Unlike its two congeners that occur only in areas warmer than 20°F (−7°C), the Mountain Bluebird survives where the minimum January temperature drops as low as 10°F (−12°C). It avoids the harsh, arid regions of the Sonoran and Mojave deserts and most other areas that receive less than 8 inches (20 cm) of yearly precipitation. The Mountain Bluebird winters where the general humidity measures 80 to 130 inches (203–330 cm) of annual pan evaporation. To the east, this means it does not occur on the coastal plains of eastern Texas. This eastern edge may also be influenced by the presence of the Eastern Bluebird, as is indicated by the rapid change in abundance from the eastern to the western species (Root, Holmgren, and Andrews 1981). (For a more complete explanation, see the text for the Eastern Bluebird.)

The preferred habitat of this species is open forests (Bent 1949), as is reflected in the location of the abundance peaks. The densest population occurs in the foothills of the Sangre de Cristo Mountains, in piñon-juniper forest that projects into the Great Plains and therefore is surrounded on three sides by grasslands, providing an excellent foraging environment. Its diet is 92% insects and other animal matter, making it the most highly carnivorous thrush in the United States (Bent 1949). Unlike its congeners, it does not forage by sitting on low perches but instead hovers while looking for food (Bent 1949), making the open habitat in southeastern Colorado ideal. Other dense concentrations occur in the piñon-juniper forest in eastern New Mexico, the open oak-juniper woodland of the Davis Mountains in southwestern Texas, and the sparse creosote bush community of southern California.

The disjunct and noncontinuous aspect of this overall distribution is due to two factors. First, the availability of fairly extensive low, open scrub forest within the necessary climatic regimes is limited. Second, the one exceptionally high abundance peak overshadows areas with low relative abundance.

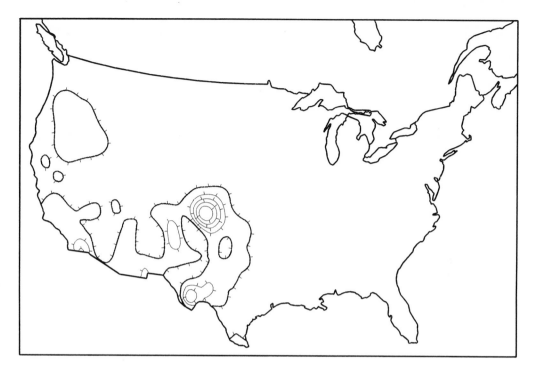

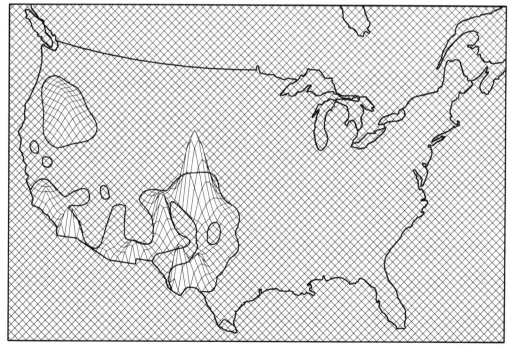

MUSCICAPIDAE

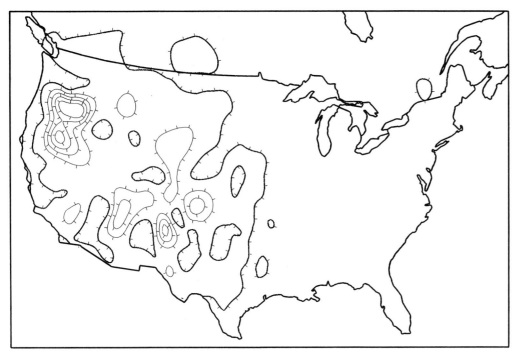

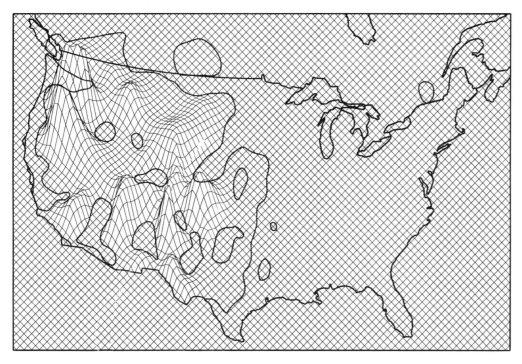

Townsend's Solitaire (*Myadestes townsendi*) Maximum: 2.00 I/Hr

The Townsend's Solitaire is normally thought to be associated with junipers. Indeed, when junipers are present, it forages extensively on the berries, which are actually cones with fleshy scales. It does, however, eat other berries such as mistletoe (Salomonson and Balda 1977) and therefore is not limited to habitats containing junipers. It feeds either on the ground or in trees. It defends feeding territories in the winter and spends much time perched on the tops of trees within these defended areas. Territory size depends on the availability of food; when berries are abundant, the territories are smaller than when food is scarce (Salomonson and Balda 1977).

In winter the Townsend's Solitaire frequents the dry mountains of the West, with the densest populations in and around juniper forests. The population of maximum abundance is in a sagebrush steppe community, but there are junipers scattered throughout. The extensive piñon-juniper forest east of the mountains near Albuquerque, New Mexico, is occupied by a fairly dense population of solitaires. This is also true for the piñon-juniper forests in Arizona and southeastern Colorado. The smaller abundance peaks scattered throughout its range, in southern California, southwestern Montana, central Colorado and Wyoming, and southwestern Texas, are not associated with stands of junipers. Instead they occur in various types of vegetation ranging from creosote bush to pine forests, often with Douglas fir mixed in.

The distribution of the Townsend's Solitaire is apparently associated with two major factors: temperature and elevation. In the North this species does not occur in areas that get much colder than 0°F (−18°C) in January, and in the South it avoids the harsh environments of the Sonoran and Mojave deserts. The eastern limit of its range is associated with the beginning of the interior plains. It does not occur in areas in this region that are lower than 1,000 feet (305 m) above sea level, and its abundance is very low at elevations under 2,000 feet (610 m), as seen from the empty areas along the Texas-Oklahoma and Kansas-Nevada borders. The small disjunct population in Arkansas occurs in the higher elevations of the Ozarks, and the obviously misplaced "population" in Quebec was due to an exceedingly rare sighting of one individual on the Montreal count in 1968.

Veery (*Catharus fuscescens*) No Map

The Veery winters outside the United States in South America (AOU 1983). There were only ten sporadic sightings of this thrush throughout the ten years examined, mostly along the Atlantic and Gulf coasts.

Gray-cheeked Thrush (*Catharus minimus*) No Map
The Gray-cheeked Thrush's main wintering ground encompasses Central and South America (AOU 1983). During the ten years of CBC data examined, there were twenty-four scattered sightings of birds along the Atlantic coast from Maine to Florida.

Swainson's Thrush (*Catharus ustulatus*) Map in Appendix B
Numerous count sites throughout the United States reported this thrush, but only five recorded it three or more times in the ten-year period examined. Its primary wintering grounds are in Mexico, Central and South America, and casually in southern Texas and on the Gulf coast (AOU 1983). The five sites were not around the Gulf, however, but on the Atlantic coast of Florida and South Carolina and on the Pacific coast in extreme southern California.

Hermit Thrush (*Catharus guttatus*) Maximum: 1.11 I/Hr
In winter the Hermit Thrush is generally absent from regions with January temperatures below 25°F (−4°C), but there are three populations surviving in areas colder than this. One of these and part of another occur in protected valleys along the Rio Grande and the Snake River. Within the areas that are suitably warm, it avoids the arid region along the California-Arizona border, perhaps because it is an extremely harsh environment, having the lowest general humidity in the country (an annual pan evaporation of 140 inches [356 cm]). This species requires open water (Bent 1949), which is rarely available in this area. The "population" in Idaho consisted of two individuals recorded on the Indian Mountain count in 1966.

This thrush prefers dense, moist forest habitats (Aldrich 1968) at lower elevations, where it feeds on insects (56% of its diet), berries, and seeds (Bent 1949). The abundance pattern reflects these preferences and the added fact that it selects warm areas; it is common only in forests that rarely get below 30°F (−1°C) in January. Within this warmer area, most of the peak abundances occur along river valleys, including the Ouachita River in Louisiana, the Red River along the Texas-Oklahoma border, and the Colorado and Guadalupe rivers in Texas. Another peak occurs in the oak woodlands in southwestern Texas. The Coast Range in the West supports a fairly dense population of Hermit Thrushes. The exception is the Klamath Mountains, which reach a higher elevation than any other mountains in the range. Other evidence that this thrush avoids higher elevations is its absence from the higher peaks of the Appalachians.

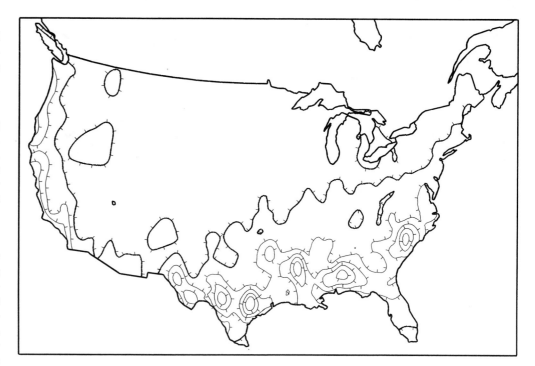

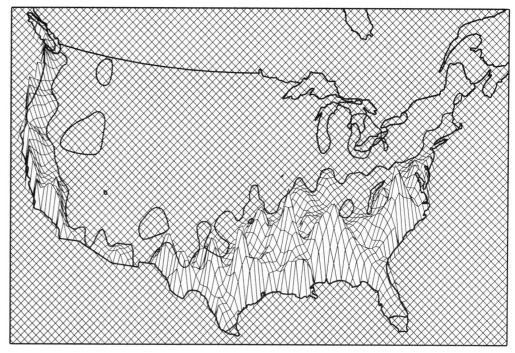

MUSCICAPIDAE

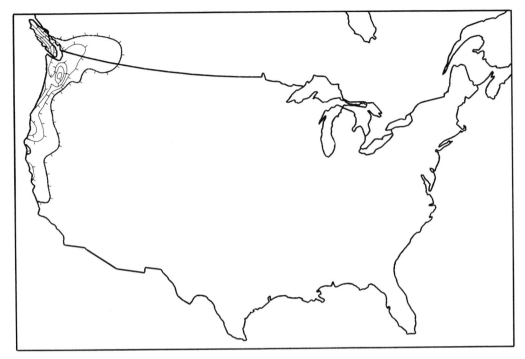

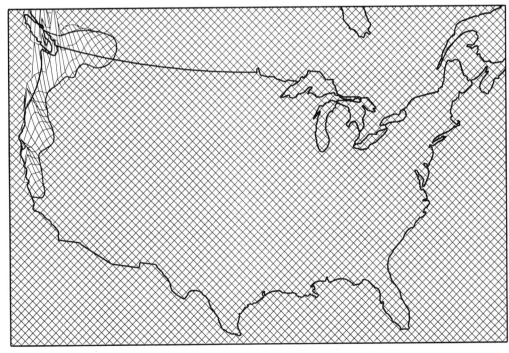

Wood Thrush (*Hylocichla mustelina*) No Map

The Wood Thrush's primary wintering area extends from southern Texas to northwestern Colombia, including eastern Mexico and Central America (AOU 1983). It has been recorded inconsistently at sporadic locations along the Atlantic coast and more regularly (four or five years out of the ten years examined) on the Gulf coast in extreme southern Texas and near Galveston.

Varied Thrush (*Ixoreus naevius*) Maximum: 20.00 I/Hr

The Varied Thrush occurs throughout the Coast Range south of the Canadian border and in the Cascade Mountains. Above the Columbia basin the range expands to the eastern slopes of the Rocky Mountains in Alberta, but the species avoids the lower elevations of the basin itself. In southern California the distribution extends east of the Cascade Range to encompass the Warner Mountains. Around the North Fork River, in the pass that divides the Cascades and the Sierra Nevada, the distribution contracts, avoiding the slopes of the latter mountains. The Varied Thrush can be found south in the Coast Range to Mount Pinos, where the southern end of the Sierra Nevada curves east and meets the Coast Range. All of this region is covered with western temperate and coastal coniferous forest or California oak woodlands. Being on the windward side of the Sierra Nevada ensures that the environment is fairly moist, with all the regions within the species' range receiving at least 24 inches (61 cm) of rain a year. The forest communities provide the secluded, shady, and moist environment in which this thrush prefers to forage (Bent 1949).

Annual precipitation is the environmental factor most strongly associated with the abundance pattern of the Varied Thrush. The area where it is at least somewhat common receives 54 inches (137 cm) of annual precipitation, and both of the highest peaks are in regions getting more than 64 inches (163 cm). One of the densest populations is on the southwestern side of Vancouver Island in Pacific Rim National Park. The other population, which is equally dense, is in Snoqualmie National Forest.

This western thrush is primarily a resident of dense, humid forest (Bent 1949). It usually forages on the ground (Law 1921), and in winter its diet is mostly vegetable matter, with fruit, weed seeds, acorns, and berries making up roughly 74% (Bent 1949). The Varied Thrush forages in dead, fallen leaves by hopping forward, grasping debris in its bill, and then simultaneously jumping backward and throwing the leaves back and to the side. It then eats exposed insects or vegetable matter (Law 1921). Significant mortality has been recorded when unusually heavy or lingering snowstorms occur. Ransom (1950) reported seeing thousands of dead and dying Varied Thrushes along a recently plowed road where they had come to forage during an unusually bad snowstorm in 1949. This thrush will use feeders particularly during severe snowstorms. Apart from the California Quail and Scrub Jay, it is the dominant diner at these feeding stations (Martin 1970).

Varied Thrush

American Robin (*Turdus migratorius*) Map in Appendix B

American Robins in the northern breeding grounds migrate south in the fall (AOU 1983) and congregate in flocks with the southern residents (Bent 1949). These flocks are large and nomadic, and thus the CBC data may not accurately represent the abundance of this species. Its range extends across the continent, but the birds avoid areas where the average minimum January temperature drops below 5°F (−15°C), areas that receive less than 8 inches (20 cm) of annual precipitation, and the higher elevations of the Appalachians, Ozarks, Rockies, and Ouachita Mountains.

Wrentit (*Chamaea fasciata*) Maximum: 2.04 I/Hr

This species, which is in a monotypic genus, is the only North American representative of the babbler subfamily Timaliinae (AOU 1983). This unique genus occurs only in the dense brush of the Pacific coastal region. Its distribution runs from the Strait of Juan de Fuca between Washington and Vancouver Island down the entire length of the coast to Mexico. Its range is bounded on the east by the high elevations of the Cascades, the Sierra Nevada, and the San Bernardino Mountains. Throughout the western part of this range the Wrentit is fairly common, with its abundance dropping off only in the North near the mouth of the Columbia River. High abundance peaks are found around Cape Blanco in southern Oregon and near Monterey, California, with a rather high concentration stretching south from this latter apex along the coast to San Diego. A small disjunct population of significant concentration is present around Porterville, at the southwestern side of the Central Valley of California.

The Wrentit primarily frequents brushland, chaparral, forest edges, and streamside environments. It prefers dense cover, which makes it difficult to see, but curiosity often drives it to an exposed branch. Open areas of only 30 to 40 feet (9–12 m) are rarely crossed. Pairs are sedentary and remain on the same territory for five years or longer. A pair will roost together on a horizontal branch in a dense area of a bush. They lean against each other, and their fluffed feathers interlace. Family members often preen each other. Year-round foraging for insects entails hopping through the foliage and hanging upside down searching for ants, wasps, beetles, caterpillars, bugs, flies, and spiders. They rarely forage on the ground. In winter berries are added to the diet, primarily poison oak because they are the most accessible (Erickson 1938).

Crypticity evidently is important to the survival of the Wrentit. Bowers (1960) found that birds in more humid areas, which have darker-stemmed vegetation, possess darker plumage. He also found that birds in warmer climates have longer extremities and smaller body mass. Thus coastal birds are darker, have longer wings and legs, and weigh less than their inland counterparts.

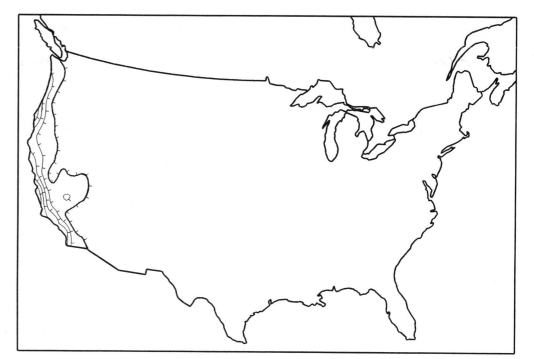

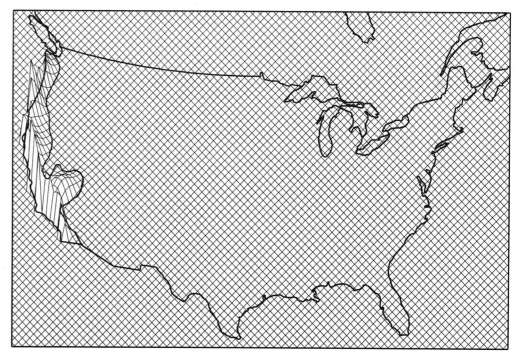

MIMIDAE

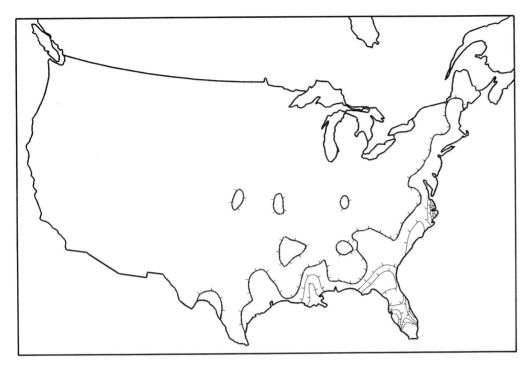

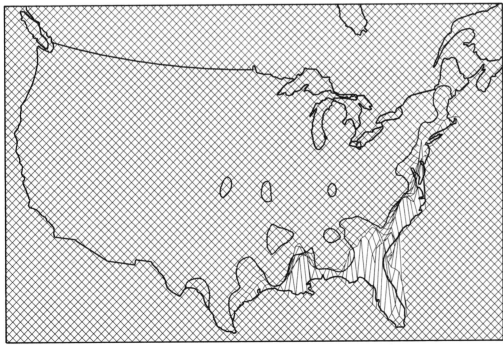

Gray Catbird (*Dumetella carolinensis*) Maximum: 1.67 I/Hr

Except for the disjunct populations, most Gray Catbirds winter along the Gulf and Atlantic coasts. In the South these areas have 240 consecutive days without frost each year, and the populations farther north along the Atlantic coast occur where the frost-free period is 210 days. Disjunct populations are primarily along the Arkansas, Ohio, Tennessee, and Missouri river valleys, where the habitat offers some protection from the harsh winter weather. At all the disjunct locations, individuals were seen in no more than three years out of the ten examined.

Swampy, warm habitats are strongly associated with dense concentrations of catbirds. The highest abundance is around the Cape Hatteras area of North Carolina, where the land is very marshy and there are several wildlife refuges. To the south of this area there is a lesser peak along the coast of South Carolina, around Cape Romain National Wildlife Refuge. Higher concentrations of catbirds occur on the border of Florida and Georgia, on the peninsula of Florida where the average minimum January temperature is over 50°F (10°C), and at the southern end of the Mississippi River and continuing down to the swampy bayous of the Louisiana coast.

The catbird cannot survive extremely cold weather and thus migrates in the winter. Except during warm winters when migration is partly curtailed, banding records show that individuals exhibit high site tenacity for their wintering areas (Bent 1948). The normal migration pattern for birds in the West is not as direct as for those in the East; as with other eastern birds that have spread westward (e.g., Veery and Red-eyed Vireo), they first migrate east and then turn south (Phillips, Marshall, and Monson 1983). Catbirds probably travel at night, because many are killed each season by hitting tall structures such as lighthouses and bridges. Their winter diet consists primarily of berries, such as mountain ash, catbrier, bittersweet, honeysuckle, poison ivy, and sumac (Bent 1948).

Gray Catbird

Northern Mockingbird (*Mimus polyglottos*) Maximum: 5.26 I/Hr

The Northern Mockingbird winters in areas that have an average minimum January temperature of at least 20°F (−7°C). On the Pacific coast, however, temperature is not directly associated with the range of this species; the climate is warm along the coast up to at least the international border, but the bird does not occur north of California. Vegetation is probably the main factor influencing this range edge, because this boundary is coincident with the beginning of the coastal coniferous forest. The disjunct population in northern New Mexico winters along the Rio Grande valley, which offers a sufficiently protected environment for these regularly observed mockingbirds.

The importance of both temperature and vegetation to the Northern Mockingbird is also evident in its abundance pattern. All the areas of higher concentration have average minimum January temperatures of at least 30°F (−1°C). The densest populations are in Texas, where the vegetation is tree and shrub savanna and scrub steppe.

"Many-tongued mimic" is a rough translation of the scientific name of the Northern Mockingbird (Gotch 1981). This name is quite appropriate because individuals regularly imitate over thirty types of birds in ten minutes, and some have been recorded as mimicking many more species than this in an even shorter time. Frequently in the fall mockingbirds sing at night, particularly when the moon is bright (Bent 1948). Birds exhibit both intra- and interspecific territoriality in summer and winter (Bent 1948), but the area defended in winter is primarily a feeding territory (Phillips, Marshall, and Monson 1983). When a pair remains together in the winter, both female and male defend their feeding area. The defense entails a hopping "dance" on the ground, the two participants facing each other with bodies and tails erect. They hop toward one another until a boundary is established (Hailman 1960). About 85% of the species' diet is wild fruits and berries, including cactus fruit when available, supplemented to a small degree by ground-dwelling insects (Bent 1948). Through time the mockingbird has expanded its range in the Southwest. Before English-speaking settlers arrived, the habitat of this bird probably included sagebrush scrub, chaparral, and desert, but the spread of trees and farmland increased its food, allowing its abundance and range to expand. The distribution of the mockingbird reached only as far north as Stockton, California, in the San Joaquin valley in 1911, but in 1978 the range had widened to Redding, California, and in 1980 it was still expanding (Arnold 1980).

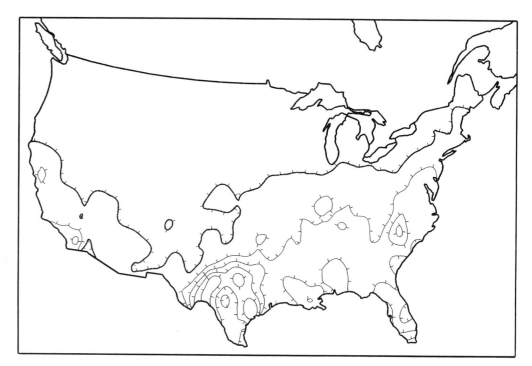

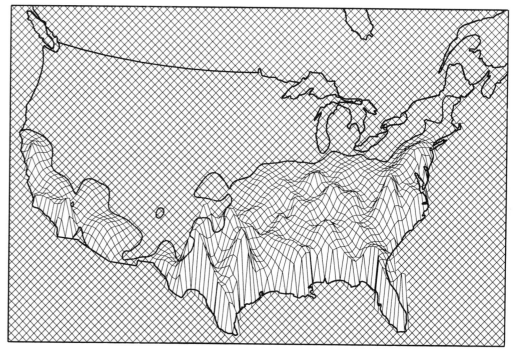

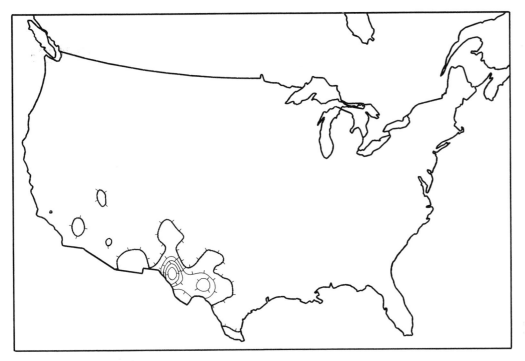

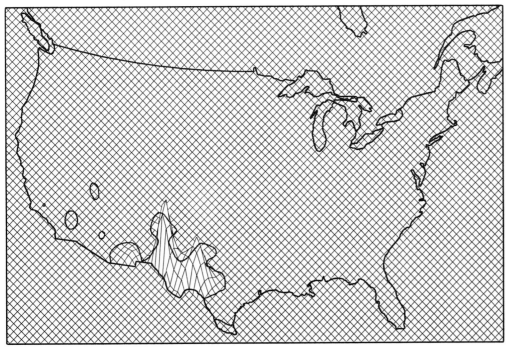

Sage Thrasher (*Oreoscoptes montanus*) Maximum: 1.45 I/Hr

The distribution shows that the Sage Thrasher is present only in semiarid regions, primarily in the sage steppe and mesquite savanna. All its disjunct populations reflect ephemeral sightings.

The rather restricted distribution of the Sage Thrasher is sympatric with that of several other mimids, but the major abundance peaks for all these species are either parapatric or allopatric. The highest abundance peak of the Sage Thrasher is in southwestern Texas, where the vegetation is scrub steppe. Going from west to east, the abundance peaks of the mimids are juxtaposed in the following way: California Thrasher, Crissal Thrasher, Curve-billed Thrasher, Bendire's Thrasher, Sage Thrasher, Curve-billed Thrasher, Northern Mockingbird, and Brown Thrasher. Such an obvious progression suggests two possible explanations. First, the environment at the location of each peak is unique, and each of the various species requires a different habitat. Hence the species are tracking the environment. Second, biotic interaction between the various groups prevents high concentrations of two species from occurring in the same location. Therefore interspecific density-dependent factors are enforcing the separation. A combination of these options is the most probable explanation. During the Wisconsin glaciation, several of the mimids speciated in separate refugia with fairly dissimilar environments (Hubbard 1973). Thus, the species evolved predilections for different habitats. Yet, interaction between them after the physical barriers between the refugia were removed probably has reinforced the juxtaposition of the abundance peaks. Field studies are needed to examine the importance of these ecological and historical factors.

Like most other mimids, in winter the Sage Thrasher eats wild berries, fruits, and the larvae and eggs of insects (Bent 1948). Other characteristics of this thrasher are similar to those of the Northern Mockingbird. When sitting, both species raise their tails rapidly and lower them slowly, and when they run both hold their tails high (Bent 1948).

Sage Thrasher

Sage Thrasher

Brown Thrasher (*Toxostoma rufum*) Maximum: 1.57 I/Hr

The primary factors associated with the winter distribution of the Brown Thrasher are temperature and vegetation. In the fall, birds in the North move south (Engels 1940) into regions where the average minimum January temperature is above 25°F (−4°C). The exceptions are along the galeria forests in the Great Plains, which presumably provide some protection from the harsh winter climate. The eastern limit of its distribution indicates that this thrasher does not frequent the grasslands and semiarid scrub and forest. Congeners may to some extent be preventing the extension of the Brown Thrasher farther west, but more in-depth study of this is needed.

The abundance pattern of the Brown Thrasher also shows a strong association with temperature and vegetation. All the areas of higher concentration, except for one spot on the Arkansas River in Oklahoma, are in regions that rarely get below freezing in January. The western boundary of the region of higher abundance stops abruptly at the edge of the mixed mesophytic and deciduous forest. The highest density of this species occurs in the swamp forest at the southern end of the Mississippi River.

Like other thrashers, the Brown Thrasher forages on or near the ground, chiefly in areas with fairly dense cover (Fischer 1981). In the winter its main staples are acorns, which it opens by hammering them with its bill (Bent 1948), and dried berries. When foraging, it pokes its bill into the ground in an up-and-down movement, probing for insects (Engels 1940). This bird does not use its feet to scratch the ground as a towhee does, but instead moves its bill in powerful side strokes to remove debris (Bent 1948). Winter territories are defended both intra- and interspecifically, and site tenacity toward winter territories in southern Texas is fairly high, with 27% of the birds returning to the same territories (Fischer 1981).

Long-billed Thrasher (*Toxostoma longirostre*) No Map

The distribution of the Long-billed Thrasher in the United States is restricted to southern Texas, with all the sightings occurring between the 99th and 95th meridians and between the 25th parallel and the Mexican border. The highest density of this thrasher was at Falcon Dam in Texas, with an average of 0.84 individuals seen per hour of count effort.

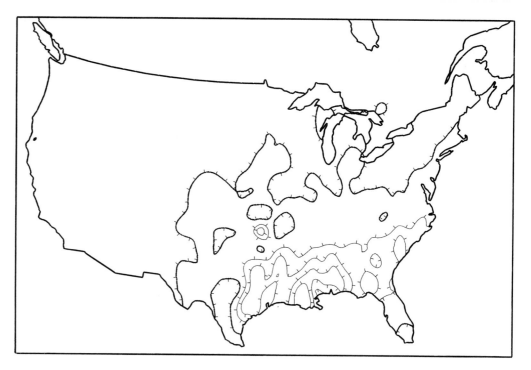

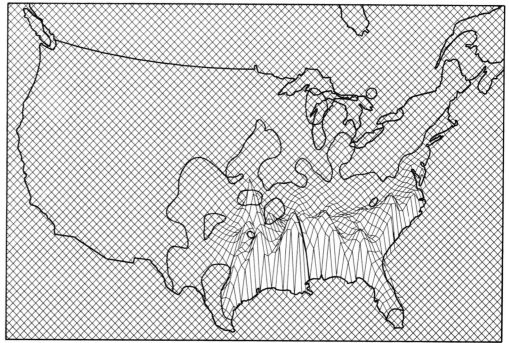

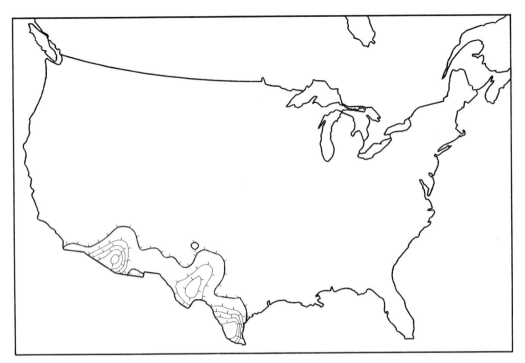

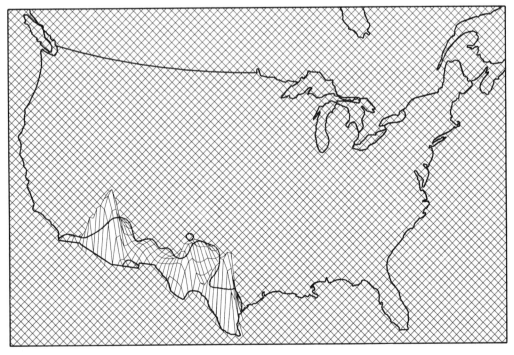

Curve-billed Thrasher (*Toxostoma curvirostre*) Maximum: 3.58 I/Hr
The Curve-billed Thrasher is a permanent resident of the semiarid desert area of the southwestern United States (Bent 1948). The distribution map shows that vegetation is one of the factors most strongly associated with its range. In southern Texas this thrasher inhabits the mesquite-acacia scrub savanna, and farther west it occurs in the scrub steppe with blackbrush and creosote bush. On a macroscale at least, the western edge of the distribution is not defined by vegetation, because the scrub steppe environment continues beyond the range limit. A high concentration of the Crissal Thrasher along the lower Colorado River valley may possibly be excluding the Curve-billed Thrasher from this area.

The abundance pattern of the Curve-billed Thrasher may be strongly influenced by the presence of the other thrashers. Studies have shown that when thrashers are sympatric various species use different microhabitats, thereby lessening competition (Engels 1940; Fischer 1981). The maps suggest that interspecific interaction is further reduced by juxtaposed peaks in species abundance. (See the Sage Thrasher account for a more detailed discussion.) The high abundance peak of the Curve-billed Thrasher in southern Arizona is wedged between that of the Crissal Thrasher to the west and a population of the Bendire's Thrasher, along with a lesser abundance peak of the Crissal Thrasher, to the east. The lesser peak of the Curve-billed Thrasher in southwestern Texas abuts high concentrations of the Sage Thrasher to the west and the Northern Mockingbird to the east. This latter peak, in turn, is north of the maximum abundance peak of the Curve-billed Thrasher in southern Texas. The vegetation in southern Texas is mesquite-acacia scrub.

The Curve-billed Thrasher usually forages in fairly open areas with little cover. Like other thrashers it is an omnivore, but it eats more insects and fewer berries than some (Fischer 1981). When foraging, it uses its bill to throw aside debris and digs holes in the ground that are frequently 2.5 inches (6 cm) deep (Engels 1940). This thrasher is not very shy and is even attracted to ranches with chollas nearby. In the 1920s it was said that this was perhaps the most abundant bird in the Phoenix and Tempe area. Pairs, which remain together over the winter, build breeding and winter roosting nests in chollas. Both members of the pair often occupy a roosting nest together (Bent 1948).

Bendire's Thrasher (*Toxostoma bendirei*) No Map
On the Christmas counts, the Bendire's Thrasher was observed throughout southern Arizona and California. In all except four locations in Arizona, however, these sightings were sporadic. This thrasher was seen in each of the ten years on both the Tucson Valley and Phoenix counts, and in six of the ten years at Nogales, Arizona, and Santa Catalina, California. The highest average density of Bendire's Thrashers was recorded at the latter count, with 0.21 individuals seen per party-hour.

California Thrasher (*Toxostoma redivivum*) Maximum: 0.54 I/Hr
The California Thrasher is aptly named, because the distribution of this nonmigratory species is restricted to California and Baja California, with only casual sightings in southern Oregon (AOU 1983). Vegetation is probably the primary factor influencing the range of this species. It frequents chaparral, California steppe, and California oakwoods. The most concentrated population is in chaparral, its preferred habitat (Grinnell 1917). This type of vegetation is open, close to the ground, with strongly interlaced branches and an evergreen, closed canopy, which provides the best environment for this shy species (Grinnell 1917).

California Thrashers forage in dense cover (Grinnell 1917), and venture out only to find water (Bent 1948). They usually forage on the ground (Grinnell 1917), moving the bill from side to side to sweep away debris (Engels 1940). The powerful bill is also used to dig in the dirt, which is "hooked" back behind the bird. Like most other thrashers, this species does not use its feet to scratch during foraging, but only for locomotion (Engels 1940). It rarely flies farther than 90 feet (27 m) (Engels 1940) and in fact rarely leaves the ground, causing Grinnell (1917) to label this bird "semiterrestrial." When foraging in a bush, it never moves higher than necessary to reach food, and it is never in an area of a bush where it would be exposed (Grinnell 1917). In winter it eats caterpillars, cocoons, moths, berries, and cactus fruit (Bent 1948).

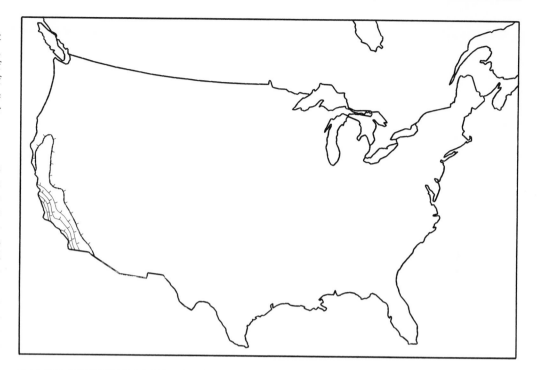

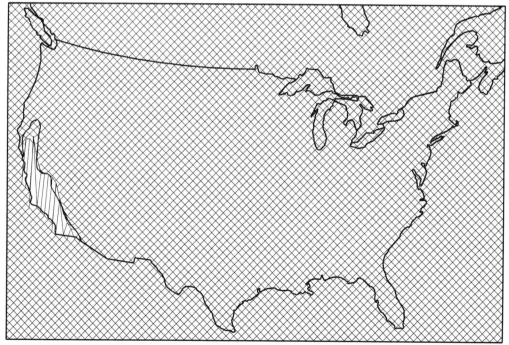

California Thrasher

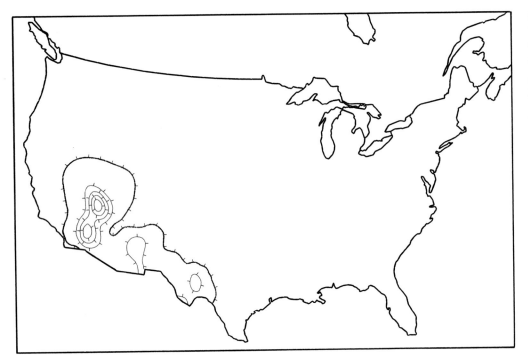

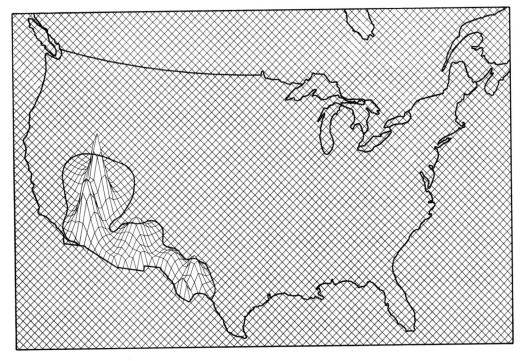

Crissal Thrasher (*Toxostoma dorsale*) Maximum: 0.78 I/Hr

The location of the overall distribution of the Crissal Thrasher is probably strongly influenced by vegetation and possibly, to a lesser extent, by interactions with other thrashers. To the east, the Crissal Thrasher avoids the grassland and the tree and shrub savanna of central and western Texas. The presence of dry-belt pine forest apparently prohibits its occurrence farther north. To the west the California Thrasher may to some extent prevent the Crissal Thrasher from invading the canyons and valleys of the chaparral country.

Even though the Crissal Thrasher is sympatric with some of the other western thrashers, the interspecific interaction is minimized because they use different microhabitats (Engels 1940; Bent 1948) and by the juxtaposition of the species' abundance peaks. The preferred habitat of the Crissal Thrasher is not desert but arroyos, valleys, canyons, and hillsides, usually with water nearby (Bent 1948). This preference is reflected in its abundance pattern, which shows the highest concentration along the southern stretches of the Colorado River valley. Two other less concentrated populations occur in the Animas valley of southwestern New Mexico and southeastern Arizona and along the Pecos River valley in southwestern Texas.

This shy thrasher usually remains hidden in dense brush and is rarely found in cacti, which provide very little cover (Bent 1948). Normally this bird will be found in small mesquite (Engels 1940; Bent 1948), creosote bush, and saltbush (Bent 1948). When foraging, it uses its bill much as the California Thrasher does; to sweep aside debris and to dig into the soil (Engels 1940). The Crissal Thrasher eats mainly berries, such as wild grapes and juniper berries, supplemented with some insects (Bent 1948). This thrasher flies little and prefers to run to cover when startled (Engels 1940). It is a permanent resident but does show some altitudinal migration during particularly severe winters (Bent 1948).

MOTACILLIDAE

Water Pipit (*Anthus spinoletta*) Maximum: 18.47 I/Hr

Most dense populations of Water Pipits are in the Southwest, with highest abundances in the Imperial Valley of southern California and along the Pecos River near the Bitter Lake National Wildlife Refuge in eastern New Mexico. Both these locations provide moist habitat along streams and ponds. To the north of the Imperial Valley, rather high concentrations of pipits occur along the Colorado River, and to the east there is a fairly dense concentration around Phoenix, Arizona. Both these environments are mesic also: along the main stream and the tributaries of the Colorado River, and in the numerous irrigated fields of central Arizona. Less concentrated populations are present in the Sacramento valley of central California and on the Edwards Plateau in southwestern Texas.

Vegetation and temperature apparently have a combined effect on the Water Pipit's distribution. The wintering grounds in the East are in areas that on average have a minimum January temperature greater than 30°F (−1°C). In the West this pipit is present where the average temperature is as low as 20°F (−7°C), but it avoids regions with large stands of dry-belt pine forest. It also avoids the harsh environments of the desert along the border of Nevada and California but is present in grasslands, savannas, and scrub steppe. The disjunct population in Iowa and Nebraska is due to an unusual sighting in 1970 at Sioux City, Iowa.

The Water Pipit is often found in fields containing little vegetation (Bent 1950). When snow blankets these barren fields, Water Pipits frequently forage along plowed roads (Phillips, Marshall, and Monson 1983). The staples of their diet are weed seeds and insects (Bent 1950), and they forage by walking across open fields. When flushed from the ground, these birds may perch on rocks, but never in leafy trees (Phillips, Marshall, and Monson 1983).

Sprague's Pipit (*Anthus spragueii*) Map in Appendix B

In general the abundance of the Sprague's Pipit was too low and sporadic for the CBC data to yield meaningful patterns. The region where this species was regularly seen was coincident with the southern distribution of *Andropogon* grass, including the area in southwestern and east-central Texas. There also were regular sightings in Arkansas and Louisiana. The highest concentrations were in extreme southeastern Texas.

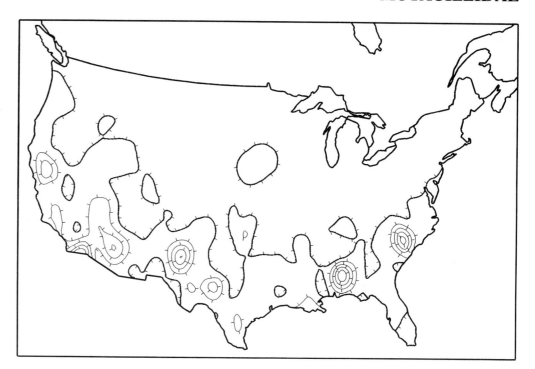

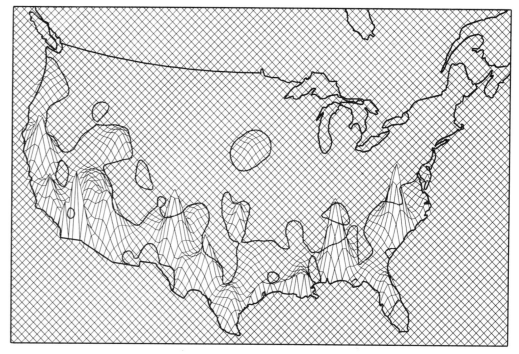

BOMBYCILLIDAE

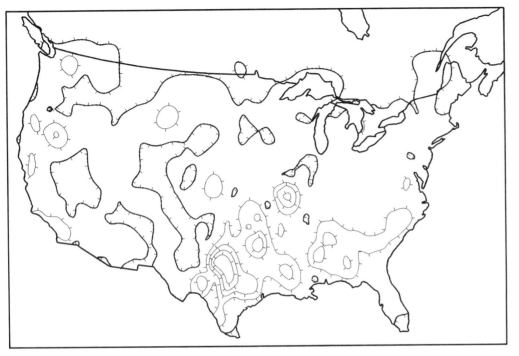

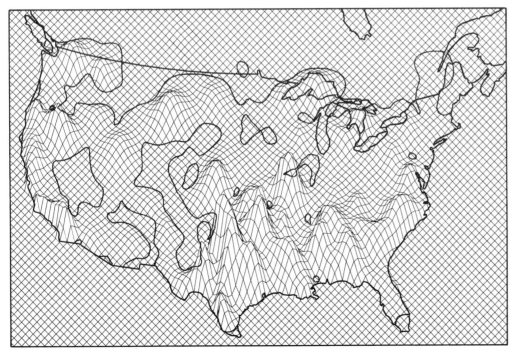

Bohemian Waxwing (*Bombycilla garrulus*) Map in Appendix B
The Bohemian Waxwing is both gregarious and nomadic. Over the years, however, consistent concentrations have been recorded in southwestern Canada and Washington State. Invasions into the South by thousands of these waxwings come at irregular intervals and have been recorded in 1909, 1917, 1920, and 1931 (Bent 1950). There is evidence in the CBC data of an irruption in 1967.

Cedar Waxwing (*Bombycilla cedrorum*) Maximum: 10.72 I/Hr
Flocks of Cedar Waxwings are nomadic to some degree, but the groups are not large enough or the wanderings sufficiently extensive to preclude the use of CBC-generated abundance patterns. These patterns show that vegetation is the main factor associated with both overall winter range and the location of dense populations. The northern distribution edge shows that this bird is absent from the boreal forest, and to some extent it avoids the mixed deciduous and coniferous forest of southeastern Canada. Grasslands, where galeria forests are not present, the deserts of Nevada, and the higher elevations of the Colorado Rockies are all environments not frequented by this bird.

The presence of junipers appears to be the primary factor defining where the Cedar Waxwing occurs in high densities. The highest abundance peak is in central Texas, corresponding almost exactly with the occurrence of the oak-juniper savanna. Lesser concentrations to the east, in eastern Mississippi and northern and southeastern Alabama, are associated with stands of junipers, liquidambar, and oaks. Junipers are also coincident with the slight abundance peaks in southern Texas along the Pecos River and at the border between California and Nevada. A fairly extensive area in central Oregon where junipers are present, however, shows no increase in abundance of waxwings. Many small abundance peaks are associated with river valleys: the Columbia River in Washington, Sacramento River in California, Missouri River in Missouri, Arkansas River in Arkansas, and Red River in Louisiana and on the border between Texas and Oklahoma.

The waxwings were given this name because of the red waxlike tips of their secondary feathers, which protect the ends of the rachis from breaking and the vanes from wear as the birds flutter in dense vegetation while foraging. Over 80% of the diet is berries and fruit, with the remainder consisting chiefly of beetles. They incessantly call softly to each other (Bent 1950) and are often seen passing berries to one another (Phillips, Marshall, and Monson 1983).

Cedar Waxwing

PTILOGONATIDAE

Phainopepla (*Phainopepla nitens*) Maximum: 6.45 I/Hr

The distribution of the Phainopepla shows a main population in the Sonoran Desert and disjunct populations in central California and southwestern Texas. The latter two locations are normally assumed to be part of only the summer range of this species (Walsberg 1977), but regular winter sightings were recorded on Christmas counts in both regions.

Temperature has little to do with the overall range of the Phainopepla except that it avoids areas with hard freezes, since freezing desiccates mistletoe berries (Anderson and Ohmart 1978). The abundance pattern, however, apparently is strongly influenced by temperature. Only areas where the average minimum January temperature is above freezing have high densities of Phainopeplas. The peak abundance is along the lower Colorado River valley, presumably in the last large stand of honey mesquite, which is in Arizona stretching from Ehrenberg in the north to Parker in the south (Anderson and Ohmart 1978).

The Phainopepla is the only member of the silky flycatchers that occurs in the United States (AOU 1983). This unusual bird has an equally unusual ecology. In the fall it migrates into the Sonoran Desert, where it winters in more mesic areas (Walsberg 1977). In the spring it breeds in this desert, seeking out areas where the vegetation is dense enough to protect nests. In late spring it moves into areas with high densities of wolfberries and insects, then it migrates north to cooler environments for the summer (Anderson and Ohmart 1978). Its winter abundance depends on the availability of its primary food, the desert mistletoe berry. This mistletoe normally parasitizes paloverde, ironwood, honey mesquite, and acacia (Walsberg 1977).

Phainopeplas' stomachs are highly adapted to allow efficient use of mistletoe berries. The gizzard is reduced in size and does not grind the berries, but instead squeezes both pulp and seed into the intestine. The berry covering, or exocarp, is stored in the gizzard until eight to sixteen accumulate, then they all are regurgitated together (Walsberg 1975). Little mounds of exocarps are a good indication of a Phainopepla's territory. In the winter females and males defend separate territories, both intra- and interspecifically. Gambel's Quails, Sage Thrashers, American Robins, House Finches, and White-crowned Sparrows are usually all displaced from clumps of mistletoe berries by the Phainopepla, but the Northern Mockingbird is normally dominant over it and thus not displaced. Western and Mountain Bluebirds often are not chased away either. At least for the House Finch, these berries are primarily only a source of water (Walsberg 1975). For the Phainopepla, however, mistletoe berries are the main food in winter. Individuals eat an average of 264 berries a day, each about 3 to 4 millimeters in diameter (Walsberg 1975, 1977). Rarely if ever is this species seen on the ground, except perhaps when drinking (Bent 1950).

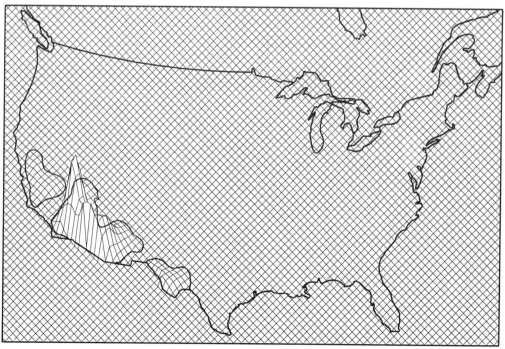

Phainopepla

LANIIDAE

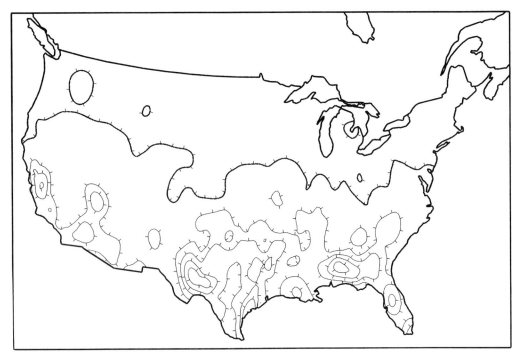

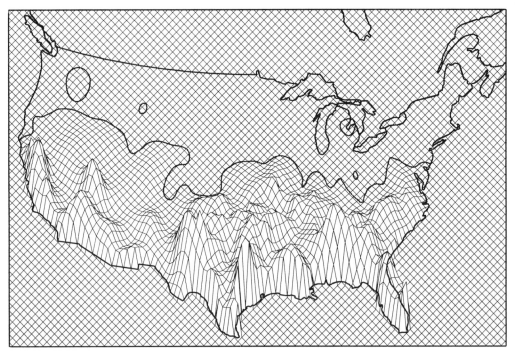

Northern Shrike (*Lanius excubitor*) Map in Appendix B

The Christmas count data from 1900 to 1935 show that on average the Northern Shrike made a southern invasion every 4.2 years (Bent 1950). After 1935 the cycle appears to disintegrate, and the irruption years of western birds are different from those in the East (Cade 1967). Examining the Christmas count data from 1963 to 1972, I found that east of the 80th meridian irruptions occurred in 1969 and 1970, and west of the 100th meridian there were southern sightings in 1965, 1966, 1970, 1971, and 1972. The overall distribution shows that this predator is present where the average minimum January temperature is below 20°F (−7°C). The warmer area, which this small predator avoids, is approximately the same region where the American Kestrel occurs in rather high concentrations. Perhaps these two ecologically similar species are avoiding each other.

Loggerhead Shrike (*Lanius ludovicianus*) Maximum: 2.80 I/Hr

None of the environmental factors examined in this study appeared to be coincident with the presence and absence of the Loggerhead Shrike. The edge of the distribution appears to correspond only roughly with the human-imposed reference line of 40° north latitude. This suggests that day length influences the northern range boundary of this predator.

This shrike occurs in high concentrations throughout areas that have less than 12 inches (30 cm) of snow a year. This includes the Southeast and areas in the West along the lower Colorado River and the San Joaquin valley of California. The highest peaks are in Texas on the Edwards Plateau, stretching from around Eldorado to Balmorhea State Park. An equally high peak is in southern Alabama, roughly around the William Dannelly Reservoir.

The Loggerhead Shrike is raptorial like its congeners. Unlike the Northern Shrike, however, the Loggerhead is reported to eat all that it kills (Bent 1950). Where prey are very common, there is a limit to the number attacked, indicating that this species does not kill just to kill (Craig 1978). This shrike normally selects prey that are easily caught rather than large in size. Items are usually 4.6 to 6.5 grams (Slack 1975). Its annual diet is 68% insects, 4% spiders, and 28% vertebrates, but in winter it eats more birds and particularly more mice (Bent 1950). Prey are captured within the winter feeding territories of solitary shrikes (Smith 1973). The size of a territory depends upon the abundance of prey in the area (Bent 1950). Sitting and waiting is the primary hunting tactic, and once it detects a prey item the shrike flies directly at it (Bent 1950). In winter hunting is most common in the afternoon, and attack rates decline with colder temperatures, probably because of a decrease in prey activity (Craig 1978). Once killed, the prey is impaled on a thorn, barb, or sharp twig while the shrike devours it (Bent 1950).

STURNIDAE

European Starling (*Sturnus vulgaris*) Map in Appendix B

The European Starling was introduced in West Chester, Pennsylvania, before 1850. Subsequent releases occurred from the 1870s to the turn of the century in Ohio, Quebec, Massachusetts, New Jersey, New York, and Oregon. Apparently the only successful introductions were of 100 birds in New York City in 1890 and another 160 in 1891 (Bent 1950). Since that time the starling range has significantly expanded. From 1963 to 1972, 1,239 Christmas count sites reported this species. Starlings form very large flocks; the maximum abundance was 8,660.00 individuals seen per hour of count effort.

Crested Myna (*Acridotheres cristatellus*) No Map

The Crested Myna is included here because it is seen regularly on counts in British Columbia; the Vancouver, Ladner, and Nanaimo counts reported it nine, eight, and five years, respectively. The highest average abundance was recorded at Vancouver, with 5.22 birds seen per hour of count effort. Luckily, this species, introduced from China about 1897, has not expanded its range as the European Starling has (Bent 1950).

VIREONIDAE

White-eyed Vireo (*Vireo griseus*) Maximum: 0.54 I/Hr

The distribution of the White-eyed Vireo increased as the forest canopy opened when American chestnut trees died out (Bent 1950). The maps show that temperature is associated with the expanded wintering grounds of the White-eyed Vireo; it does not occur in areas having a minimum January temperature lower than 40°F (4°C), except for a small extension along the coast that ends in southern North Carolina. Here the minimum temperature does not drop below freezing.

The optimum habitats for the White-eyed Vireo include old fields with small trees and low, swampy thickets (Bent 1950). The abundance peaks help confirm that these are indeed this species' preferred habitats. The highest concentration of White-eyed Vireos is in Florida around Gainesville and in the wetlands of southeastern Louisiana near the mouth of the Mississippi River. Lesser concentrations are in the Big Thicket country along the Texas-Louisiana border and on the coastal plains of southern Texas near the town of Alice.

Roughly 67% of this vireo's diet in December and January consists of insects, with most items being either lepidopteran larvae or hemipterans, and seeds make up about 23% of the diet during these two months (Nolan and Woolridge 1962). Therefore the apparent influence of temperature on the distribution of this vireo may be both a direct and an indirect effect; birds need high ambient temperatures to keep warm, but also to ensure the availability and detectability of insect prey. When insects are not available, berries, such as sumac, dogwood, wild grape, and wax myrtle, make up part of the January diet (Bent 1950).

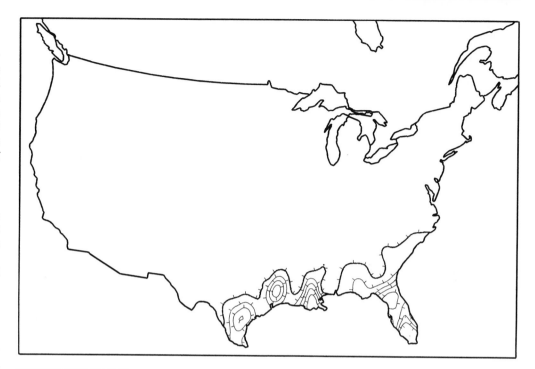

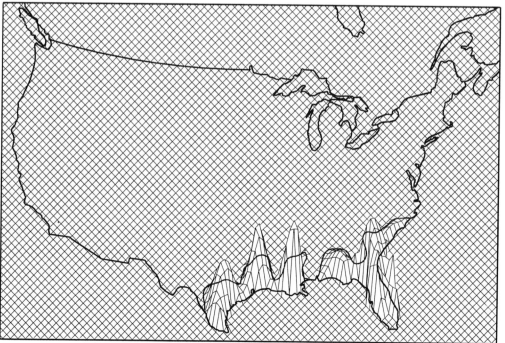

White-eyed Vireo

VIREONIDAE

Solitary Vireo (*Vireo solitarius*) Maximum: 0.33 I/Hr

From central Texas on east, the Solitary Vireo winters in areas that have an average minimum January temperature of 35°F (2°C) or more. The three disjunct populations in the West, along the Rio Grande valley of west Texas, in south-central Arizona, and in southern California, are also in warm areas, but there the average winter temperature may drop to 30°F (−1°C). This vireo is seen fairly regularly in these western areas, but this is not true of the small "population" in west-central Texas, which was due to a rare sighting of three Solitary Vireos on the West Lake Meredith count in 1967.

Temperature is also strongly associated with where this vireo is common within its overall distribution. In the areas with high concentrations, temperatures rarely dip much below 40°F (4°C). The densest population was recorded in Bastrop and Buescher state parks in Texas where, on the coastal plains along the Colorado River near the base of the Balcones Escarpment, the forest is protected and thereby provides an excellent wintering habitat.

The primary foraging activity of the Solitary Vireo is gleaning insects from twigs and leaves of trees in forests. Its annual diet is 96% spiders and insects, primarily lepidopterans at all stages in their life cycle and hemipterans. In the winter, hibernating stinkbugs are the most important food, and because the number of insects drops off during this season, berries such as wild grapes, dogwood, viburnum, and wax myrtle make up about 25% of the winter diet (Bent 1950). The name Solitary Vireo is apt but is not a unique description, since most vireos are usually found alone or perhaps in pairs.

Yellow-throated Vireo (*Vireo flavifrons*) No Map

This vireo was seen sporadically at several sites along the Gulf coast, with regular sightings only at the southern tips of Florida and Texas. The highest concentrations of Yellow-throated Vireos also were observed at these two locations, with an average of 0.02 individuals seen per hour of count effort at both locales.

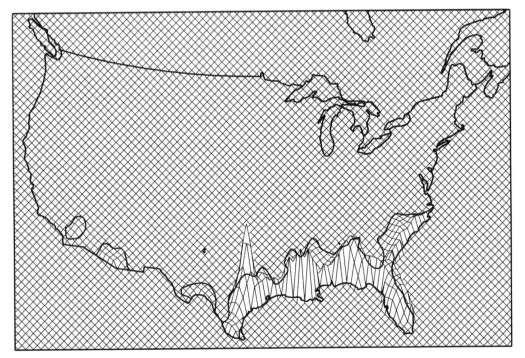

Yellow-throated Vireo

Solitary Vireo

Hutton's Vireo (*Vireo huttoni*) Maximum: 0.38 I/Hr

The Hutton's Vireo is the only nonmigratory vireo in the United States (AOU 1983). It lives primarily along the Pacific coast in evergreen forests between the ocean and the mountains, where the climate is moderated by the ocean. West of the southern half of the Sierra Nevada, this vireo frequents the California oakwoods, and along the northern half it is in the California mixed evergreen forest, which is a combination of oak, madrone, Douglas fir, and redwood. West of the Cascade Mountains this vireo is found in forests made up of spruce, cedar, hemlock, Douglas fir, and live oak. The smaller disjunct populations in southern Arizona and southwestern Texas are in evergreen oak-juniper woodlands where the average minimum temperature in January is over 30°F (−1°C).

The most concentrated population of Hutton's Vireos is in the densest stand of evergreen California oakwoods that occurs along the coast. The northern edge of this population abuts the southern end of the forests consisting of madrone, fir, and redwood species. The presence of the chaparral along the coast is coincident with the southern edge of the abundance peak.

The Hutton's Vireo often joins foraging flocks made up of small woodpeckers, White-breasted Nuthatches, Brown Creepers, Ruby-crowned Kinglets, Orange-crowned Warblers, and in Arizona, Bridled Titmice (Phillips, Marshall, and Monson 1983). Basically, its entire diet consists of insects, about half being hemipterans. Caterpillars and moths make up about 25% and beetles about 13% (Bent 1950).

Red-eyed Vireo (*Vireo olivaceus*) No Map

There were very few sightings of the Red-eyed Vireo during the ten years examined. All of these were sporadic, with each census reporting this vireo in only one or two years. The observations were along the Gulf coast, primarily at the southern tip of Florida, but not on the Keys.

EMBERIZIDAE

Tennessee Warbler (*Vermivora peregrina*) No Map

This warbler was not recorded on a Christmas count from 1963 to 1966. After that time it was observed at seventeen sites, but fifteen of these reported it in only one year, and the remaining two sites reported it in two years. All the observations were in the warm southern areas along the Gulf and Atlantic coasts.

Nashville Warbler (*Vermivora ruficapilla*) Map in Appendix B

At the forty-five sites where the Nashville Warbler was observed, it reached a maximum density of only 0.16 individuals seen per party-hour. This concentrated population was at the southern tip of Texas. Most other sightings were scattered along the Pacific coast and through the southern states between California and Texas. A few other observations were reported around the Gulf coast and along the Atlantic coast up to New Jersey.

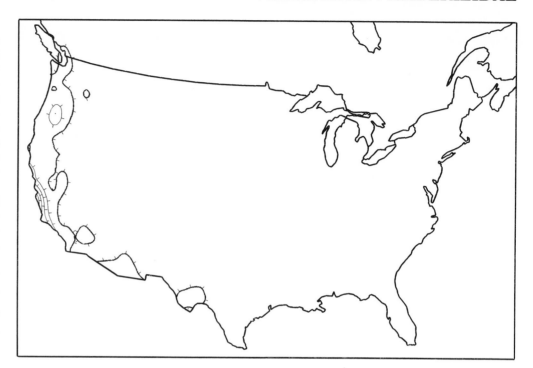

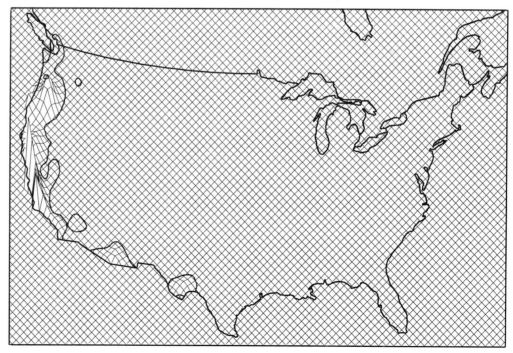

EMBERIZIDAE

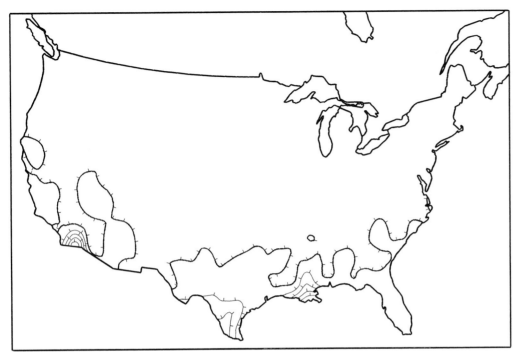

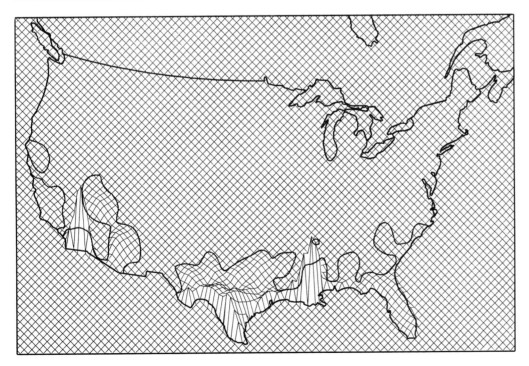

Orange-crowned Warbler (*Vermivora celata*) Maximum: 2.72 I/Hr
The winter distribution of this insectivore appears to be strongly associated with climate. The Orange-crowned Warbler migrates into the extreme southern tier of states from its breeding area, which stretches as far north as western Alaska and the central Yukon and covers most of Canada and the western United States (AOU 1983). Most of the regions within its wintering area have more than 210 consecutive days a year without frost. Warm environments allow this small insectivore to expend less energy maintaining its body temperature, and its insect prey is much more abundant and active in warmer climates (Young 1982).

The abundance pattern shows three peaks, two of which are extremely high. One of these is in southern Louisiana around the mouth of the Mississippi River, extending up the Pearl River into the state of Mississippi. The other dense population is in the Imperial Valley of California, which encompasses and stretches south of Salton Sea. A slighter concentration is in southern Texas on the Nueces Plains, extending to the southeastern part of the Edwards Plateau.

The fall migration of the Orange-crowned Warbler is fairly late and rather protracted. This warbler winters in habitats with live oaks, myrtle thickets, brushy field edges, or patches of woodland. In Florida it occurs in oaks and cabbage palms. Its diet consists chiefly of insects, but it eats some berries and fruit. This warbler also is attracted to feeders, eating suet, peanut butter, and crumbs (Griscom and Sprunt 1957).

Worm-eating Warbler (*Helmitheros vermivorus*) No Map
Around Fort Lauderdale, Florida, is the only location in the United States where wintering Worm-eating Warblers can be found with any consistency. The species was recorded there in six of the ten years, but the average abundance was fewer than 0.01 individuals per party-hour. Most of the other thirteen sites reporting this species were in Florida, with a few scattered sightings in the Rio Grande valley of Texas.

Ovenbird (*Seiurus aurocapillus*) Map in Appendix B
The Ovenbird was recorded on enough counts to warrant plotting its abundance (fifty-two sites), but its density was too low (0.11 I/Hr) to ensure reliable patterns. In general, its range extends along the Atlantic coast from North Carolina to Florida, encompasses Florida, and stretches around the Gulf coast. The most concentrated population is near West Palm Beach on the Atlantic coast of Florida.

Northern Waterthrush (*Seiurus noveboracensis*) Map in Appendix B
Observations of the Northern Waterthrush at 72% of its reporting sites occurred in fewer than five years, and many of these sites were scattered throughout the United States (e.g., in the Great Plains and along the Mississippi valley). This wandering behavior resulted in a confusing abundance map with several disjunct populations scattered across the nation. Consistent sightings were reported in Florida and at a few locations along the Gulf coast. The highest abundance was on Florida's southern Keys, with 0.32 individuals seen per party-hour.

Louisiana Waterthrush (*Seiurus motacilla*) No Map
The wintering grounds of the Louisiana Waterthrush extend from northern Mexico, southern Texas, and the Bahamas south through Central America to Panama, northeastern Colombia, and northern Venezuela (AOU 1983), but there were no consistent sightings at any of the CBC sites in the United States. All thirteen sites reported this warbler in only one year. The highest abundance was around Galveston, Texas, and the other sites were east of there, along the southern border of the United States.

Northern Parula (*Parula americana*) Maximum: 0.28 I/Hr
The Northern Parula is an eastern warbler, with breeding grounds extending from southeastern Manitoba to Nova Scotia and south to southern Texas and Florida (AOU 1983). The wintering grounds extend primarily along the Gulf coast and the southern Atlantic to central South Carolina. The migration between these two areas can be costly; many of these night travelers are killed when they hit radio beacons, tall buildings, bridges, and the like (Griscom and Sprunt 1957). The maps show what are probably late migrants rather than wintering individuals in several disjunct areas. All these disjunct populations are ephemeral and due to sightings in one or at most two years. The more regular wintering areas along the coasts are in regions that average more than 270 consecutive days a year without frost, and in January the mean minimum temperature is over 45°F (7°C).

The abundance pattern shows one major center of concentration, and this overshadows the abundance at all other localities. This dense population is on the Atlantic coast of southern Florida near Vero Beach, where the temperature rarely drops below 55°F (13°C) in January and there is no frost at all in more than 50% of the years.

The diet of the Northern Parula consists almost entirely of spiders and adult and larval insects such as beetles, moths, and flies. These prey items are caught in a manner similar to the foraging tactics of titmice and nuthatches. The warbler methodically searches cracks in the bark on limbs and trunks of trees. Occasionally it will forage on the ground and even come to feeding stations for suet and peanut butter (Griscom and Sprunt 1957).

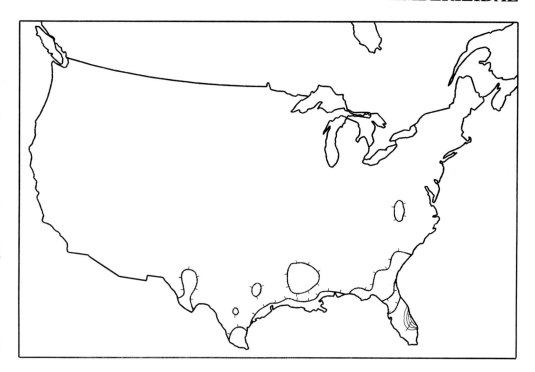

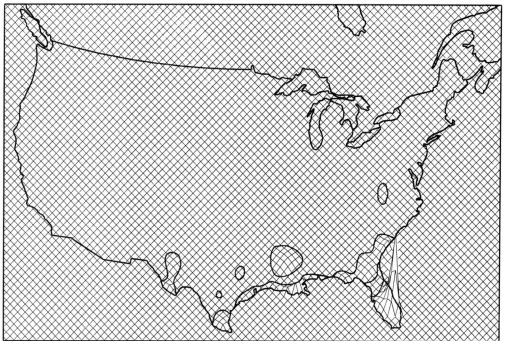

EMBERIZIDAE

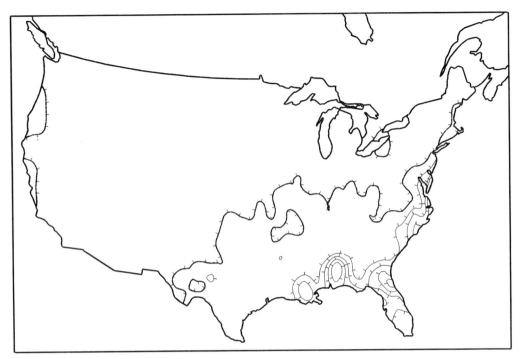

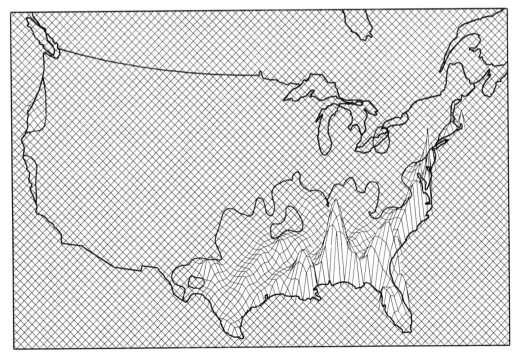

Yellow Warbler (*Dendroica petechia*) Map in Appendix B
The densest population of wintering Yellow Warblers in the United States is in the Imperial Valley of California, where on average only 0.01 individuals were seen per party-hour. The only other fairly dense population occurred at the southern tip of Texas. Its distribution encompasses the warm areas of the southern states, primarily around the Gulf, and regions along the California coast and along the Atlantic coast from Florida to New Jersey.

Yellow-rumped Warbler, Myrtle Race (*Dendroica coronata coronata*)
  Maximum: 32.75 I/Hr
The recently combined Myrtle and Audubon's subspecies of the Yellow-rumped Warbler were considered separate species when the Christmas count data examined were collected. I have provided maps for both of these forms because separately they certainly provide more information about the biogeography of this warbler than could a map of combined data.

The winter distribution of the Myrtle Warbler shows that warm temperatures strongly influence where it occurs. In most of the region where it is present, the annual length of the frost-free period is at least 180 days, and the January temperature rarely drops below 25°F (−4°C). These conditions hold true for the disjunct population in California. Other factors, however, must be limiting these western populations, because habitats with these conditions cover a much more extensive area than this warbler inhabits. Perhaps the presence of the Audubon's race restricts this subspecies, but a smaller-scale study is needed to examine this hypothesis.

This eastern counterpart of the Audubon's Warbler is appropriately named because in winter it is often associated with wax myrtle or bayberry trees and bushes. The abundance pattern shows that the highest concentrations of the Myrtle Warbler are coincident with the distribution of the evergreen bayberry, which covers the coastal plain from New Jersey to Louisiana (Brockman 1968). All of this region where the warbler is fairly common also has an average January minimum temperature above freezing.

At the northern extreme of its distribution, where temperatures are colder, the warbler eats bayberries almost exclusively. The waxy substance in the berries is primarily fat, and they also have traces of protein and carbohydrates. The berries remain on the bushes or trees, making them easy to find when snow is on the ground (Wilz and Giampa 1978). The winter diet of this subspecies consists primarily of berries of wax myrtle, cedar, yaupon, poison ivy, and sumac (Griscom and Sprunt 1957), but it also eats insects in warmer areas where they are available. A high number of Myrtle Warblers are killed during migration because at night they run into structures such as tall buildings and radio towers. Two birds have also been found dead tangled in spiderwebs, both in South Carolina (Griscom and Sprunt 1957).

Yellow-rumped Warbler, Myrtle Race

Yellow-rumped Warbler, Audubon's Race (*Dendroica coronata auduboni*) Maximum: 27.31 I/Hr

The Audubon's race is present west of the 100th meridian; the distribution appears to be associated primarily with temperature and to a much lesser extent with vegetation. Most of the area where it occurs has an average minimum January temperature of at least 20°F (−7°C). In west-central Texas, however, this warbler is absent from warm regions, presumably because the vegetation there is tree and shrub savanna and grasslands. The Yellow-rumped Warbler is present in semiarid shrub and scrub steppe habitats. The northern limit along the Washington coast is probably influenced by warm temperature too; this warbler occurs in areas that have 300 or more consecutive days a year without frost. There are two disjunct populations, both along river valleys; one is in the Columbia basin of Washington, and the other is on the Rio Grande in New Mexico.

The abundance pattern shows that a dense population of this warbler winters in the Imperial Valley of southern California, with a fairly high concentration stretching northward from the San Diego coast to around Santa Barbara. A lesser peak in abundance is present around Phoenix, Arizona. The high abundances in these areas are probably due to several factors, such as warmth and high relative humidity.

Griscom and Sprunt (1957) reported that this warbler showed only an altitudinal migration, with birds wintering as far north as the northern edge of their breeding ground in central British Columbia and southern Alberta (AOU 1983). This was not the case during the ten years of this study. There apparently was migration south and west. Such migration would be expected, since about 85% of this warbler's diet consists of insects and spiders (Griscom and Sprunt 1957) and it does not often forage in the protected crevices of bark where numerous dormant insects winter in colder environments. Thus, birds would need to migrate into warmer climates where active insects are abundant.

Magnolia Warbler (*Dendroica magnolia*) No Map

All twenty-seven sites reporting the Magnolia Warbler were east of the 100th meridian, and twenty-four of them were below the 31st parallel. The only two locations where this warbler was observed in more than five years were on the Atlantic coast between Fort Lauderdale and West Palm Beach, Florida. The most highly concentrated population also occurred here, with 0.01 individuals seen per party-hour.

Cape May Warbler (*Dendroica tigrina*) No Map

In the United States, the Cape May Warbler winters regularly only on the Florida Keys and at Cape Sable on Florida Bay, but even at these locations the density was only 0.02 individuals seen per party-hour. Nine other Florida locations and three sites along the Atlantic coast between Georgia and New Jersey reported this warbler.

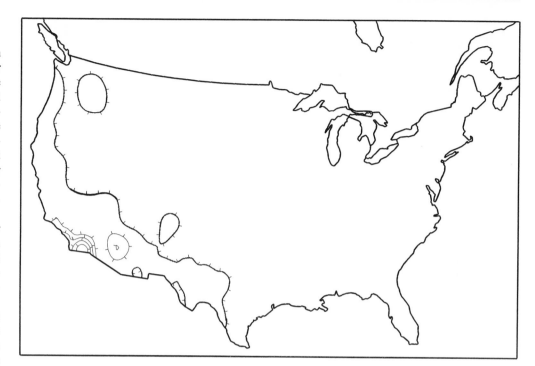

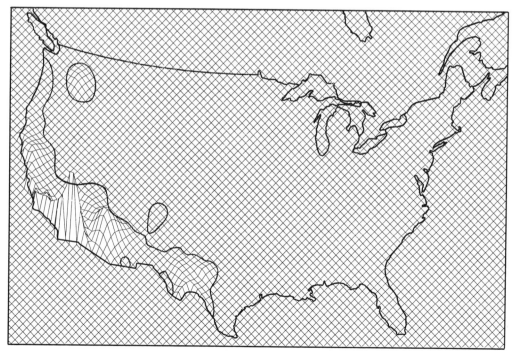

Yellow-rumped Warbler, Audubon's Race

EMBERIZIDAE

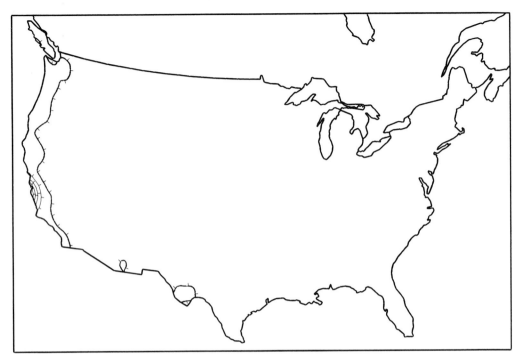

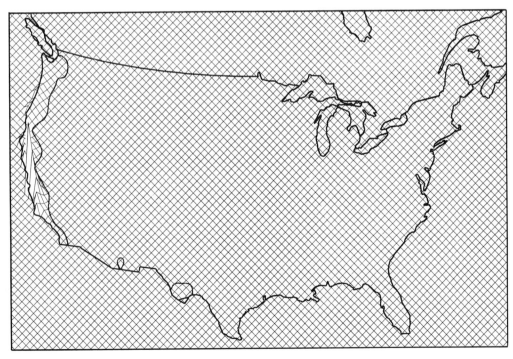

Black-throated Blue Warbler (*Dendroica caerulescens*) No Map
Most of the twenty-five sites reporting the Black-throated Blue Warbler were in Florida, with a few scattered observations north along the Atlantic coast to New Jersey. The most reliable location for finding this warbler is at Cape Sable on Florida Bay, where the densest population occurred (0.02 I/Hr) and birds were observed every year.

Black-throated Gray Warbler (*Dendroica nigrescens*) Map in
   Appendix B
Only four of the twenty-five sites reporting the Black-throated Gray Warbler noted this species in more than five years. Three of these were along the Atlantic coast of Florida; the fourth was on Florida Bay at Cape Sable, the location of the most concentrated population (0.02 I/Hr). The remaining twenty-one sites were scattered throughout Florida and along the Atlantic coast.

Townsend's Warbler (*Dendroica townsendi*) Maximum: 0.98 I/Hr
In the area examined, this active warbler winters almost exclusively in the western coastal states, from the Mexican border to Canada. The exceptions are two disjunct populations in southeastern Arizona and in Big Bend National Park of Texas. Most of the distribution of Townsend's Warbler is west of the Cascade Mountains and the southern Coast Range. The high mountain peaks seem to play a part in restricting the range of this warbler, but temperature and vegetation apparently are also important. Basically its entire range is where the average minimum January temperature is above freezing. The northern limit on the Canadian border seems to be influenced by temperatures dropping below 30°F (−1°C) in January. Even though the temperature in extreme southeastern California is above freezing, the Townsend's Warbler avoids the area, presumably because of unsuitable vegetation. It occurs in the chaparral region along the coast, which contains spiny ceanothus (California lilac), and avoids the environment farther east that is dominated by the creosote bush. There were four census sites in southeastern Arizona where this warbler was seen, but it was reported only one or two times at each of these locations over the ten years examined. The population in the Chisos Mountains of Big Bend National Park in Texas, however, was reported regularly.

Temperature seems to be the main factor associated with high concentrations of wintering Townsend's Warblers. The densest population occurs on the California coast from San Luis Obispo to San Francisco, with the apex around Monterey. All of this area has an average minimum January temperature of at least 40°F (4°C).

This insectivore obviously prefers warmer temperatures, perhaps partly because its prey are more abundant and active and thereby easier to detect (Young 1982). Spiders and insects, including weevils, engraver beetles, and caterpillars, make up 95% of its diet; the remaining 5% consists of seeds. Surprisingly, this warbler comes to feeders, eating cheese, peanut butter, and even marshmallows (Griscom and Sprunt 1957).

Townsend's Warbler

Hermit Warbler (*Dendroica occidentalis*) No Map
The Hermit Warbler was reported at fourteen sites scattered along the Pacific coast from San Diego, California, to the middle of Oregon. Only the census near Monterey, California, reported it regularly; it was observed in five years. Even there the abundance was low, with 0.01 individuals seen per party-hour.

Black-throated Green Warbler (*Dendroica virens*) No Map
In the United States, the wintering grounds of this warbler are reported to include southern and southeastern Texas and southern Florida (AOU 1983). All twenty-three Christmas count sites reporting it were in Florida, however, and only two counts, one in the lower Keys and the other near Key Largo, observed it in five or more years.

Yellow-throated Warbler (*Dendroica dominica*) Maximum: 0.50 I/Hr
The winter distribution of this warbler in the Southeast apparently is influenced by warm climate. The Yellow-throated Warbler is present in areas that annually have more than 240 consecutive days without frost, and it is recorded regularly (five or more years) where the frost-free period is longer than 270 days a year. The range stops in central North Carolina, where the environment becomes swampy and presumably lacks suitable vegetation. In the Carolinas this warbler is usually found in live oaks, and farther south in Georgia it is found in the cypress-pine–live oak association (Griscom and Sprunt 1957). Open water, however, does seem to be a necessary part of its habitat. The population extension in inland Louisiana is along the Red River. One of the disjunct populations in the West is on the southwestern end of Lake Mead in Nevada, but this, like the disjunct population on the California coast, is due only to infrequent sightings.

The most regular and abundant population is on the Florida peninsula. The apex stretches from around Yankeetown at the mouth of the Withlacoochee River to around Steinhatchee on Deadman Bay and extends inland to encompass Gainesville. A less regular but equally abundant population stretches along the southern Rio Grande valley in Texas, from the Amistad Reservoir south to the Gulf of Mexico. Within this Texas population, peaks occur just south of Eagle Pass and around Santa Ana National Wildlife Refuge.

The foraging habits of the Yellow-throated Warbler somewhat resemble those of the Brown Creeper; it methodically inspects crevices in the bark of larger limbs and trunks of trees. Its diet consists entirely of spiders and insects, such as beetles, scale insects, flies, crickets, and grasshoppers. Some spiders, however, prove deadly to this warbler. Two dead birds were reported tangled in the golden-colored web of the Carolina silk spider. Webs frequently are strung between tree trunks about 50 feet (17 m) apart. On migration, a very large number of these night travelers are killed by hitting structures such as tall buildings and bridges (Griscom and Sprunt 1957).

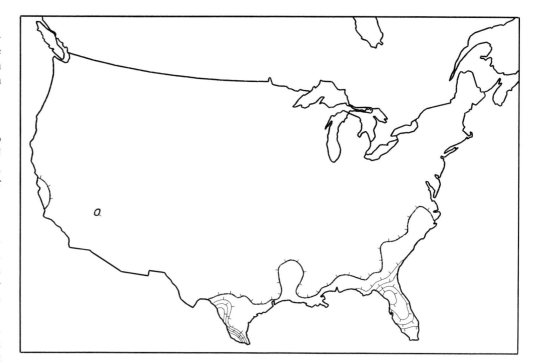

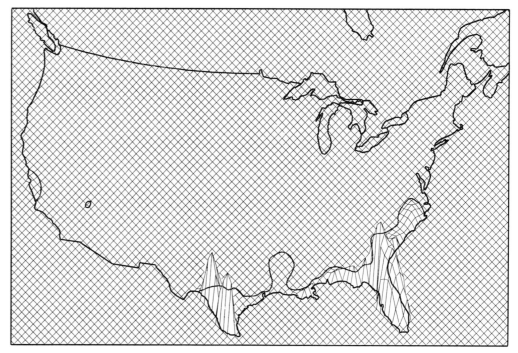

Yellow-throated Warbler

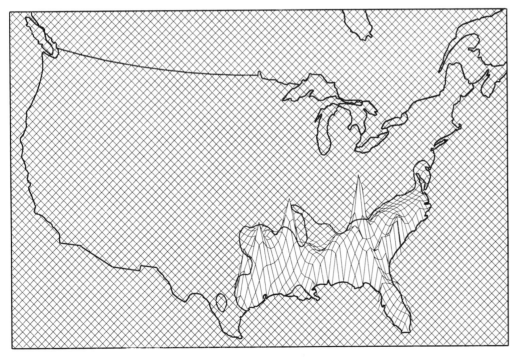

Pine Warbler (*Dendroica pinus*) Maximum: 2.78 I/Hr

The western distribution edge of the Pine Warbler appears to be associated with precipitation, while the northern boundary is coincident with temperature. The disjunct population in southwestern Texas is due to sightings in one year at several localities. The western edge of the primary wintering area in the United States is coincident with the 32 inch (81 cm) annual precipitation isopleth, suggesting that areas with less precipitation are unsuitable. To the north this warbler is absent where the average minimum January temperature drops below 30°F (−1°C), but one exception is the extension into Missouri in the Mark Twain National Forest.

As its name suggests, the Pine Warbler is usually found in pines (Griscom and Sprunt 1957). This is evident from the abundance pattern, which shows that concentrated populations occur in most of the loblolly-shortleaf pine forests in the United States. This type of forest is fairly extensive in the Southeast, and consequently the Pine Warbler is fairly common throughout its entire range, unlike any other warbler wintering in the United States. In North Carolina some factor other than vegetation is influencing its abundance; the loblolly-shortleaf pine forest continues into this region, but the abundance of the warbler drops off. The strong association with pines has proved somewhat detrimental to this species. The decline in its abundance over the years has been linked to the destruction of the pine forests by logging (Griscom and Sprunt 1957). Thus, it is to be expected that the peak abundances occur in protected areas. In southeastern Texas an extremely dense warbler population occurs in and around the Sam Houston National Forest, and just southwest of there is a less extensive and a bit less dense population around Bastrop and Buescher state parks. On the border between Louisiana and Arkansas is another concentrated population, near Felsenthal National Wildlife Refuge. Another high abundance peak is present in Georgia around Atlanta.

Pine Warblers frequently join foraging flocks with Carolina Chickadees, Tufted Titmice, Downy Woodpeckers, Brown Creepers, Brown-headed Nuthatches, and Ruby-crowned and Golden-crowned Kinglets. Normally there are approximately equal numbers of Pine Warblers and Brown-headed Nuthatches in a given flock (Morse 1967). The warbler also associates with flocks of bluebirds, Palm Warblers, and Chipping Sparrows (Griscom and Sprunt 1957). In winter the Pine Warbler normally forages on the ground (Griscom and Sprunt 1957) and on the proximal part of pine limbs (Morse 1967). In summer it eats primarily insects and spiders, but pine seeds, fruit, berries, and some weed and grass seeds make up the better part of its winter diet. Unlike most songbirds, the Pine Warbler sings throughout the winter (Griscom and Sprunt 1957).

Prairie Warbler (*Dendroica discolor*) Maximum: 1.26 I/Hr

This warbler primarily winters on the Bahama Islands and south through the West Indies to islands off the coasts of Mexico, Belize, and Honduras (AOU 1983). Within the United States it is primarily restricted to Florida. All the disjunct populations outside Florida are due to irregular sightings, and in fact this warbler is not reported very regularly in northern Florida. This species was reported in five or more years only where the average minimum January temperature is over 50°F (10°C).

Contrary to its name, the Prairie Warbler does not winter in high abundances on prairies. Instead it is common in the southern mixed forest and mangrove forest on the Gulf coast around Fort Myers, Florida. Not shown on the map is another abundant population in southern Florida around Big Pine Key, which is primarily mangrove forest.

This warbler is usually found in brushy vegetation that is less than 25 feet (8 m) high, and Griscom and Sprunt (1957) suggest that the name Scrub Warbler would be more appropriate. Because of its propensity for this habitat, the abundance of this warbler is not declining and may even be increasing, due to the clearing of woodlands and the subsequent growth of scrubby vegetation (Griscom and Sprunt 1957). A comparison of the Prairie Warbler's diet in the summer with that of birds wintering in Puerto Rico shows that their diets are similar. This warbler preys primarily on spiders and insects, including small beetles, lepidopteran larvae, and aquatic insects, along with a bit of vegetation. Its foraging behavior is fairly diverse and includes gleaning on diagonal twigs with its body parallel to the ground; flycatching from an exposed perch, usually on a flight level with the perch and infrequently flying up at about a 30° angle and gliding back to the perch; hovering under a leaf or in front of a spiderweb; hanging upside down, which it does infrequently; and while perched, seizing close-flying insects, which it may pursue if it misses the first time (Nolan 1978).

Bay-breasted Warbler (*Dendroica castanea*) No Map

The Bay-breasted Warbler winters from Panama through Colombia to northwestern Venezuela (AOU 1983). Only eleven sites reported this species in the United States, and observations at only one of these occurred in four years. Those at the remaining sites occurred in only one or two years. All these locations were in Florida or along the Gulf coast.

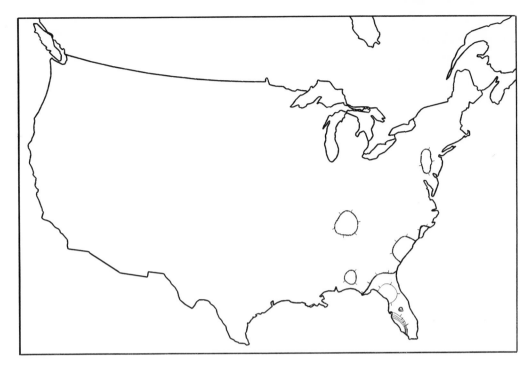

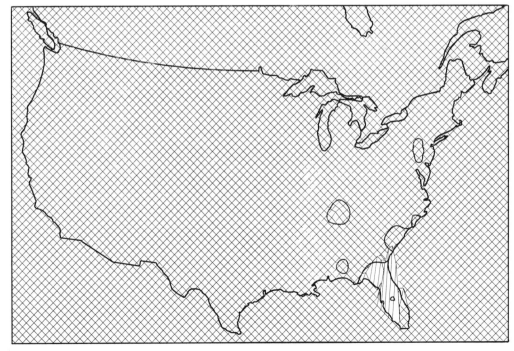

EMBERIZIDAE

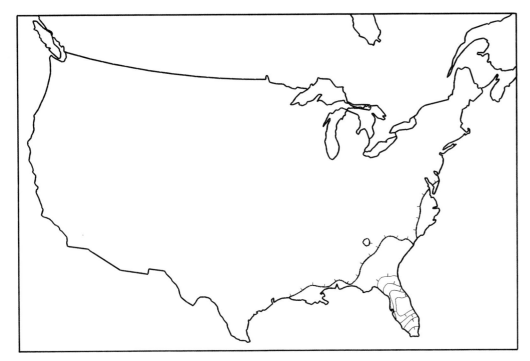

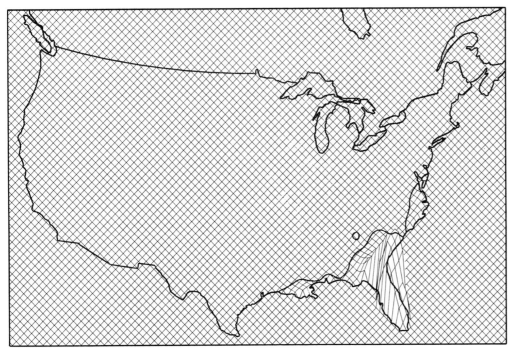

Palm Warbler (*Dendroica palmarum*) Maximum: 6.61 I/Hr
Like the Prairie Warbler, the Palm Warbler is inappropriately named. It rarely frequents palms, except perhaps the palmetto. Open fields and pastures are where it usually can be found, and it even occurs in manicured yards and parks (Griscom and Sprunt 1957). Perhaps because of its ability to survive and even thrive in disturbed environments, this warbler's distribution is not obviously associated with any of the environmental factors examined. This may also be because it winters in a restricted area and the scale used here to examine the various patterns is too coarse. Most of this species' distribution does occur where the annual frost-free period extends at least 240 days, but this is also true for the area west of south-central Louisiana, where this warbler is not present. General humidity in this vacant region may be too low, as indicated by an increase in pan evaporation to over 70 inches (178 cm). Vegetation may also be playing a role; most of the distribution occurs in areas with southern mixed forest, which is not present west of south-central Louisiana.

The most highly concentrated population of Palm Warblers is in an area where the minimum January temperature is over 45°F (7°C). The apex of this population is in the center of the Florida peninsula around several lakes and extends south from the southern edge of Ocala National Forest to around Avon Park, near the north side of Lake Okeechobee. Indeed, Griscom and Sprunt (1957) reported that the Palm Warbler may be the most common landbird in Florida during the winter. It often joins chickadee foraging flocks and hunts for beetles, ants, spiders, caterpillars, grasshoppers, and the like (Griscom and Sprunt 1957).

American Redstart (*Setophaga ruticilla*) No Map
The thirty-nine locations reporting the American Redstart stretched sporadically along the Atlantic coast but also extended along the Gulf coast and inland through the southern states to California. This warbler was observed most consistently in Florida, and the most abundant of these populations was in the lower Keys, where 0.13 individuals were seen per party-hour.

Wilson's Warbler (*Wilsonia pusilla*) Map in Appendix B
Unfortunately, the maximum abundance of the Wilson's Warbler was so low (0.09 I/Hr) that the resulting abundance pattern may not be accurate. Thus, the contour map has been placed in appendix B. This species' range generally encompasses the western part of the Gulf coast, the southern regions of the southwestern states, and the Pacific coast from California to the Oregon border. The densest population was in Louisiana at the mouth of the Mississippi River.

Common Yellowthroat (*Geothlypis trichas*) Maximum: 3.81 I/Hr
The range of the Common Yellowthroat is strongly associated with temperature and covers most of the area in North America where the frost-free period is longer than 240 days. This includes the region from the California coast near Point Arena to southwestern Arizona and from southwestern Texas to Virginia. Several of the inland extensions and disjunct populations were reported regularly, including the populations along the Colorado River on the border between California and Arizona, up the Pecos River in Texas, around Lake Texoma, and on the Tennessee River in northern Alabama. The disjunct population in Arkansas at the confluence of the Arkansas and Mississippi rivers is due to irregular sightings.

The abundance pattern shows that temperature is also the main factor associated with dense populations of this warbler. The three most concentrated populations occur in areas where the average minimum January temperature is over 45°F (7°C). The densest is in southern Florida on the Atlantic coast near West Palm Beach. The next most abundant population is on the Rio Grande in Texas near Falcon Dam State Park, and a fairly high concentration extends inland on the coastal plains in front of the Edwards Plateau in Texas. A dense population on the Louisiana coast extends inland, roughly along the Mississippi River. There is a much lower abundance peak on the Gulf coast of northeastern Florida between Crystal River and the city of Perry, extending inland to around Gainesville. A decrease in abundance occurs around Lake Okeechobee.

The Common Yellowthroat frequents dense undergrowth, which it uses for cover, but it is fairly easy to see because it is exceedingly curious and readily responds to "pishing." It can be found in both wet and dry habitats provided dense cover is available. Marshes, swamps, river edges, and the edges of woodlots all are excellent environments for this warbler. Its abundance is negatively affected by at least two factors. Large numbers are killed each spring and fall during migration when they hit structures such as tall buildings. Also, during the breeding season its nests are often parasitized by cowbirds; in fact, it is the seventh most parasitized bird in North America. As a defense, the Common Yellowthroat will build a new nest on top of a parasitized nest (Griscom and Sprunt 1957).

Yellow-breasted Chat (*Icteria virens*) Map in Appendix B
As with the Wilson's Warbler, the abundance of the Yellow-breasted Chat is too low (0.05 I/Hr) to ensure reliable maps. The 105 CBC sites reporting this warbler indicate that it ranges along the Gulf coast and up the Atlantic coast to the southern border of Maine. At all the more northerly locations, sightings occurred only once.

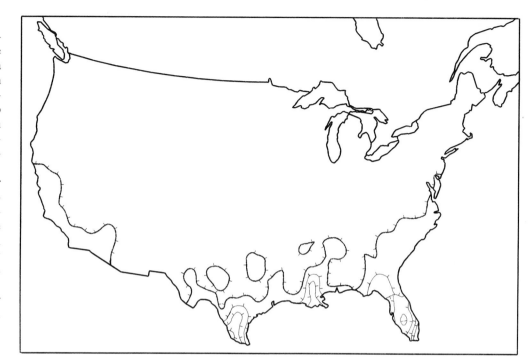

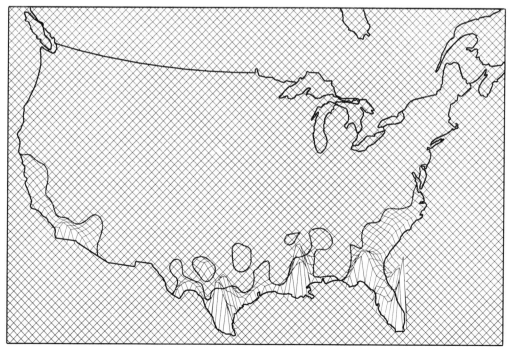

EMBERIZIDAE

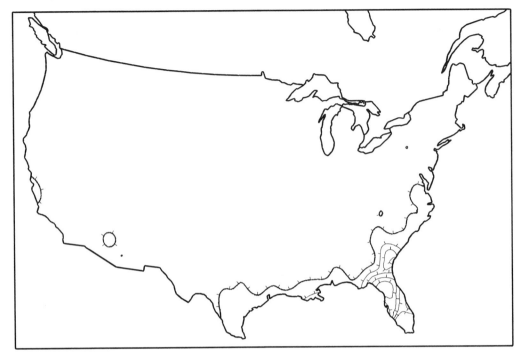

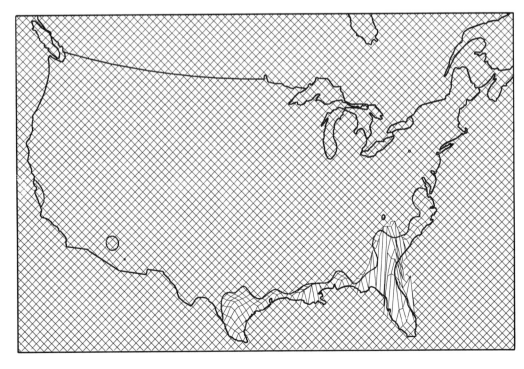

Black-and-white Warbler (*Mniotilta varia*) Maximum: 0.29 I/Hr
Temperature seems to be the major factor associated with where the Black-and-white Warbler winters. It occurs where the frost-free period is over 240 days a year. One reason this small passerine avoids cold environments is the energy cost of keeping warm (Root 1988b). All the disjunct populations of this warbler, in California, Arizona, Pennsylvania, and western North Carolina, are due to irregular sightings. Because birds often linger on their breeding grounds into late fall (Griscom and Sprunt 1957), these are probably sightings of late migrants. The data show no synchrony in these observations.

Temperature apparently also plays some part in structuring the Black-and-white Warbler's abundance pattern. Most of the regions with high concentrations have average minimum January temperatures over 45°F (7°C), even the slight concentration in southeastern Louisiana. The highest abundance occurs in Florida at approximately the same location as for the Yellow-throated Warbler—around Gainesville and extending to Yankeetown in the southwest and Deadman Bay directly west. Less concentrated populations occur in Florida around Tampa Bay and Sarasota and on the Georgia coast around Harris Neck National Wildlife Refuge, just south of Savannah.

The foraging habits of the Black-and-white Warbler resemble those of a nuthatch or the Brown Creeper. All these species methodically search the crevices of bark on trunks and larger limbs. The warbler is specifically looking for click beetles and bark beetles and hunting for moths and caterpillars in leaf clusters. Its winter distribution reportedly has expanded since 1905 when Frank Chapman, originator of the Christmas counts, reported that it was present from western Florida to southern Texas (Griscom and Sprunt 1957). The accompanying maps show that its recent winter distribution covers this area plus the region along the Atlantic coast from the southern tip of Florida to Maryland. Griscom and Sprunt (1957) suggest that the extension into northern South Carolina seen during their study was due to an increase in observers. This may be part of the reason, but it is probably only a small part.

Summer Tanager (*Piranga rubra*) No Map
The only count recording the Summer Tanager in more than five years was the site just north of the Mexican border on the coast of California. Here it was observed in six years, but the average abundance was less than 0.01 individuals seen per party-hour. The other twenty-four sites reporting this tanager were scattered throughout the southern states from California to Florida.

Western Tanager (*Piranga ludoviciana*) No Map
Most of the twenty-five sites reporting the Western Tanager are west of the 95th meridian, with a majority of those in California. Observations at only three locales occurred in five or more years, all in southern California along the coast. The abundance at all these sites was 0.01 individuals seen per party-hour.

Northern Cardinal (*Cardinalis cardinalis*) Maximum: 13.26 I/Hr

Over the years the Northern Cardinal has greatly expanded its range. In 1886 it only occasionally occurred north of the Ohio River, by 1895 its range reached the Great Lakes, and by 1910 it was in southern Ontario and along the southern portion of the Hudson River (Bent 1968). The extension into the Northwest occurred primarily along the Mississippi River and its tributaries (Dow and Scott 1971). Since 1943 and 1958, when the first nests were recorded in Connecticut and eastern Massachusetts, respectively, this species has expanded dramatically into the Northeast (Beddall 1963) and simultaneously decreased its dispersal into the Northwest (Dow and Scott 1971). To the north it occurs where the average minimum January temperature is above 5°F (−15°C). Moisture appears to influence the western edge of the main wintering area, with the cardinal frequenting only regions that receive more than 16 inches (41 cm) of annual precipitation. This is also true for the population in southern New Mexico and Arizona, but not for the birds in southern California. This far western population was introduced in Pasadena, California, in 1923 (Beddall 1963) and has not expanded much, probably because of the dryness of the surrounding environment.

The Northern Cardinal prefers woody cover (Beddall 1963), and no doubt the establishment of towns and cities with their associated parks and yards with trees and bushes has increased both its distribution and its abundance. The riparian and galeria forests along rivers provide corridors for dispersal (Dow 1970). River valleys strongly influence the abundance pattern. The densest concentrations are on the Mississippi River, both in the South and farther north, and along the Colorado and Guadalupe rivers in southern Texas. Less dense populations are present along the Ohio, Arkansas, Brazos, and Red rivers. Slight abundances occur in regions with a minimum winter temperature over 20°F (−7°C) and an annual rainfall of 24 inches (61 cm) or more.

About 90% of the Northern Cardinal's winter diet is vegetable matter, primarily seeds that have a mean size of 0.12 inch (3.1 mm) (Pulliam and Enders 1971). In warm temperatures they choose seeds that are easily husked; foxtail seeds, which are easy to handle, are preferred over hemp or ragweed seeds, which take longer to eat. At temperatures near freezing, however, birds are not choosy about which seeds they eat. When it is cold, speed of handling, caloric content, and weight do not seem to matter (Willson and Harmeson 1973). This bird forages 68% of the time while standing on the ground and picking seeds off the plant; 9% of the time it picks seeds from the ground; and 23% of the time it perches on the plant (Pulliam and Enders 1971).

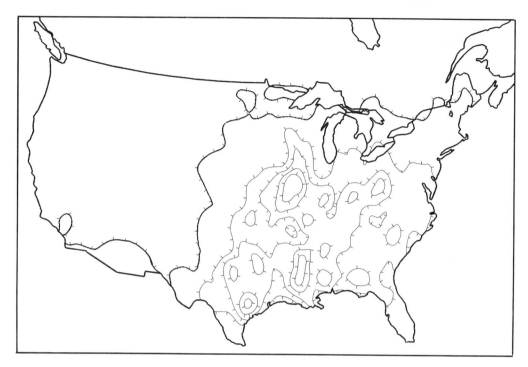

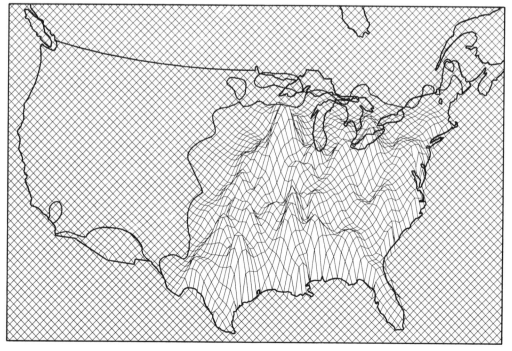

EMBERIZIDAE

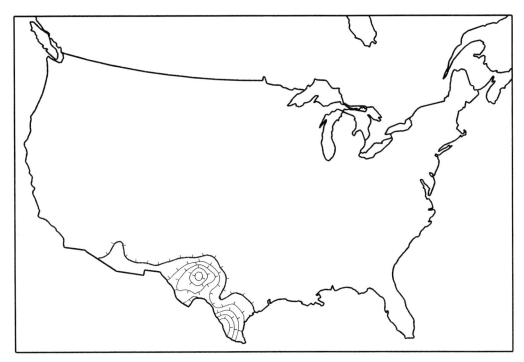

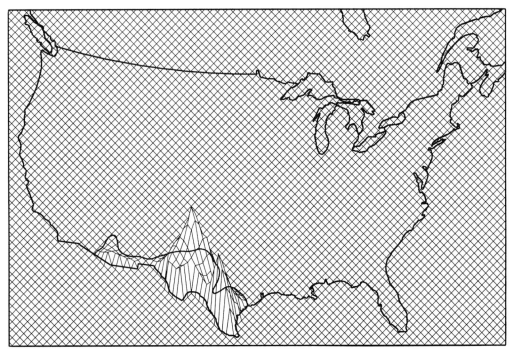

Pyrrhuloxia (*Cardinalis sinuatus*) Maximum: 9.12 I/Hr

The factors associated with the boundaries of the Pyrrhuloxia's distribution are somewhat vague. A combination of temperature and vegetation appears to indicate where this species winters. This bird occurs in habitats that have thorny bushes, such as mesquite and acacia, and a mean minimum January temperature of at least $25°F$ ($-4°C$). The ratio of thorny bushes to those without thorns also may be important, because mesquite is present to the northeast of the distribution but oak and juniper are also there. Vegetation dictates many behaviors of the Pyrrhuloxia. For example, it eats the seeds of hegari that grow up within mesquite bushes but ignores those interspersed between mesquite plants (Bent 1968).

The preferred habitat of the Pyrrhuloxia is mesquite and other thorny bushes along the edges of large arroyos and at the wider portions of canyons (Bent 1968), a predilection that is apparent in its abundance pattern. The two areas with the highest concentrations are along the Pecos River near Imperial, Texas, and along the Rio Grande near Laredo, Texas.

In winter the main staple of the Pyrrhuloxia is the mesquite bean, and when conditions are appropriate it will come to feeders (Bent 1968). Twelve or so will gather in a flock during the winter (Phillips, Marshall, and Monson 1983) and forage together where food is abundant (Bent 1968). These flocks are more mobile than wintering groups of Northern Cardinals (Phillips, Marshall, and Monson 1983), and their members feed on the ground less frequently (Bent 1968).

The unusual name of this species comes from the genus name Bonaparte gave it in 1850. He combined the genus name of the bullfinches, *Pyrrhula,* which comes from the Greek *pyrrhos* meaning flame colored or *pyrrhoulas* meaning a red bird, with *loxos,* which is Greek for crosswise (Gotch 1981) or crooked (Bent 1968). This is an apt description for this sooty red bird with a notched bill. Subsequently the Pyrrhuloxia was reclassified into the genus *Cardinalis* (AOU 1983), which happens to be the genus originally assigned by Bonaparte when the bird was first described in 1837 (Bent 1968).

Pyrrhuloxia

Rose-breasted Grosbeak (*Pheucticus ludovicianus*) Map in
   Appendix B
The forty-three Christmas count sites reporting the Rose-breasted Grosbeak
were scattered throughout the East and Southwest. This species' range
extends from the eastern border of Texas along the Gulf coast, around
Florida, and up the Atlantic coast to New Brunswick. Inland areas encom-
passed in the range include the regions along the Mississippi valley, around
the Great Lakes, and from southwestern Arizona to the coast of central
California. The most concentrated population occurred in Michigan around
the Great Lakes, with 0.12 individuals seen per party-hour.

Black-headed Grosbeak (*Pheucticus melanocephalus*) No Map
Sightings at all but one of the thirty-eight sites reporting the Black-headed
Grosbeak occurred in fewer than five years. The one exception was the
count near Santa Barbara, California, where it was seen in eight years, but
the average abundance was less than 0.01 individuals per party-hour. This
grosbeak was seen in southern Texas and at areas stretching inland across
New Mexico and Arizona to California and along the seaboard to the
border of Oregon.

Blue Grosbeak (*Guiraca caerulea*) No Map
Winter sightings of the Blue Grosbeak occurred at twenty-one locations
scattered throughout the southern tier of states from Florida to California
and along the Atlantic coast from Florida to North Carolina. The only site
where it was consistently observed was near Nogales, Arizona, where it
was seen in six years, but the average abundance was only 0.03 individuals
per party-hour.

Lazuli Bunting (*Passerina amoena*) No Map
The winter range of the Lazuli Bunting encompasses southern Baja California, southern Arizona, and the area of Mexico from southern Chihuahua
to Guerrero and central Veracruz (AOU 1983). Eleven Christmas count
sites in southern Arizona and southern California recorded this bunting.
The densest population (0.45 I/Hr) was recorded near Nogales, Arizona,
where individuals were seen in 70% of the years examined.

Indigo Bunting (*Passerina cyanea*) No Map
Indigo Buntings were seen at thirty-nine CBC sites along the Gulf coast
and in Florida south of the 30th parallel. It was recorded in more than
50% of the years examined at several sites. The most abundant population
was near Fort Lauderdale, Florida, where 0.67 individuals were seen per
party-hour.

Painted Bunting (*Passerina ciris*) Map in Appendix B
Even though this exotic-looking species was recorded at only thirty-five
sites, mapping the data provided interesting biogeographic information.
Therefore the contour map is included in appendix B. Most of the thirty-
five sites were in Florida, with a few scattered sightings along the Gulf
coast. The most reliable place in the United States to see Painted Buntings
in the winter is near Fort Lauderdale, Florida, where birds were seen each
year and the average abundance was 1.70 individuals per party-hour.

Dickcissel (*Spiza americana*) Map in Appendix B
The winter range of the Dickcissel in North America covers most of the
East. It extends along the Gulf and Atlantic coasts, along the Mississippi
valley, throughout the Northeast, and slightly into southern Canada. A total
of 153 sites recorded the Dickcissel within this area, but the maximum
average abundance at all these locations was only 0.05 individuals seen per
party-hour, which means that where Dickcissels were most common, one
bird was sighted every twenty hours on average. The densest population is
along the Mississippi River.

Olive Sparrow (*Arremonops rufivirgatus*) No Map
The Olive Sparrow, which is more closely related to towhees than to sparrows (AOU 1983), was seen at only sixteen sites in the southern United
States. All the sightings were in extreme southern Texas, below the 30th
parallel and between the 97th and 100th meridians. Of the counts where
this species was seen in seven or more years, the highest abundance was
near Alice, Texas, with 0.39 individuals seen per party-hour.

Indigo Bunting

EMBERIZIDAE

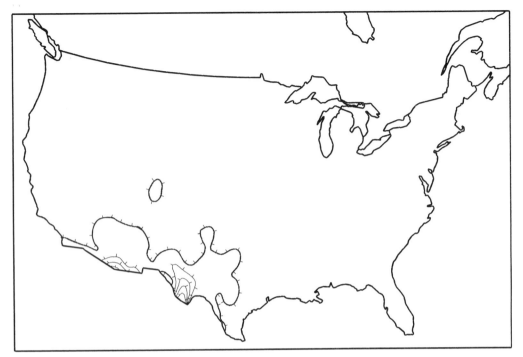

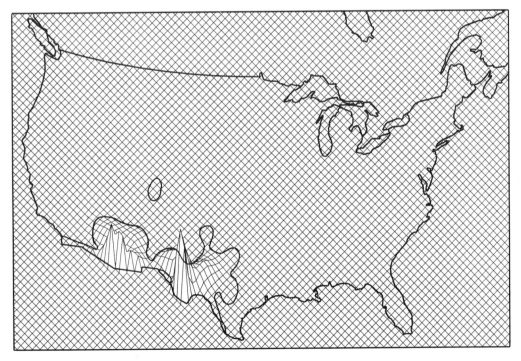

Abert's Towhee (*Pipilo aberti*) No Map

This southwestern towhee has a fairly restricted range. It was seen at only eighteen sites, all west of the 110th meridian—scattered throughout Arizona, southern Nevada, southwestern Utah, and southern California. The most regular sightings were in southeastern Arizona, around Organ Pipe Cactus National Monument in Arizona, in the Imperial Valley of California, near Zion National Park in Utah, and in the desert just southeast of Las Vegas, Nevada. The Abert's Towhee was most abundant in this last area, with the Henderson, Nevada, count reporting an average of 2.23 individuals seen per party-hour.

Green-tailed Towhee (*Pipilo chlorurus*) Maximum: 1.01 I/Hr

This strikingly colored towhee migrates in the fall, chiefly to areas south of its breeding range (AOU 1983). The wintering area appears to be associated with both temperature and vegetation. All populations, except the small disjunct one in Colorado, are in regions where the average minimum winter temperature rarely drops below $20°F$ ($-7°C$). It apparently avoids grassland and mesquite-acacia scrub vegetation and is present in oak-juniper woodlands. The vegetation where the range extends north into the panhandle of Texas around Amarillo consists of an oak-bluestem savanna, or shinnery, which traverses the western side of the Great Plains along the Canadian River. The small segregated distribution in Colorado is due to one individual seen in 1968 at Hotchkiss.

Oaks seem to be associated with high abundances of this shy bird. The highest abundance peak is in the oak-juniper woodland of southwestern Texas, which stretches north from Big Bend National Park along the Del Norte and Davis mountains. The other fairly concentrated population is in southeastern Arizona and southwestern New Mexico, where there also is oak-juniper woodland.

This towhee needs fairly dense brush for shelter (Bent 1968) and retreats into it when alarmed (Oberholser 1974). During winter it normally is found on the ground or low in bushes and will often run crouched close to the ground rather than flying (Bent 1968). When foraging it moves debris out of the way by characteristically scratching backward with both feet simultaneously (Phillips, Marshall, and Monson 1983). This behavior appears to be so ingrained that even where there is no debris—for example, at a feeder—the kicking occurs. This bird eats weed seeds and some insects (Bent 1968).

Green-tailed Towhee

Rufous-sided Towhee (*Pipilo erythrophthalmus*) Maximum: 4.12 I/Hr
The factors strongly associated with the distribution of the Rufous-sided
Towhee are not obvious. It avoids areas where precipitation is less than 8
inches (20 cm) a year, such as the desert along the California and Nevada
border. The southern trend of the distribution and the extensions along
both coasts suggest that warmth is important. East of roughly the 100th
meridian, this towhee avoids areas with an average minimum January temperature lower than 20°F (−7°C), but in the West it occurs where the minimum January temperature is under 15°F (−9°C). Perhaps the diverse
topography in the West provides protected environments that allow this
towhee to withstand lower temperatures.

Along with temperature, vegetation helps define where this towhee
occurs in high concentrations. These areas are in the mixed mesophytic
and deciduous forest and have an average minimum January temperature
warmer than about 25°F (−4°C). Most of the densest populations occur in
national forests, including the northwestern coast of Florida around the
Apalachicola National Forest and Saint Marks National Wildlife Refuge,
the Blue Ridge area of northern Georgia in the Chattahoochee National
Forest, along the South Carolina coast in the Francis Marion National Forest, and within the De Soto National Forest in southeastern Mississippi.

Hedgerows, thickets, brushy hillsides, woodlands, swamps (Bent 1968),
thickets along forest edges, and the underbrush and second growth of semiopen forests are habitats where the Rufous-sided Towhee is most likely to
be found (Oberholser 1974). Like the Olive Sparrow and the Green-tailed
Towhee, this towhee is usually found on or near the ground (Oberholser
1974), in the shadowy protection of these various types of dense undergrowth. It normally forages on the ground, where it moves debris by kicking both feet backward at the same time to expose seeds, berries, and
insects (Bent 1968). Its annual diet consists of 30% spiders, snails, and
insects such as moths, caterpillars, beetles, bugs, and ants. Beetles are its
main animal food in winter. The vegetable matter making up 70% of the
annual diet includes seeds from ragweed, foxtail, and dock and wild fruits.
Acorns are the main staple in the winter, and numerous birds congregate
where they are abundant. Even though this towhee is primarily a ground
feeder, it will frequent feeding stations in the winter (Bent 1968).

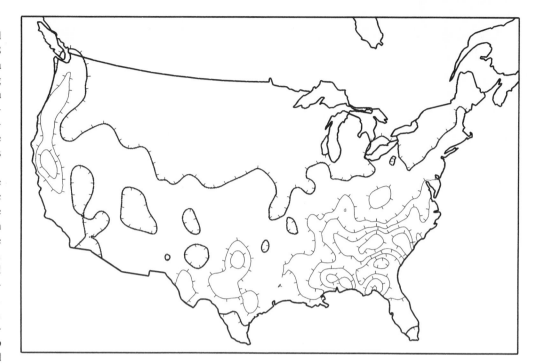

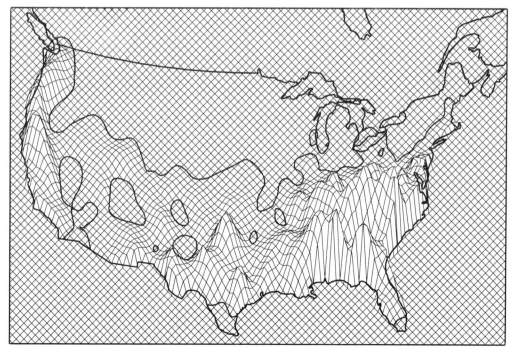

EMBERIZIDAE

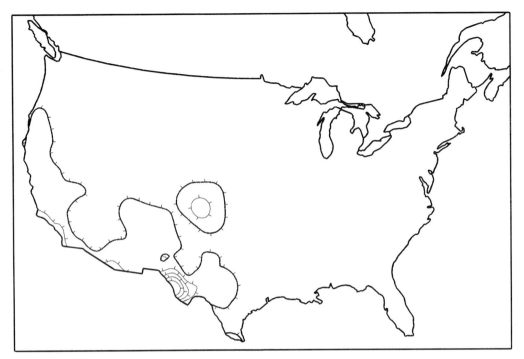

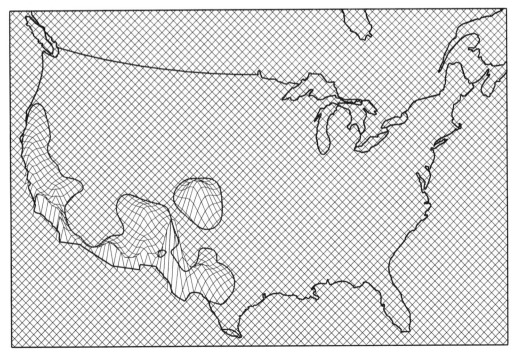

Brown Towhee (*Pipilo fuscus*) Maximum: 9.50 I/Hr

Unlike the other towhees, the Brown Towhee is often found foraging more than six feet (2 m) from cover. Brushy areas are invariably nearby, however, providing a refuge from predators or the weather (Pulliam and Mills 1977). Vegetation has been noted as limiting the distribution of this species (Bent 1968), and indeed the maps suggest this. This towhee avoids the Great Plains, where presumably the density of shrubs is too low. It also avoids large stands of creosote bush in southeastern California and western Arizona, as well as the grasslands of western Texas. To the north, both along the coast and in the Four Corners region, where Utah, Arizona, New Mexico, and Colorado meet, this towhee avoids the dense stands of tall pine forests. The disjunct population in the panhandle of Oklahoma is in an area where the average minimum January temperature is 10°F to 20°F (−12°C to −7°C). This apparently segregated population was reported regularly on counts at Clayton, New Mexico, and Kenton, Oklahoma, where the vegetation is an eastern extension of the piñon-juniper forest.

The high concentrations of the Brown Towhee apparently are associated chiefly with vegetation and elevation. The densest population occurs in the oak-juniper woodland of the Del Norte and Davis mountains in southwestern Texas. A rather high concentration in the Oklahoma panhandle area occurs in the piñon-juniper woodlands around Black Mesa, the highest point in Oklahoma (4,973 feet [1,516 m] above sea level). Other dense populations are present in the oak-juniper woodlands around Nogales, Arizona, and in the chaparral along the southern coast of California.

The Brown Towhee is resident throughout its range and is strongly territorial. Banding records have shown that a bird will remain on a given territory for five years (Bent 1968). This strong sedentary behavior enhances the opportunities for populations to exhibit significant geographic variation. Ten subspecies are present north of the Mexico border (AOU 1957). The coloration (Bent 1968) and in some cases the behavior of these subspecies vary greatly, with individuals in California foraging in gardens while Arizona birds avoid such habitats (Phillips, Marshall, and Monson 1983). In the winter, territories are still defended, but not as rigorously as during the breeding season. Birds from neighboring territories will congregate at abundant food sources, such as feeders. Often towhees join winter flocks of White- and Golden-crowned Sparrows, Song Sparrows, and House Finches (Bent 1968). Like the other towhees, this species eats seeds, berries, and insects (Oberholser 1974).

Rufous-crowned Sparrow (*Aimophila ruficeps*) Maximum: 3.88 I/Hr

The Rufous-crowned Sparrow has approximately half of its geographic distribution in Mexico (Wolf 1977). The portion in the United States appears to be restricted by the availability of appropriate vegetation. This sparrow avoids areas covered with dense woodlands, including both deciduous and coniferous forests. The mesquite-acacia scrub of extreme southern Texas and fairly pure stands of creosote bush in western Arizona are also avoided. This sparrow is present in the more open and stunted piñon-juniper and oak-juniper stands in central Texas and Arizona. In southern California it frequents the chaparral country and the scrub oaks. The distribution does not extend as far north in California as the oaks do, apparently because these northern areas are too moist. This sparrow avoids habitats to both the north and the east where the annual precipitation exceeds 40 inches (102 cm).

The maps indicate that topographic relief is a major factor associated with high densities of Rufous-crowned Sparrows. All the peak abundances occur near sloping ground, including the area in southern Texas along the Balcones Escarpment, east of the Edwards Plateau in central Texas, along the Delaware and Davis mountains in the Big Bend area of Texas, and in the Mogollon and San Francisco mountains on the border between New Mexico and Arizona.

The preferred habitat of the Rufous-crowned Sparrow is rather dry, grassy areas interspersed with boulders, trees, or clumps of low bushes (Wolf 1977). In Arizona this bird is found on foothills with scattered oaks, madrone, mountain mahogany, beargrass, and mescal plants. It prefers south-facing slopes because the northern ones are usually too densely vegetated (Bent 1968; Wolf 1977). This species forages primarily on the ground, eating seeds, grass stems, and plant shoots, and 95% to 100% of its winter diet is vegetable matter (Bent 1968). Foraging usually occurs within 7 feet (2 m), and on rare occasions 13 feet (4 m) of brushy cover, to which it retreats when alarmed (Pulliam and Mills 1977). This species does not migrate, but there is some shifting of ranges (Wolf 1977).

Bachman's Sparrow (*Aimophila aestivalis*) Map in Appendix B

Except for two unusually high counts, the average ten-year abundance at the forty-one locations where the Bachman's Sparrow was observed was under 0.20 individuals seen per party-hour. On the two high counts, birds were seen in large numbers in one or two years and none were observed in other years. Thus, the detailed information about this sparrow's abundance pattern seems unreliable, and the map was placed in appendix B. In general its distribution extends roughly from eastern Texas to Florida, but Bachman's Sparrows are absent at the southern end of Florida and from the Gulf coast to central Mississippi and in northern Alabama and Georgia. This bird was recorded in 50% or more of the years examined at five count sites in Florida and one each in South Carolina and Alabama. Of these seven sites, the Mount Dora count in Florida recorded the highest ten-year abundance, with 0.06 birds seen per party-hour.

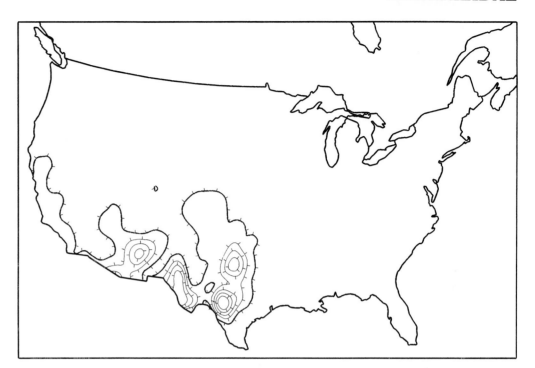

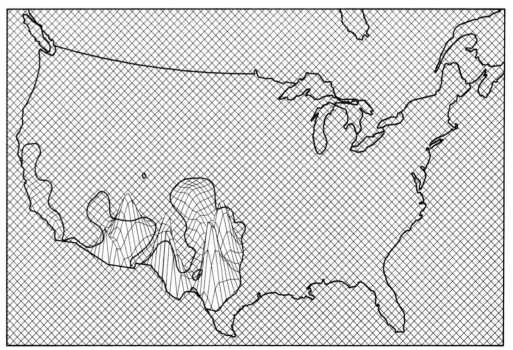

EMBERIZIDAE

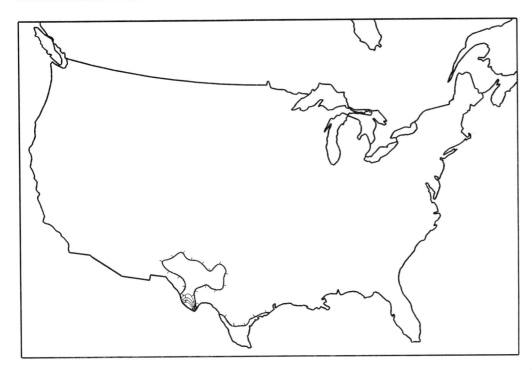

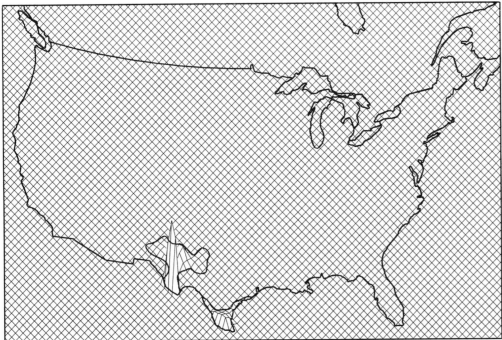

Cassin's Sparrow (*Aimophila cassinii*) Map in Appendix B
Even though the Cassin's Sparrow was recorded at forty sites, its occurrence at these locations was fairly irregular, with only nine sites reporting it in at least 50% of the years examined. All these latter counts were along the extreme southern border of the study area, stretching from southeastern Arizona to the mouth of the Rio Grande near Brownsville, Texas. The highest abundance at the locations with regular sightings was in the Big Bend area, with an average of 0.51 individuals seen per party-hour. The peak on the map centers on Portal, Arizona, where numerous birds were seen in one year.

Rufous-winged Sparrow (*Aimophila carpalis*) No Map
Most of the Rufous-winged Sparrow's distribution is in Mexico, with only the extreme northern edge extending into the United States (Wolf 1977). The CBC sightings indicate that in the United States it ranges from southeastern Arizona to the Rio Grande valley. Of the twelve count sites reporting this sparrow, it was seen regularly at only two locations in southeastern Arizona. The highest density was recorded around Tucson, with 0.10 individuals seen per party-hour.

Clay-colored Sparrow (*Spizella pallida*) Maximum: 6.48 I/Hr
The winter range of the Clay-colored Sparrow extends from central Texas south through Mexico to the Isthmus of Tehuantepec at the southern borders of Veracruz and Oaxaca (AOU 1983). The forty-eight sites recording this sparrow indicate that its range in the United States is restricted to the coastal plain and lower Rio Grande valley in southern Texas and the area around the Davis Mountains and Edwards Plateau.

The most concentrated population unfortunately is significantly denser than the others, and thus it overshadows the rest of the abundance pattern. The most abundant population was recorded around Big Bend National Park, one of only four regions where this sparrow was seen in at least 50% of the years examined. The other localities were in the lower Rio Grande valley, around Midland and Odessa, Texas, and on Merritt Island along the Atlantic coast of Florida. The average density at this last count was too low relative to the maximum abundance to be indicated on the maps.

In fall the Clay-colored Sparrow migrates in flocks with Chipping Sparrows and Brewer's Sparrows. Unlike many sparrows, these species migrate during the day. Large flocks forage in open, nonforested areas in winter, frequenting weedy fields and brushy hillsides in search of seeds from a wide variety of plants. Breeding populations have been extirpated from Iowa and Illinois, but newly established breeding grounds now occur in the East and North as dense forests are cleared (Bent 1968).

Clay-colored Sparrow

Brewer's Sparrow (*Spizella breweri*) Maximum: 30.00 I/Hr
Like that of the Clay-colored Sparrow, the range of the Brewer's Sparrow is fairly restricted in the United States. This bird occurs in the more arid environments of the Southwest; it begins farther west than the Clay-colored Sparrow and stretches to the California-Arizona border, where it avoids forests, pure stands of creosote bush (Phillips, Marshall, and Monson 1983), and the juniper woodlands of southwestern Texas.

The Brewer's Sparrow has been called the drabbest of all the North American sparrows (Bent 1968), and this helps explain why it is so difficult to identify. Most of the sightings in Texas are said to be misidentifications of immature Clay-colored Sparrows (Oberholser 1974). Assuming this is true, the high concentration in southwestern Texas should be discounted, at least to some extent, and the secondary abundance peak in southeastern Arizona and southwestern New Mexico, where the Clay-colored Sparrow does not winter, should be considered of more importance. The peak abundance in the Big Bend area of Texas is slightly north of the Clay-colored Sparrow peak, but these apexes are so close that high densities of the two species undoubtedly overlap.

The Brewer's Sparrow was named by Cassin in 1850 in honor of Thomas Mayo Brewer, a prominent Boston physician and naturalist (Bent 1968). In winter this sparrow forms foraging flocks with White-crowned, Black-throated, Vesper, Savannah (Bent 1968), Clay-colored, and Chipping Sparrows (Oberholser 1974). Vegetation makes up about 90% of its diet, the main portion being weed seeds. It migrates during the day in flocks with Chipping Sparrows and Clay-colored Sparrows. By not migrating at night, these sparrows avoid tall structures. The death rate from hitting towers and the like can be very high; for example, one night in Georgia fifty thousand birds of various species were killed (Bent 1968).

Black-chinned Sparrow (*Spizella atrogularis*) No Map
The distribution of the Black-chinned Sparrow extends from western Texas around the 101st meridian to southern California. Of the twenty-three sites reporting this sparrow, only four recorded it in five or more years. The locations of these regular sightings were scattered almost the entire length of the distribution, with two in the area around Big Bend National Park, one in southeastern Arizona, and the last in southern California. Of these sites the highest average abundance was in southwestern Texas, with 0.35 individuals recorded per party-hour.

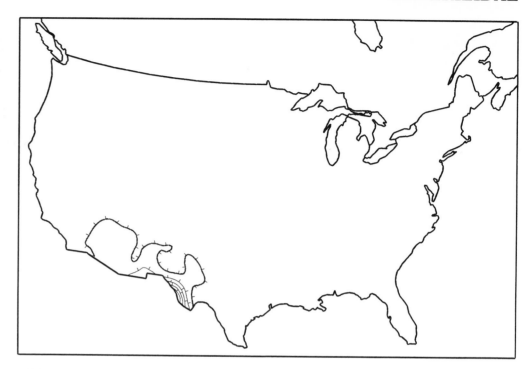

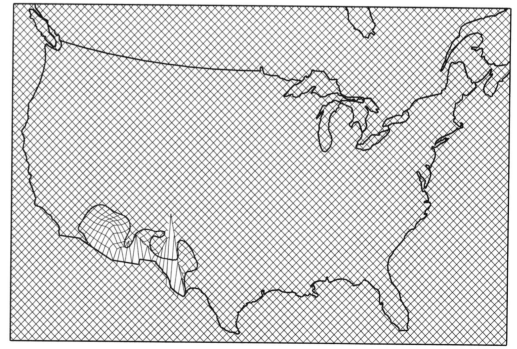

Brewer's Sparrow

EMBERIZIDAE

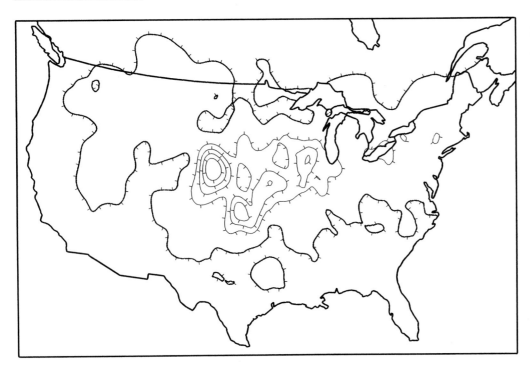

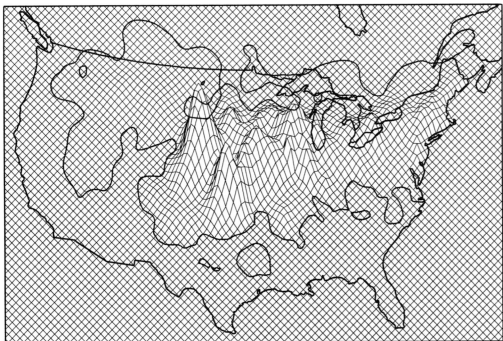

American Tree Sparrow (*Spizella arborea*) Maximum: 47.04 I/Hr

Temperature is the primary factor corresponding with the winter range of the American Tree Sparrow. The northern range limit is concomitant with the −10°F (−23°C) average minimum January isocline. The distribution of the American Tree Sparrow is unusual because it does not extend south to the Mexican border. The factors determining the southern range edge are not as obvious as those associated with the northern range limit. Interactions with the Chipping Sparrow may be preventing southern extension of the range of the American Tree Sparrow. These two sparrows are allopatric, but more localized studies are needed to determine if interspecific interactions are actual restricting either species' range. The vacant area extending through eastern Utah and western Colorado implies that the American Tree Sparrow avoids both the Colorado and the Green River valleys.

The highest abundance of American Tree Sparrows has been reported in the corn belt (Bent 1968). The abundance pattern here, however, shows a stronger association with the region where winter wheat is raised. Within the area where it is fairly common, the densest populations are primarily found along the Platte, Arkansas, Mississippi, and Missouri rivers.

The name American Tree Sparrow is somewhat misleading, because the species is more often found in bushes than in trees. It was named by the early settlers after the European Tree Sparrow because both species have rufous caps (Bent 1968). In winter, flocks of this North American species normally are found in fallow fields, along fencerows, or at forest edges. Membership in these flocks is not consistent and changes frequently. Within the flocks, birds usually maintain about a 6 inch (15 cm) distance from each other while foraging, which normally is done on the ground. About 98% of the winter diet is seeds, mainly weed seeds. Given that one of these sparrows eats about one-quarter ounce of weed seeds a day, and assuming there are about ten birds per square mile in Iowa, where they spend roughly two hundred days a year, on average American Tree Sparrows eat about 875 tons of weed seeds annually in this midwestern state alone (Bent 1968).

American Tree Sparrow

American Tree Sparrow

Chipping Sparrow (*Spizella passerina*) Maximum: 17.10 I/Hr

Chipping Sparrows that breed in the North migrate southward in the fall (AOU 1983). Their wintering grounds seem to be in areas where the American Tree Sparrow is absent, where the average minimum January temperature rarely drops below 20°F to 30°F ($-7°C$ to $-1°C$), and where pines, scrub oaks, or both are present. Finer-grained studies are needed before we can know if either or both of these species restricts the range of the other. In the East the Chipping Sparrow is found in deciduous forests with scattered pines, and in the West it avoids the dense coniferous forests and semiarid scrub but is present in the oak savanna of Texas, the oak-juniper woodland of southern Arizona and of the Big Bend and Davis Mountains area of Texas, and the California oakwoods in the southern part of that state. The three disjunct populations center on national wildlife refuges, including Minidoka in Idaho, Lake Andes in South Dakota, and Kirwin in Kansas. The protected habitat and supplemental grain provided at the refuges undoubtedly allow birds to survive the harsh winter environments in these areas.

High densities of sparrows are most strongly associated with vegetation, at least in the West. The most concentrated populations are in the oak-juniper woodlands of southern Arizona, southwestern Texas, and the Balcones Escarpment in south-central Texas. A rather high concentration also is present along the border between Alabama, Georgia, and Florida.

The abundance of this species dropped dramatically around the turn of the century. In 1841 Audubon commented that "few birds are more common throughout the United States than this [species]" (Bent 1968). The reason for the decline probably is the insurgence of the House Sparrow, which had spread throughout basically all of the United States by 1898 (Summers-Smith 1963). Since that time, the habitat in which the Chipping Sparrow is found includes pine woods, forest openings, the shores of streams and lakes (Bent 1968), and within and on the edges of oak woodlands in the Southwest (Pulliam and Mills 1977). When alarmed it will retreat into dense cover, but it often is found foraging up to 105 feet (32 m) from cover (Pulliam and Mills 1977). As trees grow back after logging and fires, the Chipping Sparrow moves in and replaces the Field Sparrow (Bent 1968). Unlike most other North American sparrows, the Chipping Sparrow feeds on unfallen seeds an average of 3 feet (1 m) above the ground, and 100% of its winter diet is vegetable matter (Allaire and Fisher 1975). Average size of seeds consumed is 0.05 inch (1.2 mm) (Pulliam and Mills 1977).

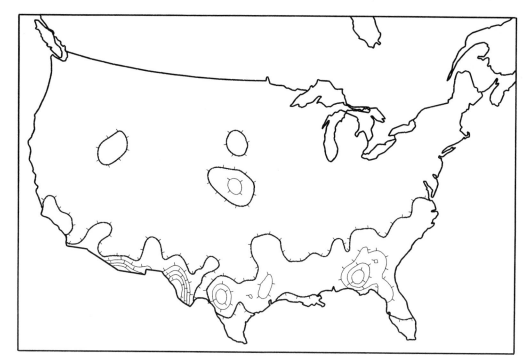

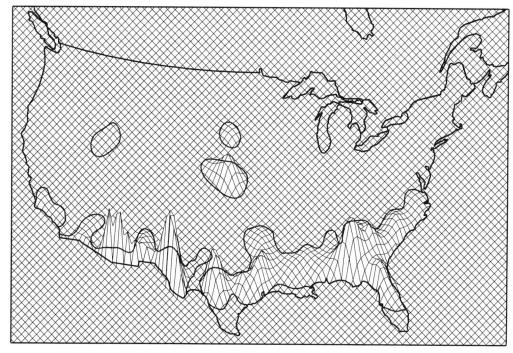

Chipping Sparrow

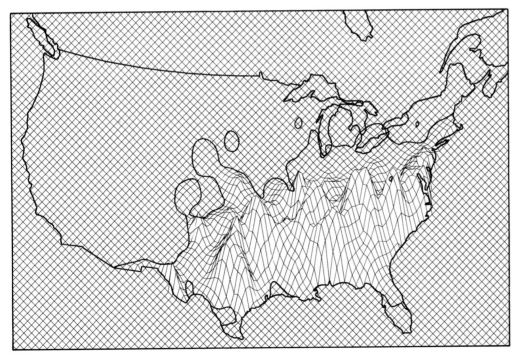

Field Sparrow (*Spizella pusilla*) Maximum: 7.44 I/Hr

Temperature is strongly associated with the wintering area of the Field Sparrow. Daily feeding rates increase in the fall to help compensate for the longer, colder nights, and metabolically it is able to acclimate to the cold, but only to a limited extent (Olson and Kendeigh 1980). Thus, as temperatures drop and nights get longer, the birds migrate south. They travel primarily at night, and mortality is high because they fly into ceilometer beams at airports, television towers, and other tall structures (Bent 1968). The wintering area includes all of the eastern half of the United States where the average minimum January temperature does not drop below 20°F (−7°C). The exceptions are the extensions into colder regions along the Platte River in Nebraska, the Arkansas River in Colorado, and up the Wabash River in Indiana to Lake Michigan.

The area where this sparrow occurs in high abundance seems to be associated with warm temperature; it lies entirely in the part of the country where it rarely freezes. The western edge of this area is concomitant with the region that receives less than 24 inches (61 cm) of precipitation a year. The species also avoids the Ozark Mountains, the coastal prairie, all of Florida, and the southern coast of Georgia.

The Field Sparrow is aptly named because it is rarely seen away from brushy fields, preferring old fields and overgrown pastures with thickets and deciduous undergrowth (Bent 1968). Its numbers greatly increase after a forest has been logged or burned, but as the trees return with time, the habitat becomes more appropriate for the Chipping Sparrow, which eventually replaces the Field Sparrow (Bent 1968). In winter it forms foraging flocks with Chipping Sparrows and other species of sparrows. The diet of wintering Field Sparrows is between 90% (Pulliam and Enders 1971) and 100% vegetable matter (Allaire and Fisher 1975), and the mean size of the seeds eaten is 0.09 inch (2.4 mm) (Pulliam and Enders 1971). It spends most of its foraging time (64%) standing on the ground eating unfallen seeds from grasses and the like, and for most of the remaining time (32%) it forages while perched on the plants themselves (Pulliam and Enders 1971).

Field Sparrow

Vesper Sparrow (*Pooecetes gramineus*) Maximum: 5.97 I/Hr

The Vesper Sparrow migrates south in the fall to its warmer winter range. East of the Great Plains it frequents regions that have an average minimum January temperature of at least 30°F (−1°C). The vegetation in this region is mixed mesophytic and deciduous forest, an inappropriate habitat for this sparrow, which prefers open areas with little tall vegetation (Bent 1968) such as prairies, savannas, weedy or grassy pastures, fields, and woodland clearings (Oberholser 1974). Thus, east of about the 95th meridian the Vesper Sparrow probably is frequenting patches of cleared land and openings within the forest. West of the eastern border of Texas, it is present in the tree and scrub savanna of the Great Plains, continuing west into the semi-arid scrub but avoiding the areas in southern Arizona and California that are covered with creosote bush. There is a disjunct population in the California steppe at the southern end of the Central Valley. The disjunct population in Iowa is due to a few birds overwintering on the Union Slough National Wildlife Refuge.

Except for the dense concentration of Vesper Sparrows along the Alabama-Georgia-Florida border, abundant populations are in areas with stunted and sparse vegetation. For example, in southeastern Arizona the species is found in the plains grassland and most commonly in areas where cover is less than 13 feet (4 m) away. When flushed, a little more than half of the birds normally fly to cover, and the others fly to the ground (Pulliam and Mills 1977), indicating that this species is not as strongly tied to habitat with cover as, say, the Chipping Sparrow or White-crowned Sparrow. A finer-grained study may find that the high concentration in the Southeast is actually in an open environment within the forest.

Nature writer John Burroughs thought the song of the Bay-winged Bunting—the previous name of the Vesper Sparrow—was much more beautiful in the evening than during the rest of the day. Thus, he used the adjective *vesper* (relating to the evening) to describe this bird (Bent 1968). From then on this sparrow has been known as the Vesper Sparrow. Indeed, in summer it often sings in the twilight after sunset, when most other birds have stopped (Bent 1968).

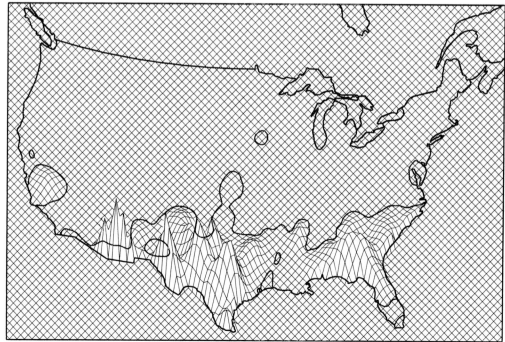

EMBERIZIDAE

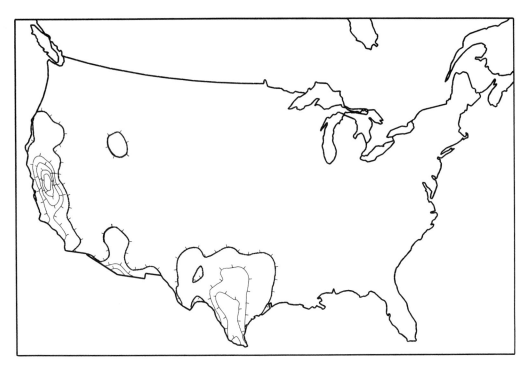

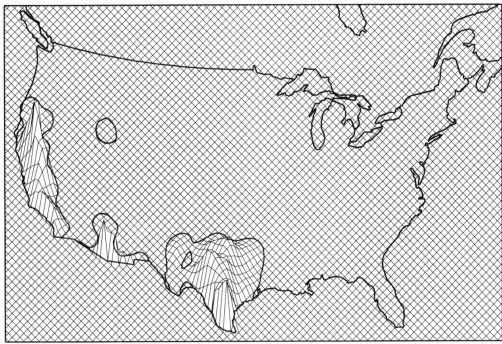

Lark Sparrow (*Chondestes grammacus*) Maximum: 13.37 I/Hr

The Lark Sparrow winters in the warm southern part of the Great Plains where the vegetation is savanna rather than pure grassland, with scattered bushes and stunted trees associated with a ground covering of herbaceous plants, primarily grasses. The range extends west into the oak-juniper habitat in southwestern Texas, the same habitat where this sparrow is found in southern Arizona and New Mexico. There is a northern extension in Arizona that encompasses the area around Phoenix. In California this sparrow is present in the chaparral and California steppe of the Central Valley. It avoids other types of vegetation, such as semiarid scrub and dry-belt pine forests. The small disjunct population in a fairly cold area is due to birds wintering on the Minidoka National Wildlife Refuge in Idaho.

The most concentrated population is in the California steppe of the San Joaquin valley, with lesser densities stretching into the California oak woodlands and chaparral. The next most abundant population is in southern Texas, where the vegetation is dominated by mesquite and acacia. From this region lesser concentrations extend north into the area where juniper and oak replace acacia. This finding corresponds with that of a finer-scaled study of this bird in Texas. Oberholser (1974) found that the optimal habitat of the Lark Sparrow is mesquite or oak savanna with scattered patches of weeds, grass, grain, and bare ground. Of less importance are the grassland, foothills, and grassy clearings in open pine woodlands. In southern Arizona a rather high concentration is present in a small area of the oak-juniper woodland around Tucson and Nogales.

In winter the Lark Sparrow, which is one of North America's largest sparrows (National Geographic Society 1983), often is found foraging in small flocks that sometimes include Field Sparrows. Interspecific fighting frequently occurs in such an association (Bent 1968). The diet of Lark Sparrows in New Mexico consists of 73% vegetable matter, such as grass seeds, waste grain, and sunflower seeds, and 27% insects, of which 14% is grasshoppers. Except for the Grasshopper Sparrow, this species eats the most grasshoppers of any sparrow.

Lark Sparrow

Lark Sparrow

Black-throated Sparrow (*Amphispiza bilineata*) Maximum: 4.25 I/Hr
The Black-throated Sparrow is one of the most elegant sparrows in North America, with its black bib accentuated by a white breast and a white malar stripe and supercilium outlining its black mask. In the summer it frequently sits on a high, exposed perch to sing, and in the winter it uses similar perches for sunning, particularly in the early morning. This is a species of warm environments, and at the first hint of cold weather birds in the northern extremes of the breeding range and at higher elevations migrate to the warmest and driest areas of the country (Bent 1968). The wintering grounds in the United States encompass all the deserts in the southwestern United States: Chihuahuan, Sonoran, and Mojave. Vegetation rather than temperature, however, best defines the winter range of this sparrow. It is present in the southern portions of the semiarid scrub, except that it avoids the chaparral in California. To the east it also occurs in the southern half of the savanna in the Great Plains. The apparently misplaced population in the panhandle region of Texas and Oklahoma is due to sightings on the Kenton, Oklahoma, count, and the other disjunct, but less aberrant population resulted from observations near the Corn Creek National Fish and Wildlife Station. Both these "populations" are ephemeral.

Concentrations of this sparrow are fairly high throughout most of its winter range. One of the densest populations is in the paloverde-cactus scrub habitat around Organ Pipe National Monument in south-central Arizona. This agrees with the findings that the Black-throated Sparrow prefers habitats with cholla cactus, creosote bush, catclaw acacia, small mesquite, artemisia, sages, and rabbit brush (Bent 1968). From Organ Pipe, high sparrow densities continue east, where a second peak of a bit lower concentration is reached along the Sulphur Springs Valley, north of Douglas, Arizona. High abundances then begin again around the southwestern edge of Texas, extending south almost to the Gulf coast, with a maximum peak in the Big Bend area, a less dense population east of there, and an even smaller peak to the south.

In winter this sparrow's diet consists only of small seeds, so water must be regularly available, though the bird does not live in riparian habitats (Bent 1968). After the fall rains water is not necessary because newly sprouting plants become a large portion of its diet (Smyth and Bartholomew 1966). It gleans the winter seeds off the ground of desert uplands, alluvial fans, and slopes where there is much exposed gravel and rock. Small mixed foraging flocks are formed with Brewer's, Chipping, White-crowned, and Sage Sparrows, Cactus Wrens, and Verdins (Bent 1968).

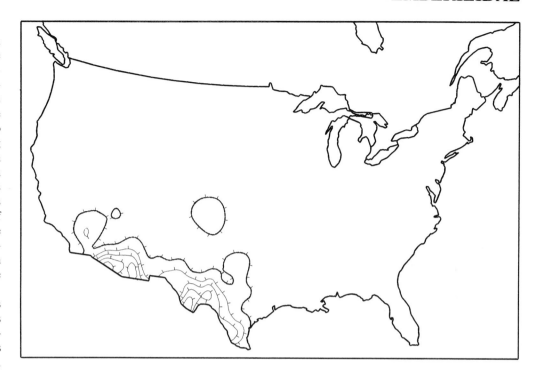

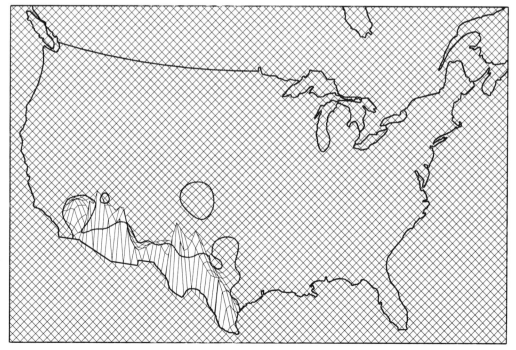

Black-throated Sparrow

EMBERIZIDAE

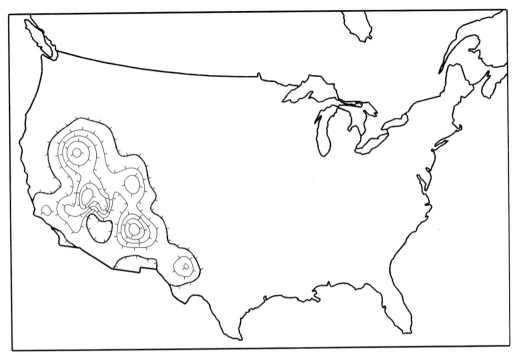

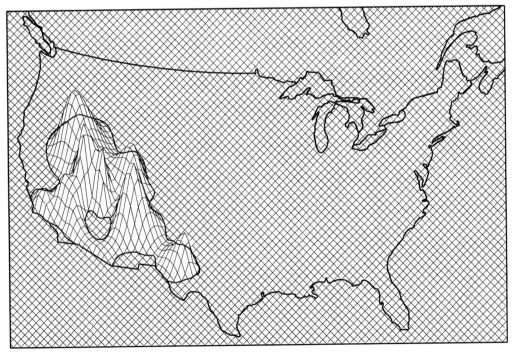

Sage Sparrow (*Amphispiza belli*) Maximum: 5.97 I/Hr

Sage Sparrows are not as strongly associated with sage or sagebrush in the winter as during the breeding season. The birds in the northern portions of the summer range migrate south into their winter range, which encompasses areas that receive less than 16 inches (41 cm) of rainfall annually. This sparrow, however, occupies only those drier regions that are covered with semiarid scrub. The maps do indicate that it occurs in the dry-belt forest of western New Mexico and central Arizona, but this is probably based on individuals frequenting openings within these forests, rather than being in the forests themselves. Unfortunately, the large scale of this study does not provide adequate information to resolve this. The southern edge of the distribution both in southwestern Texas and in southern Arizona and New Mexico suggests that this species avoids oak-juniper woodlands. The size of the distribution in Nevada may be exaggerated because the lack of counts in this region required fairly extensive interpolation of data. Given the information provided by the data, however, this is the best possible approximation of the actual distribution.

As with the Black-throated Sparrow, the abundance of the Sage Sparrow is high throughout most of its winter range. Meents, Anderson, and Ohmart (1982) found that in the lower Colorado River valley the Sage Sparrow frequents the riparian habitat, but the highest concentrations are present in honey mesquite. Closer examination showed that the reason for the high density is not the mesquite itself but inkweed, which is associated with the honey mesquite. Inkweed seeds are a favorite of the Sage Sparrow. Such subtle associations may also be the reason the high abundance peaks seen on the maps are not obviously associated with any of the environmental factors examined. The scale of this study is probably too large to detect such abstruse associations. More localized studies are needed, like the one done along the Colorado River, particularly in the areas of the highest abundance peaks in northern Nevada, southern Nevada, and along the border between Arizona and New Mexico.

In the dry environment of its winter range, the Sage Sparrow gleans seeds from the surface of the sand or gravel, under or between scattered low bushes. Infrequently this bird will scratch away debris, but the low amount of precipitation ensures that vegetation and subsequent litter will be at a minimum. In winter it eats seeds exclusively. When foraging it often runs across the ground using its tail for balance, holding it approximately perpendicular. Loose foraging flocks form during the winter (Bent 1968).

Sage Sparrow

Savannah Sparrow, Excluding Ipswich Race (*Passerculus sandwichensis*) Maximum: 8.83 I/Hr

Even though this sparrow frequents savanna environments, it was not named for this. Instead, Wilson named it after Savannah, Georgia, where the first specimen was collected (Bent 1968). The Savannah Sparrow frequents many environments other than savannas. From about the 95th meridian on east, it is present mainly where the average minimum January temperature is over 30°F (−1°C). This includes regions where the vegetation is mixed mesophytic and deciduous forest. Because it prefers more open habitat, it probably frequents cleared fields and forest openings in this region. The habitat requirements for this species are fairly diverse, ranging from cultivated fields to lightly or heavily grazed pastures (Grzybowski 1982). This sparrow also frequents areas along the Pacific coast where the minimum temperature is above freezing. From Texas on west, however, it is present where the winter temperatures may drop to almost 10°F (−12°C), but all these areas are in either savanna or semiarid shrub vegetation.

In the West the most concentrated populations are in open, savanna-type habitat. The highest density is in the Imperial Valley in southern California, which is dominated by creosote bush, bur sage, saltbush, and greasewood. A less dense population is in the California steppe of the Central Valley. In the East the abundance peaks do not correspond with vegetation or the other environmental factors examined. The scale of this study may preclude determining the factors associated with the location of these peaks.

This sparrow is usually found in fields in early successional stages, particularly in the winter. This sparrow does not require woody vegetation, and because it infrequently scratches debris out of the way, it prefers foraging on bare ground (Bent 1968). In southeastern Arizona the Savannah Sparrow is normally found in the plains grasslands at a range of 13 to 26 feet (4–8 m) from cover. Cover usually is not used as protection, because fewer than 30% of birds fly to cover when flushed. Instead, most fly to an exposed perch (Pulliam and Mills 1977). In winter over 90% of this sparrow's diet is vegetable matter, mostly seeds (Bent 1968). When water is not available it decreases its activity level to conserve body moisture (Smyth and Bartholomew 1966).

Savannah Sparrow, Ipswich Race (*Passerculus sandwichensis principes*) Map in Appendix B

At least eleven subspecies of the Savannah Sparrow winter in the United States (AOU 1957). This includes the Ipswich subspecies which was considered a separate species when the data examined were collected. Its conspecific status occurred because it interbreeds with other subspecies in Nova Scotia (AOU 1983). The Christmas counts show that this race winters along the Atlantic coast from northern Florida to Cape Cod (see map in appendix B). The highest abundance was 0.16 individuals seen per party-hour around Brigantine National Wildlife Refuge in New Jersey.

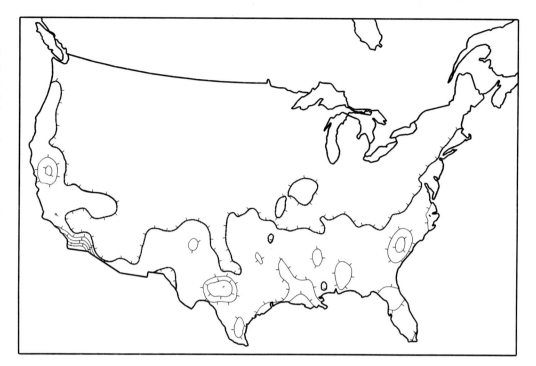

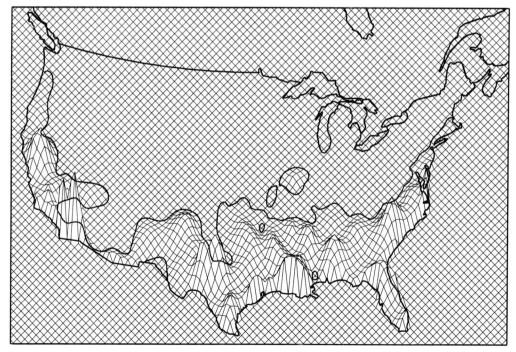

EMBERIZIDAE

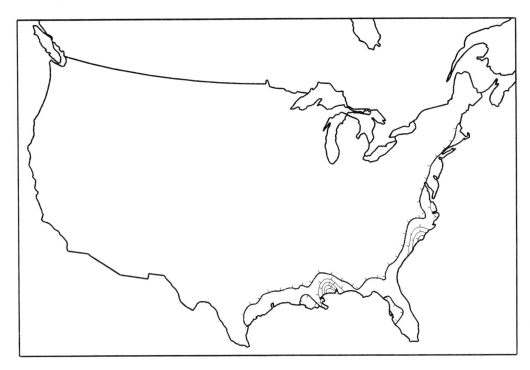

Baird's Sparrow (*Ammodramus bairdii*) No Map
In the United States the Baird's Sparrow winters primarily along the southern border from Texas to Arizona. It was recorded at twenty-four locations, but sightings at all but one were sporadic. Near El Paso, Texas, this sparrow was seen in eight of the ten years examined, but the density was very low, with an average abundance of only 0.01 birds seen per hour of censusing.

Grasshopper Sparrow (*Ammodramus savannarum*) Map in
  Appendix B
Only two of the 124 censuses reporting the Grasshopper Sparrow had average abundances over 0.20 individuals per party-hour, and both were due to sightings of large concentrations in just one year. Thus, this sparrow is too rare for much confidence to be placed in the details provided by the CBC data. Hence the map is included only in appendix B. Sightings were generally along the Gulf coast and along the Atlantic coast from South Carolina to Florida, but sporadic observations extended as far north as Maine. Populations were most regularly seen around Fort Lauderdale, Florida, where the mean abundance was 0.11 individuals per party-hour.

Sharp-tailed Sparrow (*Ammodramus caudacutus*) Maximum: 1.04 I/Hr
The Sharp-tailed Sparrow breeds as far north as the southern part of the District of Mackenzie in the Northwest Territories and as far west as British Columbia (AOU 1983), but with the onset of cold weather birds migrate south and east to their wintering grounds along the Atlantic and Gulf coasts, where the winter weather is substantially moderated by the oceans. Even so, the individuals reported on the Christmas counts in New England probably do not survive the cold (Bent 1968) and either die or move farther south later in the season. For some unknown reason, this sparrow avoids the areas along the coasts in southern Texas, central Louisiana, and west-central Florida.

There are three areas where concentrations of Sharp-tailed Sparrows are fairly high. The densest population is around the Gulf Island National Seashore near Biloxi, Mississippi. There is a slightly smaller peak on the Atlantic coast around Cape Fear and Smith Island, just south of Wilmington, North Carolina. To the north on the northern border of that same state is yet another fairly dense population, this one is centered on the Back Bay and Mackay Island national wildlife refuges.

Even though Sharp-tailed Sparrows flock in the winter, counting them can be difficult, because the species is very secretive. Birds hide among the dense grasses along the edges of salt ponds and tidal rivers. "Squeaking," however, will usually bring one or two out into the open, if only for a moment before they dive back into the grassy cover. At low tide they can be found foraging on mud flats for aquatic insects and the like. Most of the diet in winter consists of seeds from grasses and wild rice, and the more inland birds also eat weed seeds. When walking through dense grass, this sparrow frequently moves stems aside with its bill (Bent 1968).

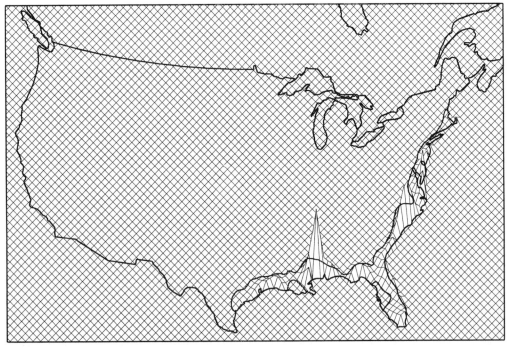

Sharp-tailed Sparrow

Seaside Sparrow (*Ammodramus maritimus*) Maximum: 3.63 I/Hr
Besides being closely related taxonomically, the Seaside Sparrow and Sharp-tailed Sparrow have very similar winter distributions. Both occur in regions of the country where the climate is moderated by the Atlantic Ocean or the Gulf of Mexico, and both avoid the warm region in southern Texas. The Seaside Sparrow is also absent from peninsular Florida.

There are three areas where dense populations of Seaside Sparrows occur. Two of these are at the same locations where there are large concentrations of Sharp-tailed Sparrows: on the Gulf Island National Seashore near Biloxi, Mississippi, and on the Atlantic coast in southern North Carolina near Cape Fear and Smith Island. The Seaside Sparrow has a less dense population along the coast of eastern Texas and western Louisiana, which encompasses the Anahuac, McFaddin, Texas Point, Sabine, and Lacassine national wildlife refuges and Rockefeller State Refuge in Louisiana. Certainly these protected areas are helping to preserve this species.

The Seaside Sparrow frequents areas within the boundaries of the tidal waters and low, rush-covered habitats. People are continually draining wetlands, which destroys these habitats, and thus the overall abundance of this sparrow has been steadily declining. Thousands of pairs use to nest around Cape May, but as of 1968 there were only a few pairs left (Bent 1968). The Dusky Seaside Sparrow, now considered a subspecies of the Seaside Sparrow (AOU 1983), is extinct. In 1980 there were only four singing males and no females left (Sykes 1980). The last male died in captivity on 16 June 1987 (Sparrow is extinct 1987). The Dusky Seaside Sparrow had a very small range—only 10 miles (16 km) in radius. After the spraying of DDT from 1942 to 1953, the population was down by 70% in 1957 (Bent 1968). The extinction on Merritt Island occurred because protection of this habitat came too late (Sykes 1980). Another subspecies of the Seaside Sparrow, the Cape Sable Sparrow, is now in danger of extirpation. While it had species status, this sparrow had the distinction of being the last avian species to be discovered in North America. It was found in 1918 among the swampy prairies near Flamingo in Everglades National Park at the southern tip of Florida. This population was completely wiped out by a hurricane in 1935, and another population on the southwest coast was significantly decreased by a fire in 1962 (Bent 1968). Certainly these evolutionarily distinct populations deserve protection from extinction. Besides making sense taxonomically, politically it would be easier to preserve these populations if they were considered full species. It is much easier to convince the public to protect a species than a subset of a species.

Henslow's Sparrow (*Ammodramus henslowii*) No Map
The thirty-eight sites where the Henslow's Sparrow was recorded stretched along the Atlantic and Gulf coasts. The most regular sightings occurred on the eastern coast of Texas, along the panhandle of Florida, and around Cocoa Beach, Florida. The highest abundance from these particular areas was at Galveston Bay, Texas, with an average of 0.01 birds per party-hour.

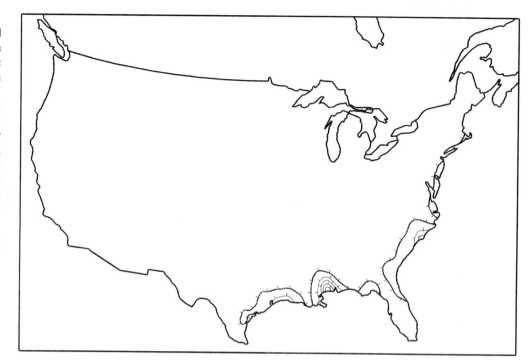

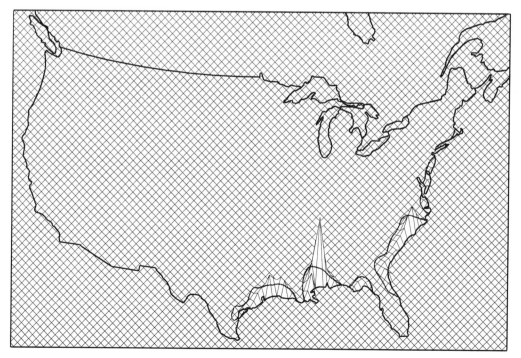

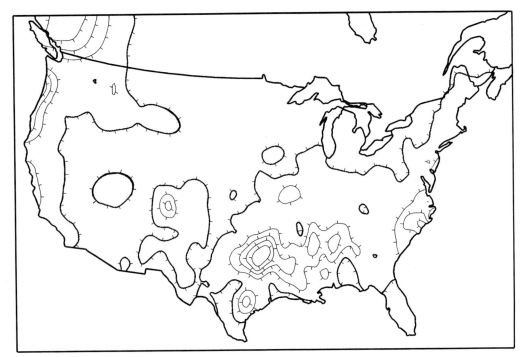

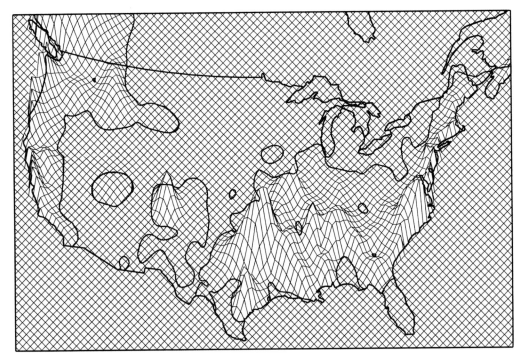

Le Conte's Sparrow (*Ammodramus leconteii*) Map in Appendix B

The Le Conte's Sparrow was seen at ninety-eight sites throughout the southeastern portion of the Great Plains and throughout the southeastern states to the center of the Florida peninsula. This region roughly corresponds to the area of the country where sorghum is grown. Of all the count locations, however, only the count near Shreveport, Louisiana, reported this sparrow regularly (ten years), and had an average abundance of 0.29 individuals seen per party-hour. Thus, the map of the Le Conte's Sparrow is included in appendix B.

Fox Sparrow (*Passerella iliaca*) Maximum: 1.59 I/Hr

The Fox Sparrow winters regularly in the mixed mesophytic and deciduous forest, in the lower Great Plains among the tree and shrub savanna, and in the West in the coastal coniferous forest and chaparral. The populations that occur in the Great Basin and western Great Plains are in the dry-belt pine forests, but most of these areas are not regularly inhabited in the winter. The eastern distribution extends north along the Atlantic coast, yet the Fox Sparrow avoids the Florida peninsula.

The most concentrated populations of the Fox Sparrow are along rivers. The highest density is near the Red River on the border between Texas and Oklahoma. From here a lesser peak stretches east to the Mississippi River and then along the Tennessee River. Less dense populations occur along the Colorado River in Texas and the Missouri River in Missouri, and there is a rather high ephemeral "population" at Monte Vista National Wildlife Refuge on the Rio Grande in Colorado. This Colorado population was due to eighty individuals seen in 1971. Besides occurring near rivers, abundance peaks occur along both the Pacific and Atlantic coasts.

The species name of this sparrow, *iliaca*, is the same as that of the Redwing (*Turdus musicus*), a European thrush. The similarities in appearance (both have extensively spotted breasts) and behavior (both are highly terrestrial) certainly influenced the naming of the Fox Sparrow. The outward appearance and other traits of this sparrow, however, vary geographically. Over geologic time, many populations of this North American endemic have evolved separately, resulting in eighteen subspecies (AOU 1957). Of all the species examined by the AOU, only the Song Sparrow and Horned Lark had more subspecies than the Fox Sparrow.

The Fox Sparrow is strongly terrestrial and feeds by scratching among fallen leaves for seeds and fruits. The scratching appears to be so automatic that it accompanies foraging even at feeders. Both feet are used simultaneously to hop forward and then are shuffled back. Foraging and most other activities occur in rather dense thickets. Presumably because of its highly terrestrial behavior, the Fox Sparrow avoids areas where there is deep snow (Bent 1968).

Song Sparrow (*Melospiza melodia*) Maximum: 7.41 I/Hr

The distribution of the Song Sparrow covers basically all of the United States, with only a relative small area in the North left vacant. The northern boundary is strongly associated with temperature. This sparrow is absent from areas that have an average minimum January temperature lower than 10°F (−12°C). This includes areas in Idaho and western Wyoming. The exception is the extension along the borders of Minnesota and the Dakotas, which may be due to birds occurring in protected habitat along the Sioux and Red rivers.

Rivers are associated with concentrated populations of Song Sparrows in the West; included are the Rio Grande, Snake, Colorado, and Arkansas. In the East most of the high concentrations are in regions that receive more than 40 inches (102 cm) of precipitation a year. The abundance peaks in this moist area also are associated with open water. In Alabama a high concentration occurs around the William Dannelly Reservoir. On the eastern side of the Mississippi River is an equally concentrated population, and lesser abundance peaks occur along the Ohio River. Populations of maximum density occur at the Santee National Wildlife Refuge in North Carolina and around Cape May, New Jersey.

The Song Sparrow has thirty-one subspecies in North America, by far the largest number for any North American bird (AOU 1957). The Horned Lark is next highest with twenty-one. The Song Sparrow occurs in a wide variety of habitats in winter. In fact only five species—Downy Woodpecker, American Robin, European Starling, American Goldfinch, and House Sparrow—were seen at more CBC sites than the 1,127 at which the Song Sparrow was recorded. Normally this sparrow is found in fairly moist areas, particularly in the brushy cover along the banks of streams and ponds, in both freshwater and saltwater marshes, in shrub-covered wet meadows, and even along coastal beaches. With irrigation many of the rivers and streams in Arizona and other parts of the West are drying up, causing a decline of this sparrow in that region (Bent 1968). Most of the birds that breed in these and other warm areas of the country remain on or near their breeding territories throughout the year, but these areas are not defended in the winter. During severe weather loose foraging flocks form, but normally foraging is a solitary activity (Nice 1943). About 90% of the winter diet is plant material, primarily seeds with an average size of 0.12 inch (3 mm) (Pulliam and Enders 1971). Birds on the coasts often concentrate on *Salicornia* seeds that have fallen into the water and then are washed ashore at high tide, forming a concentrated food source along the high-water mark (Bent 1968). In general, inland birds spend almost 75% of their time standing on the ground eating seeds off plants and about 20% foraging while perched on a plant (Pulliam and Enders 1971).

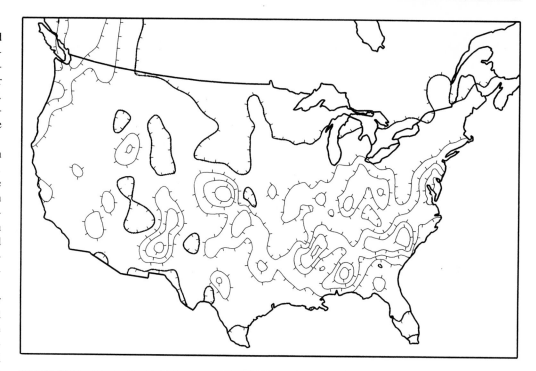

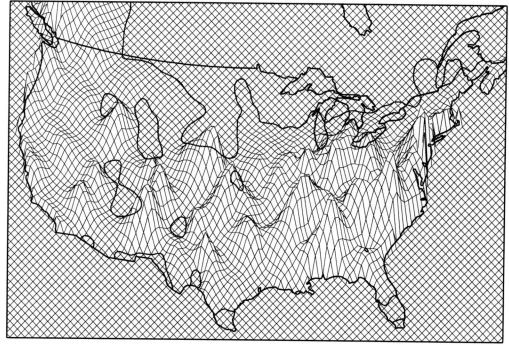

EMBERIZIDAE

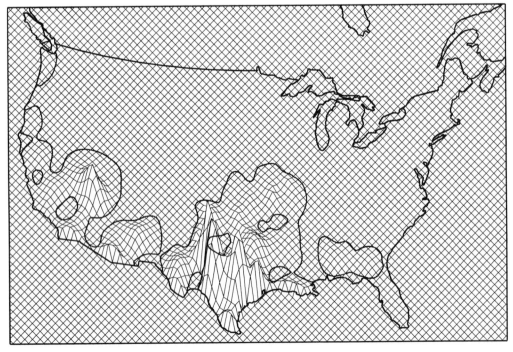

Lincoln's Sparrow (*Melospiza lincolnii*) Maximum: 4.15 I/Hr
Wintering areas of the Lincoln's Sparrow that are north of about the 35th parallel apparently are frequented only during warm winters. The entire winter range, including the irregularly occupied northern regions, occurs where the average minimum January temperature is over 20°F (−7°C), and the more regularly frequented areas are where the low temperature is 30°F (−1°C). Except for the disjunct population to the east, the main distribution stops roughly at the Mississippi River.

The concentrated populations of the Lincoln's Sparrow are densest in southern Texas, within the savanna habitat on the Edwards Plateau; several lakes and rivers in this area probably also attract this sparrow. A less dense population occurs along the Colorado River near the border of Nevada, Utah, and Arizona.

The Lincoln's Sparrow was named by Audubon after Thomas Lincoln, who was in Labrador with Audubon and was the first to collect a specimen of this elusive bird. Audubon had a hard time procuring one because of its secretive behavior, which also makes censusing difficult. In addition, there is danger that it may be misidentified because of its strong resemblance to an immature Swamp Sparrow. Normally the Lincoln's Sparrow is found in moist areas with low-growing bushes, annuals, and grasses (Bent 1968). It also frequents brush piles and patches of tall forbs. In Texas the Lincoln's Sparrow is more common than the Song Sparrow because the former is less strongly tied to moist areas (Oberholser 1974). Besides hiding in dense cover, this sparrow also forages inconspicuously on the ground and rarely is far from cover. It does use feeders, but more often it is found scratching on the ground with both feet in search of seeds under debris. It is more solitary than the Song Sparrow, and even during harsh weather loose flocks form infrequently (Bent 1968). It avoids cold climates in winter, and birds move out of all breeding areas except those along the Pacific coast (AOU 1983). Migration occurs at night, and mortality is high from collisions with television towers and the like (Bent 1968).

Lincoln's Sparrow

Lincoln's Sparrow

Swamp Sparrow (*Melospiza georgiana*) Maximum: 5.94 I/Hr

The winter range of this migratory species is unusual for a sparrow. The region frequented is concomitant with the area of the country below 1,000 feet (305 m) in elevation. This includes the inland area between the Gulf coast and the Great Lakes and along the Atlantic seaboard but excludes the Appalachians and Ozarks. The two exceptions are, first, the Swamp Sparrow does not continue on north up the Saint Lawrence valley (but here cold is probably excluding it), and second, it is present in southern Texas on the Edwards Plateau, which is a bit over 2,000 feet (610 m) in altitude.

High concentrations of the Swamp Sparrow occur near open water. The highest peak abundance is in the bayous along the Louisiana coast, with increased concentrations extending up the Mississippi River. Rather dense populations are present in Alabama around the William Dannelly Reservoir and along the Missouri River in Missouri.

The diet of the Swamp Sparrow includes a higher proportion of insects than that of any other member of the genus *Melospiza* and most other emberizids. Even in winter it eats 55% animal matter, including beetles, ants, bees, wasps, caterpillars, grasshoppers, and crickets. The rest of the diet is primarily seeds. Because of this unusual diet, its skull, jaw muscles, and bill are smaller than those of other sparrows. Also, this species often forages differently from most sparrows; it feeds in shallow water much like a sandpiper, which may help explain why its femur and tibiotarsus are longer than those of the Song Sparrow. In winter it often frequents broom sedge fields and open marshes but not salt marshes, which are frequented by the Seaside Sparrow. Censusing the Swamp Sparrow can be difficult because it is inconspicuous, and unlike most other sparrows it does not form foraging flocks (Bent 1968).

Snow Bunting (*Plectrophenax nivalis*) Map in Appendix B

The Snow Bunting is much too nomadic and gregarious to be adequately censused by the methods used in the CBC. Thus, its map has been placed in appendix B. The Snow Bunting was seen on 521 sites throughout the study area, but at many of these locations the annual abundance ranged from no individuals in one year to hundreds the next. The overall distribution extends from central British Columbia east along the international border, encompassing the Great Lakes, to the Atlantic coast. A southern extension occurs along the Atlantic seaboard to around Chesapeake Bay.

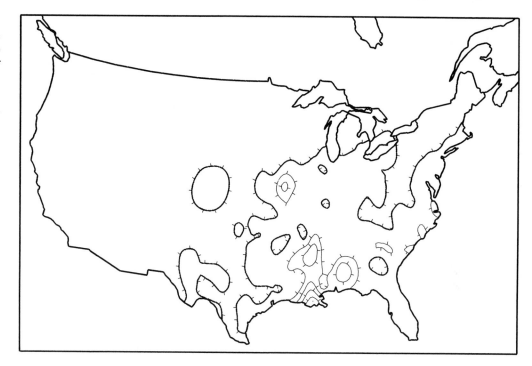

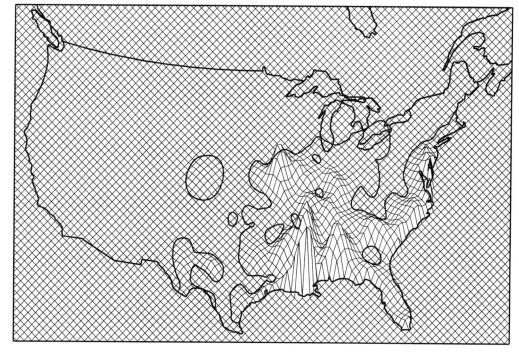

EMBERIZIDAE

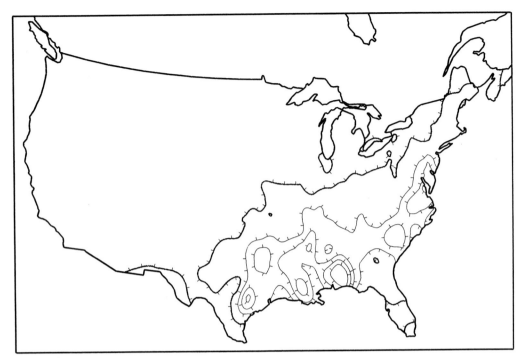

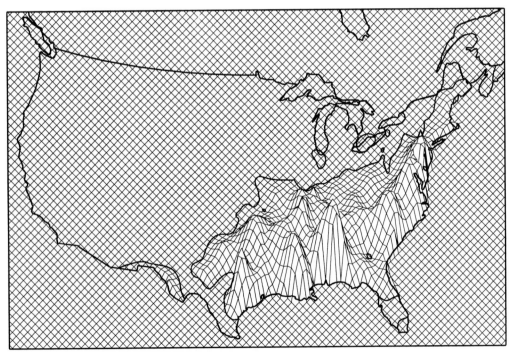

Lark Bunting (*Calamospiza melanocorys*) Map in Appendix B
Of all members of the subfamily Emberizinae, the Lark Bunting forms the largest winter flocks. Groups of over 2,000 are not uncommon. Such large flocks are almost impossible to count accurately, and site abundances are strongly influenced by the chance finding of flocks within the count circles. Thus the map of this species is provided only in appendix B. This bird was seen at sixty-nine sites that covered most of western Texas and extended into the southern portions of western New Mexico to central Arizona. The densest populations were in the Big Bend area and around Midland and Odessa, Texas.

White-throated Sparrow (*Zonotrichia albicollis*) Maximum: 21.90 I/Hr
Except for a rather small range extension west of the 95th parallel into the savanna of the southeastern Great Plains, the entire distribution of the White-throated Sparrow is limited to areas that receive 40 inches (102 cm) or more of precipitation a year. The abundance pattern is also associated with rainfall, but a stronger correspondence apparently occurs with temperature. The western edge of the area where this sparrow is fairly common stops abruptly when the average annual precipitation drops below 32 inches (81 cm). The more expansive northern boundary of these abundant populations shows that the White-throated Sparrow most often frequents habitats that have an average minimum January temperature over 30°F (−1°C). The individual abundance peaks within this region are strongly associated with open water. The population with the highest concentration is in Alabama around the William Dannelly Reservoir, and slight concentrations stretch from here to the Mississippi River, both in Louisiana and farther north along the Mississippi border. Less concentrated populations are present in the marshy area around Chesapeake Bay, along the Colorado River in southern Texas, and on the Red River between Texas and Oklahoma.

The White-throated Sparrow normally winters in sheltered areas. It frequents habitats of fairly dense brush within a semiopen canopy of balsam fir and spruces (Bent 1968). About 90% of its winter diet in the East, at least, is vegetable matter (Pulliam and Enders 1971), mainly weed seeds and small fruit (Bent 1968). The mean size of the seeds eaten is 0.13 inch (3.2 mm) (Pulliam and Enders 1971). When foraging, this sparrow rarely gleans items off the bare ground. Instead, it takes unfallen seeds directly from the plants. Eating while perched on a seed head, stalk, or branch of a plant takes about 60% of its foraging time, with the remaining time spent standing on the ground and feeding on the low vegetation (Pulliam and Enders 1971). This bird also frequently uses feeders (Bent 1968).

White-throated Sparrow

Golden-crowned Sparrow (*Zonotrichia atricapilla*) Maximum: 19.94 I/Hr

In the United States the winter distribution of this elegant sparrow is restricted to the area west of the Cascades, the Sierra Nevada, and the San Bernardino Mountains, where it frequents the coastal coniferous forest and mixed evergreen and deciduous forest. The distribution does not continue north into Canada, probably, at least in part, because of colder temperatures coupled with a lack of adequate vegetation.

At least two of the three dense populations of Golden-crowned Sparrows are associated with areas where the environment is protected. The abundance peak farthest south stretches along the coast roughly between San Simeon and Monterey Bay. Most of this area is covered by the Los Padres National Forest. High densities of Golden-crowned Sparrows continue northeast to the Sacramento valley, where the Sutter and Colusa National wildlife refuges lie. To the north a less dense population centers on Medford and Ashland, Oregon. Just south of this area is the Rogue River National Forest, which may influence the location of this peak.

Fairly dense brushland with open areas is the habitat in which the Golden-crowned Sparrow is normally found (Davis 1973)—for example, within thickets along streams, in thick garden shrubbery, and in chaparral (Bent 1968). In these areas it often flocks with White-crowned Sparrows, but the more wary Golden-crowned stays much closer to cover (Bent 1968). The flocks vary in size from ten to twenty birds (Bent 1968), are very stable, and have well-defined ranges (Davis 1973). Only rarely do the ranges of these flocks overlap, and flock members show rather high site tenacity (Pearson 1979). Over the years birds migrate back to the same winter flock territory (Bent 1968). By removal experiments, Davis (1973) showed that Golden-crowned Sparrows are aggressive enough to exclude juncos from desired habitats, particularly sources of water. Before the fall rains, the diet of this sparrow is primarily seeds, and thus water is necessary during this time. After the rains its diet still is almost 100% vegetable matter, but besides seeds it now eats sprouting annuals and buds, which significantly decrease its need for water (Davis 1973).

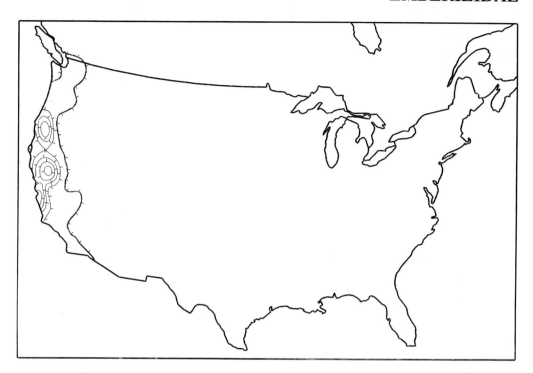

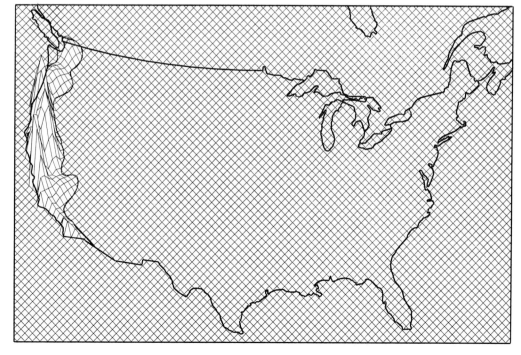

Golden-crowned Sparrow

EMBERIZIDAE

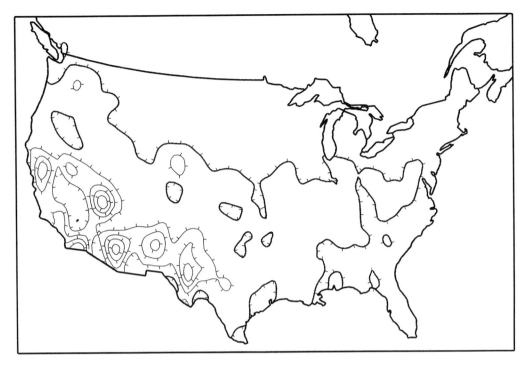

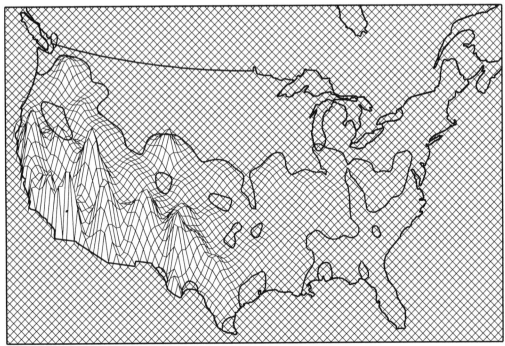

White-crowned Sparrow (*Zonotrichia leucophrys*) Maximum: 48.65 I/Hr

The White-crowned Sparrow is the western counterpart of the White-throated Sparrow. Unlike that of the White-throated Sparrow, its distribution is not strongly concomitant with precipitation and shows a stronger association with temperature. The northern range limit indicates that this sparrow is absent where the average minimum January temperature drops below 15°F (−9°C). It also avoids the southeastern corner of the country, and some, but certainly not all, of the sites east of the 100th meridian do not regularly record this sparrow. The presence of the White-throated Sparrow in this region may restrict its occurrence.

The dense populations of the White-crowned Sparrow all occur west of the 100th meridian and are sympatric with the western distributional edge of the White-throated Sparrow. Unlike this latter species, whose abundance is strongly associated with temperature, the highest abundance of the White-crowned Sparrow occurs along rivers. The abundance peak farthest east is in the warmer climates of the South, on the border between New Mexico and Texas along the Pecos River. From here slight concentrations stretch west, reaching a peak in the center of New Mexico along the Rio Grande, and continue westward to a slight concentration in Arizona, reaching an apex in the Phoenix-Tucson area. An equally dense concentration is west of this in the Imperial Valley of southern California, and another of the same density is in the southwestern corner of Utah, around Zion National Park. The maps indicate that the White-crowned Sparrow occurs in rather high concentrations across Nevada, but the environment is inappropriately dry and harsh for this species, suggesting that the interpolated values in this area are probably inaccurate because of the lack of count sites. The high concentrations in California stretch along the Pacific border from southern California to Humboldt County. A dense population is present in the Sacramento valley.

Winter foraging flocks include ten to twenty White-crowned Sparrows, and because of fairly high site tenacity, their composition is rather stable from year to year (Bent 1968). They frequent open areas as long as some type of cover, such as bushes or shrubbery, is within 7 feet (2 m), and occasionally birds will venture as far as 14 feet (4 m) from cover (Pulliam and Mills 1977). When alarmed this sparrow will always fly to cover (Pulliam and Mills 1977), usually at high speed (Bent 1968). The clearing of forests has provided more habitat that is suitable for these birds (Cortopassi and Mewaldt 1965). The winter diet is primarily seeds gleaned from the ground. When necessary they will scratch among the litter and debris to expose food (Bent 1968). Morton (1984) found that wintering Gambel's White-crowned Sparrows (*Z. l. gambelii*) exhibit a latitudinal cline in sex ratios. Males make up 80% of the population closer to the breeding grounds, whereas only 25% of the southern population is male.

Harris' Sparrow (*Zonotrichia querula*) Maximum: 26.11 I/Hr

Except for the towhees, the Harris' Sparrow is the largest of all the emberizids. It winters in the grassland and in tree and shrub savanna, and it avoids both the mixed mesophytic and deciduous forest to the east and the dry-belt pine forest to the west. Cold temperatures probably are at least partly preventing this sparrow from extending farther north. The distribution does not continue west across the entire expanse of the grassland or tree and shrub savanna. Whatever factor prevents this sparrow from occurring in the far western portion of the Great Plains is not obvious, perhaps because of the large scale of this study.

The distribution of this sparrow has changed very little over the past century. In 1884 Wells Cooke determined that the eastern edge of the winter range of the Harris' Sparrow paralleled the 96th meridian. By 1929 the winter range was described as occurring between the 28th and 41st parallels and the 94th and 100th meridians (Bent 1968). The maps presented here show that some expansion has occurred to the north and west, with the present distribution lying between the 94th and 102nd meridians and the 28th and 45th parallels. Perhaps the establishment of winter wheat in Kansas and an increased number of feeders, particularly in the North, have both aided in the slight expansion of this species.

Over 90% of this sparrow's winter diet is vegetable matter, with about 50% of that attributable to weed seeds and 25% to wild fruit. The animal matter consists of some insects, spiders, and snails. This sparrow normally feeds in the underbrush and dense shrubs along forest edges or openings. It will forage on the ground, scratching away dead leaves, but when alarmed it flies to cover and perches high in a tree. The only other sparrow that retreats to a high perch is the American Tree Sparrow. Coincidentally, these two sparrows often form foraging flocks. Sometimes juncos, goldfinches, Song Sparrows, and Northern Cardinals also join these flocks (Bent 1968).

The first recorded Harris' Sparrow specimen was collected in April 1834 by Thomas Nuttall while he was traveling across Missouri with John Townsend. They gave it the common name Mourning Finch and the scientific name *Fringilla querula*. One month later Maximilian, Prince of Wied, collected specimens in southeastern Nebraska and named the sparrow *Fringilla comata*. Nine years later, around Fort Leavensworth, Kansas, Edward Harris collected what Audubon thought was a new species. Subsequently, Audubon named it *Fringilla harrisii* with the common name Harris' Sparrow (Bent 1968). Because the earliest recorded scientific species name takes precedence over all others, the specific name remains *querula*. Audubon's common name, however, is used because that was the one he published in the sixth volume of his widely read *Birds of America*.

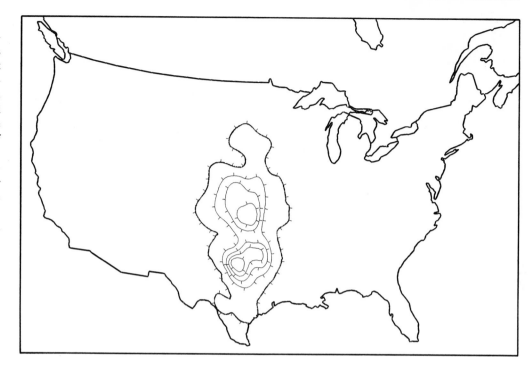

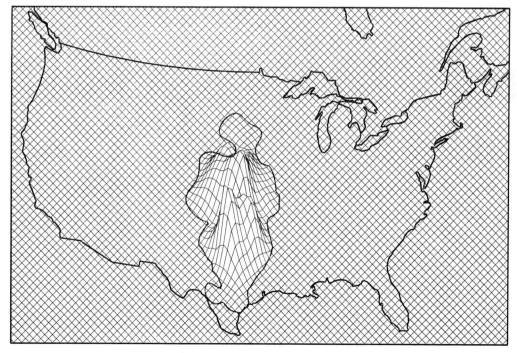

Harris' Sparrow

EMBERIZIDAE

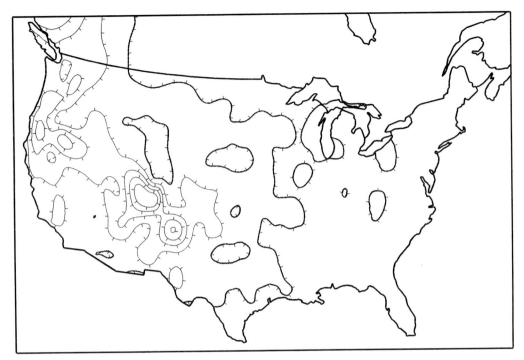

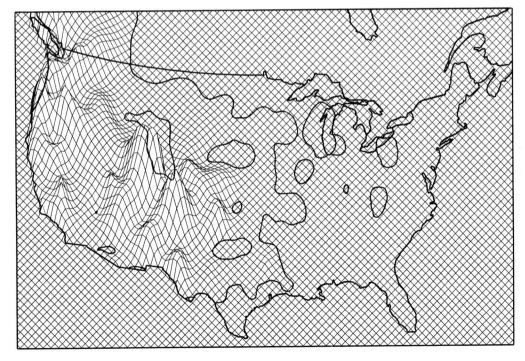

Yellow-eyed Junco (*Junco phaeonotus*) No Map

The major portion of the Yellow-eyed Junco's distribution is in Mexico, with only its extreme northern edge in the United States (AOU 1983). This junco was observed at only seven CBC sites, and all were along the Mexican border between the 108th and 111th meridians, which includes southeastern Arizona and southwestern New Mexico. This junco was seen in each of the ten years examined at the Santa Catalina Mountains count area, with an average abundance of 0.45 juncos seen per hour of count effort.

Dark-eyed Junco, Oregon Race (*Junco hyemalis oreganus*) Maximum: 31.07 I/Hr

The Oregon race is the western equivalent of the Slate-colored race. The eastern range edge of the Oregon Junco is concomitant with the eastern side of the grasslands. This boundary indicates that the western subspecies avoids the mixed mesophytic and deciduous forest. The overall western distribution and the range limit in southern Texas indicate that this race frequents areas higher than 1,000 feet (305m) above sea level, a predilection also shown by the scattered populations in the Appalachians and Ozarks. This subspecies apparently avoids areas in the North where the average minimum January temperature drops below 0°F (−18°C). The distributions of the Oregon and Slate-colored races overlap in the Great Plains.

Dense populations of Oregon Juncos occur in the more open woodlands of the dry-belt forests and in the pines along the Pacific coast. The lack of counts in Nevada combined with high counts to both the east and the west caused the interpolated values in this area to be rather high. Given that the vegetative cover is primarily semiarid scrub, these high densities may be unrealistic. Tracts of ponderosa pines, however, are scattered throughout this region. More censusing is needed.

Oregon Juncos are normally found at the edges of coniferous forest, where they use the trees for shelter and forage in the open, grassy areas. Their winter diet is primarily weed seeds, wild and cultivated oats, and barley. Stable foraging flocks form in the winter, and often joining these flocks are chickadees, Bushtits, Varied Thrushes, Ruby-crowned Kinglets, Chipping Sparrows, White-crowned Sparrows, Green-tailed Towhees, and other races of juncos (Bent 1968).

Dark-eyed Junco, Oregon Race

Dark-eyed Junco, Slate-colored Race (*Junco hyemalis hyemalis*)
   Maximum: 34.58 I/Hr

During the time when the CBC data examined here were collected, the Slate-colored Junco was considered a species, and hence its abundance information was recorded separately. The western range limit of this subspecies coincides with the western edge of the Great Plains, indicating that except for a few isolated pockets this junco avoids the semiarid scrub and dry-belt pine forest. To the north this bird avoids areas that have a minimum January temperature lower than 0°F to 10°F (−18°C to −12°C). This junco is also absent from southern Texas, areas along the Gulf coast, and peninsular Florida.

High concentrations of the Slate-colored Junco occur throughout most of its distribution. The western border of the area where it is abundant appears to be associated with precipitation, with the highest population densities occurring where the annual rainfall is over 24 inches (61 cm). The area of high concentration extends only as far south as where the minimum January temperature is under 40°F (4°C). The most densely concentrated populations are primarily in riparian habitat. This is true along the Mississippi River on the border between Iowa and Illinois and along the Red River, which forms the border between Texas and Oklahoma. The unusual peak in southern Mississippi is due to a high count at Stafford Springs in 1967, the only year that count was held.

In the winter the Slate-colored Junco eats weed, hemlock, and yellow birch seeds and will come to feeders, though it usually forages on dropped seeds rather than on the platforms. It scratches for seeds by hopping forward and then back. Holes 3 to 4 inches (8−10 cm) in diameter are scratched in the snow when necessary (Bent 1968). In deep snow juncos are forced to feed on unfallen seeds, but even then 95% of the time birds will pull seed heads to the ground rather than perching on plants (Gottfried and Franks 1975). Winter foraging flocks are usually stable (Bent 1968) and have well-defined home ranges (Gottfried and Franks 1975). A latitudinal gradient in the gender ratio of populations occurs in the winter. In the South 70% of the birds are female, but only 20% are female in the North (Ketterson and Nolan 1976). There are probably two reasons for this. First, larger birds can survive longer without food than smaller ones. Thus males, which are larger, can survive harsh weather and deep snowfalls more easily than females (Ketterson and Nolan 1976). Second, males that stay nearer the breeding areas are able to get better breeding territories. Males are dominant over the females and consequently drive them farther south (Ketterson and Nolan 1979). Unexpectedly, the annual mortality of populations wintering farther north is about the same as that for birds in the South. The overwinter fatalities are higher for the populations wintering in the North, but this is balanced by higher migration fatalities (Ketterson and Nolan 1982).

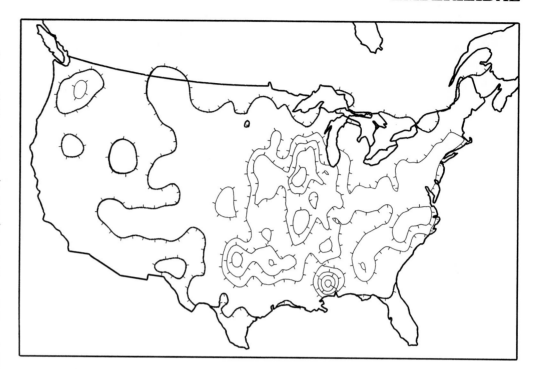

EMBERIZIDAE

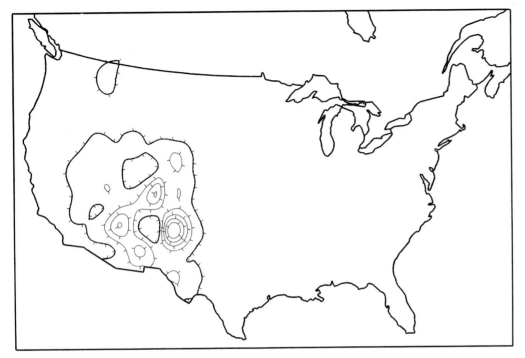

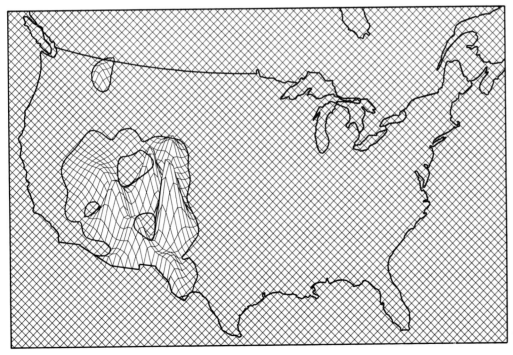

Dark-eyed Junco, White-winged Race (*Junco hyemalis aikeni*) No Map
The White-winged race of the Dark-eyed Junco was seen at twenty-seven locations, primarily along the Rocky Mountains in northern New Mexico, Colorado, and southern Wyoming. The site with the highest mean abundance, however, was in the Black Hills of South Dakota, where 5.40 individuals were seen per party-hour.

Dark-eyed Junco, Gray-headed Race (*Junco hyemalis caniceps*)
 Maximum: 11.41 I/Hr
This subspecies is present in areas where the precipitation is 16 inches (41 cm) or less annually and where there are pine or juniper pine forests. Included are the dry-belt pine forests and scattered tracts of junipers and other conifers that occur throughout the semiarid scrub. Thatcher described these habitats as being preferred (in Bent 1968).

All the most concentrated populations of the Gray-headed Junco are on conifer-covered slopes of mountains. The highest abundance peak is at the southern end of the Sangre de Cristo Mountains in New Mexico. To the north of this area there is a less dense population in the southwestern corner of Colorado around the San Juan Mountains. From here a slight concentration stretches southwest to another abundant population in the San Francisco Mountains around Flagstaff, Arizona. A slight concentration continues southeast to a small peak in the Black Range of southwestern New Mexico.

In winter, foraging flocks of the Gray-headed Junco often contain members of other junco races. Other species that join these flocks include Mountain Chickadee, Pygmy Nuthatch, Brown Creeper, and White-breasted Nuthatch. These flocks usually contain from ten to thirty birds (Bent 1968). In the winter, aggressive behavior in flocks of Yellow-eyed and Dark-eyed Juncos is temperature dependent. As the temperature drops below the birds' thermoneutral zones, the mean size of the flock increases, thereby increasing aggression. Larger flocks also form as food becomes scarcer, which again increases aggression (Pulliam et al. 1974).

McCown's Longspur (*Calcarius mccownii*) No Map
Of the twenty-seven sites where this longspur was reported, only two reported it in five years and only one in all ten years. All three of these counts were in Texas; the less regular sightings were on the Eldorado and Muleshoe national wildlife refuge counts, and Friona was where the McCown's Longspur was seen each year. The highest average abundance was also reported at Friona, with 105.20 individuals seen per hour of count effort.

Dark-eyed Junco, Gray-headed Race

Lapland Longspur (*Calcarius lapponicus*) Map in Appendix B

The gregariousness and wandering behavior of the Lapland Longspur may decrease the reliability of the CBC data to such a degree that a map of the abundance data recorded at the 384 sites is not reliable. Thus, the map is included in appendix B. The overall distribution of this longspur is roughly coincident with the region where winter wheat and oats are grown. The exception is in the colder areas of Canada, which this bird avoids. Because of its wandering, disjunct populations were seen in many states.

Smith's Longspur (*Calcarius pictus*) No Map

The Smith's Longspur was seen at twenty-one sites, chiefly between the 30th and 35th parallels and the 90th and 100th meridians. It was seen at only two sites in five or more years. These included Norman, Oklahoma, where sightings were made in seven of the ten years, and Little Rock, Arkansas, where it was seen in all ten years. The higher average abundance occurred at Little Rock, with 0.26 individuals seen per party-hour.

Chestnut-collared Longspur (*Calcarius ornatus*) Maximum: 13.74 I/Hr

The overall winter distribution of the Chestnut-collared Longspur primarily covers the southwestern portion of the Great Plains. During the fall it migrates into the tree and shrub savanna, except those areas with acacias, which are chiefly in extreme southern Texas, and the grassland region along the eastern border of New Mexico and western Texas. In the savanna, this longspur eats entirely plant material, primarily weed seeds (Bent 1968). The disjunct "population" in northern California indicates that fairly large populations do wander in the winter. In 1971 one Chestnut-collared Longspur was shown on the Honey Lake count, and on this same California count the next year, 150 were reported.

Over the years the abundance of this species has decreased along with the destruction of the grasslands from both overgrazing and farming (Bent 1968). The more concentrated populations are somewhat anomalous given what is known about the species' preferred habitat. The highest density is along the Pecos River on the border between New Mexico and Texas, and there is a less dense population on the Red River between Texas and Oklahoma. Pulliam and Mills (1977), however, found that in Arizona this longspur prefers plains-grassland habitat, is never closer to cover than 164 feet (50 m), and is more common where cover is farther than 210 feet (64 m) away. Certainly a study is needed in the area of either of the two abundance peaks to determine how close the birds are to riparian habitats.

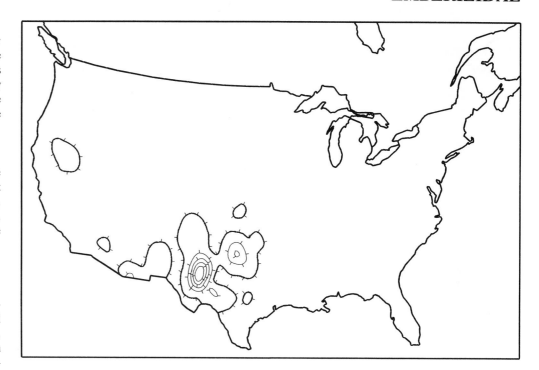

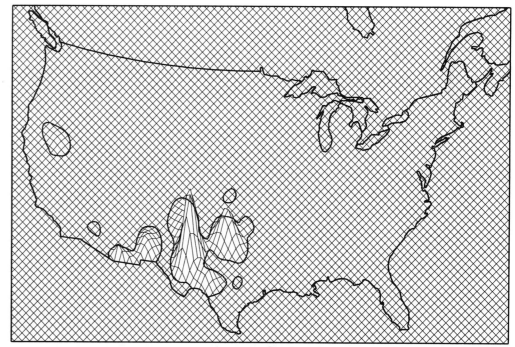

Chestnut-collared Longspur

EMBERIZIDAE

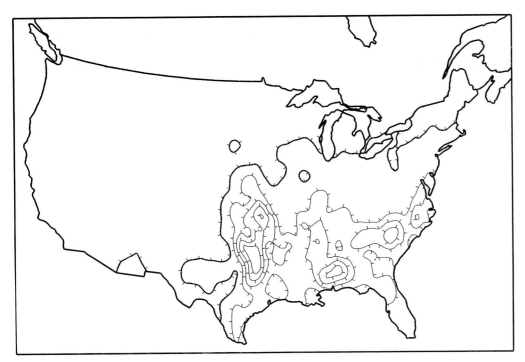

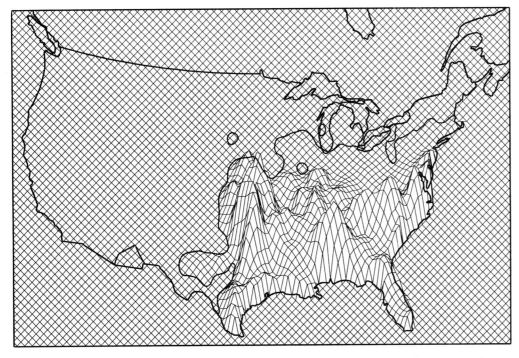

Eastern Meadowlark (*Sturnella magna*) Maximum: 17.36 I/Hr

The Eastern Meadowlark spread westward as people of European descent established settlements and thereby opened up the forest environment for farming. This expansion continued until the ranges of the Eastern Meadowlark and Western Meadowlark met. The interaction between these two species, which were officially separated in 1910 (AOU 1910), resulted in the Western Meadowlark's preventing the westward expansion of its eastern counterpart (Lanyon 1956). The accompanying maps also provide circumstantial evidence that the Western Meadowlark is more aggressive than its congener. The ranges of these species overlap to some extent. The sympatry of the distributions shows that low densities of the Western Meadowlark occur even where the eastern species is present in high numbers, but the range boundary of the Eastern Meadowlark skirts the locations where its western congener is abundant. In fact, most of the sightings of Eastern Meadowlarks west of the 100th meridian are irregular and were reported only 10% to 20% of the time. Thus high densities of the Western Meadowlark seem to exclude its eastern counterpart, but the opposite is not true for the Eastern Meadowlark. A similar situation can be seen in the maps of the Black-capped Chickadee and Carolina Chickadee.

The maps indicate that precipitation is at least partially influencing the range of these species, which supports Lanyon's (1956) hypothesis that the proximate factor limiting meadowlark distributions is precipitation. The Eastern Meadowlark occurs where the annual precipitation is 24 inches (61 cm) or more, and its western counterpart is found in drier areas. Temperature apparently helps define the northern limit of the Eastern Meadowlark, because this bird avoids regions where the average minimum January temperature drops below 15°F (−9°C).

Temperature, moisture, and vegetation are all associated with where this species winters in high densities. Most of the dense populations are in regions where the minimum January temperature is over 30°F (−1°C). The exception is the extension in the grasslands of the Great Plains. Most of the highly concentrated populations occur along rivers or lakes: around the Red River on the border between Texas and Oklahoma, near Oologah Lake in northern Oklahoma, just south of the William Dannelly Reservoir in Alabama, and along the Catawba River on the border between North Carolina and South Carolina.

In winter the Eastern Meadowlark mainly eats seeds, chiefly those of weeds, as well as waste corn, wheat, rye, and oats. Wild fruits supplement its diet to some degree. This bird normally forages on the ground and will scratch with its feet and even dig with its bill. It frequents stubble and old, weed-covered fields, and it will migrate out of areas where the snow is too deep (Bent 1958).

Eastern Meadowlark

Western Meadowlark (*Sturnella neglecta*) Maximum: 43.11 I/Hr

The distributions of the Eastern and Western Meadowlarks have a fairly large area of overlap in the Great Plains. The eastern edge of the Western Meadowlark's range coincides with the western limit of the mixed mesophytic and deciduous forest. Thus, this meadowlark apparently frequents the open habitats of the Great Plains and avoids dense forest. The northern limit of its range, like that of its eastern congener, is associated with temperature. This meadowlark is absent from regions that have an average minimum winter temperature below 10°F (−12°C), which includes the vacant areas in Wyoming, Colorado, and Utah.

The behaviors of the Eastern and Western Meadowlarks are very similar. Both forage on the ground along roadsides, on vacant land, and in cultivated fields where there is an abundance of weeds and grasses. Both species eat primarily weed seeds and waste grain in the winter (Bent 1958). Because of these strong similarities, it is not surprising that there is competition between them (Lanyon 1956). The maps of these two congeners suggest that interspecific interactions may affect their abundance patterns (see the account of the Eastern Meadowlark for an explanation). The areas where these meadowlarks occur in high density abut and do not overlap. The main distinction between the occurrence of these two species is that the Western Meadowlark prefers drier areas (Lanyon 1956). Its most concentrated populations are not restricted to moist areas around rivers and lakes as are those of the eastern species; the highest concentration of the western species is on the Great Plains in Oklahoma, around the Kirwin National Wildlife Refuge. To the south there is a somewhat lesser peak in the grasslands around Plainview, Texas. A peak of equal concentration occurs in the grasslands and tule marshes of the Sacramento valley of California.

Red-winged Blackbird (*Agelaius phoeniceus*) Map in Appendix B

This abundant, transcontinental blackbird was reported at 1,041 count sites, but its extreme gregariousness may have caused the maps to be misleading. Thus, the contour map is provided in appendix B. The abundance data are strongly influenced by the chance occurrence of a large flock within a count circle. For example, a roost of 40 million Red-winged Blackbirds was recorded at Little Rock, Arkansas, in 1965, four times the previous national record for individuals of one species reported at one location.

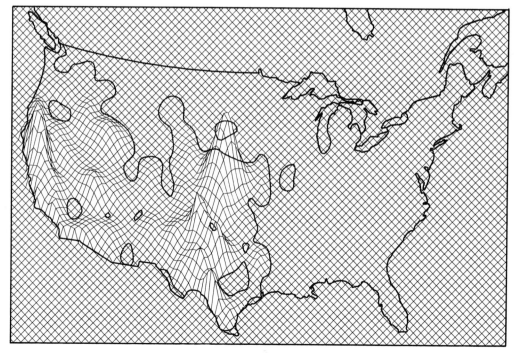

EMBERIZIDAE

Tricolored Blackbird (*Agelaius tricolor*) Map in Appendix B
The map of this species is included only in appendix B because "the outstanding characteristic of the Tricolored Blackbird is its highly gregarious behavior at all times, . . . [and] the immensity of its flocks, . . ." (Bent 1958, 186). For example, 2,000 birds were recorded on the Medford, Oregon, count in 1963, but none were seen in 1965. The forty-two sites recording this species were scattered throughout California and southern Oregon.

Yellow-headed Blackbird (*Xanthocephalus xanthocephalus*) Map in Appendix B
The gregarious and nomadic behavior of the Yellow-headed Blackbird has resulted in a wide variance of individuals being recorded at given Christmas count sites. For example, on the Salton Sea South count in California 4,500 blackbirds were seen in 1966, but in 1969 none were recorded. Thus, the contour map is included in appendix B. The one hundred sites where this species was observed were scattered throughout southeastern California, central and southern Arizona, and southern New Mexico along the Rio Grande. The highest average abundance was 167.03 individuals seen per party-hour in the Phoenix area.

Rusty Blackbird (*Euphagus carolinus*) Map in Appendix B
The Rusty Blackbird has a maximum average abundance of 811.45 individuals per party-hour. This high value not only indicates its extreme gregariousness but also causes populations of low concentration not to be included on the map. Therefore the mapped distribution looks more contracted and spotty than it actually is. The contracted range shows that fairly large numbers of Rusty Blackbirds occur east of the 100th meridian, between the 32nd and 38th parallels.

Brewer's Blackbird (*Euphagus cyanocephalus*) Map in Appendix B
Except for a few scattered locations in the Southeast, the 455 count sites reporting the Brewer's Blackbird are mainly west of the 95th meridian, which is near the eastern border of Texas. Most of these counts are in the warmer habitats of the South and up along the Pacific coast. The highest average abundance of 412.22 individuals seen per party-hour was recorded in eastern New Mexico along the Pecos River. Most of the denser populations occur along river valleys.

Great-tailed and Boat-tailed Grackles (*Quiscalus mexicanus* and *Q. major*) Map in Appendix B
These species were considered conspecific when the data examined in this study were collected. Combined, these two grackles were observed on 138 counts, most in areas along the Gulf and Atlantic coasts where the average minimum January temperature is above freezing. Sightings were also reported from along the Rio Grande and Pecos valleys. The most concentrated population was in southern Georgia, where 221.50 Boat-tailed Grackles were seen per party-hour.

Common Grackle (*Quiscalus quiscula*) Map in Appendix B
Of all wintering North American birds, the Common Grackle had the second-highest maximum average abundance value, 9,689.00 individuals seen per party-hour. This concentrated population was in southern Georgia, where the Boat-tailed Grackle also reached its maximum abundance. The winter range of this species is primarily east of the 95th meridian and south of the 40th parallel.

Bronzed Cowbird (*Molothrus aeneus*) No Map
The thirty-two Christmas count sites reporting this cowbird are chiefly west of the 95th meridian and south of the 35th parallel, but sightings were very irregular in the colder parts of this area. The highest average abundance at sites where it was seen in at least 50% of the years was near Brownsville, Texas. Here observations in ten years resulted in an average abundance of 6.02 individuals seen per party-hour.

Brown-headed Cowbird (*Molothrus ater*) Map in Appendix B
This brood parasite is gregarious in the winter, with an average of 1,265.44 individuals seen per party-hour in the densest population. This abundant population, like those of the Common and Boat-tailed Grackles, is in southern Georgia. The Brown-headed Cowbird is mainly a bird of the Southeast, except that the range extends north along the Mississippi and Ohio rivers, and birds avoid the Appalachians. Disjunct populations are scattered throughout the southern parts of California, Arizona, and New Mexico.

Orchard Oriole (*Icterus spurius*) No Map
The Orchard Oriole was recorded in fewer than five years at all eighteen sites where it was reported. Most of these sites are scattered along the Atlantic and Gulf coasts, with a few western outliers in southern California. The maximum average abundance was only 0.01 individuals per party-hour.

Hooded Oriole (*Icterus cucullatus*) No Map

A total of five sites observed the Hooded Oriole in at least 50% of the years examined. These are in southern Texas, southeastern Arizona, and southern California. All twenty-one sites recording this species, except one count in southern Texas, are west of the 100th meridian. The maximum average abundance for all twenty-one sites was only 0.02 individuals per party-hour.

Spot-breasted Oriole (*Icterus pectoralis*) No Map

This species was introduced into southeastern Florida from Central America (AOU 1983). Of the four counts on which this species was observed, those at Fort Lauderdale and West Palm Beach, Florida, reported it in all ten years. The highest abundance was 0.26 individuals per party-hour at Fort Lauderdale.

Northern Oriole, Baltimore Race (*Icterus galbula galbula*) Maximum: 1.51 I/Hr

The winter range of the Baltimore race of the Northern Oriole has been spreading farther north. In 1957 this species was reported "occasionally in winter in southeastern Canada and eastern United States from Toronto, Ontario, south to Louisiana, especially since about 1951" (AOU 1957, 534). By 1983 its winter range had expanded so that it is seen "regularly in small numbers in the Atlantic states north to Virginia, . . . and casually elsewhere in eastern North America north to the Great Lakes region, southern Ontario and New England" (AOU 1983, 738). The maps show that its wintering range encompasses more southerly areas where the climate is moderated by oceans. Regular sightings were reported primarily on counts east of the 90th meridian and south of the 37th parallel. The sporadic sightings, including that of two birds at a feeder in 1967 on the Northfield count in Minnesota, may have been of individuals migrating late because of warm weather, but a more in-depth analysis is needed to determine if this hypothesis is correct.

The two densest populations occur in areas that appear to have little in common other than a general warm climate. One of the populations stretches from around Tallahassee to Gainesville, Florida, and the other is in southeastern North Carolina, extending from around the town of Rocky Mount to Croatan National Forest near New Bern.

The primary wintering information for this oriole comes from observations in Central America. Here its diet consists of both animal and vegetable material. It eats fruit and will come to feeders for ripe bananas. When flowers are blooming, it probes them for the nectar, the insects attracted to the nectar, or both. The "small creatures" that live in the moss and lichen-covered branches are also part of its diet (Bent 1958).

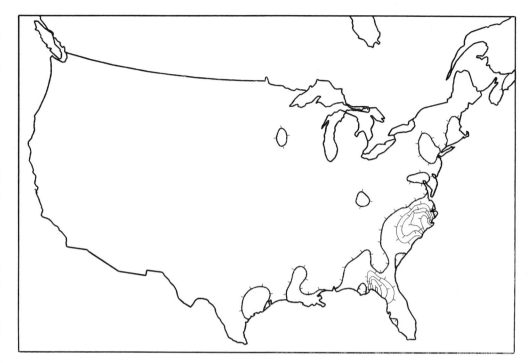

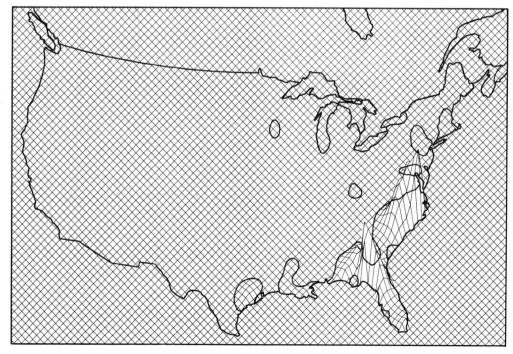

Northern Oriole, Baltimore Race

Northern Oriole, Bullock's Race (*Icterus galbula bullocki*) Map
in Appendix B

The Bullock's Oriole and Baltimore Oriole have been lumped together into the Northern Oriole (AOU 1983), but each of these evolutionarily distinct races is easily recognized over most of their ranges and the two were recorded separately on the Christmas counts. The Bullock's Oriole was seen at fifty-three sites across the United States, but the maximum average abundance was only 0.20 individuals seen per party-hour. Most of the sightings were along the Gulf and southern Pacific coasts, but there were scattered observations throughout most of the United States.

Altamira Oriole (*Icterus gularis*) No Map

The far northern extent of the Altamira Oriole's range encompasses the extreme southern part of Texas along the southern Rio Grande valley. It was reported in all ten years on counts at Bentsen State Park and Santa Ana National Wildlife Refuge. The average abundances at both these protected areas were basically identical, with 0.23 individuals seen per party-hour at Bentsen and 0.25 at Santa Ana.

Audubon's Oriole (*Icterus graduacauda*) No Map

The range of Audubon's Oriole, formerly known as the Black-headed Oriole, extends from southern Texas to Oaxaca, Mexico (AOU 1983). The ten sites recording it in the United States are in the southern Rio Grande valley. Birds were seen in each of the ten years at Santa Ana National Wildlife Refuge, but the average abundance here was only 0.04 individuals seen per party-hour.

FRINGILLIDAE

Rosy Finch, Gray-crowned Race (*Leucosticte arctoa tephrocotis*)
No Map

The three races of the Rosy Finch were classified as one species only in 1983 (AOU 1983), and thus the CBC data examined provide information on the distribution and abundance of each race. Most of the thirty-five sites recording the Gray-crowned Rosy Finch are in the Rocky Mountains from central New Mexico to Idaho. Four additional sites recorded this species in Alaska. The highest average abundance was 8.79 individuals seen per party-hour near Gunnison, Colorado, where this Rosy Finch was observed in five years.

Rosy Finch, Black Race (*Leucosticte arctoa atrata*) No Map

All twenty sites reporting the Black Rosy Finch are in the Rocky Mountains between central New Mexico and southwestern Montana. Only three sites recorded it in 50% or more of the years examined. These include the counts near Pikes Peak in Colorado, around Salt Lake in Utah, and near Dubois, Wyoming, in the Wind River Range. The last location reported the highest average abundance, 1.50 individuals seen per party-hour.

Rosy Finch, Brown-capped Race (*Leucosticte arctoa australis*) No Map

Of the three races of Rosy Finch, the Brown-capped has the most restricted range. The eleven sites reporting this Rosy Finch were all within the Colorado Rockies except for a sighting of fifty individuals on the Espanola, New Mexico, count in 1968. As with the Gray-crowned race, the highest average abundance was recorded near Gunnison, Colorado. Here these two races were seen in all five years this count was held during the period examined. Indeed, the Black race was even observed in four of these years. The average abundance for the Brown-capped race was 12.10 individuals seen per party-hour.

Pine Grosbeak (*Pinicola enucleator*) Map in Appendix B

The Pine Grosbeak's winter diet is 99% vegetable matter, primarily seeds from pines, firs, spruces, and birches (Bent 1968). It frequents the boreal and the mixed deciduous and coniferous forests in the North, but in years of bad cone crops it invades areas to the south (Bock and Lepthien 1976d). The CBC data show that Pine Grosbeaks are consistently present north of about the 50th parallel, but during irruption years birds occur as far south as the dry-belt pine forest of central Arizona. The highest concentrations of this grosbeak are in south-central Saskatchewan and just north of Lake Superior.

Purple Finch (*Carpodacus purpureus*) Map in Appendix B

Bock and Lepthien (1976d) found that the Purple Finch is irruptive. It invades more southerly areas when the northern cone crop is small. Its general winter range covers the area east of the 100th meridian, and a narrow band of the distribution extends along the Coast Range in California, Oregon, Washington, and British Columbia. In general the abundance is higher in the eastern portion of its distribution.

Cassin's Finch (*Carpodacus cassinii*) Map in Appendix B

Like its congener, the Cassin's Finch irrupts southward when the northern cone crop is small (Bock and Lepthien 1976d). Thus only the contour map is included in appendix B. This finch frequents the high, cool coniferous forests in the West (Bent 1968). The most abundant population is in the eastern foothills of the Colorado Rockies, where on average 2.99 individuals were seen per party-hour.

House Finch (*Carpodacus mexicanus*) Maximum: 76.40 I/Hr

Until 1940 the House Finch was restricted to areas west of the Mississippi River. In that year numerous birds were captured and shipped to New York, where dealers were going to sell these "Hollywood Finches," as they were glamorously renamed, as cage birds (Bent 1968). The House Finch, however, was protected by the Migratory Bird Act (Palmer 1973). To escape prosecution, the bird dealers released the finches, which successfully established themselves in New York and have been spreading since then (Bent 1968). This finch was first seen in Virginia in 1962, and it bred near Richmond in 1978 (Sprenkle and Blem 1984). The CBC data show that the eastern population grew exponentially from 1963 to 1972, except for a few fluctuations attributed to the birds' inability to prosper during extraordinarily wet years (Bock and Lepthien 1976c).

The eastern populations seem to have adapted to a much wetter climate than is tolerated by most western birds. Precipitation appears to be associated with where the western individuals are present. Except along the Pacific coast, the House Finch avoids areas that receive more than about 16 inches (41 cm) of precipitation a year, and it is present in areas with low general humidity. Vegetation and temperature seem to have little effect on where this finch winters.

Precipitation also may be associated with where finches winter in high densities. The densest concentration is in the San Joaquin valley, centered on the region that gets less than 16 inches (41 cm) of rain annually, and this high-density area is bounded on the north by the occurrence of over 24 inches (61 cm) of precipitation. In California this finch has been said to be the "most destructive bird pest in California" (Palmer 1973). Large flocks, which in the winter show strong site tenacity (Thompson 1960), eat seeds and buds off trees. Even though they are protected by the Migratory Bird Act, a provision allows their regulation to help prevent agricultural damage (Palmer 1973). A lesser concentration of finches centers on Phoenix, Arizona, which gets less than 24 inches (61 cm) of rain annually.

Both the distribution and the abundance of the House Finch have expanded with human settlement, for it prospers around towns and cities. By 1925 it had extended its range to eastern Oklahoma, and it reached northern British Columbia by 1937. Before the House Sparrow arrived in 1894, the House Finch was the only bird around buildings in Denver. Its diet reflects the association with humans in that it eats seeds, both wild and from feeders, suet, bread crumbs, and buds of trees and shrubs (Bent 1968). The eastern population uses feeders so much that the morphology of their bills has changed, allowing them to open sunflower seeds more efficiently than their western relatives (Sprenkle and Blem 1984). Unlike most other birds, the House Finch feeds its young primarily seeds rather than the more usual diet of insects (Bent 1968).

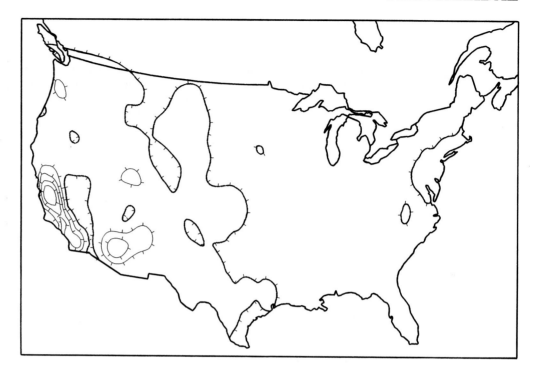

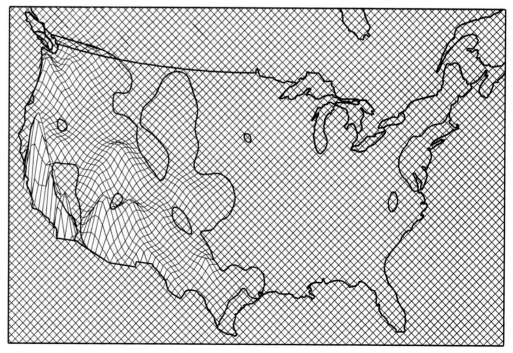

FRINGILLIDAE

Red Crossbill (*Loxia curvirostra*) Map in Appendix B
The Red Crossbill and its congener, the White-winged Crossbill, are not truly migratory, but instead wander nomadically, tracking the cone crop. Thus, both crossbills are strongly irruptive (Bock and Lepthien 1976d). Most of the 405 sites where the Red Crossbill was observed are in the northern coniferous forests where the average minimum January temperature is below 20°F (−7°C). The highest average abundances are in the forests of Washington State.

White-winged Crossbill (*Loxia leucoptera*) Map in Appendix B
The White-winged Crossbill wanders throughout the coniferous forests following the availability of pine seeds. Because of this irruptive behavior, the contour maps of both *Loxia* congeners have been relegated to appendix B. In general the range of the White-winged Crossbill is much farther north than that of the Red Crossbill. The former is present in the boreal and mixed deciduous and coniferous forests, including the southern extension in the Appalachians, and is absent from the mixed mesophytic and deciduous forest. The most concentrated populations are around the southwest tip of Lake Superior.

Evening Grosbeak (*Coccothraustes vespertinus*) Map in Appendix B
In winter this grosbeak is irruptive (Bock and Lepthien 1976d). Its abundance varies greatly from year to year, and thus its map is included in appendix B. In general the Evening Grosbeak ranges throughout the North and tracks the occurrence of pines in the West and in the Appalachians. The name Evening Grosbeak is misleading because it implies that this finch is crepuscular, which is not the case.

Common Redpoll (*Carduelis flammea*) Map in Appendix B
Like most other pine-seed specialists, the Common Redpoll invades southward when the northern cone crop is small (Bock and Lepthien 1976d). Most of the 540 sites recording this redpoll are in areas where the average minimum January temperature is below 10°F (−12°C). The highest concentrations are in southern Saskatchewan and northern North Dakota.

Hoary Redpoll (*Carduelis hornemanni*) Map in Appendix B
The Hoary Redpoll was not one of the species examined by Bock and Lepthien (1976d), but its similarities with the Common Redpoll suggest that it is indeed irruptive. By comparing the number of sites reporting this redpoll on a given year with the total number of counts held that year where this redpoll had ever been observed, I found that it invades southern areas in the same years when the Common Redpoll and other irruptive species do. In general the range of the Hoary Redpoll is farther north than that of the Common Redpoll. The former was recorded at only fifty-eight sites, primarily in southern Canada, where the average minimum January temperature drops below 5°F (−15°C). The highest concentration is roughly in the same location as that of the Common Redpoll—southern Saskatchewan.

Pine Siskin (*Carduelis pinus*) Map in Appendix B
The Pine Siskin irrupts to the south when cone crops in the North are small. In nonirruptive years (e.g., 1963, 1965, 1967, 1968, and 1971) its range is restricted primarily to the northern coniferous forest, but when it invades to the south it occurs throughout the United States and southern Canada (Bock and Lepthien 1976d). Two areas of high abundance are indicated in the CBC data; one is in the coastal coniferous forests of northwestern Washington and southwestern British Columbia, and the other is in the dry-belt pine forests of the Southwest. Presumably in nonirruptive years the more northerly location contains a high abundance, and dense populations occur in the southern areas primarily during invasion years.

Red and White-winged Crossbills

Lesser Goldfinch (*Carduelis psaltria*) Maximum: 16.96 I/Hr

The distribution of this small western goldfinch is strongly associated with vegetation. The eastern border of its distribution in Texas indicates that it avoids the mixed mesophytic and deciduous forest as well as the dry-belt pine forest of Arizona and New Mexico. The Lesser Goldfinch is present, however, in the stunted woodlands of piñon-juniper forests. Other environments where it also occurs include the savannas of southern Texas, the scrub steppe of the Great Basin, southern New Mexico, Arizona, and California, and the woodlands west of the Coast Range.

The most abundant population is in northern California's Sacramento valley. This concentrated population is juxtaposed to that of the House Finch, with the peak abundance of the red finch just south of that of the Lesser Goldfinch. A finer-grained study is needed in the Central Valley of California to determine if there is an interspecific density-dependent suppression between these two finches. Less concentrated populations of the Lesser Goldfinch are present in the chaparral of southern California and along the Rio Grande in southern Texas.

The ecology of the Lesser Goldfinch is fairly similar to that of the House Finch. Both species occur in drier, open areas with sparse trees and bushes, and both stay near open water. Their winter diets consist almost entirely of seeds, and both prefer seeds with high fat content (e.g., sunflower seeds). The goldfinch often feeds along roadsides in flocks, which sometimes include other species such as juncos and sparrows (Bent 1968).

Lawrence's Goldfinch (*Carduelis lawrencei*) No Map

This striking goldfinch can be difficult to find because it has a fairly restricted range but nomadically wanders throughout it in the winter. Of the thirty-six census sites reporting the Lawrence's Goldfinch, only ten recorded it in five or more years. Two of these sites are in southeastern Arizona, around Nogales and Tucson, and the others are in southern California below the 35th parallel. One exception is the Crystal Springs Reservoir count in California, which has a history of reporting unusual species. The highest average abundance was around Tucson, Arizona, with 1.13 birds seen each party-hour, but the variance around this mean is fairly high because of the wandering of this goldfinch.

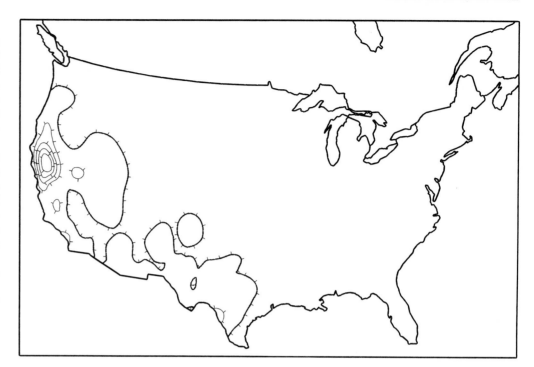

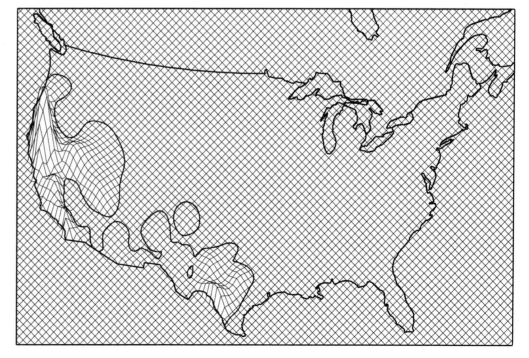

FRINGILLIDAE

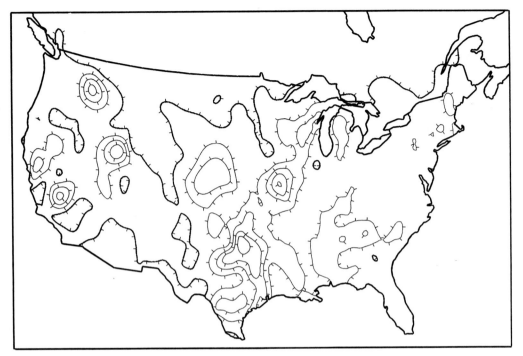

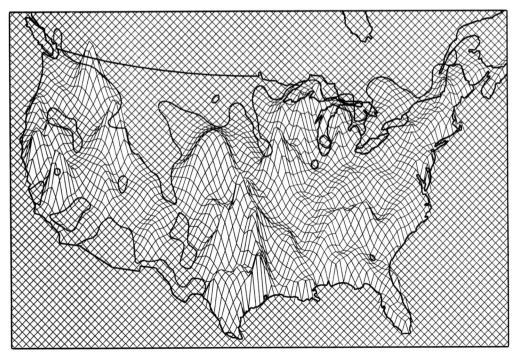

American Goldfinch (*Carduelis tristis*) Maximum: 16.67 I/Hr

The American Goldfinch is certainly an appropriate name for this transcontinental finch. The distribution shows that climate apparently is associated with where it winters. In the West it is absent from areas where the average minimum January temperature falls below 10°F (−12°C), which includes the large southern extension into the Rocky Mountain states. East of roughly the Mississippi River, this goldfinch appears to survive in areas where the average temperature drops as low as 5°F (−15°C). In addition, it avoids the harsh environments of the Chihuahuan and Sonoran deserts.

Vegetation and precipitation do not appear to strongly influence the winter range of the American Goldfinch, but both factors seem to affect the location of high population concentrations. In the West, all the abundance peaks are concomitant with the edges of forests that abut either grasslands or scrub steppe. Included are peaks in southern California, central California, northern Utah, and on the border between Wyoming and Utah. In the eastern half of the United States the highest peaks are associated chiefly with river valleys—in Missouri along the Missouri River and along the Red River on the border between Texas and Oklahoma. The populations along the Mississippi River, however, are low. This species frequently uses feeders, and the distribution of feeders in the United States may influence where it winters in large numbers. Unfortunately, there are no good data on the distribution or abundance of feeders with which to compare the biogeographic data on birds.

The American Goldfinch primarily eats seeds from plants in the composite family, including the sunflower and thistle, which are its preferred foods. When these are not available it eats seeds of birch, alder, sweet gum, and sycamore trees, along with those of evening primrose and ragweed. Foraging flocks form in the winter, at times including redpolls and siskins. If they are feeding in the snow on emergent seed heads, American Tree Sparrows often join the group. The distress call of one member of the flock will bring the entire group to its aid. Unfortunately the abundance of this finch has been negatively affected by the presence of House Sparrows, which have driven the goldfinch from several breeding areas (Bent 1968).

American Goldfinch

PASSERIDAE

House Sparrow (*Passer domesticus*) Maximum: 135.14 I/Hr

Unfortunately the House Sparrow has done very well in North America since its introduction in 1851, greatly affecting the occurrence of native birds. The sparrow was first introduced in 1850, when eight pairs were released in Brooklyn Park, New York. These all died before spring, but fifty more were introduced in 1851, and these began breeding. Supplemental introductions occurred throughout the United States and Canada, and the range expanded with the establishment of human settlements and farms. By 1898 the House Sparrow had spread over all of the United States except Wyoming, Nevada, New Mexico, and Arizona (Summers-Smith 1963).

On the Christmas counts examined here, the House Sparrow was reported at 1,244 sites out of a possible 1,282 (97%). The only distributional limit shown on the map is in southern Canada, where the counts are so sparse that the precise location of the boundary is questionable. House Sparrows do not migrate, and in severely cold winters, particularly when there is heavy snowfall, large numbers die off (Summers-Smith 1963). Johnston and Fleischer (1981) found that it is primarily small males and large females that die in stressful times. At high latitudes the larger birds are dominant over the small ones, and the medium-sized birds expend much energy fighting. The average size of individuals in different populations varies, with larger birds occurring in the North and smaller ones in the South. Also, the extremities are relatively shorter in the North than in the South (Johnston and Selander 1973).

The abundance pattern of the House Sparrow shows peak abundances in the Great Basin, around Phoenix, Arizona, and in the central United States. In the latter region the House Sparrow is undoubtedly attracted by farms and ranches. The House Sparrow was more common outside this central region before the advent of the tractor and car, because it has a commensal relationship with the domestic horse, being attracted to feed grains (Moseley 1947). The areas of high concentration have now contracted to encompass the region of the country where small grains are grown and livestock is raised or ranged.

Eurasian Tree Sparrow (*Passer montanus*) No Map

Like its North American congener, the Eurasian Tree Sparrow was introduced, but unlike the House Sparrow, its distribution has remained restricted. Only eleven sites recorded this sparrow, and only four of those reported it in five or more years. All four of these sites are within 0.5° of latitude or longitude of Saint Louis, Missouri. The highest average abundance was at Orchard Farms, northwest of Saint Louis between the Missouri and Mississippi rivers, near the Saint Charles airport, where 2.47 individuals were seen per party-hour.

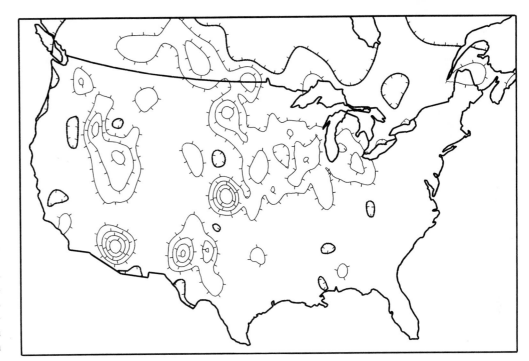

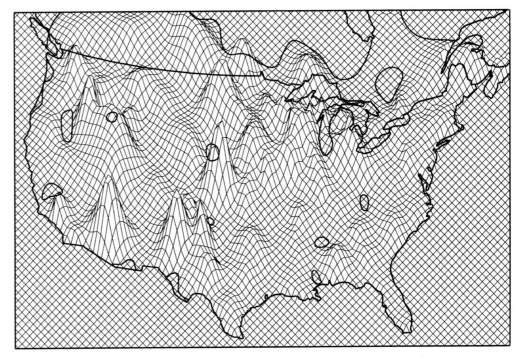

Appendix A
Species List

The common names of the 508 birds included in this atlas are listed below in the sequence followed in the text. This order follows, as closely as possible, the American Ornithologists' Union *Check-list of North American Birds* (AOU 1983). Where departures from this order have been required because of the length of the entries, species thought to be closely related (Mayr and Short 1970; AOU 1983) are grouped together. Each common name is followed by the total number of sites where the bird was recorded and the maximum abundance value used in the normalization process. The notes tell why maps of various species were included only in appendix B, or why they were excluded altogether (e.g., "too few sites"). Asterisks before species names indicate that maps are presented in the main text. Species with maps in appendix B are marked with a dash.

Map	Species	Number of Sites	Maximum Abundance	Notes
*	Red-throated Loon	168	5.30	
*	Pacific Loon	51	5.40	
−	Common Loon	391	2.15	Nomadic
	Least Grebe	19	0.39	Too few sites
*	Pied-billed Grebe	724	2.77	
−	Western and Clark's Grebes	118	90.07	Nomadic
*	Horned Grebe	449	6.00	
*	Red-necked Grebe	127	3.97	
−	Eared Grebe	210	113.05	Bad peak
	Northern Fulmar	17	3.21	Too few sites
	Sooty Shearwater	14	0.06	Too few sites
	Manx Shearwater	4	0.09	Too few sites
*	American White Pelican	86	23.34	
*	Brown Pelican	70	26.50	
−	Northern Gannet	63	10.46	Pelagic
*	Great Cormorant	73	9.53	
	Brandt's Cormorant	39	172.70	Too few sites
−	Pelagic Cormorant	40	60.15	Nomadic
*	Double-crested Cormorant	251	33.32	
	Olivaceous Cormorant	18	6.47	Too few sites

Map	Species	Number of Sites	Maximum Abundance	Notes
*	Anhinga	70	3.91	
	Magnificent Frigatebird	23	0.86	Too few sites
*	American Bittern	206	0.23	
−	Least Bittern	44	0.06	Rare
	Great Blue Heron (White Race)	23	1.88	Too few sites
*	Great Blue Heron (Blue Race)	761	2.45	
*	Great Egret	189	12.98	
*	Snowy Egret	135	14.14	
*	Little Blue Heron	109	20.41	
*	Tricolored Heron	92	4.81	
	Reddish Egret	33	0.63	Too few sites
*	Cattle Egret	104	66.67	
*	Green-backed Heron	209	1.01	
*	Black-crowned Night-Heron	240	1.98	
*	Yellow-crowned Night-Heron	72	0.99	
*	White Ibis	69	37.85	
*	Glossy Ibis	41	1.50	
	White-faced Ibis	27	24.65	Too few sites
	Roseate Spoonbill	25	2.36	Too few sites
*	Wood Stork	43	6.65	
*	Mute Swan	98	4.31	
−	Tundra Swan	222	140.76	Nomadic
	Trumpeter Swan	11	0.63	Too few sites
	Fulvous Whistling-Duck	26	0.12	Too few sites
	Black-bellied Whistling-Duck	12	0.03	Too few sites
−	Greater White-fronted Goose	115	107.87	Nomadic
−	Snow Goose (White Morph)	305	500.00	Gregarious
−	Snow Goose (Blue Morph)	216	419.89	Gregarious
	Ross' Goose	30	0.27	Too few sites
	Brant (Black Race)	32	14.06	Too few sites
*	Brant (Atlantic Race)	66	319.75	
−	Canada Goose	744	666.16	Gregarious
*	Wood Duck	543	16.08	
−	Green-winged Teal	636	214.44	Gregarious

Map	Species	Number of Sites	Maximum Abundance	Notes
	Green-winged Teal (Common Race)	14	0.01	Too few sites
*	American Black Duck	656	111.75	
*	Mottled Duck	53	8.88	
−	Mallard	1,059	2,142.86	Gregarious
−	Northern Pintail	660	714.29	Gregarious
*	Blue-winged Teal	304	15.25	
−	Cinnamon Teal	100	11.12	Bad peak
−	Northern Shoveler	454	46.13	Nomadic
*	Gadwall	561	25.06	
−	Eurasian Wigeon	57	0.09	Rare
−	American Wigeon	661	220.10	Gregarious
*	Canvasback	588	38.14	
*	Redhead	527	47.89	
*	Ring-necked Duck	609	33.86	
*	Greater Scaup	345	130.78	
*	Lesser Scaup	694	78.43	
−	Common Eider	70	266.67	Gregarious
−	King Eider	43	7.33	Bad peak
*	Harlequin Duck	63	3.35	
*	Oldsquaw	290	106.03	
*	Black Scoter	171	27.31	
*	White-winged Scoter	221	85.00	
*	Surf Scoter	174	62.22	
−	Barrow's Goldeneye	101	9.55	Bad peak
−	Common Goldeneye	795	37.25	Bad peak
*	Bufflehead	660	24.69	
*	Hooded Merganser	615	2.80	
−	Common Merganser	703	58.33	Nomadic
*	Red-breasted Merganser	450	22.22	
*	Ruddy Duck	536	153.49	
*	Black Vulture	264	7.79	
*	Turkey Vulture	435	7.56	
	California Condor	1	0.21	Too few sites
*	Osprey	135	1.02	
*	Black-shouldered Kite	59	1.22	
*	Bald Eagle	456	3.87	
*	Northern Harrier	912	1.53	
−	Sharp-shinned hawk	737	0.12	Rare
−	Cooper's Hawk	795	0.15	Rare
−	Northern Goshawk	278	0.09	Rare
−	Broad-winged Hawk	79	0.37	Nomadic
	Short-tailed Hawk	8	0.02	Too few sites
−	Swainson's Hawk	91	0.30	Nomadic
	White-tailed Hawk	11	0.08	Too few sites
−	Red-tailed Hawk (Harlan's Race)	94	0.12	Rare
*	Red-tailed Hawk	1,107	1.80	
*	Red-shouldered Hawk	616	0.56	
*	Ferruginous Hawk	142	0.75	
*	Rough-legged Hawk	779	1.02	
*	Harris' Hawk	47	1.49	
*	Golden Eagle	270	0.58	
	Crested Caracara	27	0.31	Too few sites
*	Prairie Falcon	158	0.22	
*	American Kestrel	1,094	2.04	
−	Merlin	343	0.11	Rare
−	Peregrine Falcon	240	0.11	Rare
	Gyrfalcon	20	0.11	Too few sites
	Plain Chachalaca	8	2.77	Too few sites
	Spruce Grouse	9	0.01	Too few sites
	Blue Grouse	16	0.37	Too few sites
	Sage Grouse	10	3.93	Too few sites
*	Gray Partridge	112	4.00	
	Chukar	35	2.09	Too few sites
*	Ring-necked Pheasant	698	15.47	
	White-tailed Ptarmigan	3	0.18	Too few sites
*	Ruffed Grouse	455	0.81	
*	Sharp-tailed Grouse	46	12.86	Too few sites
	Greater Prairie-Chicken	20	2.80	Too few sites
	Lesser Prairie-Chicken	3	7.58	Too few sites
*	Wild Turkey	148	3.28	
	Montezuma Quail	8	0.45	Too few sites
*	Northern Bobwhite	646	5.20	
*	Scaled Quail	59	19.65	
*	Gambel's Quail	46	10.24	
*	California Quail	104	17.20	
	Mountain Quail	30	2.04	Too few sites
	Limpkin	19	0.37	Too few sites
	Black Rail	15	0.01	Too few sites
*	Clapper Rail	115	1.43	
*	King Rail	91	0.27	
*	Virginia Rail	231	0.20	
*	Sora	179	0.66	
	Purple Gallinule	18	0.11	Too few sites
*	Common Moorhen	168	3.33	
*	American Coot	761	183.20	
−	Sandhill Crane	92	2,331.31	Gregarious
	Whooping Crane	1	0.78	Too few sites
*	Black-bellied Plover	167	6.16	
	Lesser Golden-Plover	23	0.11	Too few sites
	Mountain Plover	12	10.31	Too few sites
*	Snowy Plover	55	0.94	
*	Semipalmated Plover	113	3.13	
*	Piping Plover	58	2.12	
*	Killdeer	860	12.66	
*	Wilson's Plover	40	1.33	
	American Oystercatcher	32	41.15	Too few sites
	Black Oystercatcher	19	3.26	Too few sites

Map	Species	Number of Sites	Maximum Abundance	Notes
–	Black-necked Stilt	38	2.31	Too few sites
*	American Avocet	69	47.68	
*	Greater Yellowlegs	240	2.72	
*	Lesser Yellowlegs	167	1.43	
–	Solitary Sandpiper	43	0.10	Rare
*	Willet	109	28.96	
	Wandering Tattler	20	0.79	Too few sites
*	Spotted Sandpiper	199	0.41	
*	Whimbrel	55	7.57	
*	Long-billed Curlew	71	7.62	
*	Marbled Godwit	66	27.32	
*	Ruddy Turnstone	118	3.17	
*	Black Turnstone	38	7.50	
	Surfbird	28	2.01	Too few sites
*	Red Knot	72	5.34	
*	Sanderling	156	12.68	
–	Semipalmated Sandpiper	115	41.50	Misidentified
*	Western Sandpiper	176	45.90	
*	Least Sandpiper	251	12.53	
	Baird's Sandpiper	16	0.82	Too few sites
	Pectoral Sandpiper	27	0.07	Too few sites
*	Purple Sandpiper	81	222.22	
	Rock Sandpiper	13	0.41	Too few sites
–	Dunlin	232	231.06	Gregarious
	Stilt Sandpiper	26	0.35	Too few sites
	Wilson's Phalarope	13	0.02	Too few sites
	Red-necked Phalarope	14	2.19	Too few sites
	Red Phalarope	28	1.10	Too few sites
*	Short-billed Dowitcher	89	14.10	
*	Long-billed Dowitcher	102	11.62	
*	Common Snipe	752	2.95	
*	American Woodcock	236	0.34	
	Pomarine Jaeger	21	0.01	Too few sites
	Parasitic Jaeger	18	0.03	Too few sites
	Heermann's Gull	26	50.33	Too few sites
	Franklin's Gull	39	0.27	Too few sites
–	Iceland Gull	102	7.86	Bad peak
	Lesser Black-backed Gull	14	9.71	Too few sites
–	Western Gull	48	969.54	Gregarious
–	Glaucous-winged Gull	64	144.44	Bad peak
*	Glaucous Gull	156	8.00	
*	Herring Gull	705	279.32	
*	Great Black-backed Gull	250	42.91	
*	California Gull	96	75.56	
	Mew Gull	59	80.04	Bad peak
*	Ring-billed Gull	725	91.95	
*	Laughing Gull	128	61.13	
	Little Gull	23	0.01	Too few sites
	Common Black-headed Gull	36	0.29	Too few sites

Map	Species	Number of Sites	Maximum Abundance	Notes
*	Bonaparte's Gull	314	66.06	
–	Black-legged Kittiwake	74	324.39	Gregarious
	Gull-billed Tern	35	0.21	Too few sites
*	Caspian Tern	78	1.32	
*	Royal Tern	81	7.92	
	Elegant Tern	6	0.01	Too few sites
*	Common Tern	79	0.48	
	Sandwich Tern	34	2.96	Too few sites
*	Forster's Tern	120	7.12	
	Least Tern	17	0.12	Too few sites
*	Black Skimmer	65	19.27	
–	Dovekie	54	67.77	Nomadic
–	Common Murre	40	1,290.91	Gregarious
	Thick-billed Murre	22	0.83	Too few sites
	Razorbill	22	12.29	Too few sites
	Black Guillemot	28	44.17	Too few sites
	Pigeon Guillemot	29	11.25	Too few sites
	Marbled Murrelet	27	4.00	Too few sites
	Ancient Murrelet	19	2.67	Too few sites
	Cassin's Auklet	14	353.50	Too few sites
	Rhinoceros Auklet	17	4.99	Too few sites
	Rock Dove	—	—	No data
	White-crowned Pigeon	5	0.41	Too few sites
*	Band-tailed Pigeon	69	40.63	
	Ringed Turtle-Dove	18	0.36	Too few sites
	Spotted Dove	14	4.14	Too few sites
*	White-winged Dove	49	1.64	
*	Mourning Dove	1,076	24.67	
*	Inca Dove	52	8.38	
	White-tipped Dove	8	0.38	Too few sites
*	Common Ground-Dove	120	27.27	
	Yellow-billed Cuckoo	15	0.01	Too few sites
	Mangrove Cuckoo	5	0.01	Too few sites
*	Greater Roadrunner	149	0.32	
	Smooth-billed Ani	19	3.02	Too few sites
	Groove-billed Ani	19	0.36	Too few sites
–	Common Barn-Owl	292	0.22	Rare
*	Eastern and Western			
	Screech-Owls	678	0.31	
*	Great Horned Owl	933	0.43	
–	Snowy Owl	234	0.21	Rare
–	Northern Saw-whet Owl	165	0.12	Rare
–	Burrowing Owl	98	0.64	Rare
	Spotted Owl	13	0.04	Too few sites
*	Barred Owl	529	0.26	
	Northern Hawk-Owl	20	0.44	Too few sites
–	Northern Pygmy-Owl	70	0.17	Rare
*	Short-eared Owl	429	0.44	
*	Long-eared Owl	293	0.24	

Map	Species	Number of Sites	Maximum Abundance	Notes
	Common Nighthawk	15	0.01	Too few sites
	Common Pauraque	18	0.45	Too few sites
	Common Poorwill	19	0.03	Too few sites
	Chuck-will's-widow	29	0.07	Too few sites
	Whip-poor-will	29	0.03	Too few sites
*	White-throated Swift	55	9.09	
	Ruby-throated Hummingbird	31	0.16	Too few sites
	Black-chinned Hummingbird	22	0.02	Too few sites
*	Anna's Hummingbird	71	2.57	
	Costa's Hummingbird	22	0.09	Too few sites
	Rufous Hummingbird	23	0.07	Too few sites
	Allen's Hummingbird	10	0.42	Too few sites
	Ringed Kingfisher	3	0.10	Too few sites
*	Belted Kingfisher	985	0.90	
	Green Kingfisher	9	0.29	Too few sites
*	Lewis' Woodpecker	80	1.32	
*	Red-headed Woodpecker	616	2.54	
*	Acorn Woodpecker	72	7.96	
	Gila Woodpecker	16	2.60	Too few sites
*	Golden-fronted Woodpecker	42	1.75	
*	Red-bellied Woodpecker	720	1.89	
*	Yellow-bellied and Red-breasted Sapsuckers	761	0.87	
	Williamson's Sapsucker	26	0.18	Too few sites
*	Ladder-backed Woodpecker	125	1.55	
*	Nuttall's Woodpecker	48	1.27	
*	Downy Woodpecker	1,151	2.25	
*	Hairy Woodpecker	1,094	1.11	
	Strickland's Woodpecker	7	0.13	Too few sites
*	Red-cockaded Woodpecker	45	0.41	
	White-headed Woodpecker	16	0.56	Too few sites
*	Three-toed Woodpecker	47	0.29	
–	Black-backed Woodpecker	76	0.04	Rare
*	Northern Flicker (Yellow-shafted Race)	921	2.77	
*	Northern Flicker (Red-shafted Race)	364	4.72	
	Northern Flicker (Gilded Race)	12	1.66	Too few sites
*	Pileated Woodpecker	653	0.70	
	Eastern Wood-Pewee	18	0.03	Too few sites
*	Black Phoebe	108	1.45	
*	Eastern Phoebe	367	1.38	
*	Say's Phoebe	148	7.27	
	Ash-throated Flycatcher	31	0.81	Too few sites
	Great Crested Flycatcher	32	0.47	Too few sites
*	Vermilion Flycatcher	88	1.11	
	Dusky Flycatcher	5	0.04	Too few sites
	Gray Flycatcher	8	0.12	Too few sites

Map	Species	Number of Sites	Maximum Abundance	Notes
	Western Flycatcher	12	0.05	Too few sites
	Great Kiskadee	11	2.08	Too few sites
	Tropical Kingbird	16	0.51	Too few sites
	Cassin's Kingbird	15	0.41	Too few sites
–	Western Kingbird	47	0.06	Rare
	Eastern Kingbird	26	0.15	Too few sites
	Scissor-tailed Flycatcher	21	0.50	Too few sites
	Eurasian Skylark	2	2.77	Too few sites
*	Horned Lark	920	58.40	
–	Tree Swallow	157	223.28	Gregarious
	Violet-green Swallow	37	0.78	Too few sites
*	Northern Rough-winged Swallow	40	2.92	
	Barn Swallow	37	0.03	Too few sites
*	Gray Jay	133	1.48	
*	Steller's Jay	153	3.12	
*	Blue Jay	1,003	11.72	
	Green Jay	11	2.29	Too few sites
*	Scrub Jay	175	5.75	
	Gray-breasted Jay	14	4.54	Too few sites
*	Pinyon Jay	57	16.06	
*	Clark's Nutcracker	61	3.50	
*	Black-billed Magpie	153	18.30	
	Yellow-billed Magpie	19	17.74	Too few sites
*	American Crow	1,108	98.91	
	Northwestern Crow	23	31.25	Too few sites
*	Fish Crow	181	38.32	
	Chihuahuan Raven	39	59.29	Too few sites
*	Common Raven	329	13.02	
*	Black-capped Chickadee	803	13.46	
*	Carolina Chickadee	408	4.91	
*	Mountain Chickadee	148	16.25	
–	Boreal Chickadee	153	2.44	Irruptive
*	Chestnut-backed Chickadee	55	7.94	
	Bridled Titmouse	14	2.37	Too few sites
*	Plain Titmouse	87	4.78	
*	Tufted Titmouse	750	4.26	
*	Tufted Titmouse (Black-crested Race)	43	11.25	
*	Verdin	80	4.52	
*	Bushtit	151	9.86	
	Bushtit (Black-eared Morph)	9	0.67	Too few sites
*	White-breasted Nuthatch	1,001	2.59	
–	Red-breasted Nuthatch	894	1.83	Irruptive
*	Pygmy Nuthatch	81	7.12	
*	Brown-headed Nuthatch	136	3.20	
*	Brown Creeper	1,016	0.62	
*	Cactus Wren	92	4.09	
*	Rock Wren	142	1.42	

Map	Species	Number of Sites	Maximum Abundance	Notes
*	Canyon Wren	115	0.96	
*	Carolina Wren	614	2.45	
*	Bewick's Wren	324	1.63	
*	House Wren	344	1.06	
–	Winter Wren	669	0.58	Bad peak
*	Sedge Wren	132	0.78	
*	Marsh Wren	328	1.29	
*	American Dipper	88	0.97	
*	Golden-crowned Kinglet	967	2.71	
*	Ruby-crowned Kinglet	793	3.84	
*	Blue-gray Gnatcatcher	184	2.32	
*	Black-tailed Gnatcatcher	48	1.91	
*	Eastern Bluebird	605	4.56	
*	Western Bluebird	136	8.82	
*	Mountain Bluebird	129	19.02	
*	Townsend's Solitaire	181	2.00	
	Veery	10	0.03	Too few sites
	Gray-cheeked Thrush	24	0.13	Too few sites
–	Swainson's Thrush	79	0.27	Nomadic
*	Hermit Thrush	607	1.11	
	Wood Thrush	37	0.04	Too few sites
*	Varied Thrush	115	20.00	
–	American Robin	1,141	205.33	Gregarious
*	Wrentit	53	2.04	
*	Gray Catbird	343	1.67	
*	Northern Mockingbird	836	5.26	
*	Sage Thrasher	60	1.45	
*	Brown Thrasher	639	1.57	
	Long-billed Thrasher	18	0.84	Too few sites
*	Curve-billed Thrasher	70	3.58	
	Bendire's Thrasher	10	0.21	Too few sites
*	California Thrasher	42	0.54	
*	Crissal Thrasher	40	0.78	
*	Water Pipit	450	18.47	
–	Sprague's Pipit	56	0.68	Nomadic
–	Bohemian Waxwing	188	43.64	Nomadic
*	Cedar Waxwing	925	10.72	
*	Phainopepla	56	6.45	
–	Northern Shrike	485	0.39	Irruptive
*	Loggerhead Shrike	664	2.80	
–	European Starling	1,223	8,659.53	Gregarious
	Crested Myna	4	5.22	Too few sites
*	White-eyed Vireo	95	0.54	
*	Solitary Vireo	132	0.33	
	Yellow-throated Vireo	31	0.06	Too few sites
*	Hutton's Vireo	67	0.38	
	Red-eyed Vireo	11	0.02	Too few sites
	Tennessee Warbler	17	0.02	Too few sites
–	Nashville Warbler	45	0.16	Rare

Map	Species	Number of Sites	Maximum Abundance	Notes
*	Orange-crowned Warbler	264	2.72	
	Worm-eating Warbler	14	0.02	Too few sites
–	Ovenbird	52	0.11	Rare
–	Northern Waterthrush	43	0.32	Bad peak
	Louisiana Waterthrush	13	0.02	Too few sites
*	Northern Parula	50	0.28	
–	Yellow Warbler	43	0.01	Rare
*	Yellow-rumped Warbler (Myrtle Race)	671	32.75	
*	Yellow-rumped Warbler (Audubon's Race)	193	27.31	
	Magnolia Warbler	27	0.74	Too few sites
	Cape May Warbler	14	0.02	Too few sites
	Black-throated Blue Warbler	25	0.10	Too few sites
–	Black-throated Gray Warbler	50	0.33	Bad peak
*	Townsend's Warbler	58	0.98	
	Hermit Warbler	14	0.02	Too few sites
	Black-throated Green Warbler	23	0.06	Too few sites
*	Yellow-throated Warbler	86	0.50	
*	Pine Warbler	227	2.78	
*	Prairie Warbler	55	1.26	
	Bay-breasted Warbler	11	0.01	Too few sites
*	Palm Warbler	220	6.61	
	American Redstart	39	0.13	Too few sites
–	Wilson's Warbler	72	0.09	Rare
*	Common Yellowthroat	290	3.41	
–	Yellow-breasted Chat	105	0.05	Rare
*	Black-and-white Warbler	100	0.29	
	Summer Tanager	25	0.02	Too few sites
	Western Tanager	25	0.02	Too few sites
*	Northern Cardinal	947	13.26	
*	Pyrrhuloxia	69	9.12	
–	Rose-breasted Grosbeak	43	0.12	Rare
	Black-headed Grosbeak	38	0.19	Too few sites
	Blue Grosbeak	21	0.10	Too few sites
	Lazuli Bunting	11	0.45	Too few sites
	Indigo Bunting	39	0.67	Too few sites
–	Painted Bunting	35	1.70	Too few sites
–	Dickcissel	153	0.05	Rare
	Olive Sparrow	16	1.07	Too few sites
	Abert's Towhee	18	2.89	Too few sites
*	Green-tailed Towhee	80	1.01	
*	Rufous-sided Towhee	885	4.12	
*	Brown Towhee	117	9.50	
*	Rufous-crowned Sparrow	95	3.88	
–	Bachman's Sparrow	41	0.91	Bad peak
–	Cassin's Sparrow	40	10.53	Bad peak
	Rufous-winged Sparrow	12	0.10	Too few sites

Map	Species	Number of Sites	Maximum Abundance	Notes
*	Clay-colored Sparrow	48	6.48	
*	Brewer's Sparrow	50	30.00	
	Black-chinned Sparrow	23	0.35	Too few sites
*	American Tree Sparrow	831	47.04	
*	Chipping Sparrow	503	17.10	
*	Field Sparrow	705	7.44	
*	Vesper Sparrow	481	5.97	
*	Lark Sparrow	189	13.37	
*	Black-throated Sparrow	81	4.25	
*	Sage Sparrow	76	5.97	
*	Savannah Sparrow	600	8.83	
–	Savannah Sparrow (Ipswich Race)	47	0.16	Rare
	Baird's Sparrow	24	0.50	Too few sites
–	Grasshopper Sparrow	127	0.32	Rare
*	Sharp-tailed Sparrow	94	1.04	
*	Seaside Sparrow	74	3.63	
	Henslow's Sparrow	38	0.03	Too few sites
–	Le Conte's Sparrow	98	4.76	Bad peak
*	Fox Sparrow	716	1.59	
*	Song Sparrow	1,127	7.41	
*	Lincoln's Sparrow	309	4.15	
*	Swamp Sparrow	674	5.94	
–	Snow Bunting	521	42.69	Nomadic
–	Lark Bunting	69	200.00	Gregarious
*	White-throated Sparrow	870	21.90	
*	Golden-crowned Sparrow	102	19.94	
*	White-crowned Sparrow	809	48.65	
*	Harris' Sparrow	263	26.11	
	Yellow-eyed Junco	7	0.53	Too few sites
*	Dark-eyed Junco (Oregon Race)	570	31.07	
*	Dark-eyed Junco (Slate-colored Race)	1,109	34.58	
	Dark-eyed Junco (White-winged Race)	27	5.40	Too few sites
*	Dark-eyed Junco (Gray-headed Race)	107	11.41	
	McCown's Longspur	27	105.20	Too few sites
–	Lapland Longspur	384	66.72	Nomadic
	Smith's Longspur	21	4.01	Too few sites
*	Chestnut-collared Longspur	40	13.74	

Map	Species	Number of Sites	Maximum Abundance	Notes
*	Eastern Meadowlark	754	17.36	
*	Western Meadowlark	403	43.11	
–	Red-winged Blackbird	1,041	23,480.10	Gregarious
–	Tricolored Blackbird	42	33.53	Gregarious
–	Yellow-headed Blackbird	100	167.03	Gregarious
–	Rusty Blackbird	603	811.45	Gregarious
–	Brewer's Blackbird	455	412.22	Gregarious
–	Great-tailed and Boat-tailed Grackles	138	221.50	Gregarious
–	Common Grackle	831	9,689.00	Gregarious
	Bronzed Cowbird	32	7.92	Too few sites
–	Brown-headed Cowbird	895	1,265.44	Gregarious
	Orchard Oriole	18	0.01	Too few sites
	Hooded Oriole	21	0.02	Too few sites
	Spot-breasted Oriole	4	0.26	Too few sites
*	Northern Oriole (Baltimore Race)	213	1.51	
–	Northern Oriole (Bullock's Race)	53	0.20	Rare
	Altamira Oriole	6	0.25	Too few sites
	Audubon's Oriole	10	0.14	Too few sites
	Rosy Finch (Gray-crowned Race)	35	13.24	Too few sites
	Rosy Finch (Black Race)	20	2.78	Too few sites
	Rosy Finch (Brown-capped Race)	11	12.10	Too few sites
–	Pine Grosbeak	383	4.09	Irruptive
–	Purple Finch	879	2.90	Irruptive
–	Cassin's Finch	86	2.99	Irruptive
*	House Finch	387	76.40	
–	Red Crossbill	405	2.46	Irruptive
–	White-winged Crossbill	296	8.17	Irruptive
–	Evening Grosbeak	745	18.23	Irruptive
–	Common Redpoll	564	40.00	Irruptive
–	Hoary Redpoll	58	20.00	Irruptive
–	Pine Siskin	875	11.11	Irruptive
*	Lesser Goldfinch	149	16.96	
	Lawrence's Goldfinch	36	1.13	Too few sites
*	American Goldfinch	1,138	16.67	
*	House Sparrow	1,244	135.14	
	Eurasian Tree Sparrow	11	2.47	Too few sites

Appendix B
Maps with Possible Problems

Maps for ninety-six species are presented here. Although various aspects of these maps may be misleading (see the Introduction), they provide some valuable information about the biogeography of these species. Thus, they are included, but in a smaller format. The reasons the maps of particular species may portray inaccuracies are noted in the text and in appendix A. These reasons are enumerated below.

1. An abundance that is either very low (below 0.20 I/Hr) or very high (above 200.00 I/Hr). Censusing such species is difficult and leads to inaccuracies (Bock and Root 1981). The distribution boundaries on the maps of gregarious species (e.g., Mallard [*Anas platyrhynchos*]) may appear contracted. Range boundaries for particular species are defined as 0.5% of their maximum abundance, but actual populations at the range limits of these species may have a lower abundance than that defined boundary value. Such populations, therefore, would be excluded during the mapping process. Even though the distributional limits may be misleading, the locations of the abundance peaks provide useful information.

2. An abundance that is highly variable over the ten-year period. This includes both irruptive and nomadic species.

3. An abundance pattern that has been incorrectly interpolated (e.g., Winter Wren [*Troglodytes troglodytes*]). Most of these problems arise when one count recording large numbers of birds occurs in a region where count sites are sparse, resulting in a much more extensive peak being represented on the maps than should have been shown.

4. The Northern Gannet's (*Sula bassanus*) distribution is primarily pelagic, and the maps show only that portion abutting the coastline.

5. The Semipalmated Sandpiper (*Calidris pusilla*) is not known to winter in areas north of central Florida (Phillips 1975). The map, which shows a more northerly distribution, is based on records of misidentifications.

Maps for species seen at fewer than forty sites are not included in this atlas. The exceptions are the Black-necked Stilt (*Himantopus mexicanus*) and the Painted Bunting (*Passerina ciris*). The page format allowed for two extra maps, and the maps of these species, which are included in this appendix, provide interesting biogeographic information.

Only contour maps are presented here, and these have been reduced in size to reiterate that they may contain misleading aspects. A transparency of the state and province boundaries plotted at this smaller size is provided in the envelope inside the back cover.

Appendix B

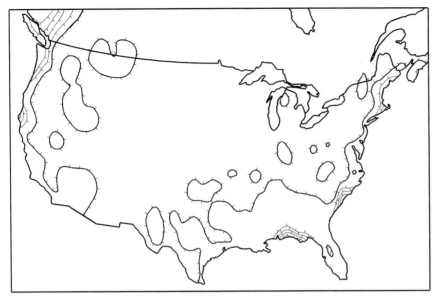

Common Loon (*Gavia immer*)

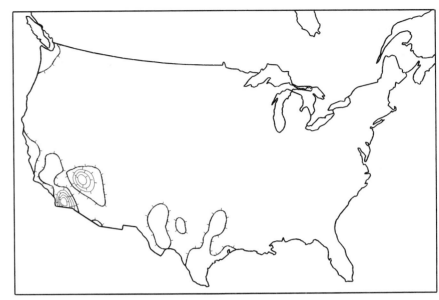

Eared Grebe (*Podiceps nigricollis*)

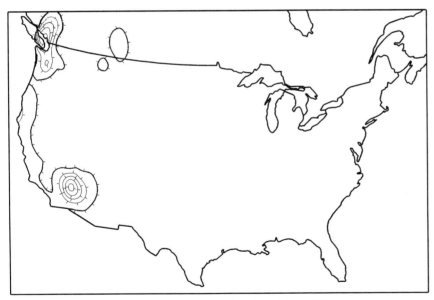

Western and Clark's Grebes (*Aechmophorus occidentalis* and *A. clarkii*)

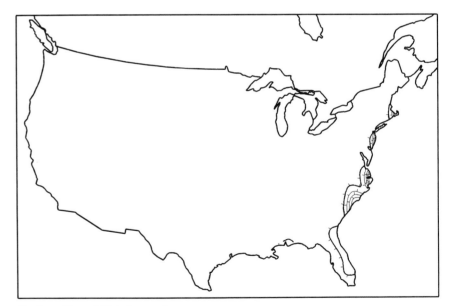

Northern Gannet (*Sula bassanus*)

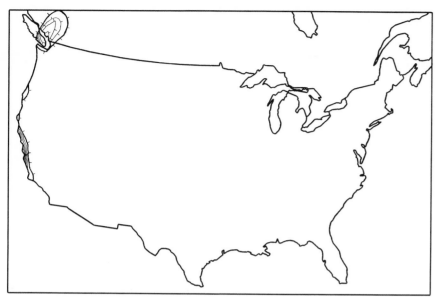

Pelagic Cormorant (*Phalacrocorax pelagicus*)

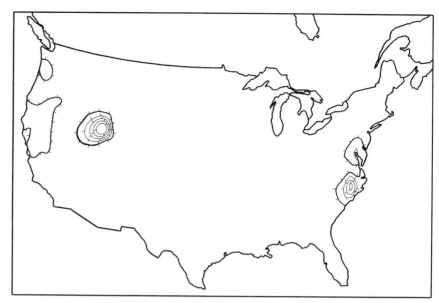

Tundra Swan (*Cygnus columbianus*)

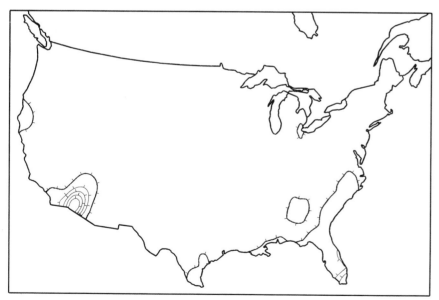

Least Bittern (*Ixobrychus exilis*)

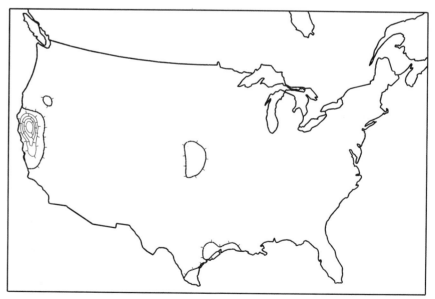

Greater White-fronted Goose (*Anser albifrons*)

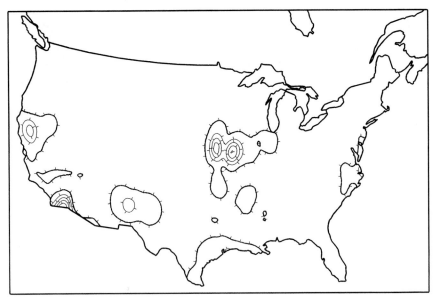

Snow Goose, White Morph (*Chen caerulescens*)

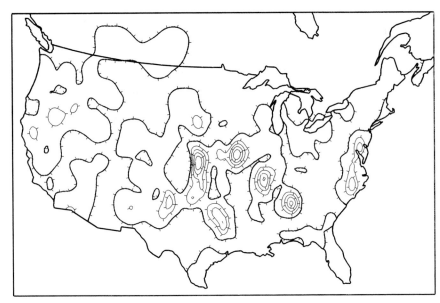

Canada Goose (*Branta canadensis*)

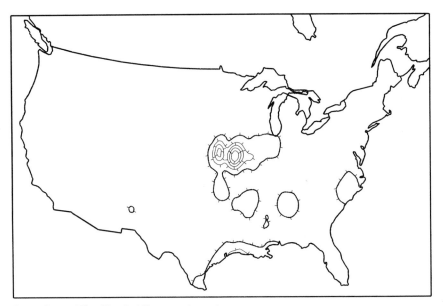

Snow Goose, Blue Morph (*Chen caerulescens*)

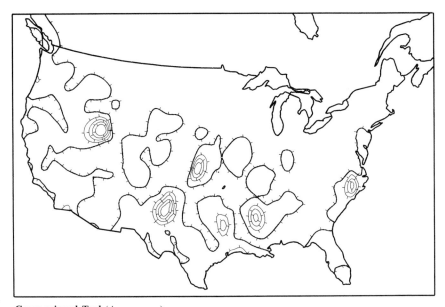

Green-winged Teal (*Anas crecca*)

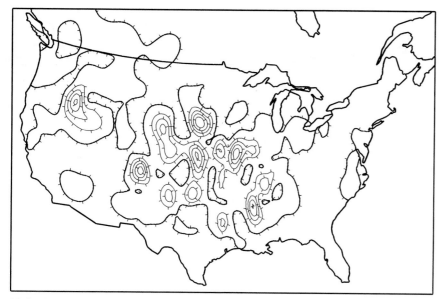

Mallard (*Anas platyrhynchos*)

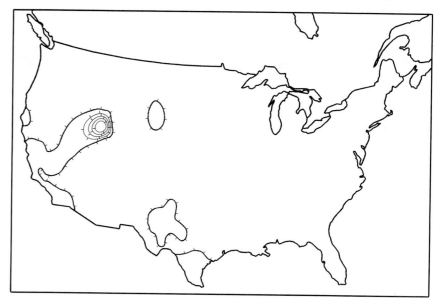

Cinnamon Teal (*Anas cyanoptera*)

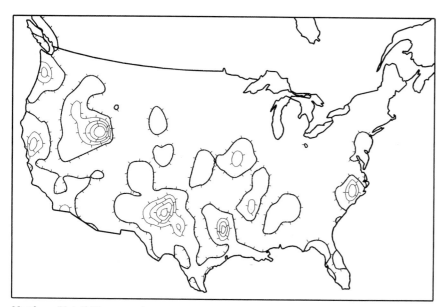

Northern Pintail (*Anas acuta*)

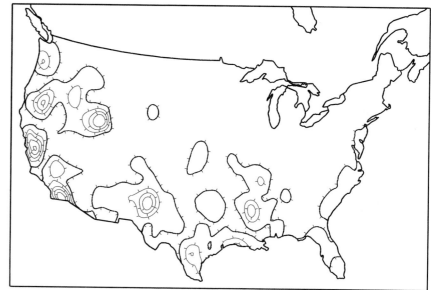

Northern Shoveler (*Anas clypeata*)

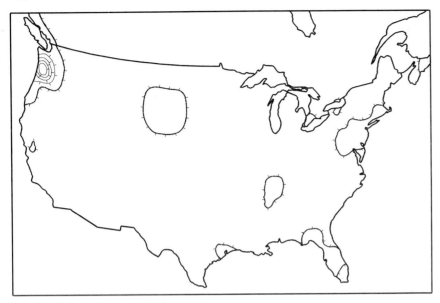

Eurasian Wigeon (*Anas penelope*)

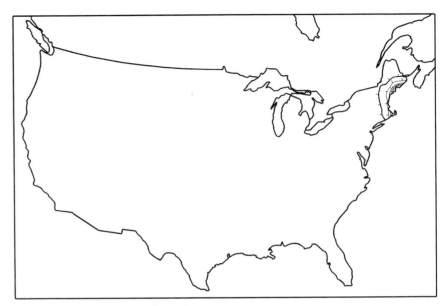

Common Eider (*Somateria mollissima*)

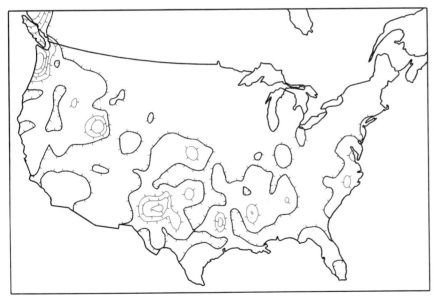

American Wigeon (*Anas americana*)

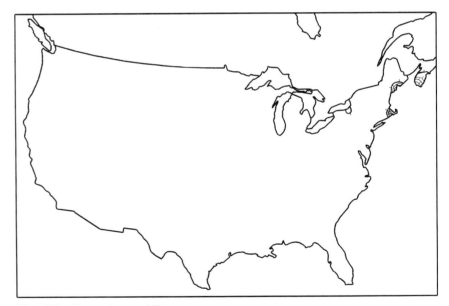

King Eider (*Somateria spectabilis*)

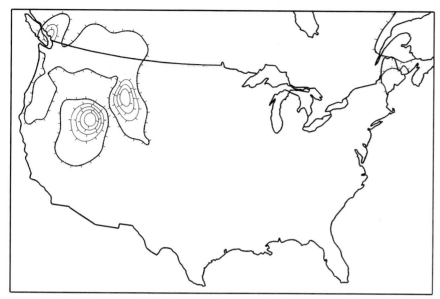

Barrow's Goldeneye (*Bucephala islandica*)

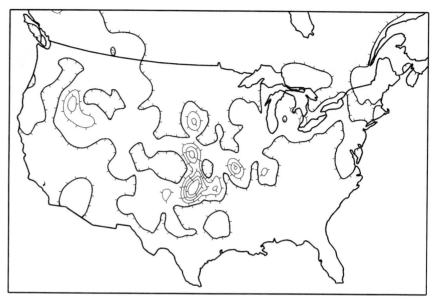

Common Merganser (*Mergus merganser*)

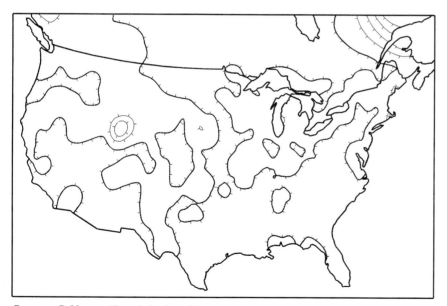

Common Goldeneye (*Bucephala clangula*)

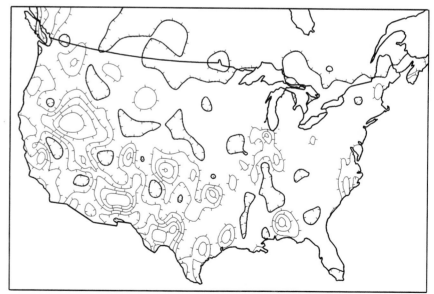

Sharp-shinned Hawk (*Accipiter striatus*)

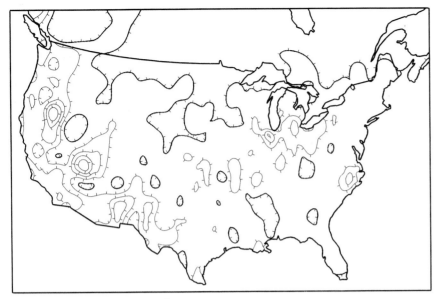

Cooper's Hawk (*Accipiter cooperii*)

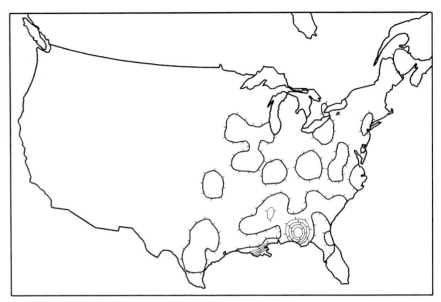

Broad-winged Hawk (*Buteo platypterus*)

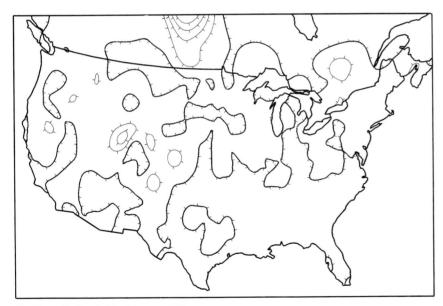

Northern Goshawk (*Accipiter gentilis*)

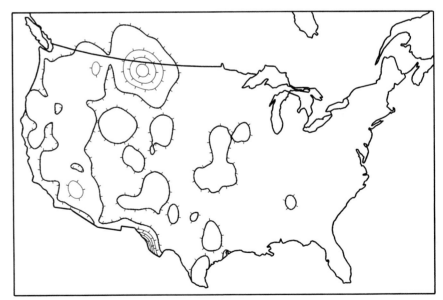

Swainson's Hawk (*Buteo swainsoni*)

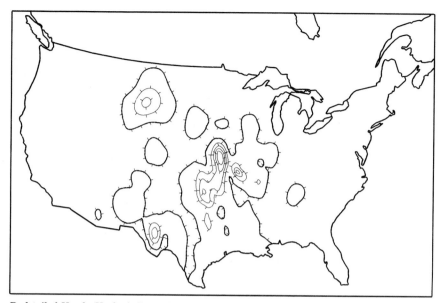

Red-tailed Hawk, Harlan's Race (*Buteo jamaicensis harlani*)

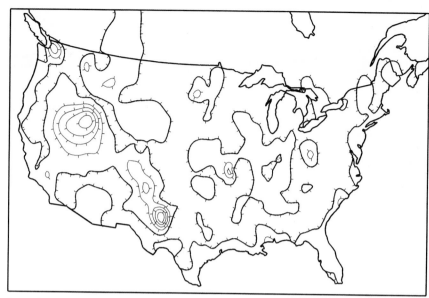

Peregrine Falcon (*Falco peregrinus*)

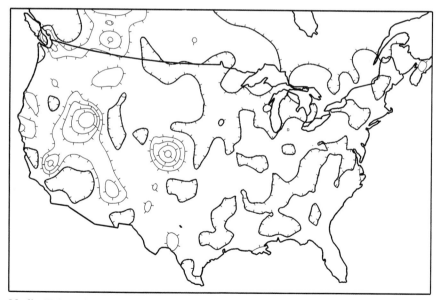

Merlin (*Falco columbarius*)

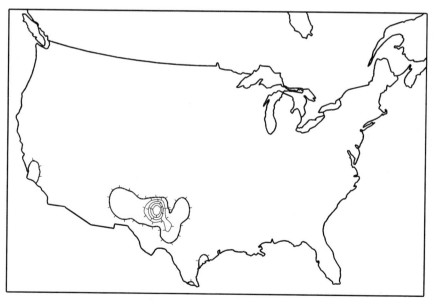

Sandhill Crane (*Grus canadensis*)

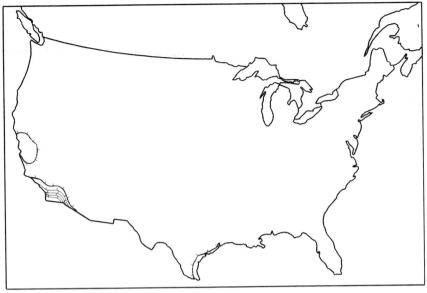

Black-necked Stilt (*Himantopus mexicanus*)

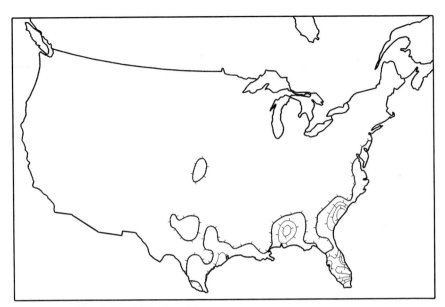

Semipalmated Sandpiper (*Calidris pusilla*)

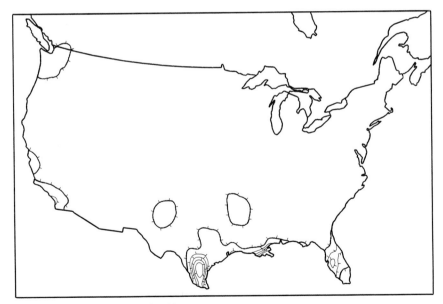

Solitary Sandpiper (*Tringa solitaria*)

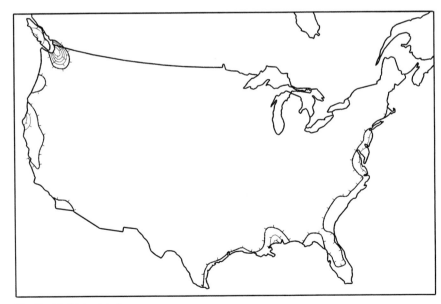

Dunlin (*Calidris alpina*)

Iceland Gull (*Larus glaucoides*)

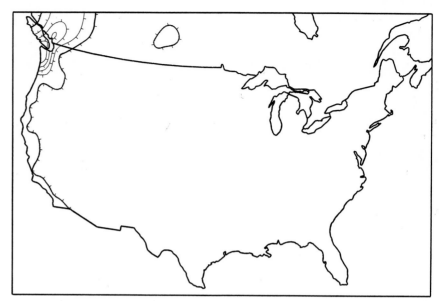

Glaucous-winged Gull (*Larus glaucescens*)

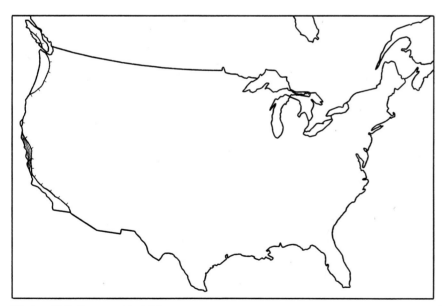

Western Gull (*Larus occidentalis*)

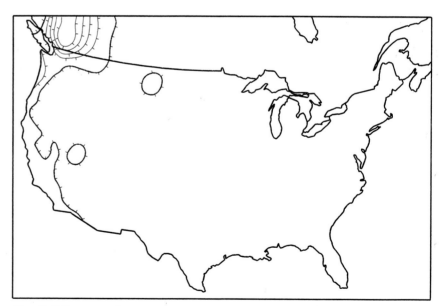

Mew Gull (*Larus canus*)

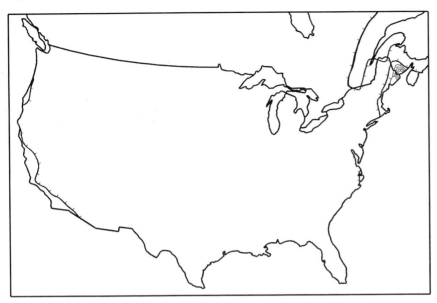

Black-legged Kittiwake (*Rissa tridactyla*)

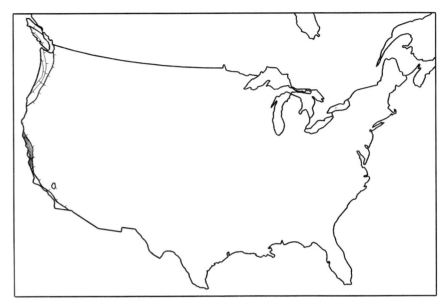

Common Murre (*Uria aalge*)

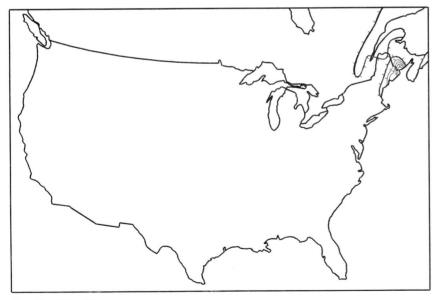

Dovekie (*Alle alle*)

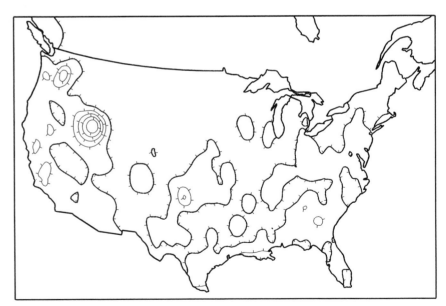

Common Barn-Owl (*Tyto alba*)

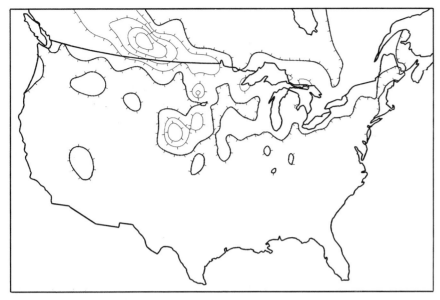

Snowy Owl (*Nyctea scandiaca*)

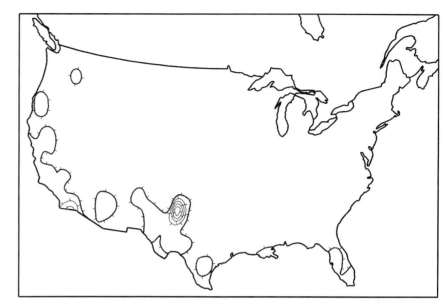

Burrowing Owl (*Athene cunicularia*)

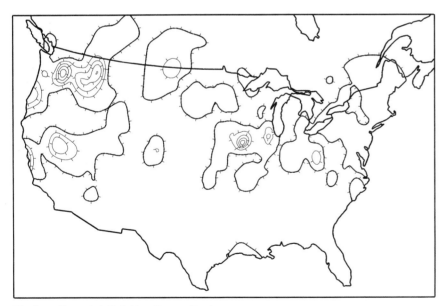

Northern Saw-whet Owl (*Aegolius acadicus*)

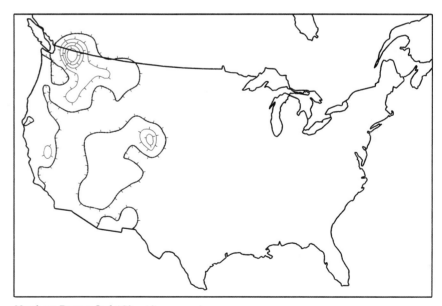

Northern Pygmy-Owl (*Glaucidium gnoma*)

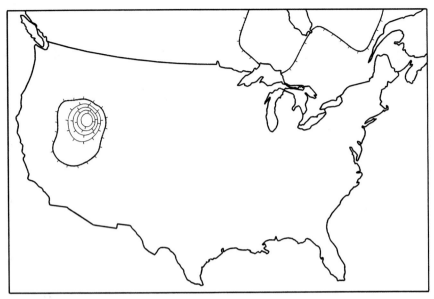

Black-backed Woodpecker (*Picoides arcticus*)

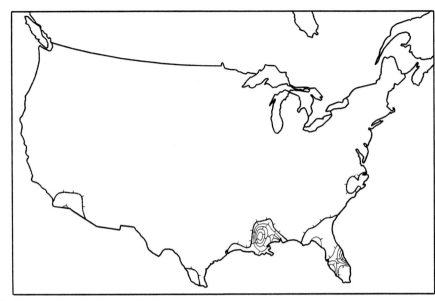

Tree Swallow (*Tachycineta bicolor*)

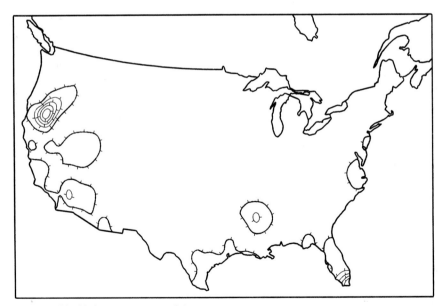

Western Kingbird (*Tyrannus verticalis*)

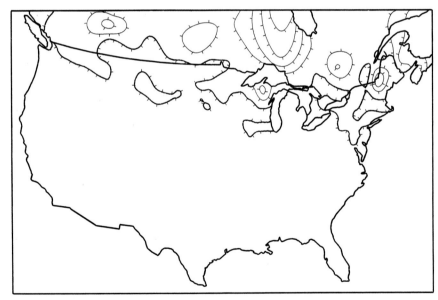

Boreal Chickadee (*Parus hudsonicus*)

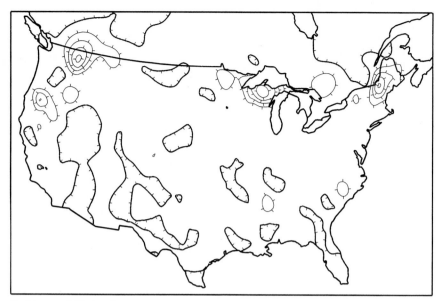

Red-breasted Nuthatch (*Sitta canadensis*)

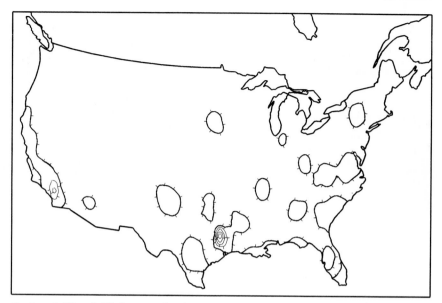

Swainson's Thrush (*Catharus ustulatus*)

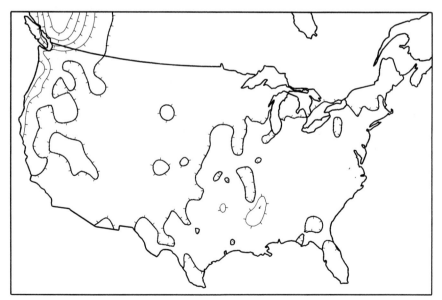

Winter Wren (*Troglodytes troglodytes*)

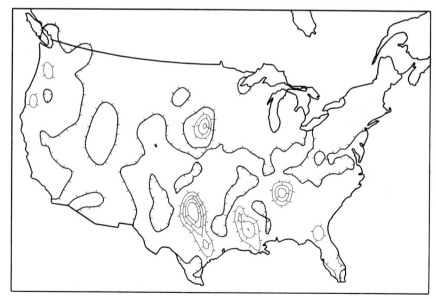

American Robin (*Turdus migratorius*)

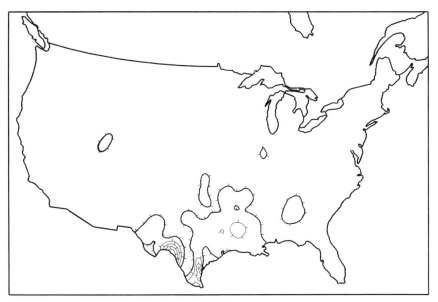

Sprague's Pipit (*Anthus spragueii*)

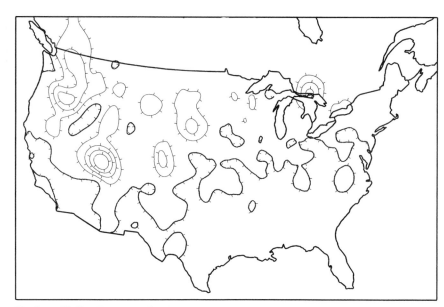

Northern Shrike (*Lanius excubitor*)

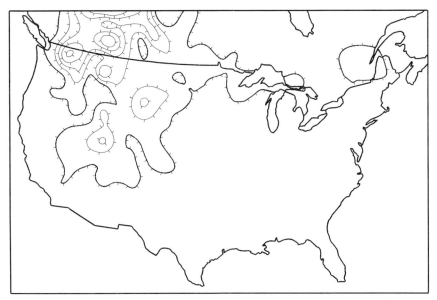

Bohemian Waxwing (*Bombycilla garrulus*)

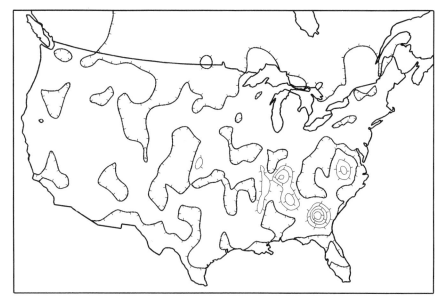

European Starling (*Sturnus vulgaris*)

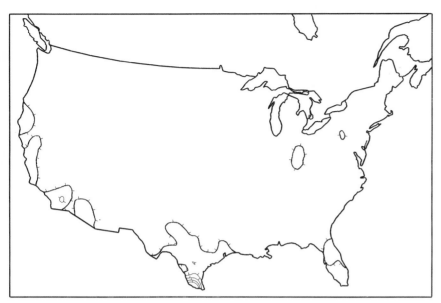

Nashville Warbler (*Vermivora ruficapilla*)

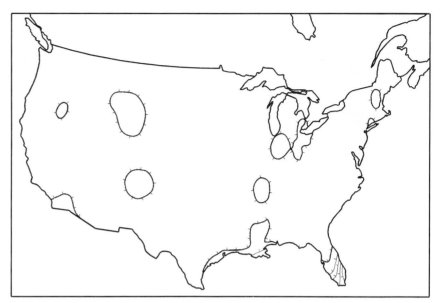

Northern Waterthrush (*Seiurus noveboracensis*)

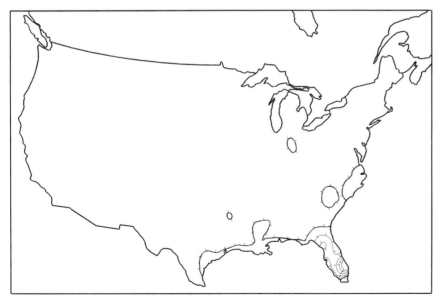

Ovenbird (*Seiurus aurocapillus*)

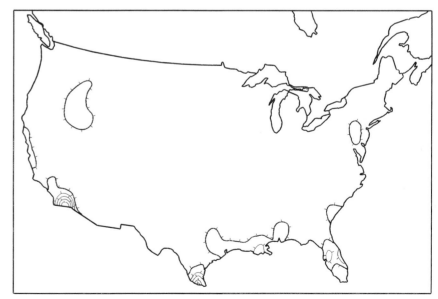

Yellow Warbler (*Dendroica petechia*)

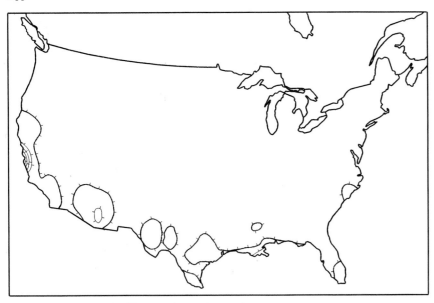

Black-throated Gray Warbler (*Dendroica nigrescens*)

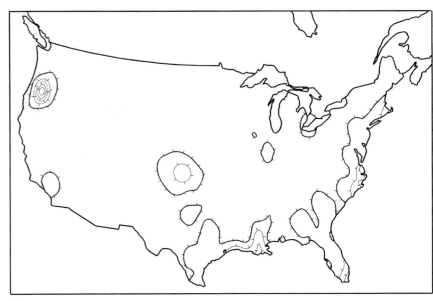

Yellow-breasted Chat (*Icteria virens*)

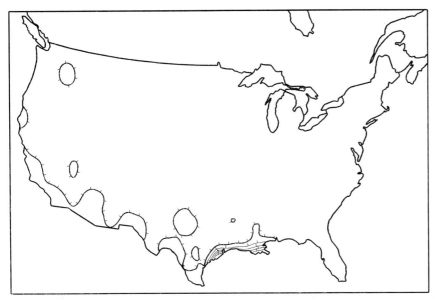

Wilson's Warbler (*Wilsonia pusilla*)

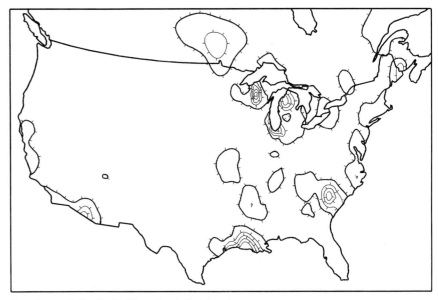

Rose-breasted Grosbeak (*Pheucticus ludovicianus*)

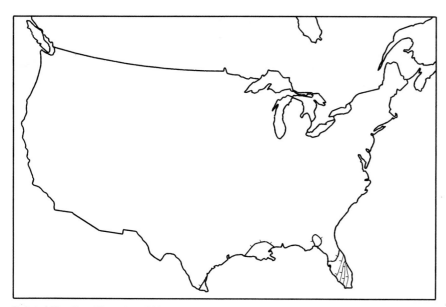

Painted Bunting (*Passerina ciris*)

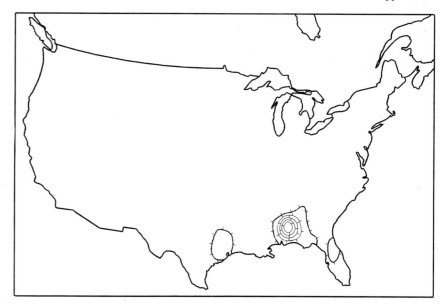

Bachman's Sparrow (*Aimophila aestivalis*)

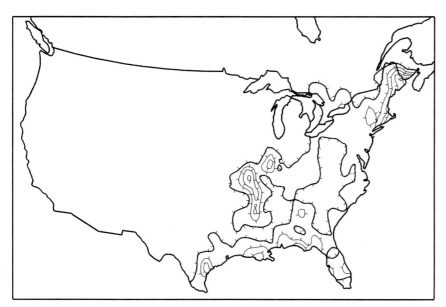

Dickcissel (*Spiza americana*)

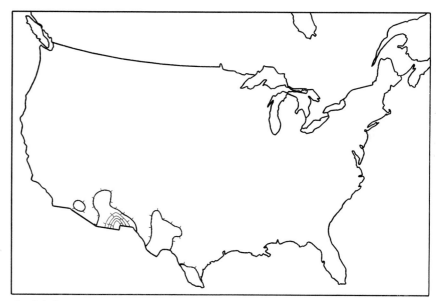

Cassin's Sparrow (*Aimophila cassinii*)

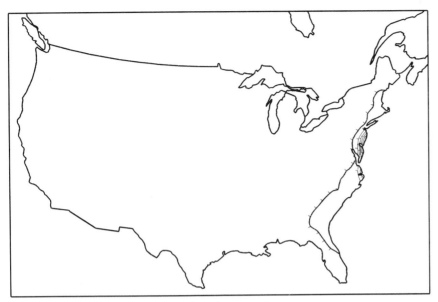

Savannah Sparrow, Ipswich Race (*Passerculus sandwichensis princeps*)

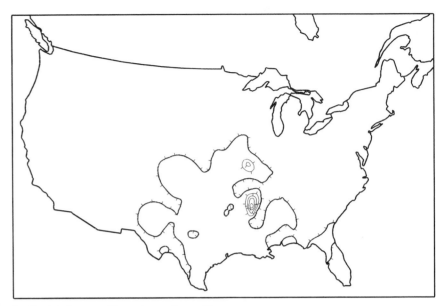

Le Conte's Sparrow (*Ammodramus leconteii*)

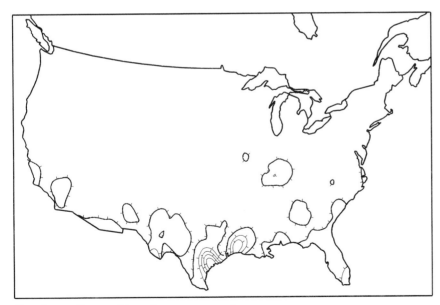

Grasshopper Sparrow (*Ammodramus savannarum*)

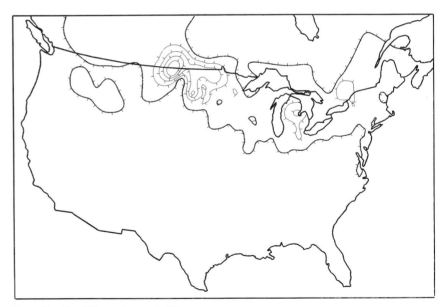

Snow Bunting (*Plectrophenax nivalis*)

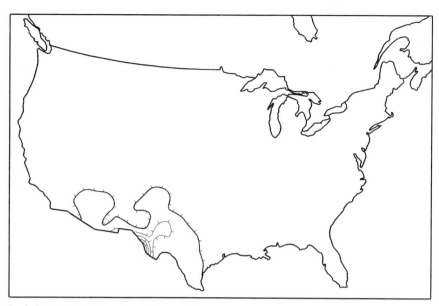

Lark Bunting (*Calamospiza melanocorys*)

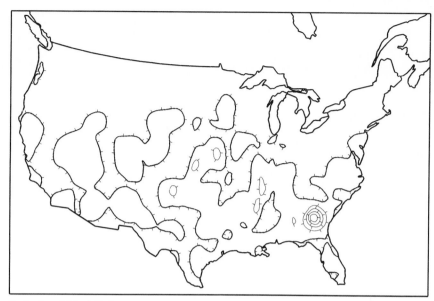

Red-winged Blackbird (*Agelaius phoeniceus*)

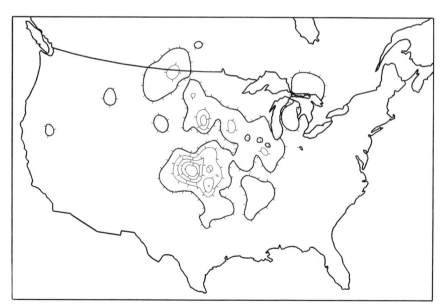

Lapland Longspur (*Calcarius lapponicus*)

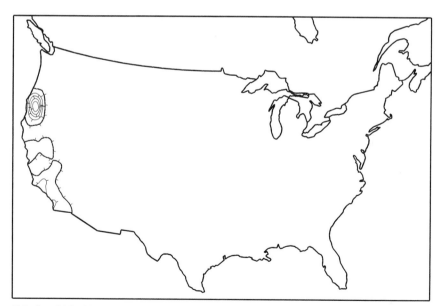

Tricolored Blackbird (*Agelaius tricolor*)

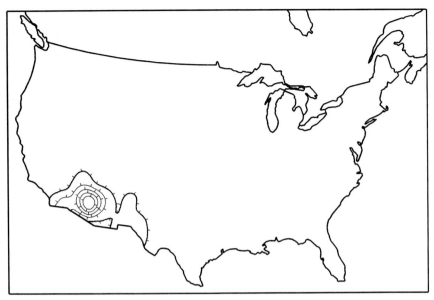

Yellow-headed Blackbird (*Xanthocephalus xanthocephalus*)

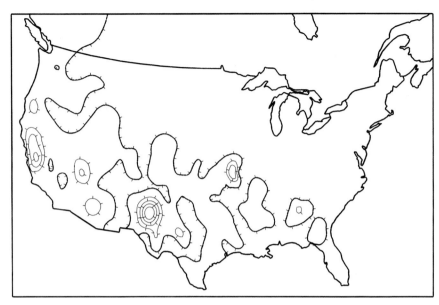

Brewer's Blackbird (*Euphagus cyanocephalus*)

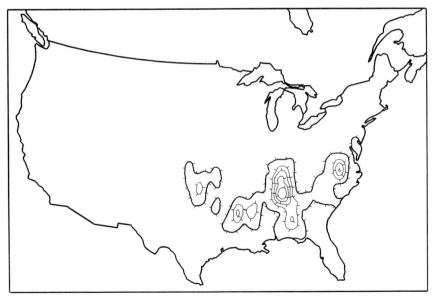

Rusty Blackbird (*Euphagus carolinus*)

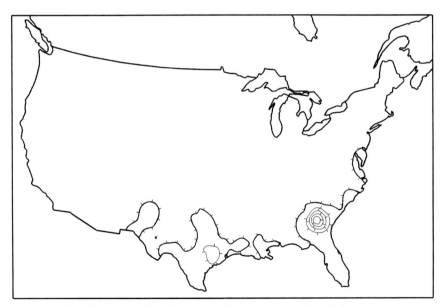

Great-tailed and Boat-tailed Grackles (*Quiscalus mexicanus* and *Q. major*)

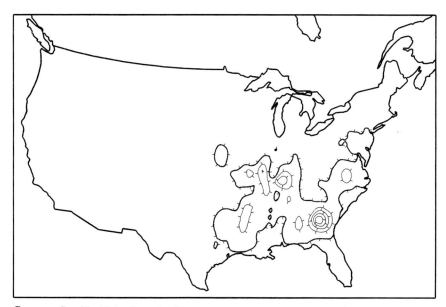

Common Grackle (*Quiscalus quiscula*)

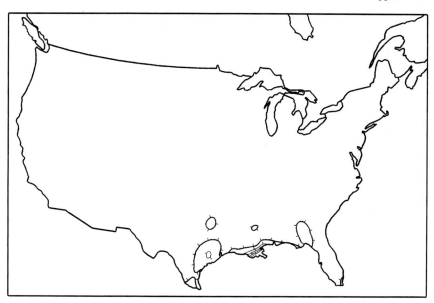

Northern Oriole, Bullock's Race (*Icterus galbula bullocki*)

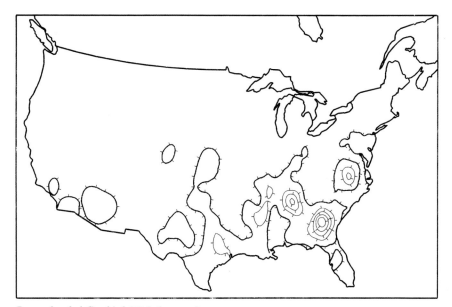

Brown-headed Cowbird (*Molothrus ater*)

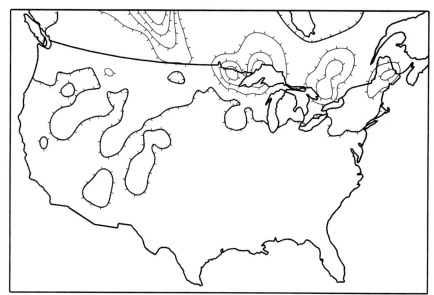

Pine Grosbeak (*Pinicola enucleator*)

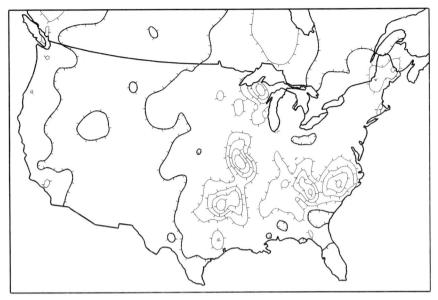

Purple Finch (*Carpodacus purpureus*)

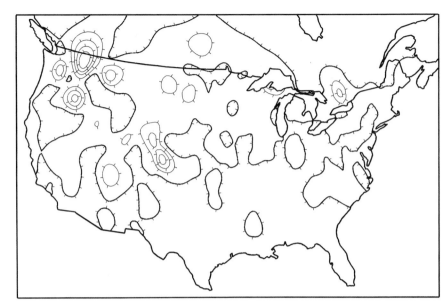

Red Crossbill (*Loxia curvirostra*)

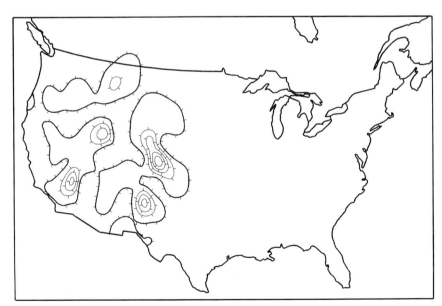

Cassin's Finch (*Carpodacus cassinii*)

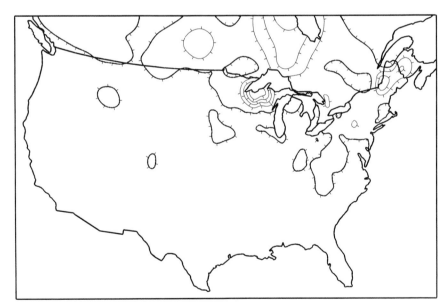

White-winged Crossbill (*Loxia leucoptera*)

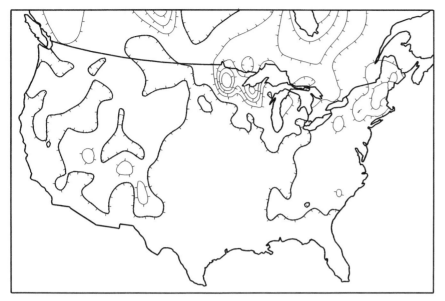

Evening Grosbeak (*Coccothraustes vespertinus*)

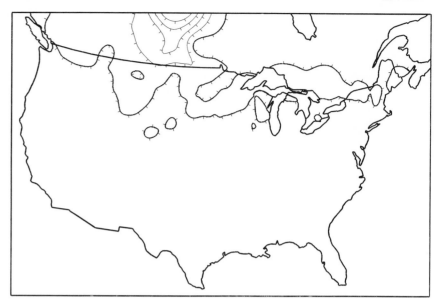

Hoary Redpoll (*Carduelis hornemanni*)

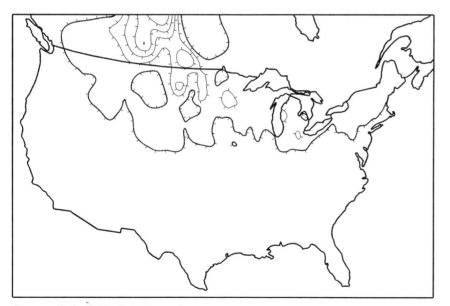

Common Redpoll (*Carduelis flammea*)

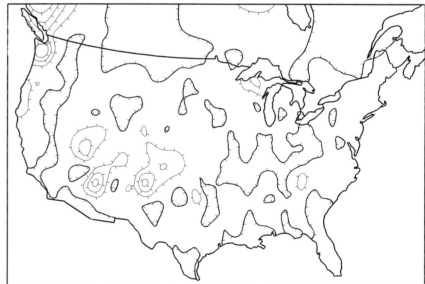

Pine Siskin (*Carduelis pinus*)

Literature Cited

Aldrich, J. W. 1968. Population characteristics and nomenclature of the Hermit Thrush. *Proceedings of the United States National Museum* 124:1–33.

Alexander, W. C. 1983. Differential sex distribution of wintering diving ducks in North America. *American Birds* 37:26–29.

Allaire, P. N., and C. D. Fisher. 1975. Feeding ecology of three resident sympatric sparrows in eastern Texas. *Auk* 92:260–69.

Amadon, D. 1984. Bare-headed vulture of California. *Living Bird* 3:4–7.

American Ornithologists' Union (AOU). 1910. *The check-list of North American birds.* 3d ed. Washington, D.C.: American Ornithologists' Union.

———. 1957. *Check-list of North American birds.* 5th ed. Washington, D.C.: American Ornithologists' Union.

———. 1983. *Check-list of North American birds.* 6th ed. Washington, D.C.: American Ornithologists' Union.

Anderson, A. H., and A. Anderson. 1957. Life history of the Cactus Wren: 1. Winter and pre-nesting behavior. *Condor* 59:274–96.

Anderson, B. W., and R. D. Ohmart. 1978. Phainopepla utilization of honey mesquite forests in the Colorado River valley. *Condor* 80:334–38.

Anderson, D. W., and I. T. Anderson. 1976. Distribution and status of Brown Pelicans in the California current. *American Birds* 30:3–12.

Anderson, S. H. 1976. Comparative food habits of Oregon nuthatches. *Northwest Science* 50:213–21.

Arbib, R. S. 1967. Considering the Christmas census. *Audubon Field Notes* 21:39–42.

Arnold, J. R. 1980. Distribution of the Mockingbird in California. *Western Birds* 11:97–102.

Ashmole, M. J. 1970. Feeding of Western and Semipalmated Sandpipers in Peruvian winter quarters. *Auk* 87:131–35.

Ashmole, N. P. 1971. Seabird ecology and the marine environment. In *Avian biology,* vol. 1, ed. D. S. Farner and J. R. King. New York: Academic Press.

Austin, G. T. 1973. Nesting success of the Cactus Wren in relation to nest orientation. *Condor* 76:216–17.

Balda, R. P., and G. C. Bateman. 1971. Flocking and annual cycle of the Piñon Jay. *Condor* 73:287–302.

Balda, R. P., M. L. Morrison, and T. R. Bement. 1977. Roosting behavior of the Piñon Jay in autumn and winter. *Auk* 94:494–504.

Baldwin, J. L. 1973. *Climates of the United States.* Washington, D.C.: U.S. Government Printing Office.

Ballam, J. M. 1984. The use of soaring by the Red-tailed Hawk. *Auk* 101:519–24.

Baltz, D. M., and G. V. Morejohn. 1977. Food habits and niche overlap of seabirds wintering on Monterey Bay, California. *Auk* 94:526–43.

Bart, J. 1977. Winter distribution of Red-tailed Hawk in central New York State. *Wilson Bulletin* 89:623–25.

Beddall, B. G. 1963. Range expansion of the Cardinal and other birds in the northeastern states. *Wilson Bulletin* 75:140–58.

Behle, W. H. 1944. Gulls as vegetarians. *Condor* 46:127–28.

———. 1973. Clinal variation in White-throated Swifts from Utah and Rocky Mountain region. *Auk* 90:299–306.

Bellrose, F. C. 1980. *Ducks, geese, and swans of North America.* Harrisburg, Pa.: Stackpole.

Bent, A. C. 1919. Life histories of North American diving birds. *United States National Museum Bulletin* 107.

———. 1921. Life histories of North American gulls and terns. *United States National Museum Bulletin* 113.

———. 1922. Life histories of North American petrels and pelicans and their allies. *United States National Museum Bulletin* 121.

———. 1923. Life histories of North American wildfowl, part 1. *United States National Museum Bulletin* 126.

———. 1925. Life histories of North American wildfowl, part 2. *United States National Museum Bulletin* 130.

———. 1926. Life histories of North American marsh birds. *United States National Museum Bulletin* 135.

———. 1927. Life histories of North American shorebirds, part 1. *United States National Museum Bulletin* 142.

———. 1929. Life histories of North American shorebirds, part 2. *United States National Museum Bulletin* 146.

———. 1932. Life histories of North American gallinaceous birds. *United States National Museum Bulletin* 162.

———. 1937. Life histories of North American birds of prey, part 1. *United States National Museum Bulletin* 167.

———. 1939. Life histories of North American woodpeckers. *United States National Museum Bulletin* 174.

———. 1942. Life histories of North American flycatchers, larks, swallows and their allies. *United States National Museum Bulletin* 179.

———. 1946. Life histories of North American jays, crows, and titmice. *United States National Museum Bulletin* 191.

———. 1948. Life histories of North American nuthatches, wrens, thrashers, and their allies. *United States National Museum Bulletin* 195.

———. 1949. Life histories of North American thrushes, kinglets, and their allies. *United States National Museum Bulletin* 196.

———. 1950. Life histories of North American wagtails, shrikes, vireos, and their allies. *United States National Museum Bulletin* 197.

———. 1958. Life histories of North American blackbirds, orioles, tanagers, and their allies. *United States National Museum Bulletin* 211.

———. 1964. Life histories of North American cuckoos, goatsuckers, hummingbirds, and their allies. *United States National Museum Bulletin* 176.

———. 1968. Life histories of North American cardinals, grosbeaks, buntings, towhees, finches, sparrows, and their allies. *United States National Museum Bulletin* 237.

Black, B. B., and L. D. Harris. 1983. Feeding habitat of Black Skimmers wintering on the Florida Gulf coast. *Wilson Bulletin* 95:404–15.

Bock, C. E. 1969. Intra- vs. interspecific aggression in Pygmy Nuthatch flocks. *Ecology* 50:903–5.

———. 1982. Synchronous fluctuations in Christmas Bird Counts of Common Redpolls and Piñon Jays. *Auk* 99:382–83.

Bock, C. E., H. H. Hadow, and P. Somers. 1971. Relations between Lewis' and Red-headed Woodpeckers in southeastern Colorado. *Wilson Bulletin* 83:237–48.

Bock, C. E., and L. W. Lepthien. 1972. Winter eruptions of Red-breasted Nuthatches in North America, 1950–1970. *American Birds* 26:558–61.

———. 1975. A Christmas count analysis of woodpecker abundance in the United States. *Wilson Bulletin* 87:355–66.

———. 1976a. Population growth in the Cattle Egret. *Auk* 93:164–66.

———. 1976b. Changing winter distribution and abundance of the Blue Jay. *American Midland Naturalist* 96:233–36.

———. 1976c. Growth in the eastern House Finch population, 1962–1971. *American Birds* 30:791–92.

———. 1976d. Synchronous eruptions of boreal seed-eating birds. *American Naturalist* 110:559–71.

Bock, C. E., and T. L. Root. 1981. The Christmas Bird Count and avian ecology. In Estimating numbers of terrestrial birds, ed. J. M. Scott and C. J. Ralph. *Studies in Avian Biology* 6:17–23.

Boeker, E. L., and T. D. Ray. 1971. Golden Eagle population studies in the Southwest. *Condor* 73:463–67.

Bovino, R. R., and E. H. Burtt, Jr. 1979. Weather-dependent foraging of Great Blue Herons (*Ardea herodias*). *Auk* 96:628–30.

Bowers, D. E. 1960. Correlation of variation in the Wrentit with environmental gradients. *Condor* 62:91–120.

Brackbill, H. 1970. Shorebirds leaving the water to defecate. *Auk* 87:160.

Brawn, J. D., and F. B. Samson. 1983. Winter behavior of Tufted Titmice. *Wilson Bulletin* 95:222–32.

Brewer, R. 1961. Comparative notes on the life history of the Carolina Chickadee. *Wilson Bulletin* 73:348–73.

Brockman, C. F. 1968. *Trees of North America.* New York: Golden Press.

Brooke, R. K. 1970. Zoogeography of the swifts. *Ostrich*, suppl. 8, pp. 47–54.

Brown, J. H., and A. C. Gibson. 1983. *Biogeography.* Saint Louis: Mosby.

Brown, J. L. 1963. Social organization and behavior of the Mexican Jay. *Condor* 65:126–53.

Brown, L., and D. Amadon. 1968. *Eagles, hawks, and falcons of the world.* New York: McGraw-Hill.

Buckley, F. G., and P. A. Buckley. 1974. Comparative feeding ecology of wintering adult and juvenile Royal Tern. *Ecology* 55:1053–63.

Bull, J. 1974. *Birds of New York State.* Garden City, N.Y.: Doubleday/Natural History Press.

Burton, J. A. 1984. *Owls of the world.* Dover, N.H.: Tanager Books.

Burton, P. J. K. 1972. The feeding techniques of Stilt Sandpipers and dowitchers. *San Diego Society of Natural History Transactions* 17:63–68.

Butts, K. O. 1976. Burrowing Owls wintering in the Oklahoma panhandle. *Auk* 93:510–16.

Cade, T. J. 1967. Ecological and behavioral aspects of predation by the Northern Shrike. *Living Bird* 6:43–86.

———. 1983. Renaissance of the Peregrine Falcon. *Living Bird Quarterly* 2:6–9.

Canada, Department of Energy, Mines, and Resources. 1974. *The national atlas of Canada.* Toronto: Macmillan.

Chapman, F. 1900. A Christmas bird-census. *Bird-Lore* 2:192.

Chapman, J. D., and J. C. Sherman. 1975. *Oxford regional economic atlas: The United States and Canada.* Oxford: Oxford University Press.

Cortopassi, A. J., and L. R. Mewaldt. 1965. The circumannual distribution of White-crowned Sparrows. *Bird-Banding* 36:141–69.

Cottam, C., and J. B. Trefethen. 1968. *Whitewings.* Princeton, N.J.: D. Van Nostrand.

Courser, W. D., and J. J. Dinsmore. 1975. Foraging associates of White Ibis. *Auk* 92:599–601.

Craig, R. B. 1978. An analysis of the predatory behavior of the Loggerhead Shrike. *Auk* 95:221–34.

Cramp, S. 1977. *Handbook of the birds of Europe, the Middle East, and North Africa,* vol. 1. New York: Oxford University Press.

————. 1980. *Handbook of the birds of Europe, the Middle East, and North Africa,* vol. 2. New York: Oxford University Press.

————. 1983. *Handbook of the birds of Europe, the Middle East, and North Africa,* vol. 3. New York: Oxford University Press.

Crawford, R. L., S. L. Olson, and W. K. Taylor. 1983. Winter distribution of subspecies of Clapper Rails (*Rallus longirostris*) in Florida with evidence for long-distance and overland movements. *Auk* 100:198–200.

Crivelli, A. J., and R. W. Schreiber. 1984. Status of the Pelecanidae. *Biological Conservation* 30:147–56.

Cruickshank, A. D. 1965. Sixty-fifth Christmas Bird Count. *American Birds* 19:85–340.

————. 1966. Sixty-sixth Christmas Bird Count. *American Birds* 20:97–384.

————. 1967. Sixty-seventh Christmas Bird Count. *American Birds* 21:81–388.

————. 1969. Sixty-ninth Christmas Bird Count. *American Birds* 23:113–432.

————. 1972. Seventy-second Christmas Bird Count. *American Birds* 26:147–530.

Davis, J. 1965. Natural history, variation, and distribution of the Strickland's Woodpecker. *Auk* 82:537–90.

————. 1973. Habitat preferences and competition of wintering juncos and Golden-crowned Sparrows. *Ecology* 54:174–80.

DeGraaf, R. M., and J. W. Thomas. 1974. A banquet for birds. *Natural History* 83:40–45.

Dixon, K. L. 1954. Some ecological relations of chickadee and titmice in central California. *Condor* 56:113–24.

————. 1956. Territoriality and survival in the Plain Titmouse. *Condor* 58:169–82.

Dow, D. D. 1970. Distribution and dispersal of the Cardinal, *Richmondena cardinalis,* in relation to vegetational cover and river systems. *American Midland Naturalist* 84:198–207.

Dow, D. D., and D. M. Scott. 1971. Dispersal and range expansion by the Cardinal: An analysis of banding records. *Canadian Journal of Zoology* 49:185–98.

Earhart, C. M., and N. K. Johnson. 1970. Size dimorphism and food habits of North American owls. *Condor* 72:251–64.

Eaton, S. W. 1983. Horned Grebes downed by ice storm. *American Birds* 37:836–37.

Eisenmann, E. 1971. Range expansion and population increase in North and Middle America of the White-tailed Kite. *American Birds* 25:529–36.

Enderson, J. H. 1960. A population study of the Sparrow Hawk in east-central Illinois. *Wilson Bulletin* 72:222–31.

Engels, W. L. 1940. Structural adaptations in thrashers (Mimidae: genus *Toxostoma*) with comments on interspecific relationships. *University of California Publications in Zoology* 42:341–400.

Ensley, P. K. 1984. Day of the condor. *Living Bird Quarterly* 3:4–7.

Erickson, M. M. 1938. Territory, annual cycle, and numbers in a population of Wrentits. *University of California Publications in Zoology* 42:247–334.

Erskine, A. J. 1972. *Buffleheads.* Canadian Wildlife Service Monograph Series, no. 4. Ottawa: Information Canada.

Erwin, R. M. 1977. Foraging and breeding adaptations to different food regimes in three seabirds: The Common Tern, Royal Tern, and Black Skimmer. *Ecology* 58:389–97.

Fischer, D. H. 1981. Winter ecology of thrashers in southern Texas. *Condor* 83:340–46.

Franzreb, K. E. 1984. Foraging habits of Ruby-crowned and Golden-crowned Kinglets in an Arizona montane forest. *Condor* 86:139–45.

Frazier, A., and V. Nolan, Jr. 1959. Communal roosting by the Eastern Bluebird in winter. *Bird-Banding* 30:219–26.

Friedmann, H. 1963. Host relations of the parasitic cowbirds. *United States National Museum Bulletin* 233.

Giuntoli, M., and L. R. Mewaldt. 1978. Stomach contents of Clark's Nutcrackers collected in western Montana. *Auk* 95:595–98.

Goodwin, D. 1976. *Crows of the world.* Ithaca, N.Y.: Cornell University Press.

————. 1983a. Behavior. In *Physiology and behavior of the pigeon,* ed. M. Abs. New York: Academic Press.

————. 1983b. *Pigeons and doves of the world.* Ithaca, N.Y.: Cornell University Press.

Gotch, A. F. 1981. *Birds—their Latin names explained.* Poole, Dorset: Blandford Press.

Gottfried, B. M., and E. C. Franks. 1975. Habitat use and flock activity of Dark-eyed Juncos in winter. *Wilson Bulletin* 87:374–83.

Graber, J. W., and R. R. Graber. 1983. Expectable decline of forest bird population in severe and mild winters. *Wilson Bulletin* 95:682–90.

Graber, R. R. 1962. Food and oxygen consumption in three species of owls. *Condor* 64:473–87.

Graber, R. R., and J. S. Golden. 1960. Hawks and owls: Population trends from Illinois Christmas counts. *Illinois Natural History Survey, Biological Notes* 41:1–24.

Grace, J. W. 1980. Cleptoparasitism by Ring-billed Gulls on wintering waterfowl. *Wilson Bulletin* 92:246–48.

Grinnell, J. 1917. The niche-relationships of the California Thrasher. *Auk* 34:427–33.

Griscom, L., and A. Sprunt, Jr. 1957. *The warblers of America.* New York: Devin-Adair.

Grossman, M. L., and J. Hamlet. 1964. *Birds of prey of the world.* New York: Clarkson N. Potter.

Grubb, T. C., Jr. 1975. Weather-dependent foraging behavior of some birds wintering in a deciduous woodland. *Condor* 77:175–82.

————. 1977. Weather-dependent foraging in Osprey. *Auk* 94:146–49.

————. 1978. Weather-dependent foraging rates of wintering woodland birds. *Auk* 95:370–76.

Grzybowski, J. A. 1982. Population structure in grassland bird communities during winter. *Condor* 84:137–52.

————. 1983. Patterns of space use in grassland bird communities during winter. *Wilson Bulletin* 95:591–602.

Gutierrez, R. J. 1980. Comparative ecology of the Mountain and California Quail in the Carmel Valley, California. *Living Bird* 18:71–93.

Hailman, J. P. 1960. Hostile dancing and fall territory of a color-banded mockingbird. *Condor* 62:464–68.

Hall, G. A. 1983. *West Virginia birds*. Special Publication 7. Pittsburgh: Carnegie Museum of Natural History.

Hamilton, R. B. 1975. Comparative behavior of the American Avocet and the Black-necked Stilt. *Ornithological Monographs* 17:1–98.

Hancock, J., and H. Elliott. 1978. *The herons of the world*. New York: Harper and Row.

Harlow, R. F., R. G. Hooper, D. R. Chamberlain, and H. S. Crawford. 1975. Some winter and nesting season foods of the Common Raven in Virginia. *Auk* 92:298–306.

Harrison, H. H. 1979. *A field guide to western birds' nests*. Boston: Houghton Mifflin.

Hatch, D. E. 1970. Energy conserving and heat dissipating mechanisms of the Turkey Vulture. *Auk* 87:111–24.

Hayworth, A. M., and W. W. Weathers. 1984. Temperature regulation and climatic adaptation in Black-billed and Yellow-billed Magpies. *Condor* 86:19–26.

Heatwole, H. 1965. Some aspects of the association of Cattle Egrets with cattle. *Animal Behavior* 13:79–83.

Heintzelman, D. S. 1979. *Hawks and owls of North America*. New York: Universe Books.

Henny, C. J., and H. M. Wight. 1969. An endangered Osprey population: Estimates of mortality and production. *Auk* 86:188–98.

Hepp, G. R., and J. D. Hair. 1983. Reproductive behavior and pairing chronology in wintering dabbling ducks. *Wilson Bulletin* 95:675–82.

————. 1984. Dominance in wintering waterfowl (Anatini): Effects on distribution of sexes. *Condor* 86:251–57.

Hespenheide, H. A. 1971. Food preference and the extent of overlap in some insectivorous birds, with special reference to the Tyrannidae. *Ibis* 113:59–72.

Hooper, R. G., and M. R. Lennartz. 1981. Foraging behavior of the Red-cockaded Woodpecker in South Carolina. *Auk* 98:321–34.

Howell, A. H. 1932. *Florida bird life*. New York: Coward-McCann.

Hubbard, J. P. 1973. Avian evolution in the aridlands of North America. *Living Bird* 12:155–96.

Ingolfsson, A., and B. T. Estrella. 1978. The development of shell-cracking behavior in Herring Gulls. *Auk* 95:577–79.

Jackson, J. A. 1974. Gray rat snakes versus Red-cockaded Woodpeckers: Predator-prey adaptations. *Auk* 91:342–47.

————. 1977. Red-cockaded Woodpeckers and pine red heart disease. *Auk* 94:160–63.

James, D. 1962. The changing seasons. *Audubon Field Notes* 16:306–11.

Jewett, S. G., W. P. Taylor, W. T. Shaw, and J. W. Aldrich. 1953. *Birds of Washington State*. Seattle: University of Washington Press.

Johnsgard, P. A. 1971. Experimental hybridization of the New World quail (Odontophorinae). *Auk* 88:264–75.

————. 1973. *Grouse and quails of North America*. Lincoln: University of Nebraska Press.

————. 1975. *North American game birds of upland and shoreline*. Lincoln: University of Nebraska Press.

————. 1981. *The plovers, sandpipers, and snipes of the world*. Lincoln: University of Nebraska Press.

————. 1983a. *Cranes of the world*. Bloomington: Indiana University Press.

————. 1983b. *The grouse of the world*. Lincoln: University of Nebraska Press.

Johnsgard, P. A., and R. DiSilvestro. 1976. Seventy-five years of changes in Mallard–Black Duck ratios in eastern North America. *American Birds* 30:905–8.

Johnston, R. F. 1960. Behavior of the Inca Dove. *Condor* 62:7–24.

Johnston, R. F., and R. C. Fleischer. 1981. Overwinter mortality and sexual size dimorphism in the House Sparrow. *Auk* 98:503–11.

Johnston, R. F., and R. K. Selander. 1973. Variation, adaptation, and evolution in the North American house sparrow. In *Productivity, population dynamics, and systematics of granivorous birds*, ed. S. C. Kendeigh and J. Pinowski. Warsaw: Polish Scientific Publishers.

Kahl, M. P., Jr. 1964. Food ecology of the Wood Stork (*Mycteria americana*) in Florida. *Ecological Monographs* 34:97–117.

Kale, H. W., II. 1965. Ecology and bioenergetics of the Long-billed Marsh Wren. *Publications of the Nuttall Ornithological Club* 5.

————. 1975. Extension of winter range of *Telmatodytes palustris waynei* to Georgia and Florida. *Auk* 92:806–7.

Kenage, E. E. 1965. Are birds increasing in numbers? *Bulletin of the Entomological Society of America* 11:81–83.

Kendeigh, S. C. 1934. The role of environment in the life of birds. *Ecological Monographs* 4:297–417.

————. 1939. The relation of metabolism to the development of temperature regulation in birds. *Journal of Experimental Zoology* 82:419–38.

Ketterson, E. D., and V. Nolan, Jr. 1976. Geographic variation and its climatic correlates in the sex ratio of eastern-wintering Dark-eyed Junco (*Junco hyemalis hyemalis*). *Ecology* 57:679–93.

————. 1979. Seasonal, annual, and geographic variation in sex ratio of wintering populations of Dark-eyed Juncos (*Junco hyemalis*). *Auk* 96:532–36.

————. 1982. The role of migration and winter mortality in the life history of a temperate-zone migrant, the Dark-eyed Junco, as determined from demographic analyses of winter populations. *Auk* 99:243–59.

Kilham, L. 1974. Covering of stores by White-breasted and Red-breasted Nuthatches. *Condor* 76:108–9.

———. 1975. Association of Red-breasted Nuthatches with chickadees in a hemlock cone year. *Auk* 92:160–62.

———. 1976. Winter foraging and associated behavior of Pileated Woodpeckers in Georgia and Florida. *Auk* 93:15–24.

Knight, R. L., and M. W. Call. 1980. *The common raven*. Washington, D.C.: U.S. Government Printing Office.

Knight, S. K., and R. L. Knight. 1983. Aspects of food finding by wintering Bald Eagles. *Auk* 100:477–84.

Koenig, W. D. 1981a. Reproductive success, group size, and the evolution of cooperative breeding in the Acorn Woodpecker. *American Naturalist* 117:421–43.

———. 1981b. Space competition in the Acorn Woodpecker: Power struggles in a cooperative breeder. *Animal Behavior* 29:396–409.

Kushlan, J. A. 1976. Feeding behavior of North American herons. *Auk* 93:86–94.

———. 1977. Foraging behavior of the White Ibis. *Wilson Bulletin* 89:342–45.

Lane, J. A. 1977. *A birder's guide to southeastern Arizona*. Denver: L and P Press.

———. 1978. *A birder's guide to the Rio Grande valley of Texas*. Denver: L and P Press.

Lane, J. A., and J. L. Tveten. 1980. *A birder's guide to the Texas coast*. Denver: L and P Press.

Lanyon, W. E. 1956. Ecological aspects of the sympatric distribution of meadowlarks in the north-central states. *Ecology* 37:98–108.

Law, E. 1921. A feeding habit of the Varied Thrush. *Condor* 23:66.

Leopold, A. S. 1973. *The California Quail*. Berkeley: University of California Press.

Lepthien, L. W., and C. E. Bock. 1976. Winter abundance patterns of North American kinglets. *Wilson Bulletin* 88:483–85.

Leukering, T. 1986. The eighty-sixth Christmas Bird Count. *American Birds* 40:589–95.

Ligon, J. D. 1968. Sexual differences in foraging behavior in two species of *Dendrocopos* woodpeckers. *Auk* 85:203–15.

Ligon, J. D., and S. L. Husar. 1974. Notes on the behavioral ecology of Couch's Mexican Jay. *Auk* 91:841–43.

Lingle, G. R., and G. L. Krapu. 1986. Winter ecology of Bald Eagles in southcentral Nebraska. *Prairie Naturalist* 18:65–78.

Ludwig, J. P. 1965. Biology and structure of the Caspian Tern (*Hydroprogne caspian*) population of the Great Lakes from 1896–1964. *Bird-Banding* 36:217–33.

McLaren, M. A. 1976. Vocalizations of the Boreal Chickadee. *Auk* 93:451–63.

McNab, B. K. 1973. Energetics and the distribution of vampires. *Journal of Mammalogy* 54:131–44.

MacRoberts, M. H. 1975. Food storage and winter territory in Red-headed Woodpeckers in north-western Louisiana. *Auk* 92:382–84.

Mader, W. J. 1978. A comparative nesting study of Red-tailed Hawks and Harris' Hawks in southern Arizona. *Auk* 95:327–37.

Marti, C. D. 1974. Feeding ecology of four sympatric owls. *Condor* 76:45–61.

———. 1976. A review of prey selection by the Long-eared Owl. *Condor* 78:331–36.

Marti, C. D., and J. G. Hogue. 1979. Selection of prey by size in Screech Owls. *Auk* 96:319–27.

Martin, S. G. 1970. The agonistic behavior of Varied Thrushes (*Ixoreus naevius*) in winter assemblages. *Condor* 72:452–59.

Mayr, E. 1963. *Animal species and evolution*. Cambridge: Harvard University Press.

Mayr, E., and L. L. Short. 1970. Species taxa of North American birds. *Publications of the Nuttall Ornithological Club* 9.

Meents, J. K., B. W. Anderson, and R. D. Ohmart. 1982. Vegetation relationships and food of Sage Sparrows wintering in honey mesquite habitat. *Wilson Bulletin* 94:129–38.

Mengel, R. M. 1965. The birds of Kentucky. *Ornithological Monographs* 3:1–581.

Mengel, R. M., and J. A. Jackson. 1977. Geographic variation of the Red-cockaded Woodpecker. *Condor* 79:349–55.

Merritt, P. G. 1981. Narrowly disjunct allopatry between Black-capped and Carolina Chickadees in northern Indiana. *Wilson Bulletin* 93:54–66.

Miller, E. V. 1941. Behavior of the Bewick's Wren. *Condor* 43:81–99.

Mills, S. G. 1976. American Kestrel sex ratio and habitat separation. *Auk* 93:740–48.

Millsap, B. A. 1986. Status of wintering Bald Eagles in the conterminous forty-eight states. *Wildlife Society Bulletin* 14:433–40.

Monroe, B. L., Jr. 1956. Observations of Elegant Terns at San Diego, California. *Wilson Bulletin* 68:239–44.

Morse, D. H. 1967. Foraging relationships of Brown-headed Nuthatches and Pine Warblers. *Ecology* 48:94–103.

———. 1968. The use of tools by Brown-headed Nuthatches. *Wilson Bulletin* 80:220–24.

———. 1970. Ecological aspects of some mixed-species foraging flocks of birds. *Ecological Monographs* 40:119–68.

———. 1972. Habitat utilization of Red-cockaded Woodpeckers during the winter. *Auk* 89:429–35.

Morton, M. L. 1984. Sex and age ratios in wintering White-crowned Sparrows. *Condor* 86:85–87.

Moseley, E. L. 1947. Variations in the bird population of the north-central states due to climatic and other changes. *Auk* 64:15–35.

Mumford, R. E., and C. E. Keller. 1984. *The birds of Indiana*. Bloomington: Indiana University Press.

Murrish, D. E. 1970a. Responses to diving in the Dipper, *Cinclus mexicanus*. *Comparative Biochemical Physiology* 34:853–58.

————. 1970b. Responses to temperature in the Dipper, *Cinclus mexicanus*. *Comparative Biochemical Physiology* 34:859–69.

Myers, J. P., and L. P. Myers. 1979. Shorebirds of coastal Buenos Aires Province, Argentina. *Ibis* 121:186–200.

National Geographic Society. 1983. *Field guide to the birds of North America*. Washington, D.C.: National Geographic Society.

Neff, J. A. 1947. Habits, food, and economic status of the Band-tailed Pigeon. *North American Fauna* 58:1–76.

Nice, M. M. 1943. Studies in the life history of the Song Sparrow: 2. The behavior of the Song Sparrow and other passerines. *Transactions of the Linnaean Society of New York* 6:1–328.

Nolan, V., Jr. 1978. The ecology and behavior of the Prairie Warbler. *Ornithological Monographs* 26:1–595.

Nolan, V., Jr., and D. P. Woolridge. 1962. Food habits and feeding behavior of the White-eyed Vireo. *Wilson Bulletin* 74:68–73.

Oberholser, H. C. 1974. *The bird life of Texas*. Austin: University of Texas Press.

Ohmart, R. D., and R. C. Lasiewski. 1971. Roadrunners: Energy conservation by hypothermia and absorption of sunlight. *Science* 172:67–69.

Olsen, D. L., D. R. Blankinship, R. C. Erickson, R. Drewien, H. D. Irby, R. Lock, and L. S. Smith. 1980. *Whooping Crane recovery plan*. Washington, D.C.: U.S. Fish and Wildlife Service.

Olson, J. B., and S. C. Kendeigh. 1980. Effect of season on the energetics, body composition, and cage activity of the Field Sparrow. *Auk* 97:704–20.

Owen, M. 1980. *Wild geese of the world*. London: B. T. Batsford.

Owre, O. T. 1967. Adaptations for locomotion and feeding in the Anhinga and the Double-crested Cormorant. *Ornithological Monographs* 6:1–138.

Page, G., and D. F. Whitacre. 1975. Raptor predation on wintering shorebirds. *Condor* 77:73–83.

Palmer, T. K. 1973. The House Finch and Starling in relation to California's agriculture. In *Productivity, population dynamics, and systematics of granivorous birds*, ed. S. C. Kendeigh and J. Pinowski. Warsaw: Polish Scientific Publishers.

Paterson, R. 1984. High incidence of plant material and small mammals in the autumn diet of Turkey Vultures in Virginia. *Wilson Bulletin* 96:467–69.

Pearson, O. P. 1979. Spacing and orientation among feeding Golden-crowned Sparrows. *Condor* 81:278–85.

Peterson, R. T. 1980. *A field guide to the birds*. Boston: Houghton Mifflin.

Peterson, S. R., and R. S. Ellarson. 1977. Food habits of Oldsquaws wintering on Lake Michigan. *Wilson Bulletin* 89:81–91.

Phelan, F. J. S. 1977. Food caching in the Screech Owl. *Condor* 79:127.

Phillips, A. 1975. Semipalmated Sandpiper: Identification, migration, summer and winter ranges. *American Birds* 29:799–806.

Phillips, A., J. Marshall, and G. Monson. 1983. *The birds of Arizona*. Tucson: University of Arizona Press.

Phillips, J. C. 1926. *A natural history of the ducks*, vol. 4. New York: Dover. Reprinted, 1986.

Pinkowski, B. C. 1977. Foraging behavior of the Eastern Bluebird. *Wilson Bulletin* 89:403–14.

Pitelka, F. A. 1950. Geographic variation and the species problem in the shorebird genus *Limnodromus*. *University of California Publications in Zoology* 50:1–108.

Pitts, T. D. 1976. Fall and winter roosting habits of Carolina Chickadees. *Wilson Bulletin* 88:603–10.

Preston, C. R. 1981. Environmental influence on soaring in wintering Red-tailed Hawks. *Wilson Bulletin* 93:350–56.

Price, F. E., and C. E. Bock. 1983. Population ecology of the Dipper (*Cinclus mexicanus*) in the Front Range of Colorado. *Studies in Avian Biology* 7:1–84.

Pulliam, H. R., K. A. Anderson, A. Misztal, and N. Moore. 1974. Temperature-dependent social behaviour in juncos. *Ibis* 116:360–64.

Pulliam, H. R., and F. Enders. 1971. The feeding ecology of five sympatric finch species. *Ecology* 52:557–66.

Pulliam, H. R., and G. S. Mills. 1977. The use of space by wintering sparrows. *Ecology* 58:1393–99.

Rabe, D. L., H. H. Prince, and D. L. Beaver. 1983. Feeding-site selection and foraging strategies of American Woodcock. *Auk* 100:711–16.

Radian Corporation. 1979. *Contour Plotting System-1, manual*. Austin, Tex.: Radian Corporation.

Ransom, W. R. 1950. Heavy winter mortality in Pacific coast Varied Thrush. *Condor* 52:88.

Rappole, J. H., E. S. Morton, T. E. Lovejoy, and J. L. Ruos. 1983. *Near Arctic avian migrants in the Neotropics*. Washington, D.C.: U.S. Department of the Interior, Fish and Wildlife Service.

Raynor, G. S. 1975. Techniques for evaluating and analyzing Christmas Bird Count data. *American Birds* 29:626–33.

Ricklefs, R. E., and F. R. Hainsworth. 1969. Temperature regulation in nestling Cactus Wrens: The nest environment. *Condor* 71:32–37.

Ripley, S. D. 1977. *Rails of the world*. Boston: David Godine Press.

Robbins, C. S., B. Bruum, and H. S. Zim. 1983. *Birds of North America*. New York: Golden Press.

Robbins, C. S., and D. Bystrak. 1974. The winter bird survey of central Maryland, U.S.A. *Acta Ornithologica* 14:254–71.

Rogers, J. P., and L. J. Korshgen. 1966. Foods of Lesser Scaups on breeding, migration, and wintering areas. *Journal of Wildlife Management* 30:258–64.

Root, R. B. 1964. Ecological interactions of the Chestnut-backed Chickadee following a range expansion. *Condor* 66:229–38.

————. 1967. The niche exploitation pattern of the Blue-gray Gnatcatcher. *Ecological Monographs* 37:317–50.

————. 1969. Interspecific territoriality between Bewick's and House Wren. *Auk* 86:125–27.

Root, T. 1988a. Environmental factors associated with avian distributional boundaries. *Journal of Biogeography* 15:489–505.

———. 1988b. Energetic constraints on avian distributions and abundances. *Ecology* 69:330–39.

Root, T. L., M. A. Holmgren, and R. W. Andrews. 1981. Winter abundance patterns of some songbirds near the 100th meridian in the southern United States. *Southwestern Naturalist* 26:95–100.

Salomonson, M. G., and R. P. Balda. 1977. Winter territoriality of Townsend's Solitaires (*Myadestes townsendi*) in a piñon-juniper-ponderosa pine ecotone. *Condor* 79:148–61.

Salt, G. W., and D. E. Willard. 1971. The hunting behavior and success of Forster's Tern. *Ecology* 52:989–98.

Schnell, G. D. 1967. Environmental influence on the incidence of flight in the Rough-legged Hawk. *Auk* 84:173–82.

Schreiber, R. W., and E. A. Schreiber. 1973. Florida's Brown Pelican population: Christmas Bird Count analyses. *American Birds* 27:711–15.

Schreiber, R. W., G. E. Woolfenden, and W. E. Curtsinger. 1975. Prey capture by the Brown Pelican. *Auk* 92:649–54.

Short, L. L. 1965. Hybridization in the flickers (*Colaptes*) of North America. *Bulletin of the American Museum of Natural History* 129:307–428.

———. 1971. Systematics and behavior of some North American woodpeckers genus *Picoides* (Aves). *Bulletin of the American Museum of Natural History* 145:1–118.

Slack, R. S. 1975. Effects of prey size on Loggerhead Shrike predation. *Auk* 92:812–14.

Smith, L. M., L. D. Vangilder, and R. A. Kennamer. 1985. Foods of wintering Brant in eastern North America. *Journal of Field Ornithology* 56:286–89.

Smith, N. G. 1966. Evolution of some arctic gulls (*Larus*): An experimental study of isolating mechanisms. *Ornithological Monographs* 4:1–99.

Smith, S. M. 1973. An aggressive display and related behavior in the Loggerhead Shrike. *Auk* 90:287–98.

Smyth, M., and G. A. Bartholomew. 1966. The water ecology of the Black-throated Sparrow and the Rock Wren. *Condor* 68:447–58.

Sparrow is extinct. 1987. *World Birdwatch* 9, no. 3:3.

Spencer, P. A. 1976. *Wintering Bald Eagles*. Washington, D.C.: National Agricultural Chemicals Association.

Sprenkle, J. M., and C. R. Blem. 1984. Metabolism and food selection of eastern House Finches. *Wilson Bulletin* 96:184–195.

Spring, L. W. 1965. Climbing and pecking adaptations in some North American woodpeckers. *Condor* 67:457–88.

Sprunt, A., Jr. 1954. *Florida bird life*. New York: Coward-McCann.

Stallcup, P. L. 1968. Spatio-temporal relationships of nuthatches and woodpeckers in ponderosa pine forests of Colorado. *Ecology* 49:831–43.

Steenhof, K. 1984. Use of an interspecific communal roost by wintering Ferruginous Hawks. *Wilson Bulletin* 96:137–38.

Stenzel, L. E., H. R. Huber, and G. W. Page. 1976. Feeding behavior and diet of the Long-billed Curlew and Willet. *Wilson Bulletin* 88:314–32.

Stiles, F. G. 1971. Time, energy, and territoriality of the Anna Hummingbird. *Science* 173:818–21.

———. 1973. Food supply and the annual cycle of the Anna Hummingbird. *University of California Publications in Zoology* 97:1–109.

Stinson, C. H. 1977. The spatial distribution of wintering Black-bellied Plovers. *Wilson Bulletin* 89:470–72.

Stone, W. 1937. *Bird studies at Old Cape May*, vol. 1. Philadelphia: Academy of Natural Science.

Stupka, A. 1963. *Notes on the birds of Great Smoky Mountains National Park*. Knoxville: University of Tennessee Press.

Summers-Smith, D. 1963. *The House Sparrow*. London: Collins.

Swenson, J. E. 1979. The relationship between prey species ecology and dive success in Ospreys. *Auk* 96:408–12.

Sykes, P. W., Jr. 1980. Decline and disappearance of the Dusky Seaside Sparrow from Merritt Island, Florida. *American Birds* 34:728–37.

Tanner, J. T. 1952. Black-capped and Carolina Chickadees in the southern Appalachian Mountains. *Auk* 69:407–24.

Tate, J., Jr. 1986. The Blue List for 1986. *American Birds* 40:227–36.

Taylor, J. M., and J. W. Kamp. 1985. Feeding activities of the Anna's Hummingbird at subfreezing temperatures. *Condor* 87:292–93.

Terborgh, J. 1971. Distribution on environmental gradients: Theory and a preliminary interpretation of distribution patterns in the avifaunas of the Cordillera Vilcabamba, Peru. *Ecology* 52:23–40.

———. 1985. The role of ecotones in the distribution of Andean birds. *Ecology* 66:1237–46.

Terborgh, J., and J. S. Weske. 1975. The role of competition in the distribution of Andean birds. *Ecology* 56:562–76.

Tewes, M. E. 1984. Opportunistic feeding by White-tailed Hawks at prescribed burns. *Wilson Bulletin* 96:135–36.

Thompson, D. 1973. Feeding ecology of diving ducks on Keskuk Pool, Mississippi River. *Journal of Wildlife Management* 37:367–81.

Thompson, W. L. 1960. Agonistic behavior in the House Finch, Part 1: Annual cycle and display patterns. *Condor* 62:245–71.

Thut, R. N. 1970. Feeding habits of the Dipper in southwestern Washington. *Condor* 72:234–35.

Tomback, D. F. 1977. Foraging strategies of Clark's Nutcracker. *Living Bird* 16:123–61.

Tramer, E. J. 1974. An analysis of the species density of U.S. landbirds during the winter using the 1971 Christmas Bird Count. *American Birds* 28:563–67.

United States Fish and Wildlife Service. 1982. *National wildlife refuges: A visitor's guide*. Map. Washington, D.C.: U.S. Printing Office.

United States Geological Survey (USGS). 1970. *The national atlas of the U.S.A.* Washington, D.C.: U.S. Printing Office.

Verbeek, N. A. M. 1972. Daily and annual time budget of the Yellow-billed Magpie. *Auk* 89:567–82.

———. 1975. Northern wintering of flycatchers and residency of Black Phoebes in California. *Auk* 92:737–49.

Verner, J. 1985. Assessment of counting techniques. *Current Ornithology* 2:247–302.

Walsberg, G. E. 1975. Digestive adaptations of *Phainopepla nitens* associated with the eating of mistletoe berries. *Condor* 77:169–74.

———. 1977. Ecology and energetics of contrasting social systems in *Phainopepla nitens. University of California Publications in Zoology.* 108:1–63.

Wardle, P. 1981. Is the alpine timberline set by physiological tolerances, reproductive capacity, or biological interactions? *Proceedings of the Ecological Society of Australia* 11:53–66.

Watson, J. W. 1986. Range use by wintering Rough-legged Hawks in southeastern Idaho. *Condor* 88:256–58.

Weller, M. W., I. C. Adams, Jr., and B. J. Rose. 1955. Winter roosts of Marsh Hawks and Short-eared Owls in central Missouri. *Wilson Bulletin* 67:189–93.

Wheeler, T. G. 1980. Experiments in feeding behavior of the Anna Hummingbird. *Wilson Bulletin* 92:53–62.

Wiens, J. A. 1981. Scale problems in avian censusing. In Estimating numbers of territorial birds, ed. J. M. Scott and C. J. Ralph. *Studies in Avian Biology* 6:513–21.

Williams, J. B., and G. O. Batzlie. 1979. Winter diet of a bark-foraging guild of birds. *Wilson Bulletin* 91:126–31.

Williams, L. E., Jr., and R. W. Phillips. 1972. North Florida Sandhill Crane populations. *Auk* 89:541–48.

Williams, O., and P. Wheat. 1971. Hybrid jays in Colorado. *Wilson Bulletin* 83:343–46.

Willson, M. F. 1970. Foraging behavior of some winter birds of deciduous woods. *Condor* 72:169–74.

Willson, M. F., and J. C. Harmeson. 1973. Seed preferences and digestive efficiency of Cardinals and Song Sparrows. *Condor* 75:225–34.

Wilz, K. J., and V. Giampa. 1978. Habitat use by Yellow-rumped Warblers at the northern extremities of their winter range. *Wilson Bulletin* 90:566–74.

Wolf, L. L. 1977. Species relationships in the avian genus *Aimophila. Ornithological Monographs* 23:1–220.

Woolfenden, G. E. 1973. Nesting and survival in a population of Florida Scrub Jays. *Living Bird* 12:25–50.

———. 1975. Florida Scrub Jay helpers at the nest. *Auk* 92:1–15.

Yahner, R. H., G. L. Storm, and A. L. Wright. 1986. Winter diets of vultures in south-central Pennsylvania. *Wilson Bulletin* 98:157–60.

Young, A. M. 1982. *Population biology of tropical insects.* New York: Plenum Press.

Yunich, R. P. 1984. An assessment of the irruptive status of the Boreal Chickadee in New York State. *Journal of Field Ornithology* 55:31–37.

Zeleny, L. 1976. *The bluebird.* Bloomington: Indiana University Press.

Zusi, R. L. 1968. "Ploughing" for fish by the Greater Yellowlegs. *Wilson Bulletin* 80:491–92.

Index